CITIZEN COWBOY

Citizen Cowboy is a probing biography of one of America's most influential cultural figures. Will Rogers was a youth from the Cherokee Indian Territory of Oklahoma who rose to conquer nearly every form of media and entertainment in the early twentieth-century's rapidly expanding consumer society. Through vaudeville, the Ziegfeld Follies and Broadway, syndicated newspaper and magazine writing, the lecture circuit, radio, and Hollywood movies, Rogers built his reputation as a folksy humorist whose wit made him a national symbol of common sense, common decency, and common people. Though a friend of presidents, movie stars and industrial leaders, it was his bond with ordinary people that endeared him to mass audiences. Making his fellow Americans laugh and think while honoring the past and embracing the future, Rogers helped ease them into the modern world and they loved him for it.

Steven Watts has written seven books, including biographies of Walt Disney, Henry Ford, Hugh Hefner, Dale Carnegie, and John F. Kennedy. He has written for *The Atlantic*, *National Review*, *Newsweek*, *Salon*, and *The American Spectator*, and has appeared on NPR, C-Span, BBC, NBC, CBS, MSNBC, Fox, and Bloomberg News. He is Professor Emeritus at the University of Missouri.

Also by Steven Watts

The Republic Reborn: War and the Making of Liberal America, 1790–1820
The Romance of Real Life: Charles Brockden Brown and the Origins of American Culture
The Magic Kingdom: Walt Disney and the American Way of Life
The People's Tycoon: Henry Ford and the American Century
Mr. Playboy: Hugh Hefner and the American Dream
Self-Help Messiah: Dale Carnegie and Success in Modern America
JFK and the Masculine Mystique: Sex and Power on the New Frontier

CITIZEN COWBOY

Will Rogers and the American People

Steven Watts

CAMBRIDGE
UNIVERSITY PRESS

Shaftesbury Road, Cambridge CB2 8EA, United Kingdom

One Liberty Plaza, 20th Floor, New York, NY 10006, USA

477 Williamstown Road, Port Melbourne, VIC 3207, Australia

314–321, 3rd Floor, Plot 3, Splendor Forum, Jasola District Centre, New Delhi – 110025, India

103 Penang Road, #05-06/07, Visioncrest Commercial, Singapore 238467

Cambridge University Press is part of Cambridge University Press & Assessment, a department of the University of Cambridge.

We share the University's mission to contribute to society through the pursuit of education, learning and research at the highest international levels of excellence.

www.cambridge.org
Information on this title: www.cambridge.org/9781108495936

DOI: 10.1017/9781108856393

First published 2024

Printed in the United Kingdom by TJ Books Limited, Padstow Cornwall

A catalogue record for this publication is available from the British Library

A Cataloging-in-Publication data record for this book is available from the Library of Congress

ISBN 978-1-108-49593-6 Hardback

Well, I don't want to be a crab, or I don't want to hinder hidden talent or art. But I just want to be modest about it, and let them practise on somebody else's life. Why pick on mine? .... There is lots of injustices in our laws, but we can at least live our lives without having them lived by some well wishing amateur man of letters .... [M]y poor little life Bernard Shaw couldent make it look like anything. But here is better still, pass a law there in Oklahoma making every biography writer join the re-forestration camps [public jobs funded by the New Deal]. That will get their minds off of writing.

Will Rogers, "Don't Write Me Up," June 11, 1933.

Contents

Plates

Author's Note

Will Rogers, in his many writings, was notorious for his haphazard use of the English language. He filled sentences with misspellings, mangled grammar, tortured syntax, promiscuous capitalization, and eccentric punctuation. This habit resulted from some combination of limited formal education, frequent haste of composition, and a determination to convey a rustic, man-of-the-people sensibility. The editor of Rogers' journalistic pieces in the 1920s and 1930s at the *New York Times* instructed proofreaders to refrain from correcting the mistakes because such action would be "taking away part of the personality he is selling to readers." This decision was undoubtedly correct. But for the modern reader, Rogers' idiosyncratic use of language, while often charming, can mislead or become off-putting.

So rather than hubristically correcting all of Rogers' errors, on the one hand, or leaving them completely as is and obscuring the narrative in a thicket of "[sic]s" and brackets, on the other, I have pursued a middle course. When quoting from Rogers' writings (and who can resist quoting abundantly from such a witty, shrewd observer of American life), I have mostly left his language undisturbed. But on occasion, if his lapses impede the flow of information or muddle understanding or create ambiguity, I have cleaned things up a bit without altering the meaning or flavor – adding a period at a sentence's conclusion or a comma after a phrase, correcting a confusing misspelling, or capitalizing the first word of a sentence. Readers who want the unvarnished version can consult the primary sources indicated in the footnotes.

Rogers was deeply committed to communicating with his readers, so I think he would understand my maneuver. Although he would probably grin, scratch the back of his head, and make some genial wisecrack about "eggheads."

Introduction

Will Rogers' America

T HE STORY BEGINS IN CONTRADICTION AND ends in tragedy. On
    November 4, 1879 William Penn Adair Rogers, the famous American
humorist, entertainer, writer, and movie star, was born near present-day
Claremore, Oklahoma, at an uneasy juncture of past and future, power and
impotence, aspiration and nostalgia. The discordant aspects of his youthful
position were striking. The son of a prominent Cherokee Indian family, he grew
up as an outsider contending with the authority and expectations of a White,
Anglo-Saxon, Protestant establishment that dominated American life. Ensconced
in a cowboy culture of horses and cattle, rifles and roping in great open spaces, he
emerged at a moment when expansion into the great American West was giving
way to a rapidly urbanizing society teeming with immigrants, factories, investment capital, and unfamiliar economic and political influences. A boy taught to
honor Victorian traditions of hard work and moral uplift, he was drawn to
enticing new ideals of consumer prosperity and commercial entertainment.
Tutored in an old-fashioned success creed postulating that character and productivity paved the road to success, he gravitated toward a newfangled ideology
insisting that personal charisma and charm led to upward mobility and prosperity. In all of these ways, the youngster from the great plains came to maturity
poised uneasily between America's vanishing rural society in the late nineteenth
century and its emerging order of urban mass culture in the early twentieth.

Fifty-six years later, Will Rogers perished in an airplane crash on August 15,
1935, while flying in the wilds of Alaska with Wiley Post, the famous pilot and a
close friend. News of his demise shocked the American public and prompted an
outpouring of grief from the highest to the lowest. John Nance Garner, the hard-
drinking, no-nonsense Vice President from Texas, adjourned the U.S. Senate and
when approached by a reporter, replied with obvious emotion, "I just can't talk
about it." President Franklin Roosevelt publicly lamented the loss of "a very old

1

friend of mine, a friend of every man, woman, and child in the United States." Newspapers throughout the country filled their pages with mournful stories, editorials, and memorials regarding the beloved entertainer, with the *New York Times* devoting four full pages to Rogers' life, death, accomplishments, and legacy the weekend after the crash. Ordinary Americans were stunned. Reports appeared of people all over the country sitting down, speechless with shock and tears welling in their eyes, upon hearing of the calamitous event. Some 50,000 people passed by Rogers' coffin at Forest Lawn Memorial Park cemetery in Glendale, California, just outside Los Angeles, on the day of his funeral (at least an equal number were waiting to do so when time ran out) while tens of thousands more filled the Hollywood Bowl for a memorial service. A Chicago newspaper editorial spoke for many when it said of the plain-spoken Oklahoman, "he exercised an influence on public sentiment perhaps greater than any political leader. He was the most widely read humorist on and off the screen and one of the very few who made intelligent comments on public affairs and issues. His homely philosophy had a tremendous influence on the public mind . . . . He came nearer to expressing the thoughts of the common man than anyone." The novelist Clarence Kelland put it simply: "Will [Rogers] was the head man of all the public figures of the day."[1]

So we are left to ponder crucial questions. What transpired in the intervening decades that carried Rogers from an early life entangled in two worlds to the status of wildly popular folk hero whose untimely death contained the stuff of national tragedy? Why did a vast audience cutting across geographical, class, gender, and ethnic lines respond so keenly to his endeavors as a vaudevillian, journalist, radio host, movie star, political critic, and humorous commentator on the foibles of American life? Put simply, what made Americans come to love him so? Part of the answer lay in an astonishing range of activity that saw him navigating nearly every tributary of popular culture in early twentieth-century America. He seemed to enter the public eye from every direction at once.

Rogers' dazzling rise to fame and influence began in the early 1900s when he traveled the country with various shows as a cowboy entertainer specializing in riding and roping tricks. He then became a mainstay on the vaudeville circuit before catapulting onto the national stage in 1916 when he joined the *Ziegfeld Follies* in New York. For the rest of his life he never left that stage; indeed, he dominated it. Rogers steadily boosted his public profile by injecting ever larger doses of comic commentary on American values and proclivities into his show while twirling his rope. Capturing the public imagination with his amusing, homespun observations on the tendencies of the age, he drew comparisons to Benjamin Franklin and Mark Twain. One wag dubbed him "The Poet Lariat." In the late 1910s he became a prominent silent film actor and made fifty movies in that genre. A decade later, with his distinctive drawl and verbal wit making him a natural, Rogers completed twenty feature films with the advent of "talkies" and became a major Hollywood star. Throughout this period, he traveled the country as a wildly popular lecturer. He wrote a weekly newspaper column, "The Weekly Article," starting in 1922, and then a shorter daily piece, "The Daily Telegram," from 1926 to 1935, both of which were syndicated nationally in some 300 newspapers. He wrote regularly on current affairs for the *Saturday Evening Post*, the *American*, and other magazines. Rogers gathered these popular journalistic writings and published several well-received volumes of collected wisdom on the American scene. His enormous public audience earned him a weekly radio broadcast, *The Gulf Headliners*, that featured his laconic, rambling thoughts on American life, some drawn from his writings and some ad-libbed.

This amazing flurry of activity made Will Rogers one of the most famous men in America, a figure whose influence ranged from the ordinary folks who adored him to the highest echelon of social and political leaders who recognized his impact. In 1918, Theodore Roosevelt declared, "This man Rogers has such a keen insight into the American panorama and the American people that I feel he is bound, in the course of time, to be a potent force in the political life of the nation." Rogers stayed at the White House in 1925 as an overnight guest of Republican president Calvin Coolidge and attended a private dinner in the same residence with Democrat president Franklin Roosevelt and wife Eleanor nearly a decade later. In July 19, 1926 Rogers graced the cover of *Time* magazine. He hobnobbed with the likes of Charles Lindbergh, Samuel Goldwyn, William Jennings Bryan, and Henry Ford. Rogers' appeal to a mass audience was astonishing. He attracted millions of radio listeners while his books, such as the *Illiterate Digest* and *Letters of a Self-Made Diplomat to His President*, sold briskly. His tremendous draw as a movie star made him the top box-office attraction in 1934 – he beat out Clark Gable, Joan Crawford, and Mae West for the honor – and one of the highest-paid actors in Hollywood. Rogers was everywhere, it seemed, and most people saw him as a national treasure. Damon Runyon, the famous writer and journalist, called him "America's most complete human document."[2]

At the heart of Rogers' popular appeal lay a unique talent for expressing what ordinary people were thinking. With a bevy of trademark mannerisms – chomping on gum, pushing his hat forward while scratching the back of his head in a perplexed manner, offering homespun homilies in a slightly stammering drawl accompanied by an infectious grin – he approached his audience as equals. In the popular imagination he appeared as a wise, witty, Lincolnesque, crackerbarrel philosopher who both amused and educated his neighbors as they sat around a woodstove in a village general store on a snowy winter afternoon. Rogers traded on a lack of pretension, beginning his commentaries with the modest disclaimer, "All I know is what I read in the papers," before going on to demonstrate quite the opposite. He offered a shrewd, but gentle, skewering of political topics ("I don't belong to any organized political faith; I'm a Democrat"), social issues (many Americans will vote in favor of Prohibition, "That is, everybody that is sober enough to stagger to the polls will"), contemporary manners ("We used to think going to see women play golf would be like going to see men crochet"), and morals (the growing popularity of divorce produced "lawyers that can cut you loose from an octopus"). Even when cracking wise, his droll comments displayed a generous sensibility, as in the famous statement he wished to be carved on his gravestone: "I never met a man I didn't like." The talented Oklahoman charmed the country as a symbol of common people, common sense, and common decency.[3]

Then there were his unique personal qualities. Throughout his engagement with nearly every new form of modern entertainment and communication, Rogers' colorful personality – a combination of wry humor, cowboy practicality, good fellowship, and skepticism of pretense and pomposity – shone through brightly. As people sensed, these characteristics were authentic, a reflection of a man who was exactly what he seemed. Yet the private man was more complicated. Like many people with a finely honed comic sense, such as Mark Twain, Rogers harbored a rather bleak, often absurd, and occasionally angry view of the world. But he mostly kept that to himself. Moreover, as his national stature and legend grew, Rogers became trapped to a certain extent by his own creation. As his friend, the writer Homer Croy, shrewdly noted, "He built himself up till he became, both on and off stage, the Will Rogers the public knew. The older he grew, and the more successful he became, the more he played this character." As a result, a few critics denounced Rogers as a panderer to the banalities of a commercialized folk culture, or merely a comic in search of laughs with no evident deeper wisdom. But the vast majority of Americans disagreed and treasured his insights. They loved the witty, plain-spoken, homespun philosopher whose grammatical lapses and inventive spelling mirrored their own.[4]

So while the facts of Rogers' ascent to the status as "the most beloved man in America" are evident, the reasons for it are much less so. Earlier and worthy treatments of his life have focused on the captivating personality and colorful endeavors of this unusual, gifted man to explain his appeal. While not ignoring these factors, this biography takes a different tack by digging deeper to uncover the cultural and social wellsprings of his tremendous popularity and influence. It examines not only what he made, but what was made of him. Rogers' life, after all, was not only fascinating but historically significant. This exploration, like the trajectory of his life, begins with the contradictions he embodied as a youth, then scrutinizes his struggle to resolve them as he matured, and ends as he is struck down at the height of his triumph. It focuses on the way in which he, like many of his fellow Americans, confronted the massive historical transformation of his age – weathering its dislocations, sometimes lamenting its cost, but ultimately promoting its new possibilities.

Rogers' life spanned the last decades of the nineteenth century and the first few of the twentieth, a period marked by one of the greatest transformations in American history. As a host of historians have detailed, the years from 1880 to 1930 encompassed a great shift away from the rural republic and toward a modern order defined by urban settlement, consumerism, mass culture, bureaucracy, and the corporate state. This transformation triggered enormous enthusiasm and aspiration, but an equal portion of anxiety, as Americans faced a vast array of unsettling changes in their lives. Rogers instinctively grasped the complexity of this historical situation and approached it with great deftness, aiming in his humorous commentary to both explore the possibilities of newfangled values and defuse the fears that accompanied them.[5]

In particular, Will Rogers' life and career were caught up in four developments central to this great wave of change in the United States. First, he represented, directly and vividly, a startling shift in the frame of the American experience, what famed historian Frederick Jackson Turner first called in 1893 "the closing of the frontier." With the settlement of the last open territories by 1900, the United States ended its more than two centuries of westward expansion and turned away from the dynamic that had shaped so many of its institutions and values since the colonial period. Influence and innovation now lay in rapidly expanding cities and the vibrant industrial economy that sustained them. Born in the "Oklahoma Territory," then the last remaining continental region to be so designated before moving on to statehood, Rogers seemed to step out of the nation's past and into its future. Outfitted in rustic clothes and delivering his jibes in a rural drawl, he presented a comforting, nostalgic image of the cowboy, a figure already disappearing into the history books amidst a booming society of urban noise and crowds, smoke-belching factories and puttering Model T's. With verbal agility and endearing wit, Rogers tiptoed along the fault line between veneration for the days-gone-by of the frontier and appreciation for modern urban dynamism. By joking about the tension he relaxed it, as when he quipped about Americans' new love affair with the automobile, "Everybody is rushing to go somewhere, where they have no business, so they can hurry back to the place where they never should have left."[6]

Second, Rogers negotiated a great change in the values of mainstream America in the late 1800s and early 1900s. This era witnessed the gradual disappearance of an old-fashioned Victorian mindset that dated back to the early nineteenth century, a stringent creed that had emphasized character formation, hard work, and emotional self-restraint as the keys to a happy and productive life. Rebelling against his father's demands that he settle into a stable, traditional career in ranching or business, a restless young Rogers abandoned the cultural tradition that informed it. He aimed for a different kind of life, vowing, "I am going to learn things that will enable me to make my living in the world without making it by day labor." Rogers first felt the pull of riding and roping contests because of his great skills riding a horse and tossing a lariat. From there it was but a short step into profitable new roles – showman, popular writer, movie actor, radio personality – that represented grand new vistas of pleasure for early twentieth-century Americans. In this modern culture, and in the economy of abundance that supported it, people valued sparkling personality over virtuous character, enjoyment over labor, self-fulfillment over self-control. To this end, Rogers mustered his enormous resources of rural charm and humor and deployed them across the entertainment landscape, in the process poking fun at a stuffy Victorian ethos and embracing a fresh culture of consumer gratification that was coming to characterize modern American life. In 1920, for instance, the Advertising Club of Los Angeles invited the Oklahoma entertainer to participate in a lighthearted debate on the relative virtues of cowboys and preachers with a popular Baptist minister who held services in a large theater. Noting how old-fashioned religion had accommodated to a modern pleasure paradigm, Rogers joked about his opponent and his hosts: "He is the only preacher that ever knew enough to not have a church but to preach in a Moving Picture Theatre, and to show you how foxy he is, he leaves the billing up there of the Picture that is playing there during the week . . . . I doubt my side will get a fair showing here as I know that Advertising and preaching [now] have much in common."[7]

Third, Rogers personified the rapidly swelling importance of celebrity in a new American culture of entertainment and media saturation. Around the dawn of the twentieth century, a great wave of new institutions devoted to leisure began to inundate the United States: amusement parks such as Coney Island, music and dance clubs devoted to ragtime and then jazz, vaudeville shows, and eventually radio and Hollywood films. Right alongside appeared a massive expansion of newspapers and slick-paper magazines that transformed print communication with the support of advertising, the same endeavor that fueled the new consumer economy. Like Theodore Roosevelt in politics and D. W. Griffith in filmmaking, Rogers grasped the essence of mass culture in the early 1900s and sensed its enormous powers of publicity and image-making. He assumed the central role in this new milieu: the celebrity. This new public figure, constantly on parade, attracted and kept attention through the mechanisms of the media and, blurring the line between public and private life, created an illusion of intimacy with a popular audience. Rogers quickly mastered such maneuvers. Appearing on the vaudeville stage, the movie screen, and over the radio waves, and trailed by newspapermen, photographers, wire-service reporters, and newsreel cameras wherever he went, he kept his image before a national audience and his finger on the public pulse. Rogers was one of the earliest, and greatest, celebrities created by America's modern mass culture. He loved the role, even as he demonstrated an awareness of its shallowness and brittleness. As he once observed wryly, his early days in the "show business" world of western-themed circuses and vaudeville meant "I was ruined for life as far as actual employment was concerned."[8]

Fourth, Rogers formulated his principles and shaped his career according to a deeply felt spirit of populism. He venerated the common man and made the standards, judgements, and status of ordinary folks a lodestar for everything he did. They were his people, and he joked about his instinctive connection to them: "You can't make any commoner appeal than I can." In a 1925 column, he declared, famously, his faith in America's "Big Honest Majority." The typical average citizen, Rogers insisted, "is not a 100 per cent American. He is not any organization, either uplift or downfall . . . . [but] an Animal that has been going along, believing in right, doing right, tending to his own business, letting the other fellows alone . . . . [H]e is just NORMAL." Rogers' populist regard for common people colored nearly everything he wrote and said, as when he sympathized with the barely educated, admitting, "I'm not sure what syntax means. But it must be bad because it's got 'sin' and 'tax' in it." Such sentiments reached a climax during the Great Depression of the 1930s. The near collapse of the economic and social system triggered an outpouring of affection for the common man who had been devastated by events, ranging from Carl Sandburg's epic poem, *The People, Yes*, to Norman Rockwell's sentimental rendering of small-town life on the cover of the *Saturday Evening Post* to John Steinbeck's novel, *Grapes of Wrath*. Will Rogers stood at the front of this populist line. He advised the newly elected Franklin D. Roosevelt by telegram to rely on ordinary citizens and be wary of elites: "The illiterate ones will all work, you will have no trouble with them. But it's the smart ones that will drive you nutty, for they have been taught in school that they are to live off the others." More sardonically, he noted that politicians usually misappropriated money because they "dident know that money trickled up. Give it to the people at the bottom and the people at the top will have it before night anyhow. But it will at least have passed through the poor fellow's hands." Rogers once claimed, in a respite from his usual comic mode, that he was exploring "the American soul." For him, clearly, that elusive quality lay in the virtues and aspirations of "just plain folks."[9]

Thus Will Rogers strode front and center stage as an influential figure who both reflected and promoted these important trends – the end of the frontier, the new culture of personality and self-fulfillment, the emergence of celebrity, and the influence of populism – in the making of modern American life. But it was the *nature* of this role that proved crucial: he acted as a historical mediator, easing Americans into the future even as he honored many of the values and institutions of the past. Rogers appeared as a reassuring figure with one foot anchored in tradition and the other in modern innovation, a man whose gentle humor and down-home wisdom helped guide his fellow citizens through a wrenching period of historical change. Perhaps his best biographer once suggested that the Oklahoman was a "beneficiary of circumstances" whose talents happened to fit the demands and opportunities of a new age. This argument shortchanges Rogers. Perhaps more than any other public figure in the early 1900s, he instinctively grasped the historical changes overturning a familiar world. Projecting his own sense of social displacement – the rural Indian cowboy traversing the media highways of an urban mass culture – onto a national screen, he deployed his humor and keen powers of observation to make sense of this transforming atmosphere. His fellow Americans, while listening to him pan the sins and praise the virtues of both the past and the present, gained the comforting thought that maybe things were not so different after all. Will Rogers, in other words, was not so much a "beneficiary of circumstance" as an active agent: a brilliant observer, translator, and negotiator of historical change.[10]

So while Will Rogers told jokes, he wasn't a jokester. Far from it. This complex, shrewd, self-effacing man played a serious role in helping Americans accommodate to modern life. He expressed many of his fellow citizens' yearnings and reservations, hopes and anxieties about the journey from a largely rural society of individualism, character, and emotional restraint to a largely urban society of bureaucratic organization, personality, and self-fulfillment. In the process, he left behind a series of incongruous but indelible images: the cowboy in chaps and wide-brimmed hat, twirling his lariat before urban vaudeville audiences; the village philosopher enchanting his listeners with a rustic style and old-fashioned wisdom as he was broadcast coast-to-coast on the radio; the man with the common touch performing "the country boy goes to the city" in movies that made him one of Hollywood's biggest draws. But playing on that ambiguity was actually his secret. By making them laugh even as he made them think, by honoring the past even as he embraced the future, Will Rogers helped ease his fellow Americans into the modern world. And they loved him for it.

1

The Final Frontier

I N MAY 1916, THE RUSTIC ENTERTAINER from Oklahoma grew highly agitated as he prepared to go on stage in Baltimore, Maryland. Now age thirty-six, but still possessing a boyish grin and shock of dark hair, Will Rogers had joined Florenz Ziegfeld's popular *Frolic* in New York City only a few months before as a novelty act, doing rope tricks while dressed as a cowboy and wisecracking with the audience about current affairs. But this was different. He had been recruited to appear in a special benefit show organized by George M. Cohan for the Friars Club, a theatrical organization. It featured a prominent cast of comics, dancers, and musicians, and Rogers, for his contribution, had put together a humorous commentary on the President of the United States and his political stance and strategies. But now, unexpectedly, the chief executive himself, Woodrow Wilson, had come up from Washington DC with his wife for the performance. As Rogers noted in his idiosyncratic syntax, no one "had ever heard of a president being joked personally in a public theater about the policies of his administration." When Wilson entered the venue, the audience stood up and applauded respect-fully. Fearing he may have blundered badly with his plan, the entertainer admitted, "I was scared to death." He nervously stalked the backstage area waiting to go on, at one point even leaving through the stage door to stand outside in a light rain to calm himself, before retreating to the dressing room.

Finally, a smart-alecky stage manager knocked on his door and deadpanned, "You die in 5 more minutes for kidding your country." A few moments later, the backstage staff nudged a reluctant Rogers onto the stage. Ambling out in front of the footlights, he stood quietly for a moment, scratched his head, grinned out at the audience from a downturned head, and drawled, "I am kinder nervous here tonight." A chuckle rippled through the crowd, and the entertainer plunged ahead. He poked fun at the loquacious William Jennings Bryan, Wilson's Secretary of State, claiming that years earlier he had been booked in his

9

hometown to follow a Bryan speech "but he [Bryan] spoke so long that it was so dark when he finished, they couldn't see my roping." A pause and quizzical expression. "I wonder what ever became of him?" Then he turned to current topics capturing newspaper headlines. On Wilson's controversial decision to send American troops into Mexico in pursuit of Pancho Villa, Rogers congratulated the U.S. Army for trapping the elusive Mexican bandit "in between the Atlantic and Pacific." On the worsening situation with warring powers in Europe that involved an exchange of threatening notes with Germany, he noted drily, "President Wilson is getting along fine now [compared] to what he was a few months ago. Do you realize, people, that at one time in our negotiations with Germany he was five notes behind?" America's woeful lack of military prepared-ness in the face of a war situation inspired him to comment, "There is some talk of getting a machine gun if we can borrow one. The one we have now they are using to train our army with in Plattsburg [military base]. If we go to war we will just about have to go to the trouble of getting another gun." On the administration's proposal for creating an army of 200,000 men: "Mr. Ford makes three hundred thousand cars every year. I think, Mr. President, we ought to at least have a man to every car."

As Rogers delivered his remarks, both he and the audience glanced anxiously at the presidential box to see Wilson's reaction. To their great relief – the president was known for being stern and moralistic – he laughed heartily. The crowd soon joined in. When Rogers completed his monologue, the audience, including Wilson, rose and applauded. The president even went backstage for a handshake and a chat with the speaker. When Cohan thanked Wilson for coming to the performance, the president replied, "I'd travel ten times that distance to listen to as wise a man as Will Rogers." In Rogers' words, it was "the proudest and most successful night I ever had on stage."

It was more than that. Wilson would go on to see Roger's act several more times, but the president's public approval of the entertainer's irreverent commen-tary in 1916 proved to be a pivot point in Roger's career. Perhaps more than any other single incident, this successful show made him a national figure – an engaging entertainer, yes, but also something more. A few days after the Baltimore triumph, Florenz Ziegfeld hired him as a full-time cast member in his famous touring company, the *Ziegfeld Follies*, where he became one of its most popular performers with his western-style roping tricks. Even more crucial to Roger's rising stature, however, was the other aspect of his act that grew larger and larger with the passage of time: a comic commentary on modern American life, the values of its citizens, and the inclinations of its leaders. His audience delighted in his witty observations and truly made him not only a star, but an influence on public opinion, for the next two decades.

Less discernably, the pivotal Baltimore show disclosed something else crucial to the makeup of Will Rogers. At the height of the backstage tension as he grew petrified at the thought of joking about President Wilson to his face, his mind traveled to an important place in his life. He confessed, "If someone had hollered, 'Next train leaving for Claremore,' I would have been on it." Claremore, Oklahoma was the site of his birth and the ancestral home to which he still returned frequently as an adult. Located in the northeastern part of the state in the heart of the Cherokee territory, this settlement had framed the early life of an Indian boy who had grown up as the scion of one of the tribe's most prominent families. Now it seemed to offer an escape to the adult nearly paralyzed by pressure as he faced a promising, yet dangerous, rendezvous with fame. But the rural town promised something more than solace; it promised a return to the place that had given him the basic emotional materials of his rise to success. It was not just fear that sent Rogers reaching for Claremore, but a yearning to return to his roots for inspiration. He sought, instinctively, to reconnect with both the vanishing frontier and the ancestral Indian homeland that provided the source of his values, attitudes, and talents.[1]

* * * * *

The Indian Territory of northeastern Oklahoma lay just west of the Ozark Plateau where small mountains and undulating hills begin to give way to the Great Plains sweeping to the horizon. Great open, rolling areas of prairie grass, particularly the bluestem variety which could grow several feet high, ran for miles and were punctuated with colorful splashes of wildflowers. Rivers such as the Verdigris and Caney sliced through the landscape while the woods buffering these meandering bodies of water were filled with oak, elm, pecan, and sycamore trees. The area teemed with wildlife as deer, wild turkeys, quail, prairie chickens, wild ducks and geese, and flocks of green parakeets populated the flatlands and the river valleys. While seldom seen in daylight, panthers and wolves rent the night air with their howls and screams.[2]

Clem and Mary Rogers, husband and wife in a prominent Cherokee family and Will Rogers' parents, had settled in this area as they raised a big family and worked as ranchers and pioneer entrepreneurs. They, along with their famous son and his siblings, were the product of a complex and fascinating background that lay intertwined with some of the key developments in the mid-nineteenth century United States.

The Cherokee Indians originally lived far to the east in the mountainous areas of the Carolinas, Georgia, Alabama, and Tennessee. But by the early 1800s, white settlers had begun overrunning their land, causing the U.S. Government to attempt to buy it while pressuring the tribe to move west of the Mississippi River. A number of Cherokee families, seeing the writing on the wall, began to voluntarily migrate westward to the Indian Territory, which consisted of much of the present state of Oklahoma. They became known as the Old Settlers. Then in 1835, a small group of Cherokees signed the Treaty of New Echota with the American government, which ceded all lands east of the Mississippi River in return for land in the Indian Territory, and they swelled the ranks of the Old Settlers. A majority of Cherokees ignored the agreement, however, and continued to resist white settlers. Led by Principal Chief John Ross, they were finally forced from their ancestral home by the U.S. Government in 1838–1839 and forcibly marched westward on the infamous Trail of Tears, a trek which saw thousands die from illness and exposure. Thus the Indian Territory contained a deeply divided Cherokee tribe, with the Old Settlers having staked out prosperous farms while the newer arrivals struggled to survive after the horrors of their overland march. Tensions regularly erupted into violence over the next decade as the two groups fought over how to reconstitute Cherokee social and political institutions. In 1839, for example, three leaders of the Treaty Party who had played key roles in negotiating the 1835 agreement were assassinated. Stark lines of division were drawn with the wealthier Old Settlers embracing intermarriage with whites, use of the English language, the pursuit of profit, and Southern-style slave labor farming while the newer arrivals were usually subsistence farmers and full-bloods who held on to the traditional Cherokee language and customs.[3]

The Rogers family figured prominently in these developments. Descended from Robert Rogers, a Scotch Irish immigrant who had married a half-blood Cherokee woman around 1800, and then his son, Robert Rogers, Jr., who likewise married a part-Cherokee woman in 1835, they were part of the Old Settlers who arrived early to the Indian Territory. Robert Jr. settled in the eastern section of the Indian Territory near the Arkansas border, and Clement Vann (Clem) Rogers, Will Rogers' father, was born there in 1839. The Rogers farm prospered with the raising of horses and cattle, wheat and corn, and a fruit orchard. As Clem grew up, he became a skilled cowboy who participated in several cattle drives herding long-horned steers to market hundreds of miles away. In 1856 he convinced his family to give him a couple dozen head of cattle, four horses, and two African-American slaves and he struck out for the western region of the Cherokee lands in the Indian Territory. He settled at a site near a tributary of the Caney River, built a small house, and started a ranch along with a trading post to make extra money. Hard-working and ambitious, Clem Rogers prospered. In 1858 he married Mary America Schrimsher, a part-Cherokee young woman from another Old Settler family, and the couple started a family, with eight children arriving at regular intervals over the next two decades. Although husband and wife were quite different in terms of temperament – Clem was quiet, serious, and stern while Mary was vivacious, personable, and light-hearted – the marriage was a solid one.

In 1861, the Rogers family and the Cherokee Nation, like nearly everyone else in the United States, was swept up in the turmoil of the Civil War. Also like the country as a whole, Cherokees in Indian Territory were deeply divided, with many of the newer arrivals and full-blood Cherokees backing the Union, while most of the Old Settlers and mixed-blood Cherokees favored the Confederacy. Clem, like many of this latter group, controlled hundreds of acres and owned a substantial house and several slaves while adopting the proud sensibility of a Southern gentleman. When war between the North and South erupted, Clem enlisted in the regiment of Colonel Stand Watie, a leading Old Settler, who went on to become a brigadier general in the Confederate Army by the end of the war. Mary's brother, John Schrimsher, also fought for the Confederacy. Clem rose to the rank of Captain while also being elected to the Cherokee Confederate Convention in 1862. The collapse of the Confederacy in 1865 was the culmin-ation of a great hardship visited upon many of the Old Settlers, including Clem. His farm had been overrun by marauding Jayhawkers from Kansas during the war, his cattle had been run off or stolen, and his slaves had been freed. Clem got back on his feet by working in "wagon freighting." He drove a six-horse team in a wagon train hauling goods throughout the region and carefully saved his money. He finally accumulated enough to establish a new ranch near the Verdigris River about seven miles away from his old place and just north of the small town of Claremore. It was here that their famous son would come into the world a few years later.[4]

William Penn Adair Rogers was born in 1879 as the youngest of seven children. He would be the family's only surviving son after the death of his older brother, Robert, a few years later. "I was born because it was a habit in those days, people dident know anything else," he later joked. "My folks looked me over and instead of the usual drowning procedure, they said, 'This thing has gone far enough, if they are going to look like this, we will stop.'" The infant was named after Colonel William Penn Adair, a distinguished Cherokee who had served with Clem in Stand Waite's regiment during the Civil War before becoming a delegate of the Cherokee Nation in Washington, DC, for fifteen years after the end of the conflict. Both Clem and Mary Rogers were roughly five-sixteenths Cherokee so Will, like his siblings, would be nine-thirty-seconds Cherokee.[5]

The boy experienced a childhood typical among prosperous farm families on the frontier in the late 1800s. As a baby and toddler, Will spent time in the company of his mother and three sisters – Sallie, Maude, and May – as they performed the daily tasks that guaranteed the family's survival and comfort: cooking and preserving food, baking, gardening, harvesting fruit from the orchard, sewing and washing clothing, housecleaning, carrying water from the well, raising chickens, and feeding the ranch hands. When his mother was preoccupied, Maude, ten years older, looked after him and, according to another family member, the two siblings "were much alike. She had his sense of humor and his warm friendly personality." When Will was old enough to walk, he ventured outdoors and wiled away the days playing on the ranch grounds and romping among the various outbuildings. He spent much time with the children of Rabb Rogers, an African-American and one of Clem's ex-slaves who lived nearby and now labored as one of his old master's hired hands. The youngsters climbed trees, went fishing, and explored the pastures and woods. Like any ranch boy, Will watched his father and his hands break horses, herd cattle, and brand calves and he took to riding at an early age when he was set atop Lummox, a gentle older horse, and delightedly plodded around for hours. A series of ponies followed as his riding skills developed and, looking back years later, he joked that "like other Oklahoma kids I was born bowlegged so I could sit on a horse." In fact, the family later recalled what may have been Will Rogers' first humorous comment when his mother admonished him for taking so long to learn how to read. Assuming a thoughtful pose, the boy replied, "I've got such a good pony that I don't want to waste my time learnin' to read." Another lifelong habit was acquired when the boy took up the lariat and developed a passion for the cowboy skill of roping.[6]

From an early age, young Will enjoyed a special relationship with his mother. Mary America Schrimsher was the daughter of wealthy Cherokee slaveholders who had been among the Old Settlers and was raised on one of the largest plantations in the Cherokee Territory. Born in 1839, she was educated at an academy in Cane Hill, Arkansas and also attended the Cherokee Female Seminary in Park Hill. Mary loved music, playing the piano and singing in a fine contralto voice, and was a good dancer. A tall, slender girl with dark hair and sparkling black eyes, she was witty and vivacious and an abundance of charm made her an attractive guest at social gatherings. Her lighthearted manner belied a religious devotion, for she was a lifelong member of the Methodist Episcopal Church South and sang in its choir.[7]

Mary married Clem Rogers in 1858 – he was a classmate of her brother at Tahlequah Seminary, and they would fight in the same regiment during the Civil War – and moved to Clem's ranch on the Caney River with its big two-room log house. When hostilities between North and South erupted in 1861, Mary and two small children were sent south to Texas to avoid the Union forces from Kansas that soon came sweeping through the Cherokee lands and destroyed the Rogers ranch. At the conclusion of the conflict in 1865, Mary and the children returned to the Indian Territory as Clem worked to rebuild his holdings. When he was able to procure a new ranch and build a new home near the Verdigris River a few miles away from their original place, Mary summoned her energy and talents to transform it into one of the finest ranch houses in the Indian Territory.

The Rogers house on the Verdigris became a showcase in the Cherokee region of the Indian Territory. Begun in summer 1873 and finished about a year and a half later, it was a two-story, white structure featuring plastered walls in the interior, clap-boards on the exterior, and a large porch at the front stretching to a roof portico supported by four large pillars. It had seven large rooms, four fireplaces, two central halls, and an open porch in the rear. An addition on the back side soon added a large dining room, kitchen, and additional bedroom. Mary was very proud of the house and installed rows of cedar trees on either side of the broad stone walkway that led from the front door down to the front gate. Very fond of flowers, she planted large beds of yellow jonquils and white and lavender hyacinths just inside the white picket fence that surrounded a spacious front yard. Even in the winter, her daughter reported, Mary festooned the house with lovely bouquets of "bittersweet from the woods, coxcomb and bachelor buttons from her lovely summer flower garden, combined with cedar and lovely dried and crystallized grasses." These "works of art" were widely admired by friends and visitors.[8]

Mary made the big house on the Verdigris a social center of the area. She was extremely hospitable and brought home guests from Sunday church almost weekly, as well as frequently hosting community socials and dances. Guests from surrounding ranches would arrive to find the Rogers lawn ablaze with light from dozens of lanterns and soon the sounds of fiddles, guitars, and piano could be heard from the parlor as dancers would begin stomping and swaying to the elaborate figures of old-time square dancing. An excellent cook and baker, Mary generously showered friends and neighbors with canned goods, pies, and meals. An amateur nurse, she frequently traveled by horseback or buggy to assist people in the area suffering sickness or going through childbirth. In her own family, Mary helped her children learn music with the piano and singing, and attended to their moral development by insisting they engage in Bible study.[9]

Mary doted on her youngest child, Willie, and he mirrored her sparkling personality. A neighbor lady described how she visited the Rogers home one day and Mary had a pan of yeast sitting on the floor letting it rise. Her young son came along, noticed the pan, and mischievously stepped right into it. The neighbor expected the toddler to get a scolding from his mother but instead Mary smiled and said, "Willie has a good idea. That'll make it sweeter. It'll be the best bread we've ever had." When Will was three years old, his older brother Robert died and that only increased the attention lavished on the only boy in the family. When he got a bit older, Will would stand next to his mother as she played the piano and both of them would sing and according to a family member, "Neighbors liked to come in and he and his mother would put on a little entertainment." A cousin recalled that the sociable Mary would hitch up a white horse to a buckboard wagon, gather up her son, and "the two of them would go visiting together. I have always thought this is where Will got his interest in going to see people. When anybody in our section saw a buckboard and a white horse coming they knew they were in for a good time." Will's wife, writing many years later, noted that "Will and his mother were very close. Her face and her voice always stayed with him . . . . [and] as far back as Will could remember, his mother's soft voice and calm, sweet, unruffled manner remained always the same."[10]

All of which made the unexpected event of 1890 particularly traumatic. In the spring, two of the Rogers girls came down with typhoid fever as it swept through the Verdigris valley and Mary nursed them tirelessly. At the same time, Will came down with the measles from another epidemic and was sent away to recuperate at the home of a friend. Worn down, Mary also was stricken with typhoid and what the local doctor diagnosed as amoebic dysentery. She died on May 28 at the age of fifty. Mary's sudden death was a blow to her family and the entire community, but it hit Will particularly hard. "He was ten years old and was disconsolate, for there had been a bond of love and understanding between them," friends of the family noted. "The two were, in main, of the same nature and it was from his mother that he got his predominant traits." The pain from this loss lingered. According to Will's wife, he "never quite got over his mother's death. He cried when he told me about it many years later. It left in him a lonely, lost feeling that persisted long after he was successful and famous." In a radio broadcast decades later, he recalled of his mother, "My folks have told me that what little humor I have comes from her. I can't remember her humor but I can remember her love and her understanding of me."[11]

The boy's close bond with his mother, and the despair triggered by her early death, only highlighted a more thorny attachment in his life. Also from an early age, Will had developed a difficult relationship with his father that only became more trying with the passage of time. Clement Vann Rogers, a leading figure in the Cherokee tribe, was a serious man and ambitious for material success and status. Through hard work and determination, this rancher, businessman, and entrepreneur had pushed to the highest levels of tribal society. He never quite understood his happy-go-lucky, charming son and vice-versa.

At his large ranch on the Verdigris, Clem presided over affairs not as an effete lord of the manor but as a no-nonsense manager of a large operation who worked right alongside his hired help. According to Ed Sunday, a long-time employee, "Clem Rogers was a ranchman any way you wanted to look at him. He wore tall top cowboy boots with his pant legs stuffed in them, leather chaps, and a western hat of medium size. He was a keen trader, knew cattle, and was one of the best riders I have ever known .... He took part in the roundups, branding, and shipping of steers and, believe me, he was the boss of his range." He became noted for his skill at handling stock and his natural horsemanship. Years later, his famous son recalled Clem's light handling of the reins and easy seat in the saddle, admitting, "Riding along with papa, I never could keep up with him." First focused on grazing cattle on some 60,000 acres of grassland, he had diversified by the 1890s to grow several hundred acres of wheat – in 1895 the Claremore *Daily Progress* dubbed him the "Oologah Wheat King" for his huge harvest – and he was one of the first rural innovators to embrace barbed-wire fencing, crop rotation, and modern farm machinery. Clem became a wealthy man and proud of his position and possessions. If he found someone on his land who did not belong "he would ride up and hit him over the head with a quirt." Some resented his stern sense of privilege, describing him as "rich and haughty – awful haughty. He thought he was monarch of all he surveyed, and he pretty nearly was." But most accorded Clem great respect, electing him as a district judge and a senator in the Cherokee Senate and approving his appointment to commissions to appraise improvements made to Indian lands and negotiate with the federal Dawes Commission on land allotment in preparation for dissolution of the Cherokee Nation. He served as a Cherokee delegate to the constitutional convention preparing for Oklahoma statehood, during which the Cooweescoowee District in which he lived was designated Rogers County in his honor.[12]

This hard-driving, ambitious man began to clash openly with his youngest child as the latter moved into boyhood and then adolescence. In certain ways they were very much alike – willful, self-possessed, determined. Maude reported that her younger brother was a stubborn little boy and Clem often would grow exasperated, shake his head, and say "There's a lot of mule in Willie." Emotionally, however, father and son seemed cut from different bolts of cloth. A kind of muted strain typified their connection. But rather than a simple story of opposition to one another on all fronts, this tale of father and son, like much else in Will Rogers' life, contained complicated elements of attraction and rejection. On the positive side of the relational ledger, the boy deeply admired Clem for his cowboy skills, intelligence, and drive and respected his authority while Clem, for his part, sought the best for his son and indulged his every desire. On the negative side, the two differed profoundly in terms of their work ethic, notion of success, and expectations about themselves and the world.[13]

At the heart of things lay a personality conflict that steadily wedged Clem and Will apart. From boyhood, the boisterous, fun-loving son baffled his hard-driving, sober-minded, ambitious father. A relation explained that Clem was well-known for being tough, gruff, and moody and in company "he would be silent for a long period of time." By contrast, Will always "was the biggest talker. He was the loudest and noisiest boy in any group. But also the best-liked. He liked everybody and everybody liked him. He was fun to be with." When he was still a child, Will's personable nature and lively intelligence caused his mother to remark that he should become a preacher. Clem did not disagree outright, but commented dourly "that so far as he could see there wasn't much money in preaching." As Will grew older, a persistent clash over work habits widened the gap. While the father demanded serious attention from his son to tasks that needed to be completed around the ranch, the younger Rogers regularly drifted off to race around on his pony and "spent more and more time roping and in working out fancy loops and throws." The boisterous Will, noted one family friend, "was a puzzle to his hard-driving father. The boy didn't like to work." The son's dismissal of something so fundamental to the father's makeup created a mutual lack of understanding. According to a family friend, "There was a barrier between Will and his father, a barrier that neither could quite breach."[14]

Ironically, Clem made matters worse by indulging Will at every turn. For all of his frustration, the elder Rogers deeply loved his only son and, according to several observers, spoiled the boy terribly. Will's wife would testify later, "the truth is that, as the only surviving son of an indulgent father, Will had everything he wanted. He had spending money and the best string of cow ponies in the country. No boy in the Indian Territory had more than Uncle Clem's boy." The father funded Will for frequent trips to St. Louis and Kansas City, bought him bicycles and fashionable clothing and fast horses, and arranged for him to get one of the first rubber-tired buggies in the Indian Territory. "Willie grew careless and untidy and his manners were those of a spoiled, impetuous boy who had inherited a natural restlessness and love of freedom that would not submit to discipline of any kind," a family member described. "Will was a restless boy who dodged his responsibilities and would not go to school."[15]

Disagreements set father and son at odds, and the most consistent one involved the boy's intense dislike for schooling in favor of riding and roping. Will had learned to ride at the age of four or five when a pillow was tucked behind the saddle horn and a cowboy would swing him up and into the saddle. His first steed was Lummox and the boy loved to spend hours parading around on the old, gentle gray horse. As his age and skill level increased, it became nearly impossible to pry Will out of the saddle. He rode constantly and fast. Ranch hands on the Rogers place described him hunting coyotes and jack rabbits "not to catch them, but to chase them on horses at top speed miles and miles across the rolling prairie. He liked it because it required fearless riding." He gained a reputation for recklessness in rounding up longhorn cattle at top speed on the open prairie, with other cowboys fearing that "his fast moving horse would hit one of those prairie dog holes and send him into eternity."[16]

Roping followed hard on the heels of riding as a great love in young Will's life. He learned to handle a lariat from Dan Walker, an African-American cowboy who worked on his father's ranch. Walker was an expert at breaking horses and herding cattle, but really excelled at roping where he would use his lariat to snare a recalcitrant steer, gather his horse in the morning, tow a cow mired in a bog, or haul firewood to the ranch house. Will grew fascinated with the veteran cowboy's skill at creating knot and loop, shaking it out, and then deftly manipulating it to fulfill many tasks. He was especially impressed by how Walker, unlike most others who whirled the loop above their head before flinging it toward the target, spread it out at his side before flipping it surely with a quick toss. Will observed him closely and then imitated his techniques. The boy would stand for hours in the back yard roping a large oak stump, and then graduated to goats and calves. He later developed his skills on horseback with similar dedication. Many times ranch hand B. T. Hoopers witnessed young Will "on his horse with rope in hand riding out on a fast trot to the nearby range, roping everything in sight." Later in life, Will explained his obsession. "[You see] the lariat-slinging business drifted into my system when I was pretty young," he wrote. "My father would send me out on the ranch, but instead of riding the range, I'd go off into a shady place and there spend the time practicing with the rope – cutting curliques and things in the prairie breeze or lassoing prairie dogs."[17]

For this energetic outdoor youth who wanted to be a cowboy, book learning held few attractions. When he was sent off to school at age seven, Will began amassing a record of poor performance probably unmatched among schoolchildren in late 1800s Oklahoma. From 1886 to 1897, he attended a series of six schools and either flunked out, was dismissed for rowdy behavior, or simply left. He began at Drumgoole School, a Cherokee elementary school near Chelsea in the Indian Territory and enrolled the following year in Cherokee National Male Seminary in Tahlequah. From 1888 to 1890 he attended the Harrell International Institute, a Methodist boarding school in Muskogee and then settled in for four years at Willie Halsell College in Vinita. He spent 1895–1896 at the Scarritt Collegiate Institute in Neosho, Missouri before leaving to spend two years at the Kemper School, a military academy, in Boonville, Missouri. As an adult, Rogers would joke that he had perfected a scam where he always informed his new teacher that he had finished *McGuffey's Third Reader* and was ready to start the *Fourth Reader*. After a couple of weeks, the teacher would marvel, "I never see you studying yet you seem to know your lessons." Said Rogers, "I had that education thing figured down to a fine point. I knew more about it than McGuffey did."[18]

At his last educational stop, Kemper, Will's antics summarized his fraught relationship with formal learning. Although highly intelligent and possessing an excellent memory, he was a mediocre student who studied when he felt like it – which was seldom – and spent most of his time having fun, racking up demerits for mischief, and yearning for the great outdoors. "I Really Try to be a good sport about this school business, but I am gaggin' at the bit," he wrote to his cousin, Spi Trent. "I can't keep myself inside a school room. I try, all right, an' I reckon my body stays put but I personally am out in the Green Pastures, an' if you ask me, I believe that's where all the learning in the world has been written, if folks wanter bother studyin' it." He liked history and got good marks in that subject and shone in elocution because, "it was impossible for Will to resist the temptation to declaim for laughs. The strange thing is that the elocution teacher, recognizing that the purpose of oratory, after all, is to sway the audience, would give Willie good marks when he succeeded in getting his laughs." Even when he attempted to honor the traditions of Kemper, things went awry. After his first year at the school, he came home and tried to show off the rifle drills and marches he had learned. According to a family report, "in obedience to his own gruff command, he grounded arms with such military snappiness that there was a deafening discharge. It was nearly a fatal accident. His hat spun in the air. The bullet had just grazed his face and he bore always on the side of his head a long white scar." Rogers later summarized his ill-fated stay at the school: "I spent two years at Kemper, one in the guardhouse and one in the fourth grade."[19]

In fact, it was Will's riding and roping addiction that often lured him into trouble at the schools he attended. He initiated one misadventure after another. At his first school at Drumgoole, he was less interested in his studies than in horses. In his words, "We got to running horse races and I had a little chestnut mare that was beating everything that any of them could ride to school and I was losing interest in what we were really there for." At subsequent schools, he constantly got into trouble with his lariat as he roped classmates, animals, and a variety of inanimate objects, usually for laughs. A series of incidents at the Scarritt Collegiate Institute typified Will's penchant for lassoing difficulties. He initially created a stir when he roped a calf in a nearby pasture and swept the bawling creature into a group of female classmates on a walk to "play havoc with their dignity." Later, to the great amusement of his friends, he roped a Grecian statue standing atop a campus fountain and yanked off one of her arms. Finally, he created a scene of hilarious havoc when he roped a colt which then bolted down the street so quickly that he lost hold of the lariat. The beast tore through the campus and passed the school president on a stroll, who unwisely grabbed the trailing rope and was promptly dragged stumbling through the backyard of a nearby house where a clothesline caught under his chin and sent him sprawling. The president did not appreciate the humor of the episode, and young Rogers departed campus at the end of the term.[20]

Will's less than stellar educational career, unsurprisingly, ratcheted up the tension with his father. Clem grew frustrated with his son's failures at school after school and saw them as a sign of his lackadaisical attitude toward life and work. A friend of the family, W. E. Sunday, recalled conversations where the elder Rogers groused that "the young scamp had been sent home [from school] again." "What for?" "Oh, arguing with the teacher." At another point, after sending off his son to military school, a grumpy Clem said, "Well, I've got Willie where he won't do any more arguing with the teachers. They'll chain him down and make him do what I want him to." The son was keenly aware of his father's disapproval and ruefully recalled it two decades later: "My father was pretty well fixed and I being the only son he tried terribly hard to make something out of me. He sent me to about every school in that part of the country. In some of them I would last three or four months." Betty Rogers, Will's wife, later wrote that her husband "always regretted that he hadn't taken advantage of his opportunities to get a good education; there wasn't a day of his life, he said, that he didn't regret it."[21]

An event occurring when he was thirteen years old, however, sealed Will's commitment to riding and roping and finalized his disdain for formal schooling. Ironically, his father arranged it. In summer of 1893, Clem set up a deal to ship cattle by rail to Chicago, took Will with him, and the two visited the World's Fair. They went through the Plaisance, a long strip of shows, booths, and restaurants near the entrance, and ate exotic dishes, rode a camel, played some games, and observed the exotic attractions. Upon entering the official fair grounds, they visited many exhibits and rode the Ferris Wheel. But the high point of the trip came last when they attended the Buffalo Bill Wild West Show. Directors of the fair had refused William F. Cody permission to be part of the exhibition because his show was "undignified," so Cody cleverly rented a fourteen-acre site near the entrance and drew sellout crowds to a horseshoe-shaped amphitheater that seated 22,000 people. Clem and Will had box seats. They saw a string of spectacular riding acts introduced by Buffalo Bill himself featuring the Pony Express, Royal Irish Lancers, French Chasseurs, Russian Cossacks, and Arabs. There was a faux battle between Indian tribes, a replication of a prairie fire, bronco riding, and a demonstration of rifle marksmanship from Cody. But the highlight for Will came in the roping demonstration by Mexican vaqueros. In gaudy outfits, they were led by the greatest roper in the world, Vincente Oropeza, who roped running horses in every way imaginable, leaped in and out of twirling loops, and wrote his name in the air one letter at a time. Will was entranced, and inspired to go home and work obsessively on improving his roping expertise. The Buffalo Bill Show in Chicago probably marked the first time he looked at riding, roping, and cowboys as not just personal amusement but commercial entertainment.[22]

After returning from Chicago, an inspired Will honed his riding and roping skills with newfound enthusiasm and was seldom seen without a lariat in hand. Within a few years, he had secured a speedy, agile cow pony, Comanche, and began entering cowboy competitions on a regular basis. These popular entertainments had emerged in the 1880s and 1890s as sites for local cowboys to show off their skills. Local leaders, seeing how rural folk flocked into town to watch and seeing the potential for promotion and profit, gradually commercialized these shows. They formalized the events, subsidized them to advertise their communities, gathered prize money from local businesses, and created the prototype of the modern rodeo. Young Rogers threw himself into these shows. On July 4, 1899 he won first place in the Claremore steer-roping contest and journeyed eastward three months later to compete in a similar contest at the St. Louis Fair. While he won no prizes, the experience before a large audience "gave me a touch of 'show business' in a way, so that meant I was ruined for life as far as actual employment was concerned," he joked later. Over the next couple of years, Will entered major contests in Oklahoma City, Des Moines, San Antonio, and Memphis as well as many minor events at county fairs, cattlemen conventions, and rural expositions in smaller towns. Clem Rogers did not approve of his son's new avocation, seeing it as just another frivolous pastime. "Willie ain't never going to amount to nothin,'" he burst out to a family member; "all he's good for is to buy up these expensive hosses and fool around [with] ropin' contests – huhhh! He's fixin' to ruin us, do you know that?"[23]

Clem and Will's long-simmering disagreements came to a boiling point when the boy suddenly left the Kemper School and bolted far to the south to find work. A fellow cadet had told Will that a large ranch near Higgins, Texas, run by Perry Ewing, was in need of cowboys to handle his cattle herd. So in March 1898, burdened with demerits, unable to face the prospect of more schooling, and, in his words, "leery of going home to my dad," Will snuck out of Boonville in the middle of the night and took the train for the Lone Star state. He made his way to Ewing's ranch, and the proprietor agreed to hire him. But recognizing that the boy came from an upstanding family, he wrote Clem to clarify that this situation had his approval. In the words of Ewing's son, "Will's father was thoroughly miffed at Will's desertion of school and wrote back for him to keep him and that if he could get any work out of Will it would be better than he'd ever done." To friends at home, Clem angrily declared, "Do you know what that damned boy has done? He's run away from school and he's over in the Texas Panhandle, digging ditches for 50 cents a day. Well, I'm going to let him stay there and rot."[24]

For the next six months, Rogers worked as a cowboy, first at the Ewing spread and then at two other Texas ranches. With each outfit he went on old-fashioned cattle drives where a handful of ranch hands herded thousands of animals over hundreds of miles to destinations in Kansas. Will loved the beauty and spaciousness of the plains, the horsemanship and roping skills required by the work, the camaraderie of the chuckwagon meals, and sleeping on the ground under the open stars. He would value this experience throughout his life. "That plains was the prettiest country I ever saw in my life, as flat as a beauty contest winner's stomach, and prairie lakes scattered all over it," he reminisced fondly upon revisiting the area in 1934. "And mirages! You could see anything in the world – just ahead of you." But as his work opportunities dried up with the onset of cold weather, the young man returned to the Indian Territory in late fall 1898 with no prospects and no plans.[25]

Setting aside his frustration, Clem tried to heal the rift with his son. Having moved to Claremore to pursue entrepreneurial opportunities as a banker, the father offered to set Will up as manager of his cattle ranch and purchase a cattle herd for him. Will agreed to the arrangement, but then quickly tired of the work. Instead of herding cattle on horseback, he was expected to plow up the plains and plant wheat and corn, cut hay to stack over the winter, and jump off his horse to open gates as his stock was moved from one fenced pasture to another. So for the next three years the young man did the bare minimum of work required to keep the ranch afloat and spent most of his time in amusements. He and his cousin, Spi Trent, built a small makeshift cabin away from the main house, where a family of renters was staying, and there they whiled away the hours as carefree bachelors. Will entered any steer roping contests that he saw and regularly competed throughout the region. Because of the nearby railroad lines, he was able to travel easily to Kansas City, St. Louis, Texas, Memphis, New York, and even San Francisco.[26]

But young Rogers spent most of his free time socializing with a group of friends and relatives his age from the area. Much of his life became one long round of parties, picnics, dancing, singing, hayrides, swimming and every manner of social gathering. He built a wooden platform for dancing in the yard of the ranch house and the group would go late into the night whirling and stomping to lively music. Will excelled at dancing and singing. A member of the group, Gazelle Lane, said of him, "What energy! He could dance all night, and when the dance was over, would be going as strong as when the dance had started." He especially loved the "cakewalk," a high-kicking, strutting dance style, and won several local competitions. Attracted to the popular music of the 1890s, he purchased sheet music for the latest ragtime and minstrel songs whenever he went to Kansas City and developed a taste for the popular "coon songs" of the era, such as "I Ain't Got a Dollar I Can Call My Own," and would sing them with great verve to the great amusement of his friends. To round out his social image, Will served as the life of the party. Seeking to impress the girls, he bought a rubber-tired buggy – the first in the area – and sported them around at every opportunity. In addition, according to a friend, "he got a derby hat and the fanciest clothes that could be procured in Kansas City and became the flashiest dresser in the Cherokee Nation." His humor appeared constantly. At a swimming party, where the boys went behind one clump of bushes and the girls another to change into old clothes before plunging into the water, he charged toward the female sanctuary shouting, "You can look now, girls. I've got my hat on." As another friend summarized, "Everybody knew him, for he was always the center of attention. He could think of more devilment in a minute than an ordinary person could in a month."[27]

But the relentless laughter and fun could not completely compensate for an obvious lack of purpose. As always, Clem stood nearby as a stern judge. Will admitted many years later that his haphazard management of the ranch severely disappointed his father once again. "Well, I dident exactly run it to suit him. I danced all my young life to the music of old country fiddlers," he noted. "Between dances and roping contests, I dident have time for much serious ranching business." A disastrous, near fatal, incident seemed to symbolize just how much of a dead-end the young man had reached in his life. After accompanying a trainload of cattle to California by rail, he and another cowboy visited San Francisco to see the sights and stayed at a small hotel. That night, either through a failure to turn off the gas after blowing out the lamp in their room (they were used to kerosene lamps) or from some kind of leak, both young men were overcome while they slept. The next morning they were discovered unconscious and rushed to a hospital where they were revived only after several hours of frantic efforts by doctors. Will staggered home in debilitated condition. "The stuff had located in my system," he explained, and Clem stepped in to help his wayward son recuperate; "papa sent me to Hot Springs, Arkansas, to take the baths."[28]

Will Rogers' youthful struggle with several highly-charged family issues – a close relationship with his mother tragically brought to a premature close, a clash of personalities and values with his father that worsened over time, a love of outdoor life and hatred for formal schooling – largely reflected the singular interaction of the boy's temperament with the Rogers family dynamic. They worked to shape the young man's independent, restless, fun-loving personality and his life-long devotion to the traditions and habits of the cowboy. But another issue emerged from his childhood to influence the mature man: coming to terms with his Cherokee heritage.

* * * * *

As one of the most famous and influential people in the United States during the two decades from the late-1910s to the mid-1930s, Will Rogers seldom talked about his background as a Cherokee Indian. When he did, he often joked about it, as when he employed this quip numerous times throughout his career: "My ancestors didn't come over on the Mayflower. They met the boat." Another joke came while performing with a circus in South Africa in 1902, where he played, in his words "blood curdling scenes of western life in America, showing encounters with Indians and robbers. I was an Indian but I screamed so loud that I liked to scared all the people out of the tent." In the late 1910s, while performing with the *Ziegfeld Follies*, he became friends with comedian Eddie Cantor, who introduced him to kosher food in New York. Rogers liked it so much that he began to partake a couple of times a week. When he left for California to make movies with Samuel Goldwyn, he said, "Eddie, they ain't never gonna believe it in Hollywood." "Believe what?" said Cantor. Replied Rogers, "That this Cherokee cowboy has become a Jewish Indian." Such comments suggested that the entertainer viewed his ancestry as little more than a comic prop.[29]

But in March 1928, Rogers displayed a radically different sensibility. Speaking in Asheville, North Carolina, after visiting the recently opened Great Smoky Mountains National Park, he appeared before 3,000 Cherokees who still lived in the area on the ancient lands of the tribe. He did a few of his popular rope tricks and told some of his trademark humorous stories. But the Indians failed to respond, looking on respectfully and stoically but not uttering so much as a chuckle. Suddenly Rogers turned serious, lambasting Andrew Jackson as the "Betrayer" who had forcibly removed much of the tribe to far-off Oklahoma and took their land many decades before. "I got no use for [Jackson] or any of his methods, for all he ever did was pounce on the Indians," he declared angrily . The novelist Ben Dixon MacNeill, who was in attendance, described a "furious" Rogers who "went into a berserk rage for about three minutes" as some "long-forgotten, in-bred memory welled up in his heart." The culmination of this outburst came in dramatic fashion as the Cherokees responded explosively and "the quiet was ripped by the screaming war cry of the tribe, while Rogers stood white, trembling, and actually aghast at himself." A bit later, the shaken speaker "said wonderingly that he didn't know what had got into him."[30]

What should be made of Rogers' divergent attitudes toward his Indian background and identity? His biographers have differed, offering diametrically opposed views that follow their subject's conflicting expression. Ben Yagoda, looking at the humorist, concluded "Other than a gag or two, and an occasional barbed reference to [Andrew] Jackson, Will Rogers did not make much of his Cherokee heritage." But Amy Ware, looking at the advocate, insisted that Rogers fully embraced his Indian background and emerged as "a Cherokee artist" who "profoundly shaped the face of American popular culture by calling upon Cherokee traditions." How can such skilled interpreters be talking about the same person?[31]

It is because, paradoxically, both are correct, just incompletely so. In fact, Rogers demonstrated a "double consciousness" about his Indian heritage that combined these divergent impulses. W. E. B. DuBois, the African-American intellectual, defined this sensibility in his 1903 classic book, *The Souls of Black Folk.* "It is a peculiar sensation, this double-consciousness, this sense of always looking at one's self through the eyes of others, of measuring one's soul by the tape of a world that looks on in amused contempt and pity," he explained. "One ever feels his two-ness – an American, a Negro; two souls, two thoughts, two unreconciled strivings; two warring ideals in one dark body." As an American Indian, another variety of outsider, Rogers displayed precisely such a conflicted emotional attitude about the background in which he grew up. On the one hand, he evinced great pride in his lineage and culture, saying, "there's nothing of which I am more proud than my Cherokee blood." But on the other, he displayed a keen awareness of how it placed him at the margins of the dominant culture and society. Rogers expressed a powerful aspiration to succeed in white America, while at the same time betraying a subtle resentment about the need to do so.[32]

Contributing to this double consciousness of his "Indianness" was Rogers' complicated personal experience as a Cherokee. The Rogers family were aristocrats within the tribe who oversaw extensive landholdings, served as political leaders in the Cherokee nation, owned enslaved African-Americans, and fought with the Confederacy during the Civil War. This created another layer of paradox in Will Rogers' background that shaped his own version of double consciousness – an outsider in the larger culture, but a privileged elite within his own community. This complicated sensibility would play out on a national stage during adulthood and feed the insights and humor that made its holder a national treasure. But it began during his youth in the Indian Territory of Oklahoma.

Will Rogers grew up in a family atmosphere where economic success and respect for American social values of individualism, ambition, and opportunity held sway. Both the Rogers clan and the Schrimshers were Old Settlers who arrived early in the Indian Territory and staked a claim to prosperity and social advancement. This heritage pushed Rogers to embrace a modernizing, assimilationist attitude formed by his family's history as part of a high-achieving tribal elite. Their point of view melded respect for Cherokee traditions with a dedicated pursuit of success – its expectations and standards – as defined by the broader Anglo-American culture. Clem Rogers proved an adept disciple as he achieved economic wealth, social standing, and political prominence in equal measure. His son, while rebelling against adopting an entrepreneurial role himself, was quite content to accept the social perks and material rewards accruing to the offspring of a rich man. Like his father, but in his own fashion, he sought to close the distance between white and Indian society.

As an adolescent, for instance, Will and several other young men were made honorary members of the Pocahontas Club, a young women's group to which his sisters and other prosperous young Cherokees belonged. This organization, in the words of a historian, sought to "find a balance between their modern, quite American lives, on the one hand, and their Cherokee traditions, on the other." Dressed in the latest fashions, these children of prosperous Cherokee families held parties and picnics, engaged in contests and games, discussed literature, and imbibed ice cream and cake. But such social activities often involved "playing Indian" to connect, however loosely, with their tribal customs and traditions. The club constructed a float for a Claremore street fair featuring some members in full warrior regalia (along with a teepee) preparing to execute Captain John Smith as Pocahontas intervened, while other members were dressed in the modern fashions of white society. Another time, the club hosted "an evening with Hiawatha" where members sat on Indian blankets and Will Rogers "made an appearance in full Indian costume – war paint, tomahawk and other paraphernalia, favoring the company with several excellent songs."[33]

Young Rogers' involvement with "stomp dances" displayed a similar assimila-tionist impulse. In the period when he half-heartedly managed his father's old ranch and threw his energy into socializing and amusements, he became an enthusiastic participant in this traditional activity among Indian youth in the area. The "stomp dance" was an English term for the vigorous "shuffle and stomp" Indian dance that usually occurs around a central fire with call-and-response songs providing music and turtle-shell rattles a rhythm. Will "was the leader of our stomp dances," a participant noted. "They were held outdoors Saturday nights on the little round knoll north of the Oowala Schoolhouse. Will always wanted us to dress up like Indians and mostly we would do that. He would dress up, too, and, now and then, would let out a war whoop that sounded like the Battle of Claremore Mound." But these dances were not pursued in a spirit of tribal purity stressing traditional religious connotations, but co-mingled with other kinds of amusement by these vivacious young people: "cakewalk" dancing, singing popular melodies, and a variety of games and frivolities. As a historian has explained, these hybrid stomp dances "fused modern U.S. pastimes with Cherokee-specific events."[34]

Will's assimilationist temper influenced his love life. When courting a young non-Indian woman in this period, Will composed letters to her that papered over the cultural differences with ironic, facetious comments about her visit to his "wild tribe," a promise to hang her photograph in his "Indian wigwam," and his determination to remain her "Injun cowboy." Later in life, as an entertainer and celebrity, Rogers often pursued a similar strategy when upholding his par-ticular heritage. Assuming a slightly defensive stance, he couched praise in terms of his tribe's adoption of Anglo-American standards, as when he told a newspaper

27

interviewer in 1906, "I'm a Cherokee and they're the finest Indians in the world. No 'blanket Indians' about them. We are civilized and educated . . . . We have our own schools, and the boys' and girls' seminaries in the Territory are just as fine as any in the country." Rogers displayed the characteristics of the pragmatic assimilationist seeking to transcend his Indian ancestry and succeed in the broader society, to meet *its* standards and beat it at its own game.[35]

This accommodating mindset, however, barely covered a subtle, persistent undercurrent of resistance and resentment. Even as a boy, Rogers nurtured a deep sense of Indian identity and grievance against white society that would shoot to the surface occasionally, but powerfully, throughout his life. At the Kemper School, his first sustained stay outside of a tribal environment, snickering cadets nicknamed him "Swarthy" and "Wild Indian." While accepting these slights in good humor, he also vigorously defended his tribal heritage when he perceived the need. "Once a classmate referred to a certain Indian chief as a thoroughbred. Will's voice rose to a high pitch in resentment as he explained that 'fullblood' was the proper term and that it spoiled his whole afternoon to hear someone call a fine Indian a thoroughbred," according to a teacher. "Again in a 'bull session' a cadet inadvertently, or perhaps purposefully remarked that Indians and Negroes were very much alike. Will lost no time in challenging the remark. With much heat and no humor he argued that the two races were wholly different in origin, ideals, characteristics, and possibilities." While at Kemper, young Rogers occasionally received a check from his father and would walk down to the Commercial Bank in Boonville to cash it. A classmate who often accompanied him reported, "Hanging on the wall was an ornate chromo of 'Custer's Last Fight.' One day Will looked at it and said, 'That's the only picture I ever saw where the Indians got the best of it.'"[36]

A strong prod to Rogers' sense of Indian identity came from his close friendship with Charley McClellan. A fellow Cherokee who grew up on a nearby ranch, McClellan went to school with Will at Willie Halsell College and shared his love of riding and steer roping. They stayed good friends throughout their adolescent years and when young Rogers was off at additional boarding schools, he wrote to McClellan grousing about his dislike of academics and yearning for the cowboy life. A one-quarter Cherokee like Will, Charley's distinguishing characteristic was his passionate embrace of traditional Indian life. He liked to dress in buckskin leggings, moccasins, and breech clout, wore his hair in a long braid, and built an authentic teepee for the stomp dances of the Pocahontas Club. He increased his knowledge of Indian culture at every opportunity. When the train carrying the Buffalo Bill show stopped in Claremore, McClellan immediately went to the Sioux Indians in the group and engaged them for the entire stay. At various times he visited with members of the Kaw and Shawnee tribes to learn their customs and dances, and occasionally he would give speeches in the

Cherokee language that Will would translate. Rogers' close friendship with this fervent Indian traditionalist undoubtedly strengthened his own identification with a Cherokee heritage.[37]

The proud, defensive, sometimes resentful portion of Rogers' Indian "double consciousness" persisted throughout his life. After becoming famous, he periodically chastised American society for mistreating the Indian people. In 1926, he pled for the preservation of a Creek Indian council house still standing near Okmulgee that was under threat of destruction from oil drillers. "Listen, you oil men . . . . Don't take that building out of the square," he told a big crowd. He reminded them that the Cherokees had "our old council house over at Tahylequah. We've got it right where it was erected and it's going to stay there . . . . The old boys that built your council house were here quite a spell before you oil and business men arrived in this neck of the woods. Remember that." In 1930, he wrote an article complaining that the federal government had purchased the Cherokee Strip in 1893 for a pittance. "I think the Government only give us about a dollar an acre for it. We had it for hunting grounds, but we never knew enough to hunt [for] oil on it." In another newspaper piece, he recalled that the government had sent the Indians to Oklahoma with "a treaty that said, 'You shall have this land as long as the grass grows and water flows' . . . . Then the Government took it away from us again. They said the treaty only refers to 'water' and 'grass'; it don't say anything about oil." On his radio show, he denounced more broadly America's unfair treatment of the Indians. "Every man in our history that killed the most Indians has got a statue built for him," he asserted. "The Government, by statistics, shows they have got 456 treaties that they have broken with the Indians. That is why the Indians get a kick out of reading the Government's usual remark when some big affair comes up, 'Our honor is at stake.'"[38]

Rogers' "double consciousness" about his Indian identity took shape during boyhood in the cultural maelstrom of America's late nineteenth-century frontier. Ultimately, it fed an adult sensibility that would prove so attractive to millions: a profound respect for mainstream American values combined with an equally profound respect for the outsider.

* * * * *

As Will Rogers' youth came to a close, several factors had clearly emerged to shape the man who would become the darling of the American people in later years. First, even as a boy, he assumed a position of mediating between divergent impulses: at the personal level, between the wit and charm and gaiety of his mother and the stern, steady, no-nonsense temperament of his father; at a broader level, between the Cherokee values and traditions of his people and the expectations of the dominant Anglo-American culture. Second, young Will personified a broader cultural shift when he rebelled against the dominant values of nineteenth-century America in an ongoing clash with his father. While Clem had pursued an agenda of hard-driving ambition, character formation, work ethic, and profit seeking characteristic of the expansive society of Victorian America, his boisterous son had sought happiness in a newer ethic of fun, amusement, and self-fulfillment. These new trends typifying a new age would carry the son to unimagined heights of popularity and influence within a couple of decades.

Most significantly, however, Will's boyhood played out amidst a social transformation in the American West that changed a centuries-long trend in the nation's history: the closing of the frontier in the late 1800s. This defining moment in American history marked the end of one era and the dawning of another as westward expansion across space lurched to a halt and the construction of a more complex society accelerated. It is tempting to see a simple reflection of this situation in the Rogers family, with Clem symbolizing a vanishing age and Will symbolizing an emerging one. But the picture was more complicated. In fact, it pitted a romantic son against a realist father. The younger Rogers reached into the past for inspiration as he plotted his way into an unknown future while the older man embraced the practical, evolving possibilities of the present.

By the end of the century, Clem had adapted to the new realities of western life where the farmer was elbowing aside the rancher, barbed wire was closing off the free-range plains, and the raising of crops was earning an equal place alongside the herding of longhorn cattle. The building of railroad lines across the Indian Territory in the 1870s and 1880s – including one that bisected Clem's ranch in 1889 – accelerated such changes and prompted the growth of small towns along the railroad stations. While Clem initially lamented the intrusion of hordes of white homesteaders and laborers and the disappearance of valuable grazing lands, he eventually made his peace with change by embracing commercial farming, feeding shorthorn cattle in fenced areas, raising hogs, growing wheat, and breeding horses. He signaled his final accommodation at century's end when he left his ranch entirely in 1898 and moved into a framed house in Claremore. The following year he joined a partnership to establish the First National Bank, for which he became vice president. The elder Rogers pressured his boisterous son to act likewise and embrace a life of the hard-working rural entrepreneur, thereby earning a steady income and, in the best family tradition, becoming a pillar of the community. But Will had other ideas. [39]

The younger Rogers cherished a romantic vision, now evaporating, of the cowboy freely riding the range and detested the confinement and drudgery of crop farming and fenced-in livestock. He confessed his inner feelings to his wife many years later. She reported that the adolescent Will was "interested only in ranching, and the open range was even then disappearing. He made his friends among the cowboys – that was the life he wanted and the life he chose to follow." When the Indian Territory was officially opened up to homestead settlement in 1889 and the open grazing lands disappeared even more rapidly, the older frontier society began to vanish. Even Clem's huge ranch shrank to the size of a "good-sized farm" and "taking care of the little bunch of cattle on what was left of his father's place was tame ranching for Willie." In later life, at the height of his fame, Will expressed these sentiments with considerable poignancy. "[A]t heart, I love ranching. I have always regretted that I didn't live thirty or forty years earlier and in the same old country – the Indian Territory," he related. "I would have liked to have gotten there ahead of the 'nesters,' the barbed wire fence, and so-called civilization. I wish I could have lived my whole life then."[40]

Rogers' intense nostalgia for a declining way of life, however, did not curdle into reactionary bitterness. It sought other means of expression. His cowboy passion initially inspired participation in the riding and roping contests that became such a large part of his life in late adolescence, but such activity only sated a portion of his hunger. So Will went off in search of new frontiers in other places where he could ride and rope and herd cattle in wide open spaces. This quest would take him to far-flung destinations around the globe – South America, Africa, Australia – where he would learn that recapturing the vanishing frontier still proved elusive. But his travels would bring an unexpected boon by opening up a new vocational world of popular entertainment. There he discovered that he could recreate the beloved cowboy of his imagination in a commercial form.

2

The Cherokee Kid

I N 1899, NEAR THE HEIGHT OF HIS REVOLT against the regimen of the
schoolroom and the drudgery of closed-field farming, Will Rogers made one of
the most important connections of his life. Amusing himself with riding and roping
contests, he had won such a July 4th event in Claremore. Subsequently, someone
submitted his name to a much larger regional contest at the yearly fair in St. Louis and,
as Rogers later explained, "the first thing I knew I was getting transportation for myself
and pony to the affair." He fared poorly in the competition – "I made the serious
mistake of catching my steer and he immediately jerked me and my Pony down for our
trouble" – but reaped a much larger dividend. He met Colonel Zack Mulhall.[1]

"Colonel" Mulhall (it was strictly an honorary moniker) was a colorful
character. Raised as an orphan, in adulthood he had become a livestock purchas-
ing agent for big railroad companies and accumulated thousands of acres of land.
He operated a large ranch near Guthrie, Oklahoma and made a lucrative living
raising cattle and breeding racehorses, in the process building a large stable and
racetrack on the property. He and his wife had five children, while he also
fathered two children with a mistress twenty-five years his junior, both of whom
were taken in by his saintly spouse and raised as legitimate members of the family.
By the century's end, Mulhall branched out and became a showman. He began
organizing cowboy competitions and put together a troupe of working cowhands
for his shows, labeling them the "Congress of Rough Riders and Ropers." Mulhall
saw something in Rogers when he competed in St. Louis and invited the young
man to join his show, where he made a handful of appearances in 1900 and 1901.
In addition to riding and roping, Rogers participated in a ruse where he pretended to be part of Mulhall's "Cowboy Band," a collection of sixty musicians
dressed in colorful outfits, and held a trombone although he couldn't play a note
on it. After the band performed a few tunes, Mulhall challenged anyone in the
audience to compete against band members in steer roping, after which Rogers

and several other ringers would display their skills to the great delight of the crowd. In addition, the young performer became a regular visitor to the Mulhall ranch, where he became very fond of the entire family and vice versa.[2]

Colonel Mulhall had a noticeable impact on young Rogers. According to Spi Trent, a cousin, the showman "was a good influence on Will as he was on many another young feller. It seems like from that time on Will was more serious about making something of himself." He felt the first tug of attraction to the world of entertainment. These appearances, he joked later, "gave me a touch of 'show business' in a way, so that meant I was ruined for life as far as actual employment was concerned." At this point in his life, however, Rogers was too restless to settle down with the Mulhall organization. The mystique of the entertainment world was alluring, but not yet compelling for this footloose young man. Rogers still yearned to lead the cowboy life and suspected that if it was no longer possible in Oklahoma, it may have survived in other areas of the world. Armed with more hope than knowledge, he left his native country and became a roustabout for nearly three years as he traveled the world. But this romantic cowboy soon discovered that the frontier was vanishing everywhere as he chased it across the globe from South America to Africa to Australia.[3]

But Rogers' journey, it turned out, was internal as well as geographical. While he failed to find those wide-open spaces where cowboys could herd cattle for weeks and sleep under the stars, he discovered other, more important things about himself. Gazing homeward from foreign climes, Rogers grew to appreciate America and its culture of freedom and opportunity. Confronting stifling hierarchies of power and privilege in more traditional societies, and doubtless drawing upon his own experience as a Cherokee, he sharpened a populist sensibility that sympathized with outsiders and ordinary people. Perhaps most importantly, he gradually embraced the vocation of entertainment, first out of desperation and then out of affinity. Will Rogers returned home after two-and-a-half years abroad with a firmer sense of himself and his future.

Thus Rogers' failure overseas, ironically, marked the beginning of his great success in his own country. For his inability to find a new frontier nudged him from the world of the working cowboy to that of the showman cowboy. There the mythos of the man with the rope and the saddle – transported from reality into the realm of the imagination – proved to be both popular and profitable. Returning to embrace the world of Colonel Zack Mulhall, Rogers became a featured attraction at the St. Louis World's Fair and then headed east to New York City to engage with the broader American entertainment world. "The Cherokee Kid," as he dubbed himself, set off on a path to fame and influence that would surpass his wildest dreams.

* * * * *

Done with schooling, dissatisfied with managing his father's shrunken ranch, and tired of frivolous social activities, Will Rogers became profoundly restless at the dawn of the new century. Like many others in the Indian Territory of Oklahoma, he heard tales and rumors about exciting opportunities opening up in Argentina, the site of a thriving cattle business. But while others were satisfied with savoring the stories, a frustrated Rogers decided to see for himself. "I had heard that the Argentine Republic was a great ranch country, so I sold a bunch of my cattle and took a boy named Dick Parris with me and we hit the trail for South America," he recalled in later years. When Will told his father about his plan, a heated argument ensued as Clem labeled this another one of his son's wild, irresponsible ideas. But he was unable to sway the young man, and with characteristic forbearance he agreed to let him go his own way and even bought back his cattle herd for 3,000 dollars.[4]

Full of confidence and unburdened by any actual knowledge, Rogers and Parris departed for New Orleans in March 1902, assuming they could easily catch a ship sailing south to Argentina. They were dumbfounded upon discovering none were available. Acting upon advice from sources in the port, they took a train to New York but were stymied once again when they learned the next ship for South America would not leave for months. Advised that the quickest way to find passage to Argentina was to go to England and catch a ship from there, the two young Americans sailed for Southampton on the *S.S. Philadelphia*. To his intense discomfort, Rogers discovered that he was extremely prone to seasickness. He reported in a letter home that they "landed after eight long days of heaving forth everything he looked at." They found lodging in a small hotel – he wisecracked that it was "a nice room almost papered [over] with pictures of Queen Victoria, who certainly had a stand in with the Photographer" – and then went up to London for some sightseeing.[5]

While touring the English capital, Rogers delighted in making fun of stuffy English tradition. In letters home he referred to King Edward VII, just about to be coronated following the death of Queen Victoria, as "his Royal Liftiness," "His Nobs," and "His Muchness" and the city constabulary as "London Robert." He had no fear of the Royal Horseguards, explaining "we was safe from that Geezer on the horse cause you would have to give him three days notice to shed some of that wardrobe so he could handle his artillery." Walking through Westminster Abbey and viewing the monuments erected to the great men of England, he joked that "I felt a curious sort of sensation creep over me while looking at this, although I knew very few of the men personally." After several days of amusement, the pair of Americans sailed for South America, going through several European ports and the Atlantic islands before landing in Buenos Aires in early May 1902. Once again, Rogers suffered from seasickness through the entire voyage.[6]

Several days in the city prefaced a trip into the interior in search of work, when Dick Parris, intensely homesick, decided to return home and Rogers paid for his passage to the United States. Left alone, the young American's hopes of finding a new frontier were soon dashed. He was able to secure a couple of brief jobs on cattle ranches over the next few weeks but it was not what he had expected. Instead of an open prairie with a vibrant cattle industry full of good-paying jobs for the skilled cowboy, he found a paternal system dominated by great landowners. Instead of opportunity, he found paltry wage labor and widespread poverty. A small group of Argentine elites owned most of the land and enhanced their economic power by keeping a firm grip on national political power. In fact, Rogers encountered the same trends in the Argentine ranch country that he had seen at home: tribal land transformed into plots of private property; fencing of open range land; landowners turning to commercial endeavors and renting ranches to tenants. The estancia owners typically lived in Buenos Aires, where they involved themselves in trade, banking, and commercial enterprises. They rented plots in their large ranches to tenant farmers, or turned them over entirely to managers. Many of these overseers were Englishmen, who often disliked Americans and were reluctant to hire them, while most of the gaucho ranch workers were part Indian.[7]

Rogers felt alienated on all fronts. In a letter home, he explained, "This is no place to make money unless you have at least $10,000 or more and then you may do some good." While admiring the skills of gauchos, he blanched at their rock-bottom pay of 7–8 dollars a month. He despaired of a cattle industry hamstrung by absentee landlords and city-bred Englishmen who didn't how to ride, how to manage a big ranch, or handle large herds of cattle. At the national level, he grew disgusted by evidence of economic and political malfeasance and concluded that Argentina had "the most corrupt and unstable of any government in the world." But even as he recoiled from the baneful behavior of the wealthy classes, Rogers felt no kinship with the thousands of immigrants streaming into Argentina from other nations and saw them as riff-raff. In a letter home, he described them as "a lot of 'dagoes' from all over the world and all having a different lingo." The daily difficulty of coping with a different language and culture exacerbated his discontent. Typically, he tried to make light of it: "I am trying to learn Spanish. I think I can say 6 words. Did know 7 and forgot one."[8]

Rogers' only solace came from indulging in popular entertainment. While in Buenos Aires, the amiable young man fell in with sailors from the U.S. battleship *Atlanta*, where he taught them the latest "coon songs" since they had not been home for two years. The sailors had a "minstrel troupe" and they urged him to enlist and join them but he declined. Rogers also accompanied the sailors to an English-speaking concert hall where he enthusiastically joined in singing.[9]

Finally, broke and without prospects, Rogers decided to leave South America. "I breezed around Argentina for 5 months till I was plum busted," he confessed. "When I went to leave the country I found I dident have enough dough to make the first payment on a soda cracker." Forced to give up his hotel room and sleep in a city park, the chastened young man wrote his sisters, "I just begin to see what little I did know about this world." He wandered down to the stockyards near the docks in search of work on a departing ship and sensed an opportunity when he spied some gauchos trying unsuccessfully to rope mules to load on a big steamship bound for South Africa. Rogers grabbed a lariat and nabbed one on the first try, which so impressed the boss that he promised the American twenty-five cents for every creature he could rope. After working all day with great success and skipping lunch and dinner, he was offered a job on the boat, in his words, "chaperoning them mules and she-cows to Africa. Figuring I might get a chance to eat, I took it."[10]

So in August of 1902 Rogers departed for South Africa working aboard a British ship, the *Kelvinside*. He had been hired as a caretaker for a huge shipment of animals – 750 mules, 300 cows, 700 sheep, 300 work horses, 50 thoroughbred race horses, 40 Shetland ponies – purchased by a wealthy farmer and horse breeder, James Piccione, who also had promised him work upon arrival. But recurring bouts of seasickness made Rogers fit only for duties as a night watchman while the crew slept. Ruefully, he described his position as "chambermaid for a parcel of mules" and promised to send his sisters something he had written on board: "a special edition of my Drama '25 days on a floating dung hill or where did he kick you.'" After a month of sailing, the steamship arrived in the port of Durban in the province of Natal, where Piccione arranged for Rogers to get a work permit. The young American then helped drive the livestock north about 150 miles to Piccione's farm just south of Ladysmith.[11]

The Piccione estate was one of the largest in Natal, and its wealthy owner not only raised cattle and sheep but trained thoroughbred horses for the international racing circuit. Rogers reported that his employer was "worth $35,000,000 [and] lives on his farm and maintains the finest racing stables in the country. He has a private race course and his stables are veritable palaces, being heated by steam and lighted by electricity. He also has a system of waterworks." During several months of labor on the Piccione farm, Rogers performed a variety of tasks. He fed, watered, and exercised the racehorses and displayed them for potential buyers when Piccione was trying to clinch a sale. Other times he worked with the veterinary caring for sick animals and occasionally with the blacksmith shoeing horses. Once, he broke a wild horse that had thrown one of the other farmhands.[12]

As in Argentina, Rogers was struck by restrictive social conditions that intensified his concern for the plight of common people. He arrived in South

Africa about three months after the end of the Boer War, which had begun in 1899 and ended in 1902 with the military triumph of the British over the Dutch settlers and the Afrikaner republics. In addition, the country was witnessing its own closing of the frontier around the turn of the century. British forces had laid waste to the Boers' houses and farms and pushed them into the interior and the evidence of destruction was still apparent in Natal when Rogers arrived. He identified with the Boers, seeing them as ordinary, hard-working citizens oppressed by a hierarchical elite. Like the Cherokees, these farmer-ranchers had been subjected to forced relocation and migration while the image of the independent, mounted Afrikaner rifleman was similar to that of the rugged American cowboy. He accused the English of always exploiting their colonies and claimed it would "only be a short time until this country will be no good, for all the English colonies have been done for, same as this will be." He argued that the Boers, in contrast, were "great fighters and very shrewd" and "as fine a lot of people as one would wish to see; peaceful, law-abiding, and friendly to all."[13]

The Boer War and triumph of British colonialism also culminated a long process of Black African dispossession begun by the Dutch. British military campaigns had destroyed many of their villages and uprooted significant portions of the native population. Rogers, while fascinated by Black Africans, was not terribly sympathetic to them. He realized they stood at the bottom of the social ladder in colonial South Africa but believed they probably belonged there. "All common labor is done by kaffirs or negroes. You have to see them to realize what wild looking people they are. All have rings, chains, and all kinds of old scrap iron in their ears and nose. Lots of them have horns tied on their heads," he wrote in a letter to the *Claremore Progress*. "As to other wearing apparel, there is little to speak of. They travel at a run all the time and are always singing. They are as crazy as snakes."[14]

As in Argentina, when Rogers turned away from social issues he frequently found amusement and solace in popular entertainment. Exchanges of letters with his sisters and friends in the United States were full of references to the latest songs from Tin Pan Alley, and his correspondents even sent him sheet music for best sellers such as "After the Ball," by Charles K. Harris. Rogers and other farm hands would gather outside of the owner's residence on many evenings where his daughter – apparently a rather plain young woman whom he described as "a damsel of some twenty winters, Which by the way must have been a bit hard" – would appear at the parlor window and lead the singing of popular songs. Rogers also attended a vaudeville show when visiting Cape Town and saw a juggler and comedian who spoke with an American accent. He went backstage afterwards and struck up a conversation with the entertainer, whom he would befriend many years later when both were on the vaudeville circuit in the United States. The man was W. C. Fields.[15]

In fact, Rogers' fondness for popular entertainment prompted a far-reaching move in late 1902. After driving a herd of mules into Ladysmith and finishing his work obligation to James Piccione, he went to the showgrounds on the edge of town and contacted Texas Jack, the impresario of a Wild West show currently playing. When the young man asked for a job, Texas Jack inquired if he had any skills. Rogers picked up a lariat and demonstrated the "Crinoline," which consisted of starting with a small loop and then letting out the rope until there was a huge circle surrounding the roper. Texas Jack immediately offered him a spot in his show but Rogers later discovered an ulterior motive. The showman had a standing offer of 50 pounds, or 250 dollars, to any audience member who could perform that trick. Hiring the young American insured that he could not collect.[16]

Texas Jack, born in 1865, had grown up as an orphan in Texas and joined a traveling circus at a young age where he performed as a sharpshooter and horseman. After journeying around the world with this outfit, he formed his own show around 1890 and toured England and South Africa, largely settling in the latter country by the end of the decade. When Rogers met him, he was the impresario of "Texas Jack's Wild West Show and Dramatic Company," which included performers from the United States, Australia, and Argentina as well as South Africa. This traveling show was part circus and part rodeo, featuring horseback tricks and races, trapeze artists, clown acts, magicians, bronco riding, historical sketches, and sharpshooting exhibitions by Texas Jack himself. The showman, along with others such as Buffalo Bill Cody, helped create the romantic image of the American cowboy and preserve it as a mainstay of commercial entertainment. As Jack wrote in a poem that appeared occasionally in one of his western sketches, "I was raised among the cowboys, my saddle is my home/ And I'd always be a cowboy no matter where I roam;/ I am a roving cowboy, I've worked upon the trail,/ I've shot the shaggy buffalo, and heard the coyote wail,/ I've slept upon my saddle, and covered with the moon,/ And I expect to keep it up until I meet my doom."[17]

Rogers quickly carved out a place for himself as a trick-rope artist and bronco rider in Texas Jack's troupe. He also took on small parts in dramatic sketches about the American West where he played Indian or African-American roles. Quickly grasping the need for a striking moniker, he christened himself 'The Cherokee Kid' and had letterheads made of the name. Within a few weeks, Rogers became a star attraction in the show. "The first time I come on to do my roping act I was called back twice and they made a big to-do over me," he explained in a letter home. "[Y]ou see, they don't use Ropes here to catch things and it is all a mystery to them to see it, and I have learned to do quite a bit of fancy Roping that they think is wonderful." A newspaper review praised him as "a champion with the lasso .... . The Cherokee Kid performed some wonderful feats with the lasso, his double act of catching first the horse and then the man with two lassos being very clever. His last performance was that of enveloping himself and horse in a crinoline letting the hoop touch the ground and then bringing it back over the horse and himself and allowing the loop to return to its former size."[18]

Rogers' life became absorbed in the details of show business life. As the Texas Jack Wild West Show toured to towns and cities throughout South Africa, myriad tasks of transportation and logistics faced the troupe of 40 performers and 30 horses. Typically, the show stayed in smaller locations for two or three days, and larger venues for several weeks. The tenure involved constant interaction with audiences. "On next Saturday afternoon we give a medal to the little boy who can throw a rope the best, so I am the Kids' ideal for they see me rope in the show and they follow me around to get me to show them," Rogers explained in a letter. "[B]ut you see, these little boys never seen a lasso before … neither did their fathers." With performances in the evening, he spent much of the daylight hours relaxing but also keeping his lariats, saddle, bridle, clothes, spurs, hat, and other tools of the trade in good working order. After several weeks with Texas Jack, he made a special request to his father: "I want about 100 feet of the best kind of hard twist rope … You can get it there, any of the boys will show you what I used to use … Pretty small but hard twist. I can't get a thing here."[19]

As Rogers settled into his role as a performer, he developed great admiration for his boss. "Jack himself is the finest old boy I ever saw and he seems to think a great deal of me," he wrote his father. "He is a much finer shot than Buffalo Bill and a fine Rider and Roper." Texas Jack also influenced the young American's maturation by conveying, and enforcing, a firm set of expectations meant to keep his performers out of trouble. Rogers quickly learned that the show was not "a wild mob like them at home, for he don't drink a drop or smoke or gamble and likes for his men to be the same." Perhaps most significantly for the future, Texas Jack was the first person to give the flighty young Cherokee a true sense of vocation. "I am going to learn things while I am with him that will enable me to make a living in the world without making it by day labor," Rogers noted only three weeks after meeting his mentor. "Texas Jack was one of the smartest showmen I ever met. It was him who gave me the idea for my original stage act with my pony. I learned a lot about the show business from him," Rogers confessed many years later after becoming one of the most famous entertainers in the world. "I used to study him by the hour and from him I learned the great secret of show business – learned when to get off. It's the fellow that knows when to quit that the audience wants more of."[20]

In fact, Texas Jack suggested that his protégé might want to consider an even larger role with the show in the foreseeable future. "Jack thinks a lot of me. I am taking his part in lots of things in the show, and he says as he is getting old I can take the show before long and do his work," Rogers wrote to his family.

He thought about settling in and eventually assuming management of the operation, but a powerful yearning to return home overwhelmed the enticements of such a position. Sometime in the late summer of 1903, the restless young man decided to leave the show – he wrote his sister that "I had had enough of Africa" – and head back to the United States by way of Australia, where he hoped to build up funds to pay for the final leg of the trip home. Texas Jack kindly wrote a glowing reference for Rogers to use when he got to Australia: "I consider him to be the Champion Trick Roughrider and Lasso Thrower of the World. He is sober, industrious, hard-working at all times and is always to be relied on."[21]

So in August 1903, Rogers caught a boat and sailed across the Indian Ocean headed for Australia. As usual, he joked about his newest enterprise – "I am heading around this old Globe to see if it really is round" – but found little humor in suffering, also as usual, from intense seasickness during the journey. He planned to stay a few weeks and informed his father he would be home by Christmas. After twenty-five days of sailing, his ship stopped first in New Zealand, which he described as "prosperous and a good little country I have ever seen." The large sheep ranches and dairy farms and great swaths of timbered country especially impressed him.[22]

Rogers continued on to Australia and arrived there in mid-September, spending time in Sydney and Melbourne before heading into the interior to see the agricultural areas. He noted the drought that had afflicted the country for the last several years, killing large numbers of livestock and harming grazing land on the vast Australian ranches. Ever the cowboy, however, he criticized the Australian ranchers for their tiny, flat saddles and use of long stock whips rather than lariats to herd livestock. He tried to use one of the cattle whips, which were about twenty feet long, "but only succeeded in tying knots around my own neck. But that wasn't so bad as the Bolos that I tried in South America. [There] I knocked knots on my head so that I could not get my hat on for a week." The Australian ranchers, he concluded, were inferior to both American and Argentinian ranchers but also "the most conceited people on the face of the globe in regard to what they can do and what they know."[23]

Rogers was fascinated by the indigenous peoples of the region, the Maoris in New Zealand and the Aborigines in Australia. He sent home postcards with pictures of these groups, describing the Maoris as "a kind of Indian" and the Aborigines as "Niggers" who had great skill with throwing the boomerang – "it will shave your hat of[f] agoing and your head of[f] acoming back." Rogers attempted to throw the device but had to admit that "the best way I could get it to come back was to send one of the little black fellows after it."[24]

In December 1903 Rogers took a job with the Wirth Brothers Circus as a lariat performer and trick rider. This well-known operation was rooted in

Australia and New Zealand but had completed several tours of South Africa, South America, England, and Asia by the time the young American joined up. Keeping his moniker as the "Cherokee Kid," he soon became a star attraction while also growing close to George and Margaret Wirth, the managers of the circus. His repertoire of lariat tricks dazzled audiences. A newspaper review praised his "splendid skills with lassoos," especially a feat where he was approached by a rider on a galloping horse and threw "two lassos encircling man and horse separately." He also elicited cheers with his riding tricks, such as hooking his feet around the saddle horn and, with his horse on the run, leaning down to pick up three handkerchiefs laying on the ground. At one show, the governor-general was so impressed that he sent a man to ask Rogers to repeat this last trick. Rather cheekily, he agreed to do it again for 150 dollars. When the government official objected, Rogers said to his emissary, "You tell the governor-general if he'll do it cheaper, I'll loan him my horse and my handkerchief." The crowd laughed, the governor-general passed the hat and raised the money, and Rogers repeated the trick.[25]

Rogers had planned to stay in Australia only a few weeks before returning to the United States, but a disastrous decision delayed his departure. Typically, it involved his cavalier attitude toward money. Apparently, several careless remarks had revealed that the young performer had amassed a substantial nest egg during his stints as a performer in South Africa and Australia, money he intended to use for the journey home. Many years later, his wife revealed the story recounted by her husband: "Will was invited into a game of cards. He was young, knew little about cards and gambling, and he lost every cent of his savings. As a result, he had to postpone his return home and stayed on with the Wirth Circus for almost eight months in order to make a stake again; it gave Will a lesson in gambling that he never forgot."[26]

By March 1904, however, Rogers had amassed enough funds to go home. He was ready to call a halt to nearly two years of traveling abroad, an experience that had been a great boon to the young man. It forced him to look inward and mature, to think about a vocation and the future instead of only living in the moment and simply pursuing pleasure. The result was a newfound confidence about forging a career in entertainment – Texas Jack and the Wirth Brothers Circus had demonstrated the real possibilities that lay in show business. Moreover, while Rogers had been unsuccessful in locating a vibrant frontier in Argentina, South Africa, or Australia to replace the one vanishing in the United States, his international experiences brought a richer dividend: prompting him to look at his own society and culture and evaluate his place in it. For the first time, Rogers confronted his own sense of what it meant to be an American. It would become a lifelong habit and a key to his enormous popularity.

From almost the first moment he landed on foreign shores, Rogers opened a dialogue – both with himself and others – about the nature and import of his native land. His earliest reflections, not surprisingly, combined appreciation with homesickness. "I have learned lots on the trip," he wrote home soon after arriving in Argentina. "[Y]ou don't know how good your country is till you get away from it." Opportunity in this South American nation, he perceived, was far more restricted than in the United States as a person with only "a small capital" had little chance of succeeding. As he explained, "Oh, it is nothing like North America. I tell you, you don't know what a good country you have till you see the others." In South Africa, Rogers expressed similar sentiments, suggesting that the dearth of Americans meant "they know a good thing and stay in a good country, and I think William [myself] will take their tip and do likewise when I again land in Yankee land."[27]

In Australia, he found it both amusing and a source of pride that anything new was identified as an American innovation: "You hear electric street cars called American tram cars. All the refreshment places are advertised in box car letters, 'American Cold Drinks, American Soda Fountain.' The bars have up drinks mixed on the American plan. The barber will advertise 'American barber chair.'" After much first-hand observation and much discussion with acquaintances made during his travels, Rogers formulated an understanding that combined pride in both his country and his Indian heritage. As he explained in a letter home, "I was always proud in America to own that I was a Cherokee and I find on leaving that I am equally as proud to own that I am an American for if there is any nation earning a *rep* abroad it is America." The common denominator was respect for, and opportunity extended to, the little guy, the average citizen. As Rogers put it, he came to realize while traveling abroad that there is not "any other place any better than the U.S. for a man with a small capital or none at all."[28]

At the same time, while abroad the youthful Oklahoman forged a deeper understanding of his own nature and proclivities. It stood in contrast to his father's demands for hard work and financial accumulation. As he prepared to leave Argentina for South Africa, he wrote a kind of confessional to Clem. It attempted to mediate their differences by explaining and defending a view of himself and a vision of personal success:

> I never cared for money only for what pleasure it was to spend it .... All that worries me is people there [at home] all say, oh he is no account, he blows all of his father's money and all that kind of stuff. Which is not so. I am more than willing to admit that you have done everything in the world for me and tried to make something more than I am out of me (which is not your fault) .... I only

write these things so we may better understand each other. I cannot help it because my nature is not like other people to make money and I don't want you all to think I am no good simply because I don't keep my money. I have less money than lots of you and I dare say I enjoy life better than any of you.

This recognition that an older model of achievement based on character, hard-work, and prosperity failed to satisfy him while a newer model stressing pleasure and self-fulfillment did, made for an important step in Rogers' life. It pointed the way to personal happiness while also providing an important foundation for Rogers' budding career in entertainment.[29]

So bolstered with a new self-awareness and a new blueprint for becoming successful in life, Rogers departed for home on March 18, 1904. He had decided to build on his achievements in South Africa and Australia and work in show business in some fashion or another. The exact nature of his plan may have been hazy, but it had a clear starting point. Possibly before he left the United States and learned that construction had begun, or possibly overseas when he got wind of its imminent opening, he became aware of a massive celebratory event already galvanizing attention in the United States. Rogers decided to take advantage. As he wrote in his last letter before catching a ship to his native land, he was determined to arrive for "certain before the opening of the St. Louis [World's] Fair."[30]

* * * * * *

The St. Louis World's Fair, or the Louisiana Purchase Exposition, as it was formally known, had its genesis in the tremendous growth of its host city. In the first years of the twentieth century, St. Louis stood as the fourth largest urban area in the United States with a population of nearly 600,000 and it proudly presented a dynamic commercial economy, a highly-ranked public school system, nine daily newspapers, and a hub for twenty-seven rail lines at the downtown Union Station. Yearning to flex its muscles, this urban giant in the American Midwest seized upon the centennial of the Louisiana Purchase, the agreement wherein President Thomas Jefferson had doubled the size of the United States by buying from France an enormous tract of land ranging from the Mississippi River in the east to the Rocky Mountains in the west. Under the leadership of businessman David Rowland Francis, who had earlier served as mayor of St. Louis and governor of Missouri, the city fathers put together a plan to host a world's fair to commemor-ate the nation's most famous land deal. They raised 15 million dollars in funding, some from the federal government and some from the states and private investors. As the largest city in the territory of the old Louisiana Purchase, St. Louis stood poised to celebrate not only its own prominence and promise but the tremendous growth of the American republic in a new century.[31]

The official groundbreaking took place on December 20, 1901 and over the next two years 12,000 workers labored to develop the fair's site on 1,100 acres in Forest Park, which sat just west of the central city. They built an elaborate network of gardens, ponds, lagoons, waterfalls, and fountains as a backdrop for a dozen enormous, lavish neoclassical palaces and exhibit halls, and dozens of other pavilions and smaller buildings that collectively became known as the "Ivory City." The main entrance funneled visitors to the Grand Basin, the center of the fair. At one end, on a hill, sat the circular Festival Hall, surmounted by a gold-leaf dome larger than that of St. Peter's Basilica and housing an auditorium seating 3,500 people along with the largest pipe organ in the world . At the opposite end sat the Louisiana Purchase Monument, a 100-foot column topped by a sculpture of Peace on a gilded globe and surrounded by base sculptures representing important historical events in the territory. Fanning out in all directions from the Grand Basin was an array of structures that put 128 acres under roof and presented exhibits from 50 foreign countries, 42 American states, and a host of private companies. Most of the structures and ornamentation in the Ivory City, despite their tremendous size, were temporary and built of staff – a strong, malleable material consisting of plaster mixed with hemp – affixed to wooden frameworks. Nonetheless, they made for an imposing sight when set along spacious boulevards and elegant canals that seemed to spread as far as the eye could see.

The St. Louis World's Fair aimed to highlight the economic power and social energy of the United States as it entered the new century. The agricultural republic of Civil War America had given way to explosive industrial development and urban growth over the following few decades, trends that had created a new sense of dynamic energy and national confidence by 1904. True, the Palace of Agriculture was the largest building at the fair, encasing twenty-one acres, but sleepy depictions of the virtuous yeoman farmer with his log cabin and forty-acres were nowhere to be found. Instead, it showcased vast displays of farm commodities, the latest models of farm machinery, and current advances in seed and fertilizer products. Symbols of production, large-scale rural enterprise, and mechanical innovations ruled the day. Even the curiosities among the exhibits – California's towering, snarling grizzly bear made of prunes, North Dakota's life-size sculpture of the personification of the strenuous life, Theodore Roosevelt on horseback as a Rough Rider, carved from butter – stressed size and strength.

Grand exhibit venues in the Ivory City reflected the same impulse. Visitors to the Palace of Electricity marveled at new-fangled electric ovens, refrigerators, wall outlets, and, at night time, multiple strings of incandescent lamps on the building's exterior. The Palace of Manufacturing covered fourteen acres and contained products from some 900 industries as well as working shops making goods for the Singer Company, Brown Shoe Company, and American Radiator Company.

The twelve-acre Palace of Machinery displayed a huge Allis-Chalmers-Bullock engine generating 6,500 horsepower along with a fully operating oil filtering and purification plant while the Palace of Transportation surveyed the history of human travel culminating in over 140 models of the newest invention sweeping the country, the automobile . On the grounds of the fair, the 265-foot-tall Ferris Observation Wheel swept riders skyward for a breathtaking view of the fairgrounds and the city of St. Louis . The DeForest Wireless Company erected a 300-foot-tall observation tower that also beamed radio messages as far away as Kansas City and Chicago. This vast technological cornucopia was intended to signal the triumph of an urban industrial society poised to make a global impact at the dawn of what would soon be termed the American Century. It expressed the nation's brash confidence in its own prosperity, growth, and energy.

The technological and industrial displays of the Ivory City implicitly marked an important historical transition: the end of the frontier as a major factor in the development of the United States. The theme of the St. Louis World's Fair – the "march of civilizations" – made the point explicitly. Permeating nearly every display and exhibit was a vision of human progress that culminated in Anglo-American achievements in technological, scientific, and economic life. The fair's official Anthropology Department, headed by W. J. McGee, an editor of *National Geographic* and former president of the American Anthropological Association, arranged displays of people from around the world according to four cultural levels: "savagery, barbarism, civilization, and enlightenment." Arranged around the periphery of the Ivory City, a series of "living exhibit" compounds, in McGee's words, aimed to show a range of humanity from "the darkest blacks to the dominant whites, and from the lowest known culture … to its highest culmination in that Age of Metal, which, as this exposition shows, is now maturing in the Age of Power." They included Mbuti pygmies from Africa living in thatched huts, Navajo Indians from the American southwest outfitted in native garb, and Patagonians from Argentina in animal-skin tents. The most spectacular ethnographic exhibit came from the Philippines. Covering 47 acres and housing about 1,100 natives from 40 different tribes, its occupants ranged from the Christianized Visayan tribe to the Igarots, who created a mild scandal with their skimpy loincloths and penchant for eating dog meat, which created a lively underground economy for stray canines in St. Louis. The fair's directors contrasted this array of "primitives" with the neoclassical, industrial Ivory City with its demonstrations of the genteel, prosperous, enlightened state of Britain and the United States. The Indian Building, federally funded through the Interior Department, performed a similar function by assuring guests that America's Indian policies that had broken tribal authority, transferred ownership of Indian lands, and encouraged cultural assimilation were an expression of progress.[32]

If the bulk of the St. Louis World's Fair served as a paean to the emergence of America's industrial civilization, one of its most popular features illustrated a profound shift in values that accompanied it. The new century pushed forward a new culture stressing the delights of leisure, entertainment, and self-fulfillment as an older Victorian ethos of hard work, moral striving, and self-control faded into the background. This boisterous new sensibility permeated "The Pike," an avenue stretching for nearly a mile along the northern edge of the fairgrounds. This midway area was designed for fun, not moral uplift or anthropological education, and within its confines visitors encountered 50 major shows and rides with some 6,000 performers and 1,500 exotic animals. Its food stands and restaurants offered cuisine from around the world as well as recent American innovations such as the ice cream cone and the hamburger. Amusement seekers could take in reenactments of the Boer War, a Chinese bazaar with silk weavers and ivory carvers, the Great Siberian Railway Ride that took passengers through Asiatic landscapes, and The Hereafter, which exhilarated riders with visions of heaven and hell. A miniature railroad system conveyed visitors to bandstands and concerts, a Moorish palace and Swiss village, an Irish castle and Persian street market, and the Magic Whirlpool water ride and Temple of Mirth fun house. Wild West shows, wild animal shows, and a reenactment of the Galveston Flood vied with one another to attract fairgoers into their seats.

The St. Louis World's Fair was a tremendous success. Americans flocked to the great exhibition, which ran from April 30 to December 1, 1904, and by the time of its closing some 19 million had passed through the turnstiles. Its impact on visitors was often profound, with *Harper's Magazine* noting that the exposition "leaves no intelligent visitor where it found him. It fills him full of pictures and knowledge that keep coming up in his mind for years afterward. It gives him new standards, new means of comparison, new insights into the conditions of life in the world he is living in." The St. Louis Fair offered a near perfect representation of the United States entering a new age with its vigorous vision of urban industrial growth, leisure and recreation, and national power and expansion. It was appropriate that President Theodore Roosevelt dedicated the exposition in April 1903 as construction kicked into high gear and then arrived again for "Roosevelt Day," held four days before its closing. The fair, like the vigorous country it celebrated, had TR's "strenuous life" inscribed all over it.[33]

Given the tremendous popularity and significance of the St. Louis World's Fair, it is little wonder that Rogers, an aspiring entertainer, rushed home from Australia to take advantage of the festivities. A rough, three-week voyage across the Pacific Ocean brought the usual bout of seasickness and his ship put in at San Francisco in early April. He then caught a train and arrived in Claremore on April 11, exhausted and out of money. Rogers later joked that on his trip around the world he had "started out 1st class . . . . Then I traveled 2nd class, then 3rd class, then when I was companion to those she-cows was what might be called no class at all . . . . I was so broke some of the boys told my dad, 'Well, Willie got back from his trip around the world and he's wearing overalls for drawers.'" After a few days spent catching up with family and friends, Rogers moved quickly to engage the matter at the front of his mind. He visited his old employer, Colonel Zach Mulhall, at his ranch near Guthrie, Oklahoma and the showman immediately offered him a position in his troupe at 60 dollars a month. Within a few weeks, Rogers headed off with Mulhall to St. Louis. In the words of his cousin, the great event in the city on the Mississippi "was a red flag before a bull to Will. In a way, you might say he had a carnival soul, for the smell of sawdust and confetti, the wheeze of calliopes and merry-go-rounds, and the bright glittery tinsel of the show business could bring a sparkle to his eyes."[34]

Rogers, along with the rest of Mulhall's group, joined one of the leading shows on The Pike: Frederick T. Cummins' "Spectacular Indian Congress and Life on the Plains." The show had begun several years earlier with a strong ethnographic emphasis on displaying the culture and practices of Indian tribes faced with the Anglo-American push into the west in the 1800s. But it had become steadily more commercialized to appeal to urban audiences. At the St. Louis World's Fair, Cummins' show maintained older elements as hundreds of Indians from various tribes created beadwork, wove baskets, made bows and arrows in the Indian Building, and demonstrated dances and religious ceremonies in a village between shows. But most of the energy went into entertainment facets of the show: fancy riding and trick roping by cowboys, stagecoach robberies, dramatic reenactments of clashes between Indians and federal forces. Two famous Indian leaders, Geronimo and Chief Joseph, actually appeared as head-liners in performances. As with many shows on The Pike, Cummins relied on grand displays, whether it was mock battles between hundreds of mounted Indians and cowboys or great parades of those same antagonists from the Old West on specially scheduled "Pike Days," when they would wind through the avenues of the fair along with Egyptians herding donkeys, flower girls from Paris, gypsies from Spain, and Chinese silk merchants.[35]

Colonel Mulhall and his cast comprised the "cowboy" portion of Cummins' popular attraction. In letters home, Rogers proudly asserted, "Our show is the biggest one at the fair." Appearing in an outdoor arena that seated a few thousand spectators, the Cummins show was a true extravaganza. It featured over 850 participants, including American Indians from over 50 tribes along with a large number of cowboys and a few cowgirls. A typical show included a grand entry of the Indians "arrayed in all the picturesque and fearsome panoply, pomp, and paint of savage foray" followed by marksmanship displays, Pony Express demonstrations, horse racing, a stagecoach robbery, cattle herding, feats of horsemanship, and roping feats. Special performances featured a reenactment of the Custer massacre at the Battle of the Little Big Horn or battles between Indian tribes. The Cummins show was among the most popular on The Pike, and Rogers attributed much of its success to Mulhall, writing that "The Colonel was a natural showman, loved the spectacular, but never had any fakes. Every boy was a real one. His Shows were of the very best."[36]

Rogers performed as a generic cowboy in the panoramic portions of the show, but made his real mark as a roping artist. Mounted on Comanche, his nimble and intelligent pony, he dazzled the crowds with many of the same feats he had developed with Texas Jack – the large crinoline loop, roping objects while at full speed on horseback, deploying two lariats at once to rope separately another rider and his horse. The cowboy and his horse worked together with perfect coordination. "Will and Comanche was almost like Siamese twins, and I reckon they loved each other like them two fellers of which one gives up his life for the other," observed a member of Rogers' family. "And you talk about smart! If you had a secret to keep, you couldn't even spell it out in front of Comanche." It was at the St. Louis World's Fair that Rogers, while still genuinely attached to ranching and cattle herding, shifted gears to embrace what one historian has called the "celebrity-style cowboy." Like Buffalo Bill Cody, the young Oklahoman increasingly shaped a cowboy image that was tinged with nostalgia even as it became an object of entertainment.[37]

It is revealing that Rogers, a Cherokee Indian, clearly chose the cowboy option over his native heritage in a show that featured both in the Old West setting. He dressed as a cowboy, performed as a cowboy, associated with the Anglo-American cowboys, and paid scant attention to the large Indian contingent at the fair. He clearly displayed the powerful assimilationist impulse in his makeup while nudging to the margins his genuine pride in his Indian background. Rogers seemed to endorse, even if implicitly, the "march of civilizations" theme that permeated the St. Louis World's Fair. The Pike, after all, offered lighthearted and entertaining versions of the ethnological view of nearly every "official" attraction and display: that modern Anglo-American industrial civilization represented the height of human development while indigenous societies represented earlier stages of barbarism. To this end, visitors to the carnival area encountered Mysterious Asia, the Cairo Bazaar, Persian Rug Weavers, Burmese musicians, singing "darkies" at the Old Plantation attraction, and the American Indians of the Cummins show as primitive oddities. Norris B. Gregg, the fair's director of concessions, explained that The Pike aimed "to make the lighter field of entertainment a pleasant vehicle of academic impression ... . Through the guise of amusement, therefore, lives and manners of peoples may be contrasted with our own, thus establishing by the most striking comparison, true ethnological values." As one observer put it simply, the World's Fair marked the beginning of Rogers' public "'Angloization,' from Cherokee Kid to Oklahoma Cowboy."[38]

Confirmation of Rogers' assimilationist tendencies came about six weeks into his tenure when Colonel Mulhall was involved in a scandal that rocked the fair's atmosphere of orderly, rational progress. Mulhall had a long-simmering disagreement with Frank Reed, the manager of the horses for the Cummins show, over treatment of the animals. A series of angry confrontations finally erupted into violence one evening after a show when both men drew pistols on the avenue outside. In the resulting gun battle Mulhall shot Reed and wounded two other men. This incident caused a deep division within the Cummins show, with the Indians expressing outrage at Mulhall's behavior while the cowboys defended him. Some 750 Indians held an "indignation meeting," presided over by Geronimo and Chief Blue Horse, and anger boiled over on both sides. A newspaper reported that "the cowboys had snapped their revolvers in the faces of the redskins after the shooting, which resulted in a pow wow [by the Indians], followed by ominous signs which bode no good for the [cowboy] ropers, and they decided in order to prevent a conflict, to retire from the grounds." A spokesman for the Cummins show said that "all the Mulhall cowboys had left the show on account of threats from the Indians." Ultimately, administrators of the fair banned Mulhall from the Cummins show or any other appearance within the fairgrounds. As a result, he quickly formed the "Mulhall Congress of Rough Riders and Ropers" and began to present shows at the Delmar Race Track a short distance away.[39]

In this controversy, Rogers took the side of Mulhall and the cowboys. "The other fellow was no good," he wrote to his family. "They can all say what they please about Mulhall but he has done more for us boys than any man on earth." Along with the rest of the cowboys, Rogers loyally joined Mulhall's Wild West Show at Delmar Gardens as he and Comanche continued performing their popular roping tricks before large crowds. A particularly dazzling moment came when he broke the world's record for roping a steer in thirty seconds. "The crowd of 20,000 cheered wildly when it was announced that Rogers had broken the record," reported a newspaper. "The steer that was selected for Rogers was a fine one. Both rider and animal get away from the pen with a running start. Rogers was on the animal at once and quickly had the lariat around his neck and the steer down on the ground and fled." Since Mulhall's shows were held on Sundays, Rogers also returned to the St. Louis World's Fair to work in a smaller Wild West Show operated by Charles Tompkins, who reported that his new employee was constantly out practicing with his lariat in the arena. "No one taught Will anything," he observed. "He got it the hard way by hard work."[40]

Full of restless energy, and in between stints with Mulhall and Tomkins, Rogers branched out to engage in other types of entertainment in St. Louis. Afflicted with "stage fever," in his words, he and a cousin, Theodore McSpadden, procured a week-long engagement at the Standard Theater with a burlesque show. Their roping act was a success and led to a second, similar engagement at the Chicago Opera House Theater a few weeks later. But when Rogers arrived, he discovered the engagement had been cancelled because he had not sent photos and publicity materials and management concluded he had cancelled. Fortunately, he was able to find a last-minute replacement gig at the Cleveland Theater and appeared for a week. During this appearance, he stumbled across an important insight when a speckled pup from a dog act ran across the stage and he roped it. The audience exploded in laughter and applause. "Well, that gave me the tip, so instead of trying to keep on with this single roping act I decided people wanted to see you catch something," he wrote later. That something, he decided, should be a horse. So when he went back to Claremore in November after the fair, he measured a plot of ground about as big as a stage, and secured a clever, agile pony from the Mulhall ranch that he named Teddy after Theodore Roosevelt. The young man and his new mount started to work out an act where he would rope a running horse on a theater stage, something never before seen.[41]

The St. Louis World's Fair marked an important step in Rogers' career. Appearing before thousands of spectators and soaking up their applause, he solidified his determination, earlier forged abroad in South Africa and Australia, to become an entertainer. This taste of accomplishment in his own country proved intoxicating. The young cowboy set his sights on success in the entertainment world and soon moved onto another, larger stage that would bring those aspirations within reach.

* * * * * * *

In the spring of 1905, Will Rogers made his way to the epicenter of entertainment in early twentieth-century America. In April he journeyed to New York City to join the "Mulhall Rough Rider Congress" for a Wild West Show at Madison Square Garden. It was an eventful trip. On the way there, he and a fellow cowboy, Jim Minnick, passed through Washington DC and were invited to the White House to give a roping demonstration for President Theodore Roosevelt's family. The president was out of town, but it is likely that the invitation came from his hands since TR was a presence in the cowboy circles in which Rogers moved. The president was a friend of Zach Mulhall and his family and had visited their Oklahoma ranch; several members of his famous Rough Rider regiment in the Spanish-American war had performed in Mulhall's shows; and Minnick had ridden in the president's inauguration parade. As the *Washington Times* reported, the two cowboys performed a number of tricks for Mrs. Roosevelt and the children, and "Rogers showed the children how a cowboy jumps the rope. Rogers is one of the few cowboys who can use two lassoes at once, and he has attained more success at this feat than any man living. He can catch a rider with one rope and the horse with the other."[42]

Upon arriving in New York, Rogers and the Mulhall "Rough Rider Congress" began a very successful one-week appearance at the Horse Association Fair in Madison Square Garden. The performers introduced themselves to the city with a cavalcade that rode up Fifth Avenue, wound its way north through Central Park and toward the Bronx on 125th Street, and then galloped back down the bridle path in the park before arriving at the venue after dark. Mulhall's troupe included his four daughters, skilled horsewomen all, especially Lucille, a fearless rider and skilled roper who served as a star attraction in the show. It also included a cowboy performer, Tom Mix, who would later go on to stardom in Hollywood acting in Western films. Rogers assumed his usual role of roping artist, and a newspaper article described the colorful aspects of the show: "cowboys and cowgirls cavorted, danced a-horseback, roped wild 'outlaw' horses and Texas steers, rode bucking broncos and threw the lariat in competition, while the Indians danced a war dance." It also praised the feats of "Will Rogers, a full blood Cherokee Indian and Carlisle graduate, [who] proved a right to his title as lariat expert. He threw it in every conceivable shape, and thought nothing of balancing a rolled lariat on his toe and throwing it over a horse's head. His final feat took the audience by storm. He threw two lariats at an oncoming rider, lassoing both horse and rider."[43]

The Mulhall show drew large and enthusiastic crowds, when several days into the engagement a startling incident earned headlines in all the city papers. It involved Rogers and made him into an instant celebrity. During one of the roping exhibitions, a steer broke loose in the arena and charged up into the seats. As nearby spectators scattered, Rogers gave chase and helped save the day. According to a breathless account in the *New York Herald,*

> Panic prevailed at the afternoon performance of the Horse Fair at Madison Square Garden, yesterday, when a wild, long-horned Texas steer leaped out of the arena, climbed two flights of stairs and ran three-quarters of the way around the Garden, back of the boxes, pursued by cowboys with ropes and leaving hysterical women and excited men in its wake .... Will Rogers, a Cherokee Indian, and three other cowboys, had joined in the chase, and "Rogers got a rope over the steer's horns just as he turned to run down into the arena. Rogers clung to the rope, but was dragged over seats and down the stairs. He was seriously bruised."

In dramatic capital letters, another newspaper blared, "STEER RUNS AMUCK IN BIG GARDEN .... INDIAN COWPUNCHER'S QUICKNESS PREVENTS HARM" before reporting how Rogers, even though "no match for the brute's strength," roped its horns and swerved it down the steps and back into the arena.[44]

Although potentially serious, the incident was probably less dramatic than it was portrayed since newspapers routinely exaggerated events to boost sales. Rogers later explained simply that a steer had jumped a railing and ran into the audience, and while a couple of the cowboys chased after him, "I saw he was going around and come out on the other side. So I headed him off and roped him, and we led him down, and no one was hurt." His friend, Jim Minnick, scoffed at the overblown newspaper coverage but admitted that Rogers got off a good quip when he saw a policeman join the chase after the steer and called out to him, "What are you going to do with it when you catch it?"[45]

Rogers enjoyed his newfound fame in New York, commenting to a friend, "I made the biggest hit here I ever dreamed of in my roping act and finished my good luck by catching the wild steer that went clear up into the dress circles of the garden among the people." Typically, he also joked about his hero status, telling another friend, "I was quite a hit in Madison Sq. Garden and I am letting my head return to its normal size before going home." At the same time, Rogers realized that the publicity was invaluable – he later admitted that the steer-roping incident "didn't do me any harm from a newspaper standpoint" – and could be an enormous boost to his fledgling career as an entertainer. It was no coincidence that a few days later he decided to leave the Mulhall show after its run at the Garden, stay in New York, and break into the theater circuit. In a letter to Clem, he wrote that he resolved to "do some work on the stage as I made a great success the week I worked here."[46]

Believing that integrating a live horse into his stage act would punch his ticket to success, Rogers practiced intensely with his new pony, Teddy. He enlisted Jim Minnick as a sidekick, found a bit of ground in New Jersey where he once again staked out a stage-size plot and began to develop a new theater act based on roping and a live horse. Rogers, well aware that a theater's wooden stage and a horse's hooves did not mix well, bought some felt and had special carpet slippers made for Teddy. After several weeks of intense rehearsal, he was satisfied with his new act and had a successful dry run at an outdoor venue for the Orange Horse Show, where he earned additional laughter and applause for two spontaneous incidents. According to a local newspaper, he was galloping around on Teddy waving his lariat when "suddenly he swerved along close to the judges' stand. In an instant he had one of the judges in the rope." A short time later a dog slipped into the ring and Rogers instantly "threw the lariat and caught the animal by its hind legs." The audience loved both maneuvers.[47]

Rogers started haunting managers, who were reluctant to take him on, and booking agents, who were reluctant to hire him, because neither believed you could do a stage act with a live horse. He was so annoyingly persistent, however, that a booking agent finally rang up Keith's Union Square Theater, a big vaudeville venue, and said, in Rogers' words, "Put this nut and his pony on at one of your supper shows and just get rid of him." He was given a trial in the least popular slot reserved for new acts and tryouts. So Rogers and Teddy, aided by Minnick, went on before a handful of customers. Minnick rode Teddy onto the stage and Rogers roped the pony around his feet. After several more lariat tricks, with Rogers now riding Teddy, Minnick remounted and Rogers took two lassos and roped each of them simultaneously as they dashed across the stage. The young Oklahoman closed the show by taking an 80-foot rope and spinning a huge crinoline over the heads of his audience. The small audience applauded vigorously. Rogers joked, "I think they took pity on that poor pony and figured if we didn't make good, both of us would have to ride back to Oklahoma. So to the surprise of everyone and the disgust of the manager, we were pretty good . . . and the people sorter liked it." This successful audition earned Rogers a contract on June 8, 1905, to appear at the venue for one week, three performances a day, at a salary of 75 dollars per week. Rogers was thrilled, writing to a friend, "I open June 12 at the swellest Vaudeville house in NY. I think I can make good. I am on a fair road to success in my line, am having a swell time."[48]

Despite Rogers' progress in focusing his talents and making a living, one problem persisted. His father remained skeptical of his son's career path. According to a cousin, "back at Claremore when you would mention Will's name, Uncle Clem would just look grim-faced and ashamed. In his secret heart, he was wishing Will was still the size where he could take him across his knee and whip the show business out of him and the cattle-raising business in." But Rogers was not deterred. Sensing a pivotal moment in his adult life, he forged ahead and bet everything on his future as a theatrical entertainer. In a letter to his sister, he vowed, "it is either [the] stage and make a good living, or no show business at all for me. Never [will I go] to the Wild West show any more."[49]

In such fashion, Will Rogers navigated a crucial transition in his life. In the space of a few years he had gone from directionless youth to aspiring young man, from frustrated student to real-life cowboy to itinerant showman cowboy, and now to the cusp of a steady career as a professional entertainer. With his first foray onto the New York stage, he began a decade-long apprenticeship that would take him to theaters throughout the United States and Europe. There Rogers would hone the skills that would launch his climb to national prominence.

3

The Vaudeville Romance

IN THE DECADE AFTER LEAVING THE WORLD of Wild West shows and open-air performances where he had launched his career as a cowboy lariat artist, Will Rogers fell in love with theater entertainment. Having completed successful appearances at the St. Louis World's Fair and Madison Square Garden, he now moved indoors to a world of wooden stages and seated audiences, props and stage lights, comics and singers, showgirls and pit orchestras. This new atmosphere restricted the physical space in which he worked, but it expanded his sense of possibility about entertaining, or even informing and bestirring, those who flocked to see him. New doors beckoned the talented young Oklahoman and he walked through them. The first one opened on the dynamic world of vaudeville, and he eagerly embraced its frenetic potpourri of fast-paced variety shows and nearly non-stop travel on a theater circuit. Rogers served an extended apprenticeship in this genre that took him to every nook and cranny in the United States, as well as two forays to Europe. "Those were great old days," he recalled in later years. "I regret the loss of vaudeville. It was the greatest form of entertainment ever conceived. Nothing in the world takes the place of a good vaudeville show."[1]

As Rogers evolved to become a major figure first on the theater stage and then on the national stage, his identity took on a new coloration. He promoted, indeed embodied, the cult of the cowboy in early twentieth-century America, which associated him with an increasingly mythologized, romanticized figure that flourished in popular culture even as the disappearing frontier of the Old West made it a relic in real life. This cultural process involved a strong personal element for Rogers as he gradually abandoned his ethnic identity as the "Cherokee Kid" to embrace a popular image as the "Oklahoma Cowboy," an Anglicized, All-American icon. In addition, during his lengthy training with vaudeville, Rogers found his true voice, first as an entertainer and then as something more – a comic commentator on the foibles, values, and possibilities of American life. This important evolution in his career could be glimpsed in the three-stage development of his theater presentations. He began as a "dumb act" lariat artist who performed tricks without speaking; then he gradually modified his stage show to present roping feats punctuated with a stream of humorous comments; finally, he emerged as a comic observer who used the lariat occasionally as a stylistic prop to accent his commentary and persona. He created the initial iteration of Will Rogers, the homespun, wise-cracking, rustically charming citizen cowboy who became one of the most beloved figures in American life.

* * * * *

Will Rogers walked on stage on opening night of a variety show in a theater in the American hinterland. He twirled his lariat and tickled the audience with a couple of casual jokes before introducing his sidekicks waiting in the wings, Buck McGee, and Teddy the horse. Then he gave the signal for the pair to join him. McGee jumped on Teddy and dashed onstage in the usual manner to serve as foils for Rogers' roping tricks. Unbeknownst to horse and rider, however, a comic-barber routine had preceded them and a significant amount of lather remained slathered on the floor boards. Teddy's hooves, encased in felt slippers, hit a patch of the slick foam and his feet went out from under him. The horse went down and slid toward the orchestra pit, slamming into the trough lights and knocking out half a dozen of them with a great crash. Teddy ended up poised precariously at the front of the stage with his head hanging over the lip and McGee's leg pinned under him. The orchestra musicians scattered in every direction as did the front-row customers, many of them screaming.

Rogers responded to this scene of bedlam with decisive action. He sprang forward and threw his lariat around Teddy's head and pulled him backwards with one hand, while he reached out and seized McGee with the other, helping to extricate him from under the horse. Then both men grabbed Teddy and managed to haul the terrified animal to his feet. As the two victims stood trembling from the close call, Rogers called out to the audience in his best bemused drawl, "No cause for alarm, folks. This is just a little something extry we put in today to see how you'd like it!" He said it with such calmness and humor that the audience laughed and the orchestra musicians and front-row attendees came back to their seats, some of them even chuckling. A stage hand mopped up the lather, and the act went on as if nothing had happened.[2]

Here was vintage Will Rogers in the decade after the St. Louis World's Fair. The incident revealed a number of qualities – wit, spontaneity, quick thinking on his feet, a knack for connecting with the audience, an ability to turn just about anything into entertainment – that had become central to his professional persona. They had been forged in trial-and-error fashion during countless live performances as Rogers gained a feel for what worked and what did not, what conveyed his talents in authentic fashion and what seemed false, what different audiences might require at different times and places. He had honed these skills over the past several years in an entertainment venue uniquely suited to reading and reaching audiences: American vaudeville.

Vaudeville had taken shape as the first mass-culture, national, commercial entertainment right before the turn of the century before spreading throughout the United States in the early 1900s. Entertainment entrepreneurs who had won their spurs in the circuses, concert saloons, and dime museums of the mid-nineteenth century, such as Benjamin F. Keith, Edward F. Albee, and Martin Beck began to establish novel storefront venues in the late 1880s and 1890s. They presented a collection of diverse acts in a common show, often relying on a "continuous" principle – bringing the opening attraction back on stage as the final one exited – to keep the performance going before a steady crowd over many hours. As audiences grew and larger theaters were established, "vaudeville" – the word seems to have been derived from *vaux-de-Vire*, a French term denoting traditional light plays and satirical songs presented by traveling entertainers – became a recognizable genre and chains were established that linked venues and performers. By 1906 the Keith Circuit dominated vaudeville east of Chicago with some eighty theaters by the following year, while Beck's Orpheum Circuit prevailed west of the Windy City.[3]

Several factors fueled the growing popularity of vaudeville entertainment. Its variety format proved crucial as managers proved determined to present "something for everybody." A typical vaudeville show presented about a dozen acts mostly derived from earlier entertainment styles: acrobats and animal acts from the circus, comedians and satires from musical comedy, blackface sketches and dances from minstrel shows, magicians and physical freaks from the dime museums, classical musicians and opera singers from serious music, even boxers and baseball players from the professional sports world. "In rapid succession, female impersonators, song and dance men, operatic sopranos, jugglers, dancing bears, storytellers, pantomimists, masters of prestidigitation, strongmen, whistlers, banjo players, acrobats, and comedy teams tumbled on and off the stage," one historian of vaudeville has described. "If you were bored by 'Del Bartimo, the great fire king, in a new and novel fire act entitled 'The Devil's Care,' all you had to do was sit back and await 'Miss Flora Story, the queen of the African harp.'"[4]

Vaudeville relied on relentless advertising to attract attention and cheap prices to get audiences into seats. Theater managers flooded local newspapers with large, flashy notices that highlighted ticket prices and listed every act that would be appearing on the bill. Within a short time, press agents and publicists were writing publicity stories about performers and popular acts that were often accompanied by photographs. In turn, newspapers, and eventually magazines, responded by establishing sections devoted to entertainment "news" and "reviews." They featured interviews with vaudeville stars, critiques of the latest shows, and gossip about the comings-and-goings of performers. The result was a flurry of publicity in towns and cities throughout the country that glamorized the world of entertainment and nourished a cult of celebrity for leading vaudeville figures. Inexpensive ticket prices also figured prominently in this barrage of enticement. For a quarter, audiences of modest means could receive hours of entertainment, an appeal that brought urban dwellers streaming into vaudeville theaters.[5]

A final factor buttressing the appeal of vaudeville was its wholesome but pragmatic moral sensibility. While earlier popular entertainments had aimed at working-class audiences with rowdy, saucy, and risqué shows often lubricated with alcohol consumption, vaudeville was determined to widen its appeal to include middle-class amusement seekers. It successfully walked a fine line between rejecting stuffy Victorian sensibilities of an earlier age and endorsing lewd, lascivious immorality. Vaudeville's moral calling card promised patrons a display of respectability, decency, and manners as signs outside theaters proclaimed "ladies welcome" and "family entertainment." Acts would occasionally skate to the edge of indecency with mildly off-color jokes, irreverent attitudes, or sensual music or drama but they never crossed the line. Theater managers insisted that performers adhere to moral guidelines, even posting notices in dressing rooms: "You are hereby warned that your act must be free from all vulgarity and suggestiveness in words, actions, and costume .... Such words as Slob, Son-of-a Gun, Devil, Sucker, Damn, and all other words unfit for the ears of children and ladies, also any references to questionable streets, resorts, localities, and bar-rooms, are prohibited under fine of instant discharge." The Keith chain was so strict that it became known among performers as the "Sunday School Circuit."[6]

Rogers yearned to enter the world of vaudeville in the aftermath of his triumph at the Madison Square Garden Wild West show where his roping of a runaway steer had earned newspaper headlines throughout New York. Taking advantage of this publicity, he had remained in the city after the Mulhall show left town and secured a billing at Keith's Union Square Theatre before going on to perform at Oscar Hammerstein's Victoria Theatre and its Paradise Roof Garden. His success at these venues led to steady engagements on the Keith Circuit, the large east-coast vaudeville chain, where he was advertised as the "Lariat King." He appeared at large Keith's theaters in Boston and Philadelphia as well as the venerable Union Square Theatre in New York. Audiences responded enthusiastically as did reviewers, such as the New York critic who noted, "He is remarkably expert with his rope and does some seemingly impossible feats with it," or the Boston critic who described him as "the applause hit of the entire bill." In such fashion, Rogers became a journeyman entertainer in the vaudeville world, albeit a fortunate one since he launched his career in big-time theaters and skipped the small-time, poor-paying, four-shows-a-day venues in which novices usually began.[7]

While Rogers focused his efforts on the continental United States, his success led to a geographical interlude. In the spring of 1906, he journeyed to Berlin to entertain at the famous Wintergarten Theater. Audiences and critics loved his act. Since there were no matinees at this venue, Rogers would go riding every afternoon at a local park and often would observe German army officers doing likewise. One day, he noticed one figure riding ahead of the others who turned, looked at Rogers' cowboy clothes, and nodded. The American did likewise, but was stopped a little farther on by a man who asked sternly why he had not saluted. When Rogers asked whom he should have saluted, the man said, "Why, the Kaiser; don't you know that was him you just met on the bridle path?" Rogers saw the monarch several more times and they exchanged nods, with the American confessing, "I never did salute him . . . . I didn't know anything about saluting. I might have used the wrong hand or something." After a month, Rogers went on to perform for the equally famous Palace Theatre in London, where he again won rave reviews. As one critic enthused, "it is going some when a Palace audience can be made to shout bravo, and more than once, too."[8]

Bolstered by these foreign triumphs, Rogers returned to the United States and resumed his vaudeville career. He hired a new agent, Mort Shea, who bolstered his bookings up and down the East Coast and the entertainer's popularity climbed steadily. Wherever he appeared, the basis of Rogers' appeal lay in his roping skills. In the first few years of his vaudeville career, he depended upon his tried-and-true talents as a lariat artist performing a variety of tricks. Added to this was his unique use of a live horse on stage, something that no other act had ever featured. After his friend, Jim Minnick, decided to go back to his ranch in Texas after a few weeks of shows in New York, Rogers hired Buck McGee, an Oklahoma cowboy who had appeared with Colonel Mulhall at Madison Square Garden, to take his place and they would work together for many years. The other key performer was Teddy, the highly intelligent, well-trained, dark-coated little horse who seemed to relish life on the stage. He was trained to leave his boarding stable just before showtime and follow McGee up the street without a halter. They would stop at the theater door, turn to face astounded onlookers who had gathered, and then walk into the venue. This clever maneuver enticed people to come see the show, and Teddy rewarded their enthusiasm by learning to bow "his acknowledgement of applause."[9]

In his early vaudeville act, Rogers would walk on stage silently to the musical accompaniment of several Western tunes, toss the lariat and hop through a loop or two. Then Teddy would dart out from the wings with McGee in the saddle, and Rogers would rope the running horse and catch him by all four feet. Then he would perform other lariat tricks – throwing two ropes at once to catch both horse and rider; a three-rope catch on McGee that would secure his head, hands, and torso; roping Teddy by the nose and then by the tail; and creating a figure-eight with the lariat. The climax of the act came when Rogers tossed the end of his rope to an usher, who would walk it up the center aisle to its full length of ninety feet. Rogers then would mount Teddy, draw in the rope, twirl a small loop, and then gradually extend it until it was swishing above the heads of the audience nearly to the back of the theater. He would conclude the famous "Crinoline" by backing Teddy to the rear of the stage, drawing in the heavy loop and letting it fall to the floor with a bang, letting out a cowboy whoop, and dashing into the wings.[10]

For all of his experience with Wild West shows, however, Rogers initially suffered from his unfamiliarity with the theater stage. He had to learn the ropes, so to speak. In one of his first appearances at Hammerstein's, he was a big hit and the audience applauded enthusiastically but Rogers simply bowed and walked offstage and headed for the dressing room as the clapping continued. Ernest Hogan, the famous African-American comedian, grabbed him and shoved him back out in front of the curtain. "Boy, don't overlook any of them, they ain't bows," he told Rogers. "Them's curtain calls and there is damn few of them up here."[11]

More importantly, Rogers learned how to engage the audience by utilizing one of his untapped talents: talking. It was a slow process. Again, he was on the bill at Hammerstein's when a fellow entertainer suggested that he should build anticipation by announcing to the audience the nature of his next roping trick. Rogers took the advice, and before his famous stunt of using two lariats at once to catch a horse and rider, he said, "I don't have any idea I'll get it, but here goes." He said it so disarmingly that the audience laughed. Rogers misinterpreted, believing they were making fun of him and left the stage in a huff after the trick. But after his fellow vaudevillians made him understand that patrons were laughing with him and not at him, he began to slip in more and more quips. When he got his lariat snarled about his feet, he wisecracked, "A rope ain't bad to get tangled up in if it ain't around your neck." Another time, after he failed on a couple of trick throws, he leaned out toward the audience and confided bemusedly, "I was a bit handicapped up there because the manager wouldn't allow a fellow to cuss when he misses." The ripples of laughter soon had him tangling and missing on purpose for the opportunity to make the jokes.[12]

As his comic commentary expanded, Rogers began making extensive notes about funny cracks he might make during his lariat routine. If he missed roping Teddy, he was prepared with, "If that ol' Pony had been trained properly he would of stuck his head in there." If he missed roping McGee, he was prepared to address him with mock indignation: "It wouldent have been much trouble to put your hands in." At the start of the big conclusion of his act where he spun the enormous crinoline out over the seats, if his toss missed the page boy in the aisle who was supposed to stretch out the entire length of the rope to impress the audience, Rogers was prepared to hand it to him easily and whisper loudly, "Rehearsal at 10 tomorrow." According to a friend, "a bit to his astonishment, Will found that he was a comedian; it was exhilarating. He had always liked to have fun when he was in a crowd and to make people laugh; and here he was merely standing in front of the crowd and having fun. And getting paid for it."[13]

In addition to tightening the nuts-and-bolts of his act, Rogers burnished an image that became crucial for his appeal to vaudeville audiences: the cowboy. It began with his appearance. As the orchestra played a western song, Rogers ambled on stage dressed in chaps, a broad-brimmed hat, and a colored shirt with a kerchief around his neck. His astonishing skills with the lariat underlined the cowboy connection, as did his verbal style, which featured a western drawl and folksy rural word choice. Audiences loved the cowboy image, and local newspaper critics invariably highlighted it. A review of his performance in Philadelphia described him as "a Western cowboy, who did some wonderful work with the lasso . . . . Rogers is a typical man of the Far West. He is a character who has lots of character." The *Boston Herald* described him as "a typical western plainsman." Reviewers competed to illuminate his cowboy characteristics, with one claiming, "Mr. Rogers has a set of teeth which carry him through an Indian massacre without a scratch, so attractive are they in a rakish smile. He is a tanned-up, lean, and richly witty cowboy who does not lose his ranch manners in an opry house." Another review focused on his language: "Isn't that the greatest line of ranger conversation ever heard? That plumb good lingo of Texas and the plains. The man has temperament, too, and magnetism and every word he says, every glance of his keen eye, every swift curve of his magic rope, comes over the footlights with a flash of power."[14]

Publicity stories took the same tack, characterizing Rogers as a *genuine* cowboy, not just someone playing a part. As a piece in the *Minneapolis Journal* declared, "Once in a while a real cowboy emerges from fiction and song into real life. Such is Will Rogers from Oklahoma, who performs a series of astonishing maneuvers with a lariat." An article in the *Rochester Union and Advertiser* did likewise: "The speaker was a slender built chap, square shouldered and with the keen eyes, alert look and clear complexion that mark the man accustomed to outdoor life, . . . a native of the southwestern section of the country where the cowpuncher still flourishes." It quoted Rogers describing his lariat tricks as a trifle, saying "If I did just a lot of that rope spinning the boys [at home] would say, 'Well, can you catch anything?'" In an interview with a Cleveland newspaper, Rogers observed that real cowboys dismissed the common wisdom claiming that a great rider was also a great roper. "A man that rides well don't rope well. And if he is great with the rope he is no shakes as a rider," he told the journalist. "You see, he just goes in and devotes himself to one thing and makes a success of it." It also became a stock story that Rogers was only doing vaudeville to make money to finance his real objective: "he will go back to ranching, on which his heart is set."[15]

At the same time, discussions of Rogers' cowboy persona puffed up its strong mythical element. In the popular culture of early twentieth-century America, the cowboy represented a vanishing breed in an urbanizing society. He had become a symbol of the individualist, honorable, freedom-loving, industrious figure from an earlier age who had conquered the continent and subdued nature in the vanguard of advancing civilization. A cult of the cowboy had drawn rapturous public attention at the dawn of the early twentieth century, as evidenced by the popularity of "Buffalo Bill" Cody and his Wild West shows, the war-hero status of Theodore Roosevelt and his Rough Riders during the Spanish-American War, and the vogue for western artists such as Frederic Remington and Charles M. Russell. Rogers was drawn into this orbit. He was smitten with Russell's drawings and paintings and became lifelong friends with the artist. In 1910, Rogers appeared with Buffalo Bill for his farewell performance in New York, where *Variety* noted that "the Oklahoma cowboy was in his element at the finish ... when he raced around the ring spinning his wide 'crinoline' loop." The *New York Times* stressed the show's mythologizing of the American cowboy, describing it as "a classic ethnological exhibit of the manners and customs of a certain period in American history and of a race which is fast disappearing from the earth."[16]

One of the most compelling expressions of the cowboy myth appeared in popular literature with the publication of Owen Wister's novel, *The Virginian* (1902). This bestseller recounted episodes in the life of a tall, handsome cowboy in Medicine Bow, Wyoming. The protagonist, a man of few words with a strong moral code, struggles with a ruthless enemy, wins the heart of a pretty school-teacher from the east, and prevails in a shootout at story's end. As the template for the American "western" in books and on screen, *The Virginian* romanticized the old West and presented the cowboy as a heroic, mythical figure who sturdily upheld old-fashioned virtues of honesty, integrity, and self-reliance. As Rogers ascended through the ranks of vaudeville entertainment, observers consistently compared him to Wister's protagonist. "To meet Rogers and talk with him is as good as reading a half dozen chapters of Owen Wister's 'Virginian,'" observed one newspaper. Another noted that the entertainer "has the fascinating drawl in speech of that creation of Owen Wister's, 'The Virginian.'" A lengthy publicity story in the *Detroit Free Press* underlined the connection in terms of masculine sex appeal. Its headline capitalized Rogers' "Heart-Armor Piercing Manner" and how his "Slim Legs in Careless Chaparrals, and a Fetching Drawl, Seems to Fit That Femininely Adored Type of Wister Virginian." The story went on to describe his "half slouching length of limb encased in leather, the blue flannel shirt open at the throat, the soft, worse-for-wear hat and the devil-may-care, good-humored smile" and concluded that he was "immensely like the posters that hang in half the girls' rooms in the country."[17]

Indeed, Rogers himself addressed the comparison. Sitting for an interview with the *Baltimore World*, this "real cowpuncher" talked about *The Virginian*. He confessed to reading part of the novel, but didn't find it very realistic or convincing, especially the part where the Virginian hanged his friend for cattle rustling. He scoffed at the idea of "stringin' [up] your pal for a few measly calves what wasn't worth hardly anything at all . . . . There ain't no such West as them fellers what wrote say there are. The law out there is every man for himself. Just so long as you don't bother me then I ain't going to bother you." He asserted that there were still cowpunchers who herded cattle, rode the fence lines, avoided liquor, and even saved their money. "You have got that book idea of the West. Tain't nothing like you think." Rogers, in the popular imagination, came off as both more authentic and more virtuous as a cowboy than the Virginian because he knew the "real" west and he believed that camaraderie and loyalty among cowpunchers was more important than upholding some abstract laws of property.[18]

So bolstered with a cowboy persona and a yen for humorous quips, Rogers solidified his position as an appealing entertainer within a short time of entering the vaudeville circuit. He became one of the star performers on a typical bill, and traveled widely throughout the United States. Working the Keith Circuit east of the Mississippi for his first two years, in 1908 he embarked on a western vaudeville theater tour, first with the Orpheum Circuit, the largest circuit west of Chicago, and then on the Sullivan and Considine Circuit. Western vaudeville was more stressful because of the huge distances between cities, but was more morally flexible and less refined than its eastern counterpart in its toleration of risqué acts and lewd jokes. By the early 1910s, Rogers traveled the entire country on a steady basis, appearing in dozens of theaters in a host of towns and cities. His entertainment persona, however, required an additional element, one that he worked assiduously to develop.[19]

* * * * *

As his vaudeville career unfolded, Rogers devoted increasing energy to honing his skills as a comic commentator. He sensed that his talent lay not in jokes but in wit; not in buffoonery but in humorous observations about the surrounding world. After much trial and error, he slowly learned that it was his style of delivery, the way he said things, rather than the gags themselves, that delighted audiences. So he labored to develop a "natural" delivery, as ironic as that seems, that was understated, self-deprecating, shrewd, folksy, and (deceptively) spontaneous that was conveyed to the audience in a charming, hesitating drawl. Typical of the Rogers approach was a quip he employed when messing up a relatively simple trick of jumping with both feet inside a spinning loop. Grinning at the audience, he observed off-handedly, "Well, got all my feet through but one." Rogers also developed mannerisms – the mock-confused look, the perplexed scratching of the head – that fleshed out his persona and style. He began to comment on his own act in a casual manner as if he had just noticed some amusing discrepancy, as when he would miss a couple of lariat tosses and observe, "I've got jokes for only one miss. It looks like I've either got to practice up and be a better roper, or learn more jokes." He came across his trademark gum-chewing by accident when he was late to a show and rushed on stage chomping away. When the audience chuckled, he realized his mouth was full of gum, so he stopped and stuck it on a fancy arch soaring over the stage. The audience roared with laughter, and as an observer reported, "Laughs didn't have to happen twice to Will. So, after that, the little wad of gum went into his act as a standard prop."[20]

Rogers' success, however, produced an uncharacteristic misjudgment about entertainment in 1910. Apparently triggered by a one-off appearance with his old mentor, Zack Mulhall, in a Wild West show in St. Louis, he decided to utilize that energy and create something new: a miniature Wild West show for the vaudeville stage. The unique twist in the "Big Act," as Rogers informally called it, would be its cast of all-female performers. He recruited the famous cowgirl, Goldie St. Clair, for fancy riding; the lariat artist, Florence LaDue; rope dancer, Hazel Moran; and trick rider, Tillie Baldwin. His role would be that of a wisecracking master of ceremonies. Focusing on his new persona as humorist and personality, Rogers would introduce the performers and then stand to the side and deliver a running commentary while doing a few lariat tricks of his own. The show premiered in New Jersey, did a several-month run on the East Coast. The Big Act, however, proved to be unwieldy and expensive to maintain. It also generated only lukewarm reactions among audiences, partly because Rogers himself seemed to linger on the margins of the entertainment. One evening at Keith's Theater in Philadelphia, Harry Jordan, the manager, asked, "why does Will carry all those horses and people around with him? I would rather have Will Rogers alone than that whole bunch put together." The all-female show fizzled.[21]

So in 1911, Rogers rebounded with one of the most happily consequential decisions of his professional life. He left behind both the old lariat-and-pony act and the Big Act to go solo as a vaudeville entertainer. This gamble reflected the growing attraction of Rogers' entertainment persona and was encouraged by his new agent, Max Hart. Hart represented some of the leading big-time vaudevillians – Fanny Brice, George Jessel, Buster Keaton, Eddie Cantor, W. C. Fields – and now he took on Rogers. Hart was a master of publicity who took out large newspaper and magazine ads for his clients, and had a knack for selling their talents to booking agents and theater managers. Under this masterful agent, Rogers consistently received a billing as "The Oklahoma Cowboy," leaving behind the earlier Cherokee associations for a new connection to the archetypal western cowboy with his individualism, rustic wisdom, plainspoken integrity, and homespun wit. This became the centerpiece of Rogers' public appeal and it would stay with him for the rest of his life.[22]

Now as a single act, Rogers made giant strides in creating his unique comedic style. Drifting steadily away from quips and jokes played strictly for laughs, he devoted himself to the creation of a larger entertainment persona – the down-home cowboy with the homespun observations, the rustic metaphors, the southwestern drawl, and the understated delivery. This set him apart in vaudeville, which was dominated by comics who employed slapstick clowning, urban ethnic satire, and risqué comments. Instead, Rogers drew more upon the cracker-barrel, tall-tale literary tradition stretching back to Benjamin Franklin's "Poor Richard" in the late colonial period, Artemus Ward in the 1800s, and even Mark Twain in more recent decades. Rogers still used the deadpan quip to poke fun at himself, as after a lariat mistake when he would comment, "I got it good the other night, you should have been there then." With growing frequency, however, Rogers turned toward topical humor rooted in everyday life. He took note of new kinds of entertainment, informing the audience, "I am going to get a moving picture of this trick and just stand and tell about it." He commented on political affairs with a light touch, noting, "If you make any money the government shoves you in the creek once a year with it in your pockets and all that don't get wet you can keep." He addressed the dangerous topic of religion with equal deftness: "If you go to church the preacher will spend an hour and a half trying to keep you awake by cussing the other denominations."[23]

With this growing arsenal of skills, Rogers' solo act proved even more popular than his old lariat-and-pony show. After appearing at the Majestic Theater in Chicago, a newspaper review offered a headline, "The Droll Oklahoma Cowboy In His New Single Offering, All Alone, No Horse," and then extolled his performance by noting, "This is the second time in the history of this playhouse that an act originally booked for one week was held over because of its success." A manager's report from a Keith's Theater in Columbus, Ohio said, "The Oklahoma Cowboy ... was a riot. His inimitable bits of talk in conjunction with his dexterity with rope and lariat made the biggest kind of a hit. He went like a cyclone throughout and could hardly get away [from the audience]."[24]

Rogers' growing popularity as a performer brought new opportunities. He briefly joined the cast of a new musical comedy, *The Wall Street Girl*, in 1912 at the George M. Cohan Theater in New York. Its story line featured a wealthy eastern woman, played by the musical star Blanche Ring, who went west and fell in love with a Nevada mining manager. A reflection of the Wild West fad in American popular culture, the show marked the first time Rogers appeared on the Broadway stage. While the show received mixed reviews, the Oklahoman earned praise for his appearance in the second act, where he performed a roping-and-comedy routine. The *New York Times* noted that he "did his regular vaudeville act, but undoubtedly scored the success of the evening, doing things with ropes and conversing in his quaint way with the audience." The *New York World* gushed that he "threw a rope over *Wall Street Girl* and dragged off the first honors of the performance . . . . Aside from his [lariat] skill, Rogers displayed a sense of humor as fresh as a breeze from the Western prairie." The show opened in April and ran for fifty-six performances in New York until June 1, and then after a summer hiatus, Rogers rejoined the cast in September for a tour of the East, Midwest, and South. [25]

Over the next two years from 1913–1915, Rogers toured the Orpheum Circuit in the western half of the country and made brief forays into Canada. The *San Francisco Bulletin* offered typical praise, noting that alongside his roping skills "he is also a humorist with as keen an insight into human nature as many of the world's most famous comedians." He appeared alongside stars such as Eddie Cantor and George Jessel, with whom he became close friends. Cantor later recalled, "This cowboy was the first guy I'd ever met from west of the Bronx and I worshipped him." He joked to Jessel that two years earlier Rogers was appearing with a trained horse "and now all he does is talk, chew gum, and do tricks with a rope, and he's getting $1,000 a week." In January 1914, Rogers performed at New York's famous Palace Theater, probably the most renowned vaudeville venue in the United States. Again, he received excellent reviews as he "hove into view with his inimitable fun-making . . . . he went over big," in the words of *Variety*. Over the next two weeks Rogers appeared at New York's Colonial Theater, Keith's Orpheum Theatre, and Hammerstein's Victoria Theatre. *Billboard*'s headline read, "WILL ROGERS MAKING RECORD," while the caption explained, "The only act that ever played three theaters in one week." He had become a genuine vaudeville star. [26]

But it was not only New York that loved the cowboy humorist. As Rogers toured vaudeville theaters throughout the United States, rave reviews poured in. "The Oklahoma Cowboy might be a division of vaudeville all by himself," said the *San Francisco Chronicle*. "Rogers' work all through is refreshingly different." In Los Angeles, a local newspaper described him as "the pet of the programme" and noted that "what tickles his audience is the stage demeanor that he assumes ... . [H]is running, half-preoccupied, gum-punctuated talk is worth listening to. It is shrewd and humorous, and entertains us quite as much as his remarkable dexterity with the rope." A Salt Lake City newspaper described how "Will Rogers, the cowboy comedian, the only animal of his kind in captivity, convulsed the audience with his droll remarks. Rogers does some clever tricks with a rope, but the tricks are only a foil for his comedy." A review of his performance in Kansas City asserted, "Will Rogers, plain Oklahoma cowboy, outshines them all. Easily he is the big hit of the show." The *Minneapolis Journal* marveled at "the bashful cowboy who ducks his head at the end of every trick. Rogers knows the value of his own personality and his own individual kind of humor, but he is one of the most modest and likable persons one could meet."[27]

Rogers' success in vaudeville paid an unexpected personal dividend. He finally achieved a reconciliation with his father as Clem came to appreciate his son's achievements and growing stature in the entertainment world. But the process had been long and difficult. Clem remained suspicious of his son's initial ventures into vaudeville, and when the paychecks rolled in he asked a friend, "do you suppose Will is making all of that money honestly?" He was not reassured when, after some of his cronies had seen Will perform in New York, they returned home and described his act as "Oh, just acting the fool like he used to do around here." Clem himself traveled to Washington DC to see Will perform and, initially, came away mystified. "Why, he ain't actin'; he's just being himself," he declared. "He was always cuttin' up and carryin' on – and now he's gettin' paid for it." But gradually Clem grew proud of his son's success even if he didn't quite understand it. Ever the businessman, he surveyed the size of the audiences and became indignant, telling his son that "the managers are not payin' you enough" and he needed to demand more money. According to a family member, Clem began to carry around newspaper clippings about Will and show them to friends. When visiting his son and attending performances, he would proudly talk to patrons in the theater lobby and take them to the dressing room door to introduce them to his son, the star performer.[28]

By the mid-1910s, after a decade in vaudeville, Rogers had carved out a secure place for himself as a popular entertainer. More importantly, he had cemented into place the basic elements of an entertainment persona that would persist for the rest of his career and make him a beloved figure in America. This persona was one part nostalgic image of the cowboy in an urbanizing age; one part homespun, cracker barrel humorist and sage; and one part modest, charming "personality" standing at the cusp of modern celebrity. Having succumbed to the romance of vaudeville and having forged an affectionate relationship, this unique and talented entertainer now sought a bigger stage and eyed the bright lights of

Broadway theater. However, there was more than his own desire and ambition at stake. Another kind of romance, this one personal rather than professional, loomed large. Will Rogers had fallen in love, married a young woman from back home, and now had family obligations to consider.

* * * * *

On September 23, 1908, Will Rogers poured out an emotional confession to Betty Blake. In a lengthy, distraught letter he admitted that he had acted terribly toward her and pleaded for her forgiveness and love:

> I have not treated you square .... [I]t seems that I haven't treated anyone square. I have *lived a lie* and now I am reaping the harvest of it. Please make a little allowance for me, dear. I am not myself now and seem to have no mind of my own.
>
> I am *scared* and don't know what to do. Betty, this is all of what comes of doing wrong. I done the greatest wrong that any one could do and I have wished and prayed a thousand times since that I had not done it.
>
> No, I am no man. I am the weakest child you ever saw. If you knew me better, [you would know] I am easily led and can be pulled into almost anything. I have no mind of my own. I just drift and drift. God knows where to.
>
> Now listen, don't you think of deserting me in all this. I need you and want you and I am hoping that this will all soon be at an end and I will be my old self again .... I'm *bad*, dearie, all bad, but I am trying to do better and live better.

Prompted by the couple's bungled efforts to make one another jealous and Rogers' long record of misadventures with women, this remarkable opening of the heart proved to be the turning point in a difficult and complex relationship that had begun nearly a decade earlier. The couple would marry some two months later and remain devoted for the rest of their lives. But like so much else with the personable but emotionally erratic young man, Rogers' journey to romantic happiness was lengthy, uncertain, and rooted in his youthful experience in the Indian Territory.[29]

As a young man from a prosperous, prestigious Cherokee family, Rogers' adolescence had been one long record of enthusiastic socializing and hijinks. With an overdeveloped sense of fun and an underdeveloped sense of responsibility, the youth had cavorted with other young people from the tribe's elite families in the Claremore and Oogolah area. From cakewalk parties to late-night gatherings of the Pocahontas Club, Rogers and his circle enjoyed the freedom of youth. Constantly joking, laughing, dancing, playing pranks, and singing the latest popular songs, the youth had taken the lead in creating an atmosphere of devil-may-care amusement. Invariably, this involved trysts and flirtations between young men and women, and Rogers took the lead here as well. With his dapper wardrobe procured in Kansas City, rubber-tired buggy, slim good looks, and charming, fun-loving nature, he cut an attractive figure. According to Jim Hopkins, a young cowhand and friend, he was "the greatest ladies' man you ever saw."[30]

Rogers had a number of girlfriends during his youthful, carefree days in eastern Oklahoma. An early romantic pursuit got off to a rocky start when, while attending the Scarritt Collegiate Institute in Neosho, Missouri, he invited a local girl, Maggie Nay, to a party. As she recounted many years later, usually a group of teenagers would meet and go out together and then "pair off after we got to our destination and, in that way, I'd be with Bill." When he asked her for a formal date, however, she was thrilled but her mother immediately refused permission. It seems a local German family made and sold wine, and Will and a few of his friends had gotten their hands on a couple of bottles, become tipsy, and created a public spectacle by falling off their bicycles on a public street. In Nay's words, "my mother wasn't sure about these *wild Indian boys from the territory*, hence her refusal to let me go." Rogers was deeply offended by the mother's accusations and wrote an indignant letter to the girl. He accepted the turndown with a sarcastic admission: "I know I drink and am a wild and bad boy and all that .... I am an outcast, I suppose." He wished her and her mother well before closing sourly, "Well, I suppose you have heard enough of this *Drunkard* that they call Will Rogers."[31]

Back in the Claremore area, Rogers courted Mary Bullette, the daughter of a prosperous Claremore merchant and rancher. The couple were active in Pocahontas Club activities and liked dancing, winning a cakewalk contest at a local minstrel show contest in March 1901. Rogers also casually dated Belle Price, another local girl, and had a more involved relationship with Ada Gray. Apparently, he rebuffed her when he left the Indian Territory to travel the world, and she wrote a pleading letter while he was working in South Africa declaring her love. "Do you withhold your self from me longer, and will you refuse to write to me after I have made you this confession?" she penned. "You shouldn't deny me this plea of my heart .... Will, when you come home I shall be the happiest person the world holds."[32]

But Rogers' most serious girlfriend was Kate Ellis, the daughter of the proprietor of the hotel in nearby Oologah. Many considered her to be the prettiest girl in the area, and according to Bill Hoge, a young man who was friends with both of them, she was Rogers' "first sweetheart .... He was quite gone on her." The couple courted for several years and there was much talk that they would get married, but Jake Ellis, her father, was opposed to the match because he thought the young man was too wild. One night when Rogers brought Kate home too late, Jake, who had reached the end of his patience, pounced on the young man, chewed him out, and forbade him from seeing her again. Affronted by the bitter attack, Rogers backed away and cooled down the relationship. Nonetheless, his family seems to have assumed that the pair were still a couple while he was abroad. His sister wrote him in South Africa that she had seen Ellis at a lecture and she "looked so well in a white silk waist[coat] and the black silk collar" Will had gifted her. In a letter to his family, the young traveler inquired, "By the way, how is Kate? I hope she has not married, too." Indeed, Will and Kate corresponded while he was abroad. She wrote a playful, flirtatious letter thanking him for his latest missive that had arrived on February 14, 1903, observing, "quite a nice valentine, wasn't it?" She noted that she was still signing herself "Kate Ellis, spinster" and chided him for joking that she was likely to take a husband in his absence: "if you hadn't been you never would have written to me." Two attractive young women had arrived in the area, she informed him, and "all of Claremore's swells go down on their knees to them. Guess you would, too, if you were here – if I'd let you???" Kate closed on a note of assurance, telling Will that if he arrived home changed unrecognizably from his world travels, when he presented himself for "your *handout*, in some manner let me know who thou art and you'll get two *hands out*."[33]

Rogers' lingering attachment to Kate Ellis did not stop him from falling into, and then fleeing, romantic entanglements while working and traveling abroad. In Cape Colony, South Africa, in June 1903, a young woman named Annie Greenslade wrote a pleading letter to "My Dearest-loveing boy." She declared, "I do love you so much. I really don't know what to do when you are going to leave me. My heart will break all over." A few weeks later in Pretoria, "Mamie S." wrote to Rogers complaining that he had stood her up for an afternoon assigna-tion, noting that if he had followed her instructions "you would have been quite safe as it is the back entrance to the hotel & nobody would have seen us." She implored him to visit her in the evening, adding, "Perhaps it is not my place to tell you how I love you but I can't help it." Mamie concluded on a desperate note: "Oh, my darling, don't say no to this, then I will really begin to believe you don't love me."[34]

After returning to the United States and devoting himself to entertainment, Rogers continued to see a variety of young women in the show business world. Early on, he formed a close bond with Lucille Mulhall, the talented daughter of Colonel Zach Mulhall and the star of his Wild West show. The two performed together sporadically from 1899 to 1902, and then again at the Louisiana Purchase Exposition in 1904 and at Madison Square Garden in 1905. Eighteen years old at the time of the St. Louis World's Fair, she had blond hair, a deeply suntanned complexion, and large blue-grey eyes. A talented horsewoman and roper, she was widely considered to be the first "cowgirl" in the United States and

Rogers described her later as "the only Girl that ever rode a horse exactly like a man (I mean a real [ranch]hand)." But she also projected an image of elegant restraint. In Rogers' admiring words, she did not dress in garish loud colors, big hats, and short leather skirts but wore a divided skirt that hung "long, away down over her patent-leather boot tops, a whip-cord grey, or grey broadcloth small, stiff brim hat, and always white silk shirt waist." Rogers' cousin, Spi Trent, asserted that he "sure was an admirer" of the young woman – "she wasn't hard on the eyes, and for another it was said she was the best woman roper that ever came down the pike" – while several of the Mulhall ranch hands concluded he had a crush on her. In one photograph, Will and Lucille stood next to one another smiling as he enclosed them both in a lariat "wedding ring."[35]

In his early years on the vaudeville circuit, Rogers had affairs with several women, a common occurence in this itinerant show business world. Buck McGee, his sidekick in the act, observed first-hand the culture of promiscuity in vaudeville, writing cynically to his wife that they were "at least one couple who are on the level with each other. That is why I am so sensitive on that point." Young, talented, and personable, Rogers moved easily in this eroticized atmosphere and had little trouble attracting and reciprocating female attention. The details remain scanty, however, because on the eve of his wedding, according to a friend, he destroyed numerous letters, photographs, and mementos from girlfriends he "now thinks very little of as he has torn and burned up two & one half bushels." Evidence has survived on one dalliance, however, with a young singer named "Nina" who performed with an act called The Electric Crickets on the same bill in New York. Rogers described her as a "nice little girl friend of mine" and admitted they went out a number of times after the show and "she got a bit stuck on me." He apparently broke things off and she took it well, writing that "the Girl that wins your love may consider herself very fortunate."[36]

A much more serious relationship developed with singer and comedienne Louise Henry. The two first appeared on the same bill in 1905 and then many times thereafter. They enjoyed shared interests. They both loved horses and would ride together whenever the opportunity appeared. In fact, Rogers joked that Teddy the horse had introduced Henry to him and, in Henry's words, "said Teddy was my horse as I was the only girl Teddy would let ride him with one exception – Lucille Mulhall." In addition, Henry played a comic country woman in her act – "Sal Skinner" – that paralleled Rogers' down-home cowboy persona. The two were often in New York at the same time and would take walks and dine together at a variety of restaurants patronized by vaudeville performers: the dining rooms at the Putnam House and Metropole Hotel, Joel's, and the Italian eateries Roversi and Tony Pearl's. Henry was smitten with Rogers, later describing him in a reminiscence as "a tall, lean, lanky, shy cowboy with sky-blue eyes and dark-brown straight hair, with his same winning smile which later became so famous." Their relationship, however, proved hard to sustain due to their disparate travel schedules on the various vaudeville circuits. To further complicate matters, Henry was married.[37]

Looming in the background of Rogers' numerous romantic escapades, however, was a relationship with a young woman from back home that never quite gelled but never quite disappeared. He had first met Betty Blake in the fall of 1899 when she had come from her hometown just over the Indian Territory border in Rogers, Arkansas to visit her sister in Oologah. Her brother-in-law was the station master at the depot there for the Missouri Pacific Railroad, and Blake was helping out one evening when a young man swung down from a train and walked up to the ticket window. Blake stepped to the window to ask what he wanted but he turned and left before she could say a word. It was Rogers, who wanted to pick up a banjo that had been shipped to him, but was too shy to ask. A couple of days later, a friend announced excitedly that Will Rogers was back in town and "had brought with him all the new popular songs from Kansas City." Betty was invited to the Oologah hotel for dinner by Mr. and Mrs. Ellis, the proprietors, along with their daughters Kate and Lil, to meet him and hear the songs. While Rogers was "awkward and very still during supper," Blake later recalled, he loosened up afterwards when they retired to the sitting room. He sang many of the new songs he had brought, including *Hello, My Baby, Hello, My Honey, Hello, My Ragtime Gal.* Upon leaving, Rogers gave Blake the sheet music and asked her to learn them on her sister's piano, one of the only ones in town. He came to her house a few days later, and they spent the evening immersed in music, him singing and her playing piano and banjo as accompaniment.[38]

Betty returned home at Christmas, and on January 5, 1900 she received an unexpected missive from her new musical friend. Granting that she would be "madly surprised on receipt of this Epistle," Rogers expressed his hope that she would return to Oologah soon where he would show her a "hot time" with dances, skating, sleigh riding, horseback riding, and "every kind of amusement on the face of God's footpiece." He made clear his romantic interest, asking her to "take pity on this poor heartbroken Cowpealer" by replying with a few words. At the same time, he conveyed considerable self-consciousness about his Indian status, noting her time in Oologah among the "Wild Tribe" in an "Indian Wigwam." He closed the letter, "I remain your true friend and Injun Cowboy." She wrote back to Rogers, and received another letter from him dated March 14 that was more intensely expressed, both on the romantic front and the self-conscious front. He declared, "I am yours as far as I am concerned" and vowed, "I would give all I possessed if I only knew that you cared something for me." He signed off, "I am yours with love." At the same time, having learned that she was being teased by friends about her Cherokee suitor, he noted defensively that while he would like to visit her "I know it would be a slam on your Society career to have it known that you even knew an ignorant Indian Cowboy."[39]

The nervous quality of Rogers' courtship flowed from a keen awareness of Blake's prominent social status in her Arkansas hometown. Betty was part of a large family of seven girls and two boys. Her father, the operator of a grist-and-sawmill, had died when she was young and left the family considerable funds, and her mother was able to buy a large house in Rogers and support her children as a dressmaker. The girls were active in the town's social affairs and the family was considered to be among its most respectable. Betty had been educated at the Rogers Academy, a Congregationalist school, and then worked at a newspaper and a number of local stores. Fun-loving and charming, she smiled easily and presented a pretty visage with large brown eyes, dark blond hair, and a pert expression on her oval face. Betty possessed abundant musical talent, learning to play several instruments and performing with a local "Young Ladies Orchestra." Rogers also valued her as a classy, genteel young woman with a steady temperament, telling his cousin that she "would always talk things over with me so calm-like and she had such a clear way of judging things .... I reckon she was what I had been needing all my life. Sort of a balance wheel."[40]

They saw one another twice at wide intervals. They attended, separately, a rodeo in Springfield, Missouri, where Rogers competed in the steer roping and then joined Blake and her friends in the grandstand where, in her words, he became "timid and shy." A few weeks later the pair crossed paths at a street fair in Fort Smith, Arkansas and conversed several times over a few days. But at the ball held to honor the queen of the fair at its conclusion, Rogers appeared but never approached Blake. She finally saw him through the window of the ballroom wandering among guests out on the lawn. "He was watching the dancers and sometimes glancing in my direction," she reported. "But he did not come in and I did not go out." Shortly thereafter, Rogers left home to seek his fortune in Argentina and the pair did not see one another for two years while he circled the globe.[41]

Their reacquaintance came by accident at the St. Louis World's Fair in 1904. Blake had come up to visit a sister, who lived in the city, and take in the exhibition. While wandering through the Oklahoma exhibition building, she overheard someone mention Will Rogers and his performance at the Cummins Wild West Show on the Pike. She sent a note to him at the venue, and he replied quickly, inviting the Blake sisters and Mary Quisenberry, one of their hometown friends, to a matinee performance the next day and then dinner. Will attempted to impress Betty, but it backfired badly. He appeared in the arena outfitted in a tight-fitting red velvet suit covered in gold braid. "He looked so funny, and I was so embarrassed when my sister and Mary gave me sidelong glances and smiled at the costume, that I didn't hear the applause or find much joy in Will's expertness with the rope," a horrified Blake said. She later found out that Mrs. Wirth from the circus in Australia had made it for him and it was one of his prize possessions. He had worn it for her benefit, but was so chagrined at her discomfort that he never wore it again. After the show, Will and Betty got away from her companions, had dinner, toured the midway, and heard the famous Irish tenor, John McCormack, sing at a special performance. Basking in their enjoyable evening, the young couple agreed to meet the next morning. Rogers, however, sent her a last-minute note saying he had been called back to the Claremore ranch by his father on some business and could not meet her. It is also possible that he had been seeing Lucille Mulhall during the fair and wanted to avoid any recriminations. In any event, this abrupt departure surprised and annoyed Blake.[42]

The schizoid quality of their encounter at the St. Louis World's Fair became all too characteristic of their subsequent courtship as missteps and frustration, misunderstandings and bungled opportunities prevailed. For the next several years, Rogers and Blake performed a romantic dance where he alternately pursued and ignored her and she alternately rejected and enticed him. In a letter meant to amuse her, for instance, Rogers joked that "according to form we both should have matrimonied long ago. It wouldent do for this young gang to look at our teeth, you know." Blake let him know she was not amused by this crack about advanced age, and he quickly backtracked, apologizing for being "so unthoughtful as to refer to something that you could in the least get offended at, but it was all a joke." A bit later, Rogers was still repairing the damage, asking Blake for a letter but "not one that I will have to take my overcoat to read for the other was on the chilly order." As he pressed his romantic case and she demurred, his appeals ranged from pleading to demanding. In a 1905 letter, Rogers asked Blake to "tell me that you could sometime learn to love me just a little" then, a short time later, he announced, "Now, you better give me an outline of my prospects in the next letter and it must come pretty soon."[43]

Mixed signals and misunderstanding continued when Rogers' sisters invited Blake for a visit in 1906. Things got off on the wrong foot when Betty arrived after a lengthy, convoluted train journey from Arkansas and Will considerately came to meet her at the station before her departure point so they could ride together for a time. However, when he walked into the coach another passenger already had taken the seat next to Blake. So Rogers leaned in, shook her hand, and silently found a seat at the front of the crowded train car. When they arrived at Chelsea, Oklahoma, the Rogers sisters were waiting at the station and teased Will about his chivalry when he got off the train carrying her two bags. He grew embarrassed and withdrew. Then over the next few days, as Blake and the Rogers girls rode horseback, visited, and invited friends for dinner and parties, Will stayed on the edges of the activity. "[H]alf of the time Will wouldn't go," Betty recalled later, "and if he did, he never looked in my direction or singled me out." He only joined her when music was being performed and she played the piano. In Betty's words, "I just could not understand him . . . . So far as Will was concerned, I was a baffled young lady when I left for home."[44]

The romantic pendulum swung hard the other way when, only a week later, Rogers dropped by Blake's home on the way back to New York and proposed that they get married immediately. He gave her a lace handkerchief from Argentina, claiming that he purchased it from an "old Indian lady" who instructed him to give it to the young woman he would marry. While appreciative, Blake turned him down. She was not keen on marrying someone in the entertainment field, explaining "from my point of view, show business was not a very stable occupation . . . . I simply could not see a life of trouping the country in vaudeville. Will could not understand my attitude. Our parting was a sad one, but we promised to write." Indeed, what unfolded was a long-distance relationship tenuously held together by letters. Typically, Rogers pleaded and cajoled Blake, asking for more letters and expressions of love – "you are mine and you know I am yours. You just keep thinking that over for you will find me the most persistent Lover you ever saw" – while she received these entreaties behind a barricade of coyness and caution. In spring 1907, he again proposed marriage and she declined. Still upset several months later, Rogers declared, "When you still refused me last spring, We will both regret that for we would have been happy . . . . I have not been worth a dam[n] since and you are the direct and unwilling cause of it."[45]

Amidst this give and take of emotions, the pair introduced a poisonous element into their relationship when they tried to create jealousy with comments about admirers each was seeing. Rogers blundered badly when, trying to assure Blake that she was the only woman he was serious about, he described "a nice little girl friend of mine" named "Nina." In a terrible lapse of judgement, he even sent an actual note from Nina, who had responded graciously to his breaking things off. Not surprisingly, Blake was not reassured. For her part, Blake let Rogers know she was seeing an attorney in her hometown, which triggered the snide remark, "So you snared you a promising lawyer. What all did he promise you, and you him?" More serious was Blake's admission of a relationship with Tom Harvey, a local businessman and son of William "Coin" Harvey, the famous free-silver advocate. A spiteful Rogers pinpointed "your Dearest friend, T. H." and rejoined, "Well it's even for I have fell in love with an actorine and gone plum nutty."[46]

This lengthy exchange of barbs finally erupted in an angry confrontation in March 1908. After Blake wrote a letter chastising Rogers for his "coolness" toward her, his dalliances with other women, and his jealous suggestions that she had been intimate with other men, he exploded about her "crazy," "afful" letter. His coolness had been prompted by her Tom Harvey romance, he wrote back. "Yes, I got a lot of girls," he added, "several on and off the stage" and he had admitted it to her proudly because "I thought it showed manhood .... I had always been a bad boy and I guess I will continue to be one till you are with me and then it's all over." As for his "unpleasant insinuations" about her sexual liberties with other men, he grew indignant and denied suggesting "you acted the least bit unladylike." Moreover, he hinted that *they* – Rogers and Blake – had engaged in sexual activity and thus sealed their commitment. "Why what we done I love you for [and] if you had not of done it I would of known you did not love me," he said. "I don't think bad of you for that, 'cause I knew you was a [kind of] girl that if you hadent of loved me that wouldent of happened." Then came the usual emotional swing. At one extreme stood resentment: "I have done nothing all year but the wrong thing .... You speak as if I had a dark plot to deceive you and you (old sleuth) had discovered it." At the other extreme stood desperate love: "I tell you, you are the only girl for me [and] I mean it regardless of how I act sometimes."[47]

This roiling of the emotional waters, the mutual bickering and jealousies, served as a backdrop to Rogers' dramatic confession of September 23, 1908, when he abandoned contention for contrition. Admitting infidelities and weaknesses of character, he threw himself on Blake's mercy and asked for her forgiveness. This clearing of the air seems to have released the tension in their relationship. The fact that Rogers talked increasingly about leaving vaudeville and returning to Claremore and settling down as a rancher also swayed Blake. Thus in the fall of 1908 the couple agreed to marriage. Blake confessed, "I think we had known from the beginning that we cared for each other." Her fiancé expressed his happiness and gratitude with a characteristic flash of humor in closing a letter in October: "By-by, my Darling Sweetheart. I hope you may never regret sticking by a bum like I am."[48]

Rogers and Blake married at midday on November 25, 1908, in Rogers, Arkansas, her hometown. The ceremony took place in the parlor of her mother's home and was attended by members of both families. The bride wore a white and blue silk dress and the groom a dark traveling suit. In the afternoon, the couple caught the train for St. Louis and spent the night there at the Planter's Hotel. The next day was Thanksgiving, and Rogers ordered a special holiday meal, complete with champagne, served in their room. Blake had never imbibed champagne and did so liberally, thinking it to be a form of cider. A bit later, when they attended a performance of *What Every Woman Knows*, starring the famous actress Maude Adams, Blake complained that the theater was too hot. When the stage began to tilt and she had trouble understanding the actors, she asked her new husband if they could leave. Rogers took her back to the hotel, and cleared up the mystery of the "cider," and kidded his bride about what kind of woman he had married. Her enthusiastic drinking, he said with a grin, led him to the conclusion that "champagne drinking must be an old Arkansas custom." This minor misstep failed to dampen Rogers' love for his new wife. As he wrote many years later, "When I roped her that was the star performance of my life."[49]

After this brief honeymoon, the couple headed to New York to embark on a new and adventurous life. It took Betty a while to become accustomed to show business and its often-extravagant denizens, but to her surprise, she grew fond of vaudeville life and the excitement of urban society. She got her first taste when, over several weeks, her husband took her on guided tours of the city – the Bowery, Chinatown, Wall Street, the Statue of Liberty, the Singer Building (then the tallest in the world at forty-one stories), the Bronx Zoo, Old Trinity Church, Central Park – when he wasn't fulfilling matinee and evening theater bookings. He also indulged her with attendance at the opera to hear the legendary tenor, Enrico Caruso, an experience that made him "utterly miserable," in her words. "I had really been carried into a new world by my marriage," admitted this small-town girl from northwestern Arkansas.[50]

Betty's education-by-travel continued when she and Will hit the road, first completing a long string of engagements in the eastern United States before heading west for a long tour of the Orpheum circuit in the western states. They spent all their time together sightseeing, horseback riding in various city parks, going into the countryside for picnics. They both enjoyed this carefree, stimulating life and Betty confessed, "I soon began to wonder if the theater was so bad after all." She also learned crucial things about her husband's personality and temperament. Most obvious was his tremendous energy for experiencing life. "Will was a difficult person to keep up with," she noted. "He hated to lose a moment of his life; he wanted to do everything right now. And he nearly ran me ragged." In addition, Will disclosed that for all his humorous camaraderie, he was essentially a "lone wolf," as he described it. Outside of the actual theater shows, where he mingled easily with other performers and the audience, he kept to himself and had little to do with the social life of his fellow troupers. She attributed this trait to his youth on the Oklahoma prairie: "As a little boy on horseback, he had learned to be alone, and it had stayed with him."[51]

They also suffered a discouraging setback. Like most young married couples when launching a new life together, Will and Betty worried about money and the looming expense of houses and children. So they took a lesson from his sister, Maude, and her husband, and bought a metal box with a slit in the top. Every day they slipped a dollar or loose change into it and after several months their nest egg had grown considerably. But one afternoon in Butte, Montana, after ice skating at an outdoor rink and before Will's evening show, they returned to their hotel and found their belongings strewn about, a number of trinkets and wedding gifts stolen, and the lid pried off their strongbox with the money gone. Will tried to laugh it off but Betty was heartbroken and there was no doubt that the loss hurt.[52]

As Will's vaudeville career accelerated and his income grew steadily, talk of returning to Oklahoma to settle down on a ranch quietly faded. "I was growing reconciled to show business," Betty admitted, "and our promised return to Claremore kept being postponed." In August 1911, she informed Clem Rogers that the couple had decided to settle in New York. They had been living at the St. Francis Hotel but now took up more permanent residence in apartments, first on West 94th Street and then on West 113th Street. On October 20, their first child, William Vann Rogers, was born. Sadly, Clem Rogers died unexpectedly only eight days later and Will cancelled his engagements and left for Claremore to attend his father's funeral. A few years later, the Rogers family took up residence on Long Island, first leasing a house in Amityville and then another in Forest Hills. The family continued to grow, with Mary Amelia Rogers arriving in May 1913 and James Blake Rogers born in July 1915. Will Rogers had become a family man.[53]

* * * * *

With Betty's support, and a trio of children to support, Rogers turned his attention to new fields of opportunity in the mid-1910s. Vaudeville was exhibiting signs of decline in the face of several threatening new trends in American entertainment: the rise of motion pictures, the emergence of musical comedy fueled by dynamic young composers such as Irving Berlin and Jerome Kern, and the flourishing of lavish Broadway reviews. Rogers maneuvered to enter this world and the tipping point came when producer Lee Shubert tapped him to appear in a new musical on Broadway called *Hands Up*. During dress rehearsals, the show had appeared a bit cumbersome and tedious and the cowboy comedian was engaged to enliven the performance. On opening night, July 22, 1915, a sensational incident occurred that, much like the steer-roping occurrence at Madison Square Garden a decade before, put the Oklahoma Cowboy in the headlines.[54]

When Rogers came on stage near the end of the first act for his lariat-and-jokes segment, the audience applauded warmly. Bolstered by the reception and accustomed to a longer performance slot in vaudeville, he exceeded his allotted time. The audience was applauding enthusiastically and laughing when, suddenly, the stage lights went dark. The director had cut him off. Rogers, irritated and embarrassed, walked offstage and in the confusion a friend and fellow entertainer sitting in the audience, Fred Stone, leaped to his feet and yelled, "Don't let them do that to Will Rogers! Give the man a chance! It's a dirty trick!" The audience applauded loudly and roared for his return, stopping the show. The stage manager and show's director finally convinced him to go back on stage, where he received another rousing reception from the audience as he presented a few more rope tricks and jokes. The incident garnered headlines in all the New York papers the next day and a press release from Shubert acknowledged that the cowboy entertainer "had scored a tremendous hit at the opening" of the show and "become famous over-night." Rogers went on to perform in *Hands Up* for the next several weeks.[55]

This incident brought another unexpected dividend. The publicity surrounding Rogers' triumph drew the attention of Gene Buck, who attended a subsequent performance of *Hands Up* to see him. Buck was deeply impressed. He recommended the entertainer to his boss, the reigning king of New York entertainment, who promptly hired the young vaudevillian. Their subsequent collaboration would vault the Oklahoman to national stardom.

4

Follies and Frolics

O N DECEMBER 23, 1917, THE CURTAIN OPENED in Chicago's Illinois Theatre as the famous *Ziegfeld Follies* began its run in the Windy City. The show had debuted on Broadway's New Amsterdam Theater in New York on June 2 and ran for 111 performances before closing on September 4. Then, following its yearly tradition, the show embarked on a months-long national tour that took it to Boston, Washington, DC, Philadelphia, and Pittsburgh before landing in Chicago, where it ran for over two months and concluded on March 2, 1918. The *Follies* gathered a galaxy of talented Broadway managers, composers, and designers who combined to create a memorable entertainment experience: the legendary Florenz Ziegfeld as producer; musical direction by Raymond Hubbell and Dave Stamper; book by Gene Buck and George V. Hobart; songs by James Hanley, Jack Egan, and Jerome Kern; special lyrics by Ring Lardner and Blanche Merrill; a patriotic finale by Victor Herbert; scenic design by Joseph Urban; costume design by Lady Duff-Gordon.[1]

Now, before a packed house as the house lights dimmed, the show began with an exotic "Arabian Nights" sequence of music and dance featuring the dazzling "Ziegfeld Girls." These famous females – the very embodiment of the "new woman" of the twentieth century with their youthful good looks, sexy costumes, and career aspirations – were also featured in several other segments, including the "Garden of Girls," "Chinese Ladders," and "Ladies of Fashion." Then followed a parade of legendary musical and comic talent with the African-American comedian, Bert Williams, in "Grand Central"; singer and comedienne Fannie Brice in the "Ziegfeld Follies Rag"; comedian W. C. Fields in the "Tennis Game"; and comedian Eddie Cantor in "Songs and Observations," among others. Interspersed with the entertainment sections were a series of "historical tableaux" of Paul Revere's Midnight Ride, Valley Forge, Abraham Lincoln at Gettysburg, and Admiral Dewey at Manila during the Spanish-American War. The show culminated with

"Can't You Hear Your Country Calling," a patriotic finale that brought most of the large cast on stage for a rousing musical tribute to the American republic, which had entered World War I just a few months earlier. Throughout the show with its nineteen segments, the audience was treated to a spectacle of lavish sets, extravagant costumes, effervescent songs, and glamorous sexuality.[2]

In a prime spot in the *Follies*, three segments back from the close of the show, an act appeared that offered a sharp contrast to the show's dominant tone of urban sophistication. "Will Rogers Sayings" featured the veteran cowboy comic who was appearing in his first full season with the show. According to the program, he was "liable to talk about anything or anybody." Indeed, after ambling onstage in western garb twirling a lariat, he offered humorous observations on a wide range of people, places, and events in America. Typically, he began by poking fun at himself and the show, particularly with regard to the Ziegfeld Girls. His place in the festivities, he noted drily, was explained by the fact that "we have to do something out here while the girls change clothes, even if they don't have much to change." He added impishly, "the girls of the *Follies* wear a little less each year. I only ask that my life be spared until I see three more years of the *Follies*." Rogers then pivoted to the local situation in Chicago, poking fun at a recent crime wave that had swept over the city. It was so bad, he observed, that "if they keep arresting them at the rate the papers say they do, it is time to call a halt, as it will interfere with attendance at the theaters." The situation had put a strain on the local police because "for the risk they run they don't pay them enough money. The city tells them, 'Why, we pay you a living wage,' but the cops say, 'Yes, but few of us live to collect it.'" He noted that the public was impacted in sundry ways, such as "automobile robbers – there are so many of them! I wanted to buy a car, but I am afraid to do it as I know everybody will wonder where I got it." He concluded with mock sorrow, "If some playwright were to write a play of Chicago life and stage it real and as it is, all the actors would be dead at the end of the show and the audience would have to let down the curtain."[3]

Rogers then took up national affairs, particularly the European conflict that the United States had entered in April. He skewered America's primary enemy in World War I, commenting, "Germany should be able to make a very generous peace with her eastern foes. One thing I will say for the Germans, they are always perfectly willing to give somebody else's land to somebody else." He looked askance at one of America's allies, declaring, "Pick up the morning paper and look for Russian news and have a fear of reading the worst – you won't be disappointed." He added that somebody recently had shot at Lenin, the Russian Bolshevik leader, and missed. "If they got any shooting to do, why don't they get some American wives to do it?" he suggested. "There hasn't been a husband missed in this country in two years." Rogers then addressed the domestic political scene. "The Republicans are jealous over the way the Democrats are running the war," he observed. "I bet when peace is declared and the Republicans get in power they'll start another war to show how much better they can run one!" He finished his routine with an observation about Henry Ford and the 1915 failure of his notorious Peace Ship to end the conflict. He claimed that if Ford now "took this bunch of girls in this show, and let 'em wear the same costumes they wear here, and marched them down between the trenches, believe me, the boys would be out before Christmas!"[4]

It was a bravura performance and the Chicago audience showered him with laughter and applause. The local critics also responded favorably. The most prestigious one, Percy Hammond, wrote in the *Chicago Tribune* that Rogers was one of the greatest hits in the show. He asserted that the comic commentator, "aided by Wrigley and a lariat, in pungent editorials on the municipal and other governments, [taught] us more than all the problem plays" of the contemporary theater. Rogers' on-stage success with the *Ziegfeld Follies* in Chicago, as was true in other cities on the tour, brought other opportunities in its wake. He wrote several pieces for the *Chicago Tribune* and *Chicago Examiner* while in residence and as his popularity soared he was engaged to return the following year as a master of ceremonies for a benefit show at the Colonial Theater and an after lunch speaker for the traffic club of Chicago.[5]

In such fashion, Will Rogers stood in the national spotlight as a key performer in the *Ziegfeld Follies*. After years of seasoning in the rough-and-tumble atmosphere of vaudeville, he now traveled the country appearing in the most popular and prestigious show of the 1910s and 1920s and made himself into both a public figure whose humorous commentary on American values and proclivities aroused considerable admiration, and a celebrity whose personality attracted compulsive attention. Tens of thousands of patrons laughed at his clever commentary, countless critics praised his unique and compelling style of humor, and reporters from newspapers and magazines hounded him for information about his life. And it was all the result of Rogers' engagement with Florenz Ziegfeld, the emotionally austere but stylistically lavish impresario whose *Ziegfeld Follies* entranced a generation of entertainment seekers throughout the United States.

* * * * * * *

Florenz Ziegfeld, Jr., had a long pedigree in American show business. Born in Chicago two years after the close of the Civil War, this son of immigrants – a German father who taught classical music, a Belgian mother with an aristocratic background – originally pursued a career helping to run his father's Chicago Musical College. Ziegfeld had become entranced by popular entertainment, however, after attending *Buffalo Bill's Wild West* show in 1883 as an adolescent. Then at the Columbian Exposition a decade later, he assisted his father in putting together a show of light-classical music at the Trocadero theater on Michigan Avenue to take advantage of the crowds flocking to Chicago for the World's Fair. Flo modified his father's offering, however, by introducing the "Trocadero Vaudevilles," an agglomeration of circus acts headlined by the heroically proportioned, and barely clad, strongman, Eugene Sandow. Sandow posed and flexed and lifted, projecting a shocking sexual allure that was only enhanced when the ladies of Chicago were invited backstage after the show to feel his muscles. Audiences were mildly scandalized but loved it.

Following his success in managing Sandow, whom he took on tour and made into a national sensation with clever publicity stunts and advertising, Ziegfeld became an entertainment impresario. A turning point came while traveling in Europe in 1896, when he met the Polish-French actress, Anna Held, who, with her curvaceous figure, sultry persona, and notorious milk-baths, had made a mark with sexuality both on and off stage. Ziegfeld began a relationship with Held and she eventually became his common-law wife. They returned to the United States together where he produced several Broadway musical plays in which she starred. More importantly, she inspired a breakthrough initiative. Ziegfeld had seen Held perform in the lavish Paris revue, the *Folies Bergères*, and began to think along those lines when he returned to the United States. In his words, while in Paris "I had seen many revues, and since New York had never had a real revue I thought to avoid competition by entering this field."[6]

So in 1907 he premiered the first *Ziegfeld Follies* on the rooftop venue at the New York Theater. Its combination of sexy showgirls, extravagant costumes, opulent sets, rousing music, and amusing comedy routines proved irresistible to the public and the crowds flocked to attend. The *Follies* became an annual event over the next two decades with new shows emerging – each striving to top the one preceding – to great anticipation every year. In 1913, Ziegfeld moved his show to the beautiful New Amsterdam Theatre in Times Square, an Art Nouveau architectural masterpiece, where it drew a consistently packed house before going out on tour to various American cities. According to one observer, the years 1915 to 1925 were the "golden age" of the *Follies* in terms of popularity and innovation. Employing talented composers such as Irving Berlin, Jerome Kern, and Victor Herbert to write original music and popular comedians such as W. C. Fields, Bert Williams, Ed Wynn, and Fanny Brice, this showman put together an all-star lineup that delighted audiences throughout the nation. Florenz Ziegfeld became the king of American entertainment.[7]

In certain ways, the *Ziegfeld Follies* drew upon the traditions of vaudeville by amassing a collection of acts presented in a revue format. But it deviated sharply by weaving together those acts thematically, having performers appear and reappear in segments throughout the show, and encasing the whole in a rich, sophisticated style that mirrored the tastes and imagery of the higher echelons of society. The hallmark of Ziegfeld musical theater was its opulent atmosphere and lush ambiance – lavish costumes, glamorous atmosphere, spectacular sets, elaborate lighting, precision dancing, and sophisticated popular music, all punctuated with interludes of comic monologues and skits. These dazzling productions presented a visual and aural feast that typically consisted of fifteen or twenty acts. They varied widely. In the 1919 *Follies*, for example, which many critics considered to be among Ziegfeld's very best productions, the acts ranged from the song and dance number "The Follies Salad" to the comedy sketch "The Saloon of the Future"; the historical tableau "Melody Fantasy and Folly of Years Gone By," featuring Lady Godiva, to ethnic comedy with Cantor and Williams; the elaborate production number "Minstrel Show" to a whimsical Herbert ballet sequence set in a circus; and all leading to the patriotic grand finale devoted to "The Salvation Army." As one commentator has noted, Ziegfeld's wildly popular productions "assimilated the best of two seemingly divergent cultures: a refined European sense of style and the American frontier spirit."[8]

The hallmark of these shows, however, was the famous "Ziegfeld Girl." The showman hired several dozen attractive show girls who became vital to the appeal of the *Follies*. These beautiful young women dressed either in very little – bathing suits, short skirts, tights, sometimes appearing partially nude in the tableaux – or in elaborate costumes of silk, satin, and chiffon adorned with feathers and mink wraps. Ziegfeld's trademark became his "glorification of the American girl," a fact reflected in the 1919 *Follies* where Irving Berlin's "A Pretty Girl is Like a Melody" anchored the central segment and the elegant chorine, Rose Dolores, appeared in the legendary White Peacock dress, a fabulous sequined gown with an elaborate feathered headdress and a long, trailing tailfeather train that fanned out and upward to a height of ten feet. The Ziegfeld Girl reflected the changing moral milieu of early twentieth-century America. In this post-Victorian age, the showman had transformed the old-fashioned, seedy "girlie show" from the nineteenth century into respectable entertainment for mixed audiences by transforming the young women at its center.[9]

Ziegfeld picked his showgirls not according to the old calculus of burlesque – crude sexuality, full figures, winking availability – but for their youthful good looks, trim figures, and talents as singers and dancers. In magazine pieces such as "Picking Out Pretty Girls For the Stage," he explained his thinking. Beauty, of course, provided the initial benchmark. With several thousand applicants for each annual show, "the first thing we do is weed out those who are not pretty in face and form." But Ziegfeld, attuned to the vigorous cultural currents of early twentieth-century America with its abandonment of an old-fashioned Victorian sensibility, sought something more. "The ones who make the really big successes have beauty – *plus personality*," he explained. "And they can even be shy on beauty, if they have enough personality. Beauty is something you *see*. Personality is something you *feel*." Moreover, the Ziegfeld Girl, like many females in a new, vibrant age, needed to be active rather than merely ornamental. In his words, "the beautiful and charming girl, or woman, who can *do* something well is sure of all the popularity she wants. If she sings, or talks, or rides, or dances, or plays tennis, or entertains, or does *something* . . . she will be pushed to the front." Ziegfeld also parried the attack from some moralists that his showgirls were gold diggers by appealing to another facet of the female experience in modern America: "I have employed hundreds of chorus girls, and I think that they are much the same as other women who work, no better and certainly no worse." As one historian has observed, in the post-Victorian society of the early 1900s the Ziegfeld Girl embodied the image of "the modern girl . . . . The image of the chorus of young girls represented possibility and freedom rather than entrapment."[10]

Behind the scenes, Ziegfeld's personality dominated the *Follies*. Most photographs show him looking at the world in a studied, somber, somewhat quizzical fashion. While often reserved to the point of aloofness, Ziegfeld displayed a commanding presence and an understated charm in his professional endeavors. A dapper dresser who favored stylish suits with lavender shirts, he hired a barber to shave him daily at his home while his family joked about the extent and complexity of his toilette. Ziegfeld was given to gambling and luxurious spending in his private life. He maintained a sprawling country estate in Westchester County, Burkley Crest, that was festooned with thousands of flowering plants and a veritable zoo of animals and birds. Its Victorian manor house had a telephone booth installed under the first-floor stairs so he could be in touch with his New York office twenty-four hours a day. While this lord-of-the manor persona helped make him a taskmaster at the *Follies*, Ziegfeld also was solicitous of his employees' well-being and sent them flowers and inscribed platinum watches when pleased with their work, qualities that cemented their loyalty and affection. In 1919, the show's cast presented Ziegfeld with a fifteen-inch-high silver loving cup with an inscription describing "a token of our love and esteem."[11]

A central aspect of Ziegfeld's personality – his notorious womanizing – shaped the world of the *Follies* in complex ways. Over the years, he indulged in liaisons with a number of beautiful Ziegfeld Girls, most famously Lillian Lorraine, Marilyn Miller, and Olive Thomas. In 1913, he divorced Held and took up with showgirl and actress Billie Burke, with whom he had a tempestuous but lasting marriage beginning in 1914. She grudgingly tolerated his affairs because of her conviction that he loved her, but Ziegfeld's dalliance with showgirls often created emotional problems at home. They also triggered tensions in the *Follies* with awkward situations and veiled accusations of favoritism. At the same time, they helped create a mystique by generating publicity and contributing to the sex appeal of the Ziegfeld brand. Newspaper stories about Ziegfeld's adventurous love life kept his name before the public. In 1922, for instance, a story hit the newspapers when the showman and Marilyn Miller got into a tiff when he accused her fiancé of criminal activity and she retorted that he had wanted to leave Burke to marry her and habitually chased after every chorus girl in sight. Ziegfeld cabled Burke – it was somehow intercepted and printed in the *New York Times* – and claimed "I swear to God there is nothing to which you can take exception." When a reporter asked her for a response, Burke said, "It's all very, very personal" and threw up her hands in frustration.[12]

As a giant figure in the expanding arena of American entertainment, Ziegfeld labored diligently to uphold the image emblazoned on his business card: "Impresario Extraordinaire." Two traits proved particularly influential. First, he brought an organized, demanding, driven temperament to the creation of the yearly *Follies* and supervised every aspect of its production down to the tiniest detail. Some described him as a dictator. He held marathon rehearsals that would last nearly twenty-four hours and became legendary for shouting at performers and staff in his relentless pursuit of entertainment perfection. Ziegfeld worked insanely long hours and demanded his staff do likewise, announcing, "When I start to do a thing I don't stop until I finish it." No aspect of a *Follies* show escaped his attention. "Too many managers let their details run down after the first week or two of success. They think minor parts and little bits of business or costumes don't matter," he once described in an interview. "Details are what makes a show's personality ... . I keep my shows combed, polished, and groomed." The wife of one of his performers recalled witnessing Ziegfeld at a spring rehearsal of the *Follies* as he "sat out in front in the dimly lighted theater and gave commands as he watched every detail of costumes and movements .... [He] threw out an entire set of costumes for the finale and ordered new ones. That must have cost him some ten or fifteen thousand dollars – but Mr. Ziegfeld was an artist of the theater, rather than a businessman."[13]

Second, Ziegfeld was a master of publicity. He advertised relentlessly, planting newspaper and magazine stories and overseeing the creation of *Follies* posters featuring evocative images of beautiful young women in daring outfits (some of them were actually smoking cigarettes) and suggestive song titles such as "Making Whoopee" and "That's the Kind of Baby for Me." He fabricated stories and cooked up publicity stunts to generate interest in his productions. Near the start of his career, Ziegfeld had called in a team of doctors to draft a report saying that Eugene Sandow was "a perfect physical specimen." After the launch of the

Follies, he planted a newspaper story claiming that singing star Nora Bayes subsisted on a diet of lollipops. He informed reporters that he had discovered Fanny Brice hawking newspapers under the Brooklyn Bridge, even though she had established a solid reputation as a comedienne in burlesque. He once had the Ziegfeld Girls parade down city streets in their bathing suits to City Hall to publicize one of his shows. Ziegfeld's penchant for publicity dovetailed neatly with an instinct for personal aggrandizement. He realized that the lavish spectacle of his shows would be enhanced by a similar personal image, so upper-class "quality" became a hallmark both of the *Follies* and himself. For instance, he germinated a story in the *New York Telegraph* noting his distress over inadvertently giving an actor a 1,000 dollar bill instead of the 1 dollar bill he had intended. When the impertinent reporter asked how Ziegfeld knew it was not a 1-million dollar bill, the showman upped the ante. Adopting a haughty look, he replied, "Because I always carry those in an inside pocket." This genius for both personal and professional publicity sent both soaring by the mid-1910s. As the *New Yorker* concluded of the famous showman, "Florenz Ziegfeld, Jr. does not seem to be acquainted with himself. He thinks he is a person. He doesn't know that he is an institution." Ziegfeld, of course, knew that better than anyone since he had created it.[14]

Third, in a deeper sense, Ziegfeld had an instinctive feel for an audience abandoning Victorian verities in the changing cultural milieu of early twentieth-century America. In a new age, countless citizens were exchanging the work ethic for the leisure ethic, character for personality, scarcity for abundance, and self-control for self-fulfillment. He demonstrated an understanding of this sea-change as the author of a 1912 magazine piece entitled "Why I Produce the Kind of Shows I Do." In an exploding consumer economy, he argued, the public was "willing to pay exceedingly large prices to get the style of entertainment it most desires. I am not in business for my health. I desire to make money." Moreover, Ziegfeld grasped that Americans had tired of the old-fashioned morality of theater productions and were "sick and tired of the conventional plots." They sought lighter fare that amused and entertained rather than instructed. "For this reason, I boldly discarded every pretense of plot," he said. "That is the secret of my success with the *Follies*." Finally, of course, Ziegfeld strived to secure beautiful, alluring women for his productions. "Mere beauty alone is not sufficient, however," he added. "I endeavor to secure clever people who can act or do something out of the ordinary. People with personality of an unusual nature." Ziegfeld created a new form of entertainment tailored to the sensibility of a new age.[15]

It was this larger-than-life producer with his imposing entertainment juggernaut that Will Rogers encountered in 1915. The meeting was serendipitous. Gene Buck, a writer, talent scout, and Ziegfeld's right-hand man, saw Rogers in the

Broadway show, *Hands Up,* and immediately concluded that he would be a perfect addition to his boss's show business empire. As Buck later noted, he "saw in Will an opportunity for a comedian who represented the West and the great outdoors – a cowboy comedian, something unknown in America." When he approached Ziegfeld about hiring the Oklahoman, the powerful producer was reluctant. Buck persisted, however, and Ziegfeld finally agreed to give Rogers a try but at a minor venue on a trial basis.[16]

So rather than heading straight to the *Follies,* Rogers began at Ziegfeld's smaller New York entertainment venue, the *Midnight Frolic,* where he debuted on August 23, 1915. He began at a salary of 175 dollars a week. Situated on the rooftop "Aerial Gardens" of the New Amsterdam Theatre – Ziegfeld presented the *Follies* in the huge auditorium on the main floor – the *Frolic* was a night club that opened its doors at midnight. It drew a clientele of well-heeled New Yorkers out to enjoy the city's night life, many of them coming upstairs after taking in the *Follies* in the large theater below. The *Frolic* offered excellent food and dancing to a live orchestra, as well as lavish shows with beautiful showgirls, comedy, and variety acts. Ziegfeld had hired Joseph Urban, a Viennese artist and set designer, to remodel the New Amsterdam rooftop. He created a striking, open floor plan with a moveable platform stage reached by a glass-enclosed runway that allowed patrons to see the showgirls as they descended to the stage. The venue's chic, fantastic reputation was enhanced by dazzling sets and innovative lighting. Both the performers and the showgirls mingled with the audience in this more intimate venue, and a spirit of revelry prevailed with customers tooting on noisemakers and banging on their tables with small wooden hammers when they approved an act.[17]

Initially, after seeing Rogers perform, a skeptical Ziegfeld believed that the Oklahoman's style would never appeal to a sophisticated New York audience. "That damn cowboy has got to go," he told Buck. "I am leaving for a couple of weeks and when I return I don't want him around here." Buck disagreed and dragged his feet before finally summoning Rogers to deliver the bad news. Before the manager could speak, however, Rogers noted that his wife had recommended that he modify his act and talk about what he read in the newspapers, making that the basis of his humorous observations. Intrigued, Buck told him to try it and held off on the dismissal. So the next evening Rogers debuted what would become his trademark line, "all I know is what I read in the papers," and began joking about the news of the day. The audience loved it. When Ziegfeld returned, Buck summoned him to observe Rogers' revamped routine with its commentary on current public affairs. A rather humorless man, the impresario was puzzled by the audience enthusiasm but recognized loud applause and laughter when he heard it. Ziegfeld gradually warmed to Rogers' talent as audiences grew both in numbers and enthusiasm, kept him on, and the Oklahoman eventually became the biggest attraction at the *Frolic*.[18]

In fact, the cowboy humorist unexpectedly became a darling of the New York critics, who were impressed by his authenticity as well as his wit. *Variety* gushed over "newcomer Will Rogers," noting, "In his cowboy outfit he kids any and everyone, does a few tricks, and is a riot." The *New York Times* likened him to Mark Twain. One reviewer concluded that Rogers was "a rare soul among comics" and concluded that given "his own field to work in, and his own crowd to work for, there is no one who can approach within yards of him as an original entertainer." Another provided an admiring description of how Rogers "plays with a rope, hat on the back of his head, a bit of gum between his teeth to keep him company – a shy Westerner venturing out alone in this mass of wild New Yorkers . . . . And all the while he talks – eyes on the floor, stepping by your table on his way around the floor, cracking delicious jokes in a soft drawl." One observer captured a key part of the appeal when he noticed that Rogers "always talks to us privately and confidentially. Even before he opens his mouth to speak, the barrier of the footlights is down and we are in the same room with him."[19]

For his part, Rogers loved the *Frolic*. Joking that the venue was for "folks with lots of money. And plenty of insomnia," he described it years later as "the start of all this midnight and late style of entertainment that has since degenerated into a drunken orgy of off-color songs and close formation dancing." "It had the most beautiful girls of any show Ziegfeld ever put on, for the beautiful ones wouldent work at a matinee for they never got up that early." Indeed, much of Rogers' success came from the startling contrast he presented with the show's glamorous showgirls. As in the larger *Follies*, the chorines were the foundation of the *Frolic*'s appeal. When Rogers joined up, the show was entitled "Nothing But Girls" and one of its most popular routines was "Balloon Girls," where chorus girls sashayed among the tables with balloons affixed to their costumes and headdresses, while male customers burst them with cigarettes or cigars. Another segment called "The Girl from My Home Town" depicted pretty young women from every part of the United States flocking to New York looking for freedom and success as a chorus girl. Surrounded by this array of female beauty, the slow-talking cowboy comic was placed in a naturally funny atmosphere as a bashful foil. He took advantage, joking about the showgirls, looking embarrassed at their flirtations, and sometimes roping them as a prank. He accurately deduced in one of his notebooks, "[To] all these beautiful girls I am the contrast."[20]

In addition to this amusing contrast with the Ziegfeld Girls, Rogers built his success at the *Frolics* with his growing skill at commenting on public affairs and personalities. Many patrons of this cabaret supper club were repeat customers, and he felt the need to refresh his routine to keep them coming back. At first he did so by staying alert to opportunities that appeared during the show where he could joke spontaneously about other performers, miscues in the production, or funny possibilities in the audience. But increasingly he followed Betty's advice and turned to the affairs of the day. A dedicated newspaper reader, he began to spend hours combing through the daily papers, in his words, "trying to dope out a funny angle to the day's news, and I found that they would laugh easiest at the stuff that just happened that day. A joke don't have to be near as funny if it's up to date." Rogers proved adept at finding people and issues that warranted gentle lampooning, comic exaggeration, or shrewd assessments of absurdity. As he quipped, "I started to reading about Congress, and believe me, I found they are funnier three hundred and sixty-five days a year than anything I ever heard of."[21]

After nine months of mounting success at the *Midnight Frolic*, Rogers finally struck Flo Ziegfeld as ready for bigger things. In rehearsals the initial version of the *Ziegfeld Follies of 1916* had proved disappointing. While typically extravagant and spectacular, it seemed to lumber along and came across as dull and stodgy. So Ziegfeld invited Rogers to join the cast to lighten the atmosphere. But the humorist, under strong pressure from his wife, declined because the salary was insufficient to warrant leaving New York on tour with the *Follies* in a few weeks. The family had settled into their Forest Hills house and kept horses at a nearby stable and Betty balked at sending her husband on the road without a handsome monetary reward. Almost immediately, Rogers regretted the decision. When he and Betty and another couple attended a *Follies* show in New York a few weeks later, he watched the slow-paced performance and knew that he would have bolstered it. He began muttering, "See Blake, what did I tell you. This was my one big chance." And "Boy, I wish I could have got my crack at it." Betty agreed that his down-home, humorous act would have improved the *Follies* tremendously and that it had been a mistake to reject the offer. "I blamed myself," she confessed, and admitted that he had every right to be upset with her.[22]

So when Ziegfeld renewed his offer a few days later, Rogers leaped at the chance. He rushed home to gather Betty and dashed back to the city to join the show that very night. The result was more than they ever could have hoped for. When Will went on the stage that evening, the audience broke into applause and responded to his routine with waves of laughter. The critics in the next morning's newspapers gave him excellent notices. It was, according to Betty, "the very proudest moment of our lives." In joining the *Ziegfeld Follies* at the height of its popularity and esteem, Rogers stood poised to become a truly national figure.

* * * * *

When he joined *The Ziegfeld Follies of 1916*, an exuberant Will Rogers may have underestimated the heavy load that he would shoulder. For several weeks, he labored at both the *Follies* and the *Frolic* in New York for his regular salary, giving two performances each night plus two matinees every week. Such diligence paid off, however. When it came time to take the *Follies* on the road, Ziegfeld, who had come to appreciate Rogers' worth, offered him a two-year agreement with a substantial raise that paid 600 dollars a week for the first year and 750 dollars a week for the second year. Rogers agreed, the two men shook hands, and they entered into an entertainment relationship that would last for nearly a decade. The humorist served as a regular in the *Follies* from 1916–1919, returned in 1922, and then again in 1924 and 1925 for a final stint.[23]

Rogers had a well-defined role in a *Follies* show. He delivered a solo comic monologue that lasted from eight to twelve minutes and had different titles in the program over the years ("Will Rogers Sayings," "Timely Topics," "Yankee Philosophy," "Out West"). He also appeared in a variety of sketches, musical numbers, and skits. In *The Follies of 1918*, for instance, he took the stage in a tuxedo and top hat to sing "Any Old Time at All" with prominent showgirl and Ziegfeld favorite, Lillian Lorraine, an unlikely transformation from cowboy to playboy that delighted the audience. In 1922, he played a baseball pitcher named "Cy Walters" in a parody called *The Bull Pen*, written by Ring Lardner. The same year he starred in a hilarious skit entitled "Koo Koo Nell," a satire of western melodrama set in the dancehalls of San Francisco. Rogers appeared as the "female" lead in a plaid dress and flowered hat, complete with a mincing manner and a frequently-used powder puff. The audience howled. Eventually, Rogers wrote and appeared in his own comic sketches. In the 1924 *Follies*, for example, he authored two political skits. In *A Couple of Senators*, he played a newly elected U.S. Senator from Oklahoma who is welcomed by a longstanding member of the chamber full of pomposity and self-importance in a send-up of the famous Senator Henry Cabot Lodge. In *The Chloride Gas Room Capitol*, Congress convenes a committee devoted to investigating its own investigating committees. It is promptly dominated by a bloviating Congressman who testifies in a fifteen-minute monologue that meanders through great clouds of nonsensical verbiage that goes nowhere. Rogers, as the committee chairman, compliments him for his "lucid" statement but asks for clarification, beginning with the second word and ending with the last. As the bloviator starts again, a gas machine on stage blows clouds of vapor out over the participants.[24]

During his tenure with the *Ziegfeld Follies*, the humorist gained a reputation as an unpretentious man, someone whose head was not turned by his growing status as a star in America's most prestigious show. Marcelle Earl, one of the chorus girls in the *Follies*, described Rogers as a "plain, natural, homespun" man and told a story of how he once entered the dining car of the troupe's train and turned down an invitation to eat with the show's stars. "I'm agoin' to set with the gals over there," he told the headliners, and joined Marcelle and her friend with the comment, "Looks mighty good what you gals are eatin'. I'll have the same." After finishing, he said, "Twas nice eatin' in such good company" and picked up the check. This was not just an act for public consumption, as Betty Rogers learned to her consternation. As her husband became a star in the *Ziegfeld Follies* firmament, she decided to renovate his small, dingy dressing room on the third floor of the New Amsterdam Theatre. She put a curtain around the window looking out over a back street, added a rug and some comfortable chairs, refurbished the drab dressing table and mirror, and brought in a couch for him to lay down and relax. When Rogers saw it, however, "a roar went up," in Betty's words. He complained that he did not want his dressing room "fancied up," as he put it, and immediately sent most of the new items to other performers and reinstalled the plain furnishings that suited him.[25]

In the backstage world of the *Follies*, Rogers developed a close friendship with fellow comics Eddie Cantor and W. C. Fields. In fact, Ziegfeld dubbed the trio the "Three Musketeers." It was an unlikely alliance: the down-home cowboy from the western plains, the boisterous Jewish prankster from the lower East Side of New York, the dyspeptic juggler and hilarious misanthrope from Philadelphia. Yet they had all earned their stripes on the vaudeville circuit and shared a commitment to comedic professionalism. In Cantor's words, "Will Rogers would watch my act from the wings or W. C. Fields' skit and offer changes in the lines or situations that invariably improved the original material. We tried to do the same for him whenever possible." They played pranks on one another, as when Fields shouted for Rogers to come quickly to a backstage area, only to turn him by the shoulders to look through an open dressing room door as a beautiful, buxom, undressed Ziegfeld Girl was quickly changing into her next costume. As Rogers turned red and stumbled away, Fields bellowed, "What's the matter, Bill? A very pretty girl!" Another time during an evening show, Cantor gave an identical joke to Fields, whose act went first, and then Rogers, who came afterwards and then laughed uproariously when it fell flat for Rogers during its second telling. The trio often hung out together outside of the *Follies*. Cantor introduced Rogers to kosher restaurants during their Ziegfeld stint, and the Oklahoman became very fond of the food. Once Cantor caught him muttering, "Too late, I guess it's too late." When the New Yorker asked what it was too late for, Rogers replied, "For me to turn Jewish."[26]

When the *Follies* left New York and embarked on its annual tour, Rogers indulged several ingrained habits. Ziegfeld knew how to keep his comic star happy, so he allowed Rogers to bring along two horses in the troupe's train that were kept in the scenery car under the supervision of a cowboy friend. When they alighted in a city for a series of shows, the performer spent many happy hours at local riding academies practicing fancy roping tricks from horseback. Rogers also remained haphazard with money. According to Betty Rogers, throughout his stint with the *Follies*, her husband "was apt to carry in his pockets as many as eight or ten uncashed weekly pay checks, and then, to the horror of the Ziegfeld business office, deposit them in the bank at one time and almost break the company."[27]

As he appeared before countless audiences around the United States during his stint with the *Ziegfeld Follies*, the Oklahoma Cowboy took a crucial step in his career. He put the finishing touches on the entertainment persona that would establish his lasting reputation. As he kept listeners both laughing and thinking, he refined several techniques that became central to the man that Americans came to know and love. The humorist had been developing most of them since he first became an entertainer, but now he both sharpened them and synthesized them into a cohesive, compelling whole. He became, fully, Will Rogers.

The central feature of this persona was a style of humor, defined most obviously by its seeming spontaneity. Rogers made it appear that his comic observations were spur-of-the-moment flashes and, indeed, he had a genius for comic improvisation, a nimble wit that sensed possibilities for humor as they appeared before him. He never rehearsed his act but "liked to keep everything he had to say as fresh for the performers in the show as for the opening-night audience. As a result, the cast always crowded around the wings when Will's act was on," Betty explained. In a fascinating article entitled "The Extemporaneous Line" in the July 1917 edition of *Theatre Magazine*, Rogers reflected on how much of his best humor emerged moment-to-moment while he faced an audience. He noted that he went onstage with a theme or idea in mind, but then altered or embroidered his comments as he read the audience and thoughts appeared suddenly. "Some of the best things come to me when I am out on the stage," he noted. "I start in on a subject and if it is no good then I have to switch quick, and lots of times when I come off of the stage I have done an entirely different act from what I intended when I went on." Rogers noted a recent example of his treatment of German submarines facing the United States when it entered World War I. He told the audience, "I read that submarines could not operate in the warm Gulf Stream, so I said, 'If we can only heat the ocean we will have them licked.' That didn't get much of a laugh and I was kinda' stuck. But I happened to add, 'Of course, that is only a rough idea. I haven't worked it out yet.' This last went big and covered up the other." This gift for comic improvisation contributed much to the Will Rogers mystique.[28]

At the same time, the Oklahoman devoted many hours to preparing his routines while paying close attention to themes, approaches, and language. He worked hard at honing his craft. Rogers pored through newspapers "trying to dope out a funny angle to the day's news," as he put it. "And, I tell you, it is sure hard digging." When the *Follies* arrived in an American city, he immediately started researching local events, issues, and developments and tailored his humorous observations to them. Rogers also began compiling "gag books" that listed quips and comments that could be used in various circumstances. In one of them, for example, he listed an all-purpose claim that since "politics is the ruination of the country" the solution lay in electing politicians for life to cut down on the endless criticism, competition, and bickering. In Rogers' words, "The minute a man knows he can't get a political job, he may turn to something useful." Another gag book entry focused on the proliferation of automobiles in modern America. "What would you do with traffic, that is the big problem nowadays," he wrote. "Simply make everybody going east go on Mondays, and everybody west on Tuesdays." Underlying everything, however, was Rogers' growing reliance on reaching his listeners with some kind of basic truth. He wanted to make them think even as they laughed. In Rogers' words,

> I use only one set method in my little gags, and that is to try and keep to the truth. Of course, you can exaggerate it, but what you say must be based on truth . . . . I don't like the jokes that get the biggest laughs, as they are generally as broad as a house and require no thought at all. I like one where, if you are with a friend and hear it, it makes you think, and you nudge your friend and say, "He's right about that." I would rather have you do that than to have you laugh – and then forget the next minute what it was you laughed at.[29]

Rogers also sharpened his delivery, realizing that *how* he made the joke was as important as what was *in* it. He became convinced that his observations must be short and snappy. "Being brief somehow gives the impression of intelligence, and folks do admire intelligence," he believed. "Brevity and clarity show that you have *thought*, and that you know what you are about." Rogers refined his mannerisms – the chewing gum, the perplexed scratching of the head, the self-effacing grin, the casual taking of an audience into his confidence, the country boy who is much sharper than he first appears. He also became a master of comic timing. He developed a trademark style as, in the words of a friend, he learned "to hesitate and seem to be at a loss what to say, then to arrive at the point with smashing suddenness."[30]

These practical efforts contributed to the creation of a genuine philosophy of humorous commentary. Emerging fully during his Ziegfeld days, it transformed the Oklahoma Cowboy, roping master and vaudeville comic, into Will Rogers, humorous observer of the foibles and values of the American people. It embodied not just jokes but genuine wit; not just gags but insights presented with a funny perspective. Not only his audiences, but the critics began to take notice. In a lengthy analysis entitled "The Wit of Will Rogers," appearing in the popular

American Magazine, author George Martin declared flatly, "His meteoric rise, in four years, to a place among the few real humorists of the stage, is astonishing." The article examined the special bond that Rogers seemed to be forging with American audiences, and quoted his own common-sense words on how he had achieved it: "if he studies human nature, and grabs the chances he sees to get ahead with his work as he goes along every day, he's pretty apt to find people that'll take an interest in him."[31]

Rogers' philosophy of humor produced an outpouring of amusing observations on serious issues in public life. While Americans were a deeply religious people, he had them chuckling in Ohio about a forthcoming centenary celebration of the Methodist Church that had been advertised as attracting several hundred thousand attendees to hear a host of ministers. "It's a terrible thing for the saloons of this town that they'll have to close just before this great gathering of Methodists," he declared with mock sorrow. "And can you imagine it – seventy thousand preachers? Why, you can hardly keep awake listening to one. What will seventy thousand of 'em do to you?" Rogers liked to deflate political pretensions as well as religious piety. In Chicago, where an angry meeting of the city's traffic club had just produced a lengthy, fervent resolution demanding that the federal government return control of the railroads to local authorities, Rogers cooled the political temperature with some practical perspective. "Folks," he said, "shortly before the coronation of the late King Edward, six pickled Irishmen – one ditch digger, two hod carriers, a truck driver, and a couple of bricklayers – met in the back end of a saloon in this town to decide whether they'd permit the coronation ceremonies to proceed. Next to that, I consider this the most momentous occasion in the history of Chicago." After the 18th Amendment established prohibition in 1917, Rogers made it a favorite object of his wit. He claimed to oppose it, sometimes for personal reasons: "I do love to play to an audience who have had a few nips, just enough so that they can see the joke and still sober enough to applaud it." Other times he offered a social justification: "Some men have to drink to live with a woman. Some women have to drink to live with a man. Most generally, though, they both have to drink to live with each other."[32]

Rogers' dexterous humor often engaged with another tried-and-true theme in his *Follies* commentaries. As he had learned in the *Frolics*, the stark contrast between the beautiful, glamorous showgirls and his own drawling, homespun cowboy image created rich, endless comic possibilities. So in his *Follies* appearances he steadily joked about the Ziegfeld Girls and himself in a laconic, conversational style, a theme he highlighted in his first appearance with the show in 1916. "Mr. Ziegfeld's shows always abound in novelties and I am one here tonight. I am the only one on the stage here fully clothed. I will be a disappointment probably as I am leaving everything in regard to the architecture of my anatomy to your imagination," Rogers told the audience. "Of course, after the show should there be a demand on the feminine part of the audience for the same appeal to them that is made to the tired businessman, I might be induced, *I say might be*, for art's sake, to remove a couple of ropes." Another display of the intrinsic humor of the cowboy and the showgirls appeared later in the same show in a daring sketch entitled "A Girl's Trousseau." A singing lingerie salesman made his pitch by holding up images of young women attired in ever skimpier dress. As he sang, a succession of Ziegfeld Girls appeared on stage in dwindling outfits that matched the drawings. With the last drawing of a young woman wearing almost nothing, the audience leaned forward breathlessly to see if Ziegfeld would actually show full nudity in a show. Rogers stepped out wearing a mask and the audience exploded in laughter.[33]

The humorist frequently played with this theme in other ways, often joking about the public perception that Ziegfeld Girls indulged in flings with wealthy suitors, or succeeded in luring them into marriage. He deadpanned, "We have a hard time keeping our girls together. Every time we get to a new town some of them marry millionaires, but in a few weeks they catch up with the show again." He appeared perplexed and speculated, "Well, the summer is about over, and what will these butterflies do then? Some of these girls don't know where their next limousine is coming from." Adopting a pose of mock apology for jokes that likely would fall flat, he explained a recent preoccupation had diverted his attention: "I have been helping the girls in the *Follies* make out their income tax. A vital question came up: do presents come under the heading of salary? . . . . One girl who has been with the various *Follies* for ten years wanted to know what she could charge off for depreciation. She was absolutely right because if, after being with them for that long, and you haven't married at least one millionaire, you certainly have a legitimate claim for depreciation."[34]

But such jokes about the Ziegfeld Girls did more than juxtapose a hayseed cowboy with a bevy of beautiful young urban females. They addressed indirectly, but shrewdly, a larger theme in the culture of early twentieth-century American culture: the "new woman" bursting into society with her rejection of old-fashioned Victorian morality, her determination to enter the public arena, and her ambitions to lead a fuller and more adventurous life. Like many Americans, Rogers labored to come to terms with this new phenomenon and used humor to light the way. While he joked about her unaccustomed ambition or perplexing independence, Rogers reassured that the "new woman" was not immoral or socially dangerous. He made this clear in a backstage interview in 1922. "There's a lot of talk these days about the old-fashioned woman and the new-fashioned woman. I don't know. I take folks as I find 'em, and there's something to be said for all," he told a journalist from the *New York Times*. "[The Ziegfeld Girls] are just old-fashioned girls at heart. Most of 'em are working for their living and working darned hard, too . . . . Why, these girls in the *Follies* have hearts as big as their hat boxes. . . . Just 'cause girls are beautiful they get panned. I don't get this association of beauty and evil. Most of the bad 'uns and criminals I've seen have been as ugly as blazes. Real beauties can afford to be good . . . . Most of the *Follies* girls are home folks!"[35]

With his humorous commentary attracting hordes of new fans, Rogers' popularity soared and created another strong connection to the broader culture. A starring role in the *Ziegfeld Follies* propelled him into national view as a celebrity. In the new consumer culture of early twentieth-century America where increasing material abundance, a flourishing entertainment industry, and a growing cult of personality were marking the parameters of a new age, this new kind of public figure became a notable feature of modern life. The celebrity – illustrated by a galaxy of actors, baseball players, musicians, and even some businessmen and politicians who exploded on the national scene – was someone whose fame was itself a cultural magnet. This media-driven fascination with the private qualities and looks, charisma and image, entertainment cachet and "personal touch" of the celebrity became a hallmark of modern life. As the historian Daniel Boorstin famously noted, celebrities became "well-known for their well-knownness." Moreover, as critic Richard Shickel observed in *Intimate Strangers: The Culture of Celebrity in America*, the modern culture of celebrity created an "illusion of intimacy" between the viewer and the star that made the former believe he really knew the latter and thus cemented a bond.[36]

Rogers assumed the trappings of modern celebrity as a feature attraction of the *Ziegfeld Follies*. As he became a well-known figure throughout the country, his views, movements, and biographical background attracted growing public interest. Reporters began to approach him for interviews as they wrote profiles for popular newspapers and magazines, and his unique background – at least for hordes of readers in large eastern cities – became an object of fascination. *American Magazine*, for example, ran a long piece on Rogers in 1919 that delved into his history and personal life and told "the story of a cowboy who has become a famous comedian." A similar 1917 article in *Everybody's* magazine described his journey from Oklahoma to the summit of New York entertainment and concluded, "His is the unique personality on Broadway." Increasingly, Rogers talked to journalists about himself and his experiences, his Indian heritage and genuine cowboy background, his early jaunts through South America and South Africa, his colorful endeavors in Wild West shows and on the vaudeville circuit. As a friend observed, "He made good copy by just talking about himself." Betty Rogers, who observed her husband's evolution into a celebrity at close range, drew a succinct conclusion: "Once the people had liked Will's roping; now they liked Will."[37]

In fact, America's growing obsession with celebrity, and Rogers' keen aware-ness of it, began to shape his *Ziegfeld Follies* act and interactions with live audiences. He deliberately played the celebrity card by identifying famous people in the audience, introducing them from the stage, and on occasion roping them for a laugh. Rogers enlisted the help of the theater's ushers, who kept an eye out for prominent attendees and sent notes back to his dressing room with the location of their seats. "Picking out and talking about distinguished people in the audience I use quite a little, but never unless I know them personally and know that they will take a joke as it is meant," he explained. For example, Rogers became friends with "Diamond Jim" Brady, the famous businessman, financier, and philanthrop-ist, and when he attended the *Follies* the humorist would introduce him from the stage and joke that Brady had hired him to accompany him to other shows in New York: "He sits in the front row and I sit in the back and if anybody cops a diamond I'm supposed to rope 'em before they get away with it." Chauncey Depew, the grand old man of New York who had achieved prominence as a long-time business figure, lawyer, orator, public official, and civic organizer celebrated his 90th birthday by attending the *Follies*. Rogers had him stand up, and cracked that both of them were popular banquet speakers and could be seen "barking around town for their dinner" (Depew quipped back that while he had been amusing audiences for many decades, he "never found it necessary to use a rope"). Prominent politicians also got the celebrity treatment. In a *Follies* show in the early 1920s, Rogers spied New York Governor Al Smith in the audience and invited him onto the stage for a good-natured chat. Rogers inquired if Smith planned to run for president, and the governor replied that he would if Rogers would serve as his Secretary of State. The humorist promised to consider the offer, but balked at the thought of adopting diplomatic dignity: "Lord, I would hate those whiskers. Perhaps we can compromise on a bobbed mustache."[38]

Famous people played their part in this cultural performance, flocking backstage to talk to Rogers and be photographed with him. At a *Follies* show in Chicago, for instance, the mayor, police chief, and city councilmen, all accom-panied by their wives, were delighted to have their pictures taken alongside the grinning humorist as they stood outside his dressing room. This became such a ritual as Rogers traveled the country that he announced his plans to write a book after his retirement from Ziegfeld entitled, *My Four Years with the Follies, or Prominent Men I've Met at the Stage Door. Follies* audiences reveled in the aura of celebrity surrounding Rogers. As one observer noted, "Will saw that audiences wanted to feel that they were rubbing elbows with notables." Rogers himself, with typical shrewdness, grasped the symbiotic dynamic at work between celebrities and the common citizens who doted on them. He declared, "Your big butter-and-egg man, your author, baseball player, and especially your politician – like attention.

They eat it up. And the folks who pay the tariffs at the box offices like to realize they are in prominent company."[39]

Having sharpened his skills as a humorist and elevated his status as a celebrity, Rogers established a solid framework of popularity during his years with the *Ziegfeld Follies*. But what created a deeper bond with audiences, one that transcended other entertainers, was a subtle, lighthearted, insightful probing of modern life and values. As he traveled the country as part of these lavish shows, Rogers gradually emerged as a trusted figure who used humor to explain Americans to themselves. Whether his subject was the political landscape, changing social mores, cultural attributes, or human foibles, he compelled his chuckling listeners to ponder the society around them and their place in it. As this gift was put on national display, the critics began to sit up and take notice. Betty relished a New York newspaper critic who praised her husband as "the columnist of the theater." A long profile in *Everybody's* magazine dubbed Rogers "the philosopher with the lariat" and compared him to the late W. S. Gilbert, the dramatist and librettist of "Gilbert and Sullivan" fame who specialized in the witty skewering of formality and pretension and topsy-turvy upending of the social order. Channing Pollock, playwright and journalist, described Rogers as "a talking Thackeray" after William Makepeace Thackeray, the English satirical writer and author of *Vanity Fair* and *The Luck of Barry Lyndon*.[40]

A crucial part of Rogers' expanding role as a serious commentator was an attribute that pushed to the forefront and came to define him more than any other: an affection for, and understanding of, ordinary Americans. He emerged as a cultural populist who exhibited a powerful undercurrent of sympathy for workaday citizens, regular folks, and common people and made their well-being the measuring stick of worth and value in American life. Rogers' closest friends were struck by this impulse. "He never looked up to the mighty or spoke down to the masses," said Eddie Cantor, who saw Rogers perform countless times in the *Follies*. He described the Oklahoman as a "spokesman of the people" and gave him the title of "Mr. American Citizen." W. C. Fields, certainly no sentimentalist, asserted that "Rogers was the nearest thing to Abraham Lincoln that I have ever known."[41]

Rogers' comments during his *Follies* act certainly supported his image as a man of the people. The main idea of taxes for common citizens, he claimed, was to get someone else to pay, particularly if they were wealthy. As he put it, "Don't a rich man buy non-taxable bonds, and not have to pay any taxes, and don't the little fellow put his in his business and have to pay? Well, let him be as smart as the big fellow." During World War I, he claimed that the federal government was trying to recruit more men for the army by suggesting they could all be officers: "After they're in, they're going to reduce 'em [in rank]! Down in Washington the other day I met an honest-to-goodness private. Poor fellow, he saluted so much he was all in!'" When joking about Prohibition, which Rogers opposed, he usually portrayed it as an affront to the rights and common sense of ordinary Americans. He pointed out that they reacted by procuring liquor illegally and hiding it in their cellars, so that "If a residence gets on fire nowadays, the firemen don't run to save the children or the valuables but to the cellar to save the booze . . . .'Bout the only thing left for a poor man that can't afford his own house with a cellar is to move to a republic." Rogers' quips almost always came from the perspective of a regular citizen just striving to get by while facing daily problems. "Never a day passes in New York without some innocent bystander being shot. You just stand around this town long enough, and be innocent, and somebody is going to shoot you," he groused. "One day there was four shot. Hard to find four innocent people in New York, even if you don't stop to shoot them." Another time Rogers opined, "Everybody's talking about what's the matter with this country, and what the country needs. What this country needs, worse than anything else, is a place to park your car."[42]

Rogers bolstered his common-man image in the interviews that journalists began to conduct. "Like Abe Lincoln, I was born in a log cabin," he told one, and followed up with an assurance that the folks who flocked to hear him would decide how long he remained an entertainer. As he explained, "when I do get my [walking] papers – in the nature of the audience not liking my little act – I will not pull one of those strategic victories by saying the people don't know a good act when they see one." In another interview, Rogers insisted that he aimed his commentary at the "smartest all-round man in this country . . . the man who works all day and has to ride thirty minutes on a street car to get home at night. He reads the newspapers. He knows what you're talking about." Rogers insisted that he was no different from any other person in retail sales and "in selling a product, any sales talk that's over the average man's head is no go."[43]

* * * * *

As he did with so many things, Will Rogers often made light of his experience with the *Ziegfeld Follies*. In 1922, during a talk to a women's group in New York, Rogers quipped, "Here's what I want for my epitaph: 'Here lies Will Rogers who worked forty years in the *Follies* and when he died he had the same wife he had when he started.'" But in serious moments he quickly acknowledged the life-changing impact of this experience. "Ziggy gave me my start," he told a newspaperman. "If there is anything I can do to repay him, nothing could be too much." The facts supported this conclusion. Rogers' appearances with the *Follies* before audiences in the thousands throughout the United States, as well as the dozens of press stories on his life and humor that appeared subsequently, made him a household name.[44]

Moreover, his great success in the *Follies* opened many other doors. Rogers was soon in demand as a humorous speaker for banquets and conventions. In the early 1920s he began recording some of his Ziegfeld monologue for Victor Records, which brought his humor to an even larger audience. Accompanied by several Ziegfeld Girls, he first appeared on the radio in 1922, a medium which soon provided him another regular outlet. In 1919, Rogers collected a host of his *Follies* jokes on public affairs and published them in a pair of books, *Rogerisms: The Cowboy Philosopher on the Peace Conference* and *Rogerisms: The Cowboy Philosopher on Prohibition*. In 1922, the humorist drew upon this same material to launch a weekly newspaper column for the McNaught Syndicate, the owners of which had offices across the street from Ziegfeld's New Amsterdam Theater. Florenz Ziegfeld allowed Rogers to stroll across the national landscape displaying his unique talent and the cowboy artist never forgot it.[45]

Moreover, as Rogers evolved into one of the biggest stars in the *Ziegfeld Follies*, he became the best friend of Flo Ziegfeld. It was an unlikely pairing. Although as different as two men could be – the elegant, austere, domineering east coast impresario and the rustic, fun-loving, just-folks humorist from the great plains – they developed a strong mutual esteem while working together. Ziegfeld's daughter, Patricia, recounted years later, "My father and Will had a warm, comfortable, and rare relationship. They could ask anything of one another and it was as good as done. They had a rapport with one another and could talk about things they couldn't talk about with other people." Their close friendship had developed gradually. It probably started when Ziegfeld offered Rogers a generous salary to join the *Follies* and invited him to his office to sign the contract. The humorist replied, "I don't like contracts. You can trust me and I know I can trust you." So they shook hands and relied on a verbal agreement while working together over the years. When the Oklahoman left the *Follies* for good, Ziegfeld presented him with a platinum watch, engraved, "To Will Rogers, in appreciation of a real fellow, whose word is his bond." When Rogers finished one of his last seasons with the show, Ziegfeld sent him a letter, declaring, "I have never had anyone appear in any of my attractions that was a greater joy to be associated with than you." In 1925, Ziegfeld sent a telegram to Rogers, who had branched out into other areas of entertainment, saying he was "delighted beyond words of your great success." The following year, upon completion of the new Ziegfeld Theatre, Rogers wired his old boss from California. "Why Flo, I feel that you are just in your infancy in theater owning," he wrote with a combination of affection and humor. "Reserving for you best corner lots in both Claremore and Beverly Hills at small increase ... . You don't furnish anything but name and girls. I hope you never have to put in movie screen. Your old hired hand, Will."[46]

In the early 1930s, when Ziegfeld was in failing health with lung and heart problems, wife Billie Burke brought him to California where they spent much time with the Rogers family at their Santa Monica ranch. Will gave Patricia her own pony to ride along with the gift of a saddle. While he was able, the impresario liked to go horseback riding and Betty Rogers recalled the striking contrast between the elegant New Yorker and the raggedy Oklahoman as they rode side by side. "Mr. Ziegfeld in a handsome pair of light-colored, winged chaps, sitting straight and erect, his gray hair sleek and glistening in the sun; Will carelessly sprawled in his saddle on his old speckled roping pony, Soapsuds, wearing his faded blue overalls, his shaggy hair blowing awry in the wind," she described. "Once they had been partners in making theatrical history and now they were even closer, they were friends."[47]

In 1932, Ziegfeld's health steadily declined and he required hospitalization by mid-summer. Rogers sheltered Billy and Patricia at his home, visited his old boss regularly, and helped pay some of the hospital costs. In a newspaper story, the humorist explained the nature of his great affection for Ziegfeld. "He had given the American Public, for Lord knows how many years, an entertainment that must have given them more pleasure and happiness than any other, for they have paid more to see it than to any other man in the world," a grateful Rogers told the *Los Angeles Examiner*. "A many of us got our start, our real start with him. Those were great old days, those *Follies* days, packed houses, wonderful audiences, [and he] never bothered me as to what I was to do or say, never suggested or never cut out .... His was a gift, not an accomplishment."[48]

When Ziegfeld died on July 22, 1932, Rogers took the lead in arranging the funeral service and securing a final resting place. Eddie Cantor, who accompanied him to visit the minister and make arrangements, reported that Rogers tried to explain to the cleric what he might say but floundered for words as his eyes filled with tears. He could only muster, "He was great, he was wonderful, he wasn't just a producer. You see, he made all of us – we would be nothing without him." According to Cantor, Rogers was "inconsolable .... He had lost someone he loved, a man whom he worshipped." A few days later, Rogers gathered his thoughts about Ziegfeld into a brief but heartfelt remembrance that was published in newspapers throughout the country:

> Our world of "make believe" is sad. Scores of comedians are not funny, hundreds of "America's most beautiful girls" are not gay. Our benefactor has passed away. He picked us from all walks of life. He led us into what little fame we achieved. He remained our friend regardless of our usefulness to him as an entertainer .... And he left something on earth that hundreds of us will treasure till our curtain falls – a badge of which we were proud and wanted the world to read the lettering on it: "I worked for Ziegfeld." So goodbye, Flo, save a spot for me for you will put on a show up there some day that will knock their eyes out.[49]

It was the concluding event in a remarkable stage in the humorist's life. In the mid-1910s, following a lengthy stint in vaudeville where he had honed his craft as an entertainer, the "Oklahoma Cowboy" ascended to the elevated platform provided by the *Ziegfeld Follies* and became the Will Rogers that America came to love. Now his astounding success brought a fresh opportunity that promised to enlarge his national profile even more: the new entertainment frontier of the movies. The cowboy humorist took his talents to Hollywood.

5

The Celluloid Cowboy

I N LATE SUMMER 1918, WILL ROGERS TOOK HIS FIRST tentative steps into an unfamiliar world. Reporting for work at a film studio in Fort Lee, New Jersey, he wandered onto the lot and tried to get his bearings. The task proved difficult as he blundered into one mishap after another. In a humorous account of his bumbling performance, Rogers noted that he arrived at 8:00 am, eager to begin work, but only "woke up the night watchman." A few extras straggled in around 9:00 am and the stars only several hours later. He was convinced to put on makeup – the cowboy entertainer hated the stuff and had never used it in the theater – and claimed "even that could not disguise this old homely pan of mine." But he appreciated the makeup artist who tried to console him by saying "the day of the pretty actor is gone. You are so ugly you are a novelty."

Setting out to find his filming location, Rogers dodged thickets of movie cameras and hordes of actors, claiming "you couldent move around with out stepping on a five or six thousand dollars a week star." As he stumbled along, a big, burly crew member grabbed his coat tail and yanked him back. "You poor boob, I saved your life," he said, and explained that Rogers was about to step between a temperamental female star, Geraldine Farrar, and cameras taking close-up shots for her present film. Farrar recently had garnered headlines for violently slapping Enrico Caruso with her fan during a performance of *Carmen* at the Metropolitan Opera. In Rogers' words, "I had heard what she did to Caruso one time, and I thanked him." Finally arriving at his studio location at 10:30, he thought he was late, only to discover that shooting began in mid-afternoon. When the director asked if he had any camera experience, Rogers said, "only with a little Brownie No. 2 I used to have." The director reassured the novice that "if you are thinking a thing, the camera will show it. So I told him I would try and keep my thoughts as clean as possible." Filming began with a crucial scene where Rogers' character carried an injured friend to a doctor's office to save his life. As the director yelled instructions through a megaphone, the fledgling actor suffered the final indignity of the day:

> I was just drama-ing all over the place, holding this pal and pleading with the doctor to do something for him when my mind was more on my art than on the load I had and I dropped him . . . . He [the director] kept impressing on me that my only pal was dying. Well, he dident have anything on me – I was almost dying. He looked and saw I had tears in my eyes, and he says, "That's great." He thought I was crying about my pal, and I was crying about going into the darn thing [the movie business].[1]

In such fashion Rogers became a participant in silent films, the new and exciting field of entertainment that was capturing the imagination of the American people. In one sense, this move was the natural culmination of a career that had progressed from outdoor cowboy shows to vaudeville to Broadway and the *Ziegfeld Follies*. In a broader social sense, however, Rogers' launching of a movie career represented a departure. The movies, as probably the most powerful propagator of the new century's ethic of self-fulfillment, entertainment, abundance, and celebrity, were enmeshed in the massive changes that were sweeping away the last vestiges of Victorian tradition and opening up a vision of modernity in the early twentieth century. Silent films became an addiction for many working-class and middle-class Americans, pushing aside older forms of amusement as it held up a mirror to a rapidly changing society. By embracing the world of movie-making, Will Rogers stepped to the cutting edge of historical transformation.

* * * * *

Rogers became involved with silent films in the summer of 1918. Rex Beach, author of many western adventure tales, including a novel entitled *Laughing Bill Hyde*, and his wife were having lunch with Will and Betty Rogers at the Long Island home the Rogerses were renting. Samuel Goldwyn was planning to make a screen version of the book and Mrs. Beach commented, "Will, you are the ideal man to play Bill Hyde in Rex's new picture." Her husband agreed. Initially, Rogers resisted the idea and, years later, jokingly recalled his response. "I tried to tell the lady that I had never bothered anybody and never annoyed over one Audience at a time, and that these were war times and a man could be arrested for treason as treason meant any thing that caused pain to our people thereby giving aid to the enemy." But gradually the entertainer softened and consented to try it. This was the film that brought Rogers to his irksome first day of shooting at the Fort Lee studio in New Jersey. But it was a difficult departure from the *Ziegfeld Follies*, the venerable show that had catapaulted him to national fame. Florenz Ziegfeld, already raided of several stars by movie producers, issued a newspaper warning on August 18, 1918, claiming exclusive rights to the professional services of entertainers in his show and threatening litigation against any producers or studios who lured them away. He backed down, however, as Rogers continued to appear in the evening performances of the *Ziegfeld Follies of 1918* while filming during the day in New Jersey.[2]

When *Laughing Bill Hyde* was a financial and critical success, Goldwyn offered Rogers a lucrative, two-year contract that paid him 2,200 dollars a week for the first year and 3,000 dollars a week for the second year. These figures doubled, and then tripled, his present salary with the *Ziegfeld Follies*. But the arrangement involved an even bigger change. The Goldwyn Pictures Corporation was in the process of moving its operation from New York to the West Coast, so Rogers committed to taking his family across the country and relocating in Southern California. He left for Los Angeles, already becoming known as "The City of Dreams," in June 1919, and his family could not have been happier. As Betty explained, "We were delighted . . . with the idea of moving to California, and with the prospects of at last settling down in a home of our own."[3]

As he headed west to California – Betty and the children would follow several weeks later after he was settled – Rogers described his train journey west as part of a pilgrimage. In a special piece for the *Kansas City Star*, he suggested that Hollywood and the movies had come to represent a new dream of success for modern Americans. As always, he began with a self-deprecating joke. "I hear the call of ART to act a fool for the Bucking pictures," he said, but was convinced that the studio actually wanted to "use me as the horrible example in some picture, But you can never tell what a movie fan will fall for." He felt encouraged, however, when a porter told him that film star Mary Pickford had taken this very train when she first went to Los Angeles years earlier. In fact, Rogers noted after looking around, "everybody on this train is going to Cal to go in[to the] movies. It's the Movie Special. The Porters will tell you they are not black – they are only made up for a part. The dining car serves for breakfast what they call a Close Up. I had a Fade Out steak for dinner . . . . There is a Corona typewriter in every berth writing Scenarios." As the humorist sensed, Hollywood had emerged as a cultural oasis, a shimmering, enticing image of happiness in modern American life that inspired people to flock there.[4]

Indeed, the golden glow of Southern California seemed to illuminate a new range of possibilities for success, prosperity, and fulfillment in the new century. America had fallen in love with the movies and, subsequently, the lush geographical location where they were created. Hollywood, perched on the northern rim of Los Angeles, had transformed from a sleepy suburb in 1910 to a bustling production center by the end of the decade. Its bright, dry climate with gentle temperatures and constant sunshine allowing year-round filming, its nearness to a variety of physical settings (ocean, desert, big city, small town, rural ranch country), and its ethnic diversity (Anglos, African Americans, Hispanics, Asians) seemed to offer all the necessary ingredients for movie-making. A cluster of film studios had begun to spring up among the gently rolling hills of Hollywood – by the 1920s they would include Fox, MGM, Universal, Warner Brothers, Columbia, United Artists, RKO – under the leadership of dynamic businessmen, many of them Jewish immigrants.

The rise of Hollywood embodied another sea-change in American life, namely the emergence of mass culture with its accompanying "leisure ethic." As growing numbers of people danced away from the genteel, moralistic restrictions of a Victorian past, new kinds of entertainment – professional sports, amusement parks, music clubs, vaudeville – sped their embrace of a new cultural style. The movies, with their technological capability to reach large audiences throughout the country simultaneously, represented the apex of this trend. Full of laughter and tears, romance and adventure, excitement and thrills, the silver screen drew millions of viewers eager to abandon stuffy restraint and pursue entertainment pleasure. Films excited audiences by suggesting the adventurous possibilities of life, titillated them with images of sexual liberation, awed them with scenes of consumer abundance, and inspired them with stories about the pursuit of personal self-fulfillment. As symbols of life's possibilities in this new age, movie stars captured the public imagination as their sparkling personalities and enticing public images elevated a new culture of "celebrity." Their larger-than-life images were further enhanced by the emergence of newspaper stories, movie magazines, and fan clubs that worked to keep them before the public. When the Oklahoma humorist, radiating rustic charm and good-natured wisdom, arrived in Hollywood to take up film work, he became swept up in promoting this new ethos in American life.[5]

For millions of Americans flocking to see silent films beginning in the mid-1910s, the experience of movie-going reinforced many of these cultural tendencies. From the outset, audiences felt a sense of awe at seeing moving pictures that captured precisely the human experience and the material world that surrounded it. Movies created new ways of seeing and perceiving as, unlike live shows or plays, the silver screen presented a fantasy experience where the viewer traveled across time and space, following the camera as a mind's eye as it moved back to take in sweeping landscapes or moved forward for close-up shots that seemed to penetrate into the very psyches of characters. This new perceptual universe fostered profound regard for the modern technology that could create such wonders. The hyper-charged, wonderous depictions of charm, innocence, villainy, and heroism on the screen also drove home the power of personality in the modern world while downplaying old-fashioned rectitude of character. In addition, for many viewers, the rise of opulent movie palaces in towns and cities not only made movie watching a cherished escape from the workaday world but promoted the ethos of material abundance that had emerged by the early 1900s alongside a dynamic new consumer economy. Finally, watching films emerged as a democratizing endeavor. Audiences crossed class lines as working-class stiffs mingled with high-society matrons to see the same films in the same venues with no special seats and no special perks. It was little wonder that *The Nation* called film the "first democratic art" in 1913. Rogers, with his common-man appeal, made for a natural fit in the new world of the movies.[6]

Samuel Goldwyn, Rogers' new boss, had emerged as a key figure in the creation of the film industry. Born Samuel Goldfish in 1879 to a Jewish family in Warsaw, Poland – he changed his last name only in 1919 – he had run away to England at age eleven and worked as a blacksmith's assistant. Four years later he immigrated to the United States and found work in the glove-making industry, first as a cutter and then a salesman. Hard working and ambitious, he rose through the ranks and earned a fortune in the glove business. He became involved in the movie business in 1913 with his brother-in-law, Jesse Lasky, and they hired a young director named Cecil B. DeMille to direct a successful film entitled *The Squaw Man*. In 1916 Goldfish partnered with playwright Edgar Selwyn to form Goldwyn Pictures Company (an industry wag suggested the merged name should have been Selfish Pictures). Goldwyn produced several successful films, but it was a feather in his cap when he was able to snag Rogers from the *Ziegfeld Follies* and sign him to a movie contract. The studio head had mixed feelings about the move. "He knew that being a star on stage had nothing to do with becoming a star on screen," an associate reported. But Goldwyn believed Rogers was worth the gamble.[7]

Shortly after arriving in Los Angeles, Rogers announced his new career in the film industry with aplomb by publishing an advertisement in *Wid's Year Book*, a trade periodical published by F. C. "Wid" Gunning. *Wid's* featured current news of the movie business, film reviews, listings of film companies, and promotional advertising. In its September 1919 number, Rogers offered a tongue-in-cheek promotion of his new entertainment endeavor. Surrounded by dozens of slick ads for movies and studios, his folksy, amusing assessment of the movie industry (and his place in it) stood out. Rogers borrowed Woodrow Wilson's recent Fourteen Points proposal at the postwar peace conference in Paris as the template for his remarks. One of Rogers' points claimed, "I hold the distinction of being the ugliest man in pictures." Another observed, "Goldwyn figured by getting a good cast and good story, it would about offset the action of the star." According to another, he claimed that unlike most male movie stars "I can't roll a cigarette with one hand and can't whip but one man at a time (and he must be littler than

I am)." Rogers' fourteenth point captured his jocular skepticism regarding a new career in the movies: "It's the only business where you can sit out front and applaud yourself." Here was a different kind of movie star with a different kind of attitude.[8]

Over the next two years, Rogers made twelve silent films for Goldwyn Productions. The first one, *Laughing Bill Hyde*, told the story of a petty thief imprisoned for assaulting his brother-in-law after the latter abused the protagonist's sister. Bill breaks out of jail with his pal, who is mortally wounded in the escape, and carries him to a doctor before fleeing to the mining camps of Alaska. Given Rogers' origins in the Cherokee territory, a fascinating turn in the plot appears at this point. Bill meets Ponotah, a Native American woman who runs the camp laundry, and discovers that she is being cheated out of her gold mine by a group of unscrupulous characters. He falls in love with her and comes up with a successful scheme to foil the swindlers. Bill and Ponotah marry as the former abandons his life of burglary and dishonesty. As in many of Rogers' films, it is a story of the outsider, the "little guy" with the heart of gold who makes good and finds happiness.[9]

After arriving in Hollywood to work at the Goldwyn Studio in Culver City, Rogers appeared in his second film, *Almost a Husband*. It established a prototype for many of his silent films that might be called the "rustic melodrama" – a sentimental story focusing on a modest figure from provincial America who encounters difficulties, braves them with a good heart and solid values, and triumphs in the end. In this first film iteration, Rogers played a schoolteacher, Sam Lyman, in a small Southern town who is secretly in love with Eva, the local banker's daughter. When the pair are accidentally married as part of a parlor game – the man "officiating" turns out to be a real minister – troubles ensue when a villainous young man who desires her, Zeb Sawyer, concocts a plot to ruin both Sam and Eva's father in order to trigger a divorce. Sam foils Zeb's scheme, however, and gains enough courage to convince Eva to honor their marriage.[10]

Rogers' third effort, *Jubilo*, was one his best silent film efforts and probably his most popular. Based on a Ben Williams tale in the *Saturday Evening Post* – the Oklahoman described it as "the finest story it was ever my privilege to work in" – the movie examined a cheerful, kindly hobo nicknamed "Jubilo" by his fellows for his habit of singing the old spiritual of that title. One day he witnesses a train robbery, but fearing involvement with the law, he quietly moves on and ends up at a ranch asking for food. Grateful for the generous treatment extended by the rancher and his daughter, Rose, he takes up manual labor for the first time to help out. When the train robbers show up trying to frame the rancher for the crime, however, Jubilo takes the lead in thwarting the plot and sending the outlaws to jail. In so doing, of course, he wins Rose's love and convinces her to marry him.[11]

Rogers loved this film role as a good-hearted, down-on-his-luck hobo. "Jubilo is a tramp. Mr. Goldwyn, after seeing me several times in my street clothes, he said, 'there is the fellow to play that tramp,'" the actor joked, before adding seriously, "I like to play tramps. There is something about an old tramp that kinder hits me, especially a kind of good-natured one that don't take things too seriously." He also loved the old African-American spiritual that popped up throughout the movie. In an ad for the film, Rogers cracked that he sang the song but "fortunately the voice don't register on the film, so you needn't stay away on that account." The role fit the Oklahoman. But as Clarence Badger, the director of almost all of Rogers' Goldwyn films, related, for years afterward whenever the star entered a theater the organist would see him and strike up "In the Days of Jubilee" in honor of his memorable performance in *Jubilo*. In Badger's words, "the strains of that old hymn followed Will as a sort of aura."[12]

Indeed, Rogers seemed personally more invested in *Jubilo* than in most of his silent films. When he heard that Goldwyn was considering changing the film's title to something snappier upon its release, Rogers sent a long, angry telegram. The comedian claimed that with such a move "you are funnier than I ever was." He sarcastically suggested several new titles to Goldwyn, including "The Vagabond With a Heart as Big as His Appetite," "A Spotted Horse But He Is Only Painted," and "He Loses in the First Reel But Wins in the Last." Years later, Rogers was still annoyed about the possible title change. "They will film the Lord's Supper and when it is made, figure that it is not a good release title and not catchy enough," he groused, "so it will be released under the heading 'A Red Hot Meal' or 'The Gastronomical Orgy.'"[13]

The ten Rogers silent films that followed by the end of 1921 unfolded within a melodramatic framework, as did most Hollywood efforts in this era. Nearly every one had a sentimental love story where the protagonist won the girl in the end after numerous scrapes and delays, a feature that beckoned back to the tradition of Victorian melodrama. This hoary sentimental model also infused Rogers' silent films with virtuous and evil characters, unlikely close calls, and chance encounters that were manipulated to create emotional crises. He made fun of this traditional model in a thumb-nail sketch of one of his films: the "father, girl, villain who makes play for girl, hero dirty but honest ... . story, same as usual. Looks bad for the hero right up to the last close-up; first reel introduces hero ... . Second reel looks bad for hero; third reel looks even worse for hero; fourth reel, evidence all points to hero being robber, villain looks sleek and satisfied. End reel five: the winners – the tramp wins, 100 percent HERO."[14]

In a more modern vein, however, the medium of silent films enlarged and embroidered Rogers' public persona, the one that had first appeared in his vaudeville days and then expanded in the *Ziegfeld Follies* – the witty, commonsensical, just-folks observer who made audiences chuckle by puncturing the pomposities and absurdities of the everyday world. The humor, of course, stood out immediately. Rogers became involved with writing the "intertitles," or the words flashed on the screen in silent films, and they were full of quips and cracks. In *An Unwilling Hero* (1921), his hobo character looks at the sky and says, "Just to show you that I have as much intelligence as those geese, I'm going south, too." A bit later, he comments, "I'm one of the few men that Prohibition hasn't driven to drink." In *Almost a Husband* (1919), Rogers drafted a series of amusing, whimsical intertitles, many of which appeared in the final film: "This picture will set back moving pictures five years;" one character says, "WHO's going to kill you and drown himself," and the victim replies, "If he's going to do both, tell him to drown himself first;" "Since the last reel I have been made a lawyer. You can do it that quick in pictures;" "Through the banker's influence I am canned as teacher. From now on the children can grow up in ignorance."[15]

Along with providing a stream of amusing observations, Rogers' screen roles for Goldwyn often portrayed him as an outsider. As in *Laughing Bill Hyde*, Rogers' typical character came from a rural or village background and appeared as an average guy struggling to survive against some kind of personal travail or social imposition. In *Jes' Call Me Jim* (1920), Rogers played a simple hunter and trapper. He liberates a friend unfairly confined in an asylum and helps him recover patents for inventions stolen by a villain who has become rich. *Water, Water Everywhere* (1919) featured the Oklahoman as a cowboy trying to fend off the restrictions demanded by the local temperance society while meeting traditional conventions of love and courtship. This rural figure, honest but standing at the margins of respectable society, wholesome but often awkward and tongue-tied in his personal deportment, became a key component of the Rogers persona.[16]

The Oklahoman also frequently inhabited good-hearted, moral characters who defended others and sacrificed for them. In *Boys Will Be Boys* (1921), Rogers played an illiterate, eccentric orphan who lives in a livery stable in a small Kentucky town. After inheriting a large sum of money from an uncle in Ireland, he suddenly becomes the richest citizen in the area. He spends the money on the pleasures of childhood he never experienced – candy, picnics, games – and shares them with children from the orphanage where he once resided. *Cupid the Cowpuncher* (1920) featured Rogers as a cowboy who ignored his own happiness and delighted in matchmaking for his fellow cowpunchers, even if the results were mixed. In *A Poor Relation* (1921), Rogers' character is an impoverished inventor, and eventually a writer, who struggles to support two orphans he has adopted. Whether it is caring for abandoned children or helping others find happiness, such silent-film roles presented Rogers as a self-sacrificing, caring individual with a deep empathy for his fellow man. This, too, became part of his public persona.

In deeper and more complicated ways, Rogers' Goldwyn-era characters often displayed an ambiguous attitude about the rules, expectations, and authority of mainstream society. They tended to chafe against hidebound tradition or overweening power and either triumphed in spite of them or reluctantly came around to accept them. The clearest examples came in Rogers' many hobo roles. *Jubilo*, of course, provided a popular template of the tramp who has fled society but kept a strong moral sense that eventually brings him back to social respectability. *Honest Hutch* (1920) presented him as a shiftless loafer in a small town on the Mississippi who is forced by circumstances to work hard and become a prosperous farmer. In *An Unwilling Hero* (1921), Rogers played a good-natured hobo who discovers that some of his fellow tramps are planning to rob a plantation near New Orleans. He warns the occupants of the impending robbery, is given new clothes and offered work, but he ultimately rejects them and returns to the freedom of the open road.

As a fledgling actor during the silent film era, Rogers ultimately combined this array of characteristics and principles to forge a populist sensibility. This tradition had deep roots in American culture going back to the early nineteenth century and had been energized by the upsurge in the Populist Party in the late 1800s and early 1900s. Populism underlined the decency, dignity, and worth of ordinary people and expressed skepticism about wealth and power. It often posed the contest between social and economic privilege and the well-being of common people as a struggle between the dangerous city and the virtuous countryside. Rogers' image as an entertainer in vaudeville – the simple, common-sense cowboy entertainer pointing out social absurdities to theater audiences in the nation's largest cities – had reflected this impulse. Now his silent films promoted it more explicitly. They gently, and often humorously, presented pictures of rural goodness that were often in conflict with social power and authority rooted in urban institutions. The most complete example of Rogers' populist persona in these movies came in *The Strange Boarder* (1920). He played Sam Gardner, a widowed Arizona rancher who tries to make a better life for his son (played by his real-life offspring, Jimmy Rogers) by taking him to the city for a good education. Sam mortgages his ranch to finance the plan, but upon arriving in Chicago he is tricked out of the 10,000 dollars by con men posing as bank officials. He then runs afoul of the law when he is mistakenly arrested for murder. A sentimental plot twist gets Sam out of prison and sends him into the arms of a young woman whom he has met at his boarding house. Despite this conventional happy ending, the bulk of *The Strange Boarder* portrays this upright rural figure struggling to escape the powerful machinations and wiles of a dangerous urban America.

At the same time, Rogers served as a mediator between past and present in many of his early silent films. He excelled at bringing the best of old-fashioned ways into the future, showing that the expectations and demands of traditional society can be modified, updated, and humanized with a bit of toleration and good-natured humor. This mediating role appeared clearly in *Doubling for Romeo* (1921), a satirical look at movie-making and social norms. Rogers played Sam "Slim" Cody, a tongue-tied cowboy who falls in love with Lulu, who is also being courted by a handsome clerk from the local drugstore. After Lulu tells Slim she wants to be romanced like Douglas Fairbanks does it in the movies, Slim goes to Hollywood determined to learn lovemaking from the movie stars of the age. He gets hired as a film "double" for a villain, but is unhappy when he is battered during a fight scene. He then gains a role as a lover, but botches romantic scenes by looking at the camera and giggling compulsively. The director finally sends the cowboy packing.

Slim returns home where Lulu now tells him he must love her like Romeo loved Juliet. So the cowboy procures a copy of the Shakespeare play to study, falls asleep, and dreams of being Romeo. After a series of dreamy, movie-like romantic encounters and swashbuckling swordfights, Slim wakes up with a new confidence about how to court women. Rejuvenated, he now combines the smooth personality and charm of Romeo with the strength and fortitude of the cowpuncher. Slim approaches Lulu and her other suitor, makes his case for loving her, and marches her off to the preacher to get married. It is what she has wanted all along. *Doubling for Romeo* humorously juxtaposes the phlegmatic cowboy tradition and the stimulating, personable world of modern movie-making throughout much of the film, and then fuses the two impulses. Rogers successfully mediated the old and the new, the past and the present, and made the transition palatable through humor. In such fashion, Rogers as a silent-film actor provided a personal bridge for viewers to make a reassuring passage between a vanishing society and an emerging one.

Rogers' acting style reinforced his compelling image. It was not an intentional connection. He scoffed at his skills as a thespian, writing, "I'm not an actor, I'm a rope thrower. I can't act. I can't be nothing but myself." He professed embarrassment when watching his movies. "The thing that struck me most when I saw myself on the screen was I never knew before how homely I was. I never did think I was an Apollo, but I didn't think I was as ugly as that face that grinned at me," he wrote. "I was the homeliest man on the screen. It was unique, distinguishing! Whatever you are, be that thing just a little better than anyone else, and you are all right. So my grin came back."[17]

In fact, Rogers displayed an adroitness in portraying his characters that broadened the palette of silent film acting. While completely untrained, of course, he instinctively embraced a realistic mode of acting that stood in contrast to the intense emotionalism, physical gyrations, and histrionics of most silent film stars. Many critics noticed and approved. A reviewer of *The Strange Boarder* praised

Rogers' understated, natural style, writing, "Without the aid of facial contortions and wild gesticulations, he draws human and real characters, and by his simple and easy bearing he makes them all the more natural and understandable." A critic made a similar point about *Jes' Call Me Jim*: "Show me an actor who can play with more genuine feeling than Rogers does the basically theatrical scene in which Jim sends Benedict's little boy into the woods to pray for the recovery of his father, and I'll introduce you to one of the leaders of his profession." Despite his inexperience as an actor, the humorist inhabited his characters and presented them to viewers as real people. As a reviewer noted of his most popular silent film, "He seems to be Jubilo, instead of simply impersonating the character." The most impressive confirmation came from the legendary Erich von Stroheim, the Austrian-born auteur of silent films, who told the *New York Times* in 1923 that Rogers provided an example of the "realism" that the movies needed to cultivate.[18]

At the same time, Rogers' acting had a second important dimension that would come to characterize Hollywood movie stars. Right alongside his realistic portrayals appeared, ironically, an ability to project his own distinctive personality no matter what the role. This quality appeared intermittently among silent film actors but would dominate after the emergence of "talkie" films with figures such as Gary Cooper, Clark Gable, and Jimmy Stewart; Bette Davis, Joan Bancroft, and Jean Harlow. Such actors always shone through their characters. Rogers was a pioneer in this development whose likable, self-effacing, modest, and authentic personality colored all his roles and allowed him to outlast bigger silent film stars such as Lillian Gish, Douglas Fairbanks, and Mary Pickford whose stature faded with the advent of more sophisticated movie technology. In its various manifestations in the Goldwyn silent movies, Rogers consistently impressed viewers as a common man with uncommon gifts of observation and humor. Perceptive critics picked up on this impulse. The *New York Times* noted of his first role in *Laughing Bill Hyde*, "Those inclined to believe that all of the magnetic Rogers personality is in his conversation will realize their mistake if they see this picture. The real Will Rogers is on the reels." Critics frequently noted the impact of "Will Rogers' personality upon the screen" and concluded "There is no other man like him on the screen today." A reviewer of *Almost a Husband* praised the "inimitable Will Rogers" with his special gifts of "simplicity and spontaneity, the two highest attributes of an actor's art." This instinctive ability to imbue roles with his unique personality marked the intersection of Rogers' acting and his celebrity.[19]

In many ways, Rogers' attractive screen presence mirrored his real-life personality as a movie actor. He quickly gained a reputation in the industry as a joy to work with, a friendly, self-effacing, good-hearted, and generous colleague in a business filled with oversized egos. Rogers displayed an unusual trait among movie stars – a notorious shyness around cameras. He did not like posing for publicity stills, often deferred to fellow actors to get screen time during film shoots, and became self-conscious about close-up shots that presented "his beaded eyelashes, magnified so that they look like Zeppelins." Betty Rogers reported that while her husband cherished fans and audiences, he found the idea of sending out autographed pictures of himself to be preposterous. Despite pressure from the Goldwyn publicity department, he lagged badly in this duty. Rogers kept cast and crew laughing during the long, sometimes tedious process of filming and re-filming. In *Doubling for Romeo*, his cowboy character had ventured to Hollywood and broken into the movies as a "double." During his first job, according to the script, the film's star sat arrogantly on the sideline watching during a fight scene as Rogers took his place to be pummeled by a muscle-bound villain. As Rogers was being thrashed, according to director Clarence Badger, the actor suddenly called out, "Please, Mr. Badger! Ain't there such a thing as gettin' a double to double for a double?" The set erupted in laughter. Rogers, the greenhorn actor, also frequently chuckled at the gaffes he made in the process of learning his craft. During the filming of *Jes' Call Me Jim*, he innocently took advantage of a production break to get a haircut. "I didn't know what I was doing," he confessed with a laugh; "here I was going in one door with long hair and coming out with a haircut." His co-star, Irene Rich, related that the makeup team had to paste part of a wig on the back of his head to cover-up the error.[20]

Rogers' natural charm and good nature produced a humorous, self-deprecating view of his new status as a famous film figure, one that he frequently shared with the public. He took his work seriously but not himself. Throughout his early days in Hollywood, Rogers mocked his disappointing physical appearance on the silver screen. Making fun of the typical movie star's vanity, he claimed that "straight on I didn't look so good" but with a rear shot "the way my ear stood out from my head was just bordering on perfect . . . . That back right ear was a by-word from coast to coast." Rogers liked to point out that he received a deflating letter from a movie fan that said, "I understand you have never used a double in your pictures – now that I have seen you I wonder why you don't." In 1926, the humorist offered a facetious summary of his great impact on the development of American movies. He pointed out that he had come to Hollywood in the early days "when some of these big stars now were just learning to get married. In other words, I am what you call a pioneer. I am all right in anything while it's in its crude state, but the minute it gets to having any class, why, I am sunk . . . . Well, there is the ["mediocre"] stage that I assisted the great film industry through. The minute they commenced to getting better, why, my mission had been fulfilled."[21]

Rogers' skewering of pretension extended beyond himself to the movie industry as a whole. "Out in Hollywood, they say you're not a success unless you owe fifty thousand dollars to someone, have five cars, can develop temperament without notice or no reason at all, and have been mixed up with four divorce cases and two breach-of-promise cases. Well, as a success in Hollywood, I'm a rank failure," he wrote. "I hold only two distinctions in the movie business: ugliest fellow in 'em, and I still have the same wife I started out with." In 1920, after two years in the movie industry, Rogers wrote a satirical list of suggestions on how to improve it. Nearly every one took aim at Hollywood hype and bombast:

"Use your audience for a Press Agent instead of hiring one."

"There is only one thing that can kill the movies and that is education."

"What the Movies need is another name for an All-Star Cast."

"What the entire industry needs is a sense of humor."

"You can't spring a new plot on an audience the first time and expect it to go . . . . It takes a Movie audience years to get used to a new plot."

"Will the industry live? . . . We can't tell yet, it's like a newly born cat, we've got to wait nine days to see if it will open its eyes."

"The average life of the movie is till it reaches the critic." [22]

With typical energy, Rogers, while immersed in a demanding career as a silent film actor, took on an additional job. In 1919, he made an arrangement with Gaumont News and Graphic, maker of newsreels that had begun accompanying feature films in theaters throughout the United States and Europe. Pell Mitchell, editor of the newsreels, had written Rogers and suggested putting together a mono-logue that would "feature your sayings and your personality each week, and will make you the best known individual in the world within a short time." The humorist accepted and by May of that year his quips and image were flashing on screens throughout the country. Rogers dubbed the presentation *The Illiterate Digest*. Most of the one- and two-liners were drawn from his *Ziegfeld Follies* act and focused on public affairs. They included, "Headline in the paper says 'Bandits from other cities are coming to Los Angeles. The landlords here are going to have some competition"; and "Income tax has made liars out of more men than golf has." *The Literary Digest*, a prestigious periodical that had presented its own filmstrips for the last two years, accused Rogers of playing on its name and sent a letter threatening a lawsuit. "I never felt so swelled up in my life" at the thought of competing with a literary publication, he wrote back to the high-powered New York attorney. But his filmed monologue had run its course as Gaumont had fallen behind in its payments and "my humor kinder waned . . . . I couldn't think of a single joke." He continued, "But you inform your clients that if they ever take up rope throwing, or chewing gum, I will consider it a direct infringement of my rights and will protect it with one of the best lawyers in Oklahoma." This endeavor, even though short-lasting, worked as another powerful force bringing Rogers before a broad American audience.[23]

As Rogers carved out an important place for himself in the fledgling movie business, he and his family settled into domestic life in Hollywood. They first rented a roomy house on Van Ness Avenue but were eager to find more spacious accommodations for horseback riding. Samuel Goldwyn offered a stopgap by providing an old building on his studio lot, which was securely fenced, and Rogers converted it into a stable for the family's collection of horses and ponies. Bill and Mary rode there every afternoon, often in the company of their father when he was not filming. Tragedy struck in June 1920, however, when the three Rogers boys came down with diphtheria and the youngest, Freddie, just a few weeks shy of two-years-old, died. Will had been filming on location and rushed home but arrived too late. Devastated by their child's death, Will and Betty were even more anxious to find a real home of their own.[24]

A few months later, Rogers bought a house in the still-developing area of Beverly Hills, across the street from the new Beverly Hills Hotel. The first house they ever owned, it sat on three acres, and Will enclosed it with a high brick wall and added a stable, riding ring, swimming pool, and two log cabins. The smaller of the two cabins was a playhouse for Mary, and the larger became a retreat for the family. With a large, open fireplace, five bunks, and a barbecue grill it became the setting for countless meals and casual gatherings. When Will's sister, Maude, visited and saw the log abode, she burst out laughing and said, "Willie, you're just like an old full-blood [Cherokee]. You buy a big house, then build a little cabin at the foot of the hill and live in it." One difficulty, however, reflected Rogers' newfound career in the movies. After building the high wall around the property, he decided the bricks looked too grim and hired a landscaping company to install ivy to soften the impact. After coming home, however, he grew indignant upon seeing small ivy slips planted in the ground. The horticulturist's assurance that they would grow quickly did not assuage him. Having grown accustomed to the movie lot, where mature trees appeared and houses were built when needed for a scene, Rogers declared, according to Betty, "When I want ivy, I want ivy I can see!" He paid an enormous amount for installing ivy plants with full-blown creepers that were set on the walls.[25]

After making the break from Broadway and the *Ziegfeld Follies* and moving to the West Coast, Rogers' film career and personal life flourished between 1919 and 1921. He became a respected and popular figure in the movie capital as his silent film roles spread his name and image to an ever-larger national audience. Then a crisis slowly enveloped Rogers, one generated by factors beyond his control and then exacerbated by a bad professional decision. It threatened to undo everything.

* * * * *

Rogers' movie contract came up for another yearly renewal in May 2021, and he was shocked when Samuel Goldwyn did not renew it. The reasons behind the decision had little to do with the actor. Granted, Rogers' movies had not been runaway successes. While enjoying critical approval and earning plaudits for their star's acting, the films had made only modest profits, and sometimes less, far below what Goldwyn had anticipated when he hired the popular entertainer from the *Ziegfeld Follies*. In fact, studio salesmen reported that they were instructed to never sell a popular movie "without 'wrapping around the exhibitor's neck' three or four Rogers features." So while the unassuming humorist had become a movie star and a national celebrity, his cinematic efforts had not been particularly lucrative for his employer.[26]

More importantly, Goldwyn Pictures found itself in a precarious financial state in 1921 for reasons that went far beyond Will Rogers. Over the previous few years Samuel Goldwyn had overexpanded his operation and stretched its finances to the breaking point. He purchased land in Culver City and built an elaborate studio with 42 buildings. He launched an "Eminent Authors" project, hiring esteemed writers such as Gertrude Atherton, Rupert Hughes, Rex Beach, and Mary Roberts Rinehart to turn out movie scripts, hardly any of which produced popular films. A prominent European author, the Belgian, Maurice Maeterinck, for instance, spent two months at the studio before writing a single page and finally submitted a literary modernist script that sent Goldwyn screaming from his office, "My God, the hero is a bee!" Goldwyn spent lavishly on expensive productions that did not pay off at the box office, while also becoming the distributor for experimental films such as *The Cabinet of Dr. Caligari*, which had American audiences booing and demanding their money back. Then an economic recession swept the movie business in the spring of 1921, sending Goldwyn Pictures spiraling even deeper into debt. Samuel Goldwyn was forced to cut costs dramatically by dropping the contracts of the studio's stars, including Rogers. Under the pressure, Goldwyn collapsed from nervous exhaustion and was removed as head of the studio by its board of directors in early 1922. He would not return until 1924, briefly with the creation of Metro-Goldwyn-Mayer and then long-term as an independent producer.[27]

Although disappointed, Rogers took his release from Goldwyn Productions with customary good humor. He understood the economic problems confronting the studio and the movie industry. At a promotional appearance for his last film for the studio, a reporter asked if it had been hard for him to muster tears and cry in one of the scenes. "No, it is not," Rogers replied. "It used to be, but the way the movie business has been for the last few months [it's] no trouble to get an actor to cry. In fact, you can't hardly keep them from it. And a Producer will cry if you [just] look at him."[28]

But Rogers did face a conundrum about his career and his future. He loved making movies and, having just purchased a new home, loved the atmosphere of Southern California and wanted to settle in, as did his family. He came up with a solution to his unemployment problem. Rogers decided to make his own movies. "Will was bitten by the bug," Betty said, and "he decided to do a little small-scale producing himself." Actors Douglas Fairbanks, Mary Pickford, and Charlie Chaplin and director D. W. Griffith had set the standard for such endeavors when they bolted the standing studios to form United Artists in 1919. Now Rogers followed the same path by forming Will Rogers Productions and planning a series of short films. Soon the Rogers home was littered with books and manuscripts as Will, Betty, and even the children searched for movie ideas and family dinners became occasions for story conferences. The humorist, after much work by Arthur S. Kane, a movie sales expert whom he hired, also reached a distribution arrangement with Pathé, the largest film production and distribution company in the world.[29]

After establishing his company, Rogers made three movies in 1922. *The Ropin' Fool* featured the Oklahoman as "Ropes" Reilly, a fanatical lariat expert, who escapes a lynch mob accusing him of a fictitious crime. The thin plot provided a cover for the star to demonstrate his remarkable roping skills with humans, horses, goats, geese, a doctor's hat, and even a rat that he snares with string. To highlight his host of tricks, Rogers had painted his ropes white so they would show up on the screen with greater clarity. In an appearance to promote the initial showing of *The Ropin' Fool* in New York City's Capitol Theater, Rogers poked fun at himself. "You see . . . 90 percent of moving pictures have no story, but this is the only one [that] ever admitted it," he joked. "Theater owners tell me it's generally about the middle of the third reel when audiences go to sleep. I am going to beat them to it with this short [two-reel] picture." A second film, *Fruits of Faith*, put Rogers in a favorite role as a good-natured tramp who falls under the sway of an itinerant preacher and is led to a new life of family and productive labor. Finally, *One Day in 365* examined a day in the life of the Rogers family as plain folk surrounded by movie stars in Beverly Hills.[30]

Rogers' experiment in movie-making was a disaster. He had put up everything he owned as collateral for the financing. He "mortgaged our home . . . . his life insurance and the Liberty Bonds bought for the children," Betty reported. "He even had to borrow money on the films themselves." Rogers fell deeply in debt. Then the financial roof fell in when Pathé informed him in September 1922 that it would need several more finished films before it could follow through on the distribution arrangement. Rogers had already spent all the funds he could gather on his trio of movies, and with no prospects of profits appearing soon, he was forced to close up production.[31]

Now faced with a large personal debt as well as unemployment in the film industry, Rogers responded to the crisis with typical energy and determination. While his family remained at their home in Hollywood, he returned to the east coast to take advantage of his assets in the entertainment field. For the next year he worked doggedly. He responded to Florenz Ziegfeld's appeals to return to the *Ziegfeld Follies* and appeared in the 1922, 1924, and 1925 annual shows for a handsome salary. Rogers utilized his popularity as a humorist to secure lucrative engagements as an after-dinner speaker at dozens of gatherings in the New York area. He made enough in these venues to get back on his financial feet.[32]

At the same time, Rogers maintained ties to Hollywood by contracting to star in two independent films. The first, *One Glorious Day* (1922), produced by Jesse L. Lasky and directed by James Cruze, both major Hollywood figures, originally had been constructed as a vehicle for the prominent comic actor, Roscoe "Fatty" Arbuckle. But Arbuckle's career had been destroyed in 1921 when he was implicated in the death of a starlet after a wild party in San Francisco fueled by alcohol and aggressive sex. The script was rewritten to star Rogers in the lead role, and the result was a satirical treatment of spiritualism and politics filmed with touches of German expressionism then *au courant* in the film world. The humorist portrayed a mild-mannered professor interested in spiritualism whose body was possessed by a forceful spirit from Valhalla. Transformed, the now vigorous academic smashes a corrupt local political machine and thrashes a romantic rival. After the spirit departs, the regenerated professor wins the girl of his dreams and is elected mayor by a grateful town. The critics raved about the film. The *New York Times* praised it as "a skillful and ingenious piece of work" and described Rogers' acting as "a revelation . . . . a good deal more on the screen than just himself" and named *One Glorious Day* as the best film of 1922. A host of newspapers and magazines had it among the year's top ten films.[33]

A second independent film project, *The Headless Horseman* (1922), was less adventurous and less successful. A retelling of the familiar tale of Ichabod Crane, the Yankee schoolmaster who comes to Sleepy Hollow, the movie starred Rogers as the protagonist whose romantic aspirations led to a nighttime encounter with a rival disguised as the horrifying phantom. Deeply frightened, he fled the small town and never returned. Reviews of the film were lukewarm, as were the assessments of Rogers in the lead role. The *Motion Picture News* spoke for many when it concluded "the picture is not first-class screen material" and noted that "Rogers may not be tall and angular enough to fit the character but he manages to carry out the impression of the figure in many ways."[34]

Finally, a more stable and long-term movie opportunity beckoned. Hal Roach, one of Hollywood's foremost producers of comic films, extended an offer to Rogers and the Oklahoman accepted. On March 10, 1923, Rogers signed a movie contract with Hal Roach Productions to make a series of two-reel comedies for a salary of 2,000 dollars a week, plus 25 percent of his pictures' profits. It was the largest payout in the history of the studio. The producer launched an ad campaign with the title, "Hal Roach presents, Will Rogers, in Two-Reel Comedies" and promised viewers that in the films "The only thing missing is the drawl." The humorist was happy to return to Hollywood and depart the after-dinner circuit in New York. "I have spoken at so many banquets during the year that when I get home I will feel disappointed if my wife or one of the children don't get up at dinner and say, 'We have with us this evening a man who, I'm sure, needs no introduction,'" he told a newspaper. He also offered a rationale linked to the movie industry, joking, "You see, when I left there a year and a half ago, they were cleaning up the Morals of Hollywood and I had to get out. But now that we both have reformed, I am returning."[35]

Roach was the mastermind behind the successful Harold Lloyd comedy films such as *A Sailor-Made Man* (1921) and in the following years would achieve even greater fame with the popular *Laurel and Hardy* films and the *Our Gang* series. Roach was visiting New York in 1921, accompanied by Lloyd and Victor Shapiro from Pathé, when the trio saw Rogers appear at Ziegfeld's *Midnight Frolic*. Rogers had the audience in stitches and pulled one of his usual stunts by roping Lloyd and hauling him onstage for an informal conversation. Mightily impressed with Rogers' charm and humorous appeal, Roach met with the humorist after the show and offered to make him the star of a series of two-reel comedies. After negotiating, they agreed that Rogers would fulfill his current commitment to Ziegfeld before returning to Hollywood. A contract was sealed, and filming began in June 1923 when the humorist returned to California. Roach and Rogers would go on to become good friends as well as colleagues, with their families socializing and the pair sharing a love of horseback riding. Rogers and Roach became dedicated polo players, practicing and playing in matches together for many years.[36]

Rogers made fourteen films for the Roach Studio in 1923 and 1924, all of them brief comedies in the slapstick genre. They followed a brief, tight filming schedule that saw each short finished in two or three weeks; often, the cast would be filming two movies at once, shooting primary and fill-in scenes for each on alternating weeks. In general, these films offered broad physical comedy full of pratfalls and slapstick. The first, *Hustling Hank* (1923) featured Rogers as a wildlife cameraman who hilariously pursues a bear to get his picture and bumbles through a formal tea party. In subsequent films, Rogers parodied famous movie actors such as Tom Mix, Rudolph Valentino, and Ford Sterling from the Keystone Cops in *Uncensored Movies* (1923) and *Big Moments from Little Pictures* (1924), mocked the artistic pretensions of the Little Theatre groups in *High Brow Stuff* (1924), and illustrated the comic nightmare of urban automobile tangles in *Don't Park There* (1924).[37]

A handful of Rogers' films for Roach illustrated the development of his persona as a humorist. Perhaps the most interesting was *Two Wagons, Both Covered* (1923), wherein the closing of the American frontier became a subject of laughter rather than drama. The project stemmed from Rogers' desire to satirize an epic, acclaimed western film released by Paramount earlier that year, *The Covered Wagon*. He wrote a screenplay that Roach and director Rob Wagner both loved, and filming began a few weeks later in Lake Elsinore, a rural area southeast of Hollywood. Rogers caricatured both the myths and symbols of America's western experience and the real-estate/consumerist frenzy of early twentieth-century society. The film portrays a wagon train snaking westward through the vast expanse of the frontier – but it consisted of only two wagons, each carefully washed every morning while every location looks ridiculously identical to the one before. Then when the pioneers reach California and one wagon heads for Los Angeles, they are attacked by "Escrow Indians" – they are actually Anglo real-estate agents in disguise – who assault them with lengthy contracts and swindle them out of their belongings, including their wagons, in land development deals. Rogers played two characters in this send-up of the typical Western film: Joe Jackson, a scruffy, disreputable scout with a mangy beard, and Bill Banion, a fussy eastern hero who insists on his morning toilette and dons his Yale swimsuit when crossing a river. The film was full of Rogerian quips: it began by noting "seventy-five years before wood alcohol and Fords civilized this country, pioneering was the chief industry," and noted during the arduous journey, "Men were no different in those days than now. The women did the work while the men 'went down in history.'" *Two Wagons, Both Covered* was both a public and critical hit, with the *New York Times* describing, "It is as funny as anything we have ever seen [on film]."[38]

A trilogy of political commentaries in 1924 took up a favorite Rogers theme: the absurdities of American politics. They starred Rogers in the role of Alfalfa Doolittle, a feckless small-town man who spends most of his time hanging out with his cronies in a general store. In the first film, *Going to Congress* (1924), scheming party bosses choose him to run for Congress because he is untainted by scandal. On the campaign trail, Doolittle kisses babies and promises rain to his rural constituency but says nothing about policies or proposals. He is swept into office. Doolittle's head swells immediately and he begins comparing himself to William Jennings Bryan and accepts the fawning compliments of a young woman at the Washington, DC train station who promptly steals his pocket watch. The second film, *Our Congressman* (1924), picks up the story as the Doolittle family have settled into the national capital. Alfalfa shows off for the press, plays golf, dresses in fancy clothes, and ignores the needs of his constituents while bumbling through formal dinners and letting slip his ignorance. His wife and daughter complement his buffoonery with social snobbery as they pursue high-society parties and sneer at ordinary citizens. The final film in the series, *A Truthful Liar* (1924), takes a zany turn in relating Doolittle's post-congressional experiences as ambassador to a European nation. He meets the king dressed in cowboy garb and slaps him on the back, deals with a crazed anarchist, and participates in laying a cornerstone for the kingdom's new Home for Disabled Tenors. After the ambassador saves the king from an assassination attempt, the pair retire to a pub and the American teaches the monarch to play poker and eat hot dogs. Inept and self-important, Alfalfa Doolittle allowed Rogers a cinematic opportunity to spoof the failures of American politics that could elevate such a man.[39]

Finally, Rogers reprised his familiar "hobo" role to poke fun at social conventions in two films for Roach. In *Jus' Passin' Through* (1923), he played a tramp who spent equal time avoiding work and seeking a hot meal. The quest finally led him to seek a position in jail where he could achieve both goals. *Gee Whiz, Genevieve* (1924), Rogers' final Roach movie, showed the protagonist as a hobo who is told he can lead the easy life by marrying the prosperous sister of an acquaintance. She has been described as a former circus performer, and he imagines an athletic, attractive young woman. After agreeing to the marriage, however, he discovers she is an elderly, sour-tempered spinster. He goes through with the nuptials and reveals that his real goal was to provide a comfortable home for his dog. In such brief comic films, Rogers developed skills as a satirist in his acting and his screen persona.[40]

* * * * *

While appreciating the steady work they provided, Will Rogers never really embraced his films with Hal Roach. He quickly grew weary of the physical comedy and broad slapstick style that characterized them. When asked about his discontent by a director, Will groused, "All I ever do on the Roach lot is run around barns and lose my pants." He contributed to screenplays on some of the movies, such as *Two Wagons, Both Covered*, and to the screen placards for others, but his frustration mounted. Roach understood the deeper problem. "No one could write for Will. He put everything over with his unique personality . . . . He was always Will Rogers. He played himself," he said. "But the house style was still slapstick, our stock in trade. We tried to play up Will's folksy appeal, but our pictures depended on visual gags. Will wasn't too comfortable with that." So despite his personal friendship with Roach, when Rogers' contract expired after two years he did not pursue a renewal. He tabled his career in the movie business for a time and turned to other endeavors – humorous lectures, the *Ziegfeld Follies*, newspaper and magazine writing.[41]

A few years later, however, Rogers returned to the world of silent films and made two independent, feature-length movies. While traveling in Europe, he agreed to appear in *Tip Toes* (1927), a film for British National Pictures shot in London. It told the story of three broke vaudevillians in London, all mediocre entertainers, who impersonate wealthy socialites to make inroads among the nobility and escape their plight. Rogers then appeared as the protagonist in *A Texas Steer* (1927), which tells the tale of a wealthy, good-hearted Texas rancher, Maverick Brander, who is elected to Congress through the machinations of a disreputable group seeking graft from the construction of the massive Eagle Rock Dam. After a series of comic complications involving virtuous opponents of the project, Brander sees the light and rushes to the floor of Congress (attired in a nightgown and a formal dress coat) to foil the plot. With typical self-deprecation, Rogers explained that he was selected to play a character who is elected to go to Washington to "play dumb" and the producer told him at the outset, "Will, all you've got to do is act natural." While neither of these films was a blockbuster at the box office, they were moderately successful and received positive reviews, many noting that "Rogers now enjoys a national and international fame as a humorist and . . . a commenter on events political and social."[42]

That same year, Rogers also took on a curious silent film project that ended up boosting his image in unexpected fashion. He made a series of travelogues that took him abroad for a lengthy survey of the European scene. The opportunity appeared as the offshoot of a writing project. *The Saturday Evening Post* and its editor, George H. Lorimer, had hired Rogers to travel to Europe and write a series of articles as an American observer. So from May to September 1926, the humorist traveled extensively in England, the continent, and as far east as the Soviet Union. He authored ten pieces under the heading *Letters of a Self-Made Diplomat to His President* that were serialized in the magazine and later collected and published in a book of the same title, while Rogers' reports from Moscow and St. Petersburg were published in a separate book as *There's Not a Bathing Suit in Russia & Other Bare Facts*. Addressed to President Calvin Coolidge, these tongue-in-cheek pieces reported on the social and political scene in Europe and the morals and values of its various peoples.

Letters of a Self-Made Diplomat presented Rogers as an updated Mark Twain, an American "innocent abroad" who cast a skeptical eye on the affairs and traditions of the old world. Proudly provincial, Rogers skewered the pomp and pretensions of Europeans and contrasted them with the plainspoken, democratic qualities of the United States. In London, he visited the House of Commons and was struck by its rudeness as members "holler at each other and interrupt and yell." After several days, he concluded, "London has the best statesmen and the rottenest coffee of any country in the world. I just hate to see morning come, because I have to get up and drink this coffee." In Italy, he contended that the vaunted bay of Naples was a disappointment and "the harbor in San Francisco . . . makes it look like the Chicago drainage canal." Describing himself as an "ordinary hard-boiled American" who wanted to "see something that was alive," he found Rome disappointing and refused to "run myself ragged dragging from one old church to another, and from one old oil painting to the next." Rogers decided that France was snobby and while in Nice he noted, "It's pronounced neece, not nice; they have no word for nice in French." In Paris, he commented caustically, "A bunch of American tourists were hissed and stoned yesterday, but not until they had finished buying."[43]

But Rogers did not let his fellow Americans off the hook completely. He admitted that his countrymen could appear ill-mannered and insensitive as tourists. He confessed,

> We, unfortunately, don't make a good impression collectively. You see a bunch of Americans at anything abroad and they generally make more noise and have more to say than anybody, and generally create a worse impression than if they had stayed at home. They are throwing rocks at us, but sometimes you think it is deserved. There should be a law prohibiting over three Americans going any-where abroad together.

But Europeans, he added, had few claims of superiority regarding bad behavior. In his words, "Some of these nations have been hating each other for generations, while they are only just starting in hating us."[44]

The cinematic connection to Rogers' European jaunt came unexpectedly. Movie director Carl Stearns Clancy, who had worked with the humorist on *The Headless Horseman*, the 1922 independent film, learned of Rogers' writing assign-ment and approached him about doing a series of light-hearted film travelogues. Rogers resisted at first but eventually agreed. Clancy paid him 20,000 dollars up front, plus 1,500 a week for ten weeks, for a total of 35,000 and Rogers agreed to write the films' subtitles. So as the Oklahoman galivanted through the Old World, Clancy and his cameraman followed him around shooting footage of his experi-ences and encounters. This was then turned into twelve one-reel travelogue films released under the heading, *Strolling Through Europe with Will Rogers*, copyrighted and distributed by Pathé Exchange. Each of these one-reel movies lasted about fifteen minutes and were widely shown in American theaters as shorts before full-length movies.[45]

Publicity for the travelogues advertised Rogers as "Our Unofficial Ambassador Abroad" and, indeed, he played the innocent, untutored American to the hilt. Displaying his proud provincialism, he appeared alongside the monu-ments and institutions he was writing about for the *Saturday Evening Post*. Viewers gained visual images of his good-natured spoofing of stuffy tradition. The series depicted Rogers in cities such as Dublin, London, Paris, Geneva, and Berlin and followed him into the countryside and smaller towns in England, Holland, France, Switzerland, and Germany. Viewers saw him puzzling over wooden shoes in Holland, grinning over the kegs of whiskey at an Irish brewery, questioning what was so curious about the Old Curiosity Shop in London, grabbing a bullhorn to lead tourists on a comical tour of the grounds of the Chateau de Saint-Germain-en-Laye, and mugging in front of the Kaiser's statue in Koblenz.[46]

Significantly, Rogers did not take on the role of an actor in these films. He appeared as himself, and in so doing took another step in shaping his compelling public image. In a promotional announcement for the travelogues in the trade publication, *Exhibitor's Herald*, on March 25, 1927, he joked about his first-person appearance. "The Character I am playing here is one I tried out before. I first tried it about some forty odd years ago and it turned out good and bad, but in the long run it kept me out of the casting line looking for an extra day," he wrote, before adding, "I wanted the reels to keep myself to show at home in my old days, and I just had them make another extra print." The amplification of the Rogers persona came partly in the films' titles, every one of which featured his name, as in *With Will Rogers in Dublin* (1927), *With Will Rogers in Paris* (1927), *Hiking Through Holland with Will Rogers* (1927), and *Reeling Down the Rhine with Will Rogers* (1927). It came partly in the cinematic set-ups, which featured him encountering the great landmarks and traditions of European civilization and reacting as Americans had come to expect: with insights cloaked in humor. It came partly from the films' technique. Clancy claimed that the travel films were not only loosely based on Mark Twain's *Innocents Abroad*, but were the first to have the star face the camera and speak directly to the audience, thus making viewers feel they were actually involved in the sightseeing tour. Rogers appeared to them not as a distant performer but as a funny, friendly guide.[47]

From this array of movies – feature films, comic shorts, newsreels, blithe travelogues – and his association with early giants of Hollywood production such as Samuel Goldwyn and Hal Roach, Will Rogers emerged as a silent-movie star in the late 1910s and early 1920s. Yet the immediate impact of his early film career was complex. On the one hand, it powerfully enhanced his standing as a national celebrity, spreading his charm and humor to every corner of the country. The publicity attending movie stardom promoted his attractive personality and polished his reputation as a satirist of American life and values. Rogers acknowledged the growing power of his film celebrity when he published a mock letter to President Coolidge in a 1923 newspaper piece. America's ambassador to England had just resigned and the humorist applied to replace him. He argued that his primary qualification was "Moving Picture experience" since increasing attention was required as to how public figures looked in the newsreels. "We must not only get men with screen personality," he wrote, "but we must get men who know Camera angles and know when they are getting the worst of it in a picture and not be caught in the background." A movie star would also know tricks to get audiences' attention such as playfully kicking the king at a reception, or stepping on a bride's train at an aristocratic wedding in Westminster Abbey. Clearly, Rogers had come to appreciate the power of movie-made celebrity.[48]

On the other hand, silent films muted Rogers' career by cutting him off from a powerful source of his appeal: the ability to speak. Verbal communication, after all, had become a crucial component in his style as a humorist. While he often wrote the screen placards for his silent films, they were no replacement for the disarming drawl, the hesitating and perplexed observations, and the unsurpassed timing of his speaking style. As Hal Roach recognized ruefully, "We were still making silent films, so people couldn't hear him. On stage that's what he did, talked and joked about current events .... . So getting over Will's personality, often driven by a lot of barbed humor aimed at hypocrisy, without dialogue to put it over? That was tough .... . No matter what we did we were losing the best part of Will's comedy. Because he couldn't talk." Silent films silenced him. And a silent Will Rogers was a much less effective and appealing Will Rogers.[49]

Ultimately, however, Rogers surmounted the limitations of the silent-film genre and turned them to his advantage. He did so in two ways. First, by becoming a familiar figure among Hollywood filmmakers and projecting his name and visage to the American public in theaters everywhere, Rogers' silent films plowed the ground for future cinematic success. When "talkie" movies appeared in the late 1920s, he was prepared to take advantage of this genre much more suited to his talents and his movie career flowered. Second, Rogers' initial appearances on the silver screen helped open up additional avenues of expression and entertainment that made him a household name. Embracing these new opportunities with newspapers, magazines, and radio the Oklahoma humorist moved forward as a key figure in the media revolution of the age. Will Rogers used silent movies as a springboard to become something much more in the 1920s – a beloved national presence who was heard, read, and seen in every corner of the country.

6

An Age of Publicity

"W E ARE LIVING IN AN AGE OF PUBLICITY," Will Rogers wrote. "It used to be only saloons and circuses that wanted their name in the paper, but now it's corporations, churches, preachers, scientists, colleges, and cemeteries." While the humorist was accurate, he was less than forthcoming about publicity seekers. He knew better than anyone that entertainers stood aside for no one in seeking public attention and, moreover, that he may have stood at the front of that line. As a performer in Western shows and a vaudevillian, humorist, and silent-film star the Oklahoman had spent much of the early twentieth century becoming an expert in bringing his name before a mass audience and keeping it there. But in the mid-1920s he vastly expanded his outreach, maneuvering to place himself in the lives and homes of ordinary people on a regular, sometimes daily, basis. For millions of Americans, through such efforts, Rogers became one of the family.[1]

He benefited greatly from an informational sea-change that swept through American society in the early 1900s. This development transformed how citizens received facts and figures, images and opinions, impressions and sounds regarding the world around them. With the closing of the frontier era and the gradual withering of a traditional agricultural society in the late nineteenth century, a dynamic consumer economy began radiating outward from growing urban centers, bringing with it innovative new modes of communication that were both far-reaching and immediate, impersonal yet intimate. What historian Warren Susman has termed a "communications revolution" saw a vast expansion of media as syndicated newspapers, mass-market magazines, phonograph records, movies and newsreels, radio, and advertising inundated the public. The people who stood at the center of this media explosion – movie stars, politicians, entertainers, writers, sports stars – saw their "celebrity" status swell to immense proportions. The media revolution changed everything in terms of how

Americans learned about, and interacted with, one another, their institutions, their leaders, and the process of forging their values. Will Rogers stood at the juncture of this transition.[2]

Earlier in the century, his successes as an entertainer had prompted his first forays into diverse ways of reaching the public that took him beyond the rodeo ring or the theater stage. Rogers' endearingly haphazard way with words, especially in establishing a warm connection with ordinary citizens, found an outlet in sporadic bursts of writing in newspapers and magazines. By the mid-1920s, however, Rogers moved wholeheartedly into new areas of communication. He took on both a weekly and daily newspaper column that gained national distribution, wrote regularly for popular magazines, dipped into the advertising world, spoke via phonograph records, and appeared on a number of pioneering radio programs. Rogers became a ubiquitous figure in American life, constantly before the public and displaying the good-natured charm, lack of pretension, and shrewd humor that made him a familiar figure to a host of ordinary readers and listeners. By the end of the decade, he may have been the most famous, and was certainly the most beloved, individual in the United States. Rogers clearly understood that his media presence had underwritten his monumental national stature. "Us Birds that try to keep before and interest the public have various ways of doing it. The more you do anything that dont look like advertising the better advertising it is," he noted in 1927 of his media efforts. Then he addressed the heart of the matter: "I get paid for being fairly well known."[3]

For all of the fresh initiatives that placed him in the front ranks of the media revolution, however, Rogers began his 1920s conquest of the American public with a rather old-fashioned maneuver. He became a regular on the lecture circuit, a tradition dating back to the mid-1800s. Embracing this decades-old manner of presenting yourself and communicating your ideas to an audience, he expanded and updated its usual features and was able to create his own brand of modern publicity. His tremendous success in this endeavor helped open other doors into American households.

* * * * *

On October 1, 1925, Will Rogers walked onstage at the Park Church in Elmira, New York to deliver the first presentation in his national lecture tour. The choice of this town was no accident. For many years Elmira had been the summer home of Mark Twain, America's best-known humorist of the late 1800s, and he lay buried there. Against such a backdrop, Rogers hoped the audience would be primed for his comic commentary. In the printed program, he had written a facetious "Warning," describing himself as "the man who will come out and enthrall you with his command of the English Language, with his unmatched dignity, with an oratorical delivery that is second only to Ben Turpin [a popular, cross-eyed, slapstick silent film star]." He added a reminder: "there is an old moth-eaten Law on the Statute Books, where if a Speaker, or Actor is attacked by the audience it still constitutes a crime. Politicians have always fought the repeal of this Law."[4]

Facing a full house, Rogers admitted uncertainty about this new career venture. "I don't know what to call this thing . . . . If I were a smart man you would call me a lecturer and if I happened to be a politician, you would call me a debater," he said. "I want to say at the start that I am not trying to displace any lecturer. So we might as well call it 'With Charity for None and Malice to All' and let it go at that." Rogers plunged on to discuss an array of topics in American life with his customary humor. The recently completed "Monkey Trial" in rural Tennessee elicited the comment, "the evolution scare has quieted down. I am glad of it. After all, we are not so much concerned as to where we came from as to where we are going." He proposed that traffic problems would be eliminated by outlawing right and left turns and insisting that "if you are going to a place to keep on going straight until you get there." He disparaged modern politics, saying, "I think both parties are terrible. The one in power is usually the worst." Noting that film star Rudolph Valentino's wife had recently said of their pending divorce that a woman with "an active mind" needed a vacation, he quipped, "So you women of Elmira who have been living happily with your husbands are dumb and you don't know it." He commented on the penny-pinching of the movie industry, relating a problem with the recent filming of *The Ten Commandments*: "They ran shy of money before it was completed and one of the owners wanted to cut it off at the eighth commandment." The local newspaper reported that the audience gave the humorist a "hearty welcome" and expressed "great pleasure" at his remarks. Rogers appreciated the reception and reported, "The only ones I had any trouble with were the regular church members who were occupying their regular pews. They just naturally went to sleep out of force of habit."[5]

In such fashion Will Rogers reached out to the public following his initial stint in Hollywood, harnessing the very quality that had been hushed by silent movies: his ability to speak. He entered the national lecture circuit and quickly became a star attraction in this venue. This old-fashioned mode of reaching the public stretched back to the mid-nineteenth century, when "The Lyceum" circuit had scattered dozens of itinerant speakers around the country giving educational presentations on every topic imaginable: *Causes of the American Revolution, Life of Mohammed, The Education of Children, The Honey Bee, The Practical Man, Instinct.* Figures such as Ralph Waldo Emerson (who often left audiences vaguely uplifted but scratching their heads) and Mark Twain (wildly popular with humorous talks he advertised as "The Trouble Starts at Eight"), along with a host of lesser lights, had plied the Lyceum circuit and supplemented their writing income with speaking fees. Beginning in the 1870s and for the next several decades, the Chautauqua movement created a parallel lecture venue with speakers, often appearing in outdoor tents, who combined religious instruction, exhortations to success, educational topics, and musical entertainment. As a newcomer to this wildly diverse American lecture tradition, Rogers proved to be a natural.[6]

Rogers first pondered this move in late 1923 when the manager of a lecture bureau in New York invited him to sign on for a national tour with the assurance that it would be a "tremendous success." Discussions ensued but Rogers decided to forego the opportunity. Two years later, however, he signed with talent manager Charles L. Wagner and began a seven-month tour in the fall of 1925. Wagner's lucrative offer helped change Rogers' mind: a guarantee of sixty lectures with a payment of 1,000 dollars per night, with an option for the following year that boosted his salary to 1,500 dollars per lecture. That first season Rogers actually delivered more than seventy lectures between October 1, 1925, and April 11, 1926, and by the second season the original contract was altered: local sponsors could either guarantee the speaker a fixed amount or award him a 75 percent cut of the gate. With profits flowing steadily, Rogers crisscrossed the United States from upstate New York to New Orleans, Chicago to Daytona Beach, Philadelphia to San Diego, hitting nearly every decent size town and city between as he talked in large auditoriums, armories, high school gyms, vaudeville theaters, music halls, and civic centers.[7]

A high point came when Rogers lectured in Tulsa, Oklahoma on October 13, 1925 and a large contingent turned out from his hometown of Claremore, some thirty miles away, to boost the crowd. The Convention Hall was packed as listeners filled the seats, perched in the aisles, stood in the back, and even sat in folding seats set up at the rear of the stage itself. Rogers was extremely nervous, walking around the building a few times before stepping onto the stage to a roar of applause and the presentation of a bouquet of flowers by two little girls from Claremore. He began his remarks and gradually relaxed as the audience laughed enthusiastically at his commentary. "Well, they kept on [laughing] seeming to want more till I did two Hours and fifteen minutes. That's, I think, a Minor League record for monologists. That made all the opening nights in New York I have worried with seem like rehearsals," he wrote ecstatically a short time later. "Just think, back home and they liked you! That was a Kick .... I felt good enough that night to last me the rest of my life."[8]

Rogers capped his initial lecture tour with a triumphant appearance at Carnegie Hall. "I just want to come out and have a chat with you, a lot of old friends I haven't seen for almost a year. How's it been with you, anyway?" he began in typically disarming fashion. "I was going to speak [for] free, then I thought I better make a small charge to keep out an undesirable element. They think you aint any good if you do it for nothing." He joked about Mayor Jimmy Walker and Governor Al Smith and poked fun at New York entertainment critics, informing the audience that he always left immediately after the show and went as far away as he could so "if the critic wants to take his spite out on us, there is nobody left there to read it but himself, and that takes all the joy away from [criticizing]." Rogers spent much time contrasting his rough-hewn style with the elegance of Carnegie Hall. "This thing was dedicated to Art, and to an audience that understood Art, so we are both desecrating the Joint," he announced. Alluding to its benefactor, Andrew Carnegie, he termed it "Uncle Andy's Temple of Art" and explained that "foreign fiddlers" who came through New York usually appeared there. A friend, however, finally convinced him that he deserved the stage at Carnegie Hall because of a novelty: "You will be the only short-haired guy that ever played that joint."[9]

Rogers' lecture tours were a disorderly combination of communication and commerce. Bruce Quisenberry, the son of one of Betty's sisters, traveled with him as personal manager. Quisenberry arranged lodging and travel between lecture sites – the talks were often scheduled on consecutive nights some distance away – and would procure trains or automobiles as needed. Often they would depart quickly after an appearance to make the next lecture and Quisenberry recalled that the pair once spent seventy-five successive nights in a train sleeper car, Rogers always in the lower bunk and himself in the upper. Quisenberry also oversaw the money, dutifully checking with the house manager, counting the gate, and making sure the lecturer got his 75 percent. Typically, Rogers never asked his nephew to give an accounting or show him the books. The entertainer was far more concerned with not disappointing the fans who flocked to see him. Once, after lecturing in Oklahoma, he missed the train to make his next lecture in Wichita, Kansas. At his own considerable expense of over 1,000 dollars, he hired a special "stub train" to pick him up and make the Wichita date.[10]

Rogers' haphazard ways on the lecture circuit drove promoter Charles Wagner crazy. Wagner complained that the humorist would come into town late, fail to check in with people organizing the show, and then appear at the last minute. "I never knew where he was," said Wagner. Often the local sponsors would arrange for a local dignitary to introduce him, but an unaware Rogers would dart onstage and begin to talk without an introduction. Other times the Oklahoman, always a soft touch, would agree to do benefit shows for organizations such as the Red Cross without consulting Wagner, who already had booked engagements for him. Wagner grew so irritated that he accused Rogers of being excessively "keen to self-advertising" and threatened to sue him for lost revenues.

But the promoter's lawyer demurred, saying, "If Rogers goes on the stand, what chance would anyone have before a jury?"[11]

From the outset, Rogers' lectures defied any expectations of solemnity or profundity. He aimed to be entertaining as well as instructive, informal as well as thought-provoking. The format encouraged the style. Rogers was joined by "The de Reszke Singers," a quartet of male singers named after their teacher, the famous Polish tenor, Jean de Reszke. They opened the show by performing acapella an assortment of light classical, folk, and spiritual tunes, and then did likewise before a second segment. When Rogers came onstage, he immediately broke all the traditional rules of the public lecture. Instead of standing behind a lectern, he strolled around the stage, leaned against the wall, plopped down on a piano stool, and even sat on the front edge of the platform with his legs dangling over, all the while chewing gum and scratching his head in mock perplexity. Betty reported that on the few occasions he had to use a microphone in a very large venue, "he was acutely embarrassed by this restriction on his movements." There were the inevitable rope tricks – Rogers could not forego such an opportunity in front of a live audience – he used to punctuate his remarks at some point during the performance. He delivered talks that were usually an hour in length, but they frequently went longer when audiences refused to let him go. He would finally close up the show with a kidding remark: "'I'm tired. Now, you folks go on out of here and go home – if you've got a home." [12]

Although Rogers appeared to talk spontaneously, his off-the-cuff remarks were actually the product of meticulous preparation. Upon arriving in a new town, he immediately darted to the local newspaper office to pick up information on city problems, the personalities and maneuvers of local politics, and tidbits of local gossip. He would write down names, incidents, and controversies on envelopes or scraps of paper stuck in his pockets and study them. Once onstage, however, he never looked at his notes. Quisenberry reported that Rogers typically divided his talks into three portions. The first addressed the local themes and people he had just picked up while the second would take up state issues such as the governor and political issues. Third, he would discuss national and international material, drawing upon much-used commentary and jokes he termed his "sure-fire stuff."[13]

All alone on stage for at least an hour, Rogers touched many of the same bases as his *Ziegfeld Follies* commentaries: politics, social issues, human foibles and frailties. He often began by making fun of himself. "A lecturer is any man who can memorize enough material to come out on a stage and insult an audience's intelligence for an hour and still have lack of conscience enough to take their money," he said. "Most of our lecturers come from Europe and most of them have written a book – generally on sex. I never wrote a book on sex but as soon as

I find out something about it, I'm going to write one." Addressing the local scene, he had ready-made cracks at hand: "The children of [town where lecture is being presented] are taught two things. To fear the Lord and hate [host town's biggest rival]." In a rural state, he would comment on agricultural problems and assert, "The trouble with the farmer in America is he belongs to so many relief organizations he's not raising enough to pay his dues." He complimented America on its growing numbers of college-educated people, observing that while graduates used to have trouble getting jobs "boys that come from college now are all settled. They go to work in a filling station." Rogers praised the growth of the medical profession but complained about specialization. "When you go to a doctor nowadays and you say, 'Doctor, I believe I broke my leg.' 'Which leg is it?' 'It's my left leg.' 'I am sorry, but you'll have to go to a left leg doctor; I'm a right leg doctor.'" Moving to the political landscape, he observed of Prohibition, "There are millions of people in this country who will vote 'dry' just as long as they are sober enough to stagger to the polls." Rogers related that some people had suggested he run for president. While considering the possibility, he decided he had only one qualification: "I'd be the only President the country ever had, you know, that would be funny purposely." Then he expressed admiration for Herbert Hoover, a trained engineer, claiming he was "the only man that's been mentioned for the Presidency on either side that could make a living at something else if defeated." Near the end of his lengthy remarks, Rogers noted what he wanted on his tombstone: "I've joked about every prominent man in my time, but I never met a man that I didn't like . . . . That's one thing, don't ever form a dislike for a fellow because you don't agree with him. Don't disagree with him looking at him; walk around behind him and see the way he's looking."[14]

After his initial tour, Rogers continued on the lecture circuit for two more years, finishing up in the summer of 1928. He loved it, later telling the *New York Times* that in his long and multi-faceted career his "greatest personal pleasure" came from public lectures, adding that this endeavor had been "the hardest work, but it was the most gratifying." Betty agreed that her husband got his greatest satisfaction from lecturing because it met several personal needs. It gave him contact with a live audience that "he could see and hear and feel. It stimulated him, gave him inspiration." Moreover, it provided a focus for his vast store of nervous energy with its pressure to always be going somewhere and doing something. Several times a week he was in a new place with new people to meet, new sights to see, and more than likely an old friend or two with whom to become reacquainted. "Will was like a small boy wanting to see everything and wanting to do everything," she said.[15]

The lecture tour held another, more subtle attraction, however, that touched something deep in Rogers' makeup. It provided an opportunity for the homespun, cowboy humorist to meet and converse with ordinary Americans out in the towns, cities, and countryside of the United States. This strong populist impulse, a constant in his career, nudged him to envision the lectures in a certain way – a means to get in touch with regular citizens outside the coastal centers of power and influence and grasp their beliefs, concerns, and aspirations. Shortly before embarking on the lecture circuit, he described his new venture as a "get together tour .... I am going out among the people whom New Yorkers call rubes. But these people I am going out among are the people that just look at New Yorkers and laugh." While originally dubious about giving public talks, according to Betty, he came around because of the opportunity to engage with common folk. "I'm getting tired of talking to Broadway," he said. "I want to get away and talk to America." By all the evidence, America was delighted he came.[16]

* * * * *

By the mid-1920s, Rogers was engaging with several newfangled means of communication that steered him into the mainstream of the era's media revolution. Radio was one of the most important. Wireless telegraphy had first emerged at the turn of the century from experimental work done by figures such as Guglielmo Marconi, and was used initially to contact ships out to sea. Inventors and businessmen such as Howard Armstrong, Lee DeForest, and David Sarnoff developed this technology to broader purposes, and in 1920 Americans first encountered commercial broadcasts when home radios became available. Rogers took advantage of this novel medium, initially appearing on the radio in 1922 on the nation's first broadcasting station, KDKA in Pittsburgh, during an interlude from a *Ziegfeld Follies* tour. He soon began to appear in a growing number of radio broadcasts.[17]

On September 16, 1925, the humorist was a featured speaker in a landmark broadcast of the annual radio industry banquet in New York. Carried by twenty-six radio stations throughout the United States, it was at the time the largest broadcast ever held. However, Rogers' appearance involved some controversy. After agreeing to do the show, he became aware that his lecture tour contract with Charles Wagner forbade him from such speaking appearances. Caught between his obligation to honor his contract and the distress of the radio figures who had gone to much trouble and already advertised his appearance, he resolved the dilemma with typical charm and shrewdness. He gave the radio talk by explaining why he was not allowed to speak, and in the process promoted his lecture tour. "Ladies and Gentlemen, I [have] been forbidden to make a speech to you over the Radio tonight, by my manager who I am soon to start on a Concert tour for," he began. "He figures if you ever heard me once, you would never want to hear me again." He apologized to the listening audience for their being unable to see him and facetiously described himself: "I am 6 foot five and a half inches, horizontal weight 195 all brawn, color of eyes azure blue, Hair jet black and wavy, features strong, complexion perfect." After a few cracks about New York politicians, he declared, "Radio is a great thing – the best thing about it is that you can tune anybody out when you want to." He then signed off with a lecture plug: "I will be in every town. I don't care where you live . . . I will be there." Wagner forgave him.[18]

The following year Rogers helped make history again as a participant in the debut broadcast of the National Broadcasting Company on November 15, 1926. The broadcast involved performers at nineteen radio stations around the United States – Rogers appeared on WDAF in Independence, Kansas – and attracted some 8 million listeners. At the time it was the largest audience he had ever reached in a live appearance. The humorist used material from his lecture tour and talked about his recent European trip where he spoke with George Bernard Shaw. "I and George both know the world is wrong but we don't know exactly what is wrong with it," Rogers noted. "We're trying to fix it, all at so much a word." Politics came in for its usual thrashing, as he explained that in visiting England he became aware of its big drawback, "the dole." "If you don't work, they pay you," he reported. "I told them that wouldn't do. We've tried it with congress and the senate for years and it's a failure."[19]

On January 4, 1928, Rogers found himself at the center of a dark publicity whirlwind stemming from a national radio broadcast. Appearing on the *Dodge Victory Hour*, an entertainment program where personalities spoke from different sites around the country, he broadcast from a makeshift studio set up in his home in California. The controversy came when Rogers introduced President Calvin Coolidge, then shifted into an imitation of the chief executive's nasal New England accent, and pretended to speak from the White House. Some of the "president's" remarks were nonsensical: "I find the country as a WHOLE prosperous. I don't mean by that, that the WHOLE country is prosperous . . . . A WHOLE is not supposed to be prosperous. There is not a WHOLE lot of doubt about that." Others were satirical, as when he praised the current goodwill tour of Charles Lindbergh, whose transatlantic flight had made him a national hero: "he is down in Central America. We seem to get in wrong faster than that boy can get us out. Wish he was twins." The impersonation was so spot-on that many listeners believed it was genuine and found "Coolidge's" comments disturbingly flippant, while many newspapers and commentators, apprised of the comic deception, criticized Rogers the next day for being disrespectful. Rogers was astonished, and then horrified, to discover that people had taken his gag seriously. A few days later, he wrote a letter of apology to the Coolidges, confessing that "due to my lack of good taste, or utter stupidity . . . I have wounded the feelings of two people who I most admire." The president replied the next day, graciously assuring Rogers that he understood it was only "harmless amusement" and conveying the hope that "you will not give the affair another troubled thought." So while the embarrassing incident subsided quickly, it provided a telling lesson in the power of modern media.[20]

While Rogers understood radio's great power to communicate, and used it effectively to keep himself before a vast American audience, he was also sensitive to the medium's limitations. He often mocked its tendency to promote shallow, frivolous entertainment. In 1924, Rogers joked that as radio's reach had extended from big cities into the furthest reaches of the countryside, "[T]here's not been a chore done after supper on an American farm since the radio came in. If you go out to throw the horses some hay, you will miss the Distraction Saxophone Hounds, or Professor Broke's Essay on Thrift." The incessant advertisements also bothered him. In a 1925 newspaper piece, he told readers that he had been invited to join an expedition to the North Pole where he would present a radio report every night on the day's events. "Brother, that is the poorest inducement you have offered me yet. I can stand the cold; I can ride a reindeer; I can chew on a penguin," Rogers replied. "But I am certainly not going to the north pole to listen to ads over the radio . . . . 'This is station WHY, announcer Rum Dum speaking. The Never-Bleed Safety Razor Blade company will put on the following program: The first number will be the Never-Bleed jazz orchestra in one of their own selections." Despite such drawbacks, radio had a significant redeeming feature for the humorist: "All you have to do is turn a dial and you are rid of what you don't like."[21]

At times, Rogers contended that radio was not quite suited to his skills and talents. In private, he complained to Betty that while the medium was well-suited to a singer or someone making a straightforward talk, for someone attuned to audience reaction like himself, it was impossible to gauge if his remarks were impacting listeners because he couldn't see faces or hear laughs. Both in terms of timing and content, Rogers felt he was shooting into the darkness. As he explained to his fans, "If you are in a Theatre, you know about the type and class of people that you will face, and kinder frame up your act accordingly. But on the radio, you got every known specie in the world . . . . On the stage, when you tell anything and it gets a laugh, why naturally you kinder wait and till the laugh is over and then go on. Well, that little microphone that you are talking into, it's not going to laugh, so you don't know . . . whether to wait for your laugh, or just go right on." If silent films had removed one of Rogers' key talents, namely his voice, radio kept that while removing others: the keen physical senses that allowed him to read an audience.[22]

The mid-1920s found Rogers dabbling in other innovative media as he maneuvered to reach an appreciative American public. He made six studio recordings for the Victor Talking Machine Company during the first half of 1923 that were made into three phonograph records and put on the market that same year. He received a royalty of 5 cents per record. "I've looked out at you from the movie screen and stage, but I never got a chance to talk to you at home before," he began in a folksy introduction. "I just want to get acquainted with you and talk over the affairs of the day." The material was from his stage act and after-dinner speeches and included segments entitled *Timely Topics, Will Rogers Nominates Henry Ford for President, Will Rogers Tells Traffic Chiefs How to Direct Traffic*, and *Will Rogers Talks to the Bankers*. The Oklahoman played up the advantage of phonograph records for the consumer, saying, "if you don't like us, you just stop the machine, take the record off, and accidentally drop it on the floor. Then the only annoyance we cause you is sweepin' up."[23]

Rogers also reached his public through advertising. In summer 1924, the American Tobacco Company secured his services to compose advertisements for Bull Durham, its popular pouch tobacco for hand-rolled cigarettes. The company rewarded Rogers handsomely, with the contract stipulating that he be paid 500 dollars for each ad of 150 words, 26 total, along with an agreement that his illustration would appear alongside. The humorist launched an ad campaign called "The Bull's Eye" that cleverly finessed the fact that he was not a smoker. He admitted that he had never used tobacco in his life, but claimed that where he came from "unless a male member of the population has got that Bull Durham tag hanging from the shirt pocket, he's liable to be arrested for indecent exposure." He closed with a self-effacing observation on the moral of his case: "if you want to grow up and know nothing but telling jokes and have people laughing at you all the time, don't smoke. But who wants to go through life acting the fool?"[24]

In addition to lecturing, radio appearances, making phonograph records, and writing advertising copy, Rogers promoted another important aspect of the media revolution when he became involved with mass-market magazines. Magazines, of course, had been published since the mid-nineteenth century but the early versions had been tightly tied to the genteel sensibility of Victorian culture with its "gentle reader." Many of the most popular had been aimed at women, such as *Godey's Lady's Book*, which focused on sentimental themes of domestic life and moral instruction. Others, such as *Harper's, The Atlantic*, and *Scribner's*, appealed to a cultivated literary sensibility and ethos of "good taste" to create a refined reading experience for well-to-do audiences. These traditional publications depended on subscriptions for the bulk of their income. Around the turn of the century, however, new mass-market magazines emerged aimed at a vast audience of middle-class and working-class readers. Influenced by the explosive popularity of metropolitan tabloids, a book publishing craze for "best-sellers," the proliferation of advertising images, and the rise of mass entertainment, a new kind of venue moved to the fore. Beginning in the 1890s, magazines such as *McClure's, Ladies' Home Journal,* and *Collier's Weekly* appeared promoting an ethos of "realism" and consumer prosperity. They featured timely articles, titillating tales, and personality profiles written in a clear, direct, persuasive, and unadorned style. With most of their income coming from advertising, not subscriptions, they aimed at a national market and filled their pages with commercial appeals for a vast array of products. [25]

Rogers, as part of his media conquest in the 1920s, established important relationships with several of the most important mass-market magazines. In the late fall of 1922, Rogers agreed to supply gags to *Life,* the New York humor magazine founded in 1883 that had steadily grown to a weekly readership of around one-quarter million people. Among his comic offerings: "New York [just] had a 'Don't Get Hurt' week – Taxi Drivers couldn't hardly wait till the following Monday to run over you," and "Certainly glad to see that Women's skirts are getting longer. A lot of men on the street seem to see where they are going now." In 1923, Rogers was a featured speaker at *Life's* 40th anniversary banquet, where he kidded everyone from John D. Rockefeller to the publication itself ("I read the Jokes in [the magazine] and thought it was older"). Rogers was not always happy with *Life's* choices from his gags. "You have some man on your paper whose Genius I don't believe you fully appreciate. The way he can [read] 48 jokes and pick out the absolute poorest is positively uncanny," he once wrote the editor. "Now this time I am *fooling him*; I'm not sending any bad ones." Later in the decade, Rogers wrote a long series of articles for the magazine in 1928 when it helped him launch a facetious campaign for president as head of the Anti-Bunk Party. [26]

In the late 1920s, the Oklahoman began to write for another popular periodical, the *American Magazine*. This monthly publication had been founded in 1906 as a venue for muckraking political exposés, but by 1915 it had shifted to emphasizing human interest pieces, short stories, and treatments of social issues. By the 1920s it had a readership of 1.8 million. *The American* published six Rogers articles, beginning with the "The Hoofing Kid from Claremore" in April 1929 and continuing over the next fourteen months. Several personality sketches covered a long-distance runner from his hometown, ex-President Calvin Coolidge, industrialist Henry Ford, and the merchant, sportsman, and philanthropist, Sir Thomas Lipton. Other articles featured Rogers giving advice on "How to Be Funny" and discussing a favorite topic, Prohibition. [27]

At the top of Rogers' periodical ventures in the 1920s, however, stood his successful alliance with the most popular of the new mass-circulation magazines, the *Saturday Evening Post*. Long-standing and multifaceted, this relationship would prevail for the rest of his career. The *Post* had begun in 1897 and by the 1920s, under the long editorship of George H. Lorimer, it had achieved a circulation of 2.4 million and become a staple in many middle-class households. In the summer of 1926, Rogers began writing the popular series of articles for the magazine that covered his extended tour of Europe, which were then collected and published as two books, *Letters of a Self-Made Diplomat to His President* (1926) and *There's Not a Bathing Suit in Russia & Other Bare Facts* (1927). He would go on to publish a humorous, two-part account of his gallstone attack and operation in the *Saturday Evening Post* in late fall 1927. Rogers followed it with pieces later in the decade on his overnight stay at the White House of Calvin Coolidge, the presidential race of 1928, and his adventures flying cross-country as a passenger aboard air-mail flights (he claimed he was charged his weight in postage). George Lorimer tried to get Rogers to write an autobiography that would be serialized in the magazine. The humorist sketched out a few incidents and ideas, but never really engaged with the project. Rogers wired Lorimer that although the memoir remained uncompleted, patience would be rewarded: "THE LONGER I LIVE THE MORE LIFE YOU GET ALL AT ORIGINAL PRICE."[28]

Among Rogers' many media ventures in the 1920s, one emerged as the most impactful. His involvement with syndicated newspapers early in the decade, first with a weekly column and then with a daily "telegram," provided a durable, dependable platform that put him into constant communication with millions of Americans. It made him not just a familiar face, but a household presence for a massive, adoring audience of ordinary citizens.

* * * * *

In the late fall 1922, V. V. McNitt of the McNaught Syndicate – this organization distributed columns, comic strips, and other features to newspapers around the United States – approached Will Rogers with an offer of 500 dollars per week to write a syndicated newspaper column. The deal did not come easily. McNitt first wrote Rogers broaching the idea and suggested they meet for a discussion. McNitt never heard back, so he finally visited the entertainer in his dressing room at the New Amsterdam Theater, where he was appearing with the *Ziegfeld Follies*, and made a personal appeal. To his dismay, McNitt learned that the *New York Herald* had already made a better offer. So on a whim he asked Rogers, "Would you be interested if we could place your articles in the *New York Times*?" Recognizing the pull of the most respected newspaper in the United States, he replied, "I guess anybody'd be interested in that." McNitt was able to secure a promise from the *Times*' managing editor, Carr Van Anda, so an agreement was reached with the

Oklahoma humorist. Rogers' first column appeared in the Sunday, December 24 edition of the *Times*. It was initially picked up by twenty subscribing newspapers but its popularity soon brought many others flocking to run it. Over the next decade, as more and more newspapers adopted Rogers' column, the McNaught Syndicate raised his payment to 1,000 dollars a week. This forum provided its author with millions of regular readers throughout the United States and he became one of the most widely read columnists in the country.[29]

This journalistic venture hit a rough patch at the outset, however. In one of his few career missteps, Rogers initially submitted a hackneyed piece called "The Story of Powder River Powell and Soapy." Full of overdrawn western dialogue and structured as an awkward conversation about world affairs between a cow-puncher and his barber, the story failed both as humor and as commentary. McNaught gently rejected it and suggested that Rogers write about contemporary affairs as himself and in a more straightforward manner. Rogers pivoted in that direction, quickly catching his stride and gaining editorial approval. Upon publication of his first syndicated column, the *New York Times* noted, "The famous cowboy monologist, Will Rogers, has undertaken to write for this paper a weekly article of humorous comment on contemporary affairs. The *Literary Digest* approved the move and quoted another editorial: 'Not unworthily is Will Rogers carrying on the tradition of Aristophanes on our comic stage.'"[30]

Rogers quickly established his trademark tone of down-home humor. In his opening column on December 24, he explained apologetically, "why I am blossoming out as a weekly infliction on you all." He claimed that he needed money to raise his trio of children and promised readers that by imbibing his commentary every Sunday they were "really doing a charitable act ... by preventing these three miniature bandits from growing up in ignorance." In his next two numbers, where he continued to introduce himself to readers, Rogers claimed that the editors were looking for "a man of broad intellect, and refinement, in other words a Gentleman and a Scholar. So naturally their first thought drifted to Me." He joked about "breaking out in a rash right here in this paper every Sunday" and described a recent appearance where the Governor of Kansas had praised him as "the only man in America who was able to tell the truth about our men and affairs. When he finished I explained to the audience .... It is because I have never mixed up in politics."[31]

Rogers' column – it became known as "The Weekly Article" – quickly took root and became his greatest means of communication with, and entertainment for, the American people. He wrote it for the rest of his life. In 1924, the *New York Times* dropped the column when it was picked up by William Randolph Hearst's *New York World*, but the shift had little impact on its popularity. By the early 1930s, some 600 daily and weekly newspapers carried Rogers' weekly essay to millions of readers throughout the United States, likely making him the most popular columnist in the country. The *Weekly Article* gave a tremendous boost to its author's career on several levels. It provided him a steady income, evening out the wild financial fluctuations that had accompanied his earlier efforts with vaudeville, Ziegfeld, lecturing, and silent films. It enhanced his relationship with the national press, making him a kind of celebrity journalist who both commented on the news and served as a subject of such commentary, a unique position that he would exploit in the future. Most importantly, the weekly column gave Rogers completely free rein to comment on political, cultural, social issues of the day and a national forum in which to do so. More than anything else among his far-flung endeavors, this made him a constant, dependable voice on modern American life.[32]

As Rogers' column developed in the mid-1920s it took on several character-istics that polished and disseminated his unique voice and image. Most famously, its author developed the habit of opening many of his efforts with the self-effacing statement, "Well, all I know is what I read in the papers" and it became his calling card. Originally, the *Weekly Article* recycled material from Rogers' stage act with the *Ziegfeld Follies* or his lecture tour and tended to be punchier and gag-filled. Over time, however, the essays evolved to become longer, more reflective, sometimes rambling but always commonsensical and humorous. They expanded to take up a variety of contemporary issues as Rogers presented political, social, and cultural commentary on the developments of the day. Picking up tendencies from his earlier efforts, he poked fun at pretension and mocked hypocrisy while probing the inconsistencies and aspirations, the follies and virtues of American life. Rogers rejected the tone of Victorian gentility that still prevailed among prominent columnists such as Arthur Brisbane and Christopher Morley, instead adopting a style that jettisoned adornment for directness, moralizing for observa-tion, high-mindedness for jocularity, and sophistication for shrewdness. Establishing an atmosphere of common people talking common sense, he encour-aged an inviting, trusting relationship with his readers as if they were friends sitting around the kitchen table, drinking coffee, and comparing notes on the world around them.

Rogers' eccentric spelling, endearingly mangled grammar, inventive syntax, and enthusiastic capitalization became one of the column's most recognizable features. Filled with slang and "aint's" and "kinders," the Oklahoman's writing appeared as the rhetorical equivalent of his chewing gum and head-scratching on stage. In one of his early columns, for example, he mused about an unusual round of personal activity in New York:

> Well, this has been a kinder quiet week. One night I had to buy my own Dinner.
> And another night a friend took me out and I didn't have to make a speech for it.

In fact, that was the reason he took me. It was with the understanding that I keep quiet.

But the Newspaper Women of all the Papers formed a Newspaper Woman's Club and they give a big Ball at the Ritz Carleton Hotel, and had a big show and I was asked to announce the acts. You know what an announcer at a Benefit Show is. Instead of letting the show run along smoothly and nice one act after the other, they have somebody come in and drag the show out. He is kinder like a Train Caller, only worse. I had some jokes about the first three or four acts, then I run out of jokes and from then on I was better.[33]

After much reflection, Rogers' editors decided to leave most of his writing in its original state, cleaning up only those errors that might mystify or mislead readers. As V. V. McNitt wrote to Carr Van Anda of the *New York Times* just before the column first appeared, "I believe that the stuff will look more genuine if the copy is left as nearly as possible like the original manuscript. We are accordingly leaving in the copy some of the unnecessary capital letters, which tend to emphasize the points that Rogers makes." Betty agreed with this hands-off approach, commenting that her husband's writing "developed as his work on the stage had – it was just a question of finding some natural way of expressing himself, of presenting his particular slant on things unencumbered by any form or style." Rogers himself typically took a humorous angle: "When I first started out to write and misspelled a few words, people said I was plain ignorant. But when I got all the words wrong, they declared I was a humorist."[34]

Rogers addressed a host of topics in his newspaper column, ranging from Jack Dempsey's heavyweight boxing matches to the popular song "Yes, We Have No Bananas" to the visit of the Prince of Wales. Early on, he joked that no matter what his subject it would drive off a segment of readers: "if I write a learned article on chewing gum, I find that I lose my clientele of readers who are toothless." Nonetheless, one of Rogers' favorite topics became American politics with its attendant issues, controversies, and personalities, even though he claimed to fear that "when I write on just strictly politics, I find that the honest people are not interested." The columnist regularly surveyed the babble of competing voices in America's contentious democratic atmosphere and delighted in skewering the posturing, deception, and absurdities that often prevailed. He jokingly advocated electing government officials for life because "no matter what man is in an office the one that you put in his place is worse." He pilloried the Democrat presidential convention of 1924 as a chaotic three-week spectacle that presented sixteen official candidates, endless nominating and seconding speeches, and 103 ballots, all of which produced the nomination of an unknown former Ambassador to Great Britain, John W. Davis, who predictably was slaughtered in the general election. "Women delegates started in with Bobbed Hair and wound up being able to sit on it," he reported tongue-in-cheek of the marathon. "In number of population the convention is holding its own. The deaths from old age among the delegates is about offset by the birth rate." After his victory in the same election, the Republican victor, President Calvin Coolidge, earned a humorous crack from Rogers about "Economy," the theme of his campaign: "as soon as he got in he raised Congress' and the Senate's Salary and redecorated the White House. So away goes another Slogan!" The partisan wrangling of American politics left the columnist shaking his head. "All you would have to do to make some men Atheists is just to tell them the Lord belonged to the opposition Political Party," he wrote. "After that they could never see any good in him."[35]

But more often Rogers chose to dig beneath the political surface and excavate American life in all its bewildering variety in the early twentieth century. Experiencing the same disorienting changes as his fellow citizens brought about by the explosion of urbanization, consumerism, media, entertainment, and mechanization in the era, he brought a down-to-earth, common-sense perspective to bear and tried to size up the impact both good and bad. Rogers stepped forward as a mediator of historical change and helped Americans come to terms with the pressures and conundrums of a rapidly modernizing society. He deployed his skills as a humorist to do so, recognizing the inevitability and usefulness of modern developments while also puncturing overblown promises of progress and gauging attendant costs. His audience, nudged to chuckle at their transforming world and at themselves, found comfort in Rogers' remarks.

Technology, for example, often appeared on the columnist's comic radar. In an age where mechanical inventions from radio to automobiles to phonographs to movies profoundly changed the quality of Americans' daily lives, Rogers looked on such advances with humorous skepticism. While granting the advantages they brought in convenience and enhanced experience, he also recognized their drawbacks. For example, in 1924 he looked askance at a new invention allowing photographs to be sent by radio waves, poking fun at the modern mania for images and a change-for-its-own-sake attitude that supported it:

> What good is it? They look just as bad as the ones we used to get by mail. In fact, they don't look as good. Every one I saw that had their pictures sent by radio looked like they had the small pox .... We used to have tintypes taken and they crossed the plains by pony express. That was not hailed as a miracle. Why? Because people were smarter in those days. They didn't go cuckoo over looking at pictures in the papers. People could read in those days. They wanted to know what was going on, not what kind of hat some guy had on. Your looks meant nothing to them; it was what you did that counted .... We are getting to be a nation that can't read anymore. If the thing hasn't got a picture of it, why we are sunk .... That's why the Bible is not read any more than it is, because it's not in

the picture section. If they could see Moses in a golf suit writing his Sermon on the Mount by radio, why they would look at it.[36]

Rogers frequently probed the allure and pitfalls of America's modern consumer prosperity, which by the 1920s had reached heights unforeseen a few decades earlier. In 1923, he offered a witty take on the real estate market springing up in and around many of the nation's cities that offered homes in new residential areas to prosperous middle-class and working-class families. The appeal of such houses, the columnist contended, revolved around the bath tub, a feature extravagantly advertised:

> The ad might better have read, "Buy our home and live in a bath tub." The biggest part of city homes nowadays have more baths than beds . . . . When you visit a friend's newly finished home you will be shown through all the bathrooms, but when you leave you couldn't to save your soul, tell where the dining room was . . . . It's not the high cost of living that is driving us to the Poor House – it's the high cost of bathing . . . . Now, mind you, I am not against this modern accomplishment, or extravagance, of ours. I realize that these manufacturers of [bathroom] fixtures have advanced their art to the point where they are practically modern Michael Angelos . . . . But, in doing so they have destroyed an American institution and ruined the only calendar that a child ever had. That was the Saturday night bath . . . . In those old days he knew that the next morning after the weekly ear washing he was going to Sunday School. Now he has not only eliminated the bath on Saturday but has practically eliminated the Sunday School, for neither he nor his parents know when Sunday comes . . . . Now that was an event. It meant something. It brought you closer together. But now bathing is so common there's no kick to it.[37]

Rogers often addressed religion, a contentious subject that required an extraordinarily light touch. He pulled it off, deftly skewering moral pretense while urging for doctrinal toleration and gently suggesting that Americans mind their own spiritual business. During the great debate over evolution that roiled the pious in the early 1920s, he wrote, "Church people all over the country are divided and arguing over where we come from. Never mind where we come from, Neighbor. . . . Just let the preachers make it their business where you are going when you leave here." Rogers poked equal fun at scientists who dismissed religious tradition. He came across a scholar, for example, who insisted that the events of the Bible happened not in the Holy Land but much further to the east near India. If such a claim gained credence, the humorist predicted, "I bet you they will dig up a Scientist from some Rotary Club and he will read a paper to prove the whole thing took place just between Glendale and Long Beach, Cal[ifornia]. Then the argument will start as to whether the River Jordan was the Sacramento or the

Talhassee." Rogers reported on his most gratifying encounter with religion in 1925, when an Ohio minister asked him to deliver a few remarks from the pulpit on Sunday morning. No one was converted, he informed readers, but he had the congregation laughing. When he finished, the congregants applauded and the minister complimented him by saying making people laugh was a balm to their soul. "I hold the distinction of being the only one that ever preached a sermon in a regular church and didn't know it," the Oklahoman concluded. "And I don't even know what denomination the church was." True to his code of religious toleration, Rogers supported Governor Al Smith of New York as a presidential candidate in 1924 and 1928, despite the politician's Catholicism. "What do we care about a man's religion [in politics]," he wrote. "We don't want to be saved spiritually, we want to be dragged out of the hole financially."[38]

American manners and daily life often drew Rogers' attention and brought a flood of humorous observations. An invitation to deliver an after-dinner speech at a banquet for the Corset Manufacturers in New York inspired a piece on this "essential industry." "Just imagine, if you can, if the flesh of this country were allowed to wander around promiscuously!" he wrote of the burden facing this Victorian female accoutrement. "Why, there ain't no telling where it would wind up." He claimed to speak from first-hand experience, recalling how once he had been seated at a dinner next to a "fleshy lady" when a broken corset string wreaked havoc. "We didn't know it at first, the deluge seemed so gradual, till finally [both] the gentleman on the opposite side of her and myself were gradually pushed off our chairs." The poor woman, having arrived in "a small roadster . . . was delivered home in a bus." This old-fashioned social problem was matched by a modern one in the growing mania for makeup, particularly the female obsession with nose maintenance. "It's getting so this country only has two occupations now. One is the women pawing at their nose with a powder puff and the other is the men talking about their golf scores," he lamented. In the past, he maintained, "the nose was a thing considered just for blowing purposes, and it was never thought it would some day be used as a background for 50 million amateur female scenic artists." Rogers claimed that he was about to become wealthy from developing a "permanent nose paint" that would keep women from worrying about a shiny nose, but was utterly flummoxed by the recent trend of surgical nose jobs for men and women alike. "Every nose has a doctor all its own," he said. "They are landscaping noses just like flower gardens." In fact, he had looked into the procedure but the doctor had said "my nose was about the only thing about my face that seemed to be properly laid out."[39]

In fulfilling this role as historical mediator trying to reconcile the past and the present, Rogers often wrote about a technological innovation that was transforming American life: the automobile. As sturdy, inexpensive cars, particularly Henry

Ford's Model T, became common among the general population in the 1920s, their revolutionary impact became obvious – broadening the scope of people's daily lives, erasing boundaries between the city and the country, increasing tourism and travel, altering habitation patterns in towns and cities, creating important new industrial jobs, promoting an ethos of consumerism and credit buying. Such developments had enriched life and promoted Americans' happiness, Rogers conceded, but he worried about unintended, negative consequences. He joked that the automobile had "made more business for an Undertaker than any other one thing" while creating "the biggest problem we have in America today, and that is 'Where am I going to park it.'" Buying these vehicles sent countless consumers into debt while driving countless towns, cities, and states to borrow money for road construction so that now "we owe more for roads than we did [during World War I] to persuade the Germans to 'please leave Belgium.'" Moreover, Rogers worried that the technique of mass production used to make cars had spilled over into American society to create a creed of "think alike." "We started building our towns alike – Filling Stations on two corners and Drug Stores on the other two," the humorist wrote. "We assemble our education at a College just like they do a Car. You start through and each Teacher sticks a little something onto you as you go by their Department, the same thing on each one." Change, the humorist liked to point out, had its costs.[40]

While Rogers' weekly newspaper column brought him an audience of millions by the mid-1920s, an additional innovation enlarged his public image even more. In a serendipitous stroke of genius, he arranged to write a brief, pithy comment on public affairs that would be published daily by newspapers all over the United States. In a succinct style of mass communication that would not be replicated for nearly a century with Twitter, Rogers became a daily presence for countless Americans, someone to enjoy over morning coffee, or a subway or train ride, or early evenings on the porch after farm chores were completed.

Rogers' "Daily Telegram," as it came to be known, began in 1926 when the humorist, shortly before his departure for a tour of Europe, ran into Adolph Ochs, publisher of the *New York Times*. During their chat, Ochs said, "If you run across anything worthwhile, cable it to us. We'll pay the tolls." When in England, Rogers recalled the conversation and sent a cable to Ochs which informed him that Lady Astor, who had entertained Rogers in London, was soon arriving in New York. "She is the best friend America has here," he noted. "She is the only one over here that don't throw rocks at American tourists." The *Times* ran it on the front page on July 30 and elicited many chuckles and positive comments. Rogers continued to send daily cables for the next several weeks, and Ochs ran them exclusively through September. After getting the consent of the writer, the McNaught Syndicate stepped in to manage this new venture and quickly put it into syndication with an original group of ninety-two newspapers. Within five years, approximately 600 newspapers subscribed, making this another Rogers media triumph.[41]

The "Daily Telegrams" were brief, usually between 125–150 words and their witty, commonsensical style captured the Rogers persona perfectly. He addressed whatever was on his mind, ranging from developments in Europe to American public affairs to the cost of houses to sights he was seeing and what he was having for dinner. As with his weekly column, Rogers pushed to have his idiosyncratic writing style, inventive spelling, and hit-or-miss grammar left as they appeared. "That's the way I write it, and that's the way I want it to lay," he told the McNaught Syndicate. They agreed. It was arranged for Rogers to send his daily dispatches to the Western Union branch office in the *New York Times* building, which then conveyed them to the subscribing newspapers around the country without revision. Rogers wrote the daily telegrams for the rest of his life, and became so dedicated to the endeavor that he missed only a handful of days. Once, when undergoing an operation in the late 1920s, he hurriedly composed three entries before they wheeled him off. After recovery, the first thing he did was to write out in longhand the next day's comment.[42]

The composition and delivery of the daily telegram was a frantic process. Rogers wrote them everywhere – on the train during his lecture tours, at dinner in one of his favorite chili restaurants, sometimes at a table in a small-town telegraph office. If he was traveling or on a movie set, his automobile served as his office. Rogers would get into the back seat, thumb through the newspapers piled around him, and wrinkle his face as he searched for items and circled them with a pencil. Finally, he would heave his portable typewriter into his lap and begin pecking out a dispatch – he was a two-finger typist – that met his requirements. Typically, he would wait until the last minute and barely finish in time to meet the 1:30 pm filing deadline. Bruce Quisenberry, Rogers' personal manager on lecture tours, described Rogers' process as "dramatic." In Quisenberry's words, his boss "would watch the time, then, at the last possible moment, he would put his portable on his knees, stare into space a few moments, then begin to peck. His hands – so amazingly skillful with a rope – were all thumbs when he tackled a typewriter. Peck-peck-peck! Sometimes he would stop, turn up the page and scowl at it for a minute." When the telegram was finally ready, Quisenberry would hop off the train at the next stop, dash off to file it at the nearest telegraph station, and then run like mad to get back on the train. Rogers liked to joke upon his return, "I'll bet we lose you someday."[43]

Rogers' wide-ranging topics contributed to the appeal of his daily telegrams. The witty observations on issues and people, the commonsensical take on snippets of daily life, the good-natured joshing about life's absurdities made for a feeling of comfortable conversation with a trusted friend or good-hearted neighbor whom you would joke around with sitting on the front porch. Rogers added to this atmosphere by signing many of his dispatches "Will." He found topics all around. On a trip to the west coast, he commented, "I never saw California looking more beautiful. The tremendous rains out here have washed away all the real estate signs." One of his squibs addressed the growing popularity of college football. "Harvard and Yale played Saturday, as usual, to decide which was the worst team in America," he joked. "They got correspondence school teams out West here that they have to handcuff to keep them from going and beating Harvard and Yale."[44]

Rogers also took on more serious topics, such as the controversy over military veterans being turned down for loans by lending institutions. "I see where a lot of banks are refusing the soldier boys loans on their adjusted compensations on account of too much red tape to handle. Not quite as much tape for them as it was for him to go to war, though there is at least no bullets in it," he observed. "Thank goodness there will be no more wars. Now you tell one." Noting a recent flowery speech that President Calvin Coolidge made to a medical society, in which he claimed that a dawning era of right living, good will, and peace would put humans "in accordance with the teachings of the Great Physician," Rogers demurred. "Gee! That sounds like one of those birthday greeting cards," he joked. "With those beautiful thoughts there must have been a third term breaking through the clouds." In December 1928, he offered his own, brief "State of the Nation" speech: "The nation never looked like it was facing a worse Winter – birds, geese, Democrats, and all perishable animals are already huddled up in three or four States down South. We are at peace with the world because the world is waiting to get another gun and get it loaded. Wall Street is in good shape, but Eighth Avenue never was as bad off. The farmers are going into the Winter with pretty good radios, but not much feed for their stock."[45]

As always, social trends caught Rogers' eye and triggered humorous skepticism. He was unpersuaded by the movement for "Companionate Marriages," which sought to loosen traditional matrimony by establishing one-year trial marriages with no children and then easy divorce thereafter. "I think marriages should be companionate. I hate to see them meet and marry when they are not friends at all," Rogers cracked. "And as for divorce, I think people put too much dependence on it. You don't see many cases where the parties did any better the second time than they did the first or the third and fourth or the fifth and so on marriages. It just looks like the people are grabbing at a straw." Noting the trend of men eschewing hats to go bareheaded, he contended it was foolish for a man to let "it rain down his neck to show people that he bathes. If your head hasn't got enough in it to carry a hat, why all the sunshine on it in the world won't do it any good." The conclusion of the holiday season brought this rumination: "Well, the Xmas spirit is over now. Everybody can get back to their natural dispositions.

If there had been as many good wishes in the heart as there was on paper, the devil would have to dig up some new clients."[46]

Rogers often turned to the daily events of his own life for material to fill his daily telegrams. During a brief, and unusual, respite from work, he convinced Betty to join him to explore the Native American treasures of Arizona. He reported, "So here we are just prowling around making no speeches, doing no act, just trying to buy a Navajo blanket from a Navajo; in other words, from the producer to the ultimate consumer without a middle man." When a severe gallstone attack in June 1927 necessitated an operation, he harvested several days of commentary. "So I am in the California Hospital, where they are going to relieve me of surplus gall, much to the politicians' delight," he reported early on. The next day, laying and waiting for transport to the operating room, he wrote, "Well, here comes the wagon. I do hope my scar will not suffer in size with other, older and more experienced scars." After the successful completion of the procedure, he expressed his appreciation to President Coolidge and several United States Senators who had sent their best wishes. "Everybody that I make a living kidding about seemed to be watching for some turn in my illness," he wrote. "People couldn't have been any nicer to me if I had died."[47]

Reading Rogers' daily telegrams on contemporary life, in addition to his lengthier weekly ruminations in his Sunday newspaper column, soon became a national habit as readers throughout the United States relished their keen, witty observations and down-home style. Rogers' written observations on American life brought him into the homes of millions of ordinary people on a regular basis and made him a trusted, beloved guide to navigating the rapidly evolving world of the early twentieth century. Millions of ordinary folks came to feel that they knew him personally, an emotional identification that indelibly stamped his persona on American consciousness. Rogers had a good sense of his outreach and impact, and often expressed his gratification. As V. V. McNitt of the McNaught Syndicate commented, "I think Will was more impressed by his success as a writer than by anything else that ever happened to him."[48]

A growing number of critics, observers, and publications also took notice, observing that the influence of the Oklahoma humorist had risen in proportion to his ubiquitous presence in American life. The *San Francisco Chronicle* noted "the Rogers phenomenon" and inquired about "the secret of this platform cowboy's vogue." It then answered its own question: "he has a faculty of seeing into the heart of a social or political or economic problem and then telling us in a sentence what is there." *Everybody's* magazine pointed out that hundreds of newspapers carried his words while "numberless others echo them in editorials beginning 'Will Rogers says,' and ending with 'Will is dead right.'" *Collier's* pronounced, "Today he is almost an American institution." The *Tulsa Daily World* drew a similar conclusion, observing that as newspapers "printed his stuff and syndicated it throughout the hinterland, he had become in a very real sense an American spokesman."[49]

But it is important to remember that Rogers' success as a popular journalist did not appear from nowhere. It was the capstone of a much broader media crusade in the 1920s that provided the humorist an unprecedented outreach to a popular audience. His wide-ranging efforts in the *Ziegfeld Follies*, silent movies, magazine writing, phonograph records, lecturing, advertising, and radio provided a foundation for his tremendous success as a newspaper writer. Indeed, there was a crucial synergy at work in the 1920s that made the whole of Rogers' media endeavors greater than the sum of its parts. Again, no one understood this interconnection more deeply, nor appreciated it more fully, than the Oklahoman himself. In 1927, with his newspaper writing in full swing and his national stature reaching its peak status, Rogers jokingly surveyed how his varied media endeavors converged to underwrite a recent trip to Europe:

> The *Saturday Evening Post* [has] already payed for the trip, talking all over the country [with lectures] has made me more than I ever could have made in [motion] pictures even if I had been a real star. [The published] book of the trip has brought enough to pay for another trip, the Vitaphone staggered me to tell about it before their double-barrel contraption . . . . The radio is another by product that I just thought of that has already paid me for them, too . . . . I like to forgot Bull Durham paying me to tell also about the same trip [in advertisements]. And, oh yes, my old friend Sam Goldwyn wants the dramatic rights to the book. I sold Keystone [movie studio] the still pictures, and the syndicated strip cartoon rights are being negotiated for [rig]ht now.

Rogers' lighthearted assessment of his interlocking media achievements produced a shrewd conclusion: "I was raised on a ranch but I never knew before there was so many ways of skinning a calf."[50]

As Will Rogers soared high above the American landscape in the mid-1920s, it was not only the form but the content of his work that pushed him upward and highlighted his visibility. Unprecedented media opportunities may have given him a tremendous platform for addressing his fellow citizens, but more was required to keep him there. What Rogers actually said, while addressing a variety of themes and topics, formed the unbreakable bond with his audience. Americans liked him for his humor and lack of pretension, but they loved him for what he taught them about themselves. Digging deeply into the cultural soil of his native land, this citizen cowboy unearthed and analyzed many aspects of life in the United States. Among the most revealing was a topic to which he returned time and again: what it meant to be an American in the modern world.

7

The American Soul

WILL ROGERS FAILED TO CONVINCE NOTABLE writers William Allen White, Arthur Brisbane, or Ring Lardner to pen an introduction to his book, *The Illiterate Digest* (1924), or so he claimed. So he wrote one himself. With tongue stuck firmly in cheek and writing in the third person, Rogers contended that most people were familiar with the author's "Literary masterpieces, both in Novels and in Books of technical knowledge. I think there are few writers of Poetry or prose today who equal him .... . His jugglery of correct words and perfect English sentences is magical, and his spelling is almost uncanny." He saved the biggest piece of hokum for last. Cervantes was known for his mastery of structure and Dickens for his detailed characterizations, Rogers observed, and his own writing deserved to be in such august company because of a distinguishing feature "quite peculiar to itself. Something that for want of a better term might be called the quality of American Soul." It was a typical Rogers maneuver: using a jest to mask serious commentary. After taking a swipe at pretension to put his reader at ease and deploying humor to lighten the mood, he then subtly proceeded to do exactly what he poked fun at.[1]

For throughout his writing efforts, and many of his speaking efforts as well, Rogers indeed explored what it meant to be an American. He was well-suited to explain the "American soul." As a denizen of the Oklahoma plains who first had gone east to New York and then later westward to Hollywood to make his fortune, a Native American who exemplified cowboy culture, and a creature of the frontier who conquered many of the institutions of an emerging urban society, he straddled many divides in American life and occupied a unique position from which to survey a transforming nation in the early 1900s. Readers and listeners sensed Rogers' serious quest to illuminate the essential qualities of being an American, no matter how lighthearted such an effort appeared on the surface, and appreciated his efforts to explain his countrymen to themselves.

This endeavor to define America, however, ultimately involved not only what Rogers said about events and people and values, but what others said about him. In its final stages, his search for the American soul turned inward as a host of critics, commentators, and ordinary citizens proclaimed *him* to be the ultimate symbol of his country, its citizens, and their bedrock beliefs. Rogers' audience came to see him as the embodiment of what Americans were, but in a larger sense what they aspired to be. This personal image as the face of America became a key to the Oklahoman's growing popularity and influence. It made him a national folk hero.

* * * * *

Rogers' search for the American soul was rooted in his proud identification as a citizen of the United States. In early manhood, while working in South America, South Africa, and Australia, he had developed a keen appreciation of his own country and its virtues. While struggling to find work in Argentina, he had written home that "you don't know what a good country you have till you see the others." His travels down under had prompted him to reflect, "I was always proud in America to own that I was a Cherokee and I find on leaving that I am equally as proud to own that I am an American." These patriotic sentiments only intensified in mature adulthood. In 1926, as he spent several months traveling in England and the European continent, Rogers reiterated his fondness for the United States. Writing of a recent trip to Europe, he vowed to see even more of his native land and reflected, "I know in my own heart that they haven't got a thing to show us over here that we haven't got at home and better." When he returned from his jaunt to Russia that same year, Rogers wrote, "I am not going to pull the old gag about 'America looks pretty good to me.' It don't look good, it looks 'Perfect.' We are better off than any Nation. Why? Why just because we work more."[2]

Rogers' patriotism was rooted most deeply in his profound regard for average American citizens, the ordinary folk who worked hard, supported their families, valued their faith, identified with their geographical locales and local customs, and treated their neighbors with respect. He embraced a populist tradition in American life dating back to the 1820s and 1830s when Andrew Jackson and his acolytes trumpeted the virtues of the common man and passion- ately defended his interests. By the late 1800s, this impulse gave rise to the Populist Party itself, which promised to protect and promote the little guy – small farmers, mechanics, shopkeepers – against the "money power" represented by banks, railroads, and industrial capital. The populist mindset, however, involved more than policy decisions and political maneuvering. It identified the heart of American values as laying in rural and small-town society where independent,

property-owning citizens embraced the dignity of labor and saw property ownership and personal independence as central to citizenship. The populist impulse, in
the elegant description of the historian Richard Hofstadter, attempted "to hold on
to some of the values of agrarian life, to save personal entrepreneurship and
individual opportunity and the character type they engendered . . . . [Populism
promoted] the ideal of life lived close to nature and the soil, the esteem for the
primary contacts of country and village life, the cherished image of the independent and self-reliant man." Here was the worldview that Will Rogers, coming of
age in rural Oklahoma, articulated so memorably in his rise to public influence.[3]

As his public profile swelled in the late 1910s and 1920s, the humorist
consistently described and defended the average American citizen. "I am out to
see how America is living," he wrote during his first season on the lecture circuit.
"I mean the ones that don't go to New York . . . . I am meeting the regular Bird –
the one that lives in his town; stays in his town; is proud of his town: he offers no
apology for not having seen last year's *Follies*, or any other year's. I wanted to find
out what he was thinking about, what he was reading about." Crisscrossing the
United States as he entertained, lectured, and wrote, Rogers admitted, "I sho love
to meet 'Folks.' I mean, 'Just folks' and talk with them and get their angle." While
in Cherokee, Wyoming, he met a man and his wife who ran a Prairie Lighthouse,
which was part of a lighting system strung across the country to guide air mail
pilots at night. Rogers talked with them at length and was fascinated by their lives
and their labor. "It makes you appreciate some 'Real Folks.' I don't know when
I enjoyed two hours more," he wrote in his *Weekly Article*. "We got some great
people in this country, and they ain't all on Wall Street, or at the Luncheon
Clubs, or in the Movies or in the Senate. Some of 'em are just in the 'Light
Houses' on the Prairies."[4]

Rogers' veneration of America's common people, as was true of the mainstream political tradition of populism, featured two major elements. On the
cultural front, he emerged as a determined foe of snobbery and all forms of
elitism in music, arts, language, and creative expression. While respectful of the
fine arts, he did not believe they somehow elevated their practitioners above those
skilled in more practical endeavors. "If a man happens to take up painting and
becomes only a mediocre painter, why should he be classed above the bricklayer
who has excelled over every other bricklayer[?]" Rogers argued. "The bricklayer
is a true artist in his line or he could not have reached the top." He liked to joke
about the pretensions of the learned, once noting of a professor who won a prize
for writing a book in one day, "That's a good thing. The quicker the authors write
them the quicker they can get to some useful work." Sometimes Rogers took the
argument to the edge of anti-intellectualism, claiming that "the most real, down-
to-earth, horse-sense men in America are the ones that can't read. I'll bet you they

are more right on any question than the so-called smart fellow." The humorist's "just folks" sensibility frequently found a personal angle due to highbrow critics who chastised him for bad manners and mangling the English language. He proudly defined himself as a man of the people whose audience appreciated him as "an old country boy in a big town trying to get along. I have been eating pretty regular and the reason I have been is because I have stayed an old country boy." When an eastern critic, for example, denounced his appearance at the Boston Symphony Hall as degrading the venue, Rogers offered a good-natured defense. He replied that his critic "unconsciously paid me a Bear of a compliment when you said, 'Will is a small-town Actor.' You bet your life I am small town. I am smaller than that, I am NO town at all, and listen, that is what I am going to stay is Small Town." In typical fashion, however, he offered reconciliation with a good-hearted joke. "I bet if I met you we would like each other fine. Because in your own heart you couldn't blame an old Country boy for wanting to finally get into the Symphony Hall of Boston, and I am broadminded enough to see your angle, too," he added. "You want to see only the best in there . . . . But give me credit for one thing. Wasn't that English of mine the worst that was ever spoken in that Hall?"[5]

In addition to this cultural populism, Rogers consistently advocated financial populism. While admiring the opportunity and productivity of his native land, he had reservations about the undue power and privilege attending those who had accumulated great wealth. Ordinary, hard-working citizens were the backbone of American society, he believed, and they deserved the same economic advantages as rich businessmen and high-class members of society. If cultural elitism irked Rogers, economic elitism offended him. While no socialist with visions of a classless society, he was acutely sensitive to the influence wielded by the rich. Rogers scoffed at the scene of banking magnate J. P. Morgan sailing for Europe when the ship managers erected "a special gangway for him to go on the boat. He had dozens of policemen and officers to see that no one molested him by even looking at him. Then you will hear some bonehead say we have no classes in America like they have in England." The humorist believed that hard-working citizens deserved a decent living and the wealthy should nurture the society that produced them. "Put big taxes on everything of a luxury nature," the Oklahoman wrote in a 1924 *Weekly Article*. "You do that, and let the working man know the rich have paid before they got it and you will do more than any one thing to settle some of the unrest and dis-satisfaction that you hear every day . . . by real citizens and every day people of this country."[6]

Rogers, of course, used humor to illuminate the contrast between strivings of common folk and the privilege of the wealthy. He noted that while America's "disgustingly rich men" often confessed confusion about how to spend their money, "Funny none of them ever thought of giving it back to the people they got it from." Rogers joked about the press's habit of asking wealthy businessmen during the Christmas holidays their view of the upcoming year, a query that always brought positive predictions. "Sure, they are optimistic of the future. If we had their dough we would be optimistic, too," he quipped. "I would not only be an optimist for that much Jack, I would even be a vegetarian." The announcement of a federal government surplus in late 1927 sent both business owners and the prosperous middle-class clamoring for a refund. But the working man, Rogers claimed, "dident say anything. He just sit home with his sense of humor and said to himself, 'I guess I am pretty lucky to just be allowed to live among all this . . . . I guess what little I paid in don't count. I never asked for anything so I have never been disappointed.'"[7]

True to the populist tradition, Rogers reserved a special place for the farmer in his musings about American values and power relations. Amidst a national cornucopia of consumer prosperity, the farmer lagged behind a host of urban enterprises and the Oklahoman proudly expressed his rural, small-town sensibility to defend him. Rogers embraced the old Jeffersonian veneration of the independent, landowning farmer as the quintessential American. Like a host of populists since the late 1800s, he fingered banks as preying on farmers with exploitive interest rates and the railroads as discriminating against them with discriminatory shipping rates. Drowning under second or third mortgages, the farmer "is not only in such a position nowadays that he is grabbing at a straw, but he is really swimming out of his way looking for the straw to grab at." The sharecropper and renter struggled the most. "He is in debt from one crop to the other to the storekeeper, or the little local bank. He never has a dollar that he can call his own," he explained. "City people don't realize the poverty of poor country folks." Given this situation, Rogers was mystified that farmers could not unite nationally, with northern farmers voting Republican and southern farmers voting Democrat. He figured it must be the outdated legacy of the Civil War, but "Now, there is a real reason why farmers or country people should be in one political party and city people in another. They have different interests, different needs, different things to sell, and hundreds of different wants and customs . . . . That should be the legitimate alignment of politics . . . the country against the city."[8]

The central problem causing the rural travail, Rogers asserted, lay in the pressure to borrow money to survive. Modern, mechanized agriculture demanded growing amounts of land and machinery and bank loans were the only way to procure them. Thus reform measures usually involved easier access to credit. But this solution only made the problem worse, the Oklahoman noted, since what the farmer needed was "some way to pay back, not some way to borrow more." After visiting the Dakotas in the mid-1920s and observing a host of mortgaged farms, Rogers told his readers that "the Government has showed them every way in the world where they can borrow money and never yet introduced an idea of how to pay any of it back . . . . If your crop is a failure and you don't raise anything, why you are fortunate. Because it costs you more to raise anything than you can sell it for, so the less you raise the less you lose, and if you don't raise anything you are ahead." Buried under a mountain of debt, the typical farmer "has to have a bookkeeper to keep a set of books to keep track of when his various Notes and Mortgages' interest comes due. It's the thought of the old Mortgages that keeps him awake at night." [9]

At the heart of Rogers' populist rendering of America – again, this was characteristic of the larger populist movement – lay a belief in the "producer ethic." This principle posited the moral and economic goodness of those who made something tangible, useful, and valuable in society, as opposed to those who manipulated money, stocks, images and slogans, shuffling paper and creating impressions to make a living. The former were virtuous, the latter were parasitical. In a sense, it was ironic that Rogers, a media maven, movie star, entertainer, and celebrity would make such an argument, but as a frontier boy from Claremore, Oklahoma he believed it with all his heart. Rogers saw the American Soul shining brightly in the farmers, mechanics, factory workers, and craftsmen who comprised much of the nation's citizens and made the useful goods that allowed it to prosper.

The humorist frequently juxtaposed these common-folk producers with social and economic manipulators who merely maneuvered goods and services to their own great profit. He described the newly completed, seventeen-story Mercantile Exchange Building in Chicago as "a landmark to the progress of the Middle Man. The farmer, the producer, is lucky if he can get a new hen roost during his lifetime, and the Consumer enjoys his one egg in the poorhouse, but the Broker, or the middle man, has certainly seen that some profit was dropped on the way from the farmer to the eater." Wall Street stockbrokers offered a tempting target for the humorist's barbs. While they scrambled around the floor of the stock exchange betting millions of dollars on the buying and selling of stock, they didn't have to worry about how to "buy an individual Harvester [combine] next year when their wheat is ripe and pay for it . . . . [I]t does seem funny that these guys can sit here, produce nothing, ride in Fisher Bodies, and yet put a price on your whole year's labor." Advertisers provided another prime example of non-productive types in modern America who expropriated profits and influence from hard-working citizens. Cleverly deploying images, words, and psychology, they beguiled ordinary folk into breaking their budgets and buying goods they may not need. "Everything now is a Saying, or a Slogan. You can't go to bed, you can't get up, you can't brush your Teeth without doing it to some Advertising Slogan,"

Rogers wrote. "Everything nowadays is a Slogan and of all the Bunk things in America the Slogan is the Champ." The humorist concluded with an aphorism: "One-third of the people in the United States promote, while the other two-thirds provide."[10]

An event in 1926 seemed to demonstrate the populist divide in America. Many American elites, Rogers noted with considerable amusement, appeared wide-eyed about the visit of Queen Marie of Romania in that year. Awed by the spectacle of royalty, they lined up to pay homage during her stops around the country as "Every rich man and his wife [were] trying to beat the other rich ones to give a reception." When Queen Marie visited Kansas City, the mayor was so transported he proclaimed it the "greatest day" in the history of the city. Rogers rolled his eyes at such ostentatious, diadem-dazzled behavior and contrasted it with the honest labor and democratic habits of ordinary Americans. Rather than mooning over royalty, he argued, people should attend the American Royal Livestock Show in that same city and observe the 1,700 boys and girls in attendance who were "taking vocational training and had led their various districts back home in the studying of farming and stock raising . . . . [They were] the Kings and Queens of Cattle, Sheep, Hogs, Horses. Real Kings and Queens that produced something."[11]

Rogers' devotion to "producerism," in concert with his dismissal of paper-pushing and image manipulation, led to deeply ambivalent feelings about the American penchant for success-seeking. He respected the traditional impulse to seek opportunity, pursue prosperity, and improve your lot in life. The stream of northern migrants to Florida in the 1920s, for example, prompted him to compare it to the great convoys of settlers snaking westward across the United States to the frontier in the 1800s. For Rogers, these new pioneers were "working people . . . . They got stout hearts. When they loaded all they had in an old Ford car and went to Florida to make a home for their children they were just as game and took just as big a chance as the old Guys in the Covered wagons did years ago." But on occasion Rogers grew less enamored of this restless spirit of improvement, contending "the pioneer wasn't a thing in the world but a guy that wanted something for nothing. He was a guy that wanted to live off of everything that nature had done. He wanted to cut a tree down that didn't cost him anything, but he never did plant one, you know. He wanted to plow up the land that should have been left to grass . . . . [He] thought it was nature he was living off, but it was really future generations he was living off of, you know."[12]

Such reservations caused Rogers to question a fervently held American social formula: hard work automatically produces success. He simply saw too many counter-examples of bad luck destroying the fruits of labor. As he noted succinctly in a *Weekly Article*, "The successful don't work any harder than the failures. They

157

get what is called in baseball the breaks." Rogers saw the trope of the self-made man as devoid of context. "A made man is a finished man and I doubt if we have one in this country now. If we have, for the Lord['s sake] let's find him. A real self-made man would have to be one who had received no learning or knowledge, or assistance from any person or source," he opined skeptically in 1923. Nonetheless, he joked, "The woods are full of those birds. Every toastmaster at every 75-cent luncheon introduces from 3 to 5 self-made ones every day."[13]

Rogers also feared that America's love affair with "bigness" in the modern, industrial, urban age was undercutting prospects for the ordinary citizen. The day of the individual working for himself had passed, he concluded, as corporate mergers and business combinations increasingly dominated the economy. In the late 1800s, the earliest consolidation had taken place within the same line of industry – oil, railroads, steel, rubber – to dominate the nation's economy but by the 1920s corporations were becoming umbrellas for enormous, wildly diverse, and powerful economic endeavors. In Rogers' words, "now it's liable to be the Pennsylvania Railroad and Mennens Borated Talcum Powder ... . General Motors not only took over Chevrolet, but Frigid Air Ice Boxes." Ever-bigger economic entities were capturing ever-bigger chunks of the market. Chain stores were spreading throughout the country and putting out of business independent grocers, butchers, clothiers, and shopkeepers of every kind. Sears Roebuck, for instance, was putting a store in every American town, Rogers pointed out, and "they will sell you a Mowing Machine, Standard Oil stock, U. S. bonds, a Farm, Town lots, Ice Cream sodas, and a house all put together like blocks." And Americans loved it, he asserted, because they loved "to talk [about] and go to big things ... . the biggest Hotel, regardless of [the] service, the biggest Theater, regardless of performance, the biggest funeral, regardless of whether they knew the corpse." This habit, however, was choking off the small, independent producer, "the little fellow that has struggled along all these years and give the best he could for the money."[14]

Rogers' misgivings caused him to view modern America's consumer prosperity with considerable ambivalence. On the one hand, he respected the entrepreneurial effort of businessmen such as William Wrigley of Chicago. The gum-chomping entertainer admired the chewing-gum magnate's prosperous business and viewed him as symbolizing an American principle: "a man to succeed nowadays must have an idea." In Rogers' whimsical description, Wrigley was "the first man to discover that the American jaws must wag. So why not give them something to wag against? That is, put in a kind of shock absorber. If it wasn't for chewing gum, Americans would wear their teeth off just hitting them against each other." Borrowing Woodrow Wilson's famous wartime slogan, Rogers proclaimed that Wrigley "has made the whole world chew for Democracy."[15]

But the material abundance created by businessmen like Wrigley, Rogers pointed out, came at a heavy cost. Consumer prosperity's foundation of buying on credit, for instance, had corrosive consequences. "If we want anything, all we have to do is go and buy it on credit," he noted. "So that leaves us without any economic problem whatever, except perhaps someday to have to pay for them." When President Calvin Coolidge extolled national prosperity in a 1927 address and urged Americans to partake by buying, Rogers joked, "Why, I hadn't read the speech half way through till I paid a dollar down on half a dozen things I didn't need. We'll show the world we are prosperous if we have to go broke to do it." In the humorist's opinion, "This country right now is operating on a Dollar down and a Dollar a Week. It ain't taxes that is hurting this country; it's Interest."[16]

Rogers also worried that the flood of consumer goods had warped American values, creating ever-expanding expectations of comfort and a shallow materialism. "Say, there ain't no civilization where there ain't no satisfaction, and that's what's the trouble now, nobody is satisfied," he fretted in a *Weekly Article*. The Oklahoman found confirmation of his concerns in a lengthy magazine advertisement for men's fashion that insisted on the necessity of a stylish jacket, a double-breasted waistcoat above unpleated "mull gray trousers" subtly striped in "white and biscuit" so as "not to jar," and sophisticated boots finished with "deGniche varnish, mixed with a little claret to make the enamel more brilliant." Rogers' mirthful reaction contained a jolt of populist umbrage:

> Now you farmers that's been hollering for relief, maby that's what's the matter with you, you haven't had this "deGniche varnish mixed with a little claret" . . . . Now you Democrats that haven't got anywhere in years, maby you haven't been wearing your trousers below your waistcoat. In fact, some of you maby haven't had trousers either above or below . . . . [Y]ou got to be careful, you may have on a pair of pants, and you feel something funny and it's your pants jarring. They are just liable to jar right off, you can't tell. There is nothing worse than a jarring pair of pants . . . . Now boneheads like you and I can't imagine sane people taking all this junk serious, but they do.[17]

From his populist perch, Rogers found reason to question the confident American creed of steady, inevitable progress that prevailed in the early twentieth century. While the modern world brought advantages, it brought just as many problems. The automobile, for example, had enormously increased geographic mobility, sped up transportation, and broadened the scope of many people's daily lives. But it also created new difficulties, exemplified in the report of 22,000 annual American traffic deaths in the 1926 Chicago *Tribune*. "FOR WHAT?," Rogers asked his readers. "Why, just to get somewhere a little quicker, that is if you get there at all . . . . Now they call all these accidents PROGRESS. Well, maybe it is Progress. But I tell you it certainly comes high priced . . . . This is the age of Progress. Live fast and die quick. That's the Slogan." Rogers feared that modern Americans, with their "satisfied ease and prosperity," were missing out on challenges to conquer and authentic life experiences to savor. "The sad thing is going to be the coming generations listening to us," he wrote. "We will be raving with nothing to rave over. Our most thrilling experiences will be how we run to catch a street car and missed it one cold day, or how we lost four good golf balls in one game." America's vaunted modern progress, in other words, may have been an illusion.[18]

With this genial skepticism of American prosperity and advancement, Rogers articulated a modest vision of his country's values and prospects. Although a proud citizen, he recoiled from the super-patriotism of the "100 percent Americanism" movement which had first appeared during World War I before linking to nativism, jingoism, and the Ku Klux Klan in the 1920s. When the mayor of Chicago formed an "America First" society with dues of 10 dollars, Rogers poked fun at the venture and offered an improvement. "I hereby offer stock in a society called 'America Only' at $20 a share," he announced in his *Daily Telegram*. "Why be only first? Let's be the whole thing. Why spend $10 to be in the front when $10 more will put you in front, behind, and in the middle all at the same time? If everybody in America will give me $20 I will be more than glad to show them where we are the 'only nation in the world.'" This organization, its founder claimed, "will run around 165 or 170 percent American. It will make a sucker out of these little 100 percent organizations." Rogers blamed World War I for overheating patriotic emotions and warping perspectives. The conflict had generated enormous pressures to define and defend American values, and this crusade had overshadowed the millions who had enlisted in the armed forces simply to defend their country even though they "didn't know whether they were '100 percent Americans' or 'Better Citizens,' or what they were." The Oklahoman believed that the Declaration of Independence and the Constitution comprised the national creed and all citizens "belonged to this club called America, and all you had to do was work for it, fight for it, and act like a gentleman, that was all the by-laws there was. As long as you did that, you could worship what you wanted to, talk any language you wanted to . . . . [B]ut now we find we got to join something and announce daily that we are for it . . . . There is no real Americanism in that."[19]

Ultimately, Rogers located the essence of the American soul in a spirit of sturdy individualism and independence, the average citizen's persistent desire to be left alone to pursue his own version of happiness. Most people wanted to work a decent job, raise their families, enjoy their neighbors and communities, and ignore self-styled reformers constantly trying to improve them. When a leading public figure bowed out of a presidential race, claiming that 90 percent of Americans were satisfied with the current political situation, Rogers demurred, claiming, "It's just got so that 90 percent of the people in this country don't give a damn." The endless debates over Prohibition, for example, had so exhausted the patience of nearly everyone but competing zealots that Rogers offered to send a wire to Congress: "Eighty percent of America wish the wets would get so drunk they would be speechless for the rest of their lives. And the drys get so perfect that the Lord would call 'em away from this earth up into heaven." He hoped this might get him called before a Congressional committee "to represent America. But I doubt it."[20]

Rogers best explained his conception of the American Soul in February 1925, when the anniversary of Lincoln's birthday prompted a lengthy reflection on his countrymen, especially the ordinary folks that he so cherished. He wrote in his *Weekly Article,*

> The American Animal . . . is nothing but the big Honest Majority, that you might find in any Country. He is not a Politician. He is not a 100 per cent American. He is not any organization, either uplift or downfall. In fact, I find he don't belong to anything. He is of no decided Political faith or religion . . . . It looks to me like he is just an Animal that has been going along, believing in right, doing right, tending to his own business, letting the other fellows alone.
>
> He don't seem to be simple enough minded to believe that EVERYTHING is right and he don't appear to be Cuckoo enough to think that EVERYTHING is wrong . . . . In fact, all I can find out about him is that he is just NORMAL . . . . [T]he only conclusion I can come to is that this Normal breed is so far in the majority that there is no use to worry about the others. They are a lot of Mavericks and Strays . . . . This country is not where it is today on account of any man. It is here on account of the big normal majority.[21]

As Rogers endeavored to identify and capture the soul of America, he identified three individuals who encapsulated the characteristic features of his native land and its people. This trio most attracted his attention from among the hundreds of people he wrote and spoke about in the 1910s and 1920s. One of them, a figure rooted in the American past, symbolized Rogers' veneration of ordinary citizens. Another, gazing into the future, pioneered an innovative technology in the new frontier of the sky. The third, like Rogers a historical mediator, had earned the adulation of millions as he shaped the future of the country, honored many of its oldest traditions, and eased his countrymen into the modern era. Among these three men, the Oklahoman discerned the essential qualities of his own land and its citizens.

* * * * *

As he climbed to national prominence in the 1910s and 1920s, Will Rogers persistently encountered William Jennings Bryan, the populist Democrat who stood as a prominent national figure since the 1890s. As usual, the Oklahoman described him in a joking manner that masked a serious critique. At his break-through performance before President Woodrow Wilson in 1916, Rogers opened with a crack about Bryan's penchant for lengthy speeches. The humorist recalled that he had begun his career by booking a hometown gig for his lariat act and was set to go on after Bryan's remarks, "but he spoke so long that it was so dark when he finished they couldn't see my roping . . . . I wonder what ever became of him?" Rogers continued to make Bryan a humorous foil over the next decade, launching so many jibes that he confessed the politician had become a "meal ticket." In many ways, the Nebraska populist made an easy target with his long-windedness, moralism, and pretension that the humorist loved to mock as emblematic of outdated cultural style. At the same time, Rogers granted the prairie politician a deep respect as a defender of common American citizens whom both cherished as the backbone of the American nation.[22]

Bryan had first burst onto the political landscape in the 1890s as an eloquent spokesman for agrarian populism. A little-known Congressman from Nebraska, his fiery denunciation of the gold standard and demand for "free silver" in the famous "Cross of Gold" speech electrified the Democratic Convention in 1892 and won him the party's nomination for president. Although he lost that election, and then two more as the party's presidential nominee in 1896 and 1908, he galvanized political discontent against the economic system of modern industrial capitalism. A spokesman for hard-working producers, anti-imperialism, and stern Christian morality, Bryan wielded much influence in national Democratic politics as the leader of the party's populist wing. He mustered his legendary rhetorical skills to speak regularly throughout the United States, particularly in rural and small-town areas where large crowds flocked to hear him. Bryan reached the apex of official influence when newly elected President Woodrow Wilson chose him to be Secretary of State in 1913, although the two soon clashed over World War I and the issue of American involvement and preparedness. Bryan's opposition led him to resign from the government in 1916.[23]

Rogers was familiar with Bryan from a young age because of his father's admiration for this defender of rural values and interests. As he slowly abandoned the role of vaudeville entertainer for that of humorous commentator on public affairs, the Oklahoman found Bryan to be too good a target to pass up. Rogers adopted a running commentary on Bryan in his newspaper and magazine writing, and a favorite topic became the Nebraskan's unsullied record of losing elections. The humorist liked to joke that Bryan lost so many elections that the kiss of death came when he *endorsed* a candidate. The Nebraskan, said Rogers, could "take a batch of words and scramble them together and leaven them properly with a hunk of oratory and knock the White House door knob right out of a candidate's hand." In 1920, Rogers tied the contemporary fad for Ouija boards with the aging populist's string of electoral defeats that seemed to push him toward irrelevance: "I really do believe you can commune with the departed, as I hear some man talked with [William Jennings] Bryan the other day."[24]

For Rogers, the comic climax of Bryan's losing political record came in the 1924 presidential election. Early in the contest, Rogers claimed, "There is only one way to stop [sitting President Calvin] Coolidge now. That is to have Bryan come out in favor of him." Then, in a turn of events almost too good to be true, Charles Bryan, the younger brother of William Jennings and the governor of Nebraska, was chosen as the vice-presidential candidate at the marathon 1924 Democratic Convention. Rogers immediately wired a warning to the party's presidential nominee, John W. Davis: "HEAR ONE OF THE BRYAN BROTHERS ARE TO BE ASSOCIATED WITH YOU INDIRECTLY. FOR GOD'S SAKE PICK THE RIGHT ONE." Then Rogers wired Charles Bryan directly: "IS THERE ANY WAY WE CAN GO THROUGH THE BIRTH RECORDS, AND SHOW THAT YOU AND MY GOOD FRIEND WJB ARE ONLY COUZINS, IF SO THIS WILL HELP US IMMENSELY IN THE CAMPAIGN." Rogers was impressed with his long-time target's "good nature" when William Jennings laughed at the barb and showed it around as a joke on himself.[25]

The elder Bryan's notorious long-windedness also became a target of Rogers' comic barbs. The old populist regularly traveled throughout rural sections of the United States, appearing at any venue that would host him and presenting lengthy orations in a bid to maintain his popularity. Rogers, in his *Weekly Article*, promised to lure Bryan to a performance of the *Ziegfeld Follies* and bring him onstage "if I can get him when he's not lecturing in a tent somewhere. He wouldn't know how to act in a regular theater with no hay to walk on and no dogs running around under his feet." Jokes about Bryan's loquacious style became a staple of the humorist's newspaper column. He noted that the Bible suggested Noah lived to be over 900 years old, adding, "Outside of Methuselah and Bill Bryan's speeches, he is the only man who ever lived that long." Another time he described a recent encounter with a salesman who tried to sell him a steam-powered car that ran by burning hay, newspapers, and other combustible materials, then slipped in the punch line: "Why, the man told me you could get 100 miles out of [the text of] a Bryan speech."[26]

Bryan's well-known piety attracted Rogers' humorous attention. While he had great respect for religion, Rogers demonstrated little patience with those who used it in a pompous, self-aggrandizing manner. Bryan, an evangelical Christian given to virtuous preachments delivered in a self-righteous tone, filled that bill. Rogers quipped that the pious populist "would make an ideal Sunday President. But he would be an absolute liability on week days." Bryan's outspoken advocacy of Prohibition, for example, drew Rogers' ire. The humorist was skeptical of the national alcohol ban as a triumph of piety over practicality, moral posturing over common sense. He also caught a whiff of hypocrisy, sensing that many supposed teetotalers took a swig or two in secret. When news of a new truth serum broke, Rogers suggested Bryan should volunteer to take it "and then be asked if he hadn't had just a little nip at some time or another."[27]

Bryan's role in the much-publicized Scopes Trial of 1925 earned a barrage of comic comments. In this legal dispute that gained national attention, a teacher in rural Tennessee was prosecuted for teaching evolution in a public high school in violation of a local statute. Bryan, a religious opponent of this scientific theory of human origins and development, rushed to the trial and volunteered as a lawyer for the prosecution. Rogers mocked the politician's action as a misguided career pivot "from non-intoxication to evolution . . . He tries to prove that we did not descend from the monkey, but he unfortunately picked a time when the actions of our people prove that we did." In a long *Weekly Article*, the humorist accused Bryan of politicizing the case with his grand pronouncements about keeping America a Christian nation. "Bryan says if he fails in this case that Christianity is through," Rogers wrote. "Why even when our Savior came down to earth he didn't make it that assertive." People had different ideas about human development, Rogers asserted, and everyone should be heard. "There is a terrible lot of us who don't think we come from a monkey, but if there are some people who think that they do, why, it's not our business to rob them of what little pleasure they may get out of imagining it," he joked. For Rogers, the controversy boiled down to a central issue: "Why don't Bryan and a lot of other people let the world alone? . . . If the Lord had wanted us to know exactly how, and where, and when we come he would have let us know in the first place. He didn't leave any room for doubt when he told you how you should act when you get here." As for Bryan's suggestion to amend the Constitution to protect Christianity, Rogers deemed it ludicrous. In his words, "when those old Boys who blueprinted the Constitution decided that a man can believe what he likes in regard to religion, that's one line that is going to stay put."[28]

Rogers, with his genuine affection for people, found his attitude softening when he came to know Bryan personally in the 1920s. Their paths crossed on several occasions and the humorist was impressed with the politician's intelligence and good humor. They spent considerable time together at the Republican National Convention of 1924 where they were both writing newspaper columns. As they sat in the press box, the pair talked about the nature of their journalistic work.

According to Rogers, "When he said he wrote seriously and I said I wrote humorously, I thought afterward we both may be wrong." They ate lunch and dinner together and agreed to exchange material, with the political veteran promising to pass along any funny observations and the comic to forward any serious observations. When they returned to the auditorium from the hotel restaurant to hear a dismal keynote speech where the rhetorical high-point inexplicably occurred in the middle, followed by a lengthy, droning conclusion, Bryan turned with a twinkle in his eye and said, "The speaker suffered from a premature climax." Rogers, dumbfounded by this risqué witticism from his pious companion, stammered, "I will have to give him a couple of good serious ones to make up for that one."[29]

Ultimately, despite his recurring jibes at Bryan's political record and cultural style, Rogers found the great populist to have a huge saving grace: his unwavering advocacy of the powerless individual, the average citizen, the little guy. Upon the politician's death a few days after the conclusion of the Scopes Trial, the humorist honored his legacy. "Bryan was just a plain citizen, holding no office. Yet this country holds hundreds of thousands of people who feel that they haven't got a Soul now who will conscientiously fight for them, the plain people," he wrote. Rogers acknowledged that Bryan always tried "to do something for the Common people," fighting against "Special Privilege," advocating the vote for women, favoring an income tax, and fighting the influence of bosses in party politics. Rogers concluded with a moving personal tribute to the old populist:

> Who will be missed any more in America than Bryan? Those thousands of people who stood along the railroad track for hours just waiting to see the Funeral train whizz by and take off their hats as it did so – they were not curiosity seekers. Oratory didn't draw them there. You couldn't have been wrong all this time and fooled these Real people for 30 years. Bryan 'Savvied' the plain people, and when you 'savvy' them you must be one of them at heart . . . .
>
> I am going to miss him. I guess I have told a thousand so-called Jokes about him, some in favor, and most of them against him. Most of them I have repeated to his face. I feel and I hope he knew personally I always admired him . . . . YOU MIGHT HAVE MISSED THE WHITE HOUSE, BUT YOU DIDN'T MISS THE HEARTS OF THE PLAIN PEOPLE. [30]

Bryan, for all of his pomposity, verbosity, and moralism, stood as a key figure in Rogers' rendering of the American Soul. The old populist personified certain traits from the nation's past – sincerity, uprightness, anti-elitism – that buttressed democratic culture in the United States. For Rogers, such values needed to be nourished and protected in a rapidly changing modern world.

If Bryan symbolized for Rogers certain old-fashioned American values that needed to be cherished, Charles Lindbergh represented the vast possibilities of a dawning new world in the early twentieth century. The youthful aviator had captured the global imagination with his astounding solo transatlantic flight from the United States to France in the spring of 1927 and emerged as *the* modern American hero. He took off from a muddy airfield on Long Island on May 20 determined to be the first flyer to cross the Atlantic and thirty-three hours later triumphantly landed his small airplane, *The Spirit of St. Louis*, at the Paris airport. The tumultuous mob scene that greeted him, followed by months of adulatory media attention around the world, showcased the young aviator as a representation of everything that Americans held dear – hard work, individual achievement, self-possession, a young man from an ordinary background achieving extraordinary things. But these old-fashioned virtues faded in the bright light of an even more spectacular aspect of his achievement. Lindbergh opened the door to the future as aviation launched a new age of air transportation. Rogers, like millions of his fellow citizens, was enthralled by the young man who had blazed a trail into this emerging frontier.

During Lindbergh's dangerous solo flight over the Atlantic, Rogers abandoned his trademark comic persona, something he rarely did. "No attempt at joke today. A slim, tall, bashful, smiling American boy is somewhere out over the middle of the Atlantic Ocean, where no lone human being has ever ventured before," he wrote in his *Daily Telegram*. "He is being prayed for to every kind of Supreme Being that has a following. If he is lost it will be the most universally regretted single loss we ever had. But that kid ain't going to fail." After Lindbergh's triumphant arrival in France, Rogers enthused, "The ones of us here now will never live to see a thing that will give us a bigger kick than his flight did. It was the greatest wished-for, and prayed-for achievement that ever happened or ever will happen in our lifetime. Prayers was what he was sailing on." Only after the safety of the young aviator was assured did the humorist allow himself a joke: "Of all the things that Lindbergh's great feat demonstrated, the greatest was to show us that a person could still get the entire front [newspaper] page without murdering anybody."[31]

Rogers joined the frenzy of acclaim engulfing Lindbergh by proclaiming the young man "the greatest American since Theodore Roosevelt, and that statement don't belong in a joke column, either." He explained that "this boy is not our usual type of hero that we are used to dealing with. He is all the others rolled into one and then multiplied by ten .... Well, this lad is our biggest national asset. He is our Prince and our President combined." Lindbergh's courage and determination were impressive, of course, but his modesty and social deftness made an equal impression. Rogers quoted the flyer as saying, "The papers ought to give me a prize for getting more sensational headlines for less reason than anyone ever did before." Surveying Lindbergh's sure-footed handling of the French public, press, and dignitaries after his touch-down in Paris, Rogers marveled, "what a smart fellow he turned out to be in everything that he did after he got there! Why, we never had a diplomat that conducted himself with as fitting grace as this lad did." The aviator seemed to provide a dash of wholesomeness for a modern audience often assaulted by news of sordid activities driven by media sensationalism. A sardonic Rogers observed, people flocked to the Lindbergh story "because it's the only thing that has been in the papers in years that was clean, and no dirt connected with it in any way. People hadn't read clean stuff in so long they just went crazy over this."[32]

Rogers' appreciation of the public acclaim for the heroic aviator – "the feeling and respect for that man among people, well it just ain't human, its sorter divine. There has never been anything like it in the history of the world" – grew even larger when he met Lindbergh and became his friend. While in Los Angeles in October 1927, Rogers learned that the young flyer was coming to town and, as he wrote in his *Daily Telegram*, Lindbergh "is the one man in this world that I would stand on a soap box on the corner and try to get a peek at." Rogers grew excited at the opportunity and confessed that "I had my opinion all formed beforehand, just what I would like to think he was, and I was like the rest, crazy about him." Rogers witnessed the aviator being mobbed by movie actors, producers, and directors at the Ambassador Hotel in Los Angeles, then met him in person the following day at a huge public reception held in a San Diego stadium. The two then shared a dais at a banquet later that night. A series of speakers showered Lindbergh with praise, but when he rose for a few remarks Rogers declared unexpectedly, "Colonel, they've been tellin' you what an inspiration you are to American boys. I've got a couple of American boys and you ain't no inspiration a-tall." The audience gasped and Lindbergh looked startled. Then Rogers delivered the punch line: "It's a lot of applesauce because if our boys tried to follow you they'd be in the middle of the Atlantic Ocean. I don't want my boys tryin' to do the stunts you've been pullin' off." Then Rogers noted that for all the rhetoric about Lindbergh's records, no one had mentioned the most impressive: "you are the only man who ever took a ham sandwich to Paris." Like everyone else, the young aviator laughed.[33]

When Lindbergh, the next morning, offered to fly him and Betty, along with a few other passengers, back to Los Angeles, the Oklahoma humorist was thrilled. Rogers cemented their friendship when he joined Lindbergh in the cockpit for much of the flight. At one point he asked the young hero how he adjusted the plane for landing when he didn't know which way the wind was blowing. "Lindbergh pointed to a washing of clothes flapping on a line. 'That tells me,' he said. 'Suppose it ain't Monday [the traditional day for doing laundry]?' said Will. 'I just wait till it is,' said Lindbergh, and Will laughed." The Rogerses and

Lindberghs became friends, staying in touch and visiting on occasion. Will and Betty traveled to Charles and Anne's New Jersey home in 1932 and met their infant son with his mop of "blonde curly hair." When the baby was kidnapped several weeks later in one of the most sensational crimes of the era, Rogers wrote, "Never since the two days and a night when this same kid's father was out over the Atlantic has the attention of everybody been centered so completely on one thing." The baby's body was found and his kidnapper arrested, but the parents fled to escape the dozens of reporters and newsreel cameras who followed their every move. They accepted an invitation to the Rogers ranch in the Santa Monica hills where Will and Betty sheltered them for two weeks away from the prying eyes of the press.[34]

Even as he lionized Lindbergh as an American hero, Rogers worried that the modern culture of publicity and celebrity might overwhelm the young flyer. Having experienced some of the pitfalls of constant public attention and acclaim, the humorist fretted that his young friend might fall victim to the commingled dangers of commercialization and trivialization. In particular, Rogers warned against being lured into show business. Himself a creature of the entertainment world, the humorist had genuine respect for the talented singers, dancers, comedians, and actors. But he also knew that promoters and publicists were eager to showcase anyone who could sell tickets and draw audiences. "When a man is put on the stage or screen for nothing but sole purpose of giving someone a chance to see him, he naturally becomes nothing more than a sideshow. That's what freaks are for," Rogers warned. "This boy is too much thought of to do that." He had witnessed a bit of this in Los Angeles when Lindbergh was mobbed by movie stars and directors clamoring for his autograph. "They didn't let him eat. They didn't let him say a word, they didn't let him do a thing but sign his name to everything in Hollywood." Indeed, Rogers had to fight this impulse in himself. While appearing at a show in New York, he received a call from Lindbergh inquiring if any tickets were available. Rogers exclaimed, "Imagine Lindbergh asking if it would be 'possible to make room for him to attend anything.' But that just shows the [modesty] of the fellow." But Lindbergh asked him to refrain from introducing him or joking about his presence in the theater. Rogers reluctantly agreed, noting, "There I stood with a pocket full of Gags that I had never used and I knew the audience would laugh at . . . . But I dident say one word about him being there. Of course you couldent introduce any other Celebrity that night, for with him in the house there just ain't any more . . . . I told him I was a bigger Hero than he was, that it took more nerve for me NOT to talk about him than he showed flying the ocean."[35]

Later, after his marriage to Anne Morrow, a young woman from a prominent family, drew even more media attention, Lindbergh asked the police for protection from the press to avoid a crush of publicity on his honeymoon. Some newspapers subsequently criticized him, arguing that he was ungrateful to the very institutions that had made him a public hero. An indignant Rogers disagreed, writing, "Lindbergh was made by just two things. The Lord and a Wright Whirlwind Motor. Newspapers couldn't have flew him from one side of a razor blade to another. They reported the fact that he arrived there." If anything, Lindbergh had given a boost to the newspapers. "He gave 'em the next most publicity to the war," Rogers pointed out. "He has paid their rent for two years." The humorist's summary captured the predominant American feeling about the young hero: "He has never made a wrong move yet, everything he has done has reflected glory on his country, he has been a gentleman under some pretty trying times."[36]

If celebrity threatened entrapment, a happier aspect of modernity presented Lindbergh with a crucial and positive role. Rogers argued that the youthful flyer, more than any other single American, had shepherded America into the aviation age. Rogers, an enthusiastic advocate of airplanes as the technology of the future, saw Lindbergh as a heroic pioneer on this new frontier. In his *Daily Telegrams* and *Weekly Articles*, he constantly praised the aviator as the very embodiment of this promising new mode of transportation. Reporting on their shared flight from San Diego to Los Angeles, he noted that aviation defined Lindbergh the man: "You have never seen him at his best till you sit out in the pilot's seat by his side. When he has a plane in his hands there is no careworn or worried look. That's when he is in his glory." Rogers added, "That kid is a born Aviator. He eats, sleeps, and drinks aviation. He is not particularly interested in anything else. This is an era of specialization. He picked out aviation, and he certainly has majored in it." More importantly for Rogers, Lindbergh's "inspiration will do more for aviation than anything that has happened to us since the Wrights . . . . We have a lot of Lindberghs over here, and a lot in the making. All they need is the training and the proper financial backing." The young man had prompted increased discussion among American military experts about the development of an air force, and similar discussions among entrepreneurs about the possibilities of commercial aviation. In Rogers' view, "that old boy Lindbergh is the one that stirred the whole thing up . . . . [W]e will never get through paying that guy."[37]

Through his efforts and example in conquering the frontier of the skies, Lindbergh personified something basic in the American Soul: peering into the future, discovering opportunity, and striving for achievement. Rogers concluded that with his wonderous transatlantic flight, Lindbergh "turned America's mind to aviation, just at a time when we was on the verge of going back to covered wagon days instead of the air." In so doing, in the best American fashion, the heroic pilot demonstrated that "there is a mighty little line between do and don't, a small margin between success and failure. His exploit just give us that little push that sent us over into the aviation line, instead of [accepting] that 'it wasn't practical.'"[38]

As Rogers scanned the American landscape during his exploration of the country's basic principles and qualities, he spied another figure who stood midway between William Jennings Bryan's past and Charles Lindbergh's future and successfully mediated their competing claims. In the humorist's judgement, Henry Ford, more than any other contemporary, had his finger on the pulse of modern America and understood its people and values. Rogers constantly wrote about the automobile maker, grew to know him personally, and became a shrewd analyst of his influence.

Rogers rightly contended that Henry Ford had done more than any other individual to create modern America. The industrialist had brought a sturdy, inexpensive automobile to the masses, thereby putting the country on wheels and transforming the nature, quality, and habits of American life. In a long article for the *American Magazine*, Rogers described Ford as "The Grand Champion" and contended that he "has had more influence on the lives, habits, and customs of the people of not only his own country, but all the World, than Napoleon or Caesar.... No man ever moved humanity like Henry Ford." The car maker's "Tin Lizzie" allowed the poor to travel as far and as fast as the rich. It transported rural folks to see the city and urbanites to view farms. His inexpensive automobile "made us discover America." Rogers understood that profound social and economic change often dwarfed momentary political disputes. "Mr. Ford has done more personally to change the style of life and customs of this country than all the Presidents ever elected, or defeated," the humorist joked to a deeper end. "He dissatisfied half of America by getting them out and seeing where the other half lived. He started half the world cranking [automobile starters], and the other half dodging."[39]

Rogers frequently noted the oversized influence of Ford's automobile on American society. In 1925, Ford announced that the Model T would now come in colors as well as basic black. "Well, whistles blew, paper was thrown out of the windows, newspapers had streaming headlines," Rogers jested. "Saying a Ford is going to change its color or style is almost like saying, '[Luther] Burbank has invented a different color for grass; from now on it will grow in Lavender and Battleship Gray.'" A few years later, a mood of breathless anticipation swept through the country as Ford undertook to replace the Model T with a newer model, the Model A. According to Rogers, when he asked a man on the street whether some leading public figure might run for president, he replied, "Oh, I don't know whether he will run or not. I wonder when Ford's new car will be ready for delivery." Rogers inquired of another about Prohibition, who shrugged his shoulders and asked, "Have you heard anything about how that new Ford stands up?" With yet another citizen, Rogers raised the issue of the controversial Congressional debate over the tariff, but he pled ignorance and speculated, "I wonder if they really are as fast as Ford says?" When Rogers had lunch with Ford in Detroit and tried to discuss public affairs, he found that the automaker "was as bad as all the other people I had talked to. All HE was interested in was the new Ford car."[40]

Rogers, of course, had his fun with Ford, as he did with just about every other public figure of the era. During World War I, the entertainer joked about the futility of the automaker's "Peace Ship" venture and later paired him with Mormon leader and bigamist Brigham Young as an originator of "mass production." In 1923, Rogers made Ford the subject of one of his recordings for Victor Records and poked fun at a variety of his endeavors, including the ubiquitous Model T, which he characterized as not "a necessity. Neither would you call it a luxury. It just kinda' comes under the heading of knick-knacks." Concerning the political speculation surrounding the industrialist, the humorist concluded, "There's no reason why there shouldn't be a Ford in the White House. They're everywhere else." The following year, when Ford had instructed his factory managers to smell the breath of workers for alcohol when they came to work in the morning, the humorist claimed it was a necessity because if a worker imbibed strong drink and then breathed on a flimsy Model T he would "blow the bolts right out of it." Rogers speculated that Ford had been careful not to order his car salesmen to smell the breath of potential customers, however, because he was "smart enough to know a sober man would never buy one." When the automaker published a long series of anti-Semitic slurs in his *Dearborn Independent* and a public outcry forced him to apologize, Rogers offered a mock explanation. Ford, he wrote, "used to have it in for the Jewish people until he saw them in Chevrolets, and then he said, 'Boys, I am all wrong.'"[41]

In a more serious vein, the Oklahoman presented the automaker, in the best populist spirit, as an American success story who had produced something useful instead of just manipulating finances to become wealthy. "Our plain old friend, Mr. Henry Ford," Rogers wrote, didn't merge companies or sell stock, was ignorant of when Wall Street opened and closed, and "thinks margins are the things you leave around the edge of anything." Rogers noted a recent *American Magazine* attributing Ford's success with a new railroad project to good judgement and hard-working habits. "Now that magazine needn't have said that he was making a success out of it," Rogers commented. "We know what he has done with it. When Henry gets his hands on anything it is, what do you call that word, Superfluous . . . to say that he has made a success out of it." Ford's success habits were enhanced by his instinctive grasp of the restless nature of his fellow citizens. "Mr. Ford knows more human Nature than any business man living," Rogers contended. "He knows the American People want to be going somewhere and they don't care where, just so they are going .... . People have confidence in getting them from where they are, and that's all America wants, IS JUST TO BE FROM HERE NEXT." As a result of Ford's practices and perceptions, the humorist concluded, "You could take every nickel he had and make him start broke in some other business tomorrow, and in 10 years he would be manufacturing nine-tenths of the World's supply of bath tubs, or own eight-tenths of the Hot Dog stands in this Country."[42]

Much of Ford's success, Rogers argued, could be traced to the fact that he was, like Lindbergh, a forward-looking prophet of the future. "I think Henry Ford is the smartest man in the World today," the humorist wrote admiringly. "If Henry Ford had studied the past instead of the future, about all he would ever have invented would have been 'the Cheapest suit of Armour on the market.'" Ford's anticipation of the future had produced the groundbreaking Model T along with the mass production techniques that allowed it to be made and sold inexpensively to the masses. That same impulse, Rogers perceived, prompted the automaker to peer over the horizon and advocate the development of aviation. By the 1920s, Ford was involved with several projects: developing an inexpensive "Flivver" airplane for the American consumer, building a sturdy "Tri-Motor" aircraft for commercial use, and constructing a state-of-art airfield outside Detroit. Rogers was also intrigued by the automaker's visionary proposal to build a massive airplane akin to an ocean liner propelled by several engines, carrying over 100 people, and big enough to buck even the strongest winds and storms. When the two men visited in 1927, they talked airplanes and the entertainer concluded of the industrialist, "He done more to further Aviation than all the other rich men combined."[43]

But Rogers also respected Ford's populist spirit that, like Bryan, venerated the traditions and achievements of ordinary American citizens. For all of his technological innovations and vast wealth, the automaker remained a man of the people with common tastes and democratic instincts. With the establishment of the Henry Ford Museum and Greenfield Village in Dearborn, Ford had gathered thousands of practical items – threshing machines, farm wagons, buggies, spinning wheels, wood stoves, furniture, houses, school buildings, old mills, general stores – to preserve memories of America's agricultural past. Rogers described this little "antique business" as residing in a space "about the size of Soldier Field in Chicago, only it is roofed over." Ford's fondness for old-time music and folk dancing also earned the Oklahoman's admiring comment, "I like him because he sees more music in an old-time fiddler than he does in a long-haired one with a foreign name." Ford made a similar impression in person as someone "modest, and plain, easy to talk to and interested in everything .... .

He knows all his machinists by name and stops and they talk over what they are working on. He is a great man. Just about the greatest we have." In fact, when Rogers read a news story about additions and subtractions to the Social Register and reacted with eye-rolling disdain – "Of all the undemocratic things you can think of just offhand, that is the prize 'Hooey,' a book to tell you who is a good Parlor Hound and who is a sort of Mongrel around the tea table" – one person leapt to mind as the antithesis of such snobbery. With sarcasm in full flight, he imagined Ford's heartbreak at being left out of this high-society volume. "Transportationally he is a Giant, but socially he is a Gnat. I can imagine his embarrassment when he found that out," wrote Rogers. "For he has been so ambitious, and has strived all his life to be somebody, and now to find he didn't make it."[44]

Ultimately, Ford, with his commingled traditionalism and innovation, seemed to personify the modern dilemma of progress for Rogers. The Detroit manufacturer understood that Americans were a restless people who wanted to be in motion and had said of his automobile, "Here is the very thing for them. They can be going somewhere." Yet Ford's revolutionary automobile also brought increased danger and encouraged mindless movement. The statistics in 1925 indicated "'48 people killed by an Auto every 24 hours in the United States.' And they call that progress," Rogers wrote in a *Weekly Article*. "I have never yet seen a man in such a big hurry that a horse or train wouldn't have got him there in plenty of time. In fact, 9/10ths of the people would be better off if they stayed where they are, instead of going where they are going .... People nowadays are traveling faster, but they are not getting any further, in fact not as far as our old dads did."[45]

In Rogers' final analysis, Henry Ford, with all of his impulses, achievements, and dilemmas, seemed to represent the essential American spirit. "What some of our self-styled prominent men do, nobody ever knows or cares, but what Henry Ford does or says is always of interest to everybody," Rogers wrote in 1925. "Why? Because he is the greatest man we have in this Country. He has given real enjoyment to more people and work to more people than any man living." Ford had demonstrated that success in America did not depend on gouging others and trampling the common good. In Rogers' humorous assessment, "First thing you know that Bird will prove a theory that you can pay the highest wages, give everybody a square deal, and still wind up by being the richest man in the world."[46]

When all was said and done, the millions of readers and listeners who regularly attended to Rogers' commentary about America, its qualities, its citizens, and its heroes usually agreed with him. They reached similar conclusions about valuing common people and common sense, appreciating the past and anticipating the future, cherishing independence and interrogating progress, and treasuring the merits of Bryan, Lindbergh, and Ford. But ultimately, many of them went a step further. The nature and meaning of America, many Americans decided by the mid-1920s, appeared most clearly when Will Rogers looked in the mirror.

* * * * *

In an elegiac piece written not long after Rogers' premature death, L. H. Robbins, in the *New York Times*, asserted that the humorist had bonded with his enormous audience over a shared sense of "American" values. Rogers had established himself, Robbins wrote, as "a spokesman for a generation of his countrymen." It was partly a matter of style. This "village sage of the crossroad store and the cracker barrel" had won over millions of readers and viewers with his humor and modesty, his open-minded and genial deportment, his position as "spokesman for the nation's horse sense." Rogers had enhanced this image through his everyday manner and identification with ordinary citizens, appearing as "the apotheosis of the common man .... He was Vox Populi in person."

But Rogers' enormous popularity, Robbins continued, also touched something deeper. He embodied what millions of citizens saw as the best qualities in the national character and self-image. He appeared to many as the quintessential American. In the essayist's words:

> Analyze the Rogers body of conceptions, and you have a fairly true map of the average American mind. You have, notably, a strong faith in humanity, a social conscience, tolerance for the other fellow, sympathy for the underdog, and a passion for fair play for both dogs. You have intellectual curiosity, shrewd observation, high respect for truth, and a candor that "smiles when it says it," disarming resentment. You have beautiful modesty of judgment, strangely coupled with conservative prejudices. With uncalculating simplicity of genius, Will Rogers mixed these ingredients in his daily squibs and radio talks and produced American opinion.

Robbins grasped a basic component of Rogers' appeal: the Oklahoman came to embody what many Americans believed about themselves and their country.[47]

This widespread perception of Rogers as the essential American took shape in the flood of commentary that attended his rapid rise to national influence in the 1920s. Dozens of articles and essays appearing in newspapers, popular magazines, journals of opinion, literary reviews, and movie periodicals throughout the United States portrayed the entertainer as a symbol of the nation's fundamental values and impulses. "In my opinion, and I've met many who share it, Will Rogers is a splendid example of a representative American, even to that dash of Indian blood," noted a journalist in *Liberty* magazine. "He has courage, he has a big heart, he is a good businessman. He believes in equality." A radio journal claimed that the Oklahoman "does just what we all long to do. He lives as a citizen of a republic might be expected to live, honoring only merit, and kowtowing to no one because of fame, fortune, or social position." A movie-fan magazine asserted that he "represents to the world the honest, shrewd, human, and humorous Yankee" and nominated him as "America's most useful citizen."[48]

This popular portrait of Rogers as a symbol of America highlighted several important features. Most broadly, and most frequently, journalists and commentators described him as a man of the people, a defender of ordinary, hard-working citizens who quietly labored to support themselves and their family with few of the advantages enjoyed by the wealthy and powerful. "Rogers is always for the man beneath," wrote the *New York Times*. "He puts a pin into the pompous and jeers at the self-righteous and the self-important." The journal *Current Opinion* concluded that he was "building a secure place for himself in the hearts of the American people," while *Liberty* magazine praised him as a public figure "who takes the Constitution seriously in respect to all men being free and equal." Such discussions often became explicitly populist in tone, noting that the humorist sprang from the "agricultural population of the trans-Mississippi prairies – the lower middle class of the soil" and evinced a democratic spirit as he "spoke the language of the great plains, like a man who had nothing more than a dash of little red schoolhouse education." This rural sensibility with its independent spirit, critical view of economic privilege, and determined self-reliance, had inspired American populists since the nineteenth century and now marked Rogers. "Persons who are raised on farms think their own thoughts, reach their own conclusions," noted an analysis of the humorist in a popular magazine. "In the country, the power of observation develops; the countryman thinks for himself and has time to meditate while plowing, riding range, or digging fence-post holes." Another journal succinctly explained the humorist's growing role as a "national spokesman": "He has the instincts of the plain people, and he may even become the voice of the plain people."[49]

Rogers' role as a spokesman for America's common man, many suggested, also made him a spokesman for common sense. Regular folks facing workaday problems with their jobs, families, and communities often developed a keen sense of practicality. The humorist perfectly expressed that mindset. Dispensing with high-flying theories, ideological abstractions, and elegant language, his musings on the issues of the day focused on practical analysis and real-world consequences. Rogers had "a genius for common sense," noted the magazine *College Humor* and numerous other publications echoed that phrase. According to the *Saturday Review of Literature*, in the humorist's popular writing "the foolery is good, so is the temper, and so is the common sense." *Liberty* magazine judged that Rogers' fans "appreciate his hard common sense" while *Cosmopolitan* concluded that his wit was "bunkered in sound common sense." Other periodicals used different phrases to stress the same quality, with the *Buffalo Evening Times* praising his "first-rate practical understanding" and the *New York Times* characterizing his pragmatic approach as "horse sense."[50]

The humorist also came to symbolize the self-made man and its accompanying work ethic, another typically American impulse. Countless articles pictured him as personifying the American success story. Even though he had grown up as the scion of a leading Cherokee family in Oklahoma, most periodicals poured the entertainer's life into a rags to riches mold. His early days had seen "hardships and adversities," said *Collier's* magazine, but he had risen to become "a prosperous citizen today." In 1928, *Forbes* ran a long, admiring piece entitled "Will Rogers: The Business Man" that stressed his iconic rise to fame and fortune. This enterprising figure, in the best American tradition, had parlayed his talents into a profitable success story, first earning a healthy salary as a silent film star and lecturer but now "money galore comes to him from newspaper owners and publishers, and his name is emblazoned in huge electric lights from theatrical entrepreneurs," *Forbes* noted. Rogers then shrewdly invested his money in property, first with his estate on Beverly Hills Drive in Los Angeles and then a 250-acre ranch north of Santa Monica, moves which made him "the real estate connoisseur of California." Stories inevitably noted his strenuous work ethic. A lengthy piece in *Everybody's* magazine reported, "Writing he calls *hard* work, and you should hear Rogers say *hard*. There is a grinding pang in the word. His whole life has been *hard*. Before turning himself loose on a subject, he studies it *hard*." Another interviewer underlined Rogers' work ethic by quoting his reply to a question about reading habits: "No, I ain't got time to read, that's a fact. Takes all my time rehearsin' and talkin' and maybe gettin' in a little sleep now and then. My leisure moments, you might say, I use for authorin.'"[51]

Rogers' image as an American icon took on additional luster from his image as a man from the Great West. In the late eighteenth century, the transplanted Frenchman, Hector St. John de Crevecoeur, had asked famously, "Who is this new man, this American?" He answered his own question by describing his countrymen as an individualistic, hard-working, self-reliant, practical, freedom-loving, and often rough-hewn people who had been shaped by their endeavors as "cultivators, scattered over an immense territory." Crevecoeur's American "new man" had been forged in the wide-open spaces of the western frontier. Like a long list of figures preceding him – Andrew Jackson, Abraham Lincoln, Mark Twain, among others – Rogers personified this "new man" for a receptive public. Outfitted in his cowboy regalia, the humorist invited viewers and listeners to see him as an iconic western figure and true-blue American. Accounts of Rogers played up the theme. "To see Will Rogers without his chaps and lariat would be lamentable," noted *Current Opinion*. A 1926 cover story in *Time* claimed that he "grew to manhood on the back of a pinto" while an article in *Liberty* stressed that the Oklahoman had been shaped by his upbringing in "a new, raw country and had to learn things. He was not hampered by theories or by curricula – he had to take the things that came handiest." The *Literary Digest* underlined the new man theme when it quoted a London reviewer of a Rogers show in 1926. "Mr. Rogers is that queer mixture of comedian, lecturer, and philosopher which seems to be produced exclusively by America," argued the English critic. "He is an incarnation of the artful, absurd, bubbling energy of the Middle West, quite sure of itself, and a little contemptuous – ever so good-naturedly – of all the rest of the world."[52]

Rogers reflected another timeworn American characteristic in his proclivity for big-hearted generosity. In the 1830s, Alexis de Tocqueville had been struck by how individualistic citizens in the United States, guarding against both the lure of selfishness and the danger of aristocratic patronage, typically embraced giving and philanthropy, often through voluntary associations. This American tradition of doing good by committing to "aid each other freely" found affirmation in the Rogers image. Stories on the entertainer constantly pointed out his reputation for having "a heart as big as all outdoors .... Not only is he one of the biggest money-makers on the stage today, but he is probably the most philanthropic." *Time* reported on "the money he gives away anonymously to sick chorus girls, and rum-dums, and broken actors" and related how, during one of his performance tours, he came across a small-town baseball team about to fold because they had shoddy equipment and no uniforms so "he used a week's salary to get them the best suits, bats, and gloves that could be bought." A shining example of Rogers' philanthropy came in his much-publicized efforts to help victims of the great Mississippi flood in the spring of 1927, when the river overflowed its banks and devastated some 10,000 square miles in bordering Southern states and rendered 700,000 people homeless. Rogers, who was on the lecture circuit, held fundraisers for flood relief in New York and New Orleans and spent months alerting the nation, both in his lectures and his newspaper pieces, of the great need for donations. A grateful New Orleans awarded him the keys to the city while the Red Cross, for whom he had raised record amounts of money, made him a lifetime member.[53]

All in all, Rogers represented a set of old-fashioned American values shining through the smoke and clamor of a modern, industrialized, and consumer happy nation. Those who looked back fondly on such traditions revered the popular humorist. "This loose-jointed, gum-chewing, ex-cowhand, more than any

American alive today, links the nation with an Americanism that is unhappily passing," asserted *Cosmopolitan* magazine. But even those with more modern tastes respected Rogers for honoring this American heritage. The progressive, urban-oriented journal, *The Nation*, for example, gave Rogers his due as "a cowboy Montaigne, an all-around sly bird" who "knows much about the American mind." It explained that when visitors from the hinterland came to New York, they could not attend the *Ziegfeld Follies* and then report home that all they saw was "a lot of pretty girls wearing nothing but sheets of tissue paper." They also saw Will Rogers, who "can be discussed in Christian Endeavor circles. A genuine ranch hand, as homely as Abraham Lincoln, he ... gives a touch of virility to a performance which would otherwise be lamentably Parisian and repugnant to our sturdy pioneer virtues."[54]

Thus Will Rogers, in his climb to popularity and influence, became the keeper of the American Soul. As theater goers, lecture audiences, radio listeners, and newspaper and magazine readers chuckled at his witticisms and relished his irreverent commentary, commentators throughout the United States acclaimed him as a national symbol. The descriptions piled one upon the other: "an American institution," "representative of our native American traditions," "all that America is," "a personality that could never have blossomed in any country other than America." The *Chicago Tribune* summarized this deep connection to national wellsprings, characterizing the humorist as "the average American .... the plain homespun American, magnified hugely by his fortunate access to all the means of communication that are available in this era – the motion pictures, the radio, the newspaper syndicates, the book publishing business, and the stage."[55]

For growing numbers of citizens, however, Rogers not only represented the habits and values of his native land, but embodied the *best* of what it meant to be an American. A 1927 editorial in the *San Francisco Chronicle*, published the day after a local Rogers performance, captured the essence of this appeal:

> Will Rogers has a faculty of seeing into the heart of a social or political or economic problem and then telling us in a sentence what is there .... When he speaks we all wonder why he has so concisely said what was in our own minds. It was there all the time, but we didn't know it until Will Rogers found it. He is Confucius adapted to America. Poor Richard attuned to jazz. He is the artist holding a mirror up to homely human nature, the genius of the plain American who "turns a keen untroubled face home to the instant need of things." In other words, he has horse sense. Which suggests that the country needs more horses.[56]

The novelist and essayist, Clarence B. Kelland, in a reminiscence about his friend, made the same point when analyzing the secret of Rogers' tremendous appeal to an American audience. After much thought, he explained with a striking visual image: "If you took Will Rogers and pitched a dab of whiskers under his chin, put a red, white, and blue hat on his head, and crammed his legs into a pair of star-spangled pants, he'd be Uncle Sam." This notion of understanding Rogers not *on* America, but *as* America reveals much. As the *New York Sun* observed, "Will Rogers has a curious national quality. He gives the impression that the country is filled with such sages, wise with years, young in humor and love of life, shrewd yet gentle .... . He is what Americans think other Americans are like."[57]

So when the Oklahoma humorist made light of his work as a reflection of the "American Soul," he must have realized that like most of his humor, this jest barely concealed an underlying truth. In explaining Americans to themselves, personifying the traits they valued, and embodying what they wanted to be, Rogers offered a portrait of his native land to his fellow citizens. And he made them smile at what they saw.

8

Politics is Applesauce

ON JUNE 10, 1928, AT THE REPUBLICAN NATIONAL Convention in Kansas City, H. L. Mencken was holding forth in an improvised, after-hours canteen on an upper floor of the convention hall that was well lubricated with liquor. The acerbic, hilarious columnist for the *Baltimore Sun* and *American Mercury* had earned a towering reputation over the previous decade as a biting critic of middle-class "Babbits," uneducated rubes, religious puritans, democratic values, and the great American "booboisie," as he liked to call them. In his inimitable style, Mencken excoriated "smuthounds," Rotarians, and denizens of the "Bible Belt" and became an idol of the nation's smart set in the Jazz Age. Now, to the amusement of about a dozen fellow journalists, he trained his rhetorical guns on one of their own who was sitting in the room.

Will Rogers, Mencken announced in a loud voice with a face flushed from several drinks, had become "the most influential editorial writer in America" and a formidable political power. The result was frightening, Mencken asserted in mock-outrage:

> Look at the man. He alters foreign policies. He makes and unmakes candidates. He destroys public figures. By deriding Congress and undermining its prestige he has virtually reduced us to a monarchy. Millions of Americans read his words daily and those who are unable to read listen to him over the radio ... . I consider him the most dangerous writer alive today.

Rogers, a friend of Mencken's for many years, chuckled and remonstrated, "you know that nobody with any sense ever took any of my gags seriously." "Certainly not," the Baltimorean retorted. "They are taken seriously by nobody except half-wits, in other words by approximately 85 percent of the voting population."[1]

While overstated with his trademark combination of humorous exaggeration and flamboyant insult, Mencken's comment captured a central truth: by the

1920s Will Rogers had become a significant political force in the United States. This development was no accident. The humorist often joked that since he was born on election day, November 4, 1879, he had a special dispensation to talk about political matters in later life. Indeed, as his career took off in the late 1910s and 1920s, politics became his comedic currency. Following his familiar introduction – "All I know is what I read in the papers" – Rogers invariably launched into a humorous interrogation of public affairs and political decisions, whether in his stage show, lectures, or journalistic writing. In his trademark style of good-natured jesting and homespun wisdom, he cut a wide swath through American political culture. Rogers made fun of both major political parties ("It is getting so that a Republican promise is not much more to be depended on than a Democratic one. And that has always been considered the lowest form of collateral in the world."). He joked about the chief executive ("We shouldn't elect a President; we should elect a magician.") and the Congress ("Congress has promised the country it will adjourn next Tuesday. Let's hope we can depend on it. If they do, it will be the first promise they have kept this session."). He mocked policy making in Washington, DC, as a ludicrous combination of inflated egos, bombastic rhetoric, and runaway self-interests ("I don't make jokes. I just watch the government and report the facts.").

As Rogers liked to say, using an early twentieth-century slang word meaning "nonsense," "I tell you, folks, all politics is applesauce." This claim reflected his deep-seated aversion to pretension, dissembling, selfishness, and pomposity, qualities he saw as all-too-characteristic of American political life. Many of his fellow citizens shared this attitude and Rogers' bemused, head-shaking reflections on public affairs and his humorous skewering of politicians contributed mightily to his tremendous popularity. In 1924, while visiting the gallery of the United States House of Representatives, Rogers turned "fiery red" and bowed when the Congressmen interrupted their deliberations to give him a standing ovation. His weekly columns were read into the *Congressional Record* and when he urged readers to tell their representatives how they felt about certain political issues, thousands of letters poured into Capitol Hill. In 1927, Rogers addressed state legislatures in California, Nevada, South Carolina, Alabama, and Minnesota. As *American Magazine* observed of the 1920s, a political period dominated by Republican presidents, "If the President of the United States says a thing is so, the Democrats may doubt him. But if Will Rogers backs him up, even the Democrats believe. In Washington they say that the Senate fears Rogers more than all the editors in America."[2]

As with many other aspects of his success, Rogers' political influence came from a combination of opportunity and hard work, style and substance. He reached millions of Americans because of his multi-faceted endeavors on the stage, the silver screen, the lecture platform, and the printed page, but he labored assiduously to cement that connection by closely observing the twists and turns of American public life and then laboring to interpret them for his massive audience. Rogers' unique words then took over, conveying his thoughts and perceptions in the down-home, just-folks fashion that had propelled him to the top in the world of stage and screen. But the happy combination of venue and style told only part of the story. Rogers' humorous approach to public affairs and his joshing of political personalities may have drawn in a host of readers and listeners. But the genuine flashes of truth and compelling quality of his political ideas kept them coming back for more.

* * * * *

Will Rogers' political sensibility emerged accidentally and developed haphazardly. It had first appeared when he began speaking to the audience to spice up his roping act during his vaudeville days in the early 1910s. After discovering that humorous quips got the biggest reaction when they addressed in-the-headlines topics, he began to scour the newspapers daily in search of material, a process that inevitably unearthed events, issues, and personalities wrapped up in public affairs. In such fashion, politics became a favorite topic of Rogers' humor.

The absurdities, posturing, and hypocrisies of political life provided rich comic material, and Rogers quickly developed a genial skepticism about politicians and the political system that touched a public nerve. His breakout performance at the Friars' Club show in 1916, attended by President Woodrow Wilson, placed politics as the centerpiece of the humorist's remarks. Rogers' clever cracks about America's lagging military preparedness, the dispute with Pancho Villa and the Mexican border, and political infighting in Washington, DC, brought peals of laughter from the audience, including the president. This rousing success established a template for skewering national politics that became a mainstay of Rogers' humor over the next two decades. In his first *Weekly Article* on December 31, 1922, for instance, Rogers recounted a recent *Ziegfeld Follies* show where he brought Kansas Governor Henry Allen up on stage from the audience. Allen extolled the humorist's "impertinences" and claimed their author was the only man in America who told the truth about public affairs. Rogers leaned out toward the audience and quipped, "It is because I have never mixed up in politics." A few years later, Rogers announced in a *Daily Telegram*, "Congress meets tomorrow morning. Let us all pray: Oh Lord, give us strength to bear that which is about to be inflicted upon us. Be merciful with them, Oh Lord, for they know not what they are doing. Amen."[3]

Armed with this satirical sensibility, Rogers stood atop a powerful, multidimensional media platform by the early 1920s as he addressed the political concerns of the age. His *Ziegfeld Follies* act featured political material, as did his public lectures delivered in cities and towns throughout the nation. His weekly column and daily telegrams, often chock full of political observations, appeared in dozens of newspapers around the United States. He published a barrage of articles on political topics in popular magazines such as *The Saturday Evening Post*, *American Magazine*, and *Life*, and newspapers such as the *New York Times*. In addition, Rogers appeared in a silent-film trilogy of political satires in 1924 – *Going to Congress*, *Our Congressman*, *A Truthful Liar* – playing "Alfalfa Doolittle," a hapless character who bumbled into politics where he found abundant reward for his ineptness.

Rogers' skill at using humor to discuss and illuminate political affairs led to a plum assignment in the journalistic world. Beginning in 1920 and continuing for the rest of his life, he covered the national conventions of both the Democratic and Republican parties. These bombastic partisan gatherings provided abundant material for jokes and satirical descriptions. In one sally, Rogers explained that journalists made conventions sound exciting and colorful when, in fact, they consisted mostly of "some old long-winded Bird talking about 'getting back to the early Lincoln Democracy.' There won't be an original saying, or a new passage uttered during the entire fiesta." The humorist claimed that after returning home from several days of endless nomination speeches and overblown "save the country" rhetoric, he fully expected one of his children to ask for money to go to the movies by arising and intoning, "The great Democratic Party of which I and my forefathers for generations back have been honored members, the Party of the Common or Real people!" Rogers had a response ready: "I will raise up and desire to smite him, even if he be of my own flesh and blood."[4]

As his commentary on public life grew in volume and popularity, Rogers engaged with many of the leading political figures of the day: Theodore Roosevelt, Warren Harding, Herbert Hoover among Republicans; Woodrow Wilson, William McAdoo, Al Smith, Franklin Roosevelt among Democrats. These encounters usually were casual and intermittent, mostly providing the humorist an opportunity to link popular personalities with political issues and controversies. But in a few cases, Rogers spent considerable time with an important political figure and was able to develop a friendship while digging deeper to gauge their personalities and characteristics. In 1926, for instance, he sailed home from Europe on the *Leviathan* with Charles Evan Hughes. Over the years, Rogers had told many jokes about this formidable public figure who had served as Governor of New York, Republican candidate for president in 1916, Secretary of State in the Harding administration, and would later be Chief Justice of the Supreme Court. Nervous about meeting the dignified, patrician, bearded Hughes, the humorist joked, "When I was first introduced, I didn't know whether to hold out my hand to shake or to cover up and protect myself." But the two became good friends and partnered to host a shipboard fundraiser for victims of a devastating hurricane in Florida which took in 42,000 dollars. During the cruise, Rogers and Hughes spent hours on deck discussing political affairs, especially the recent landing of U.S. Marines in Nicaragua to prevent a leftist takeover of the government, a move the Oklahoman vehemently opposed. Rogers came to have great respect for the New Yorker's intelligence, integrity, and good humor and the two would gather periodically in the years to come. "The Secretary has been so thoroughly humanized that he has almost gotten common," Rogers recounted. "[I]f he had been running for President then he would have carried that boat, Democrats and all . . . . for if ever a man was misunderstood in regard to being a genuine good fellow it's Mr. Hughes." The distinguished Republican recipro-cated, signing off in a letter to Rogers several years later, "Yours for more and better wisecracks."[5]

Rogers also became good friends with Bernard Baruch, the influential financier and luminary in the Democratic Party. The scion of a Jewish family in South Carolina, Baruch had earned a fortune on Wall Street investing in the sugar and rubber industries before becoming an adviser on economic issues to President Woodrow Wilson, who appointed him chairman of the new War Industries Board. In Rogers' rendering, when Wilson complained that Baruch had only appointed Republicans to the Board, the chairman replied, "You told me to get prominent men from every Industry and I did. Now I can go and get you some Democrats but they won't be very prominent and won't have any Industries with them." Baruch would become a wise man in Democratic circles for several decades, serving Franklin Roosevelt during World War II and advising a number of other presidents. Rogers became acquainted with Baruch in the early 1920s and they would meet at Democratic conventions and travel to Washington, DC, in the financier's private railroad car. Baruch frequently attended the *Ziegfeld Follies* and visited with Rogers backstage afterwards, while the businessman hosted the enter-tainer at his Scottish castle in 1926 where they went grouse hunting. According to Rogers, Baruch named the birds "after some prominent Republican and with names like that he never misses." The New Yorker became a political mentor to the Oklahoman, sharing his expertise on international trade, monetary policy, financial policy, and foreign affairs on many occasions. In 1928, Baruch invited Rogers and General John J. Pershing to his brownstone home on Fifth Avenue after a performance of *Three Cheers*, where they discussed world affairs late into the night. The humorist and the financier shared a mutual admiration. Baruch described Rogers as "a Benjamin Franklin philosopher of our time . . . . You have been taking the swelling out of a lot of heads, putting joy into lives, comfort into hearts, and made many a man stand steadier upon his feet." Rogers reciprocated, lauding his friend as the "Financial Department of the Democratic Party" and praising his financial acumen, as when Baruch wisely advised the humorist to pay off his debts and stay out of the stock market before the Great Crash of 1929. "I did what you told me," the humorist told him, "and you saved my life."[6]

Perhaps Rogers' most unlikely political friendship was with Calvin Coolidge, who unexpectedly became president in 1923 upon the sudden death of Warren G. Harding. A flinty, taciturn New Englander, the former Massachusetts governor was notorious for his clipped sentences and tight-fisted political style. Rogers met him in 1925 when they both appeared at the Gridiron Club dinner in the national capital. The humorist visited the White House in advance and anticipated a pinched, close-lipped encounter but Coolidge crossed him up, talking pleasantly and deftly displaying a "kinder quiet sense of humor." When Rogers noted the prestige of the Gridiron dinners, Coolidge agreed but noted they were hard on him. When Rogers sympathized about the jokes always aimed at the president, Coolidge replied, "no, it keeps me there until after 12 [midnight]." When Rogers praised the club's reputation for putting on a great event, the president observed drily, "Yes, the singing is good." At the dinner itself, Coolidge laughed at all Rogers' jokes about him, and the humorist concluded, "He was as agreeable as an Insurance Agent." In 1926, Coolidge invited Rogers to stay at the executive mansion after his return from Europe and the pair spent a long evening discussing national politics and world affairs. Rogers admired the plain living and simple tastes of Coolidge and his family and when the New Englander ended his presidency, he concluded, "I think he has done a mighty good job." Rogers later reported, "I am personally very fond of him . . . . I know of no man connected with either party who I have ever had the pleasure of meeting for whom I have a greater regard."[7]

As he engaged the issues and individuals, opportunities and conundrums of American public affairs in the late 1910s and 1920s, Rogers consistently addressed what he liked to call the "bunk" of politics. An advocate of sincerity, common sense, and friendly good will, he recoiled from the displays of duplicity, pretense, egotism, and crude self-interest all too characteristic of America's political affairs. Ironically, Rogers illuminated the nonsense of politics in October 1922 when, as a personal favor to Theodore Roosevelt, Jr., he attended a political rally and spoke on behalf of the re-election of Republican congressman Ogden Mills in New York City. But as a non-partisan, and having never met Mills and knowing nothing about his politics, Rogers spent his time offering a humorous indictment of politics as usual:

> [T]his is my first crack at a political speech, and I hope it flops. I don't want [it]
> to go over and then have to go into politics, because up to now I have always

tried to live honest. A great many think I was sent here by Mr. Mills' opponent, but this is not the case. I don't know him. But he must be a scoundrel. From what I have read of politics, every opponent is . . . . Mr. Mills is quite a novelty. He is one of the few men that didn't go into politics through necessity. He was wealthy when he started. Not as wealthy as he is now, but he had some money, and he went into politics to protect it . . . . for they say there is honor among thieves . . . . I have no politics. I came here because a Roosevelt asked me to come here. A Roosevelt hint is the same as one of my wife's commands.

As the *New York Times* commented editorially on this bewildering political "endorsement" of Mills, who sat silently on the platform with a stolid expression, "whether the candidate whom Mr. Rogers was ostensibly supporting gained more by the performance than did his opponent it would be hard to say."[8]

Revelations of political bunk became a Rogers calling card, as he made clear in one of his first *Weekly Articles*. "You know, the more you read and observe about this Politics thing, you got to admit that each party is worse than the other. The one that's out always looks the best," he wrote. The humorist frequently claimed that the last two letters in Washington, DC, stood for "Department of Comedy." He mocked politicians' habit of proclaiming their devotion to public service when it was actually "public jobs that they are looking for." Rogers shook his head at the process of trying to pass legislation where politicians ignored the actual merits of a bill while scrambling to see if it had been introduced by the opposite political party, when they would automatically oppose it, and whether it would boost or undermine their chances for re-election. "[P]olitics and self-preservation must come first, never mind the majority of the people of the U. S.," Rogers wrote. "A man's thoughts are naturally on his next term, more than on his country."[9]

Rogers saw Republicans and Democrats as equally implicated in the practice of political bunk. "If a man could tell the difference between the two parties he would make a sucker out of Solomon for wisdom," he argued in 1928. "[T]his country runs in spite of parties; in fact, parties are the biggest handicaps we have to contend with. If we dident have to stop to play politics, any administration could almost make a Garden of Eden out of us." In Rogers' assessment, the allure of a political party increased only when it was out of power. During the administration of Democrat Woodrow Wilson, the Republicans looked appealing, and then during the administration of Republican Warren G. Harding the Democrats began to look attractive. He drew the obvious conclusion: "The only way in the world to make either one of those old parties look even half way decent is to keep them out." The Oklahoman joked about his party nonalignment. "I am just sitting tight waiting for an attractive offer, and I may have something to announce in the next few weeks. But right now I am a missionary. I am going to devote my life's work to rescue this country from the hand of the politician, and also rescue the politician to a life of Christianity."[10]

The 1924 presidential election between sitting President Calvin Coolidge, a Republican, and Democratic challenger John W. Davis struck Rogers as particularly vapid. After observing the candidates and studying their statements, he saw the only difference as being "the Democrats want the Republicans to get out and let them in, and the Republicans don't want to get out." The campaign, he wrote, was bereft of serious positions and debate:

> They are so hard up for an issue that Mr. Coolidge has just announced his policy will be Common Sense. Well, don't you know the Democrats will claim that too? Do you think they will call their campaign "Darn Foolishness?" Besides, Common Sense is not an issue in politics, it's an affliction. Davis announces that his policy will be honesty. Neither is that an issue in politics. It's a miracle, and can he get enough people to believe in miracles to elect him?[11]

As Rogers meandered through the political landscape, pointing out absurdities and joking about the peccadillos of leading figures, he occasionally stumbled into controversy. He had a dust-up with Warren G. Harding when he joked in his *Ziegfeld Follies* act about the president's fondness for golf, tendency to delegate responsibility, and the controversial actions of the Disarmament Conference. Earlier, Rogers had visited Harding in the White House and the two had hit it off. When the humorist offered to relate the latest political jokes, the president quipped, "I know 'em. I appointed most of them." After a congenial gathering, Rogers reported, "I felt just like I was shaking hands with some old cow man from Oklahoma." Thus the humorist was shocked when a White House secretary appeared in his dressing room and asked him to cut back on jokes about the president. Even though Rogers obliged by trimming his criticism when the *Follies* visited Washington, DC, a few weeks later, Harding made a point of attending another show in town to indicate his disapproval. The humorist was peeved at the president's thin skin, and during a curtain call told the audience, "I have cracked quite a few jokes on public men here, both Republicans and Democrats. I hope I have not given offense. In fact, I don't believe any big man will take offense." Noting that presidents Roosevelt and Wilson had laughed at his cracks, he jabbed, "After all, it is the test of a big man whether he can stand the gaff." In a *Weekly Article*, Rogers noted Harding's snub due to "the humorous relations between the White House and myself being rather strained." The humorist soon felt bad about this uncharacteristic hubbub, however, and he downplayed the tension between the two when Harding died unexpectedly in 1923. Rogers blamed it on newspaper exaggerations, praised Harding's sense of humor, and reiterated his fondness for the late president.[12]

A few years later, Rogers stumbled into a fiasco regarding Harding's successor, President Calvin Coolidge. On January 4, 1928, the humorist served as master of ceremonies for a national radio broadcast of the *Dodge Victory Hour*, during which he mimicked President Coolidge to deliver a statement on the state of the nation at the new year. "I am proud to report that the country as a whole is prosperous. I don't mean by that that the whole country is prosperous, but, as a whole it is prosperous," he intoned nonsensically in the New Englander's distinctive nasal twang. "A hole is not supposed to be prosperous, and we are certainly in a hole. There is not a whole lot of doubt about that. Everybody I come in contact with is doing well. They have to be doing well or they don't come in contact with me." Rogers' uncanny impersonation caused many listeners to believe it was really the president speaking and they protested the stunt when they learned the truth. More embarrassment came when a number of critics took Rogers to task for overstepping the bounds of good taste and disrespecting the nation's leader. The mortified humorist wrote a letter of apology to Coolidge and the First Lady, stating, "I find that due to my lack of good taste, or utter stupidity, I have wounded the feelings of two people who I most admire .... If there ever was a sad Comedian, I am one, and I do ask all the forgiveness that it's in your and Mrs. Coolidge's power to give." The president replied quickly and graciously, dismissing the controversy as "of rather small consequence" and the humorist's impersonation as "harmless amusement." But he did not invite Rogers back to the White House during the last year of his presidency.[13]

Despite such occasional missteps, Rogers steadily amassed immense popularity and influence from his commentary on American political affairs. As Adolph Ochs, the powerful publisher of the *New York Times*, wrote of the Oklahoman in 1926, "He has the happy faculty of presenting complex public questions in such a way as to bring them within the comprehension and understanding of the general public, whose confidence and respect he enjoys to a marked degree." Rogers gained such influence neither as a disinterested reporter on public affairs, a mere comedian riffing on the foibles of public men and public policy, nor a sophisticated analyst of political ideas and ideological tendencies. Rather, he functioned as a common-sense political guide for millions of Americans, helping them navigate the treacherous waters of a rapidly modernizing society. Although he avoided party labels, Rogers had a definite point of view, and his skill at expressing his political values and sensibility helped his fellow citizens make sense of the world around them.[14]

* * * * *

As his national profile grew, Rogers insisted, sometimes vehemently, that he was not just a jokester in his political commentary. In 1925, during a debate in the House of Representatives, a member quoted from several Rogers articles that had criticized Congress for failing to award a veteran's bonus and ignoring military preparedness and asked that they be read into the *Congressional Record*. But another Congressman objected to recording the remarks of a mere "professional joke maker." The Oklahoman found this declaration hilariously ironic and reacted with unusual emotion:

> Now can you beat that for Jealousy among people in the same line? Calling me a Professional Joke Maker! He is right about everything but the Professional. They are the Professional Joke Makers. Read some of the Bills that they have passed. I could study all my life and not think up half the amount of funny things they can think of in one Session of Congress. Besides, my jokes don't do anybody any harm. You don't have to pay any attention to them. But every one of the Jokes those Birds make is a LAW and hurts somebody (generally everybody) .... . Of course, I can understand what he was objecting to was my common sense creeping into the Record. It was such a Novelty, I guess it did sound funny.[15]

It was more than common sense, however, for beneath the veneer of humor Rogers articulated a political perspective that permeated everything he thought and wrote. But it was difficult to label. As a young man, the Oklahoman had flirted with radical political ideas. In 1908 he mailed two novels that he had read to fiancée Betty Blake: socialist writer Joseph M. Patterson's *A Little Brother of the Rich* and muckraking reformer Robert Herrick's *Together*. Both books savaged modern industrial capitalism as inhumane and accused it of fostering poverty, suffering, and wrenching social inequality. But as he grew older Rogers rejected all forms of socialism as tyrannical and unrealistic. "Communism is like Prohibition, it's a good idea but it won't work," he wrote in a *Weekly Article*. He found it grating that many American radicals proclaimed the superiority of socialist regimes while comfortably ensconced in the freedom and prosperity of the United States. "The old Communist preaches his doctrines, but he wants to do it where he is enjoying the blessings of Capitalistic surroundings," Rogers quipped. "He preaches against the Pie, but he sure eats it." When a contingent of "Reds, or Bolsheviki" held a meeting in Madison Square Garden, the humorist chuckled at their denunciations of everything American, including "heavy snow, [the] Declaration of Independence, 5 cent Street Car Fare, Floods in Georgia, Mayor Hylan's Bathing Suit, Twin Beds, and the Eclipse."[16]

Rogers' trip to the Soviet Union in 1927 clinched his disapproval of socialist schemes of reform. Upon arriving in Moscow and taking a taxi to his hotel, Rogers got his "first touch of Communism" when he asked the fare and the driver "guessed within ten cents of my total amount of money and names HALF of it." Every subsequent monetary encounter replicated this process. These "polite methods of banditry" took nearly all his money, he claimed, and "whittled me to where I was a Communist. That is, I thought I was. But I couldn't seem to guess what anybody else had . . . . Nobody was splitting with me." Rogers traveled about the country for several weeks and gathered his observations in a book published later that year, *There's Not a Bathing Suit in Russia*. Communism, the humorist concluded, was ruining the country. Russia was beset with high prices, low availability of goods, and rampant corruption as high-blown rhetoric far outpaced practical problem-solving. "Communism to me is one-third practice and two-thirds explanation," Rogers wrote. "If Socialists worked as much as they talked, they would be the most prosperous style of Government in the World." The humorist believed the origins of this problem lay in the writings of Karl Marx, who "wrote for the dissatisfied, and the dissatisfied is the fellow who don't want to do any manual labor. He always wants to figure out where he and his friends can get something for nothing."[17]

Rogers also found the Communist ethos of revolutionary violence disturbing. The Russians had made worship of Lenin their new religion and the Soviet leader, in the humorist's words, "preached Revolution, Blood, and Murder in everything I ever read of his." Amused by party officials who began criticizing Leon Trotsky as a conservative, he scoffed, "A Conservative among Communists is a man with a Bomb in only one hand; a Radical is what you would call a Two-Bomb Man." Sobered by tales of trains packed with political prisoners headed to Siberian labor camps and reeling from the relentless barrage of party slogans, injunctions, and art encountered everywhere in Russia, he told readers, "It seems the whole idea of Communism . . . is based on propaganda and blood." Ironically, it only produced a new version of social inequality, for when Rogers attended the races he noticed immediately that "the grandstand had all the men of the Party, and over in the center field stood the mob in the sun. Well, there was Bourgeois and Proletariat distinction for you."[18]

At the other end of the political spectrum, Rogers pondered the impact of fascism, an encounter that revealed more than any other the pitfalls of his unsophisticated political approach. While traveling abroad in the 1926, he met with Benito Mussolini and, like many Americans, judged the Italian dictator to be an attractive reformer. "I have never yet seen a thing that he has done that wasn't based on common sense," Rogers wrote of Mussolini. "He has done more constructive things for his country since the war than any hundred men in any other country." The Oklahoman appreciated how the Italian leader had vanquished the socialists and Communists in Italy and put an end to their violent revolutionary schemes. Rogers praised Mussolini for solving crippling labor disputes by establishing a law outlawing both strikes by workers and lockouts by owners, instead sending disagreements to a mediating body consisting of representatives from labor, capital, and the government. Through such actions the

Italian premier had "put everybody in Italy to work . . . and anybody that has ever been to Italy before knows that anyone who can put them to work, even if he never did anything else, should follow Caesar into the hall of fame."[19]

Equally important, the Italian leader was personally charming, a trait for which Rogers always fell. After a lengthy conversation filled with repartee and light-hearted observations, Mussolini grasped the Oklahoman by the shoulders and asked him to tell his American audience, "Mussolini R-e-g-u-l-a-r Guy . . . . Mussolini no Napoleon, want fight, always look mad; Mussolini laugh, gay, like good time same as everybody else, maybe more so – and he winked." With the high value he placed on personality, as well as practical achievement, Rogers failed to appreciate how Mussolini had banned opposition parties, restricted free speech and other liberties, and used violent tactics with his Black Shirts to establish his authority. In one of the most misguided sentences he ever wrote, the humorist asserted, "[The] Dictator form of Government is the greatest form of Government there is, if you have the right Dictator. Well, these folks have certainly got him." Rogers only changed his perspective in 1934 when Mussolini invaded Ethiopia and illuminated for the world the profound threat of fascism.[20]

Within the United States, Rogers' idiosyncratic political sensibility caused him to avoid identification with either the modern Democratic or Republican parties. Determinedly non-partisan, he made much comedic hay making fun of both of them. As he once cracked in a *Weekly Article*, "You know, it takes nerve to be a Democrat. But it takes money to be a Republican." Rogers described Democrats as amiable losers who would rather argue about politics than do anything to win elections, while Republicans were interested in turning a profit and saw politics as an annoying sidelight. With government patronage jobs such as the Post Office, for instance, a Republican saw himself "as independent as a bank Vice President" determined to run the operation efficiently while a Democrat envisioned "a cross between the country grocery store and the modern night club. They welcome anything in there just so it's in the shape of an argument." Even elections for the highest office in the land mattered little as to whether Democrats or Republicans triumphed. "Somebody is going to be President. It don't make any difference who it is," Rogers asserted. "None of them from any party are going to purposely ruin the country. They will all do the best they can. If weather and crops, and no wars, and a fair share of prosperity is with them they will go out of office having had a good Administration."[21]

Rogers took political positions that cut across the grain of standard-issue big-government, social reform progressivism, on the one hand, and fiscally responsible, entrepreneur friendly conservatism, on the other. He opposed Republican tax cuts in the prosperous 1920s until the large national debt was paid off. "When is the time to pay off a debt if it is not when you are doing well?" Rogers wrote.

"When we die, we want everything we have left clear and unencumbered [for our children] .... [B]ut when it comes to COLLECTIVELY, why it looks like we will break our neck to see HOW MUCH we can leave them owing." But the humorist also opposed progressive social reformers who pointed to poverty or emotional disabilities as mitigating factors in criminal behavior. "An ape can go through life and never be murdered or robbed by its own kind, but in Chicago no man has ever been able to live there long enough to die of old age," Rogers wrote. "Pork used to be Chicago's chief commodity; now automatic pistols and floral offerings are its leading industries." Criminals should be thrown in jail, he insisted, adding sarcastically, "but of course that is out of the question – that's barbarous, and takes us back, as the hysterics say, to the days before Civilization." He offered a dictum: "A liberal is a man who wants to use his own ideas on things in preference to [earlier] generations who, he knows, know more than he does."[22]

What defined Rogers' idiosyncratic political posture, one that avoided endorsing socialism and fascism, the Democrats and the Republicans? As his commentary unfolded, it gradually became clear that he stood squarely in the tradition of American populism, a movement on behalf of the ordinary citizen originating in the Jacksonian age and stretching through the Populist Party of the late 1800s into the early 1900s. The deep regard for the well-being of common people that anchored Rogers' understanding of the "American soul" had a strong political dimension, and he expressed it clearly in his views on public affairs. The humorist insisted that the interests of ordinary folk should guide American political deliberations, cheering when it did and jeering when it did not. In 1923, after attending a banquet of prominent public figures at the Waldorf in New York, Rogers told readers in his *Weekly Article*, "Nobody said a word for you but me. I tell you, the more I hear these big men talk, the more I realize I am the only one that is trying to uphold the rights of the common People." In the best populist tradition, the Oklahoman advocated for capitalism and individualism and competition, but insisted that it should work fairly. He believed in giving the little guy a fair shot at succeeding.[23]

Rogers' politics encompassed several tried-and-true populist traditions. First, he advocated curbing the "money power," those powerful institutions of modern finance that dominated modern America's economy. He believed they exerted unfair influence on competition and achievement and placed banks and Wall Street financiers at the top of the list. Rogers often disparaged the "Wall Street millionaire." He once noted that a newspaper headline described three men being arrested for racehorse betting while an adjoining column blared "Wall Street stock market reaches another four million; call money is the highest in its history." His caustic conclusion: "You don't have to look much further in the paper for humor than that." Bankers fared little better in his assessment due to their encouragement of easy credit and debt. "If you think it ain't a Sucker Game, why is your Banker the richest man in your Town? Why is your Bank the biggest and finest building in your Town," the humorist noted. "You will say, what will all the Bankers do? I don't care what they do. Let 'em go to work, if there is any job any of them could earn a living at." In 1924 Rogers proposed a hefty sales tax on the sale of luxury items. In his words, "You do that, and let the working man know the rich have paid before they got it and you will do more than any one thing to settle some of the unrest and dissatisfaction you hear every day – not by the Reds or Bolsheviki, or even Pinks, but by real citizens and everyday people of this country."[24]

An advocate of the long-time populist belief in "producerism," Rogers decried stockbrokers and bankers as parasites who made nothing useful but shuffled paper and manipulated the system to make huge profits. Upon hearing that Wall Street was adding 275 additional seats to the stock exchange, he suggested they run an ad in the newspapers: "No training, no conscience necessary; all you need is six hundred thousand dollars, but you get it back the first good day." In 1922, when Rogers addressed a convention of bankers in New York, his humor had an unusual bite:

> Loan Sharks and interest hounds: I have addressed every form of organized graft in the United States, excepting Congress, so it's naturally a pleasure for me to appear before the biggest. You are without a doubt the most disgustingly rich audience I have ever talked to, with the possible exception of the bootleggers union, local number one .... I see where your convention was opened by a prayer. You had to send outside your ranks to get somebody that knew how to pray. You should have had one creditor here. He'd shown you how to pray. I noticed in the prayer the clergyman announced to the Almighty that the bankers were here. Well, it wasn't exactly an announcement. It was more in the nature of a warning. He didn't tell the devil, as he figured he knew where you all were all the time anyhow.

When a downward spike in the stock market caused concern in 1924, Rogers reacted with mock horror. "They had to keep open 20 minutes longer," he wrote. "Just think of the inconvenience of the brokers having to wait until 20 minutes after 3 pm in raking in more dough. It is one of the worst personal hardships that the Exchange members has gone through in ten years. Wall Street men missed golf games that hadn't missed them in years."[25]

Rogers' populist criticism of banking and finance pushed him to a broader critique of early twentieth-century American prosperity. He concluded it had been constructed on a weak foundation of widespread debt. "No nation in the history of the world was ever sitting as pretty. If we want anything, all we have to do is go and buy it on credit," he wrote in 1928. "So that leaves us without any economic problems whatever except perhaps someday to have to pay for them." Moreover, the ranks of the prosperous included too few ordinary working citizens, many of whom struggled to survive and never saw the inside of a bank. The beneficiaries of abundance simply ignored such privation, Rogers asserted, as they indulged in amusements and reveled in abundance. He described the depressing results in humorous language. "There hasent been a Thomas Jefferson produced in this country since we formed our first Trust. Rail splitting produced an immortal President in Abraham Lincoln; but Golf, with 20 thousand courses, hasent produced even a good A Number-1 Congressman," Rogers asserted. "There hasent been a Patrick Henry showed up since businessmen quit eating lunch with their families, joined a club and have indigestion from amateur Oratory." One of his *Daily Telegrams* offered a pungent conclusion: "Truly, Rome never saw such prosperity."[26]

In the best tradition of populism, Rogers paid special attention to the plight of American farmers. For decades, the industrial revolution and mechanization had squeezed tillers of the soil with pressures to buy more acreage and procure tractors and harvesters. The result was mounting debt from loans, increased production creating falling prices, and expanded fees from the railroads to bring crops to market. Rural outrage had exploded with the Populist Party in the 1890s and now Rogers continued the protest. He wrote constantly of how farmers appealed to Congress for assistance "to pay some Interest on the second or third Mortgages.... [E]very time somebody has thought of relief for him it has been to make it so he could borrow more money. That's what's the matter with him now. What he needs is some way to pay [it] back." Drowning in debt, the farmer was weighted down by an "abundance of interest .... It's the thought of the old Mortgages that keep him awake at night." At one point, Rogers suggested sarcastically that American farmers negotiate with their own government in the same manner as foreign allies (and borrowers) during World War I and to "get the same liberal terms to pay for their homesteaded land, and their grazing taxes, ... and [mortgages]." Perhaps the most debilitating rural problem was sharecropping, which put poor farmers in thrall to wealthy landowners. "The poorest class of people in this country is the renter farmer, or the ones that tends the little patch of ground on shares," Rogers noted. "He is in debt from one crop to the other to the store keeper, or the little local bank. He never has a dollar that he can call his own. City people don't realize the poverty of poor country folks."[27]

Like populists since the 1800s, Rogers argued that a corrupt political process too often failed common people. He denounced elected officials for a long list of sins. Their oversized egos demanded attention and there was "no other line of business that any of them could get in where they would get one-tenth part of the publicity that they get in public office, and how they love it! Talk about actors. Actors basking in the limelight! Say, an old Senator can make an actor look like he is hid under a barrel." Elected politicians sought shortcuts to wealth and power. Republicans, as with the Teapot Dome scandals of the Harding Administration, were "supposed to have perfected it up to the high standard that it occupies today," but Democrats had initiated political corruption "in what was called Tammany Hall. But a good thing can't be restricted and is bound to spread." Because of the spread of corruption throughout the political system, Rogers proposed establishing a "School of Public Testimony" where newly elected officials would be prepared for the inevitable investigation and subsequent appearance on the courtroom stand. The humorist promised, "We will teach 'em not to be nervous, not to let the other fellow get 'em rattled, and have 'em all trained to tell where they got every dollar they used in their campaign and how much they paid for each vote."[28]

Rogers believed that a penchant for party loyalty and partisan machinations undermined the public good and neglected the interests of ordinary citizens. In a *Weekly Article* titled "Most Politicians Are Chore Boys For Men Higher Up," he contended that most politicians were "pawns" for powerful bosses who manipulated them in the interest of the party and the "poor nut don't know if he is to be advanced from an alderman to Senator or sent back to garbage inspector. These babies at the head move him and he goes and likes it or gets out." As for legislation and public policy, it emerged not from calculations of social or economic need but "by the aid of swaps and trades. They are just a lot of horse traders. 'You help me put over my new Post Office and I will help you get your creek widened.'" Too often the politician's goal was to get "enough Government loot to be re-elected." A politician's success came from an ability to "hornswoggle the Government out of something ... for some kind of a scheme for his own district's special benefit. A man that looked after the interests of the majority in politics wouldent even be nominated the second time." Rogers concluded, "[T]his country runs in spite of parties; in fact, parties are the biggest handicap we have to contend with. If we dident have to stop to play politics any administration could almost make a Garden of Eden out of us."[29]

While Rogers' political commentary focused on socioeconomic interests and partisan competition, he occasionally touched on emerging social issues in American public life. As a typical populist, he tended to combine traditional values with a spirit of humane reformism. The Oklahoman's comments on African Americans, for instance, expressed both a casual racism, particularly in his use of language, and an enlightened desire for racial equality. It is not surprising that the son of a Confederate officer and slaveowner harbored a dismissive, sometimes disparaging view of Black citizens that peeked through his humorous cracks. As a young man visiting South Africa, he had written letters home describing "niggers," a racist pejorative he also used on occasion in letters and conversation. When Rogers visited the Tuskegee Institute in the 1920s, he was impressed by "the Harvard of the Ethiopian race" and "the glorious tradition of Booker T. Washington." But he expressed it in condescending and paternalistic language. "After 4 years there they straighten your hair and your English both," he wrote. "I met all the head men and the Professors of the Institute. No Southern Darkey talk among them. You would think you were conversing with the Boston Historical Society. They spoke such good English I couldn't understand 'em."[30]

At the same time, Rogers' humane instincts nudged him toward abandonment of racial discrimination. He had grown up nurtured by Black farmers and cowboys in the Claremore area while his vaudeville and *Ziegfeld Follies* career brought him into contact with Black entertainers such as Bert Williams, with whom he developed a warm friendship. When his sister, Maud, died in 1925, he wrote of her funeral in a *Weekly Article*, "I wish you could have seen the Negroes at her home on the day of the Funeral. Before her death, she said, 'They are my folks, they have helped me for years, they are all my friends. When I am gone I don't want you Children at my Funeral to show any preference.' That's the real South's real feelings for its real friends ... . Death draws no color line." Two years later, Rogers argued with genuine feeling that one of the worst impacts of the great Mississippi flood came with "the thousands and thousands of negroes that never did have much, but now it's washed away. You don't want to forget that water is just as high up on them as it is if they were white. The Lord so constituted everybody that no matter what color you are you require about the same amount of nourishment."[31]

Rogers spoke out against the resurgence of the Ku Klux Klan in the 1910s and 1920s, a trend that particularly roiled the Democratic Party. He pilloried Democratic Senator Tom Heflin of Alabama, who had filibustered the Senate for over five hours with a tirade against Blacks and Catholics. "That's a record for narrow views," Rogers quipped. "Tonight in his home capital I am pleading with Alabama not to exterminate all Catholics, Republicans, Jews, negroes ... . Of course my plea will do no good, for Tom knows the intelligence of his constituency better than we do." At the marathon Democratic Convention in 1924, the delegates held a heated debate over the Ku Klux Klan, which resulted in the adoption of a plank narrowly condemning "violence" in domestic politics rather than the KKK by name. A disgusted Rogers wrote, "Saturday will always remain burned in my memory as long as I live, as being the day when I heard the most religion preached, and the least practiced, of any day in the world's history." Newspaper columnist Heywood Broun praised Rogers for his stance, claiming "No man is better equipped to fight the Klan with useful weapons. He knows those people from the ground up. I think he could kid the Klan out of existence."[32]

In a similar vein, the humorist advocated for religious tolerance. During the Scopes Trial, he chastised Protestant fundamentalists such as William Jennings

Bryan for stirring up "religious hatred" and trying to impose their beliefs on the education system. Rogers observed that people around the world had different religious beliefs but a wise God "was pretty wise when he did see to it that they all do agree on one thing (whether Christian, Heathen, or Mohammedan) and that is the better lives you live the better you will finish." Rogers consistently denounced the anti-Semitism and anti-Catholicism promoted by "100% Americanism" crusaders even as he utilized certain denigrating stereotypes in doing so. In his first syndicated *Weekly Article* in late 1922, he noted that the Ku Klux Klan had appeared in New York and made it clear they "kinder got it in for the Jewish People. Now, they are wrong. I am against that. If the Jewish People here in New York hadent jumped in and made themselves good fellows and helped us Celebrate our Xmas, The thing would have fell flat. They sold us every present." In 1928, Rogers defended Democratic presidential candidate Al Smith from anti-Catholic attacks. The Oklahoman claimed that the Jewish population of New York had supported Smith for two terms as governor and "Any time they let you run their State, the State where they own 90% of the stock – if the Jews can trust you with New York where they own everything, I see no reason why us Protestants couldn't trust him." Rogers made his ultimate point when he declared of Smith, "What do we care about a man's religion? We don't want to be saved spiritually, we want to be dragged out of the hole financially."[33]

On the issue of women's rights, which had gained national attention in the drive for female suffrage, Rogers' jokes barely muffled his staunch traditionalism regarding the proper position for the sexes. He tended to value women most when they were ensconced in the home pursuing marriage and motherhood. While the "Ziegfeld Girls" were acceptable as entertainment, Rogers disapproved of youthful flappers in the 1920s who fled customary roles and adopted risqué attire. Hemlines rose so high that "It was just legs, legs, legs. The whole country had gone legs," Rogers joked. "[W]e woke up one morning with thousands of knees staring us in the face .... We would have thought much more of 'em, both morally and artistically, if they had just kept 'em covered." In contrast, he reflected on two of his sisters in small-town Oklahoma who were devoted to raising their children, bolstering their families, and bettering their communities. "They have carried on the same as thousands of Women have carried on in every small and Big Town in the World," he wrote. "They don't want credit. They do good simply because they don't know any other thing to do." He made fun of Winifred Valentino when she separated from husband Rudolf, the heartthrob actor Rudolf, declaring her need for a "marital vacation" because "a Woman with an active mind needs a wider outlet for her energy. She needs business or a profession." Rogers facetiously found a larger lesson in her action. "There you are, happily married women; this just shows you what a lot of saps you are," he claimed. "You Women at home haven't got any more mind than a Billy Goat. If your mind was active you would jump up and take a 'marital vacation' from your husband. Put on a Turban and go to France." Bringing his anti-elitism to bear, Rogers argued that "the brightest and most active brains have belonged to our everyday Women who you never heard saying very much, but if you talked with them you would soon see they had pretty sound ideas on about everything."[34]

Given such traditional views, it was not surprising that Rogers was skeptical of the crusade for women's right to vote. Once again, humor barely masked his old-fashioned paternalism. The push for the Nineteenth Amendment granting female suffrage, finally successful in 1920, Rogers wrote, "not only caused millions of men to go hungry (by their wives being away at a rally), but it is causing a lot of them to go Jobless, all because the whole thing was a misunderstanding. The men give 'em the vote, and never meant for them to take it seriously. But being Women they took the wrong meaning and did." Females, Rogers believed, were ill-suited to the political arena: "It gets 'em out and gives 'em a chance to get away from home, and wear badges. But it just seems like they havent added anything constructive to the art of Politics." Moreover, women were just as bad as men with "terrible campaign speeches .... You expect a man to make a poor speech, for he has been doing it for years, he don't know any better. He is supposed to be boring or he wouldn't be a Speaker. But we did kinder look for something out of the Women when they entered the political arena." In 1924, riffing on a recent wave of wives shooting their husbands, Rogers claimed that "Remington, and Smith and Wesson, have done more to advance the cause of women's suffrage than all the arguments of its millions of believers," he wrote. "If you see a woman or young girl at a shooting gallery . . . you will know at once that she is engaged, and is practicing for the inevitable."[35]

Rogers' political commentary was not restricted to domestic affairs. His travels abroad also produced a flood of pieces on American foreign policy and international affairs, where he emerged as an opponent of internationalism and foreign intervention. Here he stood as an heir to a populist tradition of isolationism, first articulated during the agrarian uprising in the late 1800s and recapitulated with World War I, when many populists expressed skepticism of American involvement. The populist aversion to imperialism and colonialism was wrapped up with its suspicions of the "money power" and aristocratic European governments, both of which promised to exploit foreign adventurism. As one historian has explained, "To the good Populist, imperialism was doubly accursed – appeal though it might to his national pride – because it was held to benefit the capitalist and the Wall Streeter rather than the nation at large, and because it was too strongly imitative of the British example."[36]

Rogers clearly expressed this tradition with his consistent opposition to foreign interventions by the United States, most of which he saw as protecting the financial profits of American corporations and financiers who had invested abroad. "[W]hat the Devil business is it of ours how some other Country runs their business?" he wrote. "America has a great habit of always talking about protecting American interests in some foreign Country. PROTECT 'EM HERE AT HOME! .... If America is not good enough for you to live in and make money in why then you are privileged to go to some other Country. But don't ask for protection from a Country that was not good enough for you." When certain American politicians urged the American government to cross the border and clean up Mexican border towns such as Tijuana, Rogers burst out, "For the love of Mike, why don't we let Mexico alone and let them run their country the way they want to! Americans only go there to make money .... So if you go down there, don't start yapping for America to protect you. Nobody shanghied you and took you there." When American gunboats were sent to China and the Marines landed in Nicaragua in the mid-1920s, Rogers despaired:

> Lord, if we would only let everybody live and act and do as they pleased (I mean of course as long as what they did did not interfere with any one else), why she sure would be a great old World. But every day you meet a Delegation going to some Convention to try and change the way of somebody else's life. I really believe if they took the badges off everybody and made them belong to nothing but their own homes and people, that the world would in a short time change its name from Earth to Heaven.[37]

At the same time, Rogers' views on foreign affairs, as on domestic affairs, did not always fit the usual lines of partisan division. While opposed to foreign interventions, he thought progressive peace initiatives such as the League of Nations and disarmament conferences were a waste of time. "I am only an ignorant cowpuncher, but there ain't nobody on earth, I don't care how smart they are, ever going to make me believe they will ever stop wars," he declared. "In fact, every war has been preceded by a peace conference. That's what always starts the next war." When a disarmament agreement at the Washington Conference of 1921–1922 led the United States to scuttle one of its greatest battleships, the U. S. S. *Washington*, Rogers sarcastically praised this innovation because, "You see, up to then, battleships had always been sunk by the enemy." He appealed to President Coolidge to muzzle any officials who promoted such conventions and "just for the novelty of the thing tend to our own business for a while. We take up with ideas so quick, I bet you it wouldent be any time before we would begin liking taking care of our own business." Similarly, Rogers resented that the United States' European allies did not appreciate its crucial intervention in World War I and insisted that England and France must repay their war loans. He urged the American government to tell those nations, "You don't seem to think you owe us anything . . . But listen, if we wasn't worth anything in this War, why don't expect us in the next one."[38]

So unlike many populists who agitated for reform schemes both at home and abroad, Rogers adopted a more realistic, prudential position. He believed that government should pass legislation to promote the public good, enforce the laws, guarantee equal treatment for all citizens, and keep an eye on the welfare of ordinary citizens. Inspired by a powerful faith in common people, he concluded that the best policy was to avoid partisan wrangling and let them freely pursue their own version of happiness. In a 1928 *Weekly Article* entitled "Politics is a Disease," Rogers joked that Democrats and Republicans tried to convince voters that "for either opponent to get in would return the whole country to Slavery, Free Silver, 'empty dinner pail,' long skirts, bustles, and suspenders" and bring calamity in its wake. But ordinary citizens knew better than to take politics too seriously. Neither warnings of disaster or high-minded moral appeals swayed them. As the endless debate over prohibition illustrated, most people simply "want to be let alone and are tired of listening to both sides." Rogers even praised Calvin Coolidge, contending that he was "the first president to discover that what the American people want is to be let alone." Displaying a forbearance and skepticism typical of many common folk, Rogers concluded, "Every time we have an election we get in worse men, and the country keeps right on going. Time has only proven one thing, and that is that you can't ruin this country even with politics."[39]

As the Oklahoman's shrewd, witty political commentary gained millions of adherents during the 1920s, his relationship with readers and listeners took an interesting turn. Attention began to shift away from the objects of his criticism and onto the humorist himself. Will Rogers became a political figure.

* * * * *

Rogers' political musings gained a host of favorable assessments from critics and political experts, a trend that helped send his reputation soaring in American public life. Addressing the Oklahoman's impact in 1925, the *Nation* concluded, "His droll comments on men and events have become so popular that he finds himself – probably to his surprise – a national figure." The *Buffalo Evening Times* described him as a "statesman," noting that "little by little, the sound common-sense back of his sallies has begun to attract the sober-minded attention of the country . . . . [I]f the Senate and the House and other branches of the government were manned with Americans like Will Rogers, some of the world's problems and some of ours would reach a speedy, sensible, and satisfactory conclusion." The *New York Times* pointed out that in ancient Athens, one of the high tides of democracy, politics had been illuminated by comedic commentary, a practice now adopted by the cowboy humorist who was "carrying on the tradition of Aristophanes, and not unworthily." Journalist L. H. Robbins stated flatly that Rogers was "the most potent individual influence in America in matters not only political but civic and social . . . . [and] in his daily squibs and his radio talks produced American opinion." A review of *Letters of a Self-Made Diplomat to His President,* concluded that "there has rarely been an American humorist whose words produced less empty laughter or more sober thought . . . . Will Rogers is much more than a funny man . . . . [His writing] embalms, as a fly in amber, the essence of America's involved relationship to Europe."[40]

Such acclaim eventually produced attempts to lure Rogers into the political arena as a candidate. Some were serious, others half-serious, and a few outright jokes. But they shared an underlying sense that the humorist understood ordinary American voters and had captured public sentiment on many issues and attitudes. Rogers himself occasionally joked about launching a political career. "I was born on election day, but never was able to get elected to anything," he wrote in a *Weekly Article.* "I am going to jump out some day and be indefinate enough about everything that they will call me a politician, then run on a platform of question marks, and be elected unanimously, then reach in the treasury and bring back my district a new bridge, or tunnell, or dam, and I will be a statesman."[41]

In 1924, Rogers received two votes for the presidential nomination at the 1924 Democratic convention. He relished this unexpected development for its comic implications, praising the two delegates "who showed intelligence far above their fellow inmates of Madison Square Garden last summer, and put into nomination that sterling statesman, and fearless leader, yours truly!" He lamented his failure to become the standard bearer, noting that victory would have brought a campaign between "Mr. Coolidge and common sense, versus William Penn Adair Rogers and no sense at all (which is even more prevalent in this country than common sense)." Had he been nominated, Rogers declared, he would have abandoned the traditional ploy of promising to lower taxes. Instead, he would have announced, "Folks, I don't believe I will be able to save you anything. Taxes are going to be high and the only thing I would advise you to do is not to have anything, because if you do have anything they will tax it away from you and you won't have anything anyway. So why have anything in the first place[?]"[42]

Periodically, serious talk popped up about electing Rogers to political office. In 1925, C. N. Haskell, former governor of Oklahoma, joined the Democrat Central Committee in Rogers County, where Claremore was located, in nominating the humorist for president. Their letter praised "the high character and ability of Will Rogers. He is the greatest available asset of the democratic party and of our country." In the same year, other Oklahomans publicly discussed putting him forward for the governorship of the state. As this ferment bubbled, Rogers finally felt compelled to address the situation. In a lighthearted letter to former Oklahoma Congressman James Davenport, one of his boosters, he wrote, "Why do you want to slander me? I was going along in my own way and not bothering anybody when you and some accomplices headed a black cat across my trail .... Jim, I couldn't be a Politician in a million years." In the late 1920s, talk again surfaced about putting Rogers forward for the presidency. He read a newspaper report about such activity and decided to reply publicly. Such proposals when done as a joke were "all right, but when it's done seriously it's just pathetic .... [T]he country hasn't quite got to the professional comedian stage," he wrote in his syndicated *Daily Telegram*. "There is no inducement that would make me foolish enough to ever run for political office. I want to be on the outside where I can be friends and joke about all of them, even the President."[43]

In late fall of 1926, Rogers' political popularity found a humorous, and highly publicized outlet. After returning from Europe and while busy crisscrossing the United States on a lecture tour, the humorist received a telegram from Douglas Fairbanks, the famous actor who was his neighbor in Hollywood. The message informed Rogers that local civic leaders and prominent citizens had chosen him to be honorary "mayor" of Beverly Hills. Such an office did not exist and the city fathers had cooked up the ploy as a publicity stunt, but it was played out to the hilt. When Rogers returned home with his family on December 21, he was met at the train station by a group of dignitaries and a full-blown parade, complete with a motorcade, political banners, and cheering crowds, took him to a platform erected in a park near the Beverly Hills Hotel. Amidst much gaiety and speechifying amidst a rain shower, the humorist was inaugurated as mayor and offered remarks that, predictably, made fun of the political process. He was not the first "Comedian Mayor," Rogers declared, since any mayor he had ever seen was automatically funny. He claimed that Beverly Hills had everything required of a good town – "Burglars, Poor parking regulations, shortage of water in the summer, poor Telephone service, Luncheon clubs" – except a good mayor. "Now I don't say I will give the old Burg an honest administration, but I will at least split 50-50 with you .... I'm for the common people, and as Beverly Hills has no common people I won't have to pass out any favors," Rogers told the crowd.[44]

For the next several months, Rogers pumped the comic potential attending his new political position for all it was worth. He thanked the host of national luminaries who sent him telegrams of congratulations – they included President Calvin Coolidge, Governor Al Smith, Mayor Jimmy Walker, Senator Hiram Johnson – and promised to staff the city administration with movie stars "so there will be no chance of a scandal." He mock-reviewed the city's police officers and fire fighters as they stood at attention, grinning. When Rogers left town on another lecture tour, he appointed Charlie Chaplin, who was mired in a controversial divorce, as acting mayor because he was "temporarily out of a wife, and can therefore devote all his humor to the office." After noting a political scandal in a nearby town, he described himself as the "Mayor who won't give up his seat in Beverly Hills without being bought off." Upon returning to his city filled with movie stars, he lamented that his office had become "clogged with divorces. Have to get rid of some of them before we can have any new marriages." Throughout, Rogers signed his *Daily Telegrams* with variations of his title: "His Honor the Mayor Beverly Hills," "The Meandering Mayor," "The Neutral Mayor." When the California state legislature passed a bill in late summer 1922 stipulating that in level-six municipalities such as Beverly Hills the chairman of the board of trustees would serve as mayor, Rogers was deposed from his fictitious office. Shortly thereafter he claimed to have become president of the national "Ex-Mayors' Association, an earnest bunch of men . . . all placed where they are by the honesty of the ballot. What this country needs is more ex-Mayors."[45]

Later that year, another indication of Rogers' political stature came when the National Press Club elected him "Congressman-at-Large." The humorist confessed to readers, "I knew I wouldent be out of a job long after they threw me out as Mayor." In its proclamation, the organization noted that several esteemed lawyers had concluded that according to the Constitution all powers not expressly reserved to the federal government were to be exercised by the National Press Club. So it thereby appointed "Mr. Rogers Congressman-at-large for the United States of America, his duties being to roam over the country, pry into the state of the Union, check up on Prohibition enforcement, and report at regular intervals to the National Press Club."[46]

In 1928, Rogers reached the highwater mark of his *faux* political career when he ran for president as the nominee of the Anti-Bunk Party. Robert Sherwood, editor of *Life*, a popular humor magazine in the 1920s, concocted the idea of a facetious presidential campaign and contacted the Oklahoman, who agreed to participate and suggested a name for the new political party. On May 17, *Life* ran an editorial titled "What This Country Needs is a Bunkless Party" and denounced both Republicans and Democrats for dodging issues, relying on bromides, and feathering their own nests. It concluded by suggesting the need for a third party and "a bunkless candidate who will run for President on an honest, courageous, and reasonably intelligent platform." An editorial the following week announced that a straw poll had produced an overwhelming majority for Will Rogers so the magazine offered him the nomination and urged him to embrace one purpose: "To fight Bunk in all its forms. If Rogers wants more of a platform than that, he can write it himself." The humorist completed the ploy the following week by accepting the nomination. The offer "leaves me dazed, and if I can stay dazed

I ought to make a splendid Candidate," he wrote. Rogers promised the main plank of his platform would be "WHATEVER THE OTHER FELLOW DON'T DO WE WILL" and vowed that his campaign would eliminate slogans since "Slogans have been more harmful to the country than the Bo-Weevil, Luncheon Clubs, Sand Fleas, Detours, Conventions, and Golf Pants." He concluded his acceptance remarks by pledging "IF ELECTED I ABSOLUTELY AND POSITIVELY AGREE TO RESIGN … . That's offering the Country more than any Candidate ever offered it in the entire History of its existence."[47]

Over the next six months Rogers and *Life* worked the campaign's comedy angle for all it was worth. They put forward as the primary advertising slogan "He Chews to Run," a clever combination of Calvin Coolidge's famous 1928 statement "I do not choose to run" and Rogers' equally famous affinity for chewing gum. They printed campaign posters emblazoned with the description "The only politician who is funny intentionally." *Life* published Rogers' campaign pronouncements every week and paid him 500 dollars per essay, although the candidate's interest occasionally lulled and the editor would have to imitate the Oklahoman's writing style to fill in the sketchy outlines he submitted. Rogers established the populist keynote of his campaign early on, describing his effort as an attempt to "show my touch with the common people by coming and mingling right with 'em … . But I don't care how common they are – they ain't any commoner than I am."[48]

As the campaign unfolded in the summer and fall of 1928, the humorist delighted in skewering the deceptions, ploys, and partisan bickering of the political system. Denouncing the "same old Applesauce" of parties describing their nominees as poor boys who had worked hard to overcome adversity and rise to eminence, Rogers urged a more honest statement from speechmakers: "Ladies and Gentleman, the man I am about to name is the son of a rich man. He has never done a tap of work in his life that anyone knows of. He just wants the job for it looks like the easiest one in sight." The Oklahoman vowed to eliminate all forms of "bunk" from his presidential campaign, including conventions ("if our Constituents couldent make a fool out of themselves at home, there was no reason for them to go away to places like Kansas City and Houston and practice"), badges ("Wearing badges has ruined more people than Toupees"), and sex appeal ("they'll have to stop printing my picture in the paper. That's final.") When Democrat and Republican spokesmen praised modern voters for being impervious to manipulation because of their superior intelligence and knowledge – meaning, of course, that they were too smart to vote for the opposing party – Rogers dissented. "We read more and we hear more over the radio, but the stuff we read and the stuff we hear don't make us any smarter. For the people that write it, and the ones that talk it out over the radio are no smarter than the ones that used to hand down the dope for our old forefathers," he wrote. "So the old Bunk that you can't fool the voter is the biggest Bunk there is. He has been fooled all his life and he will always be fooled." When both Democrats and Republicans tried to straddle the Prohibition issue to avoid alienating "Wets" and "Drys," Rogers offered his own solution: "Wine for the Rich, Beer for the Poor, and Moonshine Liquor for the Prohibitionists."[49]

Rogers frequently joked about the superficial, evasive statements quality of the mainline candidates, Secretary of Commerce Herbert Hoover for the Republicans and Governor Al Smith of New York for the Democrats. The humorist dismissed Hoover's claims of American prosperity, cracking "I will show where we are NOT prosperous because we haven't PAID for it YET." He noted Smith's endorsement of minimally lowering the tariff, drolly characterizing it as a case where "since the Republicans have shown the Tariff will work, why the Democrats kinder have to say, 'We are still 'agin it, but not as much as we were.'" When Hoover and Smith courted the farmer's vote, Rogers rhetorically rolled his eyes, claiming "Al can hand the farmer a couple of Subway tickets, and Hoover slip him a Blueprint [for farm reorganization], and that's all either one can really deliver to the farmer. I am the only Candidate that is running on either side that has ever looked a Mule in the face (or otherwise) down a corn row." Overall, Rogers claimed that voters faced a better alternative with the Anti-Bunk Party, an organization "for the benefit of those that want NOTHING and have a reasonable expectation of getting it."[50]

Despite its jocular tone, there was an underlying seriousness to Rogers' presidential campaign that revealed both his personal appeal and dissatisfaction with the regular course of modern American politics. Notable public figures stepped forward to back the campaign. Judge Ben B. Lindsey, a prominent progressive reformer, endorsed Rogers not "because he makes us laugh, but because he really knows us and he knows what he is talking about ... . The people trust Will. They believe in him. They love him as they did Lincoln ... . [T]hey had what this country needs: genuine honesty; freedom from cant, hypocrisy, and sham; the courage of true independence." "The joke of Will Rogers' candidacy for President is that it is no joke," wrote Henry Ford in a public letter. "It is a serious attempt to restore American common sense to American politics." A number of newspapers around the country offered editorial support. "*Life* is staging a playful campaign of Will Rogers for President, but we're not so sure the idea is only a joke. Why not put him over in earnest?" said the *Chicago Evening Post*. "His is the humor of common sense; his comments are funny because they are true." The *Wilmington News Dispatch* reflected, "Probably Mr. Rogers would get very vexed, very vexed indeed, at the implication that anyone was taking him seriously . . . . But we can't help but do just that. It is impossible to hide sound political judgment and a commonsensical outlook even under the bushel-basket of humor and levity."[51]

Perhaps the most interesting assessment of Rogers' candidacy came from the pen of the essayist, novelist, and editor, Dorothy Van Doren, writing in the pages of the esteemed political journal, *The Nation*. In place of the "stale windiness" of regular political discourse, she contended, the humorist's campaign generated "wind of a refreshing sort. The Rogers wind blows cobwebs away, cobwebs that both the major parties have been guilty of weaving." Van Doren described Rogers as a truth-teller who understood that politics had become a business, and like any other business it was implicated in the flashy, often misleading, promises characteristic of a modern culture of commerce, advertising, and entertainment:

> This is the Age of Bunk. We eat it with our cereal at breakfast, we ride to work with it posted before our eyes, we see it in movies at night, we hear it over the radio. Bunk is the American staple of existence. In love, in war, in work, in play it is busy making things seem what they almost certainly are not. Bunk greases the wheels of industry; bunk furnishes the home. Mr. Rogers . . . is not the first man to see that bunk colors politics as well as everything else in American life. The truth of the matter is that the American people like bunk, they choose it deliberately, it is the breath of life to them.

But Rogers, despite such obstacles, obviously delighted in being a "debunker" and the fact that he spared no one his barbs but delivered them evenhandedly and with great good humor made him a very popular figure. Van Doren wished him the best in his campaign, although he had no hope (or expectation) of winning. Perhaps his greatest contribution, she concluded, lay in the fact that "thousands of Americans are giving thanks to Mr. Rogers for providing the one cheerful note in an otherwise trying political campaign."[52]

As the election date drew near, Rogers admitted his chances of victory were slim, joking, "So I may be defeated next Tuesday, but if I am I can retire as a Gentleman and NOT a politician." When the returns showed that Hoover decisively defeated his opponents and won the presidency, the Oklahoman issued a statement declaring, "Well, I am not downhearted. I know that 1932 is coming and by that time they may have new plumbing in the White House . . . so it will be more desirable quarters for me and my family. In the meantime, I'm working so [you] don't need to worry. Politics is a side-line with me. It's not a business."[53]

Thus Rogers did not win any political office, and never seriously attempted to do so. And his commentary on politics never abandoned light-heartedness for high seriousness, thus depriving it of the acclaim and prestige that would attend the sober assessments of a Walter Lippman or a William Allen White. Nonetheless, Rogers did acquire a profound political influence among a host of ordinary Americans who saw in his efforts a healthy combination of skepticism and humorous good will. He promoted the well-being of common citizens in a fashion that nurtured mutual respect and forbearance in public life. While the specific issues and policy disputes of his age have faded into the historical past, Rogers' sensibility about public debate and discussion has survived. He nurtured an approach toward public issues that was critical yet charitable, principled yet magnanimous, serious in its assessment yet genial in its expression. Endorsing a civic tradition crucial to the survival of America's heritage of republican government, Rogers thought and wrote as a connoisseur of civility.

* * * * *

As a performer on stage, screen, and lecture hall and a writer for newspapers and magazines, Will Rogers ran a serious risk when he ventured into political commentary. His vast audience, like the United States itself, harbored adherents to both political parties and a host of competing social, cultural, ideological, and geographical loyalties. So political cracks, no matter their target, threatened to alienate a portion of listeners or readers and drown the humor in political contention. Betty Rogers often warned her husband to be careful with his quips about politicians and partisan issues. "I was inclined to worry over Will's informality in talking about public men," she explained. "I was afraid he would go too far and that someone would take offense, and I thought he should be more careful." Indeed, Rogers keenly appreciated that entertainers had to be careful to not take advantage of their popularity by attempting to become political gurus. "We are paid by an audience to entertain them, not to instruct them politically. While the things you say may please one part of your audience it may displease the other part, and as one pays just as much to get in as another, we want to be friendly with each," he wrote in a *Weekly Article*. "So distribute your compliments and your knocks so when the audience go out they don't know where you are politically."[54]

The Oklahoman overcame such obstacles and prospered as a political commentator because of an inner saving grace. Amid the flurry of jabs and quips about American political failings, he conveyed, consistently and genuinely, a respect for his fellow citizens and their feelings and opinions that transcended partisan disputes. As he frequently told his lecture audiences when discussing public affairs, "[D]on't ever form a dislike for a fellow because you don't agree with him . . . . Now, don't disagree with him looking at him; walk around behind him and see the way he's looking." Rogers did not make politics personal. He did not endorse hate or engage in moral condemnation. He avoided insults and steered wide of pontification. Even when they had an edge, his points were delivered with a smile that inspired chuckles, not glares; embodied a sense of human failing rather than a revelation of evil; and nurtured a belief in pragmatism and problem solving, not ideological purity or superiority. Audiences quickly grasped that for the cowboy humorist, politics was an endeavor for genial discussion, not a blood sport.[55]

Rogers once addressed politicians directly as he explained his strategy in joking about them. "I don't play any favorites," he said. "I haven't got it in for anybody or anything. They are all great sometimes and they are all terrible sometimes. None of you are perfect, and so I just lay for you till some of your little imperfections crop up and remind you of them." Moreover, the humorist made a point of kidding those on top of the partisan game rather than those struggling on the bottom. When President Harding made clear his annoyance with Rogers' jokes about him and his administration, the entertainer addressed the controversy during an appearance at the *Ziegfeld Follies*. He told the audience, "You folks know I never mean anything by the cracks I make here on politics. I generally hit the fellow that's on top because it isn't fair to hit the fellow that's down. I played here five times during the Wilson administration and every time Mr. Wilson came and laughed at the cracks I made at him more than he did at those I made against the other fellow." Then Rogers gently chided Harding for his sensitivity: "If a big man laughs at jokes on him, he's all right." But when Harding died a short time later, Rogers made a point of affirming the late president's humanity. He wrote in his *Weekly Article*, "I liked President Harding. You see, I had met him, and I don't believe any man could meet him and talk to him and not like him . . . . [H]e was a good friend to ALL kinds of people. For he had the right dope after all. Everybody is JUST FOLKS."[56]

In fact, Rogers publicly admitted to liking nearly every politician he met, despite how he may have pilloried some of their actions or attitudes. "You know I like to make little jokes and kid about the Senators. They are a kind of a never ending source of amusement, amazement, and Discouragement. But the Rascals, when you meet 'em face to face and know 'em, they are mighty nice fellows," he confessed to readers in 1929. "When you see what they do officially you want to shoot 'em, but when one looks at you and grins so innocently, why you kinder want to kiss him." Rogers spoke similarly a year earlier when he poked fun at several prominent politicians in a public lecture and then admitted to the audience, "I like all of them, that's the thing. There ain't a candidate I could mention that ain't a good friend of mine. I go around and tell jokes about all of them, but ... I hate to see anyone get defeated ... . Here's what I want on my tombstone: 'I've joked about every prominent man in my time but I never met a man that I didn't like.'" He remained committed to approaching politics with a combination of good will and good humor. "I don't think I ever hurt any man's feelings by my little gags. I know I never willfully did it," he wrote in 1923. "When I have to do that to make a living I will quit. I may not have always said just what they would have liked me to say but they knew it was meant in good nature."[57]

So while Rogers took politics seriously, he never made it the centerpiece of existence. Rather than politicizing every issue that came before the American public, he encouraged his fellow citizens to spend their energy on the meaningful stuff of life – family, friends, community, rewarding work, fulfilling hobbies – and realize that most politics was an annoying, often amusing, distraction that mattered little in the long run. Most politicians were trying their best, he argued, and the citizenry should celebrate their successes and laugh at their shortcomings. And much comfort came from the American Constitutional order that kept bad impulses in check and guaranteed basic rights. In Rogers' words,

Election is here in a couple of days and a lot of people lose a lot of sleep and get all heated up over it, and Politicians will spout off to you that if such and such a man is not elected that will mean sure destruction to the whole country. Now just stop and figure, ever since we have had this Government why some man has been in there as President. Sometimes he belonged to one party and sometimes to another. Now what I want to know is what difference did it make to the country? Every man America has ever had in that high exalted position has done the very best he possibly could, and to their credit not a one has ever done bad. We haven't been ruined under a single one of their administrations . . . . There is no less sickness, no less Earthquakes, no less Progress, no less Inventions, no less morality, no less Christianity under one than the other . . . .

Our government is so arranged that no President could do any harm even if he wanted to. We have a Congress that is all powerful. We have in addition a Supreme Court, to see that Congress don't go on a tear . . . . [The candidates] are all good Americans and have the interests of this country at heart . . . . I don't think we will be ruined Tuesday no matter who is elected, so the Politicians will have to wait four more years to tell us who will ruin us then.[58]

So for Rogers, politics was not an arena for displays of moral superiority, smugness, and condescension or the settling of scores or the reaping of advantages. It was a human activity much like any other that was fraught with foolishness and idealism, fragility and purpose, squandered opportunities and delightful achievements. Politics, in the Oklahoman's view, demanded a recognition of others' humanity and a respect for their views, even if you disagreed with them. In the end, what lay at the heart of Rogers' civility was his humor. He always delivered his political jabs with a smile, thereby removing the sting from what otherwise might have angered or offended. After the predictably huge win for President Calvin Coolidge in the 1924 contest, for example, Rogers noted, "they just held an election but nobody knows WHY. It cost this country millions of dollars just to see how many votes Mr. Coolidge could beat Mr. Davis and Mr. LaFollette by. It would be just like putting me in the ring with [heavyweight champion] Jack Dempsey. Everybody would say, 'Why Dempsey will knock him clear out of the ring,' and the promoter would say, 'Yes, but come and pay your money and see how far out of the ring he will knock him.'" As the *Nation* noted of such jibes, "It is just as well for Mr. Rogers that his caustic observations are wrapped in humor. If they were delivered without the funny tags, his audience would set the dogs on him."[59]

But of course, it was not just political commentary that featured Rogers' comic touch. Humor permeated all of the many endeavors – stage shows, Hollywood movies, documentary films, radio broadcasts, magazine and news-paper writing – through which he reached his massive audience. A brilliant talent for finding mirth in nearly every nook and cranny of American life was crucial to making him a folk hero to so many of his fellow citizens. This genius for comedic observation stamped the entertainer as a unique and compelling figure. But Rogers' humor can only be understood, like nearly every aspect of his life and career, by examining the complex elements that went into it.

Plate 1 "Clem Rogers, Will Rogers' father and a prominent figure among the Oklahoma Cherokees, never quite reconciled his hard-working, ambitious mindset with that of his fun-loving, personable son." (Courtesy of Will Rogers Memorial Museum)

Plate 2 "Mary America Schrimsher Rogers, Will Rogers' mother, conveyed her charming personality and keen sense of humor to the youngest among her five children." (Courtesy of Will Rogers Memorial Museum)

Plate 3 "A youthful Will Rogers with his cousin, Charlie McClellan, a devotee of traditional Cherokee customs and values." (Courtesy of Will Rogers Memorial Museum)

Plate 4 "Rogers as a cadet at the Kemper School, a military academy, before his antics led to one among many early departures from academic institutions." (Courtesy of Will Rogers Memorial Museum)

Plate 5 "Rogers (far right) with Texas Jack (far left), the cowboy entertainer in South Africa who first drew the young American into the show business world as a lariat performer." (Courtesy of Will Rogers Memorial Museum)

Plate 6 "Rogers on Comanche (left), the first of his stalwart show horses, with Colonel Mulhall's troupe at the St. Louis World's Fair in 1904." (Courtesy of Will Rogers Memorial Museum)

Plate 7 "Rogers' awkward courtship of Betty Blake was reflected in this Claremore youth outing, where she remained seated head-on-hand in the front seat of the wagon while he perched uneasily at the far rear." (Courtesy of Will Rogers Memorial Museum)

Plate 8 "Rogers amuses his fellow performers by encasing the entire cast of a vaudeville show in his trademark 'big crinoline' lariat throw." (Courtesy of Will Rogers Memorial Museum)

Plate 9 "In this publicity photo, Rogers appears as the winsome cowboy star of the vaudeville stage." (Courtesy of Will Rogers Memorial Museum)

Plate 10 "Florenz Ziegfeld, the suave, forceful impresario whose wildly popular shows featured lavish sets, entertainment revues, and alluring images of 'the American girl.'" (Courtesy of Archive PL/Alamy Stock Photo)

Plate 11 "Rogers surrounded by the beautiful females of the *Ziegfeld Follies*, the show that first brought the Oklahoma entertainer before a national audience." (Courtesy of Will Rogers Memorial Museum)

Plate 12 "Rogers in *The Ropin' Fool*, a silent cinematic short that showcased his formidable lariat skills." (Courtesy of Will Rogers Memorial Museum)

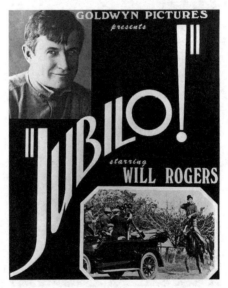

Plate 13 "Rogers' burgeoning career in silent films produced publicity photos such as this for *Jubilo*, his most popular silent movie effort." (Courtesy of Will Rogers Memorial Museum)

Plate 14 "Following his move to Hollywood as a silent film star, Rogers and his family took up residence in this Beverly Hills home, complete with playground and riding ring." (Courtesy of Will Rogers Memorial Museum)

Plate 15 "Will and Betty Rogers with their three children (l to r), Jim, Will Jr., and Mary." (Courtesy of Will Rogers Memorial Museum)

Plate 16 "The Rogers' sprawling home on their 350-acre ranch in the Santa Monica Mountains." (Courtesy of Will Rogers Memorial Museum)

Plate 17 "The living room of the Rogers ranch home with its colorful western décor." (Courtesy of Will Rogers Memorial Museum)

Plate 18 "Rogers in the heat of a polo match, here dressed in the sport's traditional garb instead of his usual haphazard cowboy attire." (Courtesy of Will Rogers Memorial Museum)

Plate 19 "A recurring scene of Rogers pounding out a newspaper column in his car while taking a break on the set of one of his movies." (Courtesy of Will Rogers Memorial Museum)

Plate 20 "Rogers chatting with William Jennings Bryan, the humorist's admirable symbol of a vanishing American past, at the 1924 Republican convention." (Courtesy of Will Rogers Memorial Museum)

Plate 21 "Rogers attending the 1933 World Series with Henry Ford (center), the industrialist who best reflected the Oklahoman's view of a dynamic American present, and the automaker's son, Edsel (right)." (Courtesy of Will Rogers Memorial Museum)

Plate 22 "Rogers with Charles Lindbergh, the heroic pilot he admired as a representative of America's promising future." (Courtesy of Will Rogers Memorial Museum)

Plate 23 "Rogers preparing to address a studio audience during the national broadcast of his popular radio show for NBC, *The Gulf Headliners*." (Courtesy of Will Rogers Memorial Museum)

Plate 24 "Rogers joking with the large, boisterous crowd who gathered to proclaim him the honorary Mayor of Beverly Hills." (Courtesy of Will Rogers Memorial Museum)

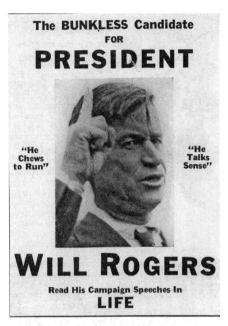

Plate 25 "A flyer promoting Rogers' facetious run for the presidency as candidate of the Anti-Bunk Party ticket in 1928." (Courtesy of Will Rogers Memorial Museum)

Plate 26 "Rogers cracks up Democratic presidential candidate Franklin Roosevelt (far left) and other political dignitaries in 1932 with a humorous introduction at a large political rally in Los Angeles." (Courtesy of Will Rogers Memorial Museum)

Plate 27 "Rogers socializing with John Nance Garner, the hard-drinking, no-nonsense Texan whose long Congressional career prefaced his service as FDR's vice-president." (Courtesy of Will Rogers Memorial Museum)

Plate 28 "Rogers chatting with his best friend, the dynamic, multi-talented entertainer, Fred Stone." (Courtesy of Will Rogers Memorial Museum)

Plate 29 "Rogers with Blue Boy, his porcine co-star, in *State Fair*, one of the talking films that propelled the Oklahoman to Hollywood stardom in the 1930s." (Courtesy of Will Rogers Memorial Museum)

Plate 30 "In the movie, *Handy Andy*, an outlandishly outfitted Rogers indulged one of his favorite comic themes, mocking America's fondness for golf." (Courtesy of Will Rogers Memorial Museum)

Plate 31 "Rogers conferring on set with two good friends, the humorist Irvin S. Cobb (middle), and director John Ford (right), all of whom worked together on the films *Judge Priest* (1934) and *Steamboat 'Round the Bend* (1935)." (Courtesy of Will Rogers Memorial Museum)

Plate 32 "One aspect of the beloved Rogers image – the personable, good-natured humorist who never met a man he didn't like." (Courtesy of Will Rogers Memorial Museum)

Plate 33 "Another aspect of the Rogers image – the wise village sage who explained America to itself." (Courtesy of Will Rogers Memorial Museum)

Plate 34 "Rogers on his first, exhilarating airplane flight in Atlantic City in 1915." (Courtesy of Will Rogers Memorial Museum)

Plate 35 "This cover illustration for one of Rogers' books underlined his vision of airplane flight as a modern frontier full of opportunities for a new kind of cowboy." (Courtesy of Will Rogers Memorial Museum)

Plate 36 "Rogers (standing on the wing) and the legendary pilot, Wiley Post, (autographing while standing on the pontoon) greeting admirers during their final, fateful flight in Alaska in 1935." (Courtesy of Will Rogers Memorial Museum)

9

The Unfunny Business of Trying To Be Funny

HUMOR IS A FUNNY THING. WE KNOW IT WHEN WE SEE or hear it, but beyond making us smile or laugh it is hard to pin down exactly what it is. Mirth may be a basic human impulse, but what *is* it that makes something funny? Other human reactions are relatively straightforward – we howl in pain, hug or kiss in love, run in fear, fight or shout in anger – but why we chuckle or belly-laugh at something or someone seems much tougher to characterize. What is funny to one person is not to another. What is funny in some contexts is not in others. What is funny in some cultures is not at all in others. Robert Darnton, in his brilliant examination of popular culture during the Enlightenment, *The Great Cat Massacre*, related that Parisian apprentices in the 1730s rounded up every cat they could find, held mock trials, and then beat and hanged the defenseless animals, an exercise they found so hilarious they reenacted it several times to gales of laughter. What modern eyes see as horrifying they saw as amusing because, Darnton explained, cats had become a special affectation of the bour-geoisie in the eighteenth century and killing them was a humorous, indirect way for mistreated workers to mock their hated masters and mistresses. Clearly, humor is a very elusive human trait.[1]

Even trying to make sense of humor can be self-defeating. Long ago Jonathan Swift warned about the difficulty in analyzing mirth, writing "What Humor is, not all the Tribe/Of Logic-mongers can describe." E. B. White agreed, asserting, "Humor can be dissected, as a frog can, but the thing dies in the process and the innards are discouraging to any but the purely scientific mind." Groucho Marx expressed this incongruity with typical pithiness: "Humor is reason gone mad." Nonetheless, psychologists, philosophers, and anthropologists have put their shoulders to the task and posited several explanations for the appeal of humor: "Superiority Theory," which locates humor in others' misfortunes and shortcom-ings; "Relief Theory," which suggests that it provides a release valve for our deepest emotional desires; "Incongruity Theory," which argues that humor arises from surprising situations or personalities that violate our expectations; and "Benign Violation Theory," which roots humor in situations that initially seem unsettling or dangerously wrong but turn out to be harmless, a realization that relieves stress. Each of these theories might explain one or two of the many varieties of humor – wit, put downs, sarcasm, slapstick, satire, burlesque – but a universal paradigm remains unrealized.[2]

Whatever its essence, the impulse to joke and laugh, many commentators agree, has played a special role in the cultural development of the United States. "We have one priceless universal trait, we Americans," William Faulkner noted. "That trait is our humor." Indeed, the uniquely fluid qualities of American social and cultural life – social mobility, democratic norms, anti-elitist impulses, free speech – has fostered a persistent irreverence regarding traditions, institutions, and authority. Wits and raconteurs have consistently subjected government, religion, education, the law, moral codes, and social norms to satire, joking dismissal, and mockery. Observing this panorama of riotous jocularity, Constance Rourke, in her groundbreaking *American Humor: A Study of the National Character* (1931), concluded, "There is scarcely an aspect of the American character to which humor is not related, few which in some sense it has not governed." Many other studies have explored the influence of the absurd, pluralism, the frontier, and ethnicity on why Americans laugh and what they laugh at.[3]

All of which suggests the complex problems facing anyone trying to make sense of the most constant feature of Will Rogers' multi-faceted career: humor. Several questions demand attention. What made him so funny for so long to so many of his readers and listeners? What was the nature of his humor and what kind of functions did it perform? Did Rogers' humor follow in well-worn paths of earlier comedic practitioners or did it branch off to become something new and unique? The answers to these queries were woven into the fabric of Rogers' life, from his boyhood in the Cherokee Territory of Oklahoma through his days in vaudeville and the *Ziegfeld Follies* through his stint in Hollywood and writing for a national audience of newspaper and magazine readers. They tell us much about Rogers, but even more about his fellow Americans in the early twentieth century.

* * * * *

As Rogers' career took off in the late 1910s and he became one of the best-known and most popular figures in the United States, many observers rushed to anoint him the leading American humorist of the early twentieth century. Publications competed in portraying his comic genius. The *Nation* described Rogers as "a humorous philosopher, a cowboy Montaigne and all-around sly bird . . . . Mr. Rogers never forgets he is a licensed fool at the court of Prosperity, and he takes all the liberties which are allowed a king's jester." *Everybody's* magazine observed that while Mark Twain had taught Americans to jeer at Europeans and H. L. Mencken had taught them to jeer at themselves, the Oklahoman avoided such maneuvers and never "abused his power, and perhaps that is one of the chief reasons he possesses so much of it." The *Dearborn Independent* termed him "one of the few original comedians on the stage" while *Current Opinion* contended, "Back of his droll exaggerations there lurks a soundness of judgment which cuts deeply into the most sacred superstitions and exposes with genial sarcasm a good many human frailties. Will Rogers is a clown, but he is also a philosopher." After seeing Rogers perform in person, the *New York Times* concluded, you realized "he put it over in the only language and intonation possible, and he said something keen and penetrating and true. All in the name of gawky, innocent, country-jake amateurishness." "He is the greatest monologist America has ever known . . . . a philosopher who has given the wise-crack the dignity of a Socratic maxim," concluded the *Tulsa Daily World*.[4]

As for Rogers himself, he modestly shied away from acclaiming his comedic efforts. "I have been over 20 years trying to kid the great American Public out of a few loose giggles now and again," he wrote in a 1925 *Weekly Article*. "Somebody had to act the fool, and I happened to be one of the many that picked out that unfunny business of trying to be funny." Likewise, he avoided waxing philosophical about the deeper meaning or import of his humor. When an earnest college reporter asked Rogers how one prepared to be a humorist, the Oklahoman replied, "Recovery from a mule kick is one that's used a lot. Being dropped head downward on a pavement in youth has been responsible for a lot. And discharge from an asylum for mental cases is almost sure fire." His assertion in 1923 – "The way to judge a good Comedy is by how long it will last and have people talk about it" – was about as deeply as he ever delved into the significance of his humorous endeavors.[5]

Yet for Rogers the creation of comedy was more than a lark. As he declared in 1924, "[N]othing is so funny as something done in all seriousness." While Rogers wanted to make people laugh, he also wanted them to think. His friend, Homer Croy, reported that in one of Rogers' films, there was a humorous scene based on the Oklahoman putting on and taking off a series of women's hats. In rehearsal, the director oversaw several versions of the scene but none of them worked. Finally, a frustrated Rogers declared, "I can't be funny with 'props.' I can only be funny with ideas." The scene was cut, and Croy concluded that the actor's comment "was the very bedrock of his comedy. He could be funny only with ideas." In a spate of interviews and off-hand remarks, Rogers discussed the elements that went into his conception of comedy. Most of his comments pertained to his live appearances on the stage or lecture platform, where he appeared deceptively spontaneous, seeming to deliver a steady stream of off-the-cuff quips and jibes when, in fact, enormous work went into creating the appearance that a joke just came to him. In a 1917 reflection in *The Theatre* magazine titled "The Extemporaneous Line," Rogers disclosed how he scoured the newspapers daily unearthing material and then painstakingly prepared a large number of gags. He then went before the audience with a rough idea of what he wanted to say, but if the response was "no good then I have to switch quick and lots of times when I come off the stage I have done an entirely different act from what I intended." Years later, at the height of his career, Rogers was interviewed by a staff writer for the *New Republic*, who noticed in his dressing room a sheet in the typewriter containing seven or eight versions of the same quip. But once on stage, the writer related, Rogers stopped during monologue and "chuckled as though a thought suddenly struck him at that minute and repeated the final version of the joke verbatim."[6]

Two years later, in the *American Magazine*, Rogers explained the comic elements that he mixed into the jokes for his vaudeville and the *Ziegfeld Follies* acts. First, he relied upon topical humor, and the more recent the better, because "I found that they would laugh easiest at the stuff that had just happened that day. A joke don't have to be near as funny if it's up to date." Second, in his observations he always endeavored "to try and keep to the truth. Of course, you can exaggerate it, but what you say must be based on truth." Third, he tried to avoid jokes that were "broad as a house and require no thought at all. I like one where, if you are with a friend and hear it, it makes you think and you nudge your friend and say, 'He's right about that.'" Fourth, he went for concise quips and cracks and avoided meandering stories because "Being brief somehow gives the impression of intelligence and folks do admire intelligence. Brevity and clarity show that you have thought, and that you know what you're about." Finally, he aimed his humor at common folk and not sophisticates and anything "over the average man's head is no go." If the jokes don't come across, Rogers told the interviewer, he doesn't blame the audience "but gives himself a pretty careful looking over to see if maybe the fault doesn't happen to be with him."[7]

In 1923, Rogers spoke with *Popular Science* magazine, where the interviewer probed for his thoughts on "The Science of Laughter." Next to a medical drawing showing the human torso and the "Laughter Machinery" of the human body, complete with "elevating" and "depressing" muscles attached to the rib cage and the diaphragm, the Oklahoman mused on the why's and wherefore's of laughter. "People need to laugh to keep their minds and bodies in good running order. It's a relaxation," Rogers said. "It gives people a fresh start, with the slate wiped clean of past aches and worries, that is to say the physical and mental atmosphere is wiped clean." Rogers also discussed his live-appearance tactic of creating suspense in his audience and then leading them to the punch line. In his words, "The best humorist is the one who knows just when to open the safety valve of laughter." Upon reflection, the humorist recalled that perhaps his most receptive audience ever came at Sing Sing Penitentiary, where the inmates kept him on stage for an hour-and-a-half and laughed uproariously at his quips. The imprisoned criminal "is ready to laugh. He needs to laugh," Rogers ventured. "A loud guffaw is a relief from his oppressive surroundings." *Popular Science* noted that Rogers fell in line with the most recent scientific findings about laughter, which stressed that laughter "gives vent to emotions that have long been repressed .... . Psychologically laughter interrupts gloomy trains of thought and morbid preoccupations. It uses up our reserve stores of energy, both muscular and nervous. It rebuilds worn cells in our system. It relieves our nervous tension."[8]

Talking with Henry Ford's *Dearborn Independent* and *Everybody's* magazine in 1925, Rogers expanded upon certain aspects of his comedic technique. He noted that he never used "profane" or "malicious" jokes in his act and explained that long-winded, meandering stories about "Scotchmen, traveling salesmen, stage-door Johnnies, and the rest of the stock characters are on my blacklist .... . Every time I see a story-teller coming I try to sneak away and if I can't make it I shut both ears. You can't stop 'em once they get the habit of repeating stories." Rogers explained that he was able to address bankers, scientists, businessmen, and politicians and joke about their foibles without hurting their feelings because his comments always contained a kernel of truth but were delivered with a light touch. "I don't jump on them and bawl them out the way a lot of public speakers do," he said. "I just sort of kid 'em along – as if I knew all their secrets and there wasn't any use for 'em to try to keep anything back on me." Finally, Rogers rejected the humorist-as-fool image. "A comedian is not supposed to be serious nor to know much. As long as he is silly enough to get laughs, why, people let it go at that," he remarked. "But I claim you have to have a serious streak in you or you can't see the funny side in the other fellow."[9]

The humor of Rogers' stage performances depended heavily on stylistic elements – the down-home observations made with a drawl and a grin; a scruffy appearance augmented by a head-scratching, gum-chewing, head-shaking manner; a habit of walking around the stage, sitting on its lip, and establishing a conversational intimacy with the audience. In addition, as with most skilled entertainers, he possessed an innate sense of comic rhythm in making a joke to an audience. "Will had a wonderful sense of timing and never hurried into the middle of a laugh," a lecture assistant noted. "[He] makes a statement, then another, then a third. All together, they make perfectly good sense, and are often funny, so that your mouth widens toward a smile. Then, after the briefest pause, comes a sudden final thrust of wit which explodes the whole business as if it were gunpowder." Admiring these on-stage skills, a newspaper critic noted that with the Oklahoman, "the written word does not have the effectiveness of the spoken word. Will Rogers' deliberately slow and easy-going drawl and his very confidential tone of voice makes his remarks sound much funnier than they seem in type."[10]

Nonetheless, the greatest impact of Rogers' humor came from his voluminous writing in newspapers and magazines. He reached thousands of people in his vaudeville and *Ziegfeld Follies* acts, lectures, and tens of thousands in his silent movies of the 1920s, talking movies of the 1930s, and radio show. But he reached millions of readers on a recurring basis in his syndicated *Daily Telegrams* and *Weekly Articles* and numerous magazine articles, and it is there that his humor flowered most effectively for a mass American audience. Readers got the best taste of the cowboy humorist's themes and tactics, and it was in the pages of newspapers and magazines where he most tickled the nation's funny bone.

* * * * *

Rogers seemed to find humor in nearly every aspect of American life. As he addressed a massive audience of readers with short daily quips and longer weekly essays beginning in the early 1920s, he joked about the weather and toothaches, the Ku Klux Klan and women's makeup, advertising slogans and sermon topics, the stock market and the World Series. Politics and public affairs, of course, provided much grist for his comic mill as he ransacked the newspapers for events and personalities at which he could poke fun. Presidents and Senators, disarmament experiments and federal agriculture policy, urban political machines and political party maneuvers fell under his comic spotlight. But amidst this avalanche of humorous observation the habits, inclinations, and preoccupations of Americans in their daily life provided perhaps the purest topics for Rogers' comic imagination. Examining his fellow citizens with a keen eye and a chuckle, he made them laugh at many of their own peculiarities.

Rogers, for instance, frequently touched upon the subject of golf, which seemed to epitomize for him the silliness, even absurdity, of modern life. In a *Weekly Article* entitled "What America Needs Is Better Putters," he confessed that he had grown up knowing nothing of the game and first encountered it when he rented a house on Long Island and saw people walking around in a beautiful field "following a boy carrying a gunny sack full of bats, and they were always changing. They never seemed able to make up their minds just which bat to use constantly." When Rogers moved to California and bought a house near a Golf Club, the real estate agent explained this as a sign "we were exclusive, and we have been. We have never been in the place." So one day he decided to watch a golf tournament and upon arriving at the course and seeing some friends, hollered out a greeting. In his words, "you would have thought I had tried to assassinate President Coolidge. There were many hands layed on me, and 500 SHUSHES, for me to be quiet. If a fellow had done the Charleston at a funeral he could have committed no worse social blunder." Then Rogers saw everyone staring at him and discovered "It was my clothes. I had attended the game in long pants. I was as out of place as if I had on a ballet skirt." As for the game itself, he was baffled to learn that each player had his own ball, which compared to every other sport he had ever seen seemed to muddle the competition. In his words, "It's the only game outside Solitaire where you play alone." Rogers never quite got the hang of how the game was played, and decided that watching a player on a golf course "is just like seeing somebody handling a Ukalalie. You can't tell whether they are playing it or just monkeying with it." The humorist was struck ultimately by "the amount of skill [players] had developed in getting near the hole, and how little they displayed getting into it." For a cowboy who grew up breaking horses and herding cattle, whacking a little white ball and then chasing it through the countryside epitomized America in the throes of prosperity and frivolity. He succeeded in prompting Americans to laugh at this example of their new leisure culture.[11]

In another essay, Rogers alighted on divorce, another feature of modern life that seemed to be occurring with ever greater frequency. But the Oklahoman was particularly interested in a wrinkle he had noticed in this larger social trend: divorced individuals returning to their first spouses. He envisioned men being motivated by a pang of conscience while women said, "Where is old John? He was too ornery to kill, but at that he was better than the last ones." Rogers predicted that if the trend reconciling first spouses gathered steam, a chaotic social scene would ensue similar to the mad railroad scramble of "changing cars at a Union Station." But, given the proclivities of modern Americans, it was probably inevitable. As Rogers explained, "I bet you every woman that was first married to a man believes in her own heart that she is still the only one he ever really loved, and he, poor conceited thing, thinks the same about her." Rogers predicted that once they were back together, however, original married couples would quickly face a dilemma. In his words, "So who will be the first one to start the original fight over again? You have had all these years to think up an answer." Typical of the cowboy humorist, this piece poked fun both at human nature and, more slyly, the present's assumption of its superiority over the past.[12]

Rogers addressed another travail of modern society when he penned a *Weekly Article* called "How a Murder Should Be Advertised." American cities, he suggested facetiously, were missing an opportunity to take advantage of the surge in urban violence to showcase themselves. In Detroit, he claimed that city luminaries complained that while their crime statistics were just as big as Chicago's they were "not getting one tenth the publicity out of it. They were becoming discouraged." Rogers quoted one of them: "What's the use of having all these robberies and killings? No one ever reads about them. Chicago seems to be the only place most people think that can put on a murder." Rogers informed them that it was a matter of advertising. In the past, Chicago had been celebrated for its massive stock yards in the same way that Detroit was known as a producer of motor cars. As the Oklahoman put it, "When you thought of Chicago you thought of a dead cow, or a stuck pig, and when you think of Detroit it's of Henry Ford's Incubator, and a stuck customer." But more recently the Windy City had begun to play up its murder rate and especially underlined its "Machine Guns . . . [since] the novelty of the weapon has as much to do with it as the prominence of the ones annihilated. Detroit is still shooting with pistols." Rogers suggested that Detroiters pick out their most colorful murders and promote them, and it would be best to find ones involving women, church members, and scandal, and follow that up with plenty of photographs for the tabloids. "Then you will have it on Chicago," the humorist declared about this scheme. "This is a day and time of progress, and new things . . . . and you just notice from now on if you don't see an improvement in publicity with Detroit's crime. They won't have to increase it. It's just getting it known."[13]

In 1929, Rogers devoted a *Weekly Article* to the modern penchant for science and statistics. In "The Lady Mosquito is Busy, Thanks," he examined a recent speech by a prominent scientist but quickly turned matters into a humorous reflection on men and women. The chief entomologist ("I don't know what it means, either," said Rogers) for the state addressed a convention of the New Jersey Exterminators' Association ("If they have got such a Society, what have they been doing?") and the Oklahoman was struck by his statement, "The normal productivity of one lone Female house Mosquito in one year is 159,875,000,000 offspring." Rogers noted, first, that this figure reflected a modern tendency where "everything is figured out down to a Gnat's tooth according to some kind of statistics," and second, that the figure was in the "BILLIONS." But the entomologist's next assertion – that half of the mosquito population were "the active, buzzing, biting, and egg-laying females" while the other half were inactive males – illuminated the human condition, Roger claimed. "You Mothers that think you have done something for your race when you have brought into the World 2 to 8 or 10 young Hyenas, you certainly can't boast after reading what the Female Mosquito has done to leave her imprint on the ankles of humanity," he wrote. At the same time, the inability of the masculine mosquitos to bite, buzz, and annoy "makes me proud I am a Male." Rogers saw two problems in this entire situation: an inability to distinguish between male and female mosquitos for extermination purposes (the former has "gone through life acting in a

Gentlemanly way, and here it is killed"), and the crying need to distribute "Pamphlets for the Female Mosquitos on Birth Control. Show them that they are not only doing their part but they are going over their Quota." Meanwhile, people should try their best to examine mosquitos closely. Rogers offered guidelines: if it bites, sings, or lays an egg it is a female mosquito; "if [it] just sits around all day and don't do anything, why about the only conclusion we can come to is that it is a HE. Don't kill him, he does no harm, he just sits and revels in the accomplishments of his Wife."[14]

Rogers turned to a familiar site for a humorous piece on the Sulphur springs near his hometown of Claremore, Oklahoma. Immersion in these therapeutic waters, he declared in a send-up of promotions for miraculous remedies, would heal all maladies, "just name your disease and dive in." Rogers noted that if you were from Minneapolis "it will cure you of everything but your Swedish accent." Those from Kansas City, being used to the awful odors of the stockyards, could embrace the sulphurous smell and "take this wonderful water home as a per- fume." If you were a southerner and "afflicted with a cotton crop under a Republican administration, or with the Klu Klux Klan, or with the hookworm, we guarantee to rid you of either or all of these in a course of 24 baths." He provided helpful directions for pilgrims seeking this miracle site from different parts of the United States. Those journeying from the east would find Claremore 1,700 miles southwest of New York City just past "Sos McClellan's place;" from the north it was 847 and a half miles from Gary, Indiana, Chicago, [where] many people come [to] from Chicago seeking recovery from gunshot wounds; if from the west, 1,900 miles from Mojave, California, "one of the few towns" not swallowed up by Los Angeles; and from the south, only 905 miles from the "mint beds in Mississippi." For those interested in how these miracle waters were discovered, Rogers informed them that years ago a man arrived "who had been raised in Kansas and he had heard in a round-about-way of people bathing, although he had never taken one." This individual was one-armed, having lost his limb "in a rush to get into a Chautauqua tent to hear [William Jennings] Bryan speak," and decided to immerse himself in the water. Upon getting out, "he noticed that he was beginning to sprout a new arm" and excitedly spread the word of the water's curative powers. Thus use of the springs was credited to a man now famous as "the pioneer of bathers in Kansas, as they now tell me it's no uncommon thing to have a tub in most of their larger towns." At the same time, caution was in order because one visitor arrived "entirely legless and stayed a week too long and went away a centipede." Rogers concluded with a personal testimonial. He had been tongue-tied as a young man, but after taking a dozen baths he was soon in New York making after-dinner speeches. But "had I taken 24 baths I would have been a politician, so you see I stopped just in time."[15]

In such fashion, Rogers joked about the vagaries and eccentricities, troubling trends and intriguing inclinations of modern American life. But he did not do so in a comic vacuum. A long tradition of American humor preceded the Oklahoman's efforts as a battery of comic writers and performers in the 1800s and early 1900s established a style that consistently amused a national audience. Rogers followed the precepts of this tradition in many ways but departed from them in others. His vast audience appreciated both.

* * * * *

Americans, since their colonial days, loved humor and accorded it a prominent place in their culture. "Ours is a land of kidding," noted the *New York Times*. "We laugh things off. We get square with the iniquities of reality by grinning at them, and we make prophets and privileged characters of those who assist us in grinning." In a country ruled by flux and change, by a penchant for individual liberty and a skepticism of institutions, scoffing at sacred cows and laughing at life's oddities were national pastimes. Jokes became an American language. Citizens of the youthful, energetic republic looked at humor with such awe and respect, even reverence, that the *Nation* concluded, "Most of us would rather be funny than rich."[16]

The great river of American humor displayed various streams and tributaries. In *American Humor: A Study of the National Character* (1931), Constance Rourke identified three comic types that rooted themselves early on in the national consciousness: the Yankee peddler, the backwoodsman, and the blackface minstrel. In various ways, their humor worked to undermine tradition, level obstacles, and subvert moral codes and social expectations. L. H. Robbins, longtime writer and critic for the *New York Times*, argued a few years later that such figures had converged to create an "American brand of humor" with several distinctive features:

> *First*, a good-natured but somewhat disillusioned point of view; *second*, spiritual emancipation from conventionality, and a boisterous, iconoclastic impudence toward self-conscious propriety, coupled with a decent respect for things and persons really respectable; *third*, a humane partiality for plain folk and the crowd, and a disposition to take robust liberties with the dignity of their superiors; *fourth*, 'studied idiocy,' or a deliberate leaning toward unconscious humor; *fifth*, spontaneous association of incongruities; *sixth*, shocking drops from the sublime to the ridiculous; and *seventh*, keen perception of truth, offset by exaggeration amounting to mendacity.[17]

In the early 1900s, under the influence of urban growth, massive immigration from eastern and southern Europe, and the popularity of vaudeville, some American humorists were seeking laughs in the ethnic tribulations and high-pressured demands of city life. Yet an old-fashioned strain of mirth-making kept a powerful hold on many Americans: the homespun, cracker-barrel tradition, which summoned images of the rustic sage sitting around the woodstove with his cronies cracking wise about the foibles, peculiarities, and pretensions of society and its inhabitants. Walter Blair, scholar of American folklore and humor, described it as "horse sense" jocularity, one that emerged as the United States expanded west and south in the nineteenth century and spread by word-of-mouth and in newspapers before finding its way into books and on-stage by the late 1800s. This native humor relied on common-sense observation, homespun philosophy, and practical experience to fuel its pungent quips, rollicking scorn, and gumptious cracks. Horse-sense was the opposite of book-sense and a humorous off-shoot of what De Tocqueville identified as the unspoken "philosophical tradition" of Americans: "to evade the bondage of system and habit, of family maxims, class opinions . . . to accept tradition only as a means of information . . . . to seek the reason of things for oneself, and in oneself alone, to tend to results without being bound to the means." The *Saturday Review of Literature* agreed, declaring that in terms of humor, "We Americans have had a long tradition of philosophers in homespun."[18]

Several popular figures exemplified America's native homespun humor. In the eighteenth century, Benjamin Franklin's "Poor Richard" appeared as a small-town sage whose aphorisms mixed practical advice on success ("A penny saved is a penny earned") with funny reflections ("Keep your eyes wide open before marriage; half-shut afterwards"). "Major Jack Downing," the Yankee villager and observer created by journalist Sheba Smith in the 1830s, set Americans laughing with his impudent cracks about the problems and possibilities of American democracy. Boston Brahmin James Russell Lowell's invention, the New England farmer "Hosea Biglow," employed Yankee dialect to humorously criticize politics in verse form. "Artemus Ward," the *nom de plume* of humorist Charles Farrar Browne and a favorite of President Abraham Lincoln, was an uneducated bumpkin who specialized in misspellings, malapropisms, and bad puns in parodies of public life and political disputes. David Ross Locke, under the pseudonym "Petroleum Vesuvius Nasby," drew laughs by employing this crude, ignorant figure to spout ardent, but nonsensical support for Southern slavery. Henry Wheeler Shaw's character, "Josh Billings," used slang and eccentric spelling in shaping folksy jokes about commonplace problems in American life. Finley Peter Dunne's "Mr. Dooley," the Irish saloonkeeper in Chicago who amused countless readers in the 1890s with his down-home wit, honored the tradition of the common-man quipster while replacing the rustic rube with a recently Americanized foreigner.[19]

The greatest exemplar of the homespun humorist appeared in the persona of Mark Twain, the pen name of Samuel Langhorne Clemens. His earliest comic pieces appeared during the Civil War and many of them were stamped with the influence of the American West, particularly the mining camps and mushrooming towns of Nevada and California. Subsequent books such as *Innocents Abroad* (1869), which satirized Americans traveling to foreign lands, and *Life on the Mississippi* (1883), a reminiscence of his time spent as a steamboat captain while a young man, continued his evolution as a humorist. Turning to long-form fiction, Twain came to rely upon his native Missouri and the Mississippi River, where he grew up, as the scene for the most beloved of his many novels, *The Adventures of Tom Sawyer* (1876) and *The Adventures of Huckleberry Finn* (1884), which were filled with humorous interludes, characters, and reflections, all coming to life in provincial settings. In addition, Clemens became a mainstay on the lecture circuit in the late 1800s where he polished his personal comic persona of Mark Twain, entertaining countless audiences around the United States emblazoned with white-hair, white-suit, and white-mustache, and brandishing an ever-present cigar while delivering a stream of funny stories and quips with impeccable timing. In almost all of his work, Twain relied upon the tradition of homespun humor with its down-home sensibility and practical mind set. It appeared in the provincial American traveler, in *Innocents Abroad*, who believed he encountered the tomb of Adam in the Holy Land and reported, "I leaned upon a pillar and burst into tears. I deem it no shame to have wept over the grave of my poor dead relative." It appeared when Huck Finn reflected, "What's the use you learning to do right when it's trouble-some to do right and ain't no trouble to do wrong, and the wages is just the same?"

This American parade of rustic, wise-cracking sages often adopted a favorite comedic tactic, what the cultural historian David Reynolds has termed the "little big man" pose. The humorist pretended to be a humble, ignorant hayseed as a ruse to disarm one's audience before delivering a comic gut punch. Reynolds noted that Abraham Lincoln, a noted devotee of homespun humor, frequently employed this tactic in politics to present himself as an uneducated, inexperienced, country bumpkin who could not possibly contend with a sophisticated political opponent shortly before skewering him, usually with a humorous jab, and making him appear elitist, foolish, or corrupt. For example, in his 1858 debates with Stephen Douglas, Lincoln described the influential, egotistical senator as a figure where his backers saw "in his jolly, fruitful face post offices, land offices, marshalships, cabinet appointments, and foreign missions sprouting out in wonderful exuberance ready to be laid hold of by their greedy hands." In contrast, the railsplitter continued, "in my poor, lean, lank face nobody has ever seen that any cabbages were sprouting out." The audience laughed and cheered.[20]

Nearly all of the homespun humorists adopted this effective ploy. Franklin established the tradition with "Poor Richard," a man of little book learning but much practical sense, and his successors embroidered it. "Jack Downing," his creator explained, was "a green, unsophisticated lad from the country" who came into town and illuminated its strange doings for "his friends at home in his own plain language." "Artemus Ward," while appearing the uneducated buffoon with his outlandish misspellings and half-digested knowledge, nonetheless offered nuggets of insight such as "The Puritans nobly fled from a land of freedim, where they could not only enjoy their own religion, but could prevent everybody else from enjoying his." "Mr. Dooley" modified the "I'm just a country boy" persona by substituting "I'm just an ignorant Irishman," and scattering wisdom from his Archey Road saloon: "There are no friends at cards or world politics" and "There's only one thing that would make me allow mesilf to be a hero to the American people, and that is it don't last long." Mark Twain, of course, apotheosized this tactic with his most famous character, Huckleberry Finn, the ragamuffin son of the town drunkard whose provincial attitudes and crude speech generated keen insights into himself as well as the people and society around him. As Huck noted after observing the Duke and the King, two con men encountered on his flight down the river, "All I say is, kings is kings and you got to make allowances, they're a mighty ornery lot. It's the way they're raised." Thus the horse-sense humorists masterfully provided cover for their humorous, yet shrewd, observations about American life and values by having their characters act the fool.[21]

Beginning in the 1910s and continuing over the next two decades, Will Rogers assumed a prominent place in this native comic tradition. He joked his way into the hearts of millions of Americans by developing his own version of the down-home, cracker-barrel style of humor and making it central to his comic commentary. While some American humorists of this era, under the influence of vaudeville and the rapid growth of cities, drifted in the direction of urban sophistication and hard-boiled cynicism in their comedy following World War I, much of the popular taste remained rooted in the past. As one observer concluded after pondering both the written and verbal successes of the Oklahoman's humor, "the old, genial, ingenuous, home-ready sort still wins the big laughs, as Rogers demonstrated." Another magazine critic agreed, arguing that "Will Rogers bred true and was the perfect upcountry philosopher .... To the last dash and comma his tricks were the same and his mind was the same – that combination of a shrewd human philosophy as broad as human nature with a fundamental distrust of everything not made in America." Still another suggested, "He might have been a cracker-barrel philosopher in the hometown grocery store; a local wit whose observations and cynicisms regarding Congress made other loiterers cackle" and whose appeal lay in "definite back-to-the-soil flavor."[22]

Like his predecessors, Rogers mastered the "little big man" pose as a key element in his horse-sense humor. He persuasively, and charmingly, presented himself as a wise fool, a barely literate cowboy who, it gradually became clear, saw into and understood just about everything he encountered. The ruse unfolded with his opening statement first used on stage – "All I know is what I read in the newspapers" – that soon became a defining feature of his *Weekly Articles*. This modest declaration established a self-deprecating tone before the cowboy philosopher deftly moved to illuminate the topic or personality at hand. Talking to a live audience, he utilized a number of famous mannerisms that reinforced the image of the untutored rustic in over his head: the shy grins, vigorous gum chewing, confused gestures, head-scratching, feigned confusion, all of which barely masked the keen intelligence and shrewdness that soon became evident. In his writing, Rogers translated these physical cues into misspellings, awkward sentence constructions, meandering colloquial language, and confessions of ignorance. "Grammar and I get along," he once wrote, combining disclosure with national prejudice, "like a Russian and a bathtub." But he gave some of his game away when he reproved a New York critic with, "I am just an old country boy in a big town trying to get along. I have been eating Pretty regular, and the reason I have been is because I have stayed an old country boy." Similarly, he responded to someone who condemned his poor use of the English language, "Shucks, I didn't know they was buying grammar now. I'm just so dumb I had a notion it was thoughts and ideas." Lowell Thomas, the newsreel star and writer, pointed out the obvious: "The only pose in Will Rogers was the pretense that he was an ignorant and illiterate fellow."[23]

Rogers' success caused many observers to note an especially close kinship with several earlier cracker-barrel American humorists. Some compared him to "Artemus Ward" because of their common tendency to poke fun at politicians, political disputes, and office-seekers and portray them all as absurdities. Others highlighted his similarity to "Mr. Dooley" due to a general lack of reverence for established institutions and a willingness to criticize both political parties and their leaders. Walter Blair underlined the Oklahoman's affinity with "Jack Downing" since both liked to use their encounters with prominent figures as a subject of humor, although the former's were real and the latter's imaginary.[24]

But Rogers was most frequently compared to Mark Twain, perhaps because they stood only a generation apart and both enjoyed mass popularity. Rogers, in fact, had a deep respect for Twain and paid homage to the legendary writer at several points in his career. The younger man began his lecture career by speaking in Elmira, New York, Twain's long-time summer residence and burial place, while his 1926 European travelogue film series was styled loosely on the older man's *Innocents Abroad*. According to Rogers' sons, their father's favorite book was Twain's *Life on the Mississippi*, which he kept on his bedside table. In New Orleans in November 1925, the mayor welcomed Rogers at a lecture stop and compared him to Twain, who had spent much time in the Southern city as a young man and remembered it fondly. In his remarks, Rogers reflected at length on the Missourian's fondness for New Orleans and drew a laugh with his declaration, "I bet you he is the only man in the world that ever moved from Louisiana to Connecticut." Rogers concluded, "I unfortunately can't describe your benefits and your beauty like dear Mark Twain did, but I like you as much." When the *Hannibal Courier* in Missouri asked Rogers to contribute to a special edition honoring Twain, its hometown hero, the Oklahoman insisted on his unworthiness. "Me [participating] in your Mark Twain edition would be like Sister Aimee [Semple McPherson, an evangelist mired in scandal] being asked to the Lord's Supper. Why, I would be a Huey Long in a Supreme Court robe," he replied. "There is one thing that ought to be eliminated in this country and that is every time somebody gets a laugh of some small dimensions, why, he is called the modern Mark Twain ... . [When that actually happens, a pair] will arrive together, one will be to replace Abraham Lincoln and the other to replace Mark Twain."[25]

Despite Rogers' protestations, he and Twain displayed similar characteristics. The two popular humorists shared an impatience with pretense and hypocrisy in American life, what one journalist described as a "common grasp of the bunk and fatuity surrounding most human affairs." They shared a talent for utilizing a natural style of slang and colloquialisms that appeared authentic, not contrived as with some other homespun humorists, and used it to convey mirth through charm, not ludicrous exaggeration. Tom and Huck and Will spoke in an unpretentious provincial manner that millions of their fellow citizens found familiar. Finally, Twain and Rogers surmounted all of their horse-sense predecessors in shaping reputations as the most typical, most native in-the-grain of American humorists, an achievement that won them a massive national audience.[26]

But as several observers noted, Twain and Rogers diverged in important ways. The Missourian usually went after his targets with a sustained campaign of comic shock-and-awe, whereas the Oklahoman adopted a sniper approach. As one critic wrote in 1927, "Where Twain laid down satire and burlesque like a barrage, Will Rogers employs against tawdriness and complacency in a futile world the single-shot rifle and both hit their target and ring the bell." In turn, this led to a difference in tone where, in the words of one observer, Twain "turned against whatever he disliked with a hate that was ferocious; Rogers had no hate." In terms of format, the two differed markedly. Twain was a book writer who occasionally produced essays and lectures; Rogers was a stage monologist turned newspaper essayist who occasionally gathered his short pieces and strung them together into books. "In sustained work, Will Rogers is infinitely the inferior of Clemens. He is by nature a paragrapher," Frederick Van de Water, critic for the

New York Herald Tribune pointed out. "Page by page there can be no comparison between Rogers and Twain. But paragraph by paragraph will not always bring the elder humorist the victory. There is no one, we think, who can say so much in so few words as Will Rogers."[27]

Yet however smoothly Rogers may have operated within the well-worn traditions of American homespun humor, he also emerged as a compelling innovator. Unlike his predecessors, only a couple of whom ventured from the printed page into the lecture hall, he presented his humor in an astonishing variety of media – onstage in vaudeville and *Ziegfeld Follies* shows, silent movies, travelogues, newspaper articles, magazine pieces, radio shows, Hollywood "talkie" films – that carried it to every nook and cranny of the United States. In sheer volume of work, Rogers also overwhelmed his comic forebears. Nearly all of them had committed comic pieces to the newspapers but on a spaced-out schedule of no more than one-per-week, at most, and sometimes one per month. And their popularity seldom lasted more than a decade. Twain stretched the norm as he became a serious literary figure and turned out a number of popular novels along with his periodical writing. But Rogers put them all in the shade with his tidal wave of comic writing consisting of a weekly newspaper column for thirteen years, a daily column for eight years, and numerous magazine articles, along with the stage-show appearances, radio monologues, and movie roles.

But Rogers' most important and lasting innovation was the voice in which he delivered his humorous commentary. In every case, the homespun humorists of the 1800s and very early 1900s created fictitious figures to deliver their comic goods. Dunne's "Mr. Dooley," Browne's "Artemus Ward," Lowell's "Hosea Bigelow," and Locke's "Petroleum V. Nasby" set their audiences to laughing by telling the jokes and making the light-hearted or sarcastic observations. Tracing Samuel Clemens' creative provenance was often more complicated as one first encountered the literary persona of "Mark Twain," then Twain's creations "Tom Sawyer" and "Huckleberry Finn" as the figures who prompted the chuckles. But in every case, the characters served as mouthpieces for the comic intelligence lurking behind and feeding them lines. A distinction remained between the flesh-and-blood creator and the fictitious creation. In contrast, Will Rogers never wrote a funny jibe or uttered a joke except as Will Rogers. The creator and the creation were one and the same, and the vast national audience that laughed at the quips and gently elbowed one another in appreciation of the underlying truth of the witticisms, understood that fact. It was not a character, but the man himself they came to love and appreciate.[28]

So Rogers emerged in the 1910s and 1920s as a prototypically American humorist, both refining the national tradition of homespun amusement and enhancing it with a unique and innovative voice. But he also connected with millions of his fellow citizens in another important way. Like them, the Oklahoman confronted a rapidly transforming society in the early twentieth century that could appear invigorating or disorienting, or some combination of both. In his own special fashion, this cowboy entertainer and writer mustered humor and put it in the service of helping Americans accommodate to new and challenging conditions.

* * * * *

Humor frequently reflects the age in which it occurs. It addresses tensions, aspirations, frustrations, and absurdities in the world around and seeks to memorialize them or relieve them through laughter. In their authoritative study, *America's Humor: From Poor Richard to Doonesbury*, the literary historians Walter Blair and Hamlin Hill observed, "As probably the most popular creative achievement of our countrymen, our humor reveals a great deal about America's history." They point out that the Jacksonian era, with its westward expansionism and boisterous acclaim of the common man, saw a coming together of elements – comic exaggeration and tall tales, anti-intellectualism, native characters with outlandish language styles – to create a national style of humor. The enormous disruptions wrought by the sectional dispute and Civil War encouraged the growth of cynicism, political criticism, regionalism, and nostalgia in American humor. Urban growth and industrial development by the dawn of the twentieth century pushed many humorists in the direction of a more urbane style expressed in glossy magazines, books, and mass media. By the 1920s, publications such as the *New Yorker* were revamping humor in a more sophisticated style influenced by psychoanalysis where the non-heroic individual reacted to the pressures of modern life with neuroses, fantasies, and escapist daydreams. [29]

Will Rogers, in his own unique fashion, provides a case study of history as humor. Emerging from a unique place at the intersection of many conflicting impulses – both cowboy and Indian, western provincial and coastal urbanite, traditional success-seeker and innovative entertainer, character acolyte and charming personality – he had a keener appreciation than most of the tremendous changes remaking the United States in the late 1800s and early 1900s. And he was able to use his special gift of humor to ease the strains and dislocations of modernizing change among an anxious citizenry. Sometimes intentionally, sometimes half-consciously, sometimes accidentally, Rogers addressed many of the concerns of his age and brought laughter, not anger or bitterness or fear, to bear. He did so in a practical-minded and comforting way. As the critic Clive James once observed, "Common sense and a sense of humor are the same thing, moving at different speeds. A sense of humor is just common sense, dancing." With his commonsensical sense of humor, Rogers danced across the American landscape to the delight of a mass audience.[30]

Rogers' laughter-inducing skill lay partly in his down-home style, partly in his charming personality, and partly in his God-given talent for seeing the funny aspects of day-to-day life. But digging deeper, one discovers that a great portion of the rapturous reception accorded him from a huge audience stemmed from his role as a mediating agent. Put simply, Rogers used humor to help millions of his readers and listeners come to terms with the enormous historical changes affecting their lives. He did so by honoring the past and embracing the future while according neither utter devotion. In a tone of joking irreverence, he made gentle fun of old-fashioned shibboleths and habits that had outlived their usefulness, thereby clearing the air of devotional smoke. At the same time, he poked fun at threatening new trends and departures, thereby expressing widely-shared frustration and stripping them of their fearfulness. In Rogers' hands, humor became a species of benign social criticism, a soothing poultice applied to promote the release of festering unhappiness. He understood that joking about something disarms it. "No country on earth will go Bolshevik as long as there are millions of people to laugh at it and love it with men like Will Rogers," noted a 1927 newspaper piece. "He is one of the safety valves in America's social and political engine, and we can't go far wrong when we admit our absurdities, as Will Rogers does with a quip and a jest." Rendering Americans' past and present with comingled affection and skepticism, the cowboy humorist offered laughter as a soothing way to help navigate the daunting obstacles of the age.[31]

Rogers' humor frequently alighted on some aspect of the great changes of his day. It might be the disappearance of the frontier and the rise of urban life; or the demise of Victorian moralism with its demands for self-control in the face of an emerging culture of self-fulfillment; or the replacement of the old-fashioned character ethic with the newfangled personality ethos in a media-driven commercial culture; and the persistence of populism in the face of challenges from a rapidly bureaucratizing, industrializing, and modernizing set of social values. "In highly flavored civilizations like our own – full of meat and bread, and perfumes and silk stockings – appetite and personality gradually melt together," the *Nation* observed in 1925. "Now, on the borders of the epoch appear a few jolly matadors who circle around the gorged bull and plant their darts into his hide . . . . Will Rogers is one of the circling matadors." The Oklahoma humorist, by encouraging laughter at certain aspects of the past, made it seem less constraining and stultifying; by encouraging laughter at certain aspects of the newly unfamiliar made change seem less intimidating and frightening. Laughter, in Rogers' hands, encouraged a healthy perspective on a transforming world because, as *Liberty* magazine observed, he was "one of the few men in the world who can make people laugh at themselves."[32]

On the one hand, Rogers consistently poked fun at modern trends in American life. Automobiles, golf, advertising, divorce, real estate booms, and statistics fell under his comic gaze and he prompted his fellow citizens to laugh at the silliness such developments often created. Rogers never wanted for topics in this vein. He humorously highlighted the frustrations of modern bureaucracy, for example, when he told of trying to procure a passport before his 1926 European trip. Rogers filled out the appropriate form at the New York office of the State Department but was told by the woman at the desk that he needed to produce a birth certificate or a signed affidavit from someone who knew his parents and had direct knowledge of his birth. Rogers replied that they did not have birth certificates in the 1879 Oklahoma Territory. In his words, "You being there was certificate enough. We generally took it for granted that if you were there you must have at some time been born." And producing a witness was impossible because his ancestors "were of a rather modest and retiring nature and being born was a private affair, and not a public function." The young woman insisted that she needed proof he was an American citizen, and refused to accept his claim that he had been "on the Cherokee rolls since I was named." She then asked Rogers if he was in *Who's Who*, and he replied, "My Lord, I am not even in the New York Telephone Directory." Rogers politely inquired if he "needed to be born again, and if so what procedure would you advise for me doing so?" He recalled that he once heard evangelist Billy Sunday saying we must all be born again but "I dident take it so literally until now. Billy had evidently been to Europe." Rogers finally procured a manager from the *Ziegfeld Follies* to attest to his birth and citizenship, but the bureaucratic standoff left its mark. The humorist ruefully concluded, "if you Foreigners think it is hard to get in here, you ain't seen nothing. You ought to be an American and try to get out once."[33]

Yet just as often, Rogers made fun of old-fashioned habits and attachments as he took aim at narrow-minded religion, moralistic busybodies, old-money elites, and long-standing social prejudices. He jokingly defined a prohibitionist as "a Man or Woman, who is so satisfied with himself that he presents himself with the 'Croix do Perfect He.' He gives himself this Medal because he is now going to start to Meddle in Everybody's business but his own." In 1924, Rogers skewered the pretensions of the nation's hoary, stuffy intellectual establishment in a *Weekly Article* account of his visit to Princeton University. He had performed in a show near this prestigious school and its president invited him to drop by the following day, in the humorist's facetious words, to provide "an intellectual treat . . . . It's a beautiful school, and I am sorry now that I chose [to attend] Harvard instead." Rogers expected to be enlightened by a host of brilliant minds but quickly discovered more earthy instincts at work. While walking across campus with a group of serious, dignified students "the first whiff of College Atmosphere I got was, 'Boy, she is Hotsy Totsy! Some frame that Gal's got!'" Then he stumbled across a bunch of students "matriculating in Algebra" as they tossed around a pair of dice "trying to figure out the cube root of Seven and Eleven. They were even so interested in it that they seemed to be making wagers on which was the most proficient." The Oklahoman capped off his day by attending a seminar with two professors and a dozen students. One of the teachers introduced himself as a specialist in "Early Reformation," to which Rogers replied, "Don't you think you should be in Grammar school or at least High School if you want to accomplish any Early Reformation? Personally, I think you are too late here." The other professor introduced his expertise as "Modern Political Science," which caused Rogers to wonder, "I was anxious to hear what the Science was to Politics." When the discussion started, the humorist was startled when a barrage of questions came at him and none of them involved intellectual topics. A professor asked, "What has become of [Ziegfeld showgirl] Ann Pennington?" The other professor followed, "Does [showgirl] Gilda Gray shake like that offstage?" A student piped up, "Are these Dames in the movies as Dumb as everybody says they are?" Rogers concluded, "Well, things drifted along like that from one political and scientific question to another" before he finally departed to appear in that evening's show. Even the hoariest of intellectual traditions, he suggested with a chuckle, were falling prey to the enticements of modern entertainment culture.[34]

Throughout these comic interrogations of past and present, however, Rogers scrupulously followed a code of civility. His jokes could be sharp but were seldom mean-spirited. This held true even with politics, the most tempting topic for harsh recriminations. In 1925, when the United States sent Marines to Nicaragua, Rogers quipped, "You can't pick up a paper without seeing where the Marines were landed to keep some Nation from shooting each other, and if necessary, we shoot them to keep them from shooting each other." In the aftermath of the 1923 Washington Conference on disarmament, the United States sank several of its battleships as part of an international agreement. Rogers found this absurd, but pilloried the situation with wit rather than bile. "You see, up to then Battleships had always been sunk by the enemy, and when he [Secretary Hughes] proposed to sink them yourself, it was the most original thought that had ever percolated [in] the mind of a statesman," he wrote. When another agreement a few years later stipulated the destruction of still more battleships, Rogers again employed jokes to suggest that the United States had been hoodwinked by other powers. "England is to sink three battleships that competed against the Spanish Armada. Japan is raising two that the Russians sunk and will re-sink them for the treaty," he claimed. "We are building two to sink." The whole effort to foster international peace through disarmament was a pipe dream, Rogers believed, because of national animosities. After touring Europe, he noted that "England and France think just as much of each other as two rival gangs of bootleggers. A Frenchman and an Italian love each other just about like Minneapolis and St. Paul ... .

Russia hates everybody so bad it would take her a week to pick out the one she hates the most. Poland is ararin' to fight somebody so bad that they just haul off and Punch themselves in the jaw to keep in practice."[35]

Ultimately, much of Rogers' success as a humorist reflected another important shift in early twentieth-century America: the redefinition of individualism in terms of "personality." In a consumer society increasingly dominated by commercial transactions and bureaucratic institutions, the stern moral demands of character formation were growing archaic while the magnetic traits of personality were becoming increasingly attractive. In 1924, *Liberty* magazine captured this important quality in Rogers. It observed that the cowboy entertainer reflected this trend when he accidently delivered the first quip in his career. Missing a rope trick, Rogers commented, "Swingin' a rope is all right if your neck isn't in it" and the audience burst into laughter, to his surprise. "He did not know he possessed that priceless something called 'personality.'" As his career unfolded, it became clear that people responded to Rogers the human being as well as to the words he was saying. *Liberty* described him as "the most popular and beloved of all comedians" and attributed it to his self-effacing manner, his obvious affection for his fellow man, and his willingness to treat everyone, whether manual laborer or high-society matron, the same. "There is something about him – his wholesome, grinning face, his wad of chewing gum, and his friendliness – that makes everyone feel as if they knew him well. He talks to them, about them and himself. Half the people in the house get the impression that Rogers is talking to them alone," the magazine noted. "Rogers is real, healthy, normal, honest." Americans laughed at the Oklahoma humorist because they liked him.[36]

Thus Rogers' practice of humor as mediation constructed a bridge from the past to the present, and his role as a comforting, amusing personality proved crucial to leading Americans across it. But was Rogers the personality in the public realm one and the same with Rogers the human being in the private realm? Did the celebrity image match the man at home in his daily interactions with friends and family? Or was the first an invention, a contrivance, created and maintained by the second as an instrument of success? As is often the case with human beings, especially talented and high-achieving ones, the answers do not come easy. Because, in fact, there was a very complex relationship between "Will Rogers," star of stage, screen, and the printed page, and William Penn Adair Rogers of Claremore, Oklahoma.

10

The Private Man

I N THE EARLY SUMMER OF 1927, AMERICANS ENCOUNTERED perhaps the most publicized illness of the decade. Will Rogers had been suffering from recurring stomach aches the last few weeks, and when a particularly severe attack sent him reeling in pain, his wife, Betty, made an appointment with their family physician, Dr. Percy G. White. He called in his associate, Dr. E. Clarence Moore. An extensive examination disclosed that Rogers was suffering from gallstones, and the two doctors determined surgery was necessary. The procedure took place on June 17 and was successful, but complications arose afterwards. The incision failed to drain properly and the patient's temperature shot up to a dangerous level. "Most people never knew how grave Will's illness was," Betty wrote later, and Will, Jr., recalled that his mother gathered the children in the parental bedroom and, with tears in her eyes, told them of their father's serious condition and "we all knelt and prayed for Daddy's life." After three weeks of hospitalization, Will recovered.[1]

Typically, the humorist worked the incident both for publicity and laughs. He devoted two installments of his *Weekly Articles* and several *Daily Telegrams* to the episode, joking that the doctors "are going to relieve me of surplus gall, much to the politicians' delight" and remarking of his host of well-wishers, "People couldn't have been any nicer to me if I had died." After his recovery, in November 1927, the Oklahoman wrote a two-part account of his medical ordeal in the *Saturday Evening Post* that was later turned into a book *Ether and Me or 'Just Relax.'* There Rogers claimed that his ignorance of medical issues stemmed from his upbringing in frontier Oklahoma, where people suffered mainly from gunshot wounds while "anything that hurt you from the lower end of your neck on down as far as your hips was known as a bellyache." He kidded that his physician looked disappointed after discovering he couldn't perform an appendectomy but then "brightened up" when further investigation revealed he would get to operate for

248

gallstones. Rogers joked that after a second doctor was consulted and a team of nurses appeared "The only other man he can possibly work with is the undertaker." Administered ether as he entered the operating room, the Oklahoman related a humorous description of his bizarre, drug-induced dream filled with mysterious figures jack-hammering through the hospital wall, singing birds and shipwrecks, Chinese missionaries coming to America seeking converts to Buddha, and rehearsing for the *Ziegfeld Follies* with Calvin Coolidge as floodwaters rose around them. After his recovery, Rogers pondered the cause of his gallstones. After rejecting several possibilities – "Republicans staying in power too long"; "seeing the same ending to Moving Pictures" over and over; "a wife driving from the rear seat" prompting gastric juice to congeal into a stone "as she keeps hollering" – he ultimately decided the malady was linked to his medical insurance. He had paid a big premium for years while never getting sick, so Betty reduced the coverage. When he claimed he might get hurt from falling off a horse, she dismissed it: "No, you have fallen off so much, you've got used to it. So I have no more hopes along that line." The gallstones appeared a short time later, of course, and a rueful Rogers concluded, "if you can't have any luck getting sick, have the policy cut down, and before six months you'll be saying, 'Doctor, the pain is right there.'"[2]

The beloved humorist's medical crisis attracted national attention. As news of it appeared, telegrams and letters poured in from well-wishers, including common folk and prominent figures alike. One from fellow journalist and radio commentator, Nellie Revell, declared, "A rolling gall stone gathers no gas. When a man has Heart, Brains and Guts like you have, he doesn't need Gall." The mayor of Miami, Florida, sent another saying, "All I know is what I read in the papers, and I see that your gall isn't what it used to be. Hope you won't be disappointed in the scar and that they didn't take any of the funny part out of you." The actor, adventurer, and horseman Irving O'Hay wrote, "I knew that Banquet grub would get you." Even President Coolidge wired, "I am sincerely sorry to hear of your illness and trust that your recovery may be speedy and complete."[3]

Rogers' medical crisis conveyed a significance beyond the state of his health. The intense public interest in his medical travail, and his willingness to share it, highlighted the bond between the entertainer and his mass audience. Even more, it cast light on the fascinating intersection of Rogers' public presence and his private life. This illumination suggested the growing power of celebrity in modern American culture where, as the critic, Richard Schickel, has pointed out, ordinary folk yearn for, or even assume, a knowledge of the private experiences of larger-than-life figures they encounter in public life. But with Rogers the connection went much deeper. Because of his regular-guy image and beloved status, Americans had a deep affection for the man they so loved to read in the newspapers, witness on stage, or listen to on the radio. A great host of people liked, even cared about, the witty, unassuming Oklahoman who made them ponder, and laugh at, the changing world around them. He was like a valued member of their community and they wanted to know more about the real Will Rogers. What was he like out of the spotlight? Was he the same witty, plain-spoken, commonsensical person who was so amazingly popular around the country? Were his democratic qualities genuine?

A spate of newspaper and magazine articles tried to answer such questions by digging into his personality and investigating his home life. Some of this journal-istic work simply spread superficial, glittering generalities but much of it conveyed underlying hints of complexity and ambiguity. It revealed that Rogers was more in some ways, and less in others, than his public image suggested, a conclusion reinforced by the comments and observations of those who knew him best. Not surprisingly, this cowboy and Indian, roper and stage comedian, rural rancher and city entertainer, evinced authenticity but one that was deeper, even murkier, than his "aw shucks," country boy, all-I-know-is-what-I-read-in-the-newspaper image. His family life, friendships, hobbies, and personal characteristics revealed these complications. They showed that "Will Rogers" was not an act performed by Claremore's favorite son, but neither did it embody the whole man.

* * * * *

"He has a deep and abiding sense of his obligation to his family and his home, and is thoroughly wrapped up in them," Betty Rogers said of her husband to a reporter from *Better Homes and Gardens* in 1928. Indeed, the private Will Rogers, first and foremost, was a devoted family man. Following their marriage in 1908, the couple had four children over the next decade: Will, Jr., in 1911, Mary in 1913, James in 1915, and Fred in 1918 (he died tragically from diphtheria in 1920). Given that Will and Betty both came from large, close-knit families, it is not surprising that they embraced domestic life and made it the center of their adult existence. The humorist, despite his appearances all over the country and his crushing schedule of writing, stage, and lecturing endeavors, always yearned to come home to his wife and children. As Betty told another journalist, "My husband is a man of marked domestic tendencies. He loves his home. He loves his family. He wants to spend as much time with us as he can."[4]

Granted, the physical setting for the Rogers household changed more than most. Following their marriage, the couple spent several years living out of a suitcase as Will traveled the national vaudeville circuit and Betty accompanied him. Her first pregnancy prompted them to settle in New York City in 1911. They spent several weeks in a midtown hotel before moving into an apartment on

West 113th Street in Morningside Heights. A few years later the family moved to a rented house on Russell Street in Queens but spent most summers at a rented house in Amityville, Long Island. In 1919, when Will's silent-movie career brought a contract with Samuel Goldwyn Studios, the family moved to Los Angeles and lived in several residences before Will purchased the family's first home in Beverly Hills in 1921.[5]

The Beverly Hills home provided a delightful environment for Rogers and his family. It featured a spacious house sitting on eleven acres that was decorated western-style with open oak beams, a big desk and easy chairs, Navajo rugs, and an enormous stone fireplace. After the family moved in, Will added a horse barn, riding ring, large swimming pool, and two log cabins, one a rustic getaway with an open fireplace, five bunks, and barbecue grill where the family gathered for many outdoor meals and holiday celebrations, and the other a play house for the children. He also enclosed several acres with a high brick wall.[6]

While Rogers loved the family's Beverly Hills home, the cowboy in him grew restless as the area grew more crowded. Yearning for the wide-open spaces of his Oklahoma childhood where he had ridden horses and roped cattle, in 1925 he began to purchase land a few miles to the west, nearer the Pacific Ocean, in the Santa Monica Mountains. Initially, Rogers bought 160 acres of undeveloped land in the Rustic Canyon area off Beverly (later Sunset) Boulevard in what is now Pacific Palisades. Over the next few years he bought several adjacent tracts and eventually accumulated 350 acres. For several years the family split time between their Beverly Hills home and the Santa Monica ranch, living in the former during the week and spending weekends and summers at the latter. Will fell in love with the rural property, however, and in 1930 they moved there permanently after a rehab project on their Beverly Hills home went awry. When adding a new bathroom for Mary, carpenters discovered the house was infested with termites and Will decided to make a move. As Betty explained to reporters from *American Magazine* and *McCall's*, the family adored the Santa Monica property and approved the decision to make it their full-time residence.[7]

The Santa Monica ranch became the Rogers clan's Shangri-La. Will, in particular, loved the property. He recreated his boyhood existence on this idyllic site where, while nestled in the Santa Monica mountains, one could also enjoy a picturesque view of the Pacific Ocean and, on a clear day, faraway Catalina Island. A long drive, lined with eucalyptus trees, curled uphill from the road to a plateau. There, on a gentle rise, Will arranged the construction of a small ranch house with an expansive living room, three small bedrooms, and an adjoining patio built around two live oaks. Over the next few years the structure was enlarged with the piecemeal addition of guest rooms, a larger bedroom for Will and Betty, and a study for Will. The roof was raised over the living room, a balcony was added, and a large picture window, a present from Florenz Ziegfeld, was installed at one end of the living room. The house was furnished western-style throughout with Navajo rugs, a light fixture made from an old wagon wheel, several paintings by his favorite Western artists, and a longhorn steer head mounted over the fireplace mantle. An old wooden Indian sat next to a barrel of ropes in one corner, which Will dipped into whenever he felt the urge to practice his roping. The abode reflected the Oklahoma humorist who oversaw its development – rambling, comfortable, unpretentious, and relaxed.[8]

In the 350 acres surrounding the house, Rogers happily supervised a host of projects. He and several hired workmen cleared sagebrush, leveled the ground for a polo field, and erected a roping corral. He purchased pieces of a large barn from the San Fernando Valley and had them transported to the ranch where they were reconstructed into a structure with two wings on each side of a tall rotunda. The new barn featured a stable with a large number of stalls for horses, while cattle and goats occupied several surrounding pastures and dogs romped in the yard. An orphaned Brahma calf named Sarah, a gift from a friend at the King Ranch in Texas, was raised on a bottle and became a family pet, often walking into the house or curling up at the feet of anyone sitting on the patio or in the yard. The Oklahoman cleared numerous riding trails through the surrounding hills that allowed for long, leisurely horseback rides through the countryside for family and friends. He even put in a small, four-hole golf course for his friends next to the polo field, although they were unnerved when their host followed them on horseback as they played and joked good-naturedly about the silliness of a game where you chased around a little white ball. Periodically, the humorist would visit a local nursery and come home with a truck full of flowers, shrubs, and trees and then supervise each one's planting around the ranch. According to Betty, "the work went on and on. Will kept adding a new fence, a new corral, a new bridle trail; he cut out new roads; he changed this and that; and the digging, clearing, building, and pounding never slowed down while he was here."[9]

Rogers' demanding work schedule kept him away from home for lengthy periods of time, but he always hungered to return to his rural home. "His interest in returning to the ranch was like that of a child with an ever-new toy," his wife reported. "The very first thing he would go to the stable, saddle a horse and either go to the polo field for a work-out or head for the trails back in the hills." Even when away lecturing or entertaining, the humorist was thinking about the ranch and various improvement projects. In 1928, while on tour in the east, Rogers sent a letter to one of his sons. "We will have a lot of roping this summer, Fancy and Calf and Goats. We will get us some goats and keep 'em up in a small pen all the time," he wrote excitedly. "I wish you would look after some things down there at the Ranch for me. Get 'em to build the back part on the barn . . . . Get those Logs put around on the outside of the east hill. Then if they have time move the old Stables, and fix up a bunk house out of part of the old one. Now see what luck you can have on this." Betty simply summed up her husband's attitude: "The ranch was the joy of his life."[10]

For Rogers, however, home meant more than a comfortable material setting and a hospitable rural atmosphere. It encompassed the sturdy ties that bound him tightly to his wife and children. His marriage to Betty Blake Rogers laid the foundation for his devotion to family. Following their somewhat tumultuous courtship, the pair quickly settled into a life together and proved to be well matched. They prospered emotionally from a strong combination of similar backgrounds and values and complementary personalities, his impulsive and energetic and hers calm and organized. Will and Betty were at ease in one another's company and completely loyal; there was never a hint of infidelity, even though they lived in the notoriously permissive atmosphere of Hollywood and Will had worked closely with a host of beautiful young women in the risqué *Ziegfeld Follies*. Will liked to joke, with an underlying pride, that he was an outlier because "I am the only motion picture actor who has the same wife he started out with. My wife is not bragging about it but I am." He clearly believed that much of his personal happiness and the family's stable, comfortable domestic life was due to Betty's even-tempered presence and solid judgement. He often declared, "The day I roped Betty Blake was the best catch of my life." While on the road in 1925, the humorist sent a telegram to his wife on their wedding anniversary and said of their marriage, "This is one bargain we made where we didn't sell out too quick. The longer we hold it the more [valuable] it seems to become."[11]

Betty preferred to stay behind the scenes and avoid the spotlight, but as Will's fame skyrocketed by the early 1920s the press sought her out to explore the home life of one of the most famous men in America. Occasionally she submitted to interviews, and as her husband noted, "People often come out to our house to see me, and when they go away, they remember only Betty." She made an initial impression with her quiet, gracious manner and understated, elegant physical presence. Of medium height with hazel eyes, wavy brown hair usually piled up toward the back of her head, a slim, athletic build, and minimal makeup she favored simple but smart clothing and spoke clearly in a resonant, low-pitched voice. "The keynote of her attire – and her personality, for that matter – is simplicity. She is without affectations of any kind," wrote one reporter." Betty projected an image of someone interested in finding "a new and delightful experience right around every corner" while also remaining "a home-loving woman, thoroughly engrossed in her husband and her children and everything that pertains to their interests."[12]

Like her husband, Betty was proudly provincial and embraced solid, mid-western values. She loved small-town life with its simple tastes and friendly manners. This quiet woman was "keenly interested in everything – except sham and pretense and hokum," noted *American Magazine*. "The moment I met her I believed she was glad to see me and that she felt it was mighty good of me to come out." This small-town sensibility carried over into her child-rearing philosophy. Betty described herself as "just an average wife and mother" who wanted her children to grow up "clean-minded and good," a task that required care and companionship, discipline and teaching. "Our parents were wholesome country people – and that's the kind of life we like," Betty explained. "And the kind we want our children to like."[13]

While Betty was devoted to her children, she also performed another labor of love – serving as a calming, guiding influence on her husband. "I think most men who lead the very active, very busy, very exciting life that my husband does need the kind of wives who can act as balance wheels," she said. "Men who lead strenuous lives and are always before the public are always keyed up. Certainly they must be helped to tone down at home." To that end she read many of Will's columns and magazine pieces and commented on them before submission; listened to his jokes and quips to assess if they were too risky and truly funny; and screened his political references to make sure she understood them as an average reader or listener should. More generally, she strived to help her impulsive husband maintain an emotional equilibrium and even out the highs and lows that were common to life in the entertainment world. Will clearly valued her opinions and trusted her levelheaded judgement. When a reporter visited the Rogers home and suggested that without Betty, Will Rogers would not have gained the achievements and fame he had, she modestly demurred. But he replied immediately, "You're right, brother!"[14]

Ultimately, much like her husband, Betty Rogers appeared to the American public as a figure successfully mediating between the past and the present. She was, at the same time, an old-fashioned woman completely comfortable as a wife and mother and a modern female who traveled widely, navigated the treacherous waters of Hollywood, and said of her daughter, "I believe in a college education for girls as well as boys." After talking with Betty at length about domestic life with her famous husband, a magazine reporter concluded, "They're living the way they want to live – a simple existence in the midst of jazzed-up Hollywood – because they have the strength of character to do as they like." A newspaper journalist noted a similar juxtaposition of traditional and modern in this woman managing a household and family in the heart of the nation's movie capital. "There is about her an old-fashioned motherliness, a lack of artificiality, that in this 'land of make-up' is especially striking," he wrote. "She is a born wife and mother; a clever hostess; an all-round sportswoman, who swims and rides with her family every day; an executive who runs a big establishment without letting it run her."[15]

While Will's marriage with Betty was the bedrock of his adult life, his relationship with their children provided much of the emotional structure erected on that foundation. As everyone who knew him testified, much of the Oklahoman's private time was taken up with Will, Jr., Jim, and Mary Rogers. He was a devoted father fully engaged with his children and determined to give them a good life. Rogers threw himself into activities with his kids. From the time they could walk, for example, he had them on horses and the trio of siblings became expert riders and ropers. As early as 1917, at a benefit event for American soldiers stationed in France, Will and the children, ages two through six, rode into the Polo Grounds in New York where the father proceeded to gently lasso and then gently release them before doing the same with their ponies "by one foot, two feet, all four feet." After this demonstration, father and children galloped around the periphery of the space to the delighted shouts and applause of the crowd in the stands.[16]

At the family's Beverly Hills home in the early 1920s, Rogers made a large riding ring where the children could ride and rope. As he told an interviewer, "sometimes we have had as many as thirty horses cavorting around in the place." A bit later at the ranch, of course, everyday life became life on horseback. Will and the children spent hours roping calves and goats, practicing riding tricks, and playing polo. Sometimes accompanied by Betty, they spent hours on leisurely rides on the many trails that Will and his hired hands cut through the beautiful rolling hills of the property.[17]

But activities on horseback were only the beginning of Will's activities with his kids. When the family first moved into the Beverly Hills house, neighbors counseled him to convert its big amphitheater front yard into a sunken garden, then fashionable on big estates. But as the entertainer told *Better Homes and Gardens*, "they didn't know what I wanted out of a garden. I wanted a playground for the kids." So he had installed sand boxes, gymnastic equipment, swimming pool, and a variety of children's yard toys such as swing sets and slides. "We all play," he reported delightedly. "We all have a lot of fun out of it, and that's what a garden is for, isn't it?" Inside the house, Rogers fixed up a playroom and a stage in the basement, including a curtain that was raised and lowered with ropes. After work he and the children would perform raucous amateur theatricals and plays. At Christmas, the humorist became legendary for organizing elaborate celebrations for the children. One year, he fixed up Mary's pony with holiday trappings, affixed a huge sack filled with presents, and had her ride the animal into the house to distribute gifts to the rest of the family. Every year, according to Betty, her husband waited until the last minute and then rushed off to the stores to buy a mountain of toys, clothing, and trinkets for the children – "he never asked the price of anything" – and then spent Christmas Eve wrapping packages for the next morning. Betty described Will as "a wonderful father" and noted that their children "hang on every word he says or writes to them."[18]

Both family and close friends and detached observers noticed, however, the special quality that colored the father–children dynamic in the Rogers household. It was obvious that Will, full of enthusiasm and spontaneity, was as much sibling as parent in the relationship. "It often seemed to me that I had four children instead of three, and that Will was the greatest child of all," Betty later wrote. "Will is only a child himself. He would much rather play with the kids than sit around and talk with grown-ups," Betty chuckled to a writer for *American Magazine*. "He never has become an adult – and in that lies much of his charm." When another reporter once asked if her husband was a disciplinarian, she laughed. "In the first place, he wouldn't know how to start disciplining them and he wouldn't have the inclination to do it," she reported. "But, if he should get started, they would either laugh or argue or coax it out of him." Son Jim reported that his father's method of discipline involved a special, silent look of censure that conveyed deep disappointment rather than anger, a look that was effective because "you wanted his approval and if you didn't have it that was the worst thing that could happen to you .... You didn't want him to feel disappointed in you." Will was so averse to being an authority figure, however, that when Betty started to actively reprimand one of the children, he fled the scene. And if he could not escape, when Betty was at the high point of dressing down the miscreant he would look up from his bowed head while standing behind her, convey just the touch of a smile, and wink.[19]

As the Rogers children grew up, they proved to be a varied lot. Will, Jr., often called Bill, was bookish and, while he rode horses and played polo, did not share his father's enthusiasm for ranch life. Bill attended Culver Military Academy in Indiana from 1926 to 1928, graduated from Beverly Hills High School in 1931, and throughout his youth accompanied his parents on several trips to Europe and Asia. He graduated from Stanford University in 1932, where he excelled in public speaking and debate. Bill could be outspoken, sometimes to the annoyance of his father, as when he told dinner guest Will Durant that his Stanford professors disparaged Durant's *The Story of Philosophy* as a mere popularization. As an adult, Bill became active in Democratic politics and journalism. Mary Rogers had a close relationship with her father, who nicknamed her "Meme." As the daughter of a movie star and former cowboy, she enjoyed a Hollywood childhood that involved meeting Charlie Chaplin, Douglas Fairbanks, and Joan Crawford while also riding at the Los Angeles National Horse Show. Mary traveled widely with her family in the United States and Europe, and after graduating high school in Beverly Hills she studied drama at Sarah Lawrence College in 1932–1933. She then returned to Los Angeles to pursue an acting career in films and on the stage.

Jim Rogers, like his siblings an early rider of horses, developed a passion for ranch life at the family's Pacific Palisades ranch. He loved being on horseback, roping calves, and playing polo, endeavors which created a special bond with his father. "I worshiped Dad . . . . I admired him tremendously because of the kind of life he lived and because of the kind of human being he was," he told a journalist in later life. As a youth, Jim appeared as a child actor in several of Will's films. He attended the New Mexico Military Institute in Roswell, graduated from the Webb School, a boarding preparatory school in Claremont, California, in 1934, and then spent one year at Pomona College. As an adult, he pursued cattle ranching while also dabbling in movie acting. Each of the Rogers children replicated part of their famous father's personality: Bill with his pursuit of journalism and politics, Mary with her strong attraction to the stage, and Jim with his quiet enthusiasm for ranch life. But each of them had their own sensibility and interests, and Will encouraged them to go their own way in life.[20]

Despite the close bond between children and father, one issue rankled the relationship. The peripatetic nature of Rogers' career created a tension over his absence that seldom burst into view but always simmered beneath the surface. His multitude of professional activities and frenetic schedule caused him to be gone from home on a regular basis. Lengthy stretches of travel were a fact of life in the Rogers household as Will traveled the country and Betty often joined him. As a journalist noted in 1926, since the beginning of their marriage the wife had been on the road with the husband "making a home for him in hotels or rented houses in any city where they remained long enough. Home has always been where Will was, and vice versa. Their roaming life has never lost its adventure for Mrs. Rogers, although she looks forward to the day when Will can ... take up permanent abode at home." Will appreciated Betty's willingness to travel. "She's a real trooper," he told an interviewer in 1930. "She can be sittin' here in a kimono and hear the train whistle for the station, and be on it all dressed and packed, with the tickets bought, before the conductor says, 'All aboard.'"[21]

When possible, Will and Betty took the children along with them on trips, usually in the summer, and other times made sure the children were lovingly cared for. They engaged Will's niece, Paula McSpadden, for a few years to live in the Beverly Hills house and help with the children when the parents were gone. Then over a much longer period they arranged for Betty's unmarried sister, Theda Blake, or "Aunt Dick," to look after the children and manage the household and she became part of the family. Will regularly sent loving, chatty letters and postcards to his kids while he was gone and Betty told an interviewer that while her husband had to be absent for "long stretches of time, we somehow manage to keep close to him." The children understood the need for their father's frequent absences but still resented the situation. Will Jr. and Jim later recalled "their parents were away from home continually; there never seemed a time when they were growing up when their father, in particular, was not involved in something that took him away." Mary was more direct. As a girl, she told Joel McCrea, an actor friend of her father's, "You know, sometimes we resent you a little bit . . . . you take so much of our father's time."[22]

As Will Rogers' celebrity grew exponentially in the 1920s, Americans grew interested not only in the nature of his private life but the quality of his private character. Most queries concerned authenticity: was the cracker-barrel philosopher and horse-sense quipster mostly an act or did it characterize the real man? The answer, as it must be, was both yes and no. Rogers was amusing and insightful at home, his family and friends testified unanimously, but it stemmed from his natural constitution and was not a performance. "He doesn't try to be funny. He just is. He simply has a fine sense of humor," Betty explained. She added, "Will is just himself – a regular husband and father and head of the house. We find him amusing chiefly because we love him. We don't demand that he be funny the clock around." After spending some time in the Rogers household, another observer concluded that the entertainer did not play the comedian at home but was naturally lighthearted and irreverent: "He doesn't live to be funny, he merely gets a lot of fun out of living. Life isn't a huge joke with him. It's a lovely adventure and not to be spoiled with too much seriousness."[23]

Will Rogers' family experience defined a large part of his private life, but not all of it. As expected from someone famous for the declaration, "I never met a man I didn't like," friends and friendship also comprised an important part of life. Yet both the volume and the intensity of these relationships were less than one might predict. The man known by so many was, in fact, well-known by only a few.

* * * * *

During his early career in vaudeville, the *Ziegfeld Follies,* and silent films, Rogers maintained friendships with a number of fellow performers and entertainment figures – Eddie Cantor, W. C. Fields, Bert Williams, Flo Ziegfeld, and Hal Roach. By 1920, however, as Rogers' fame skyrocketed with lecture tours, radio broadcasts, after-dinner speeches, magazine pieces, and newspaper columns, he drifted away from the theatrical stage except for occasional appearances. Subsequently, many of these connections to performer friends faded into the past. Over the next decade he went his own way, settling down with his family in Southern California and usually writing and performing alone. Moreover, as Rogers himself once confessed, his career had been largely a solitary endeavor with both the goals and the energy flowing from internal sources. "Most of my life has been lived alone," he wrote in a *Weekly Article*. "I never run with a pack."

While fond of people and usually gregarious and companionable, he plotted his own course outside the parameters of a team or an organization. Rogers' sons described their father succinctly: "He was a loner."[24]

Nonetheless, Rogers cultivated a small circle of friends with whom he enjoyed spending time and sharing laughs. He enjoyed the company of several casual companions from the movie world such as Leo Carillo, a vaudeville dialect comedian and actor. Walt Disney, the rising studio head whose animated films were taking the country by storm in the late 1920s, became a regular visitor to the Rogers ranch to play polo on the weekends. Disney admired the Oklahoman and, according to a studio colleague, studied and imitated Rogers' friendly, informal, down-home style. Actor Spencer Tracy became another polo pal. Oscar Lawler, former U.S. assistant attorney general and the family lawyer, had been a neighbor and friend of the Rogers clan when they lived in Beverly Hills. Later, he visited the ranch frequently to play golf on its four-hole course.[25]

Rogers developed a deeper friendship with Guinn "Big Boy" Williams, a character actor and comedian he first met on the set of the silent film, *Almost a Husband*. When Rogers first saw the "extra" in the cast looming above his colleagues at six-foot two inches with a weight of 200 pounds, he dubbed him "Big Boy" and the name stuck. The two became friendly – in Williams' words, "Bill took to me and I took to him right away" – and the following year they appeared together in another movie, *Cupid the Cowpuncher*, where Williams got screen credit for a small part. A string of silent film co-appearances followed. Williams had grown up on a ranch in Decatur, Texas, and the two transplanted cowboys became good friends, sharing outdoor interests and a roughhouse style, as they wisecracked, wrestled, swung lariats, and rode horses. Their friendship was cemented when Rogers, after a discussion on a movie set where Williams confessed to being homesick, stuck a wad of bills in his friend's hand and said, "You take time off between this picture and the next. Go see your maw." "After that, I sorta' worshiped Bill," Williams admitted. The handsome young Texan became a regular visitor to the Rogers ranch in the 1920s and, like his famous friend, developed a passion for polo, eventually becoming an expert player with a string of 125 polo ponies.[26]

Rogers enjoyed a warm camaraderie with a circle of cowboy artists and enthusiasts who shared his frontier sensibility and whose work he began to collect. The humorist had discovered Charles M. Russell's cowboy paintings in 1908 and then met the artist a few years later in Great Falls, Montana, during a vaudeville engagement. They liked each other and would meet in New York when Russell was in the city exhibiting his work, or in Southern California, where the Russells would often spend the winter at their Pasadena home. Russell had been a cowpuncher in his youth and loved horses and he spent many an hour riding through the hills with Rogers at his California ranch. The Oklahoman loved Russell's painterly portrayals of people, events, and vistas from the American west and described him as "the greatest artist of this kind in the world." He purchased several Russell paintings and sculptures which went on display in his ranch home. On a more personal level, Rogers enjoyed Russell's company, especially his flair for humorous, self-deprecating stories. In a 1924 *Weekly Article* devoted to the artist, Rogers retold one of Russell's tales about a painting that featured a local, notoriously ugly cowboy astride a bucking horse. When he took it to his favorite saloon for a first look, most of the patrons commented on the painter's success in capturing the homely cowboy's features. But one elderly townsman, Old Yank, peered at the painting for a while with a skeptical expression before finally saying, "The horse looks a little like him." Rogers repeated another Russell tale of a cowboy friend who approached him and inquired, "Charlie, what is it that makes them pictures cost so much? Is it the brush or the paint?" When Russell died in 1926, Rogers penned a touching tribute to his friend in the artist's posthumously published book, *Trails Plowed Under.* "Old Timer, you don't know how we miss you," Rogers wrote. "It wasn't what you had done, it wasn't because you could paint a horse and a cow and a cowboy better than any man that ever lived, I don't know, it was just you, Charley . . . . Well, can't write you any more, Charley, dam [n] paper's all wet. It must be raining in this old bunk house."[27]

Like Russell, Ed Borein was another artist who specialized in nostalgic renderings of the Old West and gained Rogers' friendship. The native Californian lived up the coast in Santa Barbara and, while a watercolorist, specialized in etchings, a process wherein a sharp steel stylus is used to penetrate a copper plate after which ink is applied to reveal the design. Rogers became acquainted with Borein in the late 1910s in New York and they quickly became friends. The humorist admired Borein's artistic renderings of Western life – in a *Weekly Article* he proclaimed him "the greatest etcher of western subjects we have" – and began to collect them. The two also shared a love of horseback riding and polo, spending many afternoons on the sporting field or the hillside trails at the Santa Monica ranch. Borein became a regular visitor to the Rogers abode and contributed a funny episode to the family lore. After growing tired of Rogers' compulsive lariat throwing in the house where the visitor often found himself ensnared by a rope, Borein went to a taxidermist and had a deceased calf stuffed and mounted on a small platform and castors. On his next visit he wheeled it into the house, proclaimed Rogers "the best dead-calf roper in the world," and urged him to aim his lariat on the bovine target whenever he felt the urge. A laughing Rogers thereafter stored the calf under the stairway and used it for just that purpose.[28]

Charles F. Lummis was the most outlandish figure among Rogers' western aficionado friends, a transplanted easterner who memorialized his adopted region not as a visual artist but as a poet and writer, photographer and editor, amateur ethnographer and archeologist. Born in Massachusetts, Lummis had attended Harvard and was a classmate of Theodore Roosevelt. Like the future president, he was fascinated by the western frontier and, following a stint with a Cincinnati newspaper, he migrated to California to take a job with the *Los Angeles Times*. Astonishingly, he made the 3,500-mile journey on foot, taking six months to complete the journey and publishing a book-length account of his adventures entitled *A Tramp Across the Continent* (1892). Lummis became enamored of the Old Southwest and publicized, defended, and studied its Spanish and Native American heritage. An antimodernist critic of the overly civilized eastern United States whose complaints about cities teeming with undesirable immigrants were tinged with racism, he contended that the wide-open spaces and vibrant nature of the great west promised Americans physical and spiritual regeneration. Ironically, Lummis became an outspoken defender of Indian rights as the editor of a magazine, *Out West*, and a founder of the Southwest Museum in Los Angeles. His glorification of the West was mirrored in his eccentric personal style – he asked friends to address him as "Don Carlos" and dressed in archaic Mexican and Indian garb. Rogers met Lummis in 1907 during the former's vaudeville days and a decade later he became a frequent attendee at the latter's famous "Saturday Nights" held at his home, *El Alisel*, he had built near Pasadena. These events gathered writers, artists, actors, musicians, scientists, and public officials to share food and conversation in an atmosphere of Mexican food and songs. Rogers grew fond of Lummis for his colorful personality and appreciated his affection for both western life and American Indian traditions. Lummis liked and deeply admired the humorist. "There isn't a man alive that I value more than Will," he wrote Betty during her husband's gallstone surgery. "And there isn't a more useful American."[29]

Rogers' endeavors in the journalistic world produced two pals. First, he became good friends with Amon Carter, the businessman, newspaper editor, philanthropist, and political power broker who shared his love of a good story and all things western. Carter helped start the Fort Worth *Star-Telegram* in 1909 and became its owner, president, and publisher in 1923. The flamboyant Texan, with his flinty features, light suits, and ten-gallon hats, was a relentless civic booster of Fort Worth, to which he shepherded numerous businesses and city improvements over many decades. Notorious for his dislike of Dallas, he took a sack lunch when he visited this sister city so he wouldn't have to spend money there and often claimed that "Fort Worth is where the West begins and Dallas is where the East peters out." Rogers and Carter had met in 1922 at the apartment of New York Giants manager, John McGraw, and in subsequent years they would share a suite at 1928 Democrat convention in Houston, see each other in

Washington, DC, while covering politics, and attend prizefights together. Rogers liked to stop by Carter's ranch and his suite at the Fort Worth Club when he was in Texas. In early 1931, Rogers reached out to his good friend for support as he planned a tour through Oklahoma, Texas, and Arkansas to raise money for drought relief. Carter lent full assistance, wiring the humorist, "THINK YOUR IDEA IS BULLY AND COMMENDABLE AND THE STAR TELEGRAM WILL BE DELIGHTED TO GIVE YOU EVERY COOPERATION THROUGH PUBLICITY INCLUDING THE RADIO ... . WILL BE GLAD TO PROVIDE YOU WITH AIRPLANE AND GOOD PILOT TO COVER THE STATE AND ANYTHING ELSE PERSONALLY WITHIN MY POWER. IT IS A GENEROUS THING FOR YOU TO DO, STILL IT IS JUST LIKE WILL ROGERS." The two men grew so close that after Rogers' sudden, shocking death, Carter flew across the country from Washington, DC, to Seattle and met the plane bringing his friend's remains back from Alaska. The heartbroken Texan then sat beside the Oklahoman's body during the flight to Los Angeles. "Your going to Seattle was the sweetest and most comforting of all the loving things that was done for him. No one but you could have thought of this," wrote a grateful Betty. "I do want you to know how deeply touched we were and how each one of us appreciate your warm affection and sincere friendship for him. He loved you, we all do."[30]

Rogers' journalistic endeavors also brought him into contact with O. O. McIntyre, whose syndicated column "New York Day by Day" ran in more than 500 newspapers throughout the country from 1912 to 1938. It specialized in describing the wonders of urban life as seen through the eyes of a Midwesterner (McIntyre had been born in Ohio). Sharing the perspective of denizens of the heartland who first encountered, then conquered, the eastern power centers of the United States, Rogers and McIntyre developed a close friendship. The two men had met through Gene Buck when McIntyre was a press agent for the *Ziegfeld Follies* and Rogers was becoming one of the brightest stars in the show. Their paths crossed again when they became attached to the same newspaper syndicate. "I have seen him at his home in California, bunked with him at political conventions, gossiped with him in dressing rooms, walked with him along London's Strand, Broadway, Hollywood Boulevard and where not," wrote McIntyre in a piece on Rogers in *Cosmopolitan*. He went on to praise the Oklahoman as a representative of "Americanism," and lauded him for his genuine shyness, warm family life, common-sense wit, and ability to "adapt himself to any situation, any crowd, in a twinkle." A grateful Rogers wired, "Thanks for that piece about me in *Cosmopolitan*. You sure had to tell some whoppers to make me out a regular fellow. It may offset the terrible opinions of some of the intellectuals. Those birds have never been able to figure out why you and I haven't starved to death. If it wasn't for our own country folk we would, too." Later, McIntyre would praise Rogers as "one of the most talented men of his time" and assert, "Such rugged forthright men, just as Lincoln did, come but once to a generation."[31]

Rogers reciprocated the admiration. He appreciated his fellow-journalist's talents as a wordsmith, noting in a *Weekly Article*, "I wish I could write like that fellow McIntyre. I never miss him. Old 'Odd' can make spinach appetizing in print. Then he has got one of the biggest herds of words to ride in and out from. He is so far ahead of all other columnists there is no comparison." Rogers would visit McIntyre's apartment when he was in New York, often accompanied by Amon Carter and Irvin Cobb, and the quartet would spend the evening telling stories and trading repartee. Rogers liked to tease McIntyre about his serious demeanor, fashionable dress, and fancy New York apartment on Park Avenue. He once gave his readers an account of a visit to the columnist's abode. "I hadent seen him in a long time, and I had heard he was kinder feeble and grouchy, and was doing well enough to have the gout along with it, so for old time's sake I thought I would see if he was still living," wrote Rogers. He claimed that he became confused "trying to find at which room Odd's property stopped and Vanderbilt's started . . . . He has two dogs, one a bull dog that can't hear. Odd used to try his jokes on him and the dog went deaf purposely . . . . He has got more clothes and more different words than any writer writing outside of a book. He has suits for every sentence."[32]

Like Rogers, Irvin S. Cobb was a humorist, writer, and actor and the two developed a friendship by the 1920s. Born in Paducah, Kentucky in 1876, Cobb first worked at a local newspaper before heading off to New York to become a staff writer for William Randolph Hearst's *New York World*. As his writing skills developed, he authored a host of syndicated newspaper features and short stories, all featuring his colloquial style and ironic humor and often set in Kentucky. Cobb joined the *Saturday Evening Post* in 1911 and covered World War I for the magazine. In the postwar period, he flourished as a lecturer and after-dinner speaker and eventually headed to Hollywood where he worked as a screenwriter and acted in ten films in the 1930s. Rotund, with dark hair and complexion, a perpetually skeptical expression, bushy eyebrows, full lips, and a double chin above which protruded an ever-present cigar, Cobb immediately impressed people as a larger-than-life character.[33]

Rogers met Cobb during his vaudeville days and then in 1921 he acted in the silent film, *Boys Will Be Boys* (1921), which was based on the Kentuckian's story in the *Saturday Evening Post*. Later, Cobb's "Judge Priest" stories about nineteenth-century life in the Bluegrass State became the basis of one of Rogers' most famous films. As Rogers acknowledged, "You know, those wonderful stories are really what made him so widely known. He is the most interesting man I have heard in many a day. He does know his Civil War history." Cobb, who was on the set, was deeply impressed when Rogers stood aside at the film's conclusion and gave a veteran actor the climactic scene "practically effacing himself" to give his colleague the spotlight. The two frequently saw one another in New York and on the lecture circuit and they loved to joke and exchange witticisms. At a New York dinner where both men were scheduled to speak, Will Hays introduced Rogers by recalling how the Oklahoman had strolled into the city and people quickly learned that he had "something under his old ten-gallon hat besides hair." Cobb jumped to his feet and exclaimed, "I want to endorse from a full heart the glowing words that have just been spoken, and I want to add that it was high time somebody in this broad land of ours said a good word for dandruff." On a radio show, Rogers hosted Cobb as a guest and delighted in playing his straight man. The two humorists were working together on a movie, so Rogers quizzed the Kentuckian on his reaction to Hollywood life:

> ROGERS: You're out here, Irvin, and how do you like Hollywood?
> COBB: Well, Bill, asking a man how he likes Hollywood is like asking a man with a wen on his nose how he likes having a wen on his nose. You in time get used to a wen on your nose, but you never really care for it.
> ROGERS: Do you like the movie business, Irvin?
> COBB: I didn't know it was a business. I thought it was a racket.
> ROGERS: Do you find the nightlife down there [in Hollywood] with the movies kind of gets you?
> COBB: I haven't been up late enough yet to see.
> ROGERS: Have you ever seen Greta Garbo?
> COBB: I never saw her. I think Garbo must be like Santa Claus. Everybody talks about it; nobody ever sees one. But I'm living in the house she used to live in . . . . People who haven't heard the news drive in looking for Greta, and they see me sitting there. One old lady from the Middle West said, 'Oh, Lord, how that girl's changed,' and drove right out.
> ROGERS: Do you feel yourself kind of going Hollywood in any way?
> COBB: I find that I'm talking to myself, and worse than that I'm answering back. And I've been cutting out paper dolls at odd times . . . . I'm living in Yes Man's Land, which is worse than No Man's Land was during the war.

On another radio show, Rogers told listeners, "Mr. Irvin Cobb I consider our greatest humorist, and when they remove the mantle at some future time . . . from Mr. Mark Twain they won't have to take it very far – just from the Mississippi River right over to Paducah on the Ohio." Cobb considered Rogers to be "one of my dearest friends on this earth" and described him as "homely and clean in his thoughts, honest and kind in his dealings with his fellow men . . . . a vital, kindly, generous, simple American gentleman."[34]

Rogers, a congenial man, enjoyed his circle of friends and relished their interactions, which were full of bonhomie and creative energy. Among all of them, however, one individual stood out as a boon companion. Fred Stone, a prominent actor, dancer, comedian, and acrobat, met Rogers in 1911 when he put out the word that he needed instruction on lassoing for a new Broadway musical show in which he was appearing, *The Old Town*. Rogers showed up at the New Amsterdam Theater, found Stone sitting in the alley resting from rehearsals, and offered to show him some rope tricks. The pair were soon flinging lariats about and Stone proved a quick study. More important, the two quickly discovered a host of commonalities – great energy, multi-faceted talents, a western background, a vibrant sense of humor – that drew them together. Although Stone was a prominent entertainer and Rogers still a middling vaudevillian with a horse act, the two bonded immediately. As Stone later wrote, "From the day of our first meeting we were friends. We didn't go through a long process of 'getting to know each other.' It was more like recognizing each other. We spoke the same language . . . . [W]e loved the same things, liked doing them in the same way." In fact, within a short time Stone became the brother Rogers never had.[35]

Stone had been born in a log cabin near Valmont, Colorado, in 1873 and moved about in the Midwest as a child. He was fascinated by the circus and learned a number of tricks in late adolescence, including tightrope walking, that earned him a spot in several traveling circuses. In the mid-1890s he partnered with Dave Montgomery to form a minstrel act, the success of which earned them the opportunity to perform in shows running in Chicago and New York. In 1903, they became famous from their starring roles in *The Wizard of Oz* musical with Stone playing the Scarecrow and Montgomery the Tin Man. In the following years, the pair starred in several musical comedies on Broadway where they became notable for funny disguises, acrobatic feats, and madcap sequences of songs, stunts, and dances. Their greatest success came with *Chin-Chin* (1915), a musical loosely based on the story of Aladdin, where their varied talents came fully into play. Sadly, Montgomery fell ill two years later while on the road with the show, and lapsed into a coma and died. Stone continued as a solo entertainer, securing roles in several Broadway productions.[36]

Rogers, as he moved about in vaudeville and Broadway circles in his early days as an entertainer, had admired Stone's talents and career from afar. The first show he took Betty to see in New York after their marriage was the musical, *The Red Mill*, starring Stone and Montgomery. After their fateful meeting in 1911, Rogers and Stone began spending considerable time together and a close friendship blossomed. They shared several interests (entertainment, horses, aviation) and proclivities (hard work, energetic physical activity, humorous banter). Rogers joked that their minimal educations explained why "we always hit it off together so well, neither was liable to use a word which the other couldn't understand." Betty often observed her husband and his good friend spending time together and was struck how the pair radiated energy. "Both of them had lived eventful and adventurous lives. They were both outdoor men and always kept themselves in trim as trained athletes do," she wrote. Rogers taught Stone rope tricks, and Stone taught Rogers dance routines and they would practice together for hours. "Both Fred and Will had the work habit – which is just as real as any other habit. Once you have formed it you aren't comfortable in idleness. They both needed work and plenty of it to keep them happy," Betty noted. "Neither could sit still long." "The two were just like brothers," added Stone's daughter, Dorothy. "Daddy and Will became inseparable."[37]

Their Rogers and Stone families also grew close. In the summer of 1915, Rogers rented a house near the Stone's Chin-Chin Ranch in Amityville, Long Island, and the clans spent many pleasant days together riding, picnicking, participating in raucous theatricals, and enjoying outings on the Great South Bay. The Rogers with Will, Betty, Will, Jr., Mary, and baby Jimmy and the Stones with Fred, wife Allene, and daughters Dorothy, Paula, and Carol became nearly an extended family. Stone loved the water – he had a boat on a channel there – and tried to teach Rogers to swim. The venture was largely unsuccessful as the Oklahoman flopped and sputtered and kicked up much water while making little headway. A discouraging development occurred when one day Rogers ran to the end of the wharf and, not understanding the rhythms of the ocean, dove into the shallow water when the tide was out and jammed his shoulder, an injury that inhibited his roping endeavors for a time. When an incredulous Stone inquired why he had done that, his cowboy friend replied, "We don't have tides in Oklahoma. We have swimmin' holes that don't try to kill you." Happier activities dominated, however. Stone reported that often he would be sleeping late after a theater performance when his neighbor would appear. "Bill would come riding under my window, winding his rope, and singing a cowboy song. I'd open the window, he'd grin sheepishly, and taking less than no time to dress I'd swallow my breakfast, hustle down and join him," Stone said. "Like two cowboys we'd ride and rope all day." In subsequent years, the two men and their families would gather frequently at Rogers' Santa Monica ranch for dinners and outdoor activities.[38]

Several show business incidents illuminated Will and Fred's relationship. Stone had encouraged Rogers to try Broadway when vaudeville passed its peak and began to decline by the late 1910s. The Oklahoman took the advice. Thus in 1915, Rogers was appearing in the show *Hands Up* at the Palace Theater in New

York when the producers turned off the stage lights to get the entertainer offstage when he went on too long with his rope tricks. Stone, who was in the audience, leaped to his feet and shouted, "Don't let them do that to Will Rogers! Give the man a chance!" The audience erupted in a burst of cheering and clapping that brought Rogers back onstage and earned him a standing ovation as well as considerable newspaper coverage the next day. During a *Ziegfeld Follies* performance a few years later, Rogers caught Stone with his lariat and pulled him up on stage from the audience. The two proceeded to visit, inquiring about their families and activities as if they were conversing in one of their living rooms. The audience loved it. When Stone had an airplane accident in the fall of 1928 that left him seriously injured, Rogers dropped his plans and stepped in as a last-minute replacement in *Three Cheers*, a show also featuring Stone's daughter, Dorothy. With little time to learn the lines, the Oklahoman ad-libbed and riffed through the whole performance, dancing with Dorothy in several routines and even singing Stone's songs, although he always joked to the audience, "When I sing, I feel that is as far as any man has ever gone for a friend." Rogers performed in *Three Cheers* from October 28, 1928 to June 1, 1929.[39]

Stone described Rogers as the "one great friend" in his life and noted, "we were closer, far closer, than brothers." Many years later, he said of the humorist, "He had a brilliant mind but the softest heart in the world. Did you ever realize that, back of every remark, was the truth? He did lots of good by speaking the truth, and it didn't offend anyone because, no matter how that truth struck home, it was always said in such a humorous way that you laughed with him." Rogers appreciation of Stone ran just as deep. On March 11, 1923, the Oklahoman extolled his friend's virtues to a national audience in a *Weekly Article* entitled "We Need More Fred Stones." Stone had just embraced religion with his usual vigor, and Rogers claimed that it was "the shortest jump, from his life to a religious one, that any man ever made." In the columnist's words, "When you consider that the biggest and highest salaried and busiest man we have in our profession can stop and give some of his time to religion, it is a lesson to the rest of us." Rogers described how Stone's parent had imbued him with Christian principles as a kid, how he was devoted to his family, and how he had become "the best loved actor on the stage today" with a style of wholesome entertainment appealing to adults and children alike. Rogers observed, "Fred Stone can do more things and do them well than any man in or out of show business" – comedy, acrobatic stunts, dancing, boxing, baseball, lariat throwing, ice skating, horseback riding and polo, and marksmanship. As the Oklahoman ended his paean, if such a man "wants to knock off and go to church I don't think I will mind, and if they will let me in, I may go, too."[40]

While Rogers' family and friendships greatly enriched his private life, so, too, did an abundance of activities that engaged the interest of this energetic, curious man. At the top of the list stood his lifelong devotion to riding and roping. From the time he first learned to get around as a child, the Oklahoman was as comfortable on the back of a horse as he was walking on the ground. And he was as comfortable lassoing something as examining it, or lassoing someone as talking to him or her. Rogers' skills with a horse and a rope had brought him into the entertainment world of outdoor shows and vaudeville, of course, but the interest was a passion more than a vocation. Riding and roping served as his favorite way to relax and enjoy himself throughout his adult life. Most evenings after supper at the Santa Monica ranch, Rogers would adjourn to the roping corral, often accompanied by a couple of his children, for a roping session with the calves he had especially secured for the purpose. As these bovine targets became used to being lassoed over and over, however, they would spy the riders and immediately stroll up alongside to meet their fates. They would have to be replaced periodically. Rogers was so addicted to roping that he kept a lariat indoors to fling around household objects, or sometimes guests. As Betty reported, whenever her husband returned to the ranch from a stint on the road lecturing or entertaining, he immediately headed to the stables and saddled a horse for a ride through the property, usually lariat in hand.[41]

Not surprisingly, Rogers had a special love of, and bond with, horses. "There is something the matter with a man who don't like a horse," his wife often heard him say. Over the years, Rogers had a host of equine favorites with the first being Comanche, his boyhood mount. The dun-colored horse with black markings was a swift, agile roping pony and his master would cherish his companionship for some two decades. Then Teddy, a clever and highly trained little horse, a dark bay with black mane and tail, became his partner on the vaudeville stage for many years. Chapel was a highly intelligent horse Rogers used for stunt riding in silent films. The animal performed so flawlessly and with such awareness, scrambling up and down slopes and making every kind of jump imaginable, that he gained a reputation for being almost "wonderfully human in understanding," in the words of one observer. After settling at the Santa Monica ranch, Rogers bought Soapsuds, an older speckled roan pony, from a ranch in Texas. While unimposing on first viewing, the animal was a first-rate roping horse, quick on his feet and highly responsive to the rider's guidance. When he was home, the Oklahoman rode him nearly every day. Standing in an equine class of his own, however, was Dopey, whom Betty described as "a family institution." Rogers purchased the jet-black, personable horse in 1915 when the family was summering on Long Island and he quickly became a pampered pet, walking into the house and sometimes ascending the stairway. The Rogers clan had him for almost two decades, and when he died a heartbroken Rogers wrote a eulogy in his *Weekly Article*:

Dopey belonged to the family. Our children learned to ride at two, and during his lifetime he never did a wrong thing to throw one off, or do a wrong thing after they had fallen off. He couldent pick 'em up, but he would stand there and look at 'em with a disgusted look for being so clumsy as to fall off. He never kicked or stepped on one of them in his life .... [H]e was always naturally gentle, and intelligent. I used to sit on him by the hour, (yes, by the year) and try new rope tricks and he never batted an eye .... In a private tan bark ring we had in our old Beverly Hills home all the children learned trick riding on him, standing up on him, running, vaulting .... We still have quite a few old favorites [horses] left, but Dopey was different. He was of the family. He raised our children. He learned'em to ride. He never hurt one in his life. He did everything right. That's a reputation that no human can die with. Goodbye, Dopey, from Mama, Dad, Bill, Mary, and Jim.[42]

Given his passion for life in the saddle, it was not surprising that Rogers took up a sport that depended on riding skills. He became an aficionado of polo. Hal Roach introduced Rogers to the game during the humorist's stint in silent movies and he played on Long Island with a group of friends, including Fred Stone, who also took up the sport. Rogers joked that onlookers soon learned, upon seeing a player take a spill, "if the falling rider hit on his feet, it was Fred Stone. If he hit on his head, it was me. We were both equally safe." The humorist praised Bootlegger as his favorite polo pony. Originally trained as a roping horse and a bit on the small side, the animal possessed extraordinary speed and quickness in stopping and turning, traits that made him ideal for the game. This black horse soon became famous for speeding around the field with a flowing mane and tail since his owner, in violation of polo tradition, could not bear to crop them. Rogers, the down-home man of the people, was somewhat embarrassed by his participation in the swanky game of polo, once writing in a *Weekly Article*, "I want it distinctly understood that I did not take up polo for any social prestige, or to make myself pointed out as a man about town." But he adored the game because, as O. O. McIntyre put it, "it gives him the chance for the hell-for-breakfast riding that he loves." Rogers believed polo enhanced his skills on horseback, insisting that "it learns you to ride quicker than anything on earth for when you start hitting at the ball you forget about how you are going to stay on, you just do it unconsciously." The game also generated a family appeal, with all of his children learning to play – they would fight over who got to ride favorite ponies – and Will, Jr. and James eventually becoming accomplished polo players.[43]

However, Rogers, true to his western spirit of independence, did not play this aristocratic game in the style of his fellow enthusiasts. Particularly in the early going, he embraced an unorthodox style of cowboy polo that involved hell-for-leather riding, western-style clothing, and rough-and tumble action. As he liked to quip, "They call it a gentleman's game for the same reason they call a tall man 'Shorty.'" A fellow player in the early days on Long Island, Eddie Dowling, an actor and producer of plays, described how Rogers "tore into a game like an Apache into battle, screaming and yelling and flourishing his mallet like a scalp stick." Once, when an opposing player split open Rogers' lip with a wayward mallet stroke, the entertainer left the field and went to the stables where an on-call veterinarian sewed it up. He returned to the contest, but carried the scar for the rest of his life. As he grew older and more experienced, the Oklahoman's tactics mellowed and he adopted the typical breeches-calf boots-helmet attire, but his energetic approach did not flag. Rogers described one of his matches in California as a contest with "the 11th Cavalry from Monterey." Things were going along nicely, he said, until the new pony he was riding "suddenly reared up and fell back on me. There he was, a laying right across my intermission, my head was out on one side and my feet on the other; that was all you could see." He recovered from that mishap but later in the match was "coming lickety split down the field, when for no reason at all the horse crosses his front legs and starts turning somersaults. They picked me up just south of Santa Barbara."[44]

As an observer rather than a participant, Rogers was a fan of team sports. He liked college football and became friends with Knute Rockne, the legendary Notre Dame coach. But baseball was his favorite spectator sport. He became fond of the game while in vaudeville where, as he traveled the country, he met and became friends with professional ballplayers. Occasionally, Rogers would attend morning practices of National or American League teams where he would don a uniform and shag balls from batting practice. "He was a good ballplayer for an amateur. We kidded a lot with him, but he chased those flies like a veteran," reported a member of the Detroit Tigers. Rogers also participated in games, usually playing first base, when touring vaudevillians would organize squads and play each other. By the 1920s, he was writing regularly about America's favorite sport in his *Weekly Articles*, where he praised it for requiring skill, determination, competitive spirit, and diligent labor. "Baseball is our national game; every boy and girl in the United States should play it," Rogers opined. "It should be made compulsory in the schools." The humorist became friends with legendary players such as Ty Cobb and Tris Speaker and became a fervent fan of the great pitcher, Walter Johnson, who first pitched in the World Series after eighteen years spent faithfully, uncomplainingly toiling for the lowly Washington Senators. The pitcher was widely admired by spectators and fellow players alike for his virtues of hard work, loyalty, and perseverance. Rogers proclaimed that "the man, woman, or child in the United States that don't love Walter Johnson and admire him as a man, is not a good American." The Oklahoman delighted in the 1934 World Series, where his favorite team, the St. Louis Cardinals, played the

Detroit Tigers. He attended five of the seven games and in Detroit sat with Henry and Edsel Ford in their stadium box. The series featured Rogers' favorite player, the Cardinals' Dizzy Dean, the flamboyant, irreverent, joke-cracking, hard-throwing pitcher from the backwoods of the Ozarks. The humorist got a special thrill when he sat next to Dean at a Baseball Writer's dinner a few months later. "He is sho' chuck full of personality and he is boastful, but it's not in a fresh way. It's in a kidding way, and he is always laughing, and he is what they call a natural ball player," Rogers reported to his readers. "He can do anything."[45]

Of all his hobbies and pastimes, however, travel may have been Rogers' favorite. He was addicted to staying on the move and found going to new places exhilarating rather than exhausting. He had journeyed around the globe as a young man and then constantly crisscrossed the United States throughout his days in vaudeville, with the *Ziegfeld Follies*, and as a lecturer and speaker. If he had a free day, he liked to grab Betty and the kids, hop into a car, and head off without any plans to see what, or whom, they encountered. On one such sojourn along a California backroad, they curved up a mountain and came across a grizzled old ranger living in a log cabin. The old man recognized Rogers and called out, "Man alive! How in the world did you ever get up here?" After an extended, friendly conversation, they had to turn the car around by hand to depart because of the narrow mountain road. Rogers loved such unexpected encounters, his wife noted, because he "had a human, friendly way with strangers and a warm curiosity about what other people were doing and thinking." In the late 1920s and 1930s Rogers' travels extended to Latin America, England, Europe, Russia, and eventually the Far East, causing him to joke, "I had visited some strange places in the world, but it was always so full of Tourists by the time I got to it that the Tourists were stranger than the place." But he always seemed to relish most his trips around the United States. In January 1926, he wrote in a *Weekly Article*, "All I know is just what I observe as I flit from one end of our great Commonwealth to another." He then noted that after closing his fall lecture tour in Boston he spent the holidays in California with family and friends and was now headed to Florida for appearances at Daytona, Palm Beach, Miami, and Jacksonville. Two years later he gave an enthusiastic account of a family road trip, along with Fred Stone and his clan, to Lake Tahoe, Yosemite, Mona Lake, Virginia City, Carson City, and Reno. "If you want to have a good time, I don't care where you live, just load in your kids, and take some congenial friends, and just start out. You would be surprised what there is to see in this great Country within 200 miles of where any of us live," Rogers concluded. "I don't care what State or what town."[46]

Will Rogers led a life that was full to the point of overflowing. His multifaceted career kept him in touch with millions of his fellow citizens while domestic duties kept him immersed in family affairs. His friends and his hobbies vacuumed up any extra time. But behind this relentless schedule of activities that the Oklahoman pursued with his trademark humor, charm, and energy where lay the real human being? When Rogers was not entertaining or writing or riding horses or seeing the world being "Will Rogers," the humorist and cracker-barrel observer of American life, what was he like? What did he truly value and believe in? What were his characteristic traits, and was the man who "never met a man he didn't like" likeable himself? How did he view life and its meaning? Rogers was seldom an introspective man and answers to these questions only appeared partially and haltingly. But the fragments that came to light disclosed a complicated man.

* * * * *

For all those who knew him, or even encountered him briefly, Will Rogers' most striking trait was his intense nervous energy. Betty came face-to-face with this trait when they first married and it left her a bit stunned. "Will was a difficult person to keep up with. He hated to lose a moment of his life; he wanted to do everything right now," she noted. "And he nearly ran me ragged." She quickly came to understand that her husband habitually scurried from activity to activity and place to place, loathing rest and always eager to stay busy. Moreover, his ruling principle was spontaneity – he hated to make plans and avoided making engagements two weeks ahead if he could avoid it. If he wanted to do something, he moved immediately to make it happen. Rogers saw life as uncertain and running the risk that something might slip away was foreign to his nature. Even buying and selling horses, an endeavor he knew intimately and thoroughly, fell victim to his nervous energy and impatience. He often undersold or overpaid simply because he wanted to enjoy the horse he wanted now and refused to wait a day or two to reach a good price. "As a result living with Will had its explosive qualities," Betty admitted ruefully. "I was not made of the same kind of stuff and there were times when this life of the moment troubled me."[47]

Rogers' friends and acquaintances confirmed Betty's perspective. Charles V. McAdam of the McNaught Syndicate hosted many of the humorist's visits to his office and marveled at his nervous energy. "He wouldn't sit still. He would be in and out of his chair; he would look out the window, then come and sit on a corner of my desk, talking all the time," McAdam reported. "And chewing. Sometimes it would be a piece of string, or rubber bands. One time, just for a joke, I asked him what he was chewing today. It was a rubber sealing ring from a Mason jar." Rogers' lecture assistant, Bruce Quisenberry, observed similar traits. "I never saw such amazing energy. He never seemed to be tired. Sometimes, when I was utterly exhausted, he would say, 'Boy, what are you so draggy about? You slept till six this morning,'" Quisenberry related. Rogers' longtime friend, the journalist O. O. McIntyre, shared a writing table with the Oklahoman at the 1928 Democratic Convention in Houston and found his jittery energy to be exhausting. "Will Rogers' seat is next to mine and if there ever was a flibberty gibbety guy he is it. His jaws snap 100 times a minute and when he is not wriggling his feet he is shifting from one hip to another or rolling a lead pencil between his palms. I wasn't there a half hour before he had worked me into a spell of the jerks," McIntyre related. "'If you can't sit still, go home,' I finally told him." At home, Rogers occasionally channeled his energy into a collection of musical instruments at which he sawed or banged away with great enthusiasm but little talent. "He owns a hurdy-gurdy, piano, violin, banjo, drums, mandolin, and guitar. He has tried them all and can't play any of them. But he still tries," a magazine reporter noticed.[48]

Rogers' energy was matched by his genuine humility, a trait many observers found hard to understand in an individual so popular and successful. He never showed the slightest sign of boastfulness or pretension about himself, his career, and his remarkable achievements. To the contrary, Rogers often expressed the belief that he had been the beneficiary of luck and that everything might come crumbling down at any moment. He never thought his next project would be a great success, he did not see himself as a sage, and he often seemed surprised about his ability to make people laugh or think. "His nature was strange: he did not have an inferiority complex, but he did – and this seems to be the very core of his being – have humility," his friend Homer Croy perceived. "He knew he was an international figure, but he didn't take it seriously. It just happened to work out that way, that was his attitude." While seldom given to self-reflection, Rogers once confessed in a *Weekly Article* that "Everything I have done has been by luck, no move was premeditated. I just stumbled from one thing to another." Emotionally, Rogers seemed prepared for his life as a public figure to end at any moment. As Betty related, when they discussed his career or his future her husband would often say, "They will get wise to me pretty soon."[49]

This genuinely humble man often displayed a generosity so conspicuous that it became legendary. It colored his endeavors both large and small. When Rogers was performing in New York City, beggars often waited at the stage door for handouts and while his colleagues would dispense quarters, he would pass out dollar bills. After he became famous, down-on-their-luck entertainers from his vaudeville days would approach him asking for money and he always provided assistance. Big Boy Williams related that after Rogers shot a film in Jackson, California and became friendly with the locals, he learned several months later that a terrible mining accident took a number of lives in the community.

He promptly, and anonymously, wired several hundred dollars to be distributed to the victims' families. Rogers paid for elderly polo ponies to be put out to pasture for a comfortable retirement and lavished Christmas presents on everyone who worked for him, or with him. Fred Stone noted that Rogers often signed over sizable paychecks to charities and organizations such as the Red Cross, Salvation Army, Community Chest, and Boy Scouts. In Stone's words, "He was thrifty about his own needs, but prodigal in supplying the needs of others."[50]

A deep sentimentality accompanied Rogers' generosity. As Betty Rogers said of her husband, "he is the softest-hearted man that ever lived; he is intensely sentimental, whether over people, places, or things, and equally loyal." This quality appeared in his kindness to animals. As a boy, he would accompany his friends to go rabbit hunting, but then would refuse to kill them. Throughout his life he criticized people who bobbed their horses' tails, declaring, "Don't you know it hurts them and does no one any good? If God hadn't wanted tails on horses, he would have borned them that way." Children struck a similar sentimental chord. On one of his lecture tours, to the annoyance of his manager, he stopped the car before a group of children who were holding up a sign to welcome him to town and did a few rope tricks to entertain them. In 1928, he actually kept an audience waiting in Raleigh, North Carolina while he performed rope tricks for a group of about twenty street urchins who had gathered in the alley behind the theater in hopes of glimpsing the famous entertainer. At the close of the impromptu show, he gave them all money to go to the movies. Big Boy Williams recalled that Rogers, during the filming of one of his silent movies, called a property man, slipped him some money, and told him to buy some ice cream or candy for a bunch of raggedy-looking kids hanging around the location looking for a thrill.[51]

This soft-hearted nature caused Rogers to cry easily. When O. O. McIntyre attended the musical *Ripples* in 1930 and sat next to the humorist, during a sad segment of the performance he was startled when he "turned suddenly to find the big stiff crying like a baby." A few years earlier, Rogers learned that Fred Stone had led the audience revolt that returned him to the stage to an ovation in *Hands Up*. According to Mrs. Stone, after she related news of her husband's maneuver, Rogers "had his knee up, with his arms clasped around it, and tears were coming down his cheeks. He was so touched." Another time the humorist was visiting and entertaining wounded soldiers in a hospital when he suddenly left the ward and disappeared. When he was gone a long time, someone went in search and found him "in the men's room, leaning on the window sill, crying at the plight of those young patients."[52]

Given his humility and sentimental regard for others, it not surprising that Rogers habitually disdained the trappings of wealth and fame. Instead, he followed his natural inclination: a man of the people with uncommon talents but ordinary tastes. This populist stance was more than a pose – he truly believed in valuing the average person and he lived the message that he delivered in his talks and writings. A fellow actor described how he refused to pull rank while traveling to movie locations, instead jumping into any available automobile and "if a bunch of guys are in a comfortable rear seat, he'll pull down the dickey seat and sit on that. If you know anything about Hollywood, you know how unusual it is for a star to be so democratic." Reporters visiting the Rogers household always walked away impressed by his rumpled appearance and unassuming manner. An article in the *American Magazine* noted,

> Much of his appeal lies in the fact that he seems to be just an ordinary sort of fellow – one of the mob. He chews gum, he wears old clothes, he snorts at convention, he is homely and usually needs a haircut. His general appearance and his habits and customs are those of a simple, straightforward man. His is a guise and a demeanor that through the ages have bred confidence – so much so that successful slickers are often found in that apparel. But Will Rogers off the stage is no different from Will Rogers on. He is just what he appears to be.

A journalist with *Better Homes and Gardens* added that while the entertainer "glories in his humble beginnings . . . this is not an act, a clever piece of stage business. Will Rogers is never guilty of affectation." A writer for *Photoplay*, while looking into Rogers' private life at the Santa Monica ranch, discovered that the entertainer often stopped by "Doc Law's," a drugstore owned by former character actor Burton C. Law, which sat down toward the beach. In Law's words, Rogers "started dropping in of evenings just to talk over old times, sit a spell and discuss politics, watching the people who are continually flowing in and out of the store, remarking about this and observing that."[53]

Rogers illustrated his stance as an ordinary American through his dress, which might charitably be described as casual. Despite appearing before audiences numbering in the thousands and enjoying friendships with, and appearances alongside, some of the most notable people of his age, he never dressed the part. Rogers had a rule that he dressed only once a day – after a morning bath, he put on clean clothes and both the cleaning and the attire had to last until bedtime no matter what came up during the day. Moreover, he never concerned himself with clothes. He dressed comfortably at home, often wearing blue jeans and work-style shirts, and maintained a couple of inexpensive suits for professional endeavors. But they were often wrinkled and when they grew thread-bare he would pop into the nearest available store and buy a new one off the rack. Once, as Rogers was about to depart for Europe, he discovered he had only the suit he was wearing. So he bought a cheap, ill-fitting one at a cut-rate shop and had the trousers shortened at a cleaning-and-pressing stand on the street. He ended up wearing it to a formal party in London where his friend, the Prince of Wales, kidded him about setting a new standard in formal dinner wear. As a journalist observed, Rogers' sartorial indifference reflected his democratic spirit of individualism where "he doesn't change his own personality to suit that of others, no matter how exalted their positions may be. In fact, he doesn't even change his mode of attire." After marrying Will and discovering that "clothes mean nothing to him," Betty at first tried to make him tidier and more stylish but eventually gave up. She learned to smile at the fact that "if the Prince of Wales was across the street, even though Will might be in pajamas and slippers, he would jump up and run across the street and say, 'Hello, Prince. How are you?'"[54]

Rogers' plain taste in clothing was matched by his simple preferences in food. While he had sampled the cuisine of nearly every region and city in the United States, as well as that of many countries in Europe, Asia, and Latin America, he preferred the down-home cooking of rural Oklahoma. Chili was probably his favorite dish, and he became a connoisseur of chili parlors around the United States. He loved beans, especially navy beans, and ham smoked by a hickory fire. Ham gravy and beefsteak gravy were particular favorites, but he had a bone to pick about the preparation of steak. "All this eating raw, bloody, rare meat, like they order in big hotels – that's just city people – that ain't old western folks," he wrote. "Ranch cooks and farm women fry steak thin and hard." After returning from a trip to his sister's home in Chelsea, Oklahoma, he raved in a *Weekly Article* about feasting on chili, biscuits, string beans cooked with fat meat, and "real cornbread. Not this old yellow kind made with eggs, but cornbread, real old corn dodger, or corn pone, made with meal, hot water, and salt."[55]

Rogers' essential nature as a simple, unassuming common man was complicated, however, by several characteristics that revealed an underlying, but powerful drive to attract notice and move ahead. He craved an audience. He craved attention. He craved approval and affirmation in ways both large and small. This appeared most noticeably in his relentless showmanship. Rogers "liked audiences; big or little, he must have an audience. If an audience responded, he would give it his great talents. And he would work as hard for a little audience as for a big one. For him there was an intoxication in standing before an audience and in seeing what he could 'do' with it," a friend reflected. "To him an audience was any group that would listen. He liked to have an audience even at a chili counter, or on a train, or at an airport." When a scheduled performance did not go as well as he wished, Rogers' spirits sank, but he always recovered and came before his next audience with added determination. With small groups of friends or acquaintances, he liked to stay up late talking and swapping stories, but many noticed that he usually dominated the proceedings, projecting the sunniest disposition, telling the funniest yarns, talking the loudest. His friend, Doc Law, told a story of how he was at the Rogers ranch when Will had to leave in a hurry to go east for a performance. Doc and Betty rushed to help him pack, and he grabbed his suitcase and headed for the train station. At the gate, however, he encountered a group of autograph seekers and could not resist telling a few jokes and chatting with everyone. He missed the train.[56]

Moreover, for all of his genuine modesty about his stature and achievements, Rogers clearly enjoyed fame. As many of his friends observed, he was always testing it although he tried to do so without notice. While walking down the street, dropping into a store, or eating in a chili parlor, he would surreptitiously glance around to see if people recognized him. If they did, he was pleased. His friend, Homer Croy, had a number of meetings and conversations with Rogers concerning a film script the former had written and the latter was performing, and Croy observed an odd habit. Whenever they exited an office or a meeting room and encountered other people, Rogers "had a peculiar way of talking to you and, at the same time, looking to see if people recognized him." When they did and called out a greeting, the humorist would smile broadly and look tickled.[57]

Perhaps because of his deep need for approval, Rogers suffered from stage fright. He admitted, "I am always nervous; I never saw an audience that I faced with any confidence." Betty explained that a hidden emotional dynamic informed one of her husband's trademark mannerisms as a performer: his opening appearance where he shuffled on stage and stood there and spoke haltingly, usually self-deprecatingly as he looked at the floor, grinned, and glanced up shyly at the people in the seats. Everyone assumed it was part of the "Will Rogers" persona, perhaps exaggerated for effect, when in fact it was genuine. In Betty's words, his "nervous preliminary fumbling, though it became an accepted part of his technique, never had to be assumed. The first few minutes before an audience were agony for Will. It was hard for him to get going, and until he was warmed up, and had the people with him, he couldn't be easy." For all his nervousness as a performer, as a writer Rogers remained perfectly cool under the pressure of his slapdash routine. He typically composed his *Weekly Articles* and *Daily Telegrams* at the last moment, writing hurriedly wherever he could set up his trusty typewriter, often in the backseat of his car if he was making a film or performing on the road. Looming deadlines and at-the-wire submissions did not seem to faze him.[58]

Ironically for a genuinely humble man who cherished kindness and cultivated likeability in human relations, Rogers proved unusually sensitive to criticism. Once when he wrote a controversial column demanding that England and France immediately repay their debt to the United States from World War I, a number of readers complained to the *New York Times* that the piece was ignorant and jingoistic. So the newspaper published an apologetic, condescending editorial distancing itself from Rogers and intoning, "Let the raw, untutored voices be heard." Obviously irked, the humorist fired back in his next *Daily Telegram*, "I would like to state to the readers of THE NEW YORK TIMES that I am in no way responsible for the editorial or political policy of this paper ... . Their editorials may be put in purely for humor, or just to fill space. Every paper must have its various entertaining features, and their editorials are not always to be taken seriously, and never to be construed as my policy." When a Boston critic went after Rogers for "desecrating" the Boston Symphony Hall with crude jokes, poor diction, and bad grammar, the humorist devoted an entire *Weekly Article* to mocking him as a snob ("when you looked me over you were 'slumming'"), a freeloader ("Your seat was about the only free one; people that pay for things never complain. It's the guy you give something to that you can't please"), and lacking in perception ("He said my jokes had lost the sting they used to have; that they had mellowed. That's not my fault. The prominent men are not as bad as they used to be .... Either that, or we are just getting more used to them.") When the Lieutenant Governor of California introduced Rogers at a rally and chided him for talking to a companion during his remarks, the Oklahoman came back with a masterful putdown when he came to the lectern. First, Rogers explained that he had whispered to the lady sitting next to him, "Who is that man talking?" and she replied, "I don't know." Rogers claimed that the same question and same answer went all the way down the line before someone correctly identified the speaker. Second, Rogers claimed he then asked, "What does he do?" and his neighbor replied, "He don't do anything. He gets up every morning and asks if the Governor's any worse."[59]

Also somewhat surprisingly for a down-home philosopher and generous philanthropist, Rogers was a tough businessman. Charles L. Wagner, who managed the humorist for several seasons as a lecturer, portrayed him as "the most temperamental, and hardest-to-deal-with star that I ever handled .... He was money mad." Indeed, Rogers' populist sensibility seems to have inculcated the idea that the "money men" for whom he worked – theater owners, studio heads, newspaper and magazine owners – were always trying to get the better of him. Always on the alert, he demanded that he be paid his worth. Rogers' innate suspicion of high finance had been exacerbated during his vaudeville days when a couple of New York businessmen had hoodwinked him into buying lots on the far end of Long Island. They promised that transatlantic liners would soon be docking at a port under development, but that turned out to be a fantasy as his lots sat in the middle of an old man's cornfield. Rogers grew more savvy, however, and after locating to Southern California proved to be an astute real estate investor. A 1928 article in *Forbes*, entitled "Will Rogers: The Business Man," described him as an "enterprising" figure who had amassed considerable wealth from newspaper and magazine writing, lecturing, and stage show appearances supplemented by a Beverly Hills home worth 250,000 dollars and a 250-acre ranch likely worth several million dollars in the near future. Rogers had a complicated view of money: he liked having it and saw it as an accurate barometer of worth and success, but after working hard for monetary gain he treated it almost casually, giving large amounts away and spending substantial sums whenever the mood struck him.[60]

As his success mounted, Rogers increasingly felt the pressures of fame. By the 1920s, as silent movies, journalistic writing, lecturing, and stage shows sent him to great heights of popularity, the humorist encountered the stress typically tormenting celebrities – being approached constantly by a host of people seeking favors and attention. Moreover, continued success required continued efforts on all these fronts to keep his name before the public. Relaxation became ever more elusive. "Demands, demands from everywhere stalked his life. He met them all. But he was tired. He wanted to get off the beaten trail," Fred Stone noted of his friend. "But he couldn't write news in an isolated spot. He couldn't keep faith with his readers [by] roping calves, twirling a lariat, lying nights on the plain. He had to go places and see things so he could write about them." In a letter to sister-in-law Maud Lane, Betty observed similarly, "It is wonderful to be a big man before the public, but oh, what a price Billy pays for it." Jim Hopkins, a hired hand who helped take care of the horses at the Santa Monica ranch, noticed more troubling signs of Rogers' stress. "He talked to himself all the time. I was worried," Hopkins said. He described an occasion when the humorist was standing around conversing with a couple of acquaintances when he seemed to drift away: "The first thing I knew, his eyes were kind of asleep and he was talking to something way off." When the others left, Hopkins said, "Will, if you don't lay off, you'll go to the bughouse," and the humorist replied, "I don't know what I was doing." "He was terribly embarrassed," the hired hand related.[61]

Rogers' genuine nature as a common man, in concert with an underlying drive for achievement and stress from the pressures attending public success, made for a complex personality with competing impulses and hidden depths. This most public of men, in fact, was deeply private as he concealed a deep reticence beneath his charming personality. "His easy, boyish, open approach made people feel that he was just what they saw on the surface," his friend Homer Croy astutely observed. "In one sense this was true, but beyond this hail-fellow-well-met personality he was vastly reserved; there was a wall no one went beyond; and there were dark chambers and hidden recesses that he opened to no one." Croy was struck by the fact that Rogers seemed to have two contrasting personalities. He recalled a private conversation where the Oklahoman was personable, relaxed, and low-key but when they finished and walked out to the street "in no time a crowd was around him. And now he was a showman. He talked to me but watched the crowd, as he always did ... . I laughed, for he was immensely amusing. The crowd laughed." Croy concluded that Rogers was tremendously likeable but "had a strangely secretive side." When dealing with an audience or group of friends he was the buoyant, amusing star of the room, but when something personal came up "he said very little, became almost taciturn ... . twirled his eyeglasses in his hands and stared at the floor, saying nothing at all."[62]

Almost everyone who came to know Rogers noticed this bifurcated quality. A friend, "Alfalfa Bill" Murray, described a two-hour conversation in Rogers' office where the entertainer talked earnestly and made no jokes. Then at a banquet that evening, Murray was startled to hear Rogers speak about the same topics and have the audience in stitches. Murray "could hardly believe it was the same person." "Big Boy" Williams had similar experiences. When he and Rogers were alone they would often talk "seriously and philosophically," but when others were around Williams would be drawn into playing the straight man as Rogers would deliver comic riffs non-stop. Spencer Tracy, an actor and fellow polo player, described Rogers as "a strange paradox .... at the same time one of the best known and one of the least known men in the world, by inclination a great mixer, by instinct a humorist; when he talks about someone else he's brilliant, but about himself he's shy, ill-at-ease, embarrassed." Walt Disney, studio head and another polo friend, had his animators study Rogers as a basis for the dwarf character "Bashful" in *Snow White* because he realized the humorist was not the outgoing extrovert he seemed, but actually shy, retiring, and subject to mood swings. The journalist Ben Dixon MacNeill said that while Rogers had keen comic instincts, "I think he was more comfortable with people who didn't laugh at every sentence he uttered. At best he was serious, tremendously practical, keen in observation and comprehension .... I doubt if anybody ever plumbed his mind."[63]

Rogers's sons confirmed these contrasting traits in their father. Will, Jr., suggested the entertainer had a kind of "dual personality" that was rooted in his situation as an Indian trying to achieve in a white world, a role that demanded a public persona somewhat different from one's private sense of self. Jim Rogers ascribed it partly to an artistic temperament. "Like so many creative people, he had days when he was riding high, on the crest of the wave, and the next day he would hit bottom," he reflected. "Mother always knew when to jolly him along and how to play to his moods." But Jim also reported that from an early age, he perceived his dad as two separate figures: "a father and an entirely separate figure, using the terms we all use, 'W. R.' He became two different people .... He's dad, and he's the public man, sort of a split figure as far as I'm concerned. You see him in two entirely different lights."[64]

Rogers' complex emotional structure with its good-humored surface and darker hidden depths ultimately produced a view of life that was similarly divided: by all accounts tolerant, civil, good-humored yet only loosely connected to deep philosophical or religious beliefs. Betty Rogers contended that her husband was by nature "a deeply religious man" although he seldom attended church. She contended that his endorsement of kindness, generosity, and tolerance were simply "a part of him, coloring his whole process of living and thinking." Son Jim concurred, observing that his father endorsed no creed but was "one of the most religious people I ever knew." His father lived daily by the golden rule and had a firm belief in the afterlife, traits that flowed from the world-view of the "Indian people" from whom he sprang. As for Rogers himself, he seldom addressed the principles or bedrock beliefs that steered his conduct. He once admitted, "I got no 'Philosophy.' I don't even know what the word means." Regarding religion, he noted that he had been raised in the Methodist Church but as an adult held to no particular creed. He replied to a minister (and then reprinted it in a *Weekly Article*) who had inquired about his religion, "I don't know now just what I am. I know I have never been a non-believer. But I can honestly tell you that I don't think that any one religion is the religion . . . . I do know that I am broadminded in a religious way. Which way you serve your God will never get one word of argument or condemnation out of me."[65]

The historian, Will Durant, wrote Rogers and asked him to share his philosophy of life, indicating he had made similar requests of Hoover, Lloyd George, Gandhi, Marconi, Trotsky, Einstein, Edison, Ford, Bernard Shaw, and several other prominent figures. The humorist joked that his presence in such exalted company caused him to conclude he "better start looking into this Philosophy thing," but then he decided he had only been put on the list "to get the 'Dumb' angle." Rogers finally offered these thoughts, providing a rare glimpse into his view of life's larger questions. Its nihilistic tone probably surprised those used to hearing his irreverent, upbeat quips:

> What all of us know put together don't mean anything. Nothing don't mean anything. We are just here for a spell and pass on. Any man that thinks Civilization has advanced is an egotist. Fords and bathtubs have moved you and cleaned you, but you was just as ignorant when you got there . . . .
>
> We have got more toothpaste on the market, and more misery in our Courts than at any time in our existence. There ain't nothing to life but satisfaction . . . . Indians and primitive races were the highest civilized, because they were more satisfied, and they depended less on each other, and took less from each other. We couldn't live a day without depending on everybody. So our civilization has given us no Liberty or Independence . . . .

The whole thing is a "Racket," so get a few laughs, do the best you can, take nothing serious, for nothing is certainly depending on this generation. Each one lives in spite of the previous one and not because of it. And don't start "seeking knowledge" for the more you seek the nearer the "Booby Hatch" you get.

And don't have an ideal to work for. That's like riding toward a Mirage of a lake. When you get there it ain't there. Believe in something for another World, but don't be too set on what it is, and then you won't start out that life with a disappointment. Live your life so that whenever you lose, you are ahead.[66]

Ultimately, Will Rogers the private man was an authentic yet complicated figure. Eager to be liked but critical in many of his observations, common in his tastes but uncommon in his talents, devoted to his family while often gone from them, humble in his success but resentful of criticism, and sunny in his evaluation of most people but dark in his view of life's meaning, he balanced his internal contradictions and never attempted to be anyone other than the Oklahoma cowboy whose witty observations and insights had somehow found a popular audience. Most of the journalists covering him would have agreed with *American Magazine*: "His entire success lies in the fact that he is just himself. At no time is he an actor." Most of his friends would have agreed with Homer Croy: "One great, one tremendous asset for Will was that he was always himself . . . . Will was exactly what he was. Never in all the world . . . was there ever a person so wholly and completely himself."[67]

At the same time, this most genuine of individuals was entangled in a snare of his own creation. Rogers was caught up in the popular image of the humble, witty, down-home, cracker-barrel philosopher that he had crafted so diligently since the early 1910s. And to a certain extent, the image became larger than the man himself. Rogers the homespun humorist was never an act, dropped at the end of the work day and taken up again whenever an audience beckoned. It was the essence of the real man. Yet the Oklahoman's enormous success allowed no respite, instead obligating him to meet at all times the expectations of others, to live up to their image of him. The more famous he became, the more intense the pressure became to be the person others encountered on the printed page or stage or movie screen. "He built himself up till he became, both on and off the stage, the Will Rogers the public knew," a friend shrewdly observed. "The older he grew, and the more successful he became, the more he played this character." As with nearly all celebrities and public figures, the price of fame was a Faustian bargain exchanging a measure of authenticity for a larger measure of love and approval.[68]

Possessed of a private life almost as multifaceted, rich, and vigorous as his public life, this shrewd and gifted humorist reached a great height of fame and influence by the late 1920s. As the decade drew to a close, however, Rogers came face to face with several transformative developments. Although nearly impossible to believe in a man almost frantically busy on so many fronts, he embraced several new endeavors that tapped into his enormous stores of talent and energy. He commenced a new career as one of the most popular radio hosts in America with his own show. He became a world traveler, circling the globe while enthusiastically embracing the new frontier of airplanes and flying. After accepting a seductive offer that returned him to the world of Hollywood filmmaking, Rogers re-emerged in the new "talkie" movies and became a movie star. But first, beginning in the fall of 1929 and continuing for several years thereafter, Rogers confronted the massive economic disaster that brought the American stock market crashing down and sent the nation reeling into a gulch of unemployment, poverty, and wrenching social strain. The Great Depression not only galvanized the popular entertainer's political and social views but, as was true of nearly all Americans, became a dominating influence on his life.

11

The Little Fellow and the Great Depression

I N EARLY 1929, WILL ROGERS MET HIS OLD FRIEND, Eddie Cantor, for dinner
at Dinty Moore's Restaurant on West 46th Street in New York. The two
entertainers had first crossed paths back in their vaudeville days and formed a
mutual admiration society. The Oklahoman appreciated the talent and show
business savvy of the wisecracking, streetwise, wide-eyed comedian from the
Lower East Side while the Jewish entertainer idolized the modest, charitable
cowboy with the string of humorous observations and western drawl whom he
came to describe as the "Great American." While vastly different in terms of
cultural background, they shared a genial temperament, a natural curiosity, and
the ability to make people laugh. These commonalities brought them together
and allowed each to enjoy new experiences – kosher food and dialect humor for
Rogers, horses and lariats for Cantor. The showmen stayed in touch even after
vaudeville declined and got together when their entertainment schedules put
them in the same city, as was now the case with Rogers starring in *Three Cheers*
and Cantor in *Whoopee* on Broadway.[1]

Now, as the two old friends bent over their meal, they encountered something that separated them. Cantor had been an enthusiastic participant in the
stock market throughout the 1920s and took in a considerable profit as share
values rose steadily, sometimes spectacularly, throughout the decade. This
evening he was ecstatic, claiming that he made more in the last month than he
did in the last two years on the stage. Rogers, with a twinkle in his eye, inquired,
"Eddie, what are you doing to the stock market that's making it go up?" Cantor
replied that he had focused on buying bank stocks, and recommended one in
particular to his friend, promising an investment would make a lot of money.
Rogers hemmed and hawed and finally gave his approval and forwarded some
money to Cantor, who bought a handful of stocks in his name. For the next
several days the value of the bank shares climbed steeply but then dropped slightly

by the second week. Rogers could not stand the financial uncertainty. He called Cantor and asked him to sell the stock, declaring "actors have got no right to look for easy pickin's." Moreover, Rogers claimed, "Each night I began to get unfunnier and unfunnier. This strain of being 'in the market' was telling on me . . . . [T]he whole thing is no place for a weak hearted Comedian." So Cantor sold the shares and sent his friend a check including the modest profits from his two-week ownership. When they met again a few days later, Rogers returned to the New Yorker a check for the stock profits having endorsed it to a boy's camp that Cantor supported.[2]

A few months later, the muffled tension over this issue between two old friends tightened in the larger society before snapping explosively. On October 28, 1929, "Black Friday," the stock market declined precipitously and over the next few days crashed completely as panic swept through Wall Street. With prices plummeting and fortunes evaporating around them, stockbrokers scurried about unable to stem the tide as a number of distraught ones jumped to their death from high-rise buildings. Investors lost staggering amounts of money. Cantor was among those wiped out financially, and the comedian would struggle mightily over the next several years to recover. This scene of financial carnage steadily expanded over the next year and spread into the broader economy as manufacturing shriveled, bankruptcies multiplied, unemployment soared, foreclosed homes became common, and millions of working-class and middle-class Americans fell into financial exigency. By 1931, the United States stood amidst the worst economic downturn in its history and the Great Depression settled over the American landscape like a thick, massive grey fog. The figures were stunning: unemployment hovered around 25 percent, investment plunged to nearly 90 percent below 1929 levels, and the gross national product languished at about 25 percent below pre-crash levels. As wealth and opportunity disappeared for many, an atmosphere of despair and dread took their place. The Depression would not lift for the next decade, and throughout that period it reached into every nook and cranny of American economic, political, cultural, and social life.[3]

As one of the nation's leading chroniclers and commentators on public affairs, Rogers naturally grew preoccupied with understanding the Great Depression, assessing its impact on the United States, and pondering ways to overcome it. In his *Daily Telegrams* and *Weekly Articles*, as well as his public talks and magazine pieces, he constantly discussed the political implications, social issues, and economic strains flowing from this massive economic trauma. The Oklahoman did so with his customary folksy wit, shrewd insight, and deep concern for the plight of ordinary citizens. Americans, many of them struggling to survive and often confronting despair, found solace and inspiration in his observations and Rogers climbed ever higher in the public estimation. His ability to find humor, however rueful it often was, even in the darkest chapter of the modern national experience offered relief and hope to millions. Even more than before, they began to hang on his every word.

So while the American economic expansion and prosperity of the 1920s screeched to a halt at decade's end, Rogers' fame and popularity soared higher. Ironically, hard times for the nation brought flush times for its favorite entertainer and pundit. He became the nation's comforter during hard times and its most passionate advocate for the common people who were suffering most. The Great Depression cemented his status as a beloved figure in American life.

* * * * *

Will Rogers never had much use for Wall Street. The buying and selling of stocks, he wrote, "is all a puzzle to me. I never did mess with it." He believed it was a financial game rigged to benefit big, wealthy investors and take advantage of small ones of limited means. Rogers compared it to a giant "sieve" where "Everything and everybody is put into it, and it is shaken, and through the holes .... the little investors go. They pick themselves up, turn bootlegger or do something to get more money, and then they crawl back in the hopper and away they go again." Most often, the Oklahoman described the stock market as a reckless form of gambling where you put down your money and chanced that it would turn a profit as the financial game unfolded. But it was a fool's game. Rogers once recommended putting up traffic lights on Wall Street to help direct the gullible: "The red light tells you you better stop and wait before buying, the green light tells you that you are a sucker anyhow and you might just as well go ahead. The yellow light means, put up no more margins, let 'em sell you out." In fact, Rogers was so contemptuous of the stock market that initially he downplayed the significance of the crash in late October 1929. Two days after "Black Friday," he wrote, "What does it mean? Nothing. Why, if the cows of this country failed to come up and get milked one night it would be more of a panic .... Why, an old sow and a litter of pigs make more people a living than all the steel and general motor stock combined. Why, the whole 120,000,000 of us are more dependent on the cackling of a hen than if the stock exchange was turned into a night club."[4]

Throughout the 1920s, Rogers had worried periodically that the allure of the stock market was emblematic of a larger problem: a growing American addiction to pursuing wealth by the easiest possible way, instead of working and saving to gain it. A national mania for consumer goods, spending, and stock speculation was swelling out of control, this small-town sage feared, and propelling the United States toward some kind of economic reckoning. In 1926, one of his *Weekly Articles* warned against the rise in personal debt and national debt, concluding, "We will have prosperity and get along fine now for a couple of years and then something will happen and we won't be doing so well." In 1928, he shook his head at Americans' frenzied pursuit of a high standard of living and inquired, "just how long is that going to last? Now the way we are acting, the Lord is liable to turn on us any minute; and even if He don't, our good fortune can't possibly last any longer than our Natural resources." He embroidered the theme of divine punishment in late 1929: "We had enjoyed special blessings over other nations, and we couldn't see why they shouldn't be permanent. We was a mighty cocky nation . . . We had begun to believe that the height of civilization was a good road, bath tub, radio, and automobile . . . . I think the Lord just looked us over, and decided to set us back where we belong."[5]

So while the stock market crash shocked Rogers, it was not a complete surprise. Gambling was great when you won, but it could be disastrous when you lost. "Oh, it was a great game while it lasted. All you had to do was to buy and wait till the next morning and just pick up the paper and see how much you made, in print," Rogers told his readers. "But all that has changed . . . . For after all, everybody just can't live on gambling. Somebody has to do some work." As the market continued to spiral downwards in the final months of 1929, he commiserated with fellow citizens that economic conditions were "just about as low as they could possibly get it but here lately it's been getting still worse." Dumbfounded to observe the panic among Wall Street stockbrokers, he grimly joked that "you had to stand in line to get a window to jump out of, and speculators were selling spaces for bodies in the East River." For Rogers, this illustrated a central lesson: "there is nothing that hollers as quick and as loud as a gambler."[6]

A month after "Black Friday," Rogers commented more extensively, and sardonically, on the stock market crash. In a *Weekly Article* entitled "Whooping It Up For Wall Street," he claimed he had been trying to restore confidence in the stock market among his readers but it was a tough sell. Ordinary Americans read stock reports and were shocked because "you wouldent think there was that many 'Minus' signs in the world . . . . It was just taking all the joy out of gambling." For ordinary citizens, it induced suspicion when financial experts claimed "a good deal of the money was 'lost on paper.' That is, it was figures but it wasent real money . . . . But then everybody said it would have a demoralizing effect on the country for so many to have their paper profits all rubbed out at once. That it would have the effect of making people more careful with their money, and thereby make it bad for speculation. That if people dident trade in stocks why Wall Street couldent exist." Rogers spoke for many when he asserted, "I never could understand what the price of stock had to do with keeping the company working and turning out their product." While he was willing to help restore confidence in the market, brokers and traders needed to understand that many average people would return slowly because "They not only lost confidence but they lost money, some of them all of their money." But the United States would recover, Rogers reminded stockbrokers, because "this Country is bigger than Wall Street, and if they don't believe it, I show 'em a map."[7]

The situation became more complicated in the months after October 1929 when the stock market languished and the larger American economy experienced a full-fledged depression with skyrocketing unemployment, collapsing banks, and spreading poverty. Over the next year Rogers began to grapple with the reality of an economic crisis that involved more than a slap-down of investment bankers. When President Hoover addressed Congress in 1930 and stressed that the Depression was a global phenomenon and America was suffering along with other nations, Rogers scoffed. "Yes, and we have suffered a lot alone, too," he wrote. "You see, that's how a lot of people try to make us feel good is to tell us how bad [off] somebody else is. I don't know what kind of a streak or a complex it is in anybody that gives 'em a kind of delight to know that somebody else has lost a leg along with you, and if they happen by chance to have lost two and you only one, why then your day is just complete." Like millions of Americans, Rogers was mystified how an economic depression could strike a nation where overproduction was the order of the day as commodities sat unsold, undistributed, and unused. In November 1930 he wondered at the bizarre spectacle of celebrating Thanksgiving when "the 'bountiful harvest' is the very thing that's the matter with us. Too much wheat, too much corn, too much cotton, too much beef, too much production of everything." His final reflection captured the frustration of many of his fellow citizens: "We are the first nation to starve to death in a storehouse that's overfilled with everything we want."[8]

As he turned to search for the underlying causes of America's economic catastrophe, Rogers soon identified a long list of culprits. Standing at the top of it were investment bankers and stock speculators, whom he saw as economic elites manipulating the system to their own economic advantage. Shortly after the stock market crash, he skewered President Hoover for calling business leaders to the White House for consultation, including stock market investors who claimed their figures suggested most market losses were only on paper. In Rogers' wry observation, that dovetailed with most Americans who "at the end of the season had figures but we couldent find the money. So the Wall Street Men had nothing on us." Hoover's group also included "Bankers ... and they announced what their annual Jip would be for [the] coming year." The problem, Rogers asserted, was not so much small local bankers but big financiers who controlled the flow of capital. "The day of the little Banker in a small town is past," he wrote. "He is a Member of a chain. He is a subsidiary of some big Concern." These banking behemoths relied on manipulating the market through their massive financial power and subsidiary institutions so that, in Rogers' view, "Removing their security or holding companies is like taking the loaded dice away from a crap shooter." When their schemes went awry, as in the stock market crash, they usually avoided shouldering the responsibility. As the Oklahoman put it, "every American international banker ought to have printed on his office door, 'Alive today by the grace of a nation that has a sense of humor.'"[9]

Rogers also saw corporate consolidation as an underlying cause of economic hard times. On March 23, 1930, several months after the stock market crash, his *Weekly Article* lamented the growth of big economic entities that had removed the modern individual's control over his own ability to make a living.

> We are living in an age of "Mergers" and "Combines." When your business is not doing good you combine with something and sell more stock. The poor little fellow, he can't combine with anything but the Sheriff in case he is going broke, which he generally is. But "Big Business" merges with another that's not doing good and both do "nothing together" .... It just looks like the way of the Little Post Officeholder is over, and the little anything is over, little Newspaper Man, Little Grocer, Butcher, everything .... The Chain [Store] will sell it to you and throw in a radio set and mattress .... They buy their Coca Cola in oil tankers. They can serve your wife a case of Gin, and you a Ford Tractor and deliver it over the counter with your Apple Pie .... So in a year or so we will all be working for "Edsel and Henry, Incorporated," "U. S. Steel and Lip Rouge, Limited," or "Chicago and DuPont Powder, Consolidated."

These huge corporate entities not only undermined the individual's control over his destiny but encouraged the easy-profits ethos of the stock market. "They don't know how it will be financially, but they know that the stock will go up, and that's all they think about, never mind the dividends," he wrote of ordinary Americans facing this reality. "General Motors not only took over Chevrolet, but Frigid Air Ice Boxes .... What's a Cadillac got to do with keeping your milk cool? I don't know but Wall Street does. It knows that the stock went up."[10]

Rogers placed much blame for the economic disaster on a widening gap between haves and have-nots in American society. The growth of economic inequality was striking, in the humorist's eyes, and he expressed his concern plainly: "This is becoming the richest, and the poorest, Country in the world. Why? Why, on account of an unequal distribution of the money." The Great Depression was symptomatic of this structural problem as an economic downturn devastated hosts of ordinary working people living close to the edge even in flush times. Politicians "don't tell that what's the matter with us is the unequal division of [wealth]. Our rich is getting richer, and our poor is getting poorer all the time," Rogers wrote near the close of 1930. "That's the thing these great minds ought to work on. Not be figuring out what the cause of this depression was, but let us fix our taxes, or our government work, and our whole system so we can kinder keep it split up a little better."[11]

Rogers believed that Americans needed to look inward to find a final cause of the Depression. The popular craze in the 1920s for buying goods on credit, and the willingness to go deep into debt as a result, helped create the impetus for an economic downturn, he believed. The Oklahoman characterized Americans' pursuit of prosperity as one lengthy, self-indulgent splurge. "Why don't somebody print the truth about our present economic situation?" he exclaimed in a *Daily Telegram*. "We spent six years of wild buying on credit (everything under the sun, whether we needed it or not) and now we are having to pay for 'em under Mr. Hoover and we are howling like a pet coon. This would be a great world to dance in if we didn't have to pay the fiddler." He elaborated in a subsequent piece: "In the old days we figured the world owes us a living, now we figure it owes us an Automobile, a Player Piano, and Radio, Frigid Air, and [movie star] Clara Bow . . . . But it's all coming under the heading of higher Civilization." Rogers argued that Americans were caught between an older, prudential mindset that encouraged saving and a modern, consumerist one that encouraged spending. "We have always been taught to save and put by every dollar that we could, and not buy anything unless we absolutely needed it, and to spend no money for things we could do without. Now all at once we are advised by everybody to start spending so it will help somebody else," the Oklahoman complained. "So it's hard to tell what to believe nowadays." He made his own preference clear: "I am telling you that if you got a dollar soak it away, put it in a savings bank, bury it, do anything but spend it. Spending when we didn't have it puts us where we are today. Saving when we have got it will get us back to where we was before we went cuckoo."[12]

So even with all of the misery and economic pain caused by the Great Depression, Rogers suggested that its silver lining appeared in bringing Americans to their senses after the overindulgence of the 1920s. "It's really not depression, it's just a return to normalcy. It's just getting back to two-bit meals and cotton underwear, and off those [$]1.50 steaks and silk Rompers," he opined in October 1931. "America has been just muscle bound from holding a steering wheel. The only callus place we got on our body is the bottom of the driving toe. We are getting back to earth and it don't look good to us after being away so long." Rogers even suggested, in the guise of humor, that the Depression was a divine warning for Americans to mend their indulgent ways. "You see, in the old days there was mighty few things bought on credit. Your taste had to be in harmony with your income," he wrote, but now "Most everybody has got more than they used to have, but they havent got as much as they thought they ought to have . . . . The Lord just kinder looked us over and says, 'Wait, you folks are going too fast, slow up and look yourself over, a year of silent meditation would do you good. Then when you start again you will know you got to get it by working and not by speculation.'"[13]

Due to his own embrace of these old-fashioned values, Rogers avoided the economic pounding from the Great Depression inflicted on many Americans, including some of his affluent acquaintances and colleagues. In the late 1920s, he had been tempted to dabble in the stock market (above and beyond Eddie Cantor) because so many of his friends in public life, the entertainment world, and the business community were making great profits. But Rogers remained uncertain, and finally went to Bernard Baruch for advice in the fall of 1929. This good friend and esteemed financier inquired into Rogers' finances and noted that his enviable income was offset by a significant debt, mostly on unimproved real estate purchased in California and Oklahoma. Baruch sternly told him it would be foolish to buy stock and advised, "you go home and pay on your debts." Less than a month after their meeting in Baruch's office, the stock market crashed. For several years, the financier wrote the entertainer to inquire "how I am making out on the debts, and how much I got 'em whittled down." Rogers, in fact, floated high above the economic privation visiting millions of Americans. His real estate investments in California held steady while his take-home income from the newspaper columns, speaking engagements, radio show, and movie contract added up to a yearly income of roughly 580,000 dollars a year. Ironically, the Oklahoman flourished as never before amidst this national economic disaster.[14]

As Rogers addressed his enormous audience and wrestled with the Great Depression – its causes, vagaries, and impact – his common-sense mindset inevitably took him from the abstract exercise of identifying causes to the concrete task of finding solutions. Entering the new decade and seeing America beset with massive unemployment, bankruptcies, shuttered factories and businesses, floundering banks, mortgage foreclosures, and failing farms, he scrambled to find remedies for this economic disaster. This took him inevitably toward the political system he had been describing, interrogating, and satirizing over the last decade. In particular, Rogers examined the country's leaderships. Initially, he engaged with the president who first confronted the Depression and struggled to end it. When that national leader failed and was turned out of office, Rogers encountered his replacement, a buoyant political figure who stepped forward with an ambitious program to overcome the United States' economic woes. In each case, the popular commentator evaluated both the character of the man and the efficacy of his policies.

* * * * *

As the American economy suffered a tremendous shock in late 1929 and began crumbling over the next few years, President Herbert Hoover attempted to halt the process of disintegration. Rogers had a long acquaintance with the Republican leader stretching back to World War I, when Hoover had been tapped by

Woodrow Wilson to direct the Commission for Relief in Belgium and then the national wartime Food Administration. The young engineer performed brilliantly, and then moved on to serve as Commerce Secretary in the Harding and Coolidge administration. He became the golden boy of the Republican party as an advocate of government/business cooperation and a disciple of efficiency in government. In 1927, Hoover further burnished his reputation for problem-solving by supervising relief efforts in the Mississippi Valley after a massive flood left much of the region in ruins, securing public and private money, coordinating the delivery of food, clothing, and shelter and making recommendations for future flood prevention.

Rogers found Hoover's rather wooden personality somewhat off-putting, but greatly admired his self-made success, talent, and drive. "He did wonderful work. But that's why he is not a politician. He is too competent," wrote the Oklahoman. "Something big comes along; we look to Hoover to do it." In 1927, when Rogers was honored as a Congressman-at-Large by the National Press Club in front of 8,000 attendees at the Washington Auditorium, the humorist concluded his jocular remarks on a serious note by asking a man to stand up "whom he considered to be one of America's greatest statesmen." When the individual did so, to a tremendous ovation, Rogers told the crowd, "when a man is sick he calls for a doctor, but when the United States of America is sick they call for Herbert Hoover." But now, with the stock market crash and rapidly deteriorating economy assaulting the nation only eight months after Hoover's inauguration as president, the Oklahoman was forced to consider the Republican leader in a much larger frame of crisis. Support gradually gave way to mounting skepticism.[15]

Initially, Rogers found much to like in the performance of President Hoover. About a week after Black Friday, Rogers praised him as a "magician" when he brought groups of businessmen to the White House, explained his goal of reviving business spending and investment in the economy, and had them "come out of the conference promising to cut off a leg, quit smoking, or give up golf ... . He gathers 'em in, a little gang at a time, and when they come out, you would suspect they had some drinks, for they immediately start announcing the spending of not only millions but billions. Let's hope they don't sober up till the spending is over." Indeed, as a practical disciple of common sense, Rogers complimented Hoover on consulting with businessmen instead of politicians: "[W]hy that was such a radical move that it had never been heard of before," the humorist wrote. "It was all new and it looked mighty radical. But this fellow Hoover is kind of a queer Duck that way. He can take a bunch of business men and talk to 'em a little while and before he gets through they are eating out of his hand, and purring and rubbing all around his legs."[16]

As he witnessed the president's efforts, Rogers also expressed considerable sympathy for Hoover as a victim of circumstances. The chief executive "has had many a tough break during the many weeks he has been in," he wrote. The problem, Rogers contended, was that during the 1920s "Mr. Coolidge and Wall Street and big business had their big party, and was just running out of liquor when they turned it over to Mr. Hoover. He arrived at the picnic when even the last hardboiled egg had been consumed. Somebody slipped some Limburger cheese into his pocket and he got credit for breaking up the dance." The Oklahoman maintained a kindly view of the president, as in an April 1930 radio speech where he reminded listeners that Hoover's "wonderful character" stemmed from being an orphan, working his way through school, becoming a successful engineer, and successfully completing difficult projects around the nation and the world. "He is the kind of fellow we want," Rogers observed, but Hoover's reputation as a "fixer" may have raised unreasonable expectations that he could just step in and repair the economy.[17]

The nation's problems, however, were immense. As the Depression deepened in the early 1930s, Rogers became preoccupied with what he saw as the two great needs of the American people as he traveled about the country: jobs and relief. He wrote constantly about the bane of unemployment, once sarcastically noting that "our great political system of 'equal rights to all and privileges to none' [is] working so smoothly that 7,000,000 are without a chance to earn their living." The humorist chastised business groups for their ritual promises that good times were about to return. "If Chambers of Commerce give some worker a job instead of some speaker at a dinner, there would be no unemployment," he said. "There has been more 'optimism' talked and less practiced than at any time during our history." In 1931, he penned an anguished *Weekly Article* entitled "Let's Give Every Man a Job" that summarized his sentiments:

> If you live under a Government and it don't provide some means of you getting work when you really want it and will do it, why then there is something wrong. You just can't let the people starve, so if you don't give 'em work, and you don't give 'em food, or money to buy it, why what are they to do? What is the matter with our Country anyhow? With all our brains in high positions, and all our boasted organizations, thousands of our folks are starving, or on the verge of it . . . .
>
> But the main thing is we just ain't doing something right, we are on the wrong track somewhere, we shouldent be giving people money, and them not to do anything for it, no matter what you had to hand out for necessities, the receiver should do some kind of work in return . . . . So every City or every State should give work of some kind, at a liveable wage so that no one would be in actual want. Of course it would cost the taxpayers more money, but if you are making it, and all your fellow men are not, why you shouldent mind paying a good slice of it for the less fortunate.[18]

Beyond the need for jobs, Rogers perceived a more immediate need to relieve suffering. He mocked the announcement that Congress may meet early to discuss the problems of those without jobs. "Well, I believe if I was unemployed and hungry I would want a little more substantial help than just the thought of 'our boys' [Congressmen] being gathered in Washington," the Oklahoman wrote. "Congress might do something. They are about due." Rogers even offered two ideas for funding a national relief program. First, in 1931 he suggested "putting a higher surtax on large incomes, and that money goes to provide some public work at a livable wage . . . . You wouldent be accepting Charity. But you would be doing honest work for it, until you could get employment in some line that was not public work . . . . It would be a glorified Community Chest idea, only instead of it being doled out to you as Charity you would work for it." Second, in 1932 he proposed a national sales tax to raise revenue for relief efforts to help the homeless and hungry. He argues that this scheme "provides where the money is coming from before it is spent; there is not a soul (unless it be a politician) that would object to paying a few cents more for an article, if he knew it was going to someone who needed it worse than him."[19]

As the new decade unfolded, Rogers grew disenchanted with President Hoover's failure to find solutions for unemployment and a means to provide relief for the suffering. In January 1930, the humorist went to the White House to discuss with the president the possibility of the federal government contributing funds to the Red Cross to help with its relief efforts. Rogers reported that Hoover "sincerely feels (with almost emotion) that it would set a bad precedent for the government to appropriate money for the Red Cross. He feels that once the government relieves the people, they will always expect it, and you have broken down the real spirit of American generosity." Rogers neither endorsed nor condemned this position but signaled his frustration with that parenthetical aside. He made it more palpable when noting that Congress was debating a humanitarian relief bill at great length with no resolution in sight. He commented, "No matter what the politicians do, whether it's called a 'dole' or a 'gift,' you can't live on these speeches they are going to make about it. Oratory is an organic exercise, but a digestive failure." He chastised opponents of this measure for their argument that "it's too much like the 'dole.' They think it would encourage hunger. The way things look, hunger doesn't need much encouragement. It's just coming around naturally."[20]

Rogers tried to cooperate with Hoover, but his misgivings often leaked through. They became evident, for example, in the humorist's famous "Bacon and Beans and Limousines" speech delivered on October 18, 1931, when he appeared with the president in a joint radio broadcast in support of Hoover's Organization on Unemployment Relief. The broadcast was linked to 150 stations nationally with the chief executive speaking from the White House and Rogers from California. Hoover spoke first, telling listeners that the worst of the Depression was over and that relief for the unemployed was the responsibility of the states and local communities, not the federal government. In his following remarks, Rogers praised the president for laboring hard to solve the nation's economic problems and granted that Hoover would rather solve the unemployment problem than any other facing his administration. The humorist acknowledged that Hoover was facing "a very tough, uphill fight" and asked listeners to realize that the president, in Roger's endearingly fractured syntax, was "a very human man."

But in the meat of his comments, Rogers was more critical and less optimistic. He took a swipe at the administration, insisting to the national radio audience that the major issue facing the country was not balancing the budget, the League of Nations, or Prohibition. "The only problem that confronts this country today is at least 7,000,000 people are out of work. That's our only problem," Rogers said. "It's [our task] to see that every man that wants to is able to work, is allowed to find a place to go to work, and also to arrange some way of getting more equal distribution of the wealth in the country." Like millions of his fellow citizens, he expressed his perplexity at how economic privation had appeared in a land so full of abundance with "more wheat and more corn and more money in the bank, more cotton, more everything in the world – there's not a product that you can name that we haven't got more of than any other country ever had on the face of the earth – and yet we've got people starving." An exasperated Rogers proclaimed, "Now if there ain't something cock-eyed in an arrangement like that then this microphone here in front of me is – well, it's a cuspidor, that's all." The humorist then took a swipe at Hoover for refusing to promote governmental relief for the unemployed. Ordinary Americans, Rogers argued, "are not asking for charity, they are naturally asking for a job, but if you can't give them a job why the next best thing you can do is see that they have food and the necessities of life." Over the next few days, the popular entertainer was flooded with approving letters and telegrams from around the United States.[21]

While Rogers mildly criticized Hoover, he excoriated Congress for flailing about and failing to do anything effective to better economic conditions. Even if a legislative proposal gained enough votes for passage, there was seldom agreement on how to secure funds to pay for it, as the humorist pointed out in a hilarious send-up of a typical Senate diary:

Monday – Soak the rich.
Tuesday – Begin hearing from the rich.
Tuesday afternoon – Decide to give the rich a chance to get richer.
Wednesday – Tax Wall Street stock sales.
Thursday – Get word from Wall Street, "Lay off us or you will get no campaign contributions."
Thursday afternoon – Decide "we was wrong about Wall Street."

Friday – Soak the little fellow.

Saturday morning – Find out there is no little fellow. He has been soaked till he is drowned.

Sunday – Meditate.

Next week – Same procedure, only more talk and less results.[22]

Hoover's inability to stem the tide of economic failure understandably produced public frustration. The president's image grew tarnished, as two developments revealed. First, as economic conditions worsened, homeless and unemployed people drifted into parks in cities and towns throughout the country to huddle in makeshift shacks built from scraps of lumber, tin, or even cardboard. These sites of desperation became known as "Hoovervilles." Second, in the summer of 1932 several thousand World War I veterans, many now jobless, journeyed to Washington, DC, to demand early payment of a cash bonus promised them by the federal government at the conflict's conclusion. The "Bonus Army" camped on the outskirts of the city as its members, many of them accompanied by their wives and children, marched and agitated for redress of their grievances. Finally, units of the U.S. Army under the command of Douglas MacArthur moved in on the protesters with drawn bayonets and several tanks, putting them to rout and burning their encampment. A strong public backlash ensued, much of it directed at Hoover, deploring this maneuver as a heartless action aimed at men who had fought for their country only a few years before. In this enveloping atmosphere of despair and uncertainty, the 1932 presidential election took shape as a referendum on the Hoover Administration's failures and the Democratic Party's promises to attack economic problems more effectively.

Rogers, with his long-time passion for politics, threw himself into the electoral contest both as an analyst and, as never before, an occasional participant. In his *Weekly Articles* and *Daily Telegrams*, he argued that voters had grown skeptical of both parties in the current atmosphere of crisis: "People ain't any more interested in politics than they are in long underwear. Both sides have lied to 'em so often that we don't look on either candidate with admiration or with hate. We just pity 'em." Complaining that it was getting harder to tell the difference between the parties regarding their policies and platforms, he recommended focusing on "the way they talk. The Republican says, 'Well, things could have been worse,' and the Democrat says, 'How?'" Rogers also remained convinced that the interests of the wealthy unduly influenced the political process. "Big money only goes to the party that supports big money," he wrote cynically. "I am entering no crusade to end it. I am just telling you how it is. You go ahead and change it."[23]

Rogers came to Chicago to observe and write about the Republican National Convention, held during the second week of June in 1932, as he had done at all the major conventions since 1920. The gathering was both dispirited, given President Hoover's unpopularity because of his failure to stem the depression, and anticlimactic, given his inevitable re-nomination because of a lack of alternative candidates. Typically, Rogers made fun of the proceedings. A dull keynote speech was made worse when the loud-speaker system malfunctioned and those at the back of the hall couldn't hear. "They got mad and got to leaving," Rogers claimed, "but not as quick as those that was sitting near and could hear it." The Oklahoman joked that another speaker grew so passionate in denouncing the opposition party that one would think "Judas Iscariot was the first Democratic floor leader and Al Capone was one of the last." The same orator compared Hoover to Jesus as a savior of mankind and in Rogers' whimsical assessment "kinder give the engineer the edge over the carpenter." The only excitement came when some delegates moved to dump Vice-President Charles Curtis from the ticket in favor of a younger, more dynamic candidate. Rogers was fond of Curtis, who was part Kaw Indian, and wrote in a *Daily Telegram*, "I am strong for Charley because he's an Injun and he is close enough to Oklahoma to understand the farmers' problem." The columnist, maneuvering behind the scenes, supported the keep-Curtis forces and chatted up several party leaders and delegates. The incumbent stayed on the ticket as Rogers told his readers, "it's the same old vaudeville team of Hoover and Curtis."[24]

Rogers gave Hoover only a slim chance for reelection. In the early days of the Depression, he still believed the president would be reelected, partly because of Republican dominance over the past fifteen years. But also because "by then we will have heard him knocked so much that we will begin to feel sorry for him and figure that he hasent had a chance ... so he will walk in." Rogers could not resist adding, "There is something about a Republican Administration that it only functions one year in four. But they make sure that year is the presidential election year." But the humorist had changed his tune by 1932. Increasingly, he expressed pity for Hoover, noting right before the convention that Americans had worn out their shin bones "kicking poor Hoover alone. Maby he did need a few, but perhaps not as many as we aimed at him." During the Republican Convention, it was striking that Rogers in his dispatches said next to nothing about Hoover, his appeal, his policies, and his reelection campaign. A few weeks later, the Oklahoman gave a straightforward reading of the Republican's prospects: "If things get better, Mr. Hoover will be elected, and if it don't, why he won't. So that's all there is to politics." Rogers, as well as all of his readers, knew very well that the economic situation was far from improving. Still later, the commentator admitted that even before the president's re-nomination nearly every political observer believed that "If things don't pick up a whole lot why Mr. Hoover hasent got a ghost of chance .... If they haden't picked up in three years why were they going to pick up this fall?"[25]

Rogers approached the Democratic Convention, also held in Chicago only two weeks later, with a very different attitude. He shared the optimism and high spirits of the party's delegates and leadership, strongly sensing that its nominee would be elected president. The humorist had ties to, and friendly feeling toward, the three leading candidates: Al Smith, the 1928 nominee; John Nance Garner of Texas, the powerful Speaker of the House of Representatives; and Franklin D. Roosevelt, the party's nominee for Vice-President in 1920 and now the twice-elected Governor of New York. He was perhaps most fond of Smith, sharing with the flamboyant New Yorker a vibrant personality, a way with words, and a strong sense of humor. They had met on numerous occasions to share stories and talk politics. However, Rogers also had ties to "Cactus Jack" Garner, a grizzled veteran of national politics and a fellow westerner with a rural sensibility. Whenever the Oklahoman was in the nation's capital he visited Garner in his office – when in Texas he visited the Speaker's ranch – and the two would discuss politics for hours on end. Rogers was least familiar with Roosevelt, whom he had met and corresponded with occasionally, but he described the New York governor as "a fine high-class man."[26]

Roosevelt, however, demonstrating the keen political skills for which he would soon become famous, realized more than the others the value of Rogers' support. In the year before the convention, the New Yorker wooed the influential humorist in a series of letters. He informed Rogers that one of his films had been screened at the governor's mansion and reported, "I liked it and especially the part you take in it." He also urged the humorist to "please stop off in Albany and come and talk to me," concluding lightheartedly, "I want to see you, Oh, most excellent of philosophers!" When Roosevelt learned that a young girl from Claremore, suffering from infantile paralysis, was seeking admittance at Warm Springs where he took treatments for polio, the governor wrote Rogers and offered to help ease her way. The humorist responded positively to these initiatives, telling the New York governor in July 1931, "If people in '32 are still as hungry as they are now, and from the looks of things they will be 'Hungrier,' why the Democrats have got a fine chance. They only vote for our Gang when they are starved out; we fatten 'em up and they turn Republican again."[27]

The two popular figures also engaged on a politically sensitive topic. A number of newspaper editorialists, letters-to-the-editor, and even Democrat politicians had speculated about Rogers as a popular candidate for the party's nomination in 1932. The entertainer responded to these rumors in a *Daily Telegram*. "If you see or hear of anybody proposing my name either humorously or semi-seriously for any political office, will you maim said party and send me the bill," he declared. "I will say 'won't run' no matter how bad the country will need a comedian by that time." Nonetheless, Roosevelt was concerned enough about a groundswell of support for the Oklahoman to contact Rogers about a month before the nominating convention. In a jocular tone barely masking the serious political undertones, the governor wrote, "don't forget you are a Democrat by birth, training, and tough experience and I know you won't get mixed [up] in any fool movement to make the good old Donkey chase his own tail and give the Elephant a chance to win the race."[28]

When the Democratic Convention met, Roosevelt steadily surged to the forefront as events unfolded. On the first two nomination ballots, he held a strong lead among the delegates but support for Garner and Smith, as well as for a number of favorite son candidates, kept him from a majority. On the third ballot, serious maneuvering and horse-trading ensued as delegates began to drift away from their favorite sons and the Roosevelt managers suggested the vice-presidential nomination for Garner. The tide began to turn. On the fourth ballot, Garner decided to accept the second spot and Texas swung its votes to Roosevelt, with California and Illinois doing the same as the New Yorker swept to victory. Roosevelt flew in from Albany to give an address accepting the nomination, where he famously proclaimed, "I pledge you – I pledge myself – to a new deal for the American people . . . . This is more than a political campaign; it is a call to arms. Give me your help, not to win votes alone, but to win in this crusade to restore America to its own people."[29]

Rogers covered these events in his convention dispatches to the *New York Times* and a national syndicate of newspapers. As always, he did so with a light touch, combining a host of humorous observations with descriptions of the sweaty, energetic, contentious scene in the Chicago auditorium that brought readers a sense of the atmosphere and action. He explained that while Republicans met in an orderly fashion, largely agreed on issues and personalities, drew up a platform with little fanfare, and adjourned promptly, their opponents haggled, back bit, traded votes, and talked endlessly. "A Democrat never adjourns," Rogers wrote. "He is born, becomes of voting age, and starts right in arguing over something, and his first political adjournment is his date with the undertaker. Politics is business with the Democrat. He don't work at it, but he tells what he would do if he was working at it." The day after the convention adjourned, Rogers flew down to Claremore for a rest, but could not resist a brief postscript. It was a good thing the convention adjourned, he wrote, because a few exhausted and hungry delegates "had started eating their alternates. Cannibalism was about to be added to the other Democratic accomplishments." He also claimed that upon awakening the next morning, he heard "a mule braying a while ago at the farm and for a minute I couldn't tell who he was nominating."[30]

Rogers' most fascinating action at the Democratic Convention, however, came by accident. During a recess from the official proceedings on July 28,

Rogers was on the convention floor chatting with delegates when a group of them, according to the *Chicago American*, dragged him to the rostrum for a few remarks. He was greeted with a standing ovation as the delegates "went stark raving mad in a delirium of joy" at his appearance. Rogers spoke off-the-cuff for almost thirty minutes, complimenting the various candidates – he termed Garner "an old Texas prairie dog" – and joking that the party's position on Prohibition would be forthcoming, "As soon as they can get enough of the platform committee sober enough" to make its report. He took a shot at the recent Republican convention, declaring, "they did the best they could with what little they had." Then he concluded on a more serious note: "Now, you rascals, I want you to promise me one thing. No matter who is nominated ... . don't go home and act like Democrats. Go home and act like he was the man you came to see nominated. Don't say he is the weakest man you could have nominated. Don't say he can't win .... I don't see how he could ever be weak enough not to win. If he lives until November, he's in." This appeal for unity brought another round of cheers from the delegates and one reporter wrote, "If some fellow'd got up and nominated Rogers right then, he'd have got two-thirds of the vote as quick as a secretary could have called the roll." Indeed, when the nominating process began, on the second ballot Oklahoma cast its twenty-two votes, to great applause from the crowd, for the man from Claremore.[31]

This episode foreshadowed Rogers' more overtly partisan role in the 1932 presidential election. He had leaned Democratic since the outset of his career as a commentator on American politics, but strived to be evenhanded in his assessment while levying criticism of both major parties. In this contest, however, with the national pain of the Great Depression looming in the background, the Oklahoman made his political sympathies clearer than they had ever been. In fact, when Roosevelt appeared in Los Angeles on September 24, 1932, for a major speech to begin his West Coast campaign, Rogers introduced him. Speaking before 80,000 supporters in the Memorial Coliseum, the humorist kidded FDR for his past convention speeches nominating Al Smith for the nomination both in 1924 and 1928. Rogers claimed that he had known Roosevelt as a young politician in New York back in his *Ziegfeld Follies* days, when "I would call on you from the stage to say a few words in appreciation of our show, and you would get up and nominate Al Smith for something." He added, "I don't want you to think I am overwhelmed by being asked to introduce you. I am not. I am broadminded and will introduce anybody." Then Rogers turned serious. "I will make no mention here tonight of the governor's 'forgotten man,'" he said, referring to a stock theme in Roosevelt's speeches. "For every man in America thought he was referring to him." With some voters, Rogers added, "your platform, your policies, your plans may not meet with their approval, but your high type of manhood gains the approval of every person in this audience. So we meet not Roosevelt the candidate but just a neighbor from the other side of the mountains." The humorist concluded on a light note: "This introduction may have lacked enthusiasm and floweriness, but you must remember you are only a candidate yet. Come back as President and I will do right by you. I'm wasting no oratory on a prospect." The candidate, standing only a few feet from Rogers, threw his head back and laughed heartily.[32]

In his *Weekly Articles* and *Daily Telegrams* published throughout the fall of 1932, Rogers clearly supported Roosevelt, sometimes subtly and sometimes not-so-subtly. He made his party affiliation clear, as when he noted the lack of rancor and striking optimism among his usually contentious, cynical cohorts and quipped, "it made me almost ashamed I was a Democrat." He tended to present the challenger in a more favorable light, as when he described the two candidates during stopovers in Southern California: "Mr. Roosevelt is a fine highclass man, win, lose, or draw" with the perfunctory addition, "This is Mr. Hoover's home State, and we want to welcome him, too." Supporters of the Republican president were not amused. An editorialist in the *Los Angeles Times* dismissed the humorist as a mere "verbal caricaturist" and asserted, "most people are taking the present campaign more seriously than Rogers does, and properly so," while a letter to the editor denounced his "shameful attack on President Hoover" and his under-handed use of a "'humor' space for propaganda." However, Harry Chandler, president and publisher of the newspaper, quickly wrote Rogers to reassure him of his high regard for his syndicated column "because it deals with current events in an inimitable way" that was humorous, striking, logical, and appealing to the public. Like all good journalism, Chandler said, the Oklahoman's writings "cause discussions, arguments, and cussing matches that make a dent in the mind of a reader."[33]

Despite his enthusiasm for Roosevelt, Rogers eventually wearied of the electoral contest as less attractive aspects of American democracy moved to the fore. Staggered from the campaign's great blasts of political hot air, he insisted that whoever spoke the least would win the election. "I seem to be the only person in America that has no idea who will win this election, but I do know one thing, it will be the side with the fewest 'orators,'" Rogers wrote grumpily. Tired of overheated rhetoric, name-calling, and scare tactics, he wrote, "There should be a moratorium called on candidates' speeches. They have both called each other everything in the world they can think of ... . The high office of the President of the United States has degenerated into two ordinarily fine men being goaded on by their political leeches into saying things that if they were in their right minds they wouldn't think of saying." The country and its citizens were much bigger than the two parties and their candidates and the contest would turn,

Rogers told his readers, on "which one is the lesser of two evils to you." Neither candidate, if elected, would bring ruin or salvation and Rogers urged voters to maintain perspective: "Should Mr. Hoover lose, I don't think there is a person that wouldn't feel downright sorry for him, for he certainly has meant well and did all he could, and I expect it won't be long till we will be feeling just as sorry for Roosevelt. This President business is a pretty thankless job." Once the contest was decided, the humorist wrote, "Let's all be friends again. One of the evils of democracy is you have to put up with the man you elect whether you want him or not. That's why we call it democracy."[34]

After voters went to the polls on November 8, the result was clear. Roosevelt won a landslide victory, taking the popular vote by 12 million votes, carrying 42 states, and amassing an electoral college tally of 472 to 59. His party also won substantial majorities in both houses of Congress. Rogers publicly sympathized with the vanquished candidate. On the day after the election, he addressed Hoover in a *Daily Telegram* with his trademark combination of folksiness, generosity, and civility: "There was nothing personal in the vote against you. You just happened to be associated with a political party that the people had just lost their taste for." Rogers urged Hoover to find comfort by recalling a long-standing trend in American politics: "There is something about a Republican that you can only stand for him just so long. And on the other hand, there is something about a Democrat that you can't stand for him quite that long." In his *Weekly Article* postmortem on the election a few days later, Rogers struck another note of kindness. He told readers that Hoover had done the best he could as president in dealing with an unprecedented economic crisis and lamented the scope of his defeat in the electoral contest. "I did hate to see a man that had been as conscientious as Mr. Hoover, take a beating like that," the columnist said. "He dident deserve it." In another newspaper piece on the election results, Rogers reaffirmed his commitment to expose political foolishness wherever he saw it. He admitted that he was friends with Roosevelt and his family, but he vowed to "start in now pretty soon making a living out of the fool things that he and those Democrats will do. And I'm not worried. I know they will do plenty of them."[35]

In private, however, Rogers exulted at Roosevelt's triumph. Two weeks after the election he sent a three-page telegram of congratulation, and friendly advice, to the president-elect, joking that now all of the office-seekers had finished their entreaties "I thought maby a wire just wishing that you can do something for the country and not just wishing you could do something for me would be a novelty." Rogers urged Roosevelt to pick good men for his administration, help the needy, pressure Europe to pay its war debt, avoid the radio until you had something of importance to say, and tell those in a panic over the stock market, "those Republican organizations affairs don't interest me in the least. Most of my people don't know if Wall Street is a thoroughfare or a mouthwash." The popular commentator recommended that Roosevelt adopt a confident, positive tone: "So go in there and handle this thing like it was just another job. Work it so that when we see you in person or on the screen we will smile with you and be glad with you."[36]

Rogers rejoiced when FDR was inaugurated in March 1933. "America hasn't been as happy in three years as they are today," he wrote in a *Daily Telegram*, because "they got a man in there who is wise to Congress, wise to our big bankers, and wise to our so-called big men. The whole country is with him .... Even if what he does is wrong they are with him. Just so he does something." When Roosevelt, with strong Democratic majorities in both the House and the Senate, launched his "Hundred Days" with a flurry of government programs that soon became known as the "New Deal," the humorist marveled at the president's political skills. "That bird has done more for us in seven weeks than we've done for ourselves in seven years," Rogers exclaimed in a radio broadcast on April 30, 1933. "We elected him because he was a Democrat, and now we honor him because he is a magician. He's the Houdini of Hyde Park." Rogers praised the new president for managing Congress: providing initiatives, kidding rather than scolding its members, recognizing that they required a firm hand since "Congress is really just children that's never grown up, that's all they are." The Oklahoman concluded by urging the president to keep his forward momentum: "Now, Mr. Roosevelt, we've turned everything over to you. We've given you more power than we ever give any man .... So you take it and run it if you want to, you know, and deflate, or inflate, or complicate, or, you know, insulate. Do anything, just so you get us a dollar or two every now and again."[37]

Rogers also discussed with his readers a taboo subject regarding Roosevelt: the president's lower-body paralysis from polio, which he had contracted in 1921. FDR avoided addressing the issue, fearing it would undermine his vibrant image with voters, and also avoided the use of a wheel chair in public, preferring to stand upright with the aid of cumbersome, painful steel leg braces and moving about with the subtle assistance of his son or an aide. The press, by and large, honored Roosevelt's wishes and seldom described or photographed him in ways that revealed his affliction. Rogers, however, tremendously admired the New Yorker for his fortitude regarding polio and addressed it in his folksy, generous manner. He told readers that FDR contracted the disease while swimming on vacation, and then fought to overcome it while maintaining an attitude that was "laughing and jolly and confident." The Oklahoman explained how the president maintained a regular physical fitness regimen, especially with swimming and other water exercises, and was in first-class physical shape. "So these folks that worry about his health, and can he stand up under this strain, yes, you bet your life he can,"

Rogers reassured his readers. "He has learned through years of hard struggle, experience, and advice, just exactly how to take care of himself."[38]

The humorist and the president cemented their personal relationship after FDR took office. In May 1933 Rogers and his wife were invited to spend the night at the White House and he reported to radio listeners that FDR, despite the daunting problems facing him and the country, had been in high spirits. "He has a grin on his face," said the humorist; "he has got some kind of divine feeling. He knows that things is going to be all right." Then in February 1934, Rogers, his wife, and daughter Mary were invited to the White House to have dinner with the Roosevelts and eight other guests. They stayed for a large reception at the executive mansion for several hundred guests. Rogers noted that he had a minor disagreement with FDR between engagements when the president changed suits and "asked me into his room to show me all the things he has in there. I asked him if he dident sit down during the time the people were passing by. (It takes about an hour and a half.) Well, he said, no, that he stood. Well, then I blew up. I told him he ought to sit down. That was one time I was telling the President of the U. S. what to do . . . . I dident get away with it. He went right down and stood up all that time." A few months later on August 13, 1934, the two public figures got together when they were both in Hawaii. "Had dinner and long chat with Roosevelt in Honolulu" where they discussed foreign affairs and Japan before Rogers headed out on a trip to the Far East. According to Rogers, "The President told me, 'Will, don't jump on Japan. Just keep them from jumping on us.'"[39]

As FDR's "New Deal" got up and running, Rogers quickly emerged as one of its biggest boosters. He tried to soft peddle his support and maintain his usual posture of evenhanded commentary and analysis, but his position was unmistakable: the new president was taking action with the people's interests at heart and deserved the nation's support. The Oklahoman approved of Roosevelt's actions to regulate business endeavor and stimulate the economy to recovery. When FDR used his first "fireside chat" to outline plans for reopening financially secure banks, Rogers proclaimed that the president "knocked another home run," both comforting the American people and using plain language to address "such a dry subject as banking and . . . made everybody understand it, even the bankers." When readers and fans inquired of the humorist what the New Deal was all about, he urged them to contemplate a recent newspaper headline that said, "'Wall Street Anxiously Awaits the President's Message.' Well, in the 'old deal' it was the President that was anxiously waiting till Wall Street sent him the message to read." When Rogers contemplated the array of big-ticket programs that Roosevelt and the Democrats pushed through Congress, he sounded like a downhome Keynesian who argued that deficit spending would revitalize the economy and ultimately result in more jobs and more tax revenue. "You can't possibly spend that much money without giving a lot of people work, and you can't give a lot of people work without them spending it," Rogers told his readers. "They can't bury it, they have to spend it. The man they spend it with, the storekeeper and [the] butcher, he has to spend it. It's bound to have a beneficial effect all around."[40]

As a steady stream of legislation poured out from Capitol Hill establishing relief and jobs programs and creating an array of "alphabet soup" federal agencies to regulate all manner of business and commerce, Rogers marveled at FDR's skill at prompting Congress to take action. Since the onset of the Depression that branch of government had debated endlessly and legislated sporadically and ineffectively. But now "Mr. Roosevelt just makes out a little list of things every morning that he wants them to do (kinder like a housewife's menu list), and for the first time in their lives they are acting like United States citizens and not like United States Senators or Congressmen." The Oklahoman found it amazing that partisan wrangling seemed to have disappeared from the halls of Congress. "The boys [in the House and Senate] have been mighty fine. We haven't heard the word Republican or Democrat in a month," he wrote. "They are in there really trying to help out the country. So if you are in reach of any of 'em tomorrow buy 'em a drink and send me the bill."[41]

Taking a longer view, Rogers contended that Roosevelt's New Deal, contrary to the angry assertions of some in the business community, was striving to save American capitalism and stave off the growth of radicalism. The Oklahoman perceived that even among FDR's political opponents, there was a realization that the president was trying to regenerate the system and not destroy it. "You see the Republicans have all the money, and they would rather be saved by another Republican, but they would rather be saved by a Democrat than not saved at all," Rogers explained. "You keep a Republican getting interest on his money and he doesn't care if it's Stalin of Russia who is doing it." By trying to help those in need, FDR had "done a lot in his attitude to offset a communistic feeling." If he had only worked to protect and bolster the status of the affluent, the humorist contended, "there would be some justification of hollering for a more equal division [of wealth], but with him doing all he can, and still keeping within the bounds of fairness to all, why he offsets the old red [communist appeal]."[42]

All in all, Rogers insisted, the New Deal must be counted a success. The American people had given Roosevelt a mandate for action and he had seized the moment. In the Oklahoman's words, "the whole thing sums itself down into trusting the President to carry the thing through, and almost all of them thinks he will do it the very best way. The people trusted him by electing him, and we hollered for action. Well, brother, we are getting it now." Rogers' admiration for FDR seemed to grow week by week. "You know, I don't believe there is a thing that this man Roosevelt couldn't put over if he was a mind to. He is so strong with the people, and so convincing over the radio," the columnist told his readers. "This fellow is uncanny in knowing what to do and say under any given condition." Rogers consistently wrote that FDR was "doing a mighty fine job" and while "some schemes haven't worked out 100 percent, there has always been a constant effort to help the unemployed, and the little fellow. Roosevelt wants to see the big fellow to do well, but he wants to make sure that he gives an even break in the accumulation of his wealth."[43]

Rogers perhaps made his biggest impact as a New Deal supporter in his radio broadcasts. The entertainer had begun a weekly radio show, *The Gulf Headliners*, shortly after FDR's inauguration and over the next two years his presentations often served as a prelude to the president's famous "fireside chats," the radio talks by which Roosevelt explained his goals and policies to the American people. In the first of these joint appearances, Rogers joked, "Mr. Roosevelt and I tonight are both going to speak to you on the Depression. I will take it up first, and if there is any loose ends left, he can pick it up where I left off." He reported that he had just returned from Washington, DC, where they "are passing bills so fast down there, they don't even vote on them; they just wave at them as they go by." Rogers then settled in to a lengthy celebration of Roosevelt's political initiatives. He praised the president for speaking plainly to Americans and realizing "what the people want was relief and not rhetoric." He praised him for implementing the bank holiday and going on the radio to explain it: "He changed us from a nation of takers-out to putters-in. That speech will, when history is written, go down some day as being the detour sign where depression turned back. It was a speech of the people, for the people, delivered so that confidence would not perish from the earth." Rogers concluded, "We elected him by a tremendous majority ... and I know we all trust in him."[44]

In subsequent radio broadcasts, the humorist frequently warmed his audience to the virtues of Roosevelt and the New Deal. Rogers lauded FDR for acting speedily upon taking office, expressing a humane concern for his fellow citizens, working to bring fairness to the tax structure, and experimenting with deficit spending to stimulate the economy. He claimed that the president was "a wonder. He knows psychology .... he knows how to reach all the people." The Oklahoman even joked about their radio partnership, reminding listeners that "Roosevelt and Rogers was on the radio last Sunday night." The public perception of the chief executive and the humorist as a political team became so striking that a newspaper reporter, interviewing the Oklahoman on his radio show, asked, "Some people are wondering if the president is writing your speeches, or you're writing the president's speeches." Rogers agreed that they shared a similar political sensibility from long involvement with public affairs and wide travel, looked to improve the lot of ordinary Americans suffering from privation, and believed that business and industry should "bet on" America by investing during hard times. The humorist expressed pride that he and FDR were of a like mind on politics and policy.[45]

Despite his enthusiastic support, Rogers harbored a friendly skepticism about certain aspects of the New Deal. In a radio broadcast, he made fun of Roosevelt's Civilian Conservation Corps, the program that gathered unemployed young men and sent them into the countryside or the wilderness, at a scant wage, to engage in conservation projects. In Rogers' opinion, with city people "planting the trees, you know, they are liable to get the wrong end in the ground and in our forest of the future, the roots will be in the air and the limbs in the ground." The humorist also had reservations about the intellectuals and professors Roosevelt brought to Washington, a group popularly termed "the brain trust." He questioned their common sense. "A professor gets all of his [notions] out of a book, but the politician, as bad as he is, does have an understanding of human nature," Rogers opined. "Theories are great, they sound great, but the minute you are asked to prove one in actual life, why the thing blows up. So professors [go] back to the classroom, idealists back to the drawing room, Communists back to the soap box." The humorist found FDR's professorial advisers such as Raymond Moley and Rexford Tugwell to be among "the nicest and most pleasant fellows you ever met in your life. All of those brain trust fellows are. But don't let 'em start explaining something to you. They get you down with theories and then stomp on you with phrases ... . [such as] 'modernized process' and 'experimental approach.'" Such highfalutin discourse carried little weight with America's common-sense philosopher.[46]

In a general way, Rogers worried that FDR and the New Deal may have encouraged an upswell of labor radicalism that undermined the American work ethic. Only eight months into Roosevelt's administration, the Oklahoman grew dismayed about news of a labor strike. He shook his head that after so much "hard work to try to get people a job, to have 'em strike the minute they get it." He thought it much better "if all these dissatisfied groups instead of striking would keep on working and lay their complaints before the government [for redress]." The following spring Rogers urged the federal government to make labor arbitration compulsory to settle the bane of strikes: "Let everybody stay on the job during arbitration. If they get the raise of wages, it starts back from the day the complaint was made." In July 1934, a general strike of tens of thousands of maritime workers in San Francisco brought violence, social chaos, and commercial paralysis to the bay area. Laborers had some legitimate grievances, Rogers concluded after journeying to the city to observe the situation, but it was clear that radicals had captured the movement. He wrote that "when the people felt that the reds were running the thing, and that it wasent really done for the sole benefit of the striking men but just to raise the devil generally, why the folks turned against 'em." When trucks were allowed to travel the city streets only when they carried a sign saying it was by permission of the strike committee, "the old American spirit bobbed up, and that really was [the] beginning of the end of the general strike."[47]

Perhaps the New Deal initiative that proved the biggest conundrum for Roger was the National Recovery Administration (NRA). This huge federal agency was created to revive the economy by supervising self-regulation among the nation's major industries, each of which was expected to draft codes that set production quotas, prescribed maximum work hours and a minimum wage, and sometimes established price guidelines. Rogers discussed the agency with its director, Hugh Johnson, and with FDR in the summer of 1933 and was convinced to support it. In August, he delivered a Blue Eagle Drive Speech, named after the NRA's ubiquitous symbol, urging Americans to cooperate with the new codes of business endeavor. In a *Daily Telegram*, Rogers described the NRA as "nothing but a code of fair ethics of people doing business with each other, and . . . it was rather a slam against a nation that we have to be forced by government control and patriotic persuasion to do what's right." At the same time, he remained wary of the NRA's vast expansion of government regulation and bureaucracy. Rogers often joked about the agency's overreach into every nook and cranny of American business. He told readers that he was in a dispute with the agency's director over "a code for comedians. He claims that Senators and Congressmen come under our code. I claim theirs is a separate union, that they are professionals and in a class by themselves and that us amateur comedians should not be classed with 'em." Another time he claimed that he had been in Washington to witness the launch of "the IYGAATNRACTWAGIOOYS . . . . Now that's got more letters in it than most of the new departments, so you might not know what it is. It's the 'If you got anything against the NRA come to Washington and get it out of your system.'" But what really bothered Rogers was the NRA's complicated bureaucratic structure. He complained that the agency's mission should be kept simple and "written on a postcard:" you can't work people over a certain number of hours with extra pay, you can't pay people under a certain sum, you can't hire child labor. "The minute a thing is long and complicated it confuses. Whoever wrote the Ten Commandments made 'em short. They may not always be kept, but they can be understood," the humorist argued. "Well, that's where Moses had it on Hugh Johnson . . . . Johnson went up on Capitol Hill and come down with 24 truckloads full of codes." The Supreme Court shared some of Rogers' misgivings, declaring the NRA unconstitutional in 1935.[48]

In such fashion, Rogers spent much time in the years following the stock market crash struggling to comprehend the Depression and gauge its impact on American life. He took stock of past mistakes, assessed present realities, and contemplated future remedies regarding this national calamity. While a supporter of the New Deal, he was not a doctrinaire advocate of the liberal welfare state created by Franklin Roosevelt and his administration. Like most Americans, he simply endorsed pragmatism and experimentation to help get the nation back on track. Rogers distilled his common-sense position in a radio address on February 4, 1934, when he offered "a message on the condition of the country." "Now is this thing of havin' millions of people – you know, everybody – workin' for the government, is that a good thing?" he asked rhetorically of the New Deal. "Well, no, it's not a good thing, but it's better than starving."[49]

But Rogers frequently focused on the plight of one group as he wrestled with the Great Depression. The pressure of this titanic event in the modern American experience steadily pushed forward a key element in the mindset of the nation's most beloved figure. In that same radio broadcast he compared the nation's citizens to "a big family" and observed that while some relatives had prospered, others "maybe worked as hard, and tried as hard, but due to just breaks of the game – why, they haven't been able to make out so well." The problems and prospects of that latter group – those ordinary folks struggling to make out, with many falling short – attracted the lion's share of Rogers' attention. As never before, the Depression galvanized the humorist's populist principles and made him a tribune of the average American.[50]

* * * * *

As Rogers wandered through the economic and social wreckage of Depression-era America searching for political solutions, he turned time and again to ponder the well-being of average, hard-working citizens. Rogers did not stand alone in this impulse. This decade of crisis saw an upsurge of populist sentiment, a sympathy for "the folk" and their well-being, in many areas of American culture. It appeared in the village sentimentality of popular illustrator Norman Rockwell and the democratic optimism of folksinger Woody Guthrie. It influenced Carl Sandburg's lengthy poem, *The People, Yes*, and the literary criticism of Van Wyck Brooks, whose *Makers and Finders* series exalted the democratic tradition of American letters. It flowered in the neorealism of "regionalist" painters such as Thomas Hart Benton, Grant Wood, and Steuart Curry, whose canvases depicted the workaday heroism of rural midwesterners. It surfaced in Lewis Mumford's agenda for reintegrating industrial technology with "the culture of the folk" and composer Aaron Copland's music such as *Fanfare for the Common Man* and *Appalachian Spring*. It shaped Walt Disney's wildly popular character, Mickey Mouse, who represented the "triumph of the little guy" as he prevailed over every obstacle thrown at him by society and nature. As one historian has put it, this swelling populist sensibility reflected "a fascination with the folk and its culture, past and present . . . a kind of collective identification with all of America and its people."[51]

The populist veneration of the people in the 1930s was more than cultural, also displaying a political dimension derived from the People's Party insurgency of the 1890s. In that earlier period, populist icons such as William Jennings Bryan and Ignatius Donnelly had denounced the modern centralization of economic power engineered by scheming financiers, crafty bankers, and power-hungry corporate magnates. As a counterweight, they upheld the integrity of local institutions and community ties, the dignity of hard work and achievement, and the need for the individual to control his livelihood and destiny, a vision especially colored by a small-town, rural sensibility. Rather than promoting a socialistic denunciation of capitalism and bourgeois values and an embrace of class conflict, the populists sought to make a market society work more fairly. Both anti-Red and anti-plutocrat, they sought a polity where wealth and power were more democratically dispersed, where freedom and opportunity prevailed and everyone had a fair chance to succeed. Figures such as Huey Long with his "Every Man a King" schemes, and Father Charles Coughlin, the "Radio Priest" in Detroit who excoriated bankers and financiers for causing economic disaster, represented various manifestations of political populism during the Depression.[52]

But it was Will Rogers, with his enormous popularity and many avenues for reaching the public, who stood at the head of the line as the leading Depression-era populist. On both the cultural and political fronts, he broadcast a populist message venerating the common man, the work ethic, individual opportunity and the virtues of small-town life and honest labor over the financial machinations and elite domination of modern urban America. Rogers was not naïve – he knew the people could be fickle and selfish, commenting in 1935, "We are the only fleas weighing over 100 pounds. We don't know what we want, but are ready to bite somebody to get it." But this cynicism seldom surfaced. Much more often he declared his faith in the ordinary American, as when he wrote in 1930, "my sympathy is naturally with the little fellow that has struggled along all these years and give the best he could."[53]

Rogers' populist convictions colored every aspect of his political commentary. They influenced his analysis of the 1932 election dynamics. The Republicans, he argued, "dident start thinking of the old common fellow till just as they started out on the election tour. The money was all appropriated for the top in the hopes that it would trickle down to the needy. Mr. Hoover was an engineer. He knew that water trickled down . . . . But he dident know that money trickled up. Give it to the people at the bottom and the people at the top will have it before night anyhow. But it will at least have passed through the poor fellow's hands . . . .

No sir, the little fellow felt that he never had a chance." After traveling about the United States discussing public affairs, Rogers concluded that average Americans displayed the most good sense. He wrote, "a fashionable New York audience is the dumbest one you can assemble anywhere in this country. Small town people will make a sucker out of 'em for reading and keeping up with the news." When critics attacked him for departing from humor to call for Europeans to pay their war debt to America, he lashed out, "Those New York writers should be compelled to get out once in their lifetime and get the 'folks' angle. I know and have known all the time that the real backbone of people of America wasent going to cancel any debts . . . . [Critics] can write their economic theories that want to, but they dident know a thing about our people."[54]

Rogers often highlighted traditional populist themes. True to this tradition dating to the nineteenth century, Rogers expressed a deep distrust of, and occasionally outright hostility toward, bankers, whom he believed manipulated the system to their own economic advantage. He claimed that when he asked America's most prominent men who was responsible for the nation's economic woes, "every one of 'em without a moment's hesitation said: 'Why, the big bankers.' Yet they have the honor of being the first group to go on the 'dole' in America." In January 1932, the Oklahoman described Hoover's Reconstruction Finance Corporation, which aimed to invigorate economic investment, as a move "to relieve bankers' mistakes and loan to new industries. You can always count on us helping those who have lost part of their fortune, but our whole history records nary a case where the loan was for the man who had absolutely nothing." International bankers were even worse. While the home banker was often guilty of making mistakes, the one banking in the international market, as World War I demonstrated, was "bad through malice aforethought. His devilment was premeditated. He knew he was loaning [American money] on no security in Europe . . . . He got his commissions for peddling it out, so what does he care."[55]

Rogers, like most populists, broadened his target to take aim at the nation's economic elites. As he argued throughout the Depression, they dominated the nation's economic structure to the detriment of ordinary, hard-working citizens. Rogers blamed stock market speculators for inducing the crash, bankers for promoting financial chaos, and corporate magnates for failing to keep jobs for working people. When Hoover formed a commission to look at unemployment relief and filled it with sixty bank presidents and corporate CEOs, the humorist wrote scornfully, "He picked every bank president and corporation head who have handled their own affairs so ably in the last year and a half that it is their stockholders that constitute the present needy." The Depression had highlighted the failure of America's economic "big men," Rogers asserted. "We used to think every head of a big organization was a 'big man" . . . but when old man 'get-back-to-earth' hit us in the jaw, why we didn't have an industry that shrunk like the 'big man' industry did. Big men are just like stocks now, they are selling at just what they are worth, no more." Moreover, he argued, it seemed clear that many businesses were "in the hands of a few men, and they see that the price is kept up. It's not regulated by supply and demand, it's regulated by manipulation." In his long telegram sent to FDR after his inauguration, Rogers warned the new president about these elitist agents of economic hardship. Adopting his usual tactic of employing humor to make a serious point, he told the new president that within the American population "the higher educated they are the bigger 'hoodlums' they are and the harder to manage. The illiterate ones will all work, you will have no trouble with them, but it's the smart ones that will drive you nutty, for they have been taught in school that they are to live off the others."[56]

In another traditional populist maneuver, Rogers cast doubts on the gold standard for American currency and promoted the monetization of silver. This issue came to the fore when FDR pushed a bill through Congress in 1933 abandoning the gold standard and then ordered the government to purchase annually domestically mined silver to help support the dollar. While traditional economists, including Bernard Baruch, and many Republicans decried the move as inflationary and destructive of confidence in the currency, the humorist facetiously agreed that it "is going to be a terrible hardship to millions of us that was so used to handling gold every day .... But a lot of guys are talking and writing about it as though they had lost an old[er] brother." In a radio broadcast, he offered a prescription for those ordinary folks who struggled to understand if they were truly reliant on gold for economic security: "If you don't know, feel in your teeth. If you have none in your pocket and none in your teeth, brother, you are off the gold." The uproar over Roosevelt's action caused the Oklahoman to recall a legendary populist event in the 1890s when "a long-haired young man came riding a day coach out of the West and said something about, 'You can't crucify us on a cross of gold' .... So lying under Arlington's hallowed soil tonight must be a satisfied smile. For it's something to be thirty-seven years ahead of your government." Rogers referred, of course, to William Jennings Bryan. [57]

As he preached his populist message during the Depression, Rogers fervently defended the work ethic as the bedrock of the American way of life, and the lifeblood of ordinary citizens. Like populists since the nineteenth century, he asserted the dignity of labor and described it as central to the well-being of ordinary citizens. His mantra during this period of economic hardship became "give people work." For average citizens, he wrote, "Their living has always been made by working, by holding an honorable job, but [now] there is no job to hold. We used to think that if a man was out of a job for a few months that that was almost a record, but now it goes by the years. What can be done to relieve it? It is our only problem." Rogers took great pains to clarify that while suffering people needed temporary relief, in the long run they needed a job rather than a handout. Moreover, he insisted that a distinction should be drawn between honorable individuals seeking work and slackers seeking support from others. "Nobody can kick on honest [people] deserving relief, and nobody can be blamed for kicking on relieving somebody when they won't work," he wrote in a *Daily Telegram*. "The governments and towns have got to find some way of telling them apart." He opposed the English system of "the dole" that "just give people money that couldent work, and not make them do anything for it – just let them sit and draw enough pay to live on." Instead, he suggested tongue-in-cheek that the government should create an official classification: "INNBAWW, or 'In Need but Absolutely Won't Work.' Then cut them out from the other needy." The Oklahoman also worried that expensive tastes and too much government assistance might warp the work ethic. Americans used to be satisfied with earning enough to get by, but "now neither government nor nature can give enough but what we think it's too little . . . . [I]f we can't gather in a new Buick, a new radio, a tuxedo, and some government relief, why we feel like the world is agin us."[58]

While a supporter of the New Deal, Rogers the populist was not intrinsically a huge fan of government regulation and the corporate state. In the 1920s Betty Blake had tried to supervise the construction of a wood-burning fireplace in the family's California home and stumbled into a morass of local, state, and federal regulations. Her husband penned this hilarious account of the frustrated ordeal:

> She thought, of course, all you had to do was build it. She didn't know the City, the County, and State and . . . the Federal Authorities had to pass [approval] on any improvement . . . . One inspector made her put another window in the room. I guess that was to jump out of in case the fireplace happened to work. Another one demanded she have a fan in the room, that the thing needed artificial ventilation. Another one said the ceiling was too low and wanted her to guarantee that nobody would ever sleep in the room . . . . Some Politician jumped up in the night out here one time and bumped his head. Now every ceiling has to be padded. Low ceilings tend to narrower minds.
>
> Well, we couldn't guarantee somebody not falling to sleep in this room. I might be telling one of my Stories to some guests some time in there . . . . [S]o she got disgusted and just built the fireplace outdoors. She thought she had 'em licked. The Fire Department says, "You can't have an outdoor fire," so the poor woman had to build a house around the fireplace. And this is no joke . . . . She built a log Cabin . . . . that was just to cover up the fireplace. Now we got it, we can't build a fire in it because there is not 3 windows in it, and we can't sleep in it because the ceiling is too low, but it is a dandy fireplace; just as good as some of them you can use.

Rogers remained skeptical of the immense, complicated bureaucratic structures created under the New Deal, once entitling a *Weekly Article* on FDR's constellation of new government agencies "The Whole Alphabet Is Used Up Now." The complex labor and industrial codes of the NRA particularly frustrated him. As he concluded of the widespread confusion and intense disagreements that ensued, "It's always better to brand a calf plain the first time." Rogers was less interested in promoting big government and regulating enterprise than in simply giving average people a job and fair shot at living a dignified, comfortable life.[59]

Rogers' populist sympathies went to average working people who lost their jobs and subsequently suffered most from the Depression. Ordinary laboring citizens were the backbone of the country, he believed, and deserved better than they were getting in this massive economic downturn. "I don't suppose there is the most unemployed or hungriest man in America [but who] has contributed in some way to the wealth of every millionaire in America," he told a radio audience in 1931. "It was the big boys themselves who thought that this financial drunk we were going through was going to last forever." Two years later he praised the forbearance of "the unemployed who have grinned and took it on the chin all this time. While being a victim of our country, the unemployed have been a credit." To illustrate the painful predicament in which working folks found themselves in the 1930s, Rogers composed this mock interview with an unemployed man:

> Q: Have you ever been appointed to a commission? A: No, nor in jail, either. Q: Have you a job? A: No, I am on a diet. Q: Do you think we will get out of this depression just because we got out of all the others? A: Lots of folks drown that's been in the water before. Q: What will give the unemployed employment? A: If somebody will throw a monkey wrench into the works. Q: Won't 1933 see a change for the better? A: I don't think so. We haven't suffered enough, the Lord is repaying us for our foolishness during prosperous days. He is not quite ready to let us out of the dog house yet. Q: Well, good luck to you. A: That's what my Congressman said.[60]

The plight of poor farmers during the Depression struck a particular chord with Rogers. A severe drought struck portions of the lower Midwest and Great Plains regions in 1930, exacerbating already dismal economic conditions. In January and February 1931, Rogers spent twenty-two days flying through Missouri, Oklahoma, Arkansas, and Texas surveying the parched conditions and poverty and fundraising for the needy. He described for readers of the *Daily Telegram* looking down upon "those dejected, desolate, anemic-looking rented farm houses. Nowhere to work and no crops for six months." He explained, "It's not cities; it's poor share croppers on cotton that's hurt worst" and lamented that "the country people absolutely have nothing." Rogers threw up his hands when Congress passed a bill offering 20 million dollars for loans-on-security to these destitute farmers, declaring "Now the man and his family that are hungry down there have no security. If he had any security he wouldn't be hungry. He would have already put it up." The humorist pitched in as his fundraising tour included performances at cities such as Fort Worth, Little Rock, Wichita Falls, Abilene, and Tulsa that eventually raised 222,000 dollars for the needy. He noted that in each locale "the well to do are helping the less fortunate" while the Red Cross was helping feed the hungry in a host of counties throughout the region. As Rogers wrote in a *Daily Telegram*, "people down in these States know that there is folks that are hungry and they are going to feed 'em as long as they are able."[61]

Rogers' populism, however laudable for its humane concern for America's working citizens, suffered from some of the creed's shortcomings. It often smacked of an unthinking anti-intellectualism that disparaged people and ideas not on their merits but simply because they came from the ivory tower, the government hearing, or the corporate boardroom. It tended to romanticize the abilities and proclivities of ordinary folks, automatically elevating their workaday experience and vague "common sense" above specialized knowledge, economic and social statistics, and sophisticated analysis. Most troublingly, perhaps, Rogers, like many populists both then and since, betrayed an attraction to the strongman model: the charismatic, willful individual who will step in and bypass the messy, contentious processes of democracy to defend and promote the welfare of the average citizen. Rogers' admiration for Mussolini reflected this tendency, but so, too, did his sometimes jaundiced reading of American political culture and traditions. Rogers admired FDR's ability to both dominate and circumvent Congress and praised him as a "dictator by popular demand." In 1933, Rogers reiterated this mindset in some talking points composed to assist his son, Will, Jr., in preparing for a debate between students at Stanford and Cambridge universities over the question: "Resolved, that the political salvation of the world lies in democracy rather than dictatorship." Even taking into account his penchant for humor and hyperbole, the elder Rogers' remarks were unsettling:

> True democracy is dictatorship in its highest form, it's where one man, even though he be elected in democratic fashion, yet he dominates all. Washington was a dictator . . . . Lincoln was a dictator . . . . All great presidents were dictators. Dictatorship has its distinct place in governments the same as a doctor has in medicine. If your country is not ill you don't need him, if your country is well and going fine you don't need a strong man, the janitor can run it. But dictatorships were invented to pull nations out of holes where democracy and its janitor had got 'em into . . . . Dictatorship by the right dictator is the best form of government there is . . . . Yes, sir, dictatorship spells action, democracy spells argument. Democracy is nothing more than a well-organized minority that rule[s] a majority.

Here Rogers betrayed a shallow understanding of both democracy and dictator-ship. He wrote these words in 1933 before the actions of European dictators brought on World War II and revealed the horrors inherent in the triumph of the strong man over democratic processes. But they revealed a blindspot in Rogers' populist world view, and in populism generally, where the desire to protect and promote the common person can swamp all considerations of divergent interests, compromise, participation, and the threat of tyranny.[62]

But in a radio speech during that same year, Rogers displayed the generous, compassionate values that were more typical of his populism. He talked colloqui-ally with his listeners about the Depression, decried the unfair advantages handed to the rich guy, and praised the little guy's ability to survive daunting adversity. Rogers envisioned an America where hard work and competition prevailed in a game that was not rigged and everyone had an equal chance to win:

> This nation needs a more equal distribution of wealth – that's one thing us dumb guys knew before the economists did. And the administration is tryin' to do it .... They've already accomplished this: It's the only time when the fellow with the money is worried more than the one without it .... The little fellow can look starvation in the face and smile, but the big guy can't look uncertainty in the face and do the same thing. The little fellow – for every wrinkle he's got in his stomach, the big bird's got two in his forehead .... The little fellow – he's the best gambler, cause all his life he's done nothing but gamble. Life itself has been a gamble with him. But the rich guys ... they want to know in advance what's ahead. They want to be tipped off .... [Y]ou see, those birds is always played with marked cards, and he's always known.[63]

Rogers' populist acclaim for "the little fellow" had a massive public appeal. Disseminated throughout the national trauma of the Great Depression, his statements in defense of the average American reflected the daily struggle of millions to survive the assault of economic privation and social dislocation. Millions of readers and listeners cherished Rogers' sympathy for their plight and his faith in their resilience, and their approval sent his popularity soaring even higher. The Oklahoman's strenuous efforts to understand and shape public affairs during this extended national crisis built up a career momentum that, like steam pushed into a generator, propelled him forward into important new endeavors. While the Depression continued to blight American life, Rogers hurtled forward with dazzling energy to circle the globe, traverse the skies above it, and penetrate new regions by radio wave. As the 1930s unfolded, the Oklahoman became a man in constant motion.

12

Man in Motion

W ILL ROGERS, IT SEEMED TO MANY OBSERVERS, seldom sat still throughout his life. As a young man in search of a future, he had left home for a two-year roustabout expedition that took him to South America, Africa, Australia, and around the world. During his early career as an entertainer, he had criss-crossed the United States on a regular basis as part of the vaudeville circuit, periodically hit the road with the *Ziegfeld Follies*, and traversed the country on extensive lecture tours. When silent movies brought him to California, he settled there but frequently journeyed to New York and Washington, DC, as shows, speaking appearances, and political engagements brought him to the East Coast. If that were not enough, the humorist regularly left home at a moment's notice to take his family on vacation jaunts to spots throughout America's western regions. Finally, beginning in the 1910s and lasting for the next two decades, he supplemented this busy schedule with international travel to Europe, Russia, Latin America, and eventually the Far East. During his hectic lifetime, Rogers circled the globe three times.

The Oklahoman's populist sensibility partly inspired his travel mania. His common-sense view of the world valued practical experience over book learning and prompted a wanderlust-as-education attitude where knowledge came from firsthand encounters with people and issues, situations and problems. When someone with a college degree "talks with an old broad minded man of the world of experience, he feels lost," he argued in a *Weekly Article*. "For there is nothing as stupid as an educated man if you get off the thing that he was educated in." Rogers firmly believed that travel provided a genuine education with new settings, a flow of information, and first-hand observation. It illustrated the value of practical experience for the person seeking useful enlightenment: "No learning in the world could have made him as smart as his life has made him." Such a person should teach others, who then would be confident that the teacher's knowledge "come from a prairie and not from under a lamp." An innate store of nervous energy also fueled Rogers' compulsive traveling. As an astounded Betty learned early in their marriage, her husband always had "somewhere we should go, something we should see." In her words, "He hated to lose a moment of his life; he wanted to do everything right now. And he nearly ran me ragged." The humorist simply craved new experiences, and the more the better.[1]

Rogers' deep need to be on the go shaped his life in important ways by the late 1920s. It prompted what became one of the defining traits of his adult life – a tremendous enthusiasm for airplane transportation. From the moment of his first airplane ride in 1915, he became a tireless booster of, and participant in, this pioneering mode of transportation. For this transplanted cowboy from the Great Plains, as the western landscape became increasingly dotted with towns and fenced off by farmers, the vast open skies beckoned as a new frontier. Flying thrilled him and at every opportunity he promoted the virtues and possibilities of the airplane to his fellow Americans. Rogers' restless energy also transported him to a novel technological destination: radio. He had participated sporadically in broadcasts in the early 1920s, but later in the decade and early in the next, by dint of two weekly shows, he moved into the nation's hearts and minds via radio waves. The man with the "aw shucks," joking manner and drawling, neighborly voice appeared as if by magic and became a regular visitor in the living rooms and dens of millions of ordinary citizens. A fan letter from a woman described how at 7:00 pm on Sunday evenings she, her mother, and her father "draw up their chairs close to the radio and we all wait for that voice which will come to us in a few minutes and which we enjoy listening to so much. There is only one trouble with your talks, Mr. Rogers. They are not nearly long enough."[2]

These endeavors made Rogers a man in motion by the late 1920s, a restless citizen cowboy speeding into the national consciousness from a number of departure sites. Traveling the world, soaring into the atmosphere, and crackling over the airwaves, the Oklahoman seemed to be everywhere, and constantly so. Americans could not take their eyes off this force of nature, even if sometimes he appeared as a blur.

* * * * *

From the outset of his career, travel had provided an important foundation for Rogers' success. His involvement with western exhibitions, stage shows, and vaudeville produced performances in every region of the United States, while also taking him abroad for two brief sojourns to England and Germany, the latter of which was cut short by the outbreak of World War I. Rogers' subsequent efforts as a journalist and writer took him on a lengthier European trip in the 1920s that produced a spate of magazine pieces, books, and newsreel films that the public devoured. Eager to go on a journey at a moment's notice and unwilling to miss anything that might be happening in the country or the world, he relished seeing every aspect of life, every wonder of nature, every species of the human animal. "Will never lost his enthusiasm for traveling. From early boyhood to his last years, it seemed almost necessary for him every once in a while to be going somewhere," Betty related. "Never satisfied with second-hand information, Will wanted to find out for himself what was going on. He wanted to be there, where the thing was happening, and talk with people on the spot." The humorist joked that his mania for travel dispensed with any need for elaborate preparations. In his words, packing took him "about as long as it would most people to get ready to drive to town Saturday afternoon and stay for the picture show that night. I got one little old soft flat red grip, or bag, that if I just tell it when I am leaving it will pack itself. A few old white shirts with the collars attached, and a little batch of underwear and sox . . . . So me and my little red bag and typewriter, one extra suit in it. It's always packed the same, no matter if it's to New York or to Singapore."[3]

In the late 1920s and first half of the 1930s, however, Rogers' international travel schedule accelerated dramatically. He headed off to destinations all over the world on a regular basis and was frequently gone for weeks, sometimes months. These jaunts added another dimension to the Oklahoman's reputation by bolstering his credentials as an informed commentator on foreign affairs as well as domestic politics. Given his wealth of rustic charm and sparkling sense of humor, these trips also made him an unofficial ambassador of good will for the United States around the world.

In December 1927, Rogers journeyed to Mexico at the invitation of Dwight W. Morrow, America's ambassador to the country. This banker-diplomat wanted to improve American–Mexican relations, which had been strained for many years, and invited the humorist, along with Charles Lindbergh, to make a good-will mission. Rogers toured the country for three weeks meeting and greeting hosts of people, dignitaries and common folk alike, and observing the people, the landscape, the architecture, the social arrangements, and cultural traditions. A highlight came when he spent one week traveling by train to several regions of the nation in the company of Mexican President Plutarco E. Calles, with whom he developed a warm friendship. The trip prompted a series of articles for the *Saturday Evening Post*, "Letters of a Self-Made Diplomat," that were subsequently collected and published in book form.[4]

Rogers' account of his Mexican sojourn displayed his typical mix of humane interest, comic observation, and hunger for practical experience. "I went to Mexico to make friends. I think it's a great Country," he told readers. "I went in to enjoy the people and the Country and get some real Chili Con Carne and

Tamales, see the Mexican Ropers – the best in the world – see the Señoritas dance .... I want to write and talk and describe the people as they struck me." George Rublee, a legal adviser to the American embassy, described the humorist's salutary impact during his tour. "He was all over the place making jokes, very impertinent, making fun of everybody and getting away with it," said Rublee. "The Mexicans roared with laughter and there was much good feeling and excitement." Rogers bemoaned his fumbling attempts to use the Spanish language, claiming, "The only trouble with this country is, the verbs have too many endings." In a talk delivered before President Calles, his cabinet, Ambassador Morrow, and other officials, the humorist put a lighthearted spin on American–Mexican tensions. "I dident come down here to try and cement good relations between the two Nations .... I dident come here to tell you that Mexico needed American capital," he jested. "I come down here to laugh with you and not at you. I dident come here to tell you that we look on you as Brothers. That would be a lot of bunk. We look on you as a lot of Bandits and you look on us as One Big Bandit. So I think we fairly understand each other." After a banquet held in the American embassy and attended by the President of Mexico and other government officials – it was their first time in the embassy in that building – the Oklahoman reported to his American audience, "We had many a laugh. These are real people down here if we only knew them."[5]

Shortly thereafter, Rogers, because of his deep interest in American public affairs, attended a pair of international conferences where the United States participated. From January 16–20, 1928, he went to Havana, Cuba, for the Pan American Conference as an unofficial representative-at-large. President Coolidge addressed the opening session of this gathering of nations from North, Central, and South America. American intervention in Latin America, such as the recent dispatch of troops to quell revolutionary unrest in Nicaragua, had prompted protests in some parts of the region and generated considerable pressure on the United States to revise its policies. Rogers sympathized with opponents of American interventionism, quipping, "It takes quite a sense of humor for these people to understand us shaking hands with one hand and shooting with the other." After surviving a several-hour ordeal at the opening of the proceedings, where fulsome welcoming remarks were followed by the playing of each participant's national anthem, the humorist suggested that regional harmony would be enhanced by the adoption of a collective anthem, perhaps composed by Irving Berlin. In his words, "When you have stood in the tropical sun for twenty-one national airs, you are about ready to vote for your nation to annex the other twenty."[6]

In January 1930, Rogers made a quick trip to observe the London Naval Conference on arms limitation held for representatives of the United States,

Great Britain, France, Italy, and Japan. He was skeptical of the gathering from the outset. With the end of World War I, he told an audience, "the conferences started. When the nations quit fightin' they had nothing to do, so they started in to confer and it's always been a matter of doubt as to whether the fightin' wasn't better than the conferrin' is . . . . America has a unique record. We never lost a war and we never won a conference." The notion that nations would disarm, he argued, violated common sense. "Naturally every Nation wants to protect themselves according to their own needs. They don't want war. Neither do they want to be left entirely defenseless," he argued in a *Weekly Article*. "There has been war since the beginning of time, and we are no smarter than the people that have gone before us, so there is apt to be some more war." The conference delegates knew "they can't go back home and tell their people that they have left them unprotected . . . . You must always remember that there is more National pride in this conference to divide up than there is Ships. Nations are not there so much to protect their Little Gunboats as they are their National Prestige." Rogers' skepticism proved well-founded. He left before the conference broke up over unresolved disputes and released only a vague, extremely limited agreement.[7]

Rogers again headed southward from April 6–19, 1931, on an extensive trip that took him to Nicaragua, Panama, Venezuela, Guatemala, El Salvador, Costa Rica, Trinidad, Puerto Rico, and the Virgin Islands. He had wanted to visit Central America since studying the region in a geography class in grade school, he claimed, and this two-week flying tour did not disappoint as it brought him into contact with a variety of fascinating landscapes and sites – coffee plantations near Guatemala City, the beautiful coast of Colombia with its old Spanish ports, the natural beauty of Costa Rica, the relaxing atmosphere of Trinidad and the Virgin Islands. But the trip quickly acquired a philanthropic agenda: raising relief funds for earthquake victims in Managua, Nicaragua. The city had been struck by devastating tremors on March 31 that killed over a thousand people, destroyed hundreds of buildings, and left many inhabitants wandering the city's streets homeless and hungry. "I have finally found somebody poorer than a southern cotton renter farmer," Rogers wrote. "The poor people just walk about dazed." He spent several days in the Nicaraguan capital city inspecting the wreckage and comforting the survivors, witnessing several thousand "mothers with babies in their arms go by and get their ration of milk." Rogers appealed in his newspaper columns for relief contributions – he noted "the generosity and goodness of the American people" – and raised 20,000 dollars in donations. He personally donated 5,000 dollars to a Red Cross survivors fund and went on to perform in benefit shows in Panama and Venezuela that earned thousands more in contributions.[8]

Later that year, the humorist made two quick trips to Mexico that underlined his great fondness for that nation and its people. In September he spent several days visiting the Babicora Ranch, an enormous spread in northern Mexico owned by William Randolph Hearst, where he enjoyed the million acres of land, 60,000 head of cattle, and abundance of horses. Less than a month later, Rogers returned for a quick, four-day jaunt to Mexico City to play in several polo matches. He traveled with Hal Roach, his old friend and director of several of his silent films, and the champion polo player, Eric Pedley. In a respite from the polo matches, he visited his old friend, former president Plutarco E. Calles, who was still a powerful force in Mexican politics. Rogers loved the atmosphere and culture in Mexico, telling readers during a stop in Mexico City, "I sure do like this country, and this is one of the greatest cities in the world." The Oklahoman was optimistic that the United States and Mexico faced a future of cooperation and accord. "We are neighbors and we both see it to our advantages that we are friends," he wrote; "Roads, Aeroplanes, Sports, Schools, Exchanges of Newspapers, a hundred things that are bringing them closer to each other all the time."[9]

On November 19, 1931, Rogers headed westward over the Pacific Ocean on a much longer, eleven-week trip that would take him to the Far East and then on around the globe. He spent the bulk of his time in Japan, China, and Manchuria and then headed home by stopping briefly in Singapore, Bangkok, Malaysia, Pakistan, India, Egypt, Israel, and Greece. Once in Europe, he met Betty in Southampton, England before spending a few days in Geneva and Paris and then sailing home to New York. While abroad, Rogers reported on his trip through the *Weekly Articles* and *Daily Telegrams* as well as a series of pieces for the *Saturday Evening Post* titled *Letters of a Self-Made Diplomat to Senator Borah*. William Borah of Idaho, a progressive Republican, was chairman of the Senate Foreign Relations Committee and an influential and well-known isolationist.[10]

The genesis of this lengthy trip appears to have been a visit to the Rogers ranch by Secretary of War Patrick Hurley, a fellow Oklahoman and long-time friend, on October 21, 1931. They talked long into the night, first discussing the question of independence for the Philippines, from where Hurley had just returned. They disagreed, with Hurley contending the Filipinos were not ready for self-rule and Rogers believing they were. The two men then turned to the tense situation in the Far East where war had broken out a few weeks before when Japan invaded and occupied resource-rich Manchuria on the Chinese mainland. The American government was worried about Japanese expansionist aspirations in the Far East and Hurley, in particular, was concerned that he was getting insufficient information about Japanese intentions, the Chinese ability to defend its territory, and the possibility of Russian intervention in Manchuria to thwart Japanese ambitions. Rogers, it appears, agreed to visit the area as both an unofficial fact-finder for Hurley and a journalist seeking information for his popular columns. Hurley prepared introductions for Rogers to American officials in the region and wrote the humorist, "If you do get to where it's happening, I hope you will wear the tin hat. Take care of yourself. Good luck." Secretary of State Henry L. Stimson also dictated a general letter of introduction for Rogers to American embassies and diplomatic personnel. Accompanied by Secretary Hurley, Rogers would visit the White House to consult with President Hoover on February 11, 1932, only two days after his return to New York.[11]

As Rogers departed California, he wrote *New York Times* publisher Adolph Ochs that he was headed to visit "China and Japan to see what this war[']s all about." To his readers, he declared, this trip is "long, and it's hazardous, and it's inconvenient, but you want the facts, and that's what I'm going after for you." Indeed, after nine days at sea on the liner *Empress of Russia*, he spent the next four weeks traveling throughout the region seeking insights into the nations and governments caught up in this dangerous conflict. In Japan, he traveled to Tokyo, where he met with the Minister of War, military intelligence officers, and the Soviet ambassador to Japan, and then toured Osaka. After receiving official permission from the Japanese government, he flew to Korea and then to Mukden, the Manchurian capital. Rogers then went north to Harbin, a Manchurian city still held by the Chinese army. Following several days of observation, he journeyed to China where he toured Peking and met with the warlord of Manchuria deposed by the Japanese, and then continued to Shanghai where he interviewed officials, studied Chinese culture, philosophy, and social arrangements, and examined the escalating civil war between the Nationalists and the Communists.[12]

Rogers' travels in, and observations about, Japan, China, and Manchuria produced a number of striking conclusions. The Japanese aesthetic love of nature – artful arrangements of trees and flowers, rock gardens, drawings and woven screens featuring natural themes – impressed him as did their embrace of Western-style "progress" with manufacturing, movies, and baseball. He came to understand the Japanese as a people who were obsessed with patriotism and national unity. "Their life belongs to their Emperor, not to them or their folks at all ... and if they can give it in service of their Country they attain immortal salvation." The Oklahoman observed that the Japanese were tenacious, skilled warriors and had created a highly organized military organization that valued training and efficiency. "These Japanese run their Wars just like they do their trains – right on time. If they are billed to take a Town at ten o'clock on a certain day, if you want to see it taken you better be there at ten, for ten past ten they will be taking another one further on .... War is a business with these folks."[13]

Rogers was fascinated by China. On the cruise across the Pacific, he read Pearl Buck's *The Good Earth*, the Pulitzer-prize winning novel about village life in rural China, and as he explored the country he noticed several defining traits. The tremendous size and diversity of China, its great mosaic of regions and peoples, quickly drew his attention. He joked that "there is more breeds of Chinese than there are of Republicans" and observed that "the tremendous size of the country ... and the different Languages, even different Races, is why there is no real Public Spirit." The Chinese love of family, where generations were often born under the same roof and lived together peacefully, and the instinctive desire for a contented life provided a powerful influence. The typical Chinese "loves life, he enjoys it," Rogers wrote. "He wants to get a little piece of land, live on it, die on it, and be let alone. He is, naturally, a compromiser. He wants to trade you, he don't want to fight you." But the most striking feature of China was its people's powerful respect for the ancient lineage of its civilization. The Chinese mindset, Rogers concluded, "is based on Tradition. He has Books to show that he has lived, done Reading and Writing, and been Educated for thousands of years .... [T]hey feel that all this modern Junk you are lording it over them is just a trick, and that it will pass in time and they will be in command."[14]

In Manchuria, where the Japanese invasion had pushed the Chinese out, Rogers quickly perceived a very tangled situation. He described how the Japanese believed they had a right to Manchuria by historical precedent and had entered the country with characteristic determination – "these Japanese take this fighting business serious" – and were now entrenched in the area. "So, if you think the League of Nations or anybody else is coming in here and demand that the Japs get out, well, they better come with a gun instead of a Resolution." The Chinese, for their part, were tormented by lack of resolve and ineptitude. They were not eager to die for their country, and their military forces suffered from weak leadership, corruption, and gross inefficiency. He wrote, "I don't suppose there is an Army in the World that can have as many things wrong with it to keep it from fighting as the Chinese." Yet Rogers believed that Japanese military success in Manchuria was unlikely to prove a lasting success. Its adversary, he contended, could absorb tremendous blows and survive because "China, even if they never shot a Gun for the rest of their Lives, is the most powerful Country in the world. You could move the whole of Japan's seventy millions into the very heart of China, and in seventy years there wouldn't be seventy Japanese left." The Oklahoman offered a pithy conclusion: "China Owns the lot. Japan owns the house that's on it, now who is going to furnish the policeman?"[15]

A year later, Rogers departed on a month-long trip to South America. There was no deeper purpose than sightseeing in one of his favorite regions of the world, and perhaps returning to the site of his initial trip abroad as a young man three decades earlier. He began in Mexico – "my pet foreign country" – and continued on with stops in San Salvador, Honduras, Nicaragua, Costa Rica, Panama, Colombia, Ecuador, and Peru, and Chile. Flying over the Andes Mountains –

"a long ambition realized" – proved thrilling, as did his week-long stay in Argentina, where he spent time on a huge cattle ranch and saw the sights in Buenos Aires, which he described as being "as big as Chicago, as live as Paris, beautiful as Beverly Hills, and as substantial as Claremore, Okla[homa]." In Brazil, Rogers declared Rio de Janeiro "the prettiest city in the world from the air," marveled at the huge scale of the Amazon River, and joked that in its turbulent political atmosphere "the people vote on whether they will hold a football game or a revolution, both equal in casualties." Not surprisingly, the humorist kidded South Americans about some of their values and traits, just as he did his fellow Americans. In an after-dinner speech in Buenos Aires, he confessed his bewilderment at the Latin fixation with honor. "If you take a man's wife down here, you have done him no particular harm, but you have raised the devil with his honor," he noted. "So it's his honor he will fight you over and not the wife." He added, "Take the word 'honor' away from a Latin orator and he would be speechless." Rogers also joked about economic matters. "Argentina's principal exports is wheat, meat, and jiggilos. The first two have been hit by depression, but the last has really thrived on it," he claimed. "The fine soil of the republic is responsible for bountiful crops of grain and cattle, but the tango is solely respon- sible for Argentina's corner on the 'jiggilo industry.'"[16]

From July 22 to September 25, 1934 Rogers circled the globe a third time, on this occasion traveling with his wife, Betty, and their two sons, Will Jr., and James (daughter Mary was engaged with summer stock theater in Maine). The Rogers clan cruised to Hawaii, where Will and Betty had dinner with President Roosevelt, and after several days of sightseeing continued westward by ship for a ten-day tour of Japan and Manchuria. The most challenging portion of the trip came with an arduous journey on the Trans-Siberian Railway through the Soviet Union to Moscow. In Betty's words, "for six days we were cooped up in a tiny compartment with a big basket of oranges, a purchased stock of canned goods, and a little canned-heat outfit for brewing tea. Our luggage was piled high beside us." Her husband was awed by the vast, endless landscape – "All a beautiful prairie, not a tree, not a fence, just grass up to your stirrups" – and Russia's abundance of natural resources with its huge rivers, imposing forests, and in one region "not an inch of land the whole way that couldn't be cultivated." After touring Moscow, the Rogerses journeyed to Odessa, the Black Sea, Ukraine, and Leningrad. At this point the two boys returned home to begin school, while Will and Betty embarked on the final stage of their global tour that took them to Scandinavia, Austria, Yugoslavia, Romania, Hungary, Scotland, and London. The couple boarded the ship S. S. *Ile de France* in England on September 21 for the four-day cruise to New York City.[17]

Rogers' string of foreign journeys had a strong impact on his stature. They greatly enhanced his reputation as a keen observer of world affairs and ambassador of American values, which in turn earned him the respect of many in American government. After Rogers' trip to the site of the Nicaraguan earthquake, the American ambassador wired a note expressing appreciation and respect to the Secretary of State: "HIS VISIT BROUGHT CHEER TO THIS SADDENED COMMUNITY AND HAS GIVEN NEW HOPE TO THE DESPONDENT (PERIOD) HE HAS SNAPPED US OUT OF OUR MORBIDNESS AND HAS GIVEN US A SANER SPIRIT TO CARRY ON OUR WORK OF RECONSTRUCTION (PERIOD) WE ALL OWE HIM A PROFOUND DEBT OF GRATITUDE." The Oklahoman's 1931–1932 fact-finding trip to the Far East came at the instigation of Cabinet officers Patrick Hurley and Henry Stimson, while his 1934 global journey utilized an introduction from Secretary of State Cordell Hull, earned the admiration of American ambassador to the Soviet Union, William C. Bullitt, and carried a letter of introduction from Senator William Borah describing him as "one of the best known and best beloved of Americans . . . . He is known as one of the keenest observers and fairest and ablest of our writers." Perhaps the greatest accolade came from President Franklin Roosevelt, who wrote to Vice-President John Nance Garner, "The first time I fully realized Will Rogers' exceptional and deep understanding of political and social problems was when he came back from his long European trip a good many years ago. While I had discussed European matters with many others, both American and Foreign, Rogers' analysis of affairs abroad was not only more interesting but proved to be more accurate than any other I had heard."[18]

Rogers' extensive global travel also worked to shape his own views in critical ways. Encountering a wide variety of peoples, traditions, and issues around the world instilled in the Oklahoman a deep respect for other cultures. While the humorist deeply respected American values, and those of Western civilization, he did not believe they could, or should, be imposed on others around the world. After returning from one of his European trips, Rogers wrote, "The trouble with America is we can't ever seem to see somebody else only through our eyes; we don't take into consideration their angle or viewpoint." The idea of cultural superiority held no appeal to a man who became the defender of "so called backward countries." Rogers' trips to Mexico especially seemed to inspire humorous jabs at American hubris. On one such journey he informed readers he would "be out of touch with what we humorously call civilization . . . . They're so primitive they have never tasted wood alcohol or know the joys of buying on credit. They are evidently just a lot of heathens that are happy." Another trip caused him to declare, "What business is it of ours how Mexico acts or lives? Every Village and community in Mexico has a church (and they go to it, too), where up here [in the United States] if we have a Filling Station we think we are up to date." Rogers forcefully explained his cultural relativism in a written piece:

America and England, especially, are regular old busybodies when it comes to telling someone else what to do. We are going to get a kick in the pants some day if we don't come home and start tending to our own business and let other people live as they want to. What degree of egotism is it that makes a Nation or a religious organization think theirs is the very thing for the Chinese or the Zulus?[19]

Given this conviction, it was no surprise that Rogers' international encounters nourished isolationist impulses. He believed that the United States meddled too frequently in the affairs of other nations, particularly in Latin America and China, and urged his countrymen to stay home and concentrate on solving their own problems. The two oceans framing America provided natural protection. "You know, I don't mind telling you brothers that geography has been mighty good to us," he told a radio audience in 1930. "It's wonderful to pay honor to Washington and Lincoln, but I want to tell you we ought to lay out one day a year for the old boy that laid out the location of this country. I don't know who he was, but boy he was a sage, that bird was." Rogers' isolationist convictions lay partly rooted in the populist tradition which, since the late 1800s, had viewed American foreign entanglements as manifestations of a corrupt, greedy economic plutocracy. The sour aftermath of World War I with the ineffectiveness of the League of Nations, the resurgence of nationalist power politics, and the failure of European nations to repay their war debts, caused him, as well as many of his fellow citizens, to balk at future American intervention in the affairs of other countries, especially military intervention. Rogers' growing sensitivity to other peoples and cultures, nurtured by his extensive international travel in the 1920s and early 1930s, further encouraged this mindset.[20]

Rogers became an outspoken advocate of the United States "minding its own business," as he often put it. After American troops entered Nicaragua in 1928 to try and guarantee free and fair elections, he scoffed, "when we start out trying to make everybody have 'Moral' elections, why it just don't look like we [are] going to have Marines enough to go around." After witnessing the opening of the Pan American Conference in Havana that same year, where the United States participated in a colorful opening ceremony, he wrote in a *Daily Telegram*, "It showed what a friend we could be to the whole world if we would only let them all alone to run their various countries the way they think best." Rogers' trips to the Far East only strengthened this mindset. "America could hunt all over the world and not find a better fight to keep out of," he observed of the Japan–China war over Manchuria. Asian nations had interests, conflicts, and values the United States could never fully understand, he argued, and a bumbling intervention would likely only worsen matters. As he wrote only half in jest as he traveled throughout the region and worried about "foreign entanglements," "my business is not to increase our Foreign Relations but abolish 'em entirely." In Rogers' view, the United States had no business intervening militarily to protect its interest abroad: "America has a great habit of always talking about protecting American interests in some foreign country. PROTECT 'EM HERE AT HOME!" Nor was it wise to impose American political institutions and practices on other nations since, he noted sarcastically, "they just won't be broadminded and let us show 'em how they should live." Rogers died before his good friends, Charles Lindbergh and Henry Ford, became leading lights in the popular "America First Committee" that urged the American government to stay out of the roiling affairs of Europe in the 1930s, although he undoubtedly would have supported its efforts. He also died before the horrors of fascism in Germany and Italy, along with Japan's military expansionism, brought on the carnage of World War II and illuminated the shortcomings of American isolationism.[21]

As Rogers the inveterate traveler regularly traversed the United States and circled the globe observing, writing, joking, and reporting he grew increasingly fascinated by a technological development that had eased his favorite compulsion. For centuries human beings had utilized ships for travel across great bodies of water while, beginning in the nineteenth century, they utilized railroads for land journeys. Rogers still employed those traditional means of transportation on many occasions for his far-flung jaunts. But increasingly he turned to a twentieth-century innovation for moving people about. The humorist became one of America's biggest boosters of airplane travel.

* * * * *

In 1915, Will Rogers was playing a vaudeville engagement in Atlantic City when he and Betty took a daytime stroll along the Boardwalk and saw a Glenn Curtiss "flying boat" moored in the shallow water. An attendant was collecting five dollars a head and carrying passengers piggy-back out to the aircraft for a brief flight around the area. The humorist was fascinated and tempted to take to the skies but his courage failed him that day, as it did several other times when he returned to view the airplane taking on a string of passengers. Finally, on the last day of his engagement, he overcame his fear enough to buy a ticket, and was carried out to the craft. According to Betty, who stayed behind on the Boardwalk during his flight, when her husband landed "he was still scared, but vastly excited" and had a photograph taken of himself in the plane that he proudly showed to others for years afterward.[22]

Rogers had been bitten by the aviation bug, thus inaugurating one of the great passions of his mature life. With enormous enthusiasm for this boundary-breaking mode of transportation, he enlisted and marched in a growing crusade in behalf of its development. Since the Wright Brothers had nudged their primitive flying machine off the ground at Kitty Hawk, North Carolina, in December 1903 after several years of labor and frustration, this infant technology had developed in sophistication and possibilities. A process of evolution steadily produced more powerful and dependable machines as pilots began to fly about in the United States and Europe and the first military aircraft took to the skies over Europe during World War I. In subsequent years, a series of achievements saw air travel gain credibility and public acceptance: pioneering pilots flew over the North Pole, Charles Lindbergh flew over the Atlantic, Amelia Earhart flew from Newfoundland to Wales, Wiley Post developed a pressurized suit to fly at high altitudes, and Jimmy Doolittle landed an aircraft using only instruments. By the mid-1920s, the airplane was poised to expand dramatically as the possibility of commercial aviation became real and promised to become a part of everyday life.[23]

Rogers stood as a key figure in this process, emerging as one of America's greatest champions of air travel. Although he never became a pilot himself, he flew constantly from 1925 to 1935, both in the United States and various areas of the world, and became friends with many of the adventurous pilots who were pioneering this new mode of transportation. He wrote and spoke about aviation at every opportunity, boosting its development, praising its virtues, and imagining its possibilities to his vast public audience. The Oklahoman promoted the establishment of commercial routes, supported an air-mail service, backed the development of the aircraft's military capability, and urged people to overcome their fears and travel by air. Rogers embraced this project with such energy and enthusiasm that a 1929 article in *Scientific American* concluded that Charles Lindbergh was his only equal as a promoter of the airplane and proclaimed the humorist "Aviation's Patron Saint."[24]

Rogers certainly earned that moniker. He engaged in his first extensive air travel in Europe in 1926 when he flew to and from a number of cities: London, Paris, Rome, Berlin, Amsterdam, Zurich, Munich, Cologne, and Moscow. In his words, "I have flew around Europe so much that if I don't have an Airship I think that I am walking." After this extensive round of airplane travel, according to wife Betty, "he came home resolved to do all he could toward calling attention to our backwardness at that time in commercial aviation." Back home, he began to fly everywhere: on mail flights after getting special permission, on humanitarian trips to view flooding in the Mississippi River basin and then the Dust Bowl a few years later, on flights designed solely to publicize air travel, and on entertainment tours when the possibility arose. Usually donning a warm jumpsuit, goggles, and a leather helmet to fly in small aircraft, or a rumpled suit and well-worn fedora for the passenger planes that began to appear, he eventually would complete some twenty-five trips by air across the country, travel by air among a host of cities in Europe, Asia, and Latin America, and log over a half-million air miles.[25]

Rogers took his first deliberately publicized air jaunt in late October 1927 from Los Angeles to New York and back on a series of airmail routes, taking three and a half days and paying a total of 814 dollars in first-class postage since his fare was measured by pound of mail. He wrote about the experience in a pair of articles for the *Saturday Evening Post*, "Flying and Eating My Way East" and "Bucking a Head Wind." The pieces provided an arresting, humorous, occasionally lyrical account of what it was like to fly a long distance in an airplane, something that hardly any of his middle-class and working-class audience had experienced. The humorist described leaving Los Angeles in an open, two-seater plane where he sat in the front cockpit and the pilot in the back with their only means of communication being written notes passed back and forth. He recounted the thrill of seeing from above Pasadena, Mt. Wilson, the snow-capped "Old Baldy" mountain east of the city, the Calico Range of mountains, Death Valley, the Colorado River, Zion National Park, Bryce's Canyon, and Salt Lake City before arriving in Cheyenne, Wyoming, to change planes:

> One of the prettiest sights I ever saw is the [landing] field at Cheyenne as we circle over it. Here is the town all lighted up and then off near it is this immense big field with a row of electric lights clear around it, and big flood and arc lights playing on the field . . . . A well-lighted field at night, with planes coming in, just reminds you of a carnival, or Coney Island. It's a real kick landing on a real lighted field at night . . . . There is not much kick coming into a [train] depot. All you see is the sides of the other cars, but when you swoop down out of the darkness onto all this flood of light and efficiency – well, I will have to get somebody to write an editorial about that.

As the plane headed east, Rogers described the immense cityscape of Chicago, the well-kept farms of the Midwest, a refuel in Cleveland, and a stop in Beaver Falls, Pennsylvania, when heavy rains, thick clouds, and fog in the Alleghany Mountains proved insurmountable. After making it to New York City and then returning to Los Angeles on another series of flights, the humorist was amazed how different the landscape looked. "Here is another great thing about an Aeroplane. You go over a country going one way and come back the very same route, but the whole thing will look different to you," he wrote. "It's because you are seeing it from exactly the opposite angle, and you will swear you dident come that way before."[26]

Rogers kept up two running jokes during his account of the transcontinental flight. The first concerned eating. Flying seemed to trigger his appetite and Betty, thankfully, had sent him off with an abundance of food. The Oklahoman joked that while Lindbergh had famously crossed the Atlantic eating only a sandwich, "I have killed a whole ham and six chickens, an armful of pies and cakes, and a clothes basket full of odds and ends and haven't got to Omaha yet." The second joke concerned his series of pilots' constant complaint that "bucking a headwind" was delaying the plane's progress, no matter which direction they were going at any given moment. Rogers grew amused by this quirk, but did not allow it to dampen his enthusiasm. "I told the flyers that I was going to keep on flying till my beard caught in the propeller, or find a pilot that dident have a headwind to buck." At the end of his journey back in Los Angeles, the last pilot rejoiced that they had made excellent time because the wind was at their back. "I fell into his arms and wanted to kiss him," Rogers told his readers. "Just think, I had finally ridden with an Aviator that caught a tailwind!"[27]

Laboring as aviation's best friend in the late 1920s and early 1930s, Rogers grew friendly with a number of aviators of the day. He flew with, and then sang the praises of, pioneering pilots such as "Wild Bill" Hopson, Roscoe Turner, Frank Hawks, Casey Jones, Jimmy Doolittle, and Wiley Post. In turn, these figures grew fond of the Oklahoman and deeply appreciated how he used his influence to promote airplanes and air travel. Jones, when interviewed for an article in *Scientific American*, noted Rogers' "wit, his extraordinary publicity resources, and his genuine enthusiasm for flying" and deemed him "aviation's best press agent. The industry owes him more than he is ever likely to collect." These relationships contributed to Rogers' knowledge of aviation and bolstered his bona fides as a commentator on this technology and its possibilities. Rogers gained his greatest traction in aviation, however, from his public friendship with Charles Lindbergh, the pilot who earned a hero's acclaim with his first ever trans-Atlantic flight in 1927. The humorist had written paeans to the man and his achievement in numerous newspaper and magazine articles and, when their paths crossed shortly thereafter, the two became fast friends. Rogers flew with Lindbergh on several occasions and joined him in promoting the airplane as a modern engine of progress. "This summer will see some great strides in commercial aviation and don't forget that old boy Lindbergh is the one that stirred the whole thing up, too," Rogers wrote in 1927. "Aviation was just Blah, maby I will – maby I won't – till [he] woke 'em up to it, we will never get through paying that guy."[28]

Rogers' great enthusiasm for flying found a recurring focus. He relentlessly promoted the growth of commercial aviation in the United States in his weekly newspaper column, magazine articles, and books, as well as his lectures, radio appearances, and after-dinner speeches. He once described it as "my pet subject" and often declared, "Honest, if people knew how fast and comfortable and safe it is on a Plane they would never travel any other way." Rogers constantly preached that the United States was lagging behind European nations, and even the Soviet Union, in the development of air travel. "That field was full of Airplanes; there must have been eight or ten single-seaters up doing their stuff," he noted upon landing at the Moscow airport. "Now that is what I am trying to get you to understand. These Guys over here in Europe, no matter how little or how big the country, they have left the ground and are in the air. Nobody is walking but us; everybody else is flying." In a 1927 meeting with President Coolidge after returning from Europe, Rogers reported on his extensive flying and argued "we over here should do more to foster commercial aviation, give the companies a government subsidy so they can exist . . . . We are carrying a lot of letters and advertising circulars, but we ain't carrying any people. We must get our people used to travel by air." The best example of this problem, he pointed out, lay in the fact that "there was no regular service to get into New York, our biggest city." Rogers campaigned for establishing a municipal airport in every city and often joked that golf courses – one of his favorite examples of modern frivolity – would be put to much better use as landing strips for airplanes. A problem he encountered in 1928 suggested, ironically, the success of his mission. When he tried to secure a last-minute ticket in Los Angeles to fly to New York, he could not get a seat and was told they had been booked for weeks. Although disappointed, Rogers happily reported, "So you see, Commercial aviation is coming along fine. All they need now is just bigger planes, with more comfort and convenience for the passengers."[29]

Rogers' enthusiasm for commercial aviation once got the best of him and created a humorous entanglement. After a cross-country flight where he pondered the difficulty of identifying towns seen below, he offered a lighthearted remedy in his *Daily Telegram*: "I ask you and plead with you again, you luncheon clubbers, will you please paint the name of your town on top of your building? I will pay for the paint if you will do it." In the following weeks he was deluged with paint bills from towns and villages around the country. Rogers paid a few and then had to recant his offer. He admitted, "I stepped into paint plum up to and over my financial neck. Say, Sherwin Williams dident have enough [paint] to have supplied the demand. I started with an awful poor idea of the number of towns in this Country . . . . Now I sure did mean well, but I just gnawed off more than I could chew. Pontiac, Michigan, sent me a bill for 98 dollars. I thought somebody was going into the paint business up there."[30]

Given his embrace of commercial aviation, it was not surprising that Rogers became a strong advocate of the airplane as an effective weapon of war. This committed isolationist embraced military preparedness as a strategy to discourage attacks on the United States and saw the airplane as a vital factor in creating a strong national defense. In the Oklahoman's vision, a Fortress America protected by two oceans and a strong air force need not fear any foe and need not interfere in other countries' affairs to protect its interests. "If the rest of the world knew that we had the greatest Air Force in the world, we wouldent have to be worrying over any disarmament conferences," he wrote in a *Weekly Article*. "All we would have to do is just sit here and take care of our own business, and you can bet no one would ever have any idea of coming over and pouncing on us." Rogers became convinced that traditional armies and navies, along with traditional weapons such as battleships and artillery, "will be as obsolete in the next war as a sword was in the last one, because in the next war there ain't nobody going to shoot nothing at you. They are just going to drop it on you. So everybody better start flying or digging in." He grew frustrated that Congress failed to envision the future where an air force would be central to America's military capability, especially when other nations seemed to be moving in that direction. As Rogers observed sarcastically, Americans "hold all the records in doing everything that an Aviator ever did, and of course Congress figures that in case of a War we would just show the enemy these records and the enemy would call off their Air part of the war."[31]

Rogers' belief in the great military potential of the airplane appeared clearly in his friendship with General William "Billy" Mitchell, an outspoken advocate for the development of a strong American air force. This World War I combat pilot stirred great controversy in the post-war period when he sharply criticized both the Army and the Navy for failing to embrace air power. In 1921, he demonstrated the power of bombing from the air when he led a small formation of planes that dropped several 2,000-pound bombs on a captured German battleship sitting off the coast of Virginia and quickly sank it. Mitchell's outspoken pronouncements alienated the top American generals and admirals, however, and they decided to send him far away from the national capital in 1925. Rogers met Mitchell at just this moment when they both attended a reception in Washington, DC, honoring General George Pershing, and the airman invited the entertainer for a flight over the capital city the next morning. Rogers, still a novice flyer at this point, claimed he was afraid to look down and only stared at the sky above, thus missing many of the landmarks Mitchell pointed out such as the Washington Monument, the White House, the Capitol Building, and Mount Vernon. After they landed, the pair had a long discussion. Mitchell explained that he had just been demoted from Brigadier General to Colonel and exiled to a remote post in Texas. Nevertheless, he promised to continue advocating for a strong, independent air force in the face of opposition from many generals and admirals. A sympathetic Rogers wrote, "it does seem a strange way to repay a man who has fought for us through a war, and who has fought harder for us in peace, to be reprimanded for telling the truth. And wasn't it a coincidence that we had just flown over Washington's home, the father of our Country, whose first claim to fame was telling the truth about a Cherry Tree!"[32]

Even from his faraway post, Mitchell continued to criticize his superiors. Things reached a tipping point when he accused senior military leaders of "treasonable" incompetence for their reservations about air power. With the endorsement of President Coolidge, he was court-martialed for insubordination and his trial unfolded from October 28 to December 17, 1925. Rogers attended the proceedings in Washington, DC, and offered encouragement to the defendant during breaks in the proceedings. The Oklahoman also supported Mitchell in several newspaper pieces. In one column, he presented a mock version of Mitchell testifying before a Congressional Committee, alongside the Army and Navy brass who opposed him, about the need for a strong air force:

> MR. CHAIRMAN – Mr. Mitchell, do you think we are prepared to go to war with an enemy with our present Airships?
>
> MR. MITCHELL – Yes, Mr. Chairman, I think we could if we used good judgement in picking our enemy. I think we could defeat Switzerland, and we would have an even chance with Monaco.
>
> MR. CHAIRMAN – Then you mean to insinuate that we couldn't whip England or Japan in the air?
>
> MR. MITCHELL – Not unless it was fixed, and we bought them off.
>
> MR. CHAIRMAN – Have these other men of the Army and Navy who are appearing here against you ever been off the ground?
>
> MR. MITCHELL – They have never been high enough to get into the upper berth in a Pullman.

Rogers also said of Mitchell's trial, "If they convict him for talking too much, Let's try the Senate. The reason Mitchell is shut up is because he said something worth while, that's why the Senate never is bothered." But this defense came to naught. The military court convicted Mitchell of insubordination and suspended him from the Army for five years. He resigned from the service a few weeks later.[33]

Rogers became embroiled in another aviation imbroglio a few years later. In 1934, evidence came to light that the United States Post Office had colluded with several new airline companies – United Airlines, TWA, and American Airlines – in the awarding of very profitable airmail contracts. The Senate opened hearings to investigate the scandal, at which point the Postmaster General cancelled the civilian airmail contracts and moved delivery to the Army Air Corps. Rogers strongly criticized this move on two counts. Corruption in one section of the fledgling airline industry did not warrant punishment for all of it, as he wrote in a *Daily Telegram*: "What's all of the hundreds of airplane pilots and the thousands of people who make an honest living in the airplane business going to do? It's like finding a crooked railroad president, then stopping all the trains." Rogers also worried about the capability of the Army Air Corps, with its poorly trained pilots, outdated aircraft, and antiquated instruments, a position that was shared by Eddie Rickenbacker, America's ace fighter pilot from World War I. This concern was borne out when ten Army pilots died in airplane crashes during the first several weeks of mail delivery. The controversy escalated when Charles Lindbergh, one of the founders of TWA, believed his company had been smeared by the federal government and fired off a lengthy telegram of protest to Roosevelt, which he also released simultaneously to the press. An annoyed White House rebuked Lindbergh as a publicity seeker. As difficulties mounted, FDR invited Rogers to the White House to discuss the airmail controversy and explain his policy. Several weeks later the president ordered airmail delivery returned to private companies and civilian pilots under a competitive bidding system, a move that was confirmed by a Congressional act three months later. Pleased that a solution had been found, Rogers declared, "All I know is, I'm going to keep on buying tickets and keep on flying."[34]

So what explained Rogers' tremendous enthusiasm for airplanes and air travel that became so central to his life in the 1920s and early 1930s? Two considerations seemed to have fueled his passion. First, flight well-suited the Oklahoman's restless, on-the-go personality and his mania for traveling. He frequently described for readers how airplanes aided his frequent desire to head out and experience a wide variety of people and places. In a 1929 *Weekly Article*, for example, the humorist explained that he had a few days off between engagements and decided to enjoy "some travel, sun, and amusement. Just think, going somewhere . . . . Well, of course, my mind turned to Planes." So he boarded an aircraft in Los Angeles and flew to Wichita, Kansas, and then down to Tulsa, where he drove to Claremore to visit family. He then left Tulsa in a small, single-engine plane and went to Reno, Nevada, and then on to west Texas to visit a friend's ranch. Finally, after a couple of jaunts by car and train, Rogers departed Albuquerque for a flight to Los Angeles. As Rogers noted, "if it hadent been for Planes, I would never have been able to spare the time to make the trip." In 1931, after a last-minute flight took him to Claremore for a ceremony honoring two pilots who had flown around the world, he admitted, "I don't ever plan ahead for anything. I don't even like to have dates ahead if I can help it. I like to do anything right now. So I grabbed the old aerial rattler the next morning, wired to Tulsa to have a Special Plane meet me in Amarillo, Texas and they sent a Dandy, one of these new Low wing Lockheads, with the retractable landing gear" that whisked him home. His wife understood the connection between airplanes and her husband's fidgety temperament better than anyone. Rogers noted that after finishing a long stretch of work, he often began "looking up into the air and see what is flying over, and Mrs. Rogers, in her wise way, will say, 'Well, I think you better get on one. You are getting sorter nervous.'" Ratifying her insight, the humorist declared, "You know, the way the planes run, it's almost impossible to think of a place that you can't be to by morning or at the latest next day at noon."[35]

At a deeper level, however, aviation served as a modern expression of Rogers' frontier spirit. This transplanted cowboy, born and bred on the expansive plains of the Oklahoma Territory, still yearned for the wide-open spaces, individual freedom, and immersion in nature that characterized his youthful days on horseback in the American west. As he came upon adulthood, of course, the closing of the frontier had proceeded rapidly and the young man headed off to pursue a career in entertainment in the unfamiliar territory of urban, industrial, consumer America. But those old values and traditions still beckoned, and flight offered a way to revive them with the skies above serving as the new frontier and pilots as the new cowboys.[36]

To describe aviation experiences, Rogers regularly employed imagery evoking the cowboy roaming the frontier on his horse. After a crash landing in Cherokee, Wyoming broke the landing gear in a two-seat aircraft and spilled him out on the ground, he said, "Once in a while I've had a horse throw me where I've been underneath him and him topmost, but I've never been thrown like I was today." After observing a particularly beautiful landscape and skyscape during a portion of a trans-continental flight, he described flying as "like sitting astride a lively cloud and sailing over the earth." Hitting turbulence in flight, he told readers, had the plane "rocking and bucking like a bronc." A visually striking rendering of this theme came from the pen of cartoonist Herb Roth, who drew a cover illustration for the Oklahoman's 1927 book, *There's Not a Bathing Suit in Russia*, that depicted a grinning Rogers, outfitted with a broad-brimmed hat, chaps, spurs, and lariat, sitting astride a small biplane cowboy-style as it soared over the Russian landscape.[37]

For Rogers, airplane pilots were modern cowboys. While boarding a plane for Moscow, he observed that it was being flown by "the funniest looking old chuckleheaded, shave-haired Russian boy that dident look like he was over twenty." Initially a bit worried, the humorist quickly saw that the youthful pilot was akin to a skilled horseman who "could sure rein that thing around and make it say Uncle and play dead and roll over. He was an Aviator . . . . This little plane seemed mighty small and jumpy to me. But this old Russian boy pulled the slack out of his reins, kinder clucked to her, and I want to tell you she left there right now." Another time, while flying in the American west, Rogers drew a parallel between the pilot, appropriately named "Slim," and cowboys who encountered a host of wild animals on the great plains. Slim took the plane down and "had his left wing tip right on the tail of a Gray Wolf. He scratched that Wolf's back for him for about 100 yards . . . . All at once he makes another razee and this time it's a bunch of Antelope . . . . Well, next comes a Coyote. He run him ragged for a few seconds . . . . He knew every old rancher across Wyoming. They would all be out waving at him."[38]

MAN IN MOTION

Rogers believed these modern cowboys of the sky embodied the frontier creed of rugged independence and self-reliance. In these early days of aviation, pilot autonomy still prevailed over corporate control. "They don't have to take off unless they want to. It's up to them – they are the last word," Rogers explained. "The company knows that if it's physically possible to go, they will go, so they let them decide." After flying into a Utah airfield from Nevada during a snowstorm, he praised the pilot as "a real aviator. He circled in those mountains for hours when you couldn't see fifty feet ahead of us, but he made it in here." Pilots were prepared for any problem with an abundance of courage and skill, and Rogers claimed they "have half a dozen different things up their sleeve to do in case of any kind of danger. I will get in one and start for the Fiji Islands with an Army, Navy, or Mail pilot if he says he thinks he can make it." Fliers had demonstrated their virtues during the Mississippi flood of 1927 when they "were real heroes. They flew all over the tops of those swamps, locating people for the boats to get." Flying, Rogers argued, was luring modern young men away from the enervating frivolity of golf and speak-easies, the empty pleasures of installment buying, and the vacant experience of speeding about in an automobile by offering them the invigorating, revitalizing experience of the pilot. "One of the DuPont boys is enlisted here at Kelly [Air Field]," he noted after inspecting a California airplane facility. "You know, there is a lot of rich kids that have given up the coonskin coat and the homemade gin and are taking to the air." In a *Daily Telegram*, the Oklahoman wrote a succinct final evaluation of the cowboy airplane pilots he had encountered: "I think they are just about the highest type bunch of men we have." [39]

As Rogers' deeply-rooted enthusiasm for aviation grew ever stronger, an unfortunate consequence of this activity occasionally came into focus – accidents. Air travel, in its early days, was dangerous and Rogers suffered a number of mishaps. Betty reported that her husband's plane crash-landed at an airfield in Chicago in 1929 while on the way to attend Henry Ford's special dinner for Thomas Edison, an accident that left him bruised and battered with several fractured ribs. Another time after being roughed up in a minor accident, Rogers went to Fred Stone's house to clean up and asked them not to tell his wife because he feared she would forbid him flying. In 1931, he actually confessed to his good friend, O. O. McIntyre, that his airplane scrapes were causing marital discord and declared, "I got to give it up. It worries Betty." But almost always, especially in addressing the public, he made light of the airplane's danger because he thought it would inhibit development of this new transportation technology. Rogers often grew defensive. "Aeroplanes are twice as safe now as Automobiles," he wrote. "The only difference is that when there is an Aeroplane accident the Guy in there gets hurt, and not some poor fellow crossing the street." Media sensationalism only fed the problem. "Every time a man is killed in the air every paper in the country carries it," Rogers argued, but "six and eight can be run over [at] a crossing in an auto by a train, and there won't be a paper outside their own country have a word about it. It's so common it's just not news." As commercial aviation grew, he believed, so too would a fair, accurate perspective on its safety compared to other modes of travel.[40]

As Rogers flew across the United States and circled the globe as an aero-nautical cowboy exploring the new frontier of the skies, this activity helped sate his hunger for enjoying new experiences, viewing new landscapes, and meeting new people. In the same period, he embraced another technological innovation that transported him through the earth's atmosphere in magical fashion. This new-fangled invention utilized the transmission of sound waves to put him in contact instantaneously with far-flung audiences around the country and the world. After occasionally dabbling with this medium in the early 1920s, by decade's end the Oklahoman found a regular home for his restless spirit on the radio.

* * * * *

On April 8, 1930, Theodore Weicker, chairman of the board for E. R. Squibb & Sons wired a delighted message to Will Rogers at his home in California. It read: "The entire organization is indeed gratified with your premier performance. Your characteristic humor and the whole show was genuinely appreciated. A fine start. Keep up the good work." The telegram referred to Rogers' initial broadcast of the E. R. Squibb Radio Show the previous evening, a fifteen-minute performance from a studio at station *KHJ* in Los Angeles. This regular show was the result of a lengthy negotiation between the Oklahoman and the Columbia Broadcasting System (CBS), a new competitor in the radio industry launched in 1927. Eager to boost its listenership, CBS had approached the popular humorist to appear in a weekly program. Rogers initially declined, citing his preference for a live audience where he could gauge reactions over the empty, unresponsive broadcasting studio he had encountered in the 1920s. He also had trouble when he indulged his stage-manner of moving about and walked away from the microphone. The radio was "made to order for a singer and a person making a straight-forward speech, or a talk explaining something," he griped to Betty. "But to have to line up there and try to get some laughs, I want to tell you it's the toughest job I ever tackled." CBS came back with an offer to provide a live audience, however, and the humorist finally agreed to a contract. The network then secured sponsorship from Squibb, one of the largest pharmaceutical companies in the United States, and the deal was complete. Rogers would go on to broadcast twelve consecutive programs from April 6 to June 22 to complete his first regular radio engagement.[41]

The Squibb Radio Show featured a central theme for each broadcast. Most of them were personality sketches – Charles Lindbergh, Herbert Hoover, Al Smith, Henry Ford – but a few addressed issues (Prohibition), events (Mother's Day), and cities (Chicago, Boston). But Rogers usually drifted off-topic to tell stories and explore whatever was on his mind. His broadcast on Ambassador Dwight Morrow, for example, meandered through an analysis of the Model T automobile and its shortcomings, the differences between West Virginia and Virginia, Calvin Coolidge's early career, the dispatching of American Marines to China and Nicaragua, and Anne Morrow's marriage to Lindbergh. Rogers was paid handsomely for his efforts, taking in 77,000 dollars from E. R. Squibb & Sons for the twelve-week series, which, as the *New York Times* noted, was almost as much as Babe Ruth's annual salary.[42]

Thus began Rogers' conquest of yet another medium that brought him before a huge audience, perhaps even bigger than that tied to his newspaper pieces, magazine articles, and public lectures. After its first appearance followed by steady growth in the 1920s, radio completed its conquest of America in the 1930s as stations proliferated and a bevy of popular shows made it the most ubiquitous form of entertainment in the country. In this "golden age of radio," wildly popular programs with figures such as Amos & Andy, Jack Benny, Rudy Vallee, Kate Smith, George Burns and Gracie Allen, Edgar Bergen and Charlie McCarthy delighted a mass audience of listeners in every corner of the country. Radio became America's most popular diversion as, in a cultural ritual, families gathered around the radio in the parlor or living room and listened intently to a wide variety of humor, drama, music, and game contests. Given Rogers' enormous popularity in every other kind of entertainment communication, it seemed inevitable that he would join this parade. Despite his misgivings, radio was well-suited to his talents. The medium allowed him to deploy the analysis, humor, and folksy language of his newspaper writing, combine it with the drawling, halting voice mannerisms of his stage performances, and distribute the whole simultaneously to anyone who could pick up a radio signal around the United States.

In 1933, Rogers took on a weekly radio show that dwarfed his earlier venture. He agreed to host the *Gulf Headliners* (later the *Good Gulf Show*) on the National Broadcasting Corporation (NBC) with sponsorship provided by the Gulf Oil Corporation. Premiering on April 30, 1933, and running to June 9, 1935, it was broadcast on Sunday evenings for thirty minutes, most of them put together in a Los Angeles studio before a live audience. Rogers delivered fifty-three performances during the show's popular run as they became a tradition in many American families, whose members would sit back and listen to the most popular entertainer and humorist in the country as a relaxing way to wind up the weekend. Unlike earlier types of media which required consumers to go out to experience – lectures, stage shows, buying a newspaper or magazine, watching a silent film in a theatre – the radio was like inviting someone into your home for a cup of coffee and a visit. In the same way that FDR utilized his folksy "Fireside Chats" on the radio to explain complex political issues to voters in everyday language, Rogers used the *Gulf Headliners* to reach workaday Americans with witty conversational musings on the issues of the day. It only enhanced the Oklahoman's standing as the nation's best friend.

Rogers was paid handsomely for this project in the amount of 50,000 dollars a week for the first seven weeks and then a commensurate salary thereafter. With characteristic generosity, he donated half of the original amount to the Salvation Army and half to the Red Cross to help the poor suffering in the Great Depression, and to provide assistance to the people of Los Angeles and Orange County who had been injured or rendered homeless during a large earthquake in March 1933. He explained the donation with self-deprecating humor in a telegram:

> I did want to make a contribution to a couple of good causes that had done such fine work during our earthquake and I didn't have the dough to do it with. So Mrs. Rogers figgered it out, as she does most of the other things . . . . She says you got the wind to do it . . . with just talk, which I would be doin for nothin anyhow to anybody I could hem up and make listen to me. So I am to preach for seven Sundays, and the Gulf Company is to take all the money and send half of it to the Red Cross and the other half to the Salvation Army, both to be used for unemployment relief . . . . The only one I can see lose is the Gulf Company, that is if they don't sell enough gas to pay for the gas they bought from me.[43]

Rogers' utilized his characteristic speaking style on the *Good Gulf Show* – witty, spontaneous, full of colloquialisms and malapropisms, all delivered in a halting rural drawl – that he employed as a homespun philosopher giving a lecture or presenting a stage show. On the one hand, his digressive musings provided great freedom as network censors were stymied because they never quite knew what he was going to say. On the other hand, the Rogers style created difficulties for the rigid schedule needed in national radio broadcasting. He prepared sketchy notes for the program (as usual, he had no use for a prepared script) that provided a rough outline of the topics he wanted to address. But the Oklahoman inevitably departed from the roadmap to follow wherever his commentary led him, which included barging over the time allotment. After running long on his first broadcast and being cut off in mid-sentence, he found a humorous solution. "The hardest thing over this radio is to get me stopped," he told listeners in his second broadcast before unveiling his new prop. "I have an alarm clock here; I brought my own clock. I have the alarm clock fixed. When that alarm goes off, I am going to stop, that is all there is to it. I don't care whether I am in the middle of reciting Gunga Din or the Declaration of Independence." Rogers was true to his word. When the alarm rang signaling the end of his time, he proclaimed, "Oh, Lord! There goes that thing. Darn that thing. I wasn't through yet. The darn thing worked today. Well, so long." In fact, the alarm clock quickly became another funny symbol of the Rogers charm. It would go off, he would express surprise and scramble to conclude, and the audience would laugh.[44]

Like Rogers' other writing and speaking endeavors, the *Good Gulf Show* relied on topical material for its commentary and humor. Often adapting elements from his *Weekly Articles* and *Daily Telegrams*, the humorist addressed political issues such as the effectiveness of the New Deal relief and employment programs and the Republican denunciation of it all; social problems such as Depression-era poverty and festering class-antagonisms; international controversies such as America's refusal to recognize the Russian regime and Hitler's moves in Germany; and cultural developments with advertising, college football games, and prize-fights. Rogers frequently drew upon his rural populist sensibility. He quipped, "Country folks are smarter than city folks. You never have to explain a joke to country folks." He traded on his man-of-the-people reputation. "I had listened to so many announcers trying to talk correctly that I thought you had to do it," he told listeners. "Now I find you can get up here and use bum English just like everybody else, and you don't have to speak correctly at all, and you are understood by everybody."[45]

Perhaps the Oklahoman's most emotional broadcast came on February 25, 1934, when he emptied the studio of its audience to talk about a missing airliner in Utah whose crew he had flown with just the week before. Rogers, right before going on the air, saw a newspaper dispatch saying that a plane had been sighted: "It didn't say whether it was wrecked or anything. Nobody could tell. And that's all they've heard up until now. That's a desolate country." Only after the show did he learn that the aircraft had crashed into a mountain and the three crew members and five passengers had died. One of Rogers' most influential broadcasts came on January 27, 1935, when his criticism of the World Court was credited with helping to influence the Senate's vote a few days later to turn down United States' membership in that body. In fact, the U. S. Senate, like much of America, became fans of the Oklahoman's radio show. In August 1933, seventy-four senators signed a message of appreciation to "the poet laureate of wise-cracks" and declared, "No one in America is held in greater affection nor higher esteem and no one person's daily comment is more enjoyed than that of Mr. Rogers." That same year, when it was rumored the Oklahoman might be leaving the airwaves, Vice-President Garner and a number of senators telegrammed and urged him to continue: "What is this we hear about your retirement (STOP) Does this mean you will not preside over the Senate again (STOP) We have enjoyed your recent talks on the air and want your assurance that you will soon return with your humorous and wholesome comment on national affairs (STOP)"[46]

Rogers' *Gulf Headliners* became one of radio's most popular shows and observers and critics chimed in with a chorus of praise. An article in *Collier's* claimed, "Think of the radio voices you like and remember. Invariably there's a strong personality coming through the tones – a personality so strong that you recognize it the minute you tune in" and offered as its first example "the wise, tolerant drawl of Will Rogers." "Sunday nights Will comes into the homes of radio listeners all over America just as his own plain self," observed *What's on the Air: The Magazine for the Radio Listener.* "He is one man among us today who tells the truth about the self-important of the earth to their faces, and makes them try to like it." An assessment in *Radio Guide* noted that Rogers "commands the highest popularity in radio" and was "the highest-paid man on the air." It lauded his natural style: "Invisible though he may be over the air, he literally comes into the living room, pulls up a chair, shifts his wad of gum, and launches forth on topics dear to everyone's hearts. Listeners are minded to say, 'Hmm, he took the very words right out of my mouth.'" In analyzing "Will Rogers at the Microphone," another periodical described his radio mission as "under the guise of genial raillery, to tell us hard, blunt truths about ourselves – truths about our politics, our civic standards, and our social habits. They are the sort of truths we do not always like to hear, but we will take them with a contagious chuckle and a piece of chewing gum." *Radioland* concluded simply, "He is the biggest one-man show in radio."[47]

In one of his radio broadcasts, however, Rogers entangled himself in social and political controversy. On January 24, 1934, he was reminiscing about life on the Oklahoma frontier – commenting on cattle herding and horses, family relations and rodeos, marshals and lawbreakers – when he took up the topic of cowboy songs. After several jokes and a round of singing, Rogers told his audience that he believed many of these tunes descended from "nigger spirituals." He used the offensive word three more times while discussing his theory. After the show ended, Rogers was surprised, and deeply upset, when a backlash erupted and NBC in New York received a torrent of complaints by telephone and telegraph. The NAACP threatened a boycott of Rogers, NBC, and Gulf while black newspapers such as the *New York Amsterdam News* carried headlines reading "NBC Mum on Rogers' Slur: Protests Flood Office After Comedian Uses 'Nigger' in a Speech." Some of the complaints had an angry tone. Others were couched in the language of disappointment, such as the letter sent directly to Rogers from Charles D. Washington, a black southerner and graduate of the Tuskegee Institute now living in New York. He had long admired the

Oklahoman's work, Washington wrote, "But I was surprised and disappointed tonight when you said *nigger* spiritual. I could not believe it at first, and asked my wife to turn the radio on louder; would not believe it then . . . [until] the third time you used the expression nigger." Washington noted his understanding that white people could use the term "unconsciously and without the least feeling of prejudice" and added, "I do not believe you would intentionally and maliciously insult a group of people because of the color of the[i]r skin." But he reminded Rogers of his standing as a "public character" who would be judged as "an Emissary of either good will or bad will." Washington ended on a note of conciliation, urging Rogers to visit the Tuskegee Institute after which "I wager you that my race shall forever after be the Negro race with you."[48]

Rogers reacted with a combination of regret and defensiveness. In his next broadcast on January 28, he made matters worse when he asserted his affection for Black Americans and tried to explain its deep roots in his childhood. "I wasn't only raised among darkies down in Indian Territory, but I was raised *by* them," he said. "Lord, I was five years old out on the ranch before I ever knew there was a white child." Indignant African Americans, such as listener Carita Roane, immediately objected, "The term 'darkey' used in your last night's broadcast is just as objectionable as is the term 'nigger.' There are two acceptable words to designate Americans of African descent: 'colored' or 'Negro.'" Roy Wilkins of the NAACP, in a letter to the law firm representing NBC, noted with a touch of sarcasm, "It may not be generally known but the words 'nigger,' 'coon,' 'pickaninny' and similar references to the Negro race over the air are deeply resented by colored people and their friends." Clearly perturbed, Rogers again tried to make amends on his March 4 broadcast, apologizing to listeners for "using some word that was objectionable to some of them" and asserting that he meant no offense.[49]

In a long missive replying to a letter of complaint from Channing H. Tobias, a prominent Black civic leader and head of the Colored Department of the YMCA, Rogers gave full vent to his comingled distress and defensiveness. "If the colored race has a more sympathetic friend than I have always been, I don't know who it is," he began. In discussing music, he explained, "I reverted to the word I had used since childhood down home, with never a thought of disrespect." A frustrated Rogers then came to the heart of his defense:

> I want to just say this, Mr. Tobias, I think you folks are wrong in jumping too hastily on to someone or anyone who might use the word with no more thought of belittlement than I did . . . . I am offering no excuse for using it myself. I was wrong. But it's the intention and not the wording you must look for. What in the world, what particle of action had ever led a single Negro to believe I hadent the best wishes toward their race? . . . . A colored cowpuncher taught me how to rope, and I contributed [money] to him and his wife, and went way out of my

way to drive by and see them every time I went to my old home in Oklahoma up to the time of their deaths .... If there is a colored performer (who I might have known in the old vaudeville days, and I knew many), if there is a Negro porter, waiter, or any one of your race that I have come in contact with in all my years; if you or anyone else can find a one that will say that I ever, by action or word, ever did one thing to humiliate, or show in any way that I was antagonistic to them, I would do anything for you can't find 'em, for I never did .... You must also use tolerance toward millions of fine white people who use the word, but who at heart are the real friends to your people.[50]

In terms of actions, as opposed to words, Rogers had a point. During his adult life he demonstrated an ethic of racial goodwill as he repeatedly treated African Americans with kindness and a lack of prejudice. Indeed, he revered "Uncle Dan" Walker, the black cowboy who had taught him to ride and rope as a boy, and "Aunt Babe," his wife. He not only visited them whenever he came home to Claremore but orchestrated, and paid for, the successful legal defense of their son in 1933 when he was accused of a domestic assault and jailed. Rogers became close friends with Bert Williams, the Black comedian, during their vaudeville days. He visited the Tuskegee Institute campus several times and expressed admiration for its achievements. During his stint as a silent film actor, the humorist went to a soda fountain in New Jersey for a soft drink when a Black boy came in and sat down on the adjoining stool. Rogers suddenly remembered a task to be done, gulped down his drink, and bolted out. The forlorn boy looked at the counter attendant and said, "I know why he left. He didn't want to eat by me." The attendant reported the remark to Rogers, and a couple of days later the actor returned to the establishment, saw the youth, and said, "Say, boy, are you busy? Come on, let's take on a dish of ice cream." The pair sat down side-by-side for a treat and a chat.[51]

Rogers' campaigns to help ordinary citizens suffering from natural disasters carefully included Black Americans. In 1927, while raising money to aid victims of the great Mississippi River flood, the columnist wrote in his *Weekly Article*, "look at the thousands and thousands of negroes that never did have much, but now it's washed away. You don't want to forget that water is just as high up on them as it is if they were white. The Lord so constituted everybody that no matter what color you are you require about the same amount of nourishment." During his 1931 drought relief tour, Rogers spoke at Dunbar High School, a Black institution in Little Rock, Arkansas, to raise money and awareness. He also addressed the Black congregation at the Mount Gilead Baptist Church in Fort Worth, Texas. According to a newspaper account, the humorist was introduced by the Rev. J. H. W. Pickard, who praised him for taking time from his busy career to "devote his time and talents and that without pay, to the relief of suffering humanity, regardless of race or color." When the pastor finished, "Rogers, visibly touched by the introduction, grasped Pickard by the hand and shook it vigorously." During the Depression, as Rogers surveyed a landscape of social and economic damage, he often pinpointed poor Black farmers as among the greatest victims. "The stock market is picking up, so that makes the rich boys feel a little better," he wrote in a 1931 *Daily Telegram*. "United States Steel can go to a thousand and one ... but that don't bring one biscuit to a poor old Negro family of fifteen in Arkansas, who haven't got a chance to get a single penny in money till their little few bales of cotton are sold away next fall."[52]

At the same time, for all his racial good deeds, Rogers harbored a casual, unthinking assumption of white racial superiority that the dustup over his use of the n-word on the radio forced him to confront, perhaps for the first time. It is not surprising that the son of a Confederate army officer and former slaveholder would assume that the white race stood above Blacks, and other races and ethnicities as well, in a hierarchy of status. As a youthful student at the Kemper School, he grew angry when a classmate claimed "Indians and Negroes were very much alike" and hotly explained how the two races were different in origin, characteristics, and prospects. During his trip to South Africa as a young man, Rogers liberally used "nigger" to describe natives he encountered. In letters home, he recounted driving a herd of mules to Ladysmith and added, "I will have some of the Native Nigger boys to help me." While detailing his performance with the *Texas Jack Wild West Show* he noted, "I play a nigger in a play ... and sing a coon song." He continued the habit after heading eastward, explaining to relatives back in Claremore that while the natives of New Zealand were "a kind of Indian called the Mouira, but the natives of Australia are Niggers." When traveling in Manchuria in 1932, he became incensed upon witnessing Russian women who had fled the Communist regime being forced into prostitution and used by Asian men. His indignant racial rendering of this tragedy was revealing:

> Years ago, the White Man had a standing, especially Social, that put him apart. But since these thousands of white Women have been, for the sake of their very existence, thrown at the feet of people who, before this time, couldent have even spoken to them, why it looks like somebody is responsible .... White civilization, in days to come, is going to have a lot to answer for. For nothing has lowered your boasted superiority of the White Race like what has happened to these Women .... [I]f we are such a superior people, and our morals are one of our most cherished traditions – 'why is it that you don't do more to protect your White Women?'

As biographer Richard D. White, Jr., also points out, what Rogers did *not* say also tells much. While commenting on every possible topic and incident in American public life in thousands of journalistic pieces, public talks, and radio broadcasts for nearly twenty years, he never mentioned the hotly debated issue of lynching or the myriad race riots in American cities, including the one in Tulsa (only thirty miles from Claremore) in 1921 that saw rampaging white mobs destroy thirty-five square blocks of the city's black community, sending hundreds to local hospitals and dozens to local morgues.[53]

Thus Rogers, like the vast majority of white Americans in the late 1800s and early 1900s, harbored paternalistic, prejudicial feelings about African Americans. But like increasing numbers of whites, he was drifting away from such views as he progressed beyond his inheritance. His beneficial racial deeds were outstripping the offensive language he grew up with and signaled his growth in racial toleration and humane feeling. The radio incident of 1934 revealed, however painfully, that Rogers had made progress, but not yet achieved perfection, on this front. The fact that he was deeply upset, tried to make amends, and never again publicly uttered the n-word revealed the Oklahoman to be not a virulent racist but a white American of the early twentieth century struggling, not always successfully, to overcome social tradition with good will.

This racial controversy notwithstanding, Rogers' popular radio show brought him before a huge national audience on a weekly basis and further cemented his beloved status among ordinary Americans. The humorist's success over the airwaves, in concert with global travel and aviation, swept him up in a series of kinetic endeavors that kept him constantly on the go by the early 1930s. This frenetic man-in-motion ethos finally flung him into the world of "motion pictures," a final endeavor that capped his extraordinary career. After inking a lucrative contract with a major Hollywood studio, he embraced "talkie" films and soon became one of America's biggest movie stars. This conquest of yet another popular form of modern communications and entertainment made him a true cultural giant. Rogers' new movie-star role combined all his trademark traits as never before – the "aw' shucks" physical mannerisms and the disheveled appearance, the drawling voice and the colloquial language, the charming personality and the horse-sense humor – and projected the whole man nationwide onto the silver screen. This larger-than-life image proved indelible.

13

The Man Talkies Were Invented For

O N JUNE 10, 1928, WILL ROGERS INFORMED READERS of his *Weekly Article* about a looming transformation of the American movies. "I was just talking to some of the biggest men in the whole industry, and . . . they say that the whole business is undergoing a great change," he reported. "That in four or five years you will look back and laugh at yourself for ever having sit for hours and just looked at Pictures with no voice or no sound." The innovation of "talking Pictures" had arrived in Hollywood with a bang as the big studios "have made contracts with General Electric (I think that's the one that holds most of the patents on the sound) and they are all going in for it heavy." Other changes were arriving in the wake of the "talkie" revolution: actors were worrying about how they sounded as well as how they looked, stage actors with trained voices were pushing out some silent movie stars who had relied on melodramatic expressions and gestures, directors were having to alter their style since they could no longer yell out instructions during shooting, scripts could no longer just contain words that looked good in printed titles but had to contain "real lines that real human beings would utter," and movie studios and movie theaters alike were frantically installing new equipment for recording and projecting sound. The rapidly shifting landscape was equal parts exhilarating and frightening and the "whole business out here is scared cuckoo," the Oklahoman quipped.[1]

Rogers put his finger on one of the great watersheds in American movie history: the "talkie revolution." Following years of experimentation and the utilization of sound fragments in several films, Warner Brothers' release of *The Jazz Singer* in October 1927, starring Al Jolson in the first feature-length movie with synchronized sound, turned Hollywood upside down. Employing the Vitaphone sound system developed by Western Electric, this film's notable popularity started a stampede toward "talkies" in the movie studios that made silent films obsolete within three years. The major studios – Warner Brothers,

Fox, Paramount, Metro-Goldwyn-Mayer, United Artists, Columbia, RKO, Universal – invested heavily in technology, both with film recording and revamping theaters for sound projection. By 1930, about two-thirds of American theaters had been retrofitted for sound, the last totally silent film was released, and crowds flocked to see and *hear* their favorite movie stars. That year an estimated 110 million people attended a movie each week. Three years later, at the low point of the Great Depression, 60 to 80 million viewers a week still managed to scrape together the price of a movie ticket. As *Fortune* magazine declared breathlessly, the advent of the talkies was "beyond comparison the fastest and most amazing revolution in the whole history of industrial revolutions."[2]

Little did Rogers know that less than a year later he would be swept up in this cultural revolution. After signing a deal with a major studio in the spring of 1929, the humorist would make twenty films over the next six years and become one of the biggest stars in Hollywood. Nearly all of his movies were warm, funny, sentimental tales of ordinary rural or small-town people upholding their values and overcoming challenges confronting them. The man from Claremore played an assortment of humble, folksy, yet shrewd characters – farmer, country doctor, steamboat captain, village banker, small-town judge – that offered variations on the public figure "Will Rogers." The plots involved him overcoming a predicament or righting an injustice through a combination of homespun wisdom, common sense, and gentle humor. These films added another significant dimension to the Oklahoman's already enormous reputation as a humorous observer of American values and habits, an influential commentator on politics, and an insightful analyst of America's changing social mores. They made him a full-blown celebrity. Rogers accrued the central attribute of the movie star: a set of personal characteristics that shone through any character he played and became embedded in the public consciousness. Like other celebrities, he became a figure ordinary people thought they knew, or wanted to know; someone whose every action and utterance attracted widespread attention. As with everything he did, Rogers' conquest of Hollywood left his audience entranced and they filled theaters throughout the United States.

Rogers liked to poke fun at his latest endeavor. He jokingly referred to Hollywood as "Cuckooland" and termed the new-style films "Squawkies" and "Noisies." He observed that the film capital was awash in aspiring actors: "Everybody that can't sing has a double that can, and everybody that can't talk is going right on and proving it." But motion pictures with sound, in some cosmic fashion, seemed to have been created with him in mind. He was a natural fit for this new entertainment medium with his great verbal dexterity, keen wit, folksy appearance, and unpretentious appeal. Bringing together his full range of talents as no other endeavor ever had, and reaching a vast audience during the movie-crazy era of the Great Depression, Hollywood films played a major role in making the Oklahoma cowboy perhaps the most influential figure in American culture in the 1930s. As a critic enthused after viewing the humorist's first sound film, "Will Rogers is the man talkies were made for."[3]

* * * * *

When Fox Film Corporation first approached Will Rogers in 1929 about doing talkie films, he was reluctant. "I've had my bellyful of pictures," he groused. Rogers' silent film career earlier in the decade had been solid but not outstanding, and he was disappointed when eventually his contract was not renewed. He had little reason to believe things would be different now. But Wilfred Sheehan, general manager of the company's Hollywood studios and a friend of Rogers, persisted and the humorist finally overcame his reluctance. The contract he signed in late March 1929 explains why. It stipulated a wide-ranging role for Rogers in the making of four films over the next year: "in addition to acting, performing, speaking and singing in said four pictures you will assist us in creating and writing original matter such as dialogue, dramatic and comedy lines, and assist in the selection and construction of the stories and continuity thereof, the selection of cast, editing, criticizing, revising, adapting, composing and creating scenarios, titles and writing the text thereof." Equally important, the contract called for Fox to pay Rogers the princely sum of 600,000 dollars for his services. When the entertainer received the contract from Fox, he blanched at the prospect of examining every detail in the bulky document, so he scrawled in the margin, "I haven't read this thing, but if Winnie Sheehan says it's all right, that's good enough for me." And he signed it.[4]

In hindsight, it does not seem surprising that Rogers made the leap. An astute observer of both the Hollywood scene and American society, he had been joking in his newspaper pieces about the craze for "talkies" sweeping through the country. For countless Americans, he noted with amazement, becoming a movie star beckoned as the latest Horatio Alger opportunity to climb to success. When Rogers returned to the east coast to attend a political convention, no one seemed to care about public affairs. "Hollywood is what I am asked more about back here than all the politics," he told readers. "'How's Clara Bow?' Did you see Barrymore's new baby?' 'Who do you have to look like to get in the movies?'" Even the distinguished regionalist author, Hamlin Garland, wrote Rogers asking for assistance in helping his son-in-law land a job in the film industry. Rogers graciously complied. Such experiences led the humorist to conclude, "If you have lost anybody anywhere in the World and don't know where they are, they are in Hollywood trying to get in the Movies." With anyone and everyone clamoring to find their destiny in Hollywood, regardless of talent or training, it sounded a note of sanity that a studio would corral someone with Rogers' undeniable appeal and successful track record in entertainment.[5]

Rogers' first film offered a crucial start-up for this new chapter in his career. Initially, he had expressed interest in doing a film version of the successful play, *The County Chairman*, by George Ade. Securing the rights proved elusive, however, and the studio convinced him to film instead an adaptation of Homer Croy's novel, *They Had to See Paris*. Croy, a Missourian and a casual acquaintance of Rogers when they had lived near one another in Forest Hills in the late 1910s, specialized in portraying transplanted Midwesterners struggling with sophisticated urban culture. He and Rogers met on numerous occasions to discuss the story, its characters, and their common background. Fox assembled a strong cast of actors to surround Rogers – including Irene Rich as his wife, a role she would reprise several times in future films – and secured veteran Frank Borzage to direct the film. The company shot several opening scenes in Rogers' hometown and then filmed the rest in a Fox studio.[6]

They Had to See Paris, released in September 1929, offered a rough template for many Rogers movies to come with its story of an ordinary man from small-town America who confronts and overcomes a travail, thereby reaffirming the bedrock values of plain folk. The humorist played Pike Peters, a garage owner and automobile mechanic from, not coincidentally, Claremore, Oklahoma, who suddenly finds himself wealthy when an oil well in which he had invested hits a gusher and begins to produce prodigiously. His wife is carried away by the sudden influx of money and insists the family move to Paris to move up in society, become cultured, and find a noble husband for their daughter. Pike reluctantly agrees, and a series of comic episodes unfold as the unassuming Oklahoman confronts Parisian townhouses, aristocratic snobs, butlers and valets, and sexy showgirls. Things go sour when Pike's unsophisticated behavior ruins his daughter's engagement to a French marquis, causing his furious wife to banish him from the household. Only when the family gets the mistaken impression he has taken up with a cabaret singer do hard feelings resolve and everyone decides to return to Oklahoma and their earlier life.

In his first talkie film, Rogers clearly played a version of himself. Pike Peters was a fountain of homespun wisdom and rustic wisecracks who joked with his buddies at the automobile garage and gently instructed his family on the deeper things in life. Chewing on a wad of gum, scratching his head, tugging at a forelock always about to cover his eye, and speaking in a hesitant rural drawl, all as backdrop for the dispensing of a witty, common-sense philosophy, he could have been Rogers on any lecture stage in the country. Pike makes friends with nearly everyone, including both his valet "Gus" and a Russian Grand Duke. He quips that "marriage is like a poker game, and you just gotta play your own hand." He reminds his wife that they cannot determine their children's happiness, saying, "If parents have kept their children out of jail, they have fulfilled their obligation." When the marquis demands a dowry to marry his daughter, Pike angrily refuses with the comment, "There's one crop in America that never fails and that's the 'fool' crop. But I'm not aimin' to add to it." He reflects the Rogers' mindset when he rejects his wife's social pretension and pleads, "Let's keep our common sense, be down to earth, and think a minute." Mrs. Peters unintentionally captures her husband's Rogersian qualities when a French aristocrat archly commented on Pike's unrefined manners, and she replied, "I know, he's so thoroughly American."

Rogers was nervous about the reception of his first talkie film. In a folksy press release, he acknowledged to his public, "Well, here I am in the talkies. It had to come .... [J]ust because I got along pretty good talking my head off about anything and everything, the films decided there must be something in it .... You all been pretty patient with me up to now, and laughed in the right places. I hope you keep it up." But unsure about the success of *They Had to See Paris*, and not keen on extravagant Hollywood movie premieres, he fled the grand opening at the Fox-Carthay Theater in Los Angeles and went home to Oklahoma. As he explained in a *Weekly Article*, when the finished film was set "to appear with a sort of Ballyhoo opening, why I figured I better kinder take to the woods till the effects kinder blew over. I wanted 'em to kinder fumigate around before I appeared in person back home." According to Croy, Rogers did not return until he received a telegram from Betty: "The picture has opened and you can come home now." Samuel Goldwyn, his old silent-film producer, may have helped ease the humorist's anxiety. "I saw 'They Had to See Paris' last night and I congratulate you on your wonderful performance," Goldwyn wrote. "I have never seen an audience enjoy a performance as much as it did yours. To my mind it is the best thing you have ever done."[7]

Reviews of *They Had to See Paris* largely agreed with Goldwyn's assessment. A spate of positive assessments appeared, with one claiming Rogers was "as spontaneous and natural for the camera and the microphone as he ever was for the stage or the concert platform." "He brings the simplicity and homely sincerity of his ways to the newer form of film expression," observed the *Los Angeles Times*. "What he couldn't do on the silent screen he can accomplish most admirably with speech. He can reach his public with a directness that was not possible through the use of the subtitle. His personality comes out clearly and genuinely. He is thoroughly himself, and that is what he should be." The *New York Times* praised his "intelligent and refreshing impersonation of the Oklahoman who went to Paris just to please his wife and children" while another reviewer was surprised that Rogers was not only humorous but had "some straight dramatic scenes which he plays in a manner that would do credit to a Barrymore." The *Philadelphia Public Ledger* summed up critical sentiment: "Audiences give every indication of taking Will Rogers to their bosoms all over again in this first all-talking feature picture of his . . . . Will Rogers playing Will Rogers in *They Had to See Paris* is a genuine artistic feat."[8]

Following the rousing reception for his first film, Rogers' career in the talkies took off. Over the next six years he made nineteen more films, an output in the same range as that of the busiest and most popular Hollywood actors. Top male box office draws such as Clark Gable, Wallace Beery, and Gary Cooper, along with top female draws such as Janet Gaynor, Joan Crawford, and Marie Dressler made between nineteen and twenty-nine films each from 1929 to 1935. While impressive on this scale of leading Hollywood stars, Rogers' volume of film appearances was little short of astonishing given that he was also writing both a daily and weekly newspaper column, broadcasting a weekly radio show, and traveling widely throughout the country and the world. By any reckoning Rogers pursued a backbreakingly busy schedule.

Rogers began at a modest pace, making two movies in 1930. *So This Is London* offered another American abroad story, this time a Texas cotton mill owner who is forced to travel to England for business reasons, where his Anglophobia is put to the test when his son falls in love with the daughter of an English nobleman. *Lightnin'* featured Rogers as a liquor-loving rascal who is drawn into combatting a tangled scheme to deprive him and his family of their hotel on the California-Nevada border. Then in 1931 Rogers doubled his film production, starring in four Fox films. *A Connecticut Yankee* presented him as the time-traveling "Sir Boss" who upends King Arthur's court in an adaptation of the famous Mark Twain novel. In *Young As You Feel*, he appeared as a punctilious, hypochondriac business-man who takes up with a cabaret singer and becomes a fashionable man-about-town. *Ambassador Bill* featured Rogers in the role of an Oklahoman who is appointed ambassador to a European nation beset by weekly revolutions, where he becomes entangled both in politics and the personal lives of the royal family . In *Business and Pleasure*, Rogers portrayed a razor-blade tycoon from Oklahoma who travels to the Middle East to discover the process of making Damascus steel, only to fall victim to a scheme launched by an archrival manufacturer.

Preoccupied with traveling and busy writing about the presidential election, Rogers released only two films in 1932. *Down to Earth* offered a sequel to *They Had to See Paris*, only now Pike Peters and his family have returned to the United States where the stock market crash has eradicated his wealth and he struggles to bring his ostentatious family down to earth. Rogers reprised the character "Jubilo" from his earlier silent film in *Too Busy to Work*, where the amiable, whimsical vagabond searches to find his lost wife and daughter. The Oklahoman starred in three movies in 1933. He appeared as an Iowa hog farmer whose family endures a week of adventures and heartaches in *State Fair*, while *Doctor Bull* saw him in the role of a small-town Connecticut doctor who stands as a confidant, caregiver, and social facilitator for the whole community. *Mr. Skitch* presented the humorist as a Missouri farmer who takes to the open road with his family after losing their homestead in a bank failure.

In 1934, Fox released three Rogers films. In *David Harum*, he played a small-town banker at the turn of the century with a passion for horse-trading and solving social and romantic problems. *Handy Andy* featured Rogers as a village druggist who is forced to sell his store before surviving a raucous trip to New Orleans and then returning to the stability of his earlier life. In another turn-of-the-century story, *Judge Priest* presented the humorist as a wise judge in a small Kentucky town who pursues both justice and community comity. In 1935, Rogers' film production reached its apex with five movies distributed to theaters throughout the United States. *The County Chairman* told the tale of a homespun frontier lawyer in Wyoming who successfully manages the course of politics in Tomahawk County. Playing a local newspaper editor and advice columnist in *Life Begins at Forty*, Rogers' investigations solve a controversial bank theft from years ago that still torments his community. *Doubting Thomas* showcased a prosperous maker of breakfast sausages who must intervene to restrain his family's wildly inflated dreams of success in Hollywood. *Steamboat Round the Bend* featured Rogers as a steamboat captain and snake-oil salesman whose involvement in a river race leads to the exoneration of a friend accused of murder. *In Old Kentucky*, the Oklahoman's final film, presented him as a racehorse trainer who maneuvers to secure the racing victory of a small-time local family over his millionaire employer.[9]

This relentless schedule of filmmaking proved highly successful. Rogers' talkies consistently drew large audiences throughout the United States and within a couple of years he stood near or at the top of surveys of Hollywood's highest-drawing movie stars. According to a survey compiled by the *Motion Picture Herald* – it was based on exhibitor reports – in 1932 Rogers climbed to number nine on the list of top box-office draws of actors and actresses. In 1933, he stood as number two; in 1934, number one; and in 1935, number two. Anecdotal evidence further illuminated Rogers' great appeal as a movie actor. In 1935, the manager of the Princess Theater in Gadsden, Alabama, wrote to the humorist reporting that Mrs. Sarah Sheffield, a seventy-five-year-old farm woman living near the town, had never seen a movie until she recently attended Rogers' *Life Begins at Forty*. The manager sent along a photograph of the new movie fan, who was smiling broadly as she said "only Will Rogers could have broken this long tie [to her home]." Obviously touched, Rogers wrote a personal note to Mrs. Sheffield thanking her for viewing his film and expressing delight at seeing her happy face in the photo.

He added, perhaps thinking of his own rural background, "I envy you, living like you do, and not seeing a lot of things like a lot of us do, we see so much it don't interest us any more. Seeing never made anybody contented, it's knowing that makes things worthwhile. With all my love and best wishes."[10]

The Oklahoman's popularity was reflected in his salary. In October 1930, because of the profitability of his initial talkies, Fox renewed Rogers' contract and engaged him to star in six more films. The studio agreed to pay him a total of 1,125,000 dollars for his services, which awarded him a significant raise from 150,000 dollars per movie to 187,500 dollars per movie. This was a very lucrative arrangement, especially as the Great Depression continued to ravage the American economy, and it positioned the humorist among the top-salaried Hollywood actors.[11]

The great success of Rogers' career in the talkies was rooted partly in his well-established personality and towering reputation with the public, qualities already established by the release of his first film. Yet the movies also presented a grand new opportunity for him to articulate his ideas and broadcast his image to his massive audience. A close look at his talkie films from 1929–1935 reveals important ways in which he used the new cinema of sound – perhaps even more effectively than radio, newspaper writing, lectures, and shows – to explain America to itself.

* * * * *

As Will Rogers' talkies went pouring out into theaters all over America from 1929 to 1935, they shared several prominent characteristics: homespun humor, sentimental storylines, and the distinctive, well-known Rogers personality. They also tended to divide broadly into two groups. First, many of the Oklahoman's early talkie films were "charisma comedies" – or simply vehicles that employed the popular Rogers persona as the centerpiece of a comedic narrative. Second, many of his later talkie films appeared onscreen as "populist parables" – or stories that utilized the Rogers persona to tout the virtues of rural and small-town life, hard work and anti-elitism, the common man and common sense. Both types of Rogers movies generated a strong appeal, with the former focusing on a light-hearted send-up of human foibles and the latter on a deeper-seated exploration of the American spirit and advocacy of common people.

Rogers' early charisma comedies featured him riffing humorously on the absurd aspects of life, the uncomfortable situations people create for themselves, and the social hypocrisies they evince all too often. In *So This Is London*, Rogers' character encounters a bureaucrat who won't issue him a passport without a birth certificate and comments drolly, "I gather from you that you doubt I was born. Course out in the country if you walk up and appear before anybody in person, why we take it as fairly positive proof that you must have been born. We just kinda' trust in that way." When the diplomat protagonist in *Ambassador Bill* arrives at his posting only to encounter the nation's weekly revolution, an armored vehicle arrives to whisk him to the embassy, prompting the comment, "Well, a Chicago taxi." *A Connecticut Yankee* shows Rogers' Hank Martin, who has awakened in the era of King Arthur, struggling to comprehend both his where-abouts and the stilted old English he hears, bursts out, "Can'st thou tellest me where in the helleth I am?" When another character asks Jubilo how he can be so lazy in *Too Busy to Work*, he explains, "It's not very hard. You jes' don't do anything about it, and the first thing you know, it takes care of itself." In *Business and Pleasure*, Rogers says of male–female relationships, "No woman will ever believe a man that he's not worthy of her . . . until after they are married."

The charisma comedies also showed Rogers regularly engaging in one of the trademark endeavors of his writing, shows, and lectures: puncturing pomposity. Lemuel Morehouse, in *Young as You Feel*, pokes fun at the pretensions of modern abstract art when he claims to create his own sculpture, which is simply an odd-shaped boulder retrieved from a construction project: "This is 'Washington Crossing the Delaware.' Turn it around and it's 'Washington Coming Back.'" In *Doubting Thomas*, Rogers lampoons amateur thespians who are convinced of their inevitable ascent to stardom, saying, "Acting is just like the measles. If you catch it when you're young, why, you can get over it, but if you catch it when you're older it's sometimes fatal." *So This Is London* shows Rogers' Hiram Draper, upon entering a lavish English estate, commenting, "I had no idea there's anything like this in England. I bet it's one of those old places they moved over here from Long Island." *A Connecticut Yankee* saw Rogers' Hank Martin quip about the nobility and its obsession with lineage, "It's funny how they only find knights and lords as your ancestors. I guess they ship over [to America] all the horse thieves."

To accentuate the humorous impact of the Rogers' persona, the charisma comedies often clad the Oklahoma cowboy in ludicrous costumes that played against his down-home image. *A Connecticut Yankee* started the trend by displaying "Sir Boss" cavorting through Camelot outfitted in a medieval tunic-and-hose topped off with a modern bowler hat, and then clanking about in a full suit of armor, complete with billowing plume. *As Young as You Feel* presented the Oklahoma cowboy decked out in an evening coat with tails, fancy waistcoat, broad striped tie, and tall silk hat with his hair stylishly slicked back. Rogers appeared in *Business and Pleasure* as a swami in Damascus outfitted in a bejeweled-and-feathered turban with a full beard and flowing robes. Two of his later films adopted this same visual ploy. In *Handy Andy*, he first donned an outrageously tasteless golf outfit with clashing knickers, cap, sweater, long socks, and two-tone shoes and then appeared at a Mardi Gras ball dressed in tights and a leopard-skin tunic to dance wildly as Tarzan. The climactic scene in *Down to Earth* featured Rogers dressed as Louis XV, complete with powdered wig, brocade coat, long silk shirt with frilly cuffs, and knee breeches, at an extravagant period party thrown by his wife.

By 1932, Rogers' talkies began to change shape as they increasingly took on the trappings of populist parables. While still full of wit and sentiment, these newer cinematic stories shifted focus to the virtues of ordinary citizens standing in opposition to the cultural and economic elites who erected barriers to their happiness. Rogers, playing variations of the small-town cracker-barrel philoso-pher, stood as the dynamic force in moving these tales along and elucidating their themes. He served as a prophet of cultural populism who praised, and exempli-fied, the common sense of the common man and embodied the security, neigh-borliness, family solidarity, and basic goodness of rural, village life. At the same time, he preached the gospel of economic populism, castigating the perfidy of big economic institutions and the selfishness of financial elites. In the hands of the Oklahoman in his later films, the silver screen became a backdrop upon which to project the hopes, dreams, and struggles of ordinary Americans.

One of the earliest populist parables, *State Fair*, established a baseline with its valentine to rural life and its quiet pleasures. This sweet-tempered story focused on an Iowa farm family, the Frakes, whose members head off to the annual state fair for a week of camping, competition, and new experiences. It captures the old-fashioned excitement that accompanied these rural-oriented exhibitions as people who labored on the land for most of the year escaped their routines, and sometimes isolation, to display their rustic skills, renew friendships, and thrill to the roller-coaster and merry-go-round of the midway and the allure of dancing-girl shows. Will Rogers portrayed Abel Frake, a hog-farmer obsessed with having Blue Boy, his prized Hampshire boar, win the grand champion ribbon. His wife, Melissa, is equally intent on winning prizes for her pickles and mincemeat. Their children, Margie and Wayne, go in search of adventure and romance. As the gentle story unfolds, both Abel and Melissa triumph in their shows; the former when he discovers Blue Boy comes to life in the presence of a comely red sow, and the latter when she and her husband accidentally add a double portion of apple brandy to her mincemeat recipe, a mistake that delights the palette-weary judges. Both children find romance with alien figures, Wayne with a beautiful trapeze artist who ultimately cannot overcome their different backgrounds, and Margie with a big-city newspaper writer who finally follows her home to propose mar-riage. Their parents also get a romantic charge as they enjoy midway rides and even attend a risqué performance of scantily-clad showgirls (with mock innocence, Abel says to Melissa, "It don't mean anything to me, but I'll take you in if you like."). Replete with scenes of reading newspapers in rocking chairs on the front porch, families sharing meals and conversation in front of their tents at the fair, and the small triumphs of living happily on the land, *State Fair* presented a warm fantasy of populist virtue.

Subsequently, Rogers' populist parables dug more deeply into the American rural experience as they not only praised the virtue of small farmers and small-town producers but shone a critical light on powerful, elitist, urban-oriented forces that often thwarted them. In part, these movies focused on the cultural dimension of populism, juxtaposing good-hearted, plain-speaking, commonsensical men and women with highfalutin, highly educated, condescending snobs who disdained them. This portrait, strongly colored by Rogers' good-natured quips and humorous insights, illuminated a clash of values while critiquing barriers to opportunity facing common folk.

This idiom of cultural populism shaped both story and dialogue in these films by placing small-town decency and hard work in opposition to the impositions of elitist influence and power. Pike Peters, the village car mechanic who stumbled into oil money in *They Had to See Paris*, struggles with a snobby, dissolute European aristocracy when they reject his plainspoken, unassuming habits. *Mr. Skitch* begins with an affluent, smug young man abandoning young Emily Skitch after her family falls on hard times, a heartless gesture that is later juxtaposed with the kindness and community spirit of dispossessed people who share vegetables and meat to create a meal for everyone at a camp of migrants. David Harum, a small-town banker in upstate New York, exemplifies kindness and neighborliness by outwitting a hard-hearted church deacon bent on gaining profit at all costs. Kenesaw Clark, editor of a local newspaper in *Life Begins at Forty*, champions principles of fair play and community spirit against the degradations of the village's social elite and their corruption of the legal and financial system. Such sentimental portraits of common folk are accented with scenes of hayrides filled with singing and laughing young people, square dances drawing participants of all ages, and a rural tribe of hog-calling specialists whose hilarious shrieking make a mockery of the local power-broker's political speech at the county fair.

Rogers' characters played the central role in these stories of populist virtue. He portrayed a series of figures who served as village wise men who smoothed social disruptions, subtly encouraged youthful romances, diffused tensions with shrewd jokes, and upheld standards of decency and fairness. The Oklahoman played an unassuming car mechanic who loves trading wisecracks with friends at his shop; a ruined small businessman who tries to revive the fortunes of his family; a kindly, generous village banker who looks out for his neighbors; a small-town pharmacist who loves the quiet satisfactions of village life; a local political wizard in Wyoming with community interests at heart; the editor of a small-town newspaper who is unafraid to defend a young man unfairly accused of a crime; and a good-hearted horse trainer who befriends and assists an aged neighbor. Rogers' characters personified the best elements of America's small-town heartland and its hard-working, family-oriented residents.

A strong element of economic populism likewise colored most of Rogers' later talkies. Influenced by the widespread financial pain of the Great Depression, these films defended the economic interests of hard-working common folk struggling to feed and clothe their families against financial elites and institutions that often oppressed them. *Down to Earth*, a sequel to *They Had to See Paris*, saw the Pike family returned to Oklahoma where their economic fortune vanishes underwater in the tides of the Great Depression. In *Mr. Skitch*, Arial Skitch, the owner of a "fixit shop" in Flat River, Missouri, has his home and belongings repossessed when the local bank goes under during the Depression and takes his savings with it. As he declares to his wife after assessing their plight, "It appears the bank's on one side and the people's on the other." Skitch and his family hit the road and head for California, where he picks up odd jobs to scrape together money for food and fuel while the couple and their four children spend the night in "car parks" during the journey. *The County Chairman's* Jim Hackler struggles mightily to overcome a money-corrupted political system by managing the campaign of an idealistic political neophyte.

This same economic populism shaped many of Rogers' later films. The central plot of *Life Begins at Forty* pits small-town newspaper editor, Kenesaw Clark, against Colonel Joseph Abercrombie, the powerful, unscrupulous local banker who attempts to destroy Clark's paper when he supports a young man unfairly accused of robbery. As Clark comments disgustedly at one point, "You rich men's all alike. You spend your whole life making money, then you don't know what to do with it." David Harum, a village banker himself near the turn of the century, confesses of his profession during the Panic of 1893, "Bankers are not in very good repute." He then goes on to demonstrate his virtue by behaving in a most un-bankerly way – he pretends to find hidden funds in the account of a widow's late husband in order to stave off a foreclosure on her home. (Rogers, in a radio broadcast, had joked of the film to his Depression-era audience, "We may have to change him from a banker into something else, in order to get sympathy for him.") In *Handy Andy*, a village pharmacist struggles to maintain his corner store against the determined acquisition efforts of a wealthy drugstore-chain magnate. *In Old Kentucky* sees unassuming horse-trainer, Steve Tapley, quietly maneuvering to undermine the interests of his millionaire employer and boost those of a small-time neighbor in an important race.[12]

The culmination of Rogers' talkie career, especially in its populist coloration, came in a trilogy of films made with the famed director, John Ford. Born John

Martin Feeney in Cape Elizabeth, Maine, in 1894, this son of Irish immigrants had moved to California in 1914, adopted the professional name "Jack Ford," and slowly rose through the ranks in silent and talkie films to become one of Hollywood's most legendary movie directors. By the end of the Depression decade, Ford was poised to make a quartet of films that boosted him to a plateau of fame with their compelling storytelling, striking aesthetics, commercial popularity, and vibrant populist tone. *Stagecoach* (1939) elevated the western from its previous B-movie status with its dramatic juxtaposition of an outlaw folk hero out to avenge his murdered family, played by a young John Wayne, and a villainous, well-fed banker who absconded with a payroll, complained about bank examiners, and constantly spouted sentiments such as "The government must not interfere with business." *Young Mr. Lincoln* (1939), starring Henry Fonda, presented the youthful railsplitter and future president as a village populist hero who tells jokes, judges pie contests, throws himself into community tugs-of-war, and displays a canny, self-deprecating courtroom style as he pleads on behalf of the poorest and the humblest. *The Grapes of Wrath* (1940), also featuring Fonda, brought John Steinbeck's novel to the screen with its harrowing account of impoverished "Okies" who flee both the dust bowl and bankers who have foreclosed on their farms and bulldozed their houses, desperately shuffle through migrant camps as they follow the promise of agricultural work in California, but ultimately endure. *How Green Was My Valley* (1941), which won Academy Awards for best film and best director, told the story of a Welsh mining strike through the eyes of a mining family, adopting an elegiac, sentimental tone to evoke the dignity, virtue, and strong ties of kinship among plain, honest, hard-working folk.[13]

These movies boosted Ford to an elevated plateau of filmmaking fame that made him one of the most respected and influential names in Hollywood. His work became noted for an Americana style and substance. But it was his mid-1930s films with Will Rogers that set the foundation for his powerful populist reading of the American experience. In three productions – *Doctor Bull* (1933), *Judge Priest* (1934), and *Steamboat 'Round the Bend* (1935) – the Oklahoma humorist and the groundbreaking director joined forces to craft complex, nuanced portraits of small-town life and common folk. As one film scholar has noted, Ford's movies with Rogers "began to fully articulate an *ideal* – an ideal to be incarnated in *Young Mr. Lincoln*, ... oppressed in the Okies of *The Grapes of Wrath*, ... and lost and remembered in the valley of *How Green Was My Valley*." It was a populist ideal, one that was heartfelt yet clear-eyed, depicting the lives of common folk in a fashion that saluted their virtues and recognized their basic goodness without ignoring their faults and weaknesses. Rogers' crucial participation in this project created his most compelling and nuanced populist tales on the silver screen.[14]

Doctor Bull (1933) opened with a series of shots – an arriving locomotive and train station, snow-covered streets surrounding a village square, residents climbing a small incline to attend church services – that skillfully suggests the close-knit nature of life in the small town of New Winton, Connecticut. But any trace of sentiment quickly disappears as a group gathered at a local store gossip and backbite about their fellow townsmen, including the local physician, Dr. George Bull. This checkered view of small-town society was characteristic of the Ford-Rogers films and all the more compelling for its realism. So, too, was the film's avoidance of easy laughs in favor of natural humor flowing from circumstance, and a leisurely pace that subtly reflected the quiet existence of village life.

Dr. Bull has labored for decades as the town doctor and health officer. Delivering babies, tending the afflicted, and comforting the dying, he is a local institution and bulwark of social stability in New Winton. He sits up all night with a sick boy, fails to collect payment from those who cannot afford it, and stubbornly treats a new husband who has fallen from a considerable height and suffered paralysis in both legs. Yet Bull is no plaster saint. Possessed of a crusty personality that does not suffer fools gladly, he dismisses hypochondriacs and neglects a wealthy family in order to aid the delivery of a baby in an immigrant Italian family. Bull also confesses to being a mediocre physician, recommending castor oil as a remedy for nearly every human ailment and even stooping to treat cows on occasion. As the film unfolds, the doctor confronts two crises. First, many villagers are scandalized by his relationship with Janet Cardmaker, widow and sister of the richest and most influential man in New Winton, Herbert Banning. When his car is parked outside her house many evenings until the wee hours, tongues wag and moral aspersions are cast. Second, when a typhoid epidemic breaks out in New Winton, many of these same critics accuse Dr. Bull of incompetence for tardiness in diagnosing and stopping the disease. The elite Banning family disapproves of the down-home doctor and fuels both crises, moving to pry him away from the widow Cardmaker and engineering a town meeting to dismiss him as the town health officer.

Ultimately, however, Bull triumphs. He strides into the town meeting and denounces his critics as "scandal hounds" and "grinning baboons." He overcomes his longtime fear of romantic commitment and proposes marriage to Janet, who accepts. After his unorthodox treatment of the paralyzed young man produces a recovery, contrary to the expert opinion of every other physician, he becomes the toast of the profession as far away as New York. Finally, it emerges that the typhoid came from a construction camp's polluting water runoff, part of a project owned by Herbert Banning, who is set to earn enormous profits from building a large water reservoir in the area. This nuanced populist parable ends with George Bull's victory on both the cultural and economic front as he vanquishes both narrow-minded moralism and economic power to protect the small-town life he loves.

Reviews of *Doctor Bull* often took note of its successful populist agenda. The *Los Angeles Times* stressed that the film's emphasis on the small-town physician whose main task was caring for the ordinary residents of his community caused viewers "to be absorbed by its deeper feeling. Dr. Bull's cases are not all clinical; to him come the mentally ill and the sick at heart as well." Another reviewer described the physician as a "human philosopher tending to his neighbor's needs . . . . A country doctor loved by all in the township where he has practiced for years and sneered at only by a family of snobs." The *New York Times* sensed the ambiguity in this story of village life, seeing it as "a homey, lifelike tale, set forth in a leisurely fashion . . . . It gives a graphic conception of life in a small Connecticut town, the weaknesses of some persons and the strengths of others." Another review saw *Doctor Bull* as part of a larger populist trend with "Hollywood's back-to-the-farm movement . . . and Dr. Rogers is very likeable, homespun and – at the end – practically a savior . . . . Dr. Rogers with his 'homely cures' is made to seem superior to the dapper young doctor with his laboratories and apparati."[15]

The following year, Ford and Rogers again collaborated to make *Judge Priest* (1934). Set in a rural Kentucky town in the 1890s, the film was based on stories written by Irvin S. Cobb, Rogers' humorist friend. It focused on Judge William "Billy" Priest, played by Rogers, who has occupied the bench of the local circuit court for over twenty years. Typical of the Oklahoman's talkie characters, Priest runs his court informally, spicing the languid proceedings with homespun humor and commonsensical rulings that are wise but don't always comport with the letter of the law. Dismissive of pretense, he reads newspaper comics during long-winded presentations and rolls his eyes when lawyers make bombastic speeches. A widower for the last fifteen years, Priest is lonely and secretly talks to his dead wife at her graveside or before her framed photograph hanging in his house. Nonetheless, he enjoys frequent mint juleps and rocking on his front porch with relatives and friends.

This small Kentucky community still lives in the shadow of the Civil War, ended a quarter century earlier but far from forgotten. It is filled with veterans of the Confederate Army, including Priest, who honor the "Lost Cause" and cultivate its memory. Indeed, this memory of times gone by is the glue that holds the community together. Priest and his army buddies gather to tell war stories, debate which battles framed certain memories, lament their fallen comrades, and re-channel their long-ago prowess in raucous, argumentative croquet games in the judge's backyard. Indeed, the entire town basks in a golden glow of honest labor, regular socializing, and shared memories. The populist nature of this mythic vision of community becomes explicit in the ongoing conflict between Priest, a beloved figure in the community, and Senator Horace K. Maydew, powerful head of a prominent family who dislikes the judge and seeks to take his place on the circuit court. The senator wields the power but the common citizens side with the judge.

The strong racial element of *Judge Priest* is both striking and cringe inducing. In this sentimental rendering of Southern life, whites and Blacks live in perfect harmony but the latter are defined strictly as servants or laborers who know their place and bow to their betters. The two central Black characters exemplify these racial stereotypes. Aunt Dilsey, played by Hatty McDowell, is Priest's maid and cook, and she performs her menial duties with boisterous good cheer. Jeff Poindexter, played by Stepin Fetchit (the comic character created by actor Lincoln Perry), embodies an extreme caricature of African Americans with his profound laziness, shuffling gate, stammering speech, and evident ignorance. But at the same time, slightly beneath the surface of *Judge Priest* lay a plea for racial toleration and good will. Aunt Dilsey and Judge Priest break down barriers as they regularly sing together both publicly and privately, harmonizing on tunes such as "My Old Kentucky Home" and "Daniel in the Lion's Den." When Poindexter is accused of being a chicken thief and is brought before the court, instead of imposing jail time Priest listens to his side of the story and releases him. During their conversation it appears they both love fishing, and thereafter they regularly head out together to the local river to angle for catfish. Indeed, the two become friends, appearing as almost mirror images of one another as they converse in a stammering, drawling style. To underline the point, in one scene, Priest, hiding out of sight, takes on the voice of himself and Poindexter in a feigned conversation to scare off an undesirable visitor. Thus *Judge Priest*, despite its often appalling racial depictions, subtly suggests a future where genuine racial harmony might come about.[16]

The plot of *Judge Priest* features two intertwined threads that reveal the film's populist fabric. First, the judge encourages a romance between his nephew, Jerome, and Ella May Gillespie, an orphan whose late mother never revealed the identity of her father. This relationship defies the town's elitist strictures: Jerome's matchmaking mother plots with Virginia Maydew, daughter of the most powerful family in town, to connect him to this daughter of privilege. Second, a violent clash between a taciturn blacksmith, Bob Gillis, and the lecherous town barber, Flem Talley, who is pursuing Ella May, comes before the circuit court where Gillis is falsely accused of starting a fight and stabbing Talley. Senator Maydew, acting as prosecutor, takes advantage of the situation to unseat Priest, demanding that he recuse himself because of prejudice. The judge does so, but then undermines Maydew's case by quietly instigating the release of information that Gillis was not only a Confederate war hero during the late conflict, but also Ella May's father. The jury refuses to convict Gillis of defending his daughter's honor, the bombastic Senator Maydew is put to rout, and Ella May is united with her father and with Jerome as her husband. This triumph of community spirit over elitist domination is celebrated in the Confederate Memorial Day parade, where Priest and his mass of supporters gather together in a joyous celebration. This loving portrayal of populist virtue in a Southern setting was similarly celebrated by both director and actor. John Ford, in an interview given many years later, declared that from among his dozens of award-winning films, "my favorite picture of all time is *Judge Priest.*" Rogers, addressing his readers in a *Weekly Article* during the making of the film, simply noted his love of its story: "I hope I don't gum it up ... for the material is sure there. It's just being able to get the spirit of the character."[17]

Reviews of *Judge Priest* recognized its rootedness in the experience of common folk. The story, in the words of one critic, "weaves together all the homely, quiet, amusing, and simple incidents to be found in a small southern town" and features a judge who is "always sympathizing with the underdog." Louella Parsons, the famous chronicler of everything Hollywood, both public and private, wrote of the movie, "Only those who have lived in a little town can appreciate the veterans reunion, the parades, the political feuds, and the cronies who stick together through thick and thin. . . . Where family tradition counts and newcomers are not particularly welcome." The *Kansas City Star* praised Rogers' portrayal of the judge who is "a bench warmer – and a heart warmer, too. Will Rogers will win even more friends in *Judge Priest* . . . . A homely old codger who has occupied the bench thirty years. To him justice has always been kindliness and common sense." The *New York Times* discerned the roots of the movie in the American countryside and lauded Rogers as a "cowboy Nietzsche" whose interpretation of a "homespun Kentucky judge shows the native American humor at its best." The *New York Herald Tribune* concurred, describing *Judge Priest* as a tour de force for Rogers and "easily the best thing the great Jeffersonian Democrat has yet contributed to the screen."[18]

Rogers and Ford completed their movie trilogy with *Steamboat 'Round the Bend* (1935). Set in the 1890s, a favorite decade for Rogers' populist parables, the film told the story of Dr. John Pearly, a clever, witty snake-oil salesman plying his "Pocahontas Remedy," which is mostly alcohol, in the towns and villages along the Mississippi River. He gains profits from pulling the wool over people's eyes, funds which are badly needed to restore his broken-down steamboat, the *Claremore Queen.* After the boat is up and running, he stumbles across another money-maker when he acquires "Marvel's Wax Museum" after its owner was run out of town. Pearly installs it on his riverboat and it becomes a floating attraction with its "educational display" of historical figures, Barnumesque oddities, and Biblical recreations such as the whale that swallowed Jonah. Meanwhile, Dr. John's nephew, Duke, has fallen in love with Fleety Belle, a "swamp girl" from a bayou family whose father regularly beats her. When a brutish river worker tries to assault her, Duke defends her honor and kills the man in self-defense during a fight. The main thread of the movie follows Duke's conviction for murder, Dr. John and Fleety Belle's attempt to save him by locating a witness who witnessed his self-defense, and an exciting steamboat race between the *Claremore Queen* and the *Pride of Paducah*, captained by Pearly's rival, Captain Eli. At the conclusion, the witness is found, the river race is won, and Duke is exonerated and reunited with Fleety Belle.

The populist frame for this film was not a small town or farm, but the community of river people on the Mississippi for whom steamboats and water commerce constituted economic lifeblood. Its late nineteenth-century setting exhibits a distinct Twainian atmosphere reflective of *Life on the Mississippi* and *Huckleberry Finn*, with its stories of navigating the river, steamboat races, and colorful characters populating riverboats, commercial docks, and villages. The film also recalls Herman Melville's novel, *The Confidence Man*, with its array of shifty figures deftly squeezing money or attention from guileless local villagers and farmers: "New Moses," the half-mad temperance preacher proclaiming the evils of demon rum; the original owner of "Dr. Marvel's Wax Museum" with his outlandish claims of the delights within; and Dr. John Pearly with his high-octane "Pocahontas Remedy" that will cure any malady. These figures are depicted with a fond grin, while the film takes a swipe at the legal system with its "hanging judge" and 500-dollar lawyers. The symbolic populist triumph of ordinary folk comes when an alliance of hard-working river men, evangelicals, destitute swamp people, and Black boat hands work together to produce the victory of the ragtag *Claremore Queen* over the sleek, well-funded *Pride of Paducah* in the race to Baton Rouge.

The Americana flavor of this Rogers-Ford film is enhanced by its frequent touches of down-home humor. After Dr. John explains to a farmer that the "Pocahontas Remedy" will cure spring fever and help him prepare for farm labor, the farmer notes that he will also try it on his wife "as soon as she finishes with the plowing." When Dr. Pearly and Fleety Belle come upon a bearded preacher and ask if he is the New Moses, he raises his hands to the heavens and proclaims, "I am the New Elijah!" causing Rogers to mutter, "wrong prophet." Dr. John changes the wax figures to meet the prejudices of a provincial audience: two bearded figures from the Bible become Frank and Jesse James, George III is transformed into George Washington, Queen Elizabeth is repainted and outfitted as Pocahontas, and Ulysses S. Grant, with a different color uniform and dyeing of hair and beard, becomes Robert E. Lee ("No wonder Professor Marvel left town," quipped Pearly of the earlier proprietor). In the hotly contested steamboat race, as the *Claremore Queen* is roaring down the river but running short of wood fuel, Pearly decides to throw his many bottles of alcoholic elixir into the boiler to generate a final burst of speed, an action endorsed by the New Moses, who furiously heaves the liquor into the flames while shouting, "Into the fiery furnace!"

This warm-hearted film, with its depiction of racing steamboats on the mighty Mississippi and crowds of plain folk gathered along its banks to labor, witness the preaching of the gospel, and seek entertainment, reflected both Rogers' and Ford's sense of the American soul being rooted in its common people. This same spirit is manifested when Duke and Fleety Belle honor the tradition of marriage and family, exchanging wedding vows even as he remains in jail slated for execution, as a choir of Black and white prisoners softly sing "There's No Place Like Home" in the background. It appears when Dr. John's uses paint and new costumes to remake distant European and Biblical figures into American icons in the wax museum, an act that creates history for the edification of plain folk. As a reviewer of *Steamboat 'Round the Bend* observed, Rogers "ambles happily through one of the vigorously American folk tales to which he brought so much warmth and native wit during his career on the screen .... [I]t's in the rich comic tradition of Mark Twain ... . [and] finds one of America's favorite philosophers at his homespun best." The *Literary Digest* added an exclamation point: "Motion picture critics in the Middle West, where the film first was released, have greeted it enthusiastically."[19]

The populist appeal of Rogers' films was evident in the crowds of ordinary movie-goers who filled theaters to see them. It was impossible "to keep the fans away .... All we have to do is advertise Rogers and they flock out to see him," wrote a theater owner in a southern mining town to the *Motion Picture Herald*. "He speaks the language these boys that toil under the ground like to hear. I could sell them a Rogers picture every month." Movie critics also frequently made note of how Rogers' films struck a chord with plain folk in the American provinces. A reviewer on the east coast argued that *Too Busy to Work* "makes pretty dull entertainment for us city slickers. Out in the great open spaces it may find more appreciative audiences." Another analyst reported a similar trend regarding the Oklahoman's first talkie film: "Returns from the granger and prairie states, the cotton belt and the rural districts of America indicate that Will Rogers in *They Had to See Paris* is outdrawing the great centers of population from three to five times." Perhaps the most perceptive assessment of the Oklahoman's cinematic appeal to ordinary citizens came in a review of *Life Begins at Forty*. "They give a comfortable feeling, these Rogers comedies, about the solidity and innate common sense of this country," wrote a critic in the *New York Sun*. "Will Rogers, although very much himself in each scene and each film, has a curious national quality. He gives the impression somehow that this country is filled with such sages, wise in years, young in humor and love of life, shrewd yet gentle. He is what Americans think other Americans are like."[20]

Rogers' populist film messages spoke to ordinary Americans, who flocked to his films in huge numbers and made him into a major movie star. As one of Hollywood's top-drawing movie actors, the Oklahoman's tremendous appeal swelled his popular audience even larger than it had been for his writing, lectures, stage shows, and radio broadcasts. But as a movie celebrity, he cut an unusual figure. While he resembled his fellow stars with a generous salary, large home in Los Angeles, and abundant attention in the press, in most ways he conducted himself quite differently. But always, as in every other facet of his career, he appeared as his own person – unique, authentic, irreplaceable.

* * * * *

From the start, Rogers demonstrated a maverick style as a movie star. After signing him to a lucrative contract, Fox Films built for his use on the studio lot a Spanish-style bungalow with a living room and fireplace, a shower bath, and an office. But he saw the house as pretentious and rarely went there, preferring to use his automobile as a portable office both on the lot and when shooting on remote locations. According to Evelyn Venable, who appeared alongside Rogers in two films, he had a roadster and a "little typewriter in the back of it, and between takes and setups, he would sit there and peck at that typewriter, writing his daily column." Rochelle Hudson, another co-star, reported that Rogers was seen daily in the car surrounded by "endless stacks of newspapers and periodicals" as he worked, often at a frantic pace, to meet his late afternoon deadline. Fox also tried to provide another movie-star perk, hiring a valet to help Rogers with his personal preparation and clothing for a day's shooting, but within a couple of days, as one observer noted, the servant "was conspicuous by his absence. Investigation revealed that Will was paying the fellow five extra dollars a day to make himself scarce."[21]

While shooting on-set, the folksy humorist displayed other idiosyncrasies. Unlike most movie stars, he was consistently self-effacing and camera shy. Director Frank Borzage marveled at Rogers' penchant for avoiding the limelight, reporting that "during the photographing of the action, whenever he was able, he stayed as far from the lens as possible." Rochelle Hudson concurred: "Instead of hogging the camera, he lets you have all the breaks in photography. As long as he can do the talking, he'll let you do the posing." During the shooting of the final parade scene of *Judge Priest*, Irvin S. Cobb noted, Rogers subtly moved to the periphery and ceded the limelight to Henry Walthall, a veteran actor whose stock had faded but thereafter received a lucrative studio contract. The humorist also tried to avoid shots focused tightly on his face. In a rare show of vanity, he admitted, "I sho' do hate those close-ups. When those old wrinkles commence coming and the old mane is turning snowy, why we don't want either cameras or people to commence to crowd us." Rogers also had a peculiar habit of only wanting to do a single take of a movie scene. According to director Frank Butler, "He never liked retakes. He just wanted to do the scene, and that was that. He wanted to get back home again." But Butler quickly added, "He always wanted to get off at four-thirty, but if I'd ask him to stay longer he would. He was a nice guy and would do anything to help."[22]

Not surprisingly given the humorist's personality and style, Rogers encouraged an informal, light-hearted, democratic atmosphere on the set. When free from cinematic and journalistic obligations, he wandered among the actors, cameras, and backdrops twirling a lariat, which had been carefully attended to by a prop boy charged with the task. He clowned around with his co-stars and the staff, lassoing them or letting loose with a stream of quips and trying to make them laugh. In more serious moments, Rogers could be glimpsed walking around with his head down, muttering to himself and, according to Hudson, "That's when he manufactures those homilies of his and nobody ever interrupts him." Other co-workers reported that Rogers could fall asleep almost instantly, anytime or anywhere. He would curl up in the back seat of his roadster or sit in a chair "and go sound to sleep. Fifteen or twenty minutes later, he will wake up, full of pep and ready to go." The humorist established two silly traditions that became trademarks of his Hollywood on-set reputation. When the morning shooting schedule neared completion, he would shout, "Lunchee! Lunchee!" to the smiling crew and staff to let them know it was almost time to eat. Then when the afternoon shoot reached 4:30 or 5 pm, the humorist would start yelling, "Santa Monica Canyon! Santa Monica Canyon!" with a grin on his face, signaling to the director that he was ready to wrap things up and head off to his beloved ranch.[23]

Rogers cultivated a special regard for the ordinary staffers who worked behind the scenes in the movie-making industry. The humorist often showed up on-set early in the morning, according to director John Ford, because he "wanted to visit with the grips and the cameraman and the rest of the cast, and whiz around and chat and talk, making jokes." Hudson noticed that while the Oklahoman often received a procession of distinguished visitors while making a movie, he was apt "at any time to forget any of them for a grip or a carpenter to whom he's talking." During the production of *Business and Pleasure*, he organized a quartette consisting of himself, an electrician, and two grips and whenever there was a break in the shooting they would practice harmonizing on a wide variety of popular songs. Afterwards, he asked that the same three workmen remain on the crew for future pictures so they could continue their venture. Perhaps Rogers' most telling action came with *Handy Andy*, a film which was finished ahead of schedule and about to wrap up. According to actress Peggy Wood, on the last day of shooting the star stalled and stalled, delaying the production's wrap up in every way imaginable. When pressed, he disclosed that he wanted to make sure the movie crew got their fully accrued pay, and after receiving assurances they would, he quit dragging his feet.[24]

Rogers' concern for the well-being of ordinary people sometimes spilled over from the movie set to the surrounding community. While shooting in Sonora, California, for *The County Chairman*, the humorist was approached over several days by local groups – the chamber of commerce, the women's auxiliary, the board of education – who asked him to speak to their organizations. Rogers finally offered to address all of them at once and requested they secure the auditorium in the local high school. Accompanied by several fellow actors and cast members, he showed up there one evening and performed a two-and-a-half-hour free show, introducing each of his colleagues and then plunging ahead with his usual offering of commentary, jokes, and observations. In the words of one of his film cohort, "he was just magnificent" and the local audience was thrilled. According to cinematography director Hal Mohr, during the making of another Rogers film the cast and crew were on their way to a rural location when they stopped to eat near a rail junction town. When they finished their meal, Mohr said, "Will wandered over to the freight yards, and there were a bunch of hoboes. And he just sat down with them and talked with these fellows for over an hour, while the whole motorcade waited to proceed on location."[25]

Rogers' unique style as Hollywood's most unassuming movie star appeared with particular clarity on the set of *State Fair*. Initially, director Henry King was concerned how his leading man would interact with Blue Boy, the enormous untrained pig who appeared with him in many scenes in the film, and worried about the possibility that Rogers might be facing some danger. King's fears quickly disappeared, however, when early in the shoot he returned to the set from lunch and passed Blue Boy's pen. To his astonishment, he saw that the huge boar "was asleep, and so was Will – sound asleep, using Blue Boy for a pillow." When Rogers awakened a short time later, he announced, "I think Blue Boy likes me." Thereafter, the movie star was often seen in the pig's company, slapping him on the back, scratching his ears, leaning against him, and even sitting on him. Blue Boy also provided Rogers with plenty of comic material. When asked about his close relationship with the prize-winning boar, he replied, "Hogs is different from folks. They don't bite the hands that feed them." To a movie-magazine reporter who inquired about his porcine co-star, Rogers quipped, "Finally got a feller in the cast that can't out-act me." When the movie was completed and someone suggested that Rogers purchase Blue Boy, the humorist shook his head woefully and stammered, "No, I just couldn't do it. I wouldn't feel right eating a fellow actor."[26]

Discussion of Rogers' capabilities as an actor made for one of the most interesting aspects of his sterling career in the talkies. He always made light of his thespian skills, usually dismissing his performance as trying to "make a lot of faces at a camera. And not very good faces either." In one of his *Weekly Articles*, he wrote self-deprecatingly of his current acting effort, "I have used up all my expressions two or three times. You know us actors just got certain little grimaces that we make for hate, fear, merriment, exaltation (well, that and merriment are pretty near the same) . . . . [W]e got about the same looks we had when the pictures were silent, only now with the look we got noises that go with it." Indeed, some commentators groused about his meager acting skills. The *Literary Digest*, in a movie review, complained, "While he was attempting to be Will Rogers, the cracker-box sage, friend of the common man, and arbiter of the national destiny, rather than a portrayer of parts devised for him in the films, he seemed to many observers of the cinema merely a minor-league demagogue striving to be a good, old-fashioned Jeffersonian Democrat all over the screen." The *Film Spectator* agreed, arguing that Fox was overexposing Rogers with too many films and thereby underlining his weaknesses as an actor. "His pictures are coming out so rapidly that he is losing his status as America's most unique character, and is becoming merely a motion picture actor trying to compete in ordinary pictures with actors who have far more skill," the journal opined. "Rogers is an institution, not a movie actor."[27]

The co-stars and directors who worked with Rogers, however, came to understand that his talent and effectiveness as an actor were more striking than was first apparent. He conveyed a believability in his characterizations that was instinctive rather than learned. In Rogers' first film, *They Had to See Paris*, director Frank Borzage sensed this quality and insisted that the microphones must follow the humorist as he wandered around rather than making him stand still. "I'm not going to change Will Rogers' naturalness. Wherever he is, that's where the scene's going to be played," he instructed the sound technicians. "You put microphones in his beard if he has one . . . . Put 'em behind pictures. Put 'em under the sofa. Put 'em any place you want. And just watch him and then you play like you're playing an organ. You just tune him in." Sterling Holloway, who worked along-side Rogers in *Doubting Thomas*, astutely assessed this quality of natural magnetism in his colleague. He noted that the Oklahoman was surrounded by trained stage actors who seemed to perform circles around him during the shooting of scenes. But "when the film was shown on the screen, none of the others meant anything. You couldn't take your eyes off Will Rogers," said Holloway. "It really amazed me, because [on-set] you thought he was just shuffling through the part, that it really wasn't going to count – but it sure did. And how!"[28]

Rogers, in other words, eschewed studied gestures and actorly techniques in favor of a natural authenticity and believability. Borzage witnessed his star's special skills "in scenes where he was called upon to portray the simple, human emotions that touch the very soul of mankind. The sincerity and conviction with which he did them was what might be expected of a great tragedian." Holloway likewise described the untrained Rogers as "an intuitive performer; he knew exactly what was right. No director really ever could tell him how to do something. He knew the 'how' always." For another colleague, an appreciation of the Oklahoman's acting ability appeared only gradually. "In a sense, he was far ahead of his time," said Lew Ayres of Rogers and his loose, improvisational approach. "[H]is relaxed attitude when you watch him today in those old films is like the most modern New York laboratory school performance. There is nothing stilted, static about Will Rogers. He was alive and real .... I now maintain that that is good acting. The capacity of a man to communicate his personality – and we thought of Will Rogers as a personality – to communicate that to an audience is an art."[29]

Without question, Rogers' most striking characteristic as a movie actor was his novel approach to dialogue: he made it up as he went along. He never studied the script before shooting scenes and he didn't learn his lines as written. Instead, he discerned a general sense of the plot, perceived what his character should be doing and saying, and then expressed his character's basic sentiments in his own words. Drawing upon his long-time experience on the stage and in the lecture hall, he improvised those words on the spot. Rogers could not have embraced such a radical technique, of course, without the permission of his directors. All of them, after witnessing the happy results of his improvisation, gave him free rein. Borzage noted that Rogers "would change the lines to conform with what he thought they should be, and his version was usually better than the original script." David Butler, who directed the Oklahoman in five films, witnessed that dialogues "weren't written in his language. He improved his lines. He was remarkable that way." John Ford described the process that unfolded. "He'd read his script and say, 'What does that mean?' And I'd say, 'Well, that's rather a tough question. I don't know what it means exactly,'" Ford related. "Then we would finally figure out what it meant and I'd say to him, 'Say it in your own words!' And he'd go away, muttering to himself, getting his lines ready, and when he came back, he'd make his speech in typical Rogers fashion, which was better than any writer could write for him."[30]

For Rogers' fellow actors, dealing with improvised dialogue triggered a combination of stress, exhilaration, and appreciation. Used to dealing with a script and set lines, this free-flowing approach initially threw them off their stride. "[S]ome of us reacted with grave concern at any thought of working with someone like this," Lew Ayres confessed. "It sometimes made it difficult on actors who worked with him. It took a particular kind of personality to respond to this loosely arranged manner of carrying on dialogue with him." For Rochelle Hudson, Rogers' ad-libbed style required constant vigilance among his fellow actors. "Nobody ever knows just what he's going to do or just what he's going to say," she described. "You never know when your cue is coming or whether you're going to get it at all .... [E]ven after he's rewritten the script he changes it some more with every take." For most of Rogers' co-stars, the experience was like driving up a very narrow, winding mountain road. "You had to be on your toes. You had to dovetail what you were supposed to say into what he actually had said. You had to do that to make sense and follow the story line," related Evelyn Venable. "It was fun, because it gave a great deal of freshness to the scenes. But it was a little bit nerve-wracking, too."[31]

A fascinating sidebar to Will Rogers' career as an actor appeared in 1934 when he was approached by the producer, Henry Duffy, and asked to play the lead role of Nat Miller in a West Coast production of Eugene O'Neill's play, *Ah, Wilderness!* The original Broadway version, starring George M. Cohan, had been a great hit. Initially, the match of the improvising, down-home humorist from the talkies and the Pulitzer Prize winning playwright seemed improbable. This semi-autobiographical play told the story of a small-town family in New England on July 4, 1906, focusing on a son's youthful indiscretions in a love affair and his subsequent interactions with his family, particularly his father, Nat Miller, the wise, kindly patriarch and owner of the local newspaper. Unlike O'Neill's usual offering of angst, disillusionment, and tragedy, *Ah, Wilderness!* was filled with sentiment and comic touches and came to a happy conclusion. "Getting back on the stage now and then is good for a person; it keeps them on their toes," Rogers announced of his agreement to take the role. "I don't know whether I can get away with it at all or whether I'll be a flop but I'm certainly going to try it for all it's worth." He also declared his intention to drop his usual improvisational style, jokingly admitting, "you have to learn lines, not my lines, but Eugene O'Neill's lines. He is that highbrow writer, and I have quite a bit of trouble reading 'em, much less learning 'em." To the astonishment of many, Rogers kept his promise and delivered a compelling performance, helping to make the play a great hit. It opened in San Francisco on April 30 for a three-week run at the Curran Theatre and then moved to the El Capitan Theater in Los Angeles, where its original three-week schedule was extended to six weeks because of public demand. Some 72,000 people eventually saw the show in Los Angeles.[32]

Rogers earned rave reviews from the critics for his straight performance in *Ah, Wilderness! Newsweek* declared, "The shrewd, simple philosophy of Nat Miller might have been written for Mr. Rogers, so easily does he slip into the part and make it his own." The *New York Times* concluded that the humorist "made Nat Miller a delightful personage, and in the father's scene with his adolescent son,

Richard, he played with a simple sincerity that brought out handkerchiefs and made tears and smiles mingle." The *Los Angeles Examiner* told readers that Rogers performed his role "with a sincerity which makes the word 'actor' sound ridiculous. His earnestness and humor are all keyed to the spirit of honesty and simplicity of that period, and in his every speech and gesture the characterization is perfect." The drama critic for the *San Francisco Chronicle*, George C. Warren, praised Rogers' portrayal of Nat Miller, asserting, "Greatest of all the qualities he put into the character is the big heart of the man; his tenderness with his son, a high school lad suffering through his first love affair .... . The sincerity of the performance is one of its great charms .... . The debut of Mr. Rogers as a serious actor was a complete success." The Oklahoman's unquestioned success in this theatre production served to legitimate positive assessments of his movie acting.[33]

As Rogers' status as a movie-star skyrocketed in the early 1930s, he became a full-fledged celebrity whose every movement, utterance, and characteristic came under the public microscope. This status was steadily boosted by the promotional arm of Fox Studios, whose flood of movie advertisements and posters burnished the Rogers image. The onslaught began with his first talkie, *They Had to See Paris*. An advertising manual for the film laid out several avenues of publicity for theaters to pursue, including this one for local newspaper readers: "Will Rogers, actor, humorist and philosopher, is known to most everyone .... . Will Rogers is practically an American institution .... . This picture presents Will Rogers in a role that promises to reveal him at his very best .... . To his role Rogers imparts his drawling, homespun humor that is a delight to behold and a double delight to listen to." As the film went before the public, a host of ads pumped up the Oklahoman's celebrity image: "Will Rogers – wit, statesman-at-large, comedian, loved the world over"; "Will Rogers .... . humorist, philosopher, America's great comedian and most natural actor"; and "Will Rogers .... . Friend of Kings, Chum of Royalty .... . talking, wise-cracking, even singing, in this merry comedy of love and life." A widely distributed poster for display in theaters stressed the delight of hearing him speak, proclaiming "Will Rogers, America's Greatest Humorist, in his first All TALKING movietone picture."

Rogers' subsequent talkies brought similar waves of publicity. A poster for *So This is London* described "The Inimitable, The One and Only Will Rogers .... . America's Ambassador of Good Cheer" while one for *A Connecticut Yankee* noted, "The King of Comedy tilts his derby and parks his gum at the Round Table." An advertising flyer for *Doctor Bull* enticed movie-goers with, "A barrel of laughter, a bit of romance, plenty of suspense, with the homespun humor of WILL ROGERS, as the old-fashioned country doctor with modern ideas." "Serving out justice – humor, pathos, laughs – that's Will Rogers as Judge Priest – most lovable character that ever came to life on the screen!" said an ad for the movie of that name. *Handy Andy* brought this breathless description: "Will Rogers .... You never dreamed HE would do such things. Dress up as Tarzan! Raise pigeons in the parlor! Ruin his wife's social career! Burn up the dance floor! Land in jail – and like it!" Rogers' final film, *Steamboat 'Round the Bend*, inspired ads proclaiming, "THE GREATEST STAR AND ENTERTAINER OF THEM ALL, in this, the Undisputed Triumph of His Glorious Entertainment Career!!"[34]

A host of movie fan magazines likewise polished Rogers' celebrity status. These popular publications, which had first arisen in the 1910s, were aimed at movie devotees and fed the public appetite for information (and gossip) about the new films, the inside workings of Hollywood, and the leading personalities in the movie industry. By the time of the talkie revolution, they were in full flower and played a major role in shaping the public profiles of movie stars. Will Rogers became a popular topic in fan magazines as his career in the talkies took off, and their stories contributed greatly to his celebrity status. Some of them focused on explaining Rogers' rapid rise to prominence in the Hollywood community. An article in *Screenland* attributed his success to a strong work ethic, disclosing that "Rogers turns out more pictures than most of the important stars. Rated tops among the box-office attractions, he is the surprise of Hollywood in that he never complains about how often he works." Others attributed his ascension to the unglamorous style that many in the industry initially found baffling. "Bill has been burning up box-office records so long that Hollywood's wise people have been annually predicting he was through. However, to confound his critics Will's getting hotter all the time," wrote *Movie Mirror*. "As a result, Hollywood has given up trying to explain Rogers. It takes him and likes him, having found out he's a difficult guy to tackle." In a piece entitled, "Will Outwits the Sexy Fellows," *Photoplay* maintained that he outdrew leading men such as Clark Gable and Frederic March because of his "naturalness," evident love of people, devotion to telling the truth, dislike of pretense, and "just folks" style. As the fan magazine put it, ordinary Americans responded to Rogers because he was "a restless individual with the spirit of the pioneer cowboy surging through his blood."[35]

Rogers' personal characteristics, in fact became a favorite topic of the movie fan magazines, who were delighted to extoll them and contribute to his growing legend. *Screenland* told readers that Rogers on a movie set was "exactly as the public he reaches gets to know him – humorous, kind, trenchant, uncompromising in his hate of sham, but good-natured about it, a wit without a trace of malice in his make-up, but above all a human being." *Photoplay* described the Oklahoman as "just a typical American .... [D]eep in his veins runs the true, down-to-earth neighborliness that made 'Old Hickory' Jackson and the yarn-spinning Abe Lincoln so dear to hearts of this country." *Movie Mirror* stressed his deep-grained morality, and quoted his objection to a bedroom scene in one of his films: "Maybe I'm old fashioned, but to me, and I think to most people, there's something kind of sacred about the private lives of a married couple, and in this case the scene could just as easy be played in the dining room or the kitchen." *Modern Screen* underlined his rich and varied home life in an article entitled, "Will Rogers, Father and Husband." *Photoplay* portrayed the humorist as America's paternal ideal. "If ever a man was father, it's Will. He looks 'the old man,' he talks like him, and he is everything we would like 'the old man' to be," the magazine stated. "Any picture he has ever appeared in contains a full-sized portrait of the average head of a family . . . . His monologue is the homely, witty horse sense you expect from a father . . . . [Y]ou will never get the shivers remembering him. But if it's comfort and the caress of a friendly hand you want – he can deliver."[36]

Rogers also used his journalistic efforts to bolster his cinematic celebrity. In his daily and weekly newspaper columns, he entertained readers with humorous critiques of the film industry, just as he did with send-ups of nearly every other facet of modern American life. This good-natured criticism of movie-making by an insider was lapped up by ordinary citizens. Rogers poked at Hollywood's crass commercialism, claiming that a studio would "film the Lord's Supper and when it is made, figure that that is not a good release title and not catchy enough, so it will be released under the heading, 'A Red Hot Meal' or 'The Gastronomical Orgy.'" Tongue-in-cheek, he criticized movie advertisement for being salacious and overblown. "I thought the underwear ads in the magazines were about the limit in presenting an eyefull, but these movie ads give you the same thing without the underwear . . . . You are liable to see the wildest stuff facing you on the billboards, and then go inside and see everybody [on screen] is dressed as esquimos all through the picture," he wrote. "So the big problem of the movies now is to deliver up what the lithograph makers and ad writers have shown on the outside . . . . We just can't seem to get 'em as wild as they show'em on the outside. We got to get wilder people." Rogers joked that too many talkies took the easy road by remaking silent films. "You see, we had the silent pictures, and they did every story under the sun, then along came the talkies, and that gave 'em an excuse to do all the silent ones over," he asserted. And they usually did so by turning to younger actors: if you were a female "that means you have forgot how to act by now, and some young girl that has just looked well in a bathing suit can out-act you, and you must give way to her. Or that if it's a boy, and if he has curlier hair and looks nicer, why naturally you must pass out."[37]

In addition to taking humorous jabs at the film industry, Rogers gave his readers inside glimpses of movie-making and the workings of Hollywood studios. His audience proved eager for such information during the movie-mad 1930s. Rogers provided details about how movies were made. He explained to readers that creating films was a large undertaking: "now that we have to carry all that sound equipment and men with it, why it looks like Barnum's circus coming. We have a very small cast, about five. Yet I bet there is about 50 of us . . . . It's kind of a cuckoo business." He used an entire *Weekly Article* in 1934 to describe how filming a turn-of-the-century story involved costuming, trained dogs, huge and complicated sets, "scenic artists" to paint backdrops, skilled cinematographers, directors overseeing everything and yelling instructions, while the actors "lay around under the shade tree here when not 'shooting' and talk old time vaudeville." Rogers informed readers that most modern films were shot almost entirely "inside a stage. Street scenes, churches, homes, and all are put inside a big stage. Then they can light it as they want to." The writer added a poignant, perhaps guilty, observation that most movie casts featured actors who used to be leads or even stars who were now playing small parts. Rogers admired their resilient grace: "They never whine, never alibi . . . . [T]here is a great, what is they call it, 'Camaraderie' among the real ones who each knew the others in those happy days . . . . Never a vitriolic note. I have yet to ever hear a knock, they just sit day after day and watch inferior actors like a lot of us who have just been lucky." "I believe there is more real nerve and gameness under the most discouraging circumstances in the picture business than any other place on earth," he concluded. "It's a heart breaking racket, but they don't sit and tell you about it. Their heads are always up."[38]

Rogers' inside view frequently turned to how filmmakers labored to keep one jump ahead of audiences, who loved to pick out discrepancies on the silver screen. For example, in a movie featuring a horse the producers usually procured several similar looking horses with similar features to share the burden: "One to jump the fence, another that will open the gate, another that will make a wild run down hill. Another just for the close-ups." Audiences went along, he joked, "till somebody conceived the idea of having one of the horses white and the other black. Then they picked out a little thing like that right away." But with audiences, the fact that "one [horse] was big and one was little never seem to interest 'em. They just sleep right through that." Rogers related that filmmakers also catered to viewers by testing movies on audiences before their release. He disclosed that when a picture was finished, the studio usually took it to a suburb of Los Angeles or a nearby town for a preview. The director and studio executives attended and gauged viewer reaction, trying to discern what elements did not work and how they might be modified. Then they "take it back and work on it, maby retake scenes, add scenes, cut out scenes. Then maby they will take it out and try it again on some other defenseless audience." Rogers concluded, "A bad picture is an accident and a good one is a miracle." Ultimately, however, the Oklahoman suggested to readers that Hollywood and its denizens were not that different from other places and people. "[Y]ou see the movie side, all the paint and glitter and makeup, and make believe houses, but as you look back at it, why a lot of those houses have backs to 'em, and people live in 'em, and they don't have any makeup, and they eat and sleep and fret and worry about work, and about their children, and everything just like any other place," he wrote. "But you got to look back to see it. Yes, sir, there is a lot of pleasure in looking back, and peeping around and trying to see the other fellow's angle."[39]

As Rogers' movie career inflated his celebrity status in America, he began to pay the price for fame. As often happened with such public figures, fans began to hound him mercilessly. Homer Croy reported that hosts of people obsessed with meeting the movie star managed to find the location of Fox studios and worm their way "onto the sound stage. He was extraordinarily generous about giving up his time to them, but sometimes – especially when he wanted to get out to the ranch – he got a little more than he wanted." Groups of devoted fans even began showing up at his Santa Monica ranch. "One night he and Betty came home from a movie and there, in the drive, was a sightseeing bus with a guide telling 'em all about it," a friend reported. "This was too much for Betty .... She said that a gate must be placed at the highway." Her husband hesitated but finally agreed. Fans began to flood the Oklahoman with mail, so much that he and Betty hired a secretary, Mrs. Daisy Tyler, to handle it and rented a small office in Beverly Hills. She sorted through the great piles, picked the most interesting for her boss to view, and he tried to reply in person if possible. Rogers, who loved to meet people, was overwhelmed with autograph seekers whenever he appeared in public and began to find the experience unpleasant. "Fellow comes up and says: 'I see all your pictures,' and I ask him which ones, and he can't name a one," he complained. "Woman brings a little five-year-old girl up and says: 'Tillie wants to meet you, she reads all your little articles in the paper and enjoys 'em. Tillie says, 'Who is he, Ma?'"[40]

As a leading movie star, Rogers increasingly came into contact with official Hollywood culture. The relationship was friendly but guarded. On one occasion it produced a highly embarrassing incident when the humorist, who disliked movie premieres, accepted an invitation in April 1932 to serve as master of ceremonies for the grand opening of the Metro-Goldwyn-Mayer film, *Grand Hotel*, at Grauman's Chinese Theater in Hollywood. He stumbled badly as a result of an ill-considered prank concerning the film's star, Greta Garbo. During his light-hearted remarks to a large crowd of movie-lovers and reporters, the Oklahoman announced that the notoriously reclusive Garbo had agreed to break her common practice and come on stage to take a bow. The crowd swooned in anticipation of a glimpse of the publicity shy star, only to see Wallace Beery, her rotund co-star in *Grand Hotel*, lumber on stage in a wig and a skirt. Rogers had set up the gag but it fell flat as the crowd expressed its disappointment, even anger.

As *Variety* would note in its coverage of the event, Rogers' stunt "proved to be a misguided joke in very bad taste . . . . [The] incident constituted [a] shocking anti-climax to the classiest opening Hollywood has seen in two years." Rogers beat a quick retreat. In a press release he apologized for the "sad hoax" and admitted, "I had no idea you first-nighters took your Greta Garbo so seriously." He also confessed his chagrin and regret in a *Weekly Article*. "Sounds kinder funny, don't it? Well, it wasn't to them," he wrote of the prank. "I dident mean any harm. Gosh, us comedians must get laughs."[41]

On another occasion, however, the growing regard for Rogers within the Hollywood establishment created a triumph. In March 1934, he hosted the annual awards event for the Academy of Motion Picture Arts and Sciences, eventually termed the Oscars. He delivered a hilarious monologue, lampooning many of the giants of the film industry and forever altering the ponderous style of the event. The humorist poked fun at studio heads such as Louis B. Mayer, Jack Warner, and Samuel Goldwyn and prominent actors Leslie Howard, Charles Laughton, and Paul Muni. "They are lovely things," he said of the Oscar statuettes. "They were originally designed for prizes at a nudists colony bazar, but they dident take 'em." Rogers praised the "great acting in this room tonight, greater than you will see on the screen. We all cheer when somebody gets a prize that every one of us in the house knows should be ours, yet we [all] smile and take it. Boy, that's acting." He finished by describing some of the award categories and their standards of achievement:

Adapters – commonly known among authors as book murderers.
Original writers – men who have good enough lawyers to protect them from plagiarism.
Sound – bringing up the good lines and drowning out the bad ones.
Photography – an art where if you shoot enough weird shots that you get the audience's mind off the actors you will get a prize.
Art director – he must make it look like a room, but not a room that anyone ever lived in.

Rogers' audience of Hollywood insiders laughed their approval. As a movie trade paper noted, "Will's wit changed the big affair from the customary ceremony of long-winded speeches into a joyous riot."[42]

During the first half of the 1930s, Rogers' string of successful movies provided the capstone of his remarkable career. They put him on constant display before the American public and greatly boosted his astonishing popularity. They also did much to popularize several of the key themes that had characterized his professional course over the previous two decades – a populist veneration for the common man and his well-being, a celebration of the new entertainment culture with its ethos of self-fulfillment and personality, and an example of the power of modern American celebrity. Ultimately, however, Rogers' talkie films shouldered a heavier burden. At their best, they attempted to help viewers come to grips with a society changing rapidly around them.

* * * * *

In Will Rogers' comic lark of a movie, *A Connecticut Yankee*, King Arthur's official wizard, Merlin, challenges his new rival's powers. Hank Martin, or "Sir Boss," has arrived in Camelot and performed several feats that the backward medieval inhabitants view as magical. Now Merlin, eager to regain the monarch's favor, dares Sir Boss to predict Arthur's future. Martin replies with a telling phrase: "I feel like I'm one of the few men who can look backwards and see ahead." Armed with a knowledge of the future history of England, he then convincingly portrays Arthur as the forerunner of several centuries of glorious achievements. In fact, *A Connecticut Yankee*'s entire structure relied on a similar juxtaposition of the past and the present. The film presented humorous vignettes of King Arthur and his Knights of the Round Table riding elaborately outfitted horses, wearing clunky armor, making grand speeches, and wielding broadswords while Sir Boss's minions come to the battlefield in fleets of Model T's, driving tanks and firing guns. Similarly, when Martin takes King Arthur on a tour of the new factory he has just established, the befuddled monarch inquires about the purpose of creating such a vast volume of goods, Sir Boss tells him not to worry, he will create demand in Camelot by employing advertising, a strange endeavor that convinces people "to spend money you don't have, for things you don't need." This "looking backward and seeing ahead" impulse in *A Connecticut Yankee* became a key element in many of Rogers' talkie movies. They presented an array of stories and characters – particularly the roles played by the Oklahoman himself – that accommodated the promise of the future to the valuable traditions of the past. As with Rogers' most successful writing and stage work, these movies offered striking mediations between past and present, helping viewers come to terms with the changing world around them.

Rogers' first talkie film, *They Had to See Paris*, set the pace by developing a strong mediational dynamic throughout. Initially, Pike Peters appears as both a traditional country boy *and* a modern car mechanic attuned to the machines remaking American society. Then, after acquiring unexpected wealth when his oil well strikes a gusher, he goes to Paris at the insistence of his wife and spends the bulk of the film poised awkwardly between the American small-town traditions he loves and modern cosmopolitan culture. At the movie's end, at Pike's instigation the family decides to leave Paris and return to its Oklahoma roots. While eager to return to rural America, Pike offers a thoughtful soliloquy on the folly of worshiping the past. "We pick on our young folks too much, you know. We think every succeeding generation is goin' to the devil. Well, if they was and every generation is getting worse than the other [earlier] generation, why we'd all be in purgatory by now," he tells his family. Then, after glancing knowingly at his wife, he continues, "Automobiles, we criticize every time young folks stop and spoon by the road. But a horse would stop [too] – not only *would*, but *did*!"

Among Rogers' early charisma comedies, a striking example of his mediating role came in *Young as You Feel*. Lemuel Morehouse, an old-fashioned widower, is the founder of Morehouse and Sons, a large meatpacking business in Chicago. Devoted to a strong work ethic and a routine of unchanging habits, he has become wealthy by laboring long hours at the office and avoiding all frivolous distractions. His two playboy sons, however, habitually shirk their business duties for a life of carousing until dawn, chasing women, and golf tournaments. When Lemuel confronts them, one replies breezily, "The day has passed when business is the main idea in life. Business is only the means to an end, and the end is happiness and contentment and the chance to enjoy the spirit of living. Self-expression!" The situation goes topsy-turvy when Lemuel meets an attractive young French singer, Fleurette, who convinces him to loosen up and have fun. The lonely older man responds and, dressed in stylish tails and top hat, is soon skipping work to squire her about town to nightclubs, fancy restaurants, and the racetrack. A liberated Lemuel proclaims, "I feel just like a kid watching the only schoolhouse in town burn down." The work of the meatpacking firm falls on the shoulders of his sons, who now grow annoyed at their father's "foolish" behavior. The climax of the film comes when Lemuel saves Fleurette from being swindled out of her family money, and he reconciles with his sons. The two generations compromise around a new cultural ethos as the father trims his work schedule to have more fun, and his sons curtail their partying to take seriously their work. Lemuel concludes of this mediating maneuver to his offspring, "I was trying to teach you a lesson and learned one myself .... Now I'm fifty-one going on twenty-four. From now on, I'm growing backwards. When I die, I'll be an infant!"

Among Rogers' populist parables, examples of historical mediation abounded. In *Handy Andy*, small-town pharmacist Andrew Yates adheres to an old-fashioned regimen of sustained labor at his corner drug store. He loves his work, and when a friend inquires whether he ever takes time to relax, he replies, "I never have any fun, but I sell a lot of headache medicine to people that *do* have fun." Yates also cares deeply about his community – he knows and treats everyone in town, carefully looks after infants and counsels their mothers on medicine, and shrugs off payment from those of little means. He is forced to give up his beloved store, however, when his socially ambitious wife, Ernestine, demands that he sell out to chain store magnate Charles Norcross and retire to a life of leisure and diversion. This new life goes badly. Andy tries raising chickens until they fly amuck through the house; playing golf, outfitted in an outlandish get-up of knickers and mismatched plaid socks and shirt, until his baseball-style swing fails to connect with the ball; and even recreating his pharmacy at home to prepare prescriptions for poor neighbors until his wife forbids it. "Did you ever try doing nothin'," he asks a friend. "You'll find it's one of the hardest jobs you ever saw in your life." The tension reaches a climax when Ernestine drags her husband to New Orleans to celebrate Mardi Gras with a wealthy friend's family in the city. Andy decides to play so hard that it will teach his wife a lesson. At the city's major costume ball, he has a couple of drinks and appears outfitted as Tarzan, complete with long hair, animal-skin garb, and wielding a club while bellowing "Ahhh—eee—ahhh—eee—ah" at every opportunity. He does a wild dance with a young woman that has the crowd roaring with laughter. After starting a brawl that lands him in jail, he tells his mortified wife that these adventures have made him a convert to fun. Andy's plan works as she encourages the couple to return home where they discover the Norcross chain has gone bankrupt and Andy is able to re-purchase his corner drugstore and returns to the work he loves. But he also appoints his son-in-law as store manager, and proclaims his newfound accommo-dation of the old and the new: "I've learned a valuable lesson on this trip, that you can work and play, too. And that's what I'm going to do from now on."

Another example of Rogers' accommodation to modernity came in *Life Begins at Forty*, where Kenesaw Clark spends much of the movie disparaging modern conveniences. Observing society's growing reliance on manufactured food, he grouses, "No quicker way to starve the country than to invent a can opener that don't work." After a neighbor woman brags about the array of electric appliances in her home, he predicts, "With all this electricity, Americans one-hundred years from now will be born without arms and legs, just a thumb to push a button." By the end of the tale, however, Clark has reconciled the old ways with the new as he rehabilitates the reputation of an ex-con in defiance of village moralists who had turned to tar-and-feathers, set up the marriage of a death-obsessed elderly churchgoer with a curvaceous blond half his age, and reached a truce with the powerful banker whom he had reformed.

Rogers' films with John Ford similarly mediated between past and present, albeit in more subtle ways. Dr. George Bull defends tradition and scorns modern inventions at every opportunity. When he is threatened with dismissal as the town's health officer, he expresses gratitude for his liberation and vows to spend the rest of his days hunting, fishing, and pursuing a vocation as a "telephone breaker," thereby getting revenge on the technological gadget that had tormented him at the office and at home. At the movie's end, however, he reconciles with modernity by marrying his long-time sweetheart and leaving his beloved town for a less restrictive environment elsewhere. In the Confederate Memorial Day parade that concludes *Judge Priest*, small-town factionalism evaporates as opponents unite and the past becomes an inspiration for uniting in the present; the old guard and the new order share in a ritual of community regeneration. *Steamboat 'Round the Bend* featured Dr. John Pearly coming to terms with the modern world. After giving bad advice to his nephew that leads to the youth's conviction for murder, Dr. John confesses, "It's my fault. I thought 'cause I was older I knew more about right and wrong than you did." He adapts to the "new woman," teaching Fleety Belle how to maneuver a steamboat and promising she will become "the best pilot on the river, except for me." The movie's most striking historical mediation concerns the "Marvel's Wax Museum." When Dr. John first reconstructs the exhibit on his steamship, he quickly changes its appearance by transforming Old Testament and European figures into American heroes to attract audience favor. Then, during the steamboat race, the entire collection of historical personages is thrown into the furnace to generate speed for victory. Much as history here goes up in flames to support a modern mechanized craft hurtling down the river, the Rogers-Ford trilogy amended its sentimental view of the past to accommodate the needs of the present.

Rogers' string of popular movies projected a larger-than-life portrait of the man, his words, his humor, and his sensibility to the great American public as never before. By the summer of 1935, the Oklahoman was a pervasive presence in American life. Anywhere in the United States you could open your morning newspapers and read his words; flip on the radio in the evening and hear his voice; pick up a magazine at the newsstand or the local drugstore and encounter his reflections; attend a show in New York or a lecture in your local hall and see the humorist in the flesh; or attend a movie at your local picture palace and view him on the screen, cracking jokes, dispensing common-sense wisdom, and puncturing pretense, all while scratching his head, looking at the floor, and grinning in mock consternation. In unprecedented fashion, Rogers had become a symbol of the United States and its most cherished values of democratic equality, the opportunity to become successful, and civil behavior in a community of citizens. It seemed that he had become America itself.

No one envisioned how quickly this tale of triumph would come to a shocking conclusion.

Epilogue

Thy Will Be Done

A s THE 1930S REACHED THEIR MIDPOINT, Will Rogers began to show signs of aging and weariness for the first time. Betty noticed the drop-off and commented, "He was in his middle fifties now and the heavy schedule he was carrying had begun to pall on him a little." His friend and film collaborator, Homer Croy, also sensed the change. "His great physical activity was beginning to tell on Will. He complained about feeling tired, but he kept up the pace," said Croy. "He would fall asleep reading his [news]paper." Rogers' eyes had begun to give him trouble. He had always valued his keen eyesight – he liked to joke about what he called his "Injun' eyes" – but now he often held the newspaper at arm's length to read and would often stop and rub his eyes. Typical of his down-home habits, he went to Woolworth's and picked out glasses off the shelf that seemed to sharpen his sight and laid in a supply. Thereafter, when talking to people, he often removed the glasses and twirled them around in his hand. Rogers, with his nervous energy, also developed the habit of gnawing on the ends of the side pieces. When they became too gnarled and twisted to use, he would toss them in the drawer of his desk and grab a fresh pair.[1]

Rogers was also growing sensitive about his age. One day the family was eating dinner when Mary mentioned the vitality and endurance of a polo player they knew, adding, "And think – he's forty-two." Rogers replied sourly, "That's not old. I can play polo and I'm a lot older'n forty-two. I guess you kids think of me as an old man hangin' around the house and gettin' in people's way." When he was set up to do the racing scene in *David Harum*, he reacted in a similar fashion. "Y'see, they've got me rigged out to drive a trottin' horse to a sulky. I never saw a man under eighty drive a trottin' horse," he complained. "That's the reason they picked me." On occasion, Rogers granted the inevitable toll exacted by father time. As early as 1931, while on his lengthy cruise to Japan on the *Empress of Russia*, he had confided to fellow passenger George Riedel that he felt worn down. Rogers, according to Riedel, confessed he "wanted to get away from things, wanted to be alone on his own" and "it was the first time in years he had felt free from care."[2]

Despite the complaints, age and health related annoyances failed to alter Rogers' relentless schedule of activity. An idea of his frantic pace can be seen in his activity from the summer of 1934 to that of 1935, when he engaged in a relentless round of traveling, radio broadcasting, speaking, filmmaking, and writing that was little short of astonishing. In this single year he went on a three-month round-the-world trip that took him to Hawaii, Japan, China, the Soviet Union, Scandinavia, England, Austria, Yugoslavia, Hungary, Romania, and Scotland. He traveled the United States on several trips that took him from his Los Angeles home to Texas, Oklahoma, Washington, DC, Maine, Massachusetts, New York, Michigan, Oklahoma, Texas, Nevada, Indiana, Pennsylvania, Ohio, Missouri, New Mexico, Louisiana, Arizona, Illinois, and Colorado (he visited some of these states several times). He attended four World Series games and the Rose Bowl, and played in numerous polo matches. During his American trips he spoke to Democratic Party functionaries in Claremore, the Los Angeles Chamber of Commerce, a national radio audience in behalf of the Salvation Army, Notre Dame University's annual football banquet, the Los Angeles Realty Board, a national radio audience for the American Foundation for the Blind, Philadelphia's Poor Richard Club, the Indiana General Assembly, Washington's Alfalfa Club, the Texas Society for Crippled Children, the Real Estate Board of New York City, and a British radio audience for the Jubilee Celebration of King George V. During this same twelve-month period, Rogers broadcast twenty-eight segments of the *Gulf Headliners* radio show from Los Angeles and several other American and European locations. He made five movies in Hollywood: *The County Chairman, Life Begins at Forty, Doubting Thomas, Steamboat 'Round the Bend,* and *In Old Kentucky.* He wrote over fifty "Weekly Articles" and over 360 "Daily Telegrams" for the newspapers as well as an article for *Good Housekeeping.* It is not hard to understand why his energy was flagging.[3]

This taxing schedule of endeavors paid dividends by elevating Rogers to a pinnacle of popularity and influence by 1935. The acclaim was nearly unanimous, but a few refused to embrace the legendary status of Oklahoma's citizen-cowboy. A handful of critics denounced both Rogers and his vast audience. Some did so from the intellectual high ground, writing critiques in highbrow journals and magazines that dismissed Rogers as a manipulative, lowest-common-denominator huckster who parlayed his appeal to the great unwashed into popularity and wealth. In *Partisan Review*, film critic and cultural commentator James Agee argued that figures such as Rogers had commercialized, corrupted, and "bourgeoizified" genuine "folk art" in modern America. Agee condemned the musical, *Oklahoma!* for peddling "pseudo-folksy charm," attacked Mark Twain for plying a "professional Americanism," dismissed John Steinbeck for promoting a simple-minded cult of the "Common Man," and claimed that Rogers "is wholly explained by our national weakness for congratulating ourselves upon our special forms of disgracefulness."[4]

In "An Open Letter to Will Rogers" in *Vanity Fair*, John Riddell, the pen name of provocateur Corey Ford, castigated Rogers as a fraud. (Ford also published mocking put-downs of Sherwood Anderson, Theodore Dreiser, and Ernest Hemingway.) The Oklahoman's homespun observations, ungrammatical writing, and laconic manner were not authentic but an elaborate act, argued Riddell, and he mimicked the humorist's style in an attempt to expose him. Rogers liked to appear as

> the Spokesman of the common people, and I kinder figgered it might be quite a relief for a feller like that to find out that his ain't the case at all . . . and as for the common people, most of them I ever talked to think he is really pretty much of a Snob . . . . Course I may not always remember to spell my words wrong, but that shouldent mean I ain't being just as quaint and homespun as you are. . . . [Rogers is a] Drug Store Cowboy [who] has got quite a reputation as a wit, in fact, because whenever anybody walks by him he always makes some wisecrack about them out loud, and all the crowd hanging around him laugh . . . . In fact, [these wisecracks] are kind of Sad, and he wouldent want people to find out that he was maybe just a boor who got his laughs by being Rude . . . . [Y]ou keep on pretending you are just one of us Common People, and you go around Europe chewing gum and acting like Just Folks, when all the time you are hobnobbing with Kings and Princes and people that Matter.

Riddell concluded sarcastically, "it's been real nice to have this friendly little chat and let you know how a lot of us here in America feel about you."[5]

Several political leftists launched attacks on Rogers for demonstrating insufficient devotion to revolutionary change and political activism. "Will Rogers likes to pose as 'home folks,' but the truth is he's a millionaire. He has never written a word in support of a worker on a strike. He has never spoken a sentence that doubted the divine justice of the capitalist system," editorialized the *American Freeman*, a socialist newspaper. "Many of his wisecracks reveal a hidden sympathy for the Fascist type of Demagogue. The great Mark Twain was a real humorist who wasn't afraid to utter some bitter truths about the mountebanks of religion, militarism, and politics." A youthful Dwight Macdonald, political and cultural commentator for several leftwing journals, skewered the Oklahoman at a symposium: "At a time when the American farmer is faced with ruin, when the whole Middle West is seething with bitterness and economic discontent, a movie like *State Fair* is an insulting 'let 'em eat cake' gesture. The vaudeville rusticity of millionaire Will Rogers, the 'cute' doll face of Janet Gaynor – thus Hollywood embodies the farmer."[6]

Two leading journals of leftist opinion likewise tried to knock Rogers off his perch. The *New Republic* characterized the Oklahoman as a mere showman whose commentary appealed mainly to an audience of "national boobies." The editors catalogued his numerous failings:

> His vivid likableness, his unfailing gift of humor covered a multitude of sins. He was, in fact, a truculent nationalist and isolationist . . . ; he was Nietzschean in his ultimate reliance on brute force. With his incessant hammering upon Congress he probably did something to accelerate the decline of faith in the democratic process . . . . He selected the objects of his stinging barbs of wit with discretion; no one knew better than he which side of his bread was buttered. What he did, of course, was to drift along with the currents of prevailing opinion in the groups where he found himself or to which he aspired.

Similarly, the *Nation* claimed that so many people loved Rogers "because of his very lack of strong or clear convictions or any single-minded purpose . . . . His comments on public affairs was almost always amusing; they became increasingly reactionary and chauvinistic; they remained always the unpredictable and irresponsible 'cracks' of a professional amateur. To call him a philosopher . . . is to credit him with order and vision, the two qualities which he most conspicuously lacked and most often spurned." Rather than using his gifts to promote social and political change, the journal concluded, Rogers simply "made a large fortune letting off steam for the American people."[7]

As events would soon disclose, such critics stood in a tiny minority. A vast majority of Americans, both ordinary citizens and cultural commentators, scoffed at these harsh assessments and revered Rogers as a national institution. In fact, the Oklahoman's triumphant conquest of American life by the mid-1930s was so complete that it seemed like nothing could stop him except his own weariness. No one foresaw that the popular humorist and cowboy philosopher, like Icarus, the mythological figure who flew too close to the sun, would lose his buoyancy and come plunging down to earth.

* * * * *

The end came suddenly and unexpectedly. Rogers had finished a spate of movies for Fox by mid-summer 1935 and with some free time, true to his travel lust, was eager to take a trip. He considered flying to Rio de Janeiro and catching the German Zeppelin for a flight to Africa, but after a visit from Wiley Post, dropped that plan in favor of a flying adventure in the far north. Post, a fellow Oklahoman and one of the great aviation pioneers, had established a reputation from a record-setting eight-day trip around the globe and several attempts to set a high-altitude record for flight. With his trademark eyepatch covering an injury suffered as a young man working in the oilfields, the pilot cut a swashbuckling figure. He and Rogers had become acquainted in 1925. The humorist greatly liked and admired Post and, according to Betty, "felt that his achievements had never been properly recognized" and wanted to boost his career. Now Post had come up with the idea of establishing a mail-and-passenger air route between the United States and Russia, but instead of a long flight across the Pacific he wanted to go on a northward route from Alaska across the Bering Sea and then Siberia. He suggested a flight that would survey this route. Will and Betty had been forced to go across Siberia by train only the year before, and Will had been frustrated by only seeing this vast land through a train window. So he was intrigued by Post's proposal. Betty was apprehensive about the trip. She worried not about the pair flying around Alaska, but the next stage where they would "cross the Bering Sea and fly over the great Siberian waste, where they might be forced down and be out of touch with the world." Nonetheless, her husband could not refuse the chance for a flying adventure over a wild, beautiful part of the globe and a departure date was set for the first week of August.[8]

There were other roads not taken. After the completion of their film, *Steamboat 'Round the Bend,* in late June, director John Ford asked Rogers to join him on a vacation cruise to Hawaii slated for early August. But the actor declined. "You keep your duck and go on the water," he jokingly replied. "I'll take my eagle and fly." In addition, Metro-Goldwyn-Mayer had vigorously sought a contract with Rogers to appear in a movie version of *Ah! Wilderness!* The humorist considered the offer and initially committed to the project, but then backed out. If he had accepted, it is likely that the movie would have been in production by August 1935. In both cases, Rogers would have been elsewhere and not flying to Alaska with Wiley Post.[9]

To prepare for the flight, Post arranged for the construction of a hybrid plane. Early in 1935 he purchased a Lockheed Orion, a six-passenger monoplane, and oversaw several modifications completed at the airport in Burbank, California: a more powerful engine, a heavier propeller, a solid-version wing that could accommodate the pontoons added for water landings, and larger fuel tanks. These changes added considerable weight to the aircraft and, in particular, made it nose heavy. In the last week of July, Post and his wife, along with Rogers, took a four-day test flight in the hybrid plane from California to New Mexico and Utah, where everything went smoothly. On August 4, Will and Betty spent the morning riding around the family ranch and stopped at a small log cabin in a canyon that he had just ordered constructed. "I tried to persuade him to postpone his trip for a few days. We'd take our bedrolls down and camp for the night," Betty reported. But he said, 'No, let's wait till I get back.'" Later that day they took in a polo game, and in the evening attended a rodeo at Gilmore Stadium in Los Angeles.

Will took a late flight to San Francisco and then went on to Seattle the next day, where he met up with Post.[10]

After three days in Seattle making final arrangements, the pair flew to Juneau, Alaska. From August 9 to August 14 Rogers and Post flew to several sites, including two towns in Canada, then Anchorage, Mount McKinley, and Fairbanks in Alaska. After these jaunts, the two Oklahomans departed Fairbanks on the morning of August 15 destined for Point Barrow, a small settlement nestled on the coast of the Arctic Ocean and the farthest town north on the North American continent. As they flew across the vast wilderness landscape, the weather grew increasingly difficult with fog setting in and visibility shrinking to near zero. Post got lost and flew in concentric circles searching for the coast line to orient himself and find Point Barrow. Finally, around 5 pm Post set the plane down through a break in the clouds in a lagoon near a tiny Inuit village of a few huts. Rogers climbed out and, pointing and exchanging phrases in pidgin English with a native named Clare Okpeaha, learned that Point Barrow was about fifteen miles northeast. He got back in the plane and Post took off, climbing steeply and banking hard to the right. At a height of about 200 feet, the plane's engine stalled and the craft somersaulted downward and hit the shallow water of the lagoon head-on with terrific force, shearing off the right wing and breaking the pontoon floats before falling over onto its back. Horrified, Okpeaha and several others ran to the wreckage and called out to the two men. There was no answer.[11]

Okpeaha immediately set out on foot to Barrow, a village with about 500 native Inuit and nine white people, and after an exhausting trek of three hours made contact with Stanley Morgan, an army sergeant stationed there, Frank Daugherty, a schoolteacher, and Charles D. Brower, a United States Commissioner and representative of the territorial courts. They obtained a whaleboat along with two other craft and returned to the scene of the crash with a crew of Inuit to find Rogers and Post dead, killed instantly with crushing injuries sustained upon impact. The bodies were extracted from the wrecked plane, wrapped in sleeping bags, and returned to Barrow as the Inuit softly sang a mourning song in their native language. Once back in Barrow, Dr. Henry Greist and his wife, a nurse, conducted a post-mortem on the victims, cleaned the bodies, and wrapped them in sheets. The next day a plane arrived from Fairbanks and picked up the bodies to begin their long journey home to the United States. Charles Lindbergh had procured the services of Pan American Airways, for whom he was working as a consultant, to perform the task.[12]

Meanwhile, news of the calamity traveled back to the continental United States. By August 16, following a radio message from Barrow to Seattle, the wire services had picked up the story and it began appearing on news outlets. Betty was in Maine with Mary as the daughter had just opened a play in summer stock theater, *Ceiling Zero*, co-starring Humphrey Bogart (ironically, the play was about a young woman whose father was killed in an airplane accident). Bogart heard the news of Rogers' death and rushed to the cottage where Betty and Mary were staying. When he gently broke the news to the wife, she "doubled up for a minute as though I'd hit her," the actor related. "Then she straightened up and said, well, there's a lot of work to be done." Betty spoke to her daughter and "Mary seemed stunned." Bill Rogers learned of his father's death from a cousin while working on a Standard Oil tanker in the port of Los Angeles and "looked stunned as though struck." Jim Rogers was told of the Point Barrow tragedy at his hotel in New York City, where he was staying after driving across the country and preparing to join his mother and sister in Maine.[13]

Rogers' funeral service was held on August 22 at Forest Lawn Memorial Park, a huge cemetery located in Glendale, a suburb of Los Angeles. The casket was first taken to the Little Church of the Flowers, a chapel on the grounds, the evening before. Then at 7 am it was moved outside into a glen of fir trees and placed on a bier adorned with red, white, and blue flowers for viewing by the public. At 1 pm the closed casket was carried to another small chapel at Forest Lawn, the Wee Kirk o' the Heather, for a smaller, private funeral service. In addition to members of the Rogers family, attendees included close friends the Stone family, Ziegfeld widow Billie Burke, and Irvin Cobb. Many among Hollywood's movie royalty also filled the pews – Clark Gable, Daryl Zanuck, Spencer Tracy, Walt Disney, Charlie Chaplin, Eddie Cantor, Mary Pickford, Will Hays, Sam Goldwyn. A few political leaders, such as James A. Farley, attended the service. Concurrent with the private funeral, all of the major Hollywood studios – Twentieth Century-Fox, Metro-Goldwyn-Mayer, Universal, Paramount, Warner Brothers, United Artists, RKO, Columbia – suspended work so employees could attend memorial services organized on each lot. Throughout the Los Angeles area, motion picture theaters darkened their screens for two minutes before the showing of films on that date in tribute to the Oklahoman. The NBC and CBS national radio networks observed a half-hour of silence.[14]

But the greatest indicator of Rogers' beloved status occurred during those hours when his casket sat outside at Forest Lawn for the public to view. A throng had begun gathering in the middle of the night on August 22, and from 7 am to noon some 50,000 people passed in front of his bier. An additional 100,000, according to some estimates, failed to gain entrance because of time constraints. Blistering heat had reached 98 degrees by noon and a number of people fainted in the heat, but the crowd persisted. An honor guard of eight noncommissioned flyers from March Field stood at attention as people streamed by, many of them in tears. Another 10,000 people went to the Hollywood Bowl for a memorial service in the afternoon. This gathering of citizens from every walk of American life seemed to reflect the honoree's populist spirit. "A pure democracy, the friends of Will Rogers, gathered yesterday on a high, sun-beaten hill in Forest Lawn and bade America's wise and gentle critic goodbye. There were the high and the low, the mighty and the humble, the socialite and the cowboy," described the *Los Angeles Daily News*. "It was the Great American Melting Pot, such a cross-section as probably never had been gathered in one place."[15]

Indeed, the public outpouring of grief throughout the United States following Rogers' untimely death was unprecedented since the assassination of Abraham Lincoln seventy years before. The fatal crash in Alaska stunned Americans. Flags flew at half-mast around the country, airplanes flew over major cities trailing black streamers, and strangers gathered quietly to discuss the national tragedy at newsstands, churches, street corners, and feed stores. Even the *New Republic*, a persistent critic of the Oklahoman, admitted that on a hot Saturday in mid-August, 1935, most Americans "were talking about Will Rogers. The restaurant waitress, the streetcar conductor, the filling-station attendant spoke of his death the day before as though each had lost a dearly loved personal friend."[16]

For weeks after Rogers' death, tributes flowed in from every direction as newspapers and magazines were filled with eulogies, remembrances, and accounts of his life and achievements. Many simply mourned the death of someone whose presence and commentary had been part of national life for the past twenty years. *The San Francisco Monitor* proclaimed, "The death of Will Rogers is a national calamity" while the *Spectator* described him as "almost the only American voice which carried over the whole country and was listened to by everybody" and concluded, "If anyone can be called a truly representative man of a nation or an epoch, it is such a man as Will Rogers." The *Tulsa Daily World* ran a cartoon of a large, uprooted tree with "Will Rogers" emblazoned on the trunk, with the caption "A Mighty Oak Has Fallen." A cartoon in *Variety* depicted a dejected Uncle Sam, head bowed, holding a newspaper in which the headline blared news of Rogers' death, and the caption read, "All I Know Is What I Read in the Papers." The *Minneapolis Journal*'s simple eloquence spoke for many:

> We all loved Will Rogers ... . Poets we have had, and philosophers, and humorists of note; but not one among them all so endeared to the heart of the whole people. None was ever mourned with such genuine grief, none will be so missed from our common life ... . For his was the rare gift of simplicity, of transparent genuineness, of all forgiving tolerance, coupled with native wisdom and quaint humor that went far to keep the world sane despite the madness of this bewildering age.

A few years later, John Ford would present a poignant, if silent, memorial in his award-winning film, *The Grapes of Wrath* – as the dispossessed Okies fled the Dust

Bowl for California, the camera lingered on a road sign reading "Will Rogers Highway."[17]

But in addition to voicing these general laments, many of the elegies recognized the specific, and powerful, bonds that had connected America's most beloved citizen to his America and its people. Many stressed how Rogers hearkened back to the nation's recently vanished frontier. "Will Rogers never allowed his public to forget that he came from Oklahoma," said one. "He was a pure product of the cattle country." *Commonweal* noted the humorist's "cowboy mannerisms and choice of the vernacular" that placed him "in the pioneer tradition of our country .... [T]here was a certain appropriateness in the news of his death being brought by an Indian who had run fifteen miles to the nearest settlement." The *World Digest* observed, "In his unhurried drawl there was the echo of the vast American plain .... He always talked with the lazy tones of the Southwest and thought the thoughts of its people." In New York, Eddie Rickenbacker, the famous fighter pilot from World War I, was quoted as saying the key to understanding Rogers' connection to his audience was simple: "He never forgot to be a cowboy."[18]

Numerous eulogies, at some point, also alighted on Rogers' celebrity status, particularly with its "illusion of intimacy" wherein ordinary people saw the person in the public spotlight as a personal companion. "It is difficult to suggest any death that could deeply and sorrowfully affect as many Americans as does the death of Will Rogers. He was the intimate friend, literally, of tens of millions of Americans," the *New York Daily Mirror* contended. A cartoon in a small midwestern newspaper depicted a smiling Rogers, with cowboy hat and lariat, walking into the sunset as he turns to wave at a father, mother, and two children standing sadly outside their house. The caption read, "Almost Like One of the Family." The *Christian Century* wrote, "One wonders whether the sudden death of any other American could have affected the public in quite the intimate and shattering fashion that this has .... This deep sense that a personal friend, a boon companion of those off-hours when one sits slippered and relaxed before one's own hearthfire, has gone."[19]

Many of Rogers' posthumous tributes pegged his popularity and influence to the central place he occupied in the entertainment and media nexus that had taken shape in modern America. The *Chicago Daily Tribune* suggested that the humorist was "the plain, homespun American, magnified hugely by his fortunate access to all means of communication that are available in this era – the motion pictures, the talking pictures, the radio, the newspaper syndicates, the book publishing business, and the stage." Analyzing his career success, the *Spectator* argued that Rogers was already well known as a stage humorist when he became "stupendously famous" from a "triple combination" of newspaper syndication, radio, and talking movies. *Variety* concluded that Rogers' renown had come from the extraordinary convergence of many entertainment endeavors: "On the stage, in pictures, and on radio he went as far as anyone can go. As a writer he was equally successful. He tackled everything and failed at nothing."[20]

Finally, nearly every assessment of Rogers in the aftermath of his death stressed his deep connection to the plain folk of America. "Will Rogers was friend, mental companion, spokesman for the average, common sense American," observed the *New York Evening Journal*. The *Chicago Tribune* concurred, observing, "He spoke the language of the great plains . . . . [A]nd when he cracked a joke, it was the sort of remark that the average American might have made if he had a humorous inspiration." L. H. Robbins, in the *New York Times Magazine*, described the Oklahoman as "the apotheosis of the common man . . . . He was Vox Populi in person." Damon Runyon depicted Rogers as the "unofficial prime minister of the people" and "the closest living approach to what we like to call the true American . . . . Behind his jesting was nearly always the expression of the thought of the people."[21]

These evaluations illuminated the underpinnings of Rogers' special place in the hearts of the great mass of Americans – as not just a popular writer, beloved humorist, radio personality, and movie-star but as a genuine folk-hero. The historical bad-timing of his death – occurring a few years before the earthquake of World War II hurled the United States out of the Great Depression and onto the international stage with a new appreciation of the nation's global responsibilities – made it seem as if he had inhabited another world. It caused his towering reputation to subside over the next few decades. Memories of what Rogers had meant to so many, for so long, faded steadily by the era of the Baby Boom, the Cold War, and the rebellion of the 1960s. Brief revivals of interest flared up thereafter, such as with James Whitmore's one-man show, *Will Rogers' USA*, which debuted in 1970, and the musical, *The Will Rogers Follies*, which ran on Broadway and then took a national tour, in the early 1990s. By and large, however, for most Americans by the end of the twentieth century, Will Rogers had become a shadowy figure from the nation's past.

But in his own time, the self-effacing Oklahoman captured the attention, and affection, of his fellow citizens by pursuing a life course that replicated the larger journey of modern America. A significant historical figure, Rogers represented the trends that defined the United States in an age of transformation from the 1890s to the 1930s: the end of the frontier, the shaping of a fresh culture of personality and self-fulfillment, the emergence of celebrity, and the sharpening of a populist world-view. With engaging humor and abundant good will, he helped hosts of ordinary people navigate the treacherous journey from a rural republic steeped in local traditions of hard work, stern morality, and individual ambition to a modern urban society devoted to consumer comfort, corporate organization, mass culture, and amusement.

But this common man of uncommon talents did more than just explore the substance of a great era of change in American history. He skillfully shaped the process by which it happened. As a beloved guide across shifting social terrain and a skilled arbiter of conflicting cultural demands, he eased his fellow citizens into a new world by using humor to soften the wrenching aspects of the transition. Rogers nourished a reverence for tradition even as he punctured its shibboleths and exposed its poses and pomposity. At the same time, he encouraged appreci-ation of modern advances, whether it was the automobile or the movies or consumer prosperity, even as he proposed a healthy skepticism about grand claims of progress. And he did all of this with a common touch that preached civility and respect for others' points of view.

Franklin D. Roosevelt, ever the shrewd diagnostician of American life, sensed Rogers' important labors in bridging past and present. In remarks not long after the Alaskan tragedy, he observed that the humorist promoted an understanding that "the way to make progress is to build on what we have, to take from the lessons of yesterday a little more wisdom and courage to the tasks of today." Rogers himself illuminated this mediational role, and its humane underpinnings, in a thoughtful *Weekly Article* he wrote just a few months before his death. A visit to a university prompted him to ponder the situation of young people entering the world who looked askance at a society ravaged by the Great Depression. While their criticism often reflected the bombastic certainty of youth, Rogers observed, older readers, including himself, needed to hear them out with sensitivity and understanding. After all, this generational encounter embodied the larger process of historical change and the human struggle to deal with it. In Rogers' view, the typical young adult in the 1930s

> looks out over the wreck, of which he had no making, and says, "So this is the old folks' way, yeah?" So he starts looking for the keyhole in the dark, too, and with his young enthusiasm he thinks he can find it before you can . . . . They [youth] feel that they are the ones to right it. We [older folks] feel we are the ones that lost it, and that we are the ones that will find it. It's just a difference of opinion, it's not a difference of nature. They are absolutely the same as we are . . . . We look at it from the old days, they look at it from the new. We are looking in different directions. We can't help but look back, they can't help but look forward. But we are both standing on the same ground, and their feet is there as firmly as ours.

This reflection on the young and the old, the past and the present, exemplified the wise and humane advice the Oklahoman often offered to his fellow citizens.[22]

Will Rogers' role in American life might be visualized in terms of a favorite rope trick from his stage act in the early 1910s. The cowboy showman, flashing his winsome grin to the audience and stammering a self-deprecating comment, would casually begin twirling two lassos simultaneously. When a horse and rider dashed out of the wings and across the stage, he flicked his twin lariats and deftly ensnared, at the same time, the swiftly-moving horse with one rope and the rider with the other. The audience invariably gasped in amazement and burst into applause. Symbolically, Rogers did much the same thing throughout his mature career when confronting the complex, challenging way in which tradition and innovation, stasis and change, figure prominently in the never-ending cycle of historical evolution. The Oklahoman faced the onrushing process of transformation in early twentieth-century America and, flinging out his verbal lariats, captured simultaneously both a disappearing past and an emerging present. With great skill and insight, and a generous portion of shrewd humor and humane feeling, Rogers drew past and present together, lessening the distance between them and making the transition seem easier for his vast number of readers, listeners, and viewers.

Rogers' enormous success in explaining modern America to itself was confirmed, tragically, by the outpouring of affection following his sudden death. But that does not mark the end of his impact. Now, almost a century later, his experiences and achievements still resonate. They suggest much about the dilemmas of our own time. His triumph in various fields of entertainment illustrates how the values of self-fulfillment and sparkling personality maintain such a hold in modern America. His climb to prominence illustrates the problems and the possibilities facing someone from a mixed-race and marginal background who labors to succeed in America's society of opportunity. His immense popularity, achieved largely through the mechanisms of mass media, suggests the virtues and limitations of celebrity as it impacts the leaders of modern society. Rogers' style of communication and way of being illuminates the salutary role played by civility and charm in discussions of public issues. His embrace of ordinary people confirms that their values and aspirations can, and should, do much to shape the nature of our society. Finally, his use of gentle, good-natured wit to probe the issues of the day reminds us that such a thing is possible, as we view it from an age where public discourse specializes in the vicious put-down, the mocking characterization, and the condescending assertion of others' stupidity. To understand this remarkable humorist, in other words, is to understand more about our historical journey to the present – what we have gained and what we have lost.

Acknowledgments

It is a pleasure to acknowledge the many people who have provided me aid and comfort in the writing of this book. Several colleagues at the University of Missouri offered their expertise and discerning eyes in reading and critiquing the manuscript. Jonathan Sperber and John Wigger, old friends and comrades from the Department of History, deployed their considerable skills to suggest a number of revisions and reconsiderations while Nancy West, from the Department of English, provided a close reading and many useful suggestions in the early going. Lauren Jackson, my research assistant for several months, did excellent work compiling and classifying a large number of newspaper and magazine pieces on Rogers and his career. Also in my mid-Missouri stomping grounds, good friends from our free-ranging book club – Marty Townsend and Clark Swisher, Barbara Rupp and Neil Minturn, Julia and Thor Norregaard – kindly read an early version of the book and devoted an evening to discussing, from the perspective of the general reader, its attractions and shortcomings while also catching a number of mistakes. My longtime friend, Cindy Sheltmire, reviewed the text and found a number of mistakes and infelicities. While they did nothing directly to influence the book for good or evil, my talented bandmates in *Flyover Country* – Soren Larsen, Doug Whitworth, Neil Minturn, Monte Safford – provided much friendship, distraction, and relaxation while providing a creative outlet away from the writing desk.

The staff of the Will Rogers Memorial Museum, especially archivist Jennifer Holt and director Tad Jones, offered a warm welcome and much help in making available materials and sources during several research jaunts to the heart of Rogers country in Claremore, Oklahoma. Jennifer also assisted greatly by digitally conveying quite a number of Rogers films and photographs for my use. The film historian Richard Bann, in Los Angeles, generously shared a cache of materials on Rogers and silent film director Hal Roach from his own considerable holdings of movie records. As the book moved toward publication, the Cambridge University Press staff eased the process of getting the manuscript knocked into shape and into print, especially my editor, Cecelia Cancellaro, and editorial assistant, Victoria Phillips.

My long-time literary agent, Ronald Goldfarb, did his usual fine job of setting up the contract with Cambridge and providing support during the writing of the book. I owe a special debt of gratitude to Steven K. Gragert, editor of several multi-volume series –*The Papers of Will Rogers, Will Rogers' Weekly Articles, Will Rogers' Daily Telegrams* – and long-time (now retired) director of the Will Rogers Memorial Museum. Steve cheerfully brought to bear his unparalleled knowledge of Rogers and his milieu to painstakingly review every line of the book manuscript. He made countless corrections and saved me from many boneheaded errors while bolstering my spirits with kind words of encouragement.

My greatest thanks, of course, go to my family. Levon let me use his office and Robbie enthusiastically greeted me every morning before I trudged upstairs to write. My daughter, Olivia, took time away from homework and her own efforts as a writer to patiently endure her father's yammering on about some old cowboy comedian from the ancient past. My wife, Patti, provided a sounding board for my endless reflections on Rogers and his significance, carefully read the manuscript with her usual acumen, and asked many probing questions, all of which greatly improved the final product. She is a star.

Abbreviations

Abbreviations of frequently cited sources:

Autobiography	Donald Day, ed., *The Autobiography of Will Rogers* (New York: Houghton Mifflin Co., 1949)
Daily Telegrams	*Will Rogers' Daily Telegrams* (Stillwater: Oklahoma State University Press, 1978–1979), vols. 1–4, James M. Smallwood and Steven K. Gragert, eds.
Folks Say	William Howard Payne and Jake J. Lyons, eds., *Folks Say of Will Rogers: A Memorial Anecdotage* (New York: G. Putnam's Sons, 1936)
Our Will Rogers	Homer Croy, *Our Will Rogers* (Boston: Little, Brown, and Co., 1953)
Papers	*The Papers of Will Rogers* (Norman: University of Oklahoma Press, 1996–2006), Arthur Frank Wertheim and Barbara Bair, eds., vols. 1–3; Steven K. Gragert and M. Jane Johansson, eds., vols. 4–5.
Political Life	Richard D. White, Jr., *Will Rogers: A Political Life* (Lubbock: Texas Tech University Press, 2011)
Radio Broadcasts	*Radio Broadcasts of Will Rogers*, Steven K. Gragert, ed. (Stillwater: Oklahoma State University Press, 1983)
Rogers at Follies	Arthur Frank Wertheim, ed., *Will Rogers at the Ziegfeld Follies* (Norman: University of Oklahoma Press, 1972)
Rogers in Hollywood	Bryan B. Sterling and Frances N. Sterling, *Will Rogers in Hollywood* (New York: Crown, 1984)
Story of His Life	Betty Rogers, *Will Rogers: The Story of His Life, Told By His Wife* (Garden City, NY: Garden City Publishing, 1943)
Weekly Articles	*Will Rogers' Weekly Articles* (Stillwater: Oklahoma State University Press, 1980–1982), James M. Smallwood and Steven K. Gragert, eds., vols. 1–3; Steven K. Gragert, ed., vols. 4–6.

WR Biography   Ben Yagoda, *Will Rogers: A Biography* (New York: Alfred
A. Knopf, 1993)

WRM   Will Rogers Memorial, a museum and archive in Claremore,
Oklahoma that holds Rogers' papers, scrapbooks of newspaper
clippings, interviews with family and friends, and a wide
assortment of materials related to his career.

Notes

INTRODUCTION

1 Garner quoted in *Chicago Tribune*, August 16, 1935; Franklin D. Roosevelt remarks in *Folks Say*, 6; *Chicago American*, August 19, 1935; and Clarence Kelland in *Folks Say*, 198.
2 Theodore Roosevelt quoted in L. H. Robbins, "Portrait of an American Philosopher," *New York Times* (November 3, 1935), and Damon Runyon in *Folks Say*, 207.
3 Notes for October 1930 speech, WRM; *Daily Telegrams*, 1: 22, and 2: 226; *Weekly Articles*, 3: 13, and 2: 310.
4 Homer Croy, *Country Cured* (New York: Harper and Brothers, 1943), 224.
5 For just a few works that explore the vast changes remaking the United States in the late 1800s and early 1900s, see Jackson Lears, "From Salvation to Self-Realization: Advertising and the Therapeutic Roots of the Consumer Culture, 1880–1930," in Lears and Richard Wightman Fox, eds., *The Culture of Consumption: Critical Essays in American History, 1880–1980* (New York: Pantheon, 1983); Olivier Zunz, *Making America Corporate, 1870–1920* (Chicago: University of Chicago Press, 1990); Lary May, *Screening Out the Past: The Birth of Mass Culture and the Motion Picture Industry* (Chicago: University of Chicago Press, 1980); and Lewis A. Erenberg, *Steppin' Out: New York Nightlife and the Transformation of American Culture, 1890–1930* (Chicago: University of Chicago Press, 1981).
6 *Daily Telegrams*, 2: 56.
7 *Papers*, 1: 387, and 4: 206–208.
8 *Weekly Articles*, 5: 76.
9 *Weekly Articles*, 1: 341 and 5: 184, and *Papers*, 5: 369.
10 The "beneficiary of circumstances" assertion appears in *WR Biography*, xiii.

CHAPTER ONE

1 For descriptions of the pivotal event in Baltimore, see *Weekly Articles*, 1: 193–196, and *WR Biography*, 146.
2 Ellsworth Collins, *The Old Home Ranch: Birthplace of Will Rogers* (Claremore, OK: Will Rogers Heritage Press, 1986), 1, 10, 19, and *Story of His Life*, 163–165.
3 *Papers*, 1: 31–32, and Charles McCloughlin: *Cherokee Renascence in the Early Republic* (Princeton, NJ: Princeton University Press, 1984) and Charles McCloughlin, *After the Trail of Tears: The Cherokees' Struggle for Sovereignty, 1839–1880* (Chapel Hill: University of North Carolina Press, 1990).

4 On the Rogers and Schrimsher families up through the Civil War, see *Papers*, 1: 32–37; Amy M. Ware, *Cherokee Kid: Will Rogers, Tribal Identity, and the Making of an American Icon* (Lawrence: University Press of Kansas, 2015), 21–30; and *Story of His Life*, 37–38.

5 *Autobiography*, 1–2; *Story of His Life*, 38; *Papers*, 1: 482–484.

6 *Old Home Ranch*, 24–25; *Story of His Life*, 43; and Homer Croy, *Our Will Rogers*, 21.

7 *Papers*, 1: 543–544, and *Story of His Life*, 36.

8 *Old Home Ranch*, 19–21, and *Story of His Life*, 40–41.

9 *Papers*, 1: 545–546, and *Old Home Ranch*, 24.

10 *Our Will Rogers*, 18–19, 17, 24, and *Story of His Life*, 41–42, 39.

11 *Papers*, 1: 547; *Our Will Rogers*, 26; *Story of His Life*, 47, and *Radio Broadcasts*, 28.

12 *Old Home Ranch*, 39; *WR Biography*, 32; Fred Roach, Jr., "Will Rogers' Youthful Relationship with his Father, Clem Rogers: A Story of Love and Tension," *Chronicles of Oklahoma*, vol. 58 (1980), 327–328; *Story of His Life*, 34, 36–38; and *Papers*, 1: 539–541.

13 *Story of His Life*, 44.

14 *Our Will Rogers*, 21–22, 24.

15 *Story of His Life*, 27, 29, 47–48, 27.

16 *Ibid.*, 41, and *Old Home Ranch*, 25–26, 42.

17 Harold Keith, *Boy's Life of Will Rogers* (New York: Thomas Y. Crowell, 1937), 37–38; *Old Home Ranch*, 25–26, 38, 42; *Papers*, 1: 154; and *Autobiography*, 7–8.

18 *Papers*, 1: 72–80, and *Autobiography*, 5.

19 *Papers*, 1: 79, and *Story of His Life*, 50–52.

20 *Story of His Life*, 45, 48, and *Our Will Rogers*, 31, 33–34.

21 "Youthful Relationship with his Father," 330–331; *Autobiography*, 5; and *Story of His Life*, 292.

22 *Boy's Life of Will Rogers*, 62–72, and *Papers*, 1: 154. On the Chicago World's Columbian Exposition, see Robert Rydell, *All the World's a Fair: Visions of Empire at American International Expositions, 1876–1916* (Chicago: University of Chicago Press, 1984), 38–71.

23 *Papers*, 1: 153–154, 158–159; *Weekly Articles*, 5: 6; and Spi M. Trent, quoted in *WR Biography*, 41.

24 *Our Will Rogers*, 46, and "Youthful Relationship with his Father," 331.

25 *Weekly Articles*, 6: 139.

26 *Papers*, 1:151–152, and *WR Biography*, 35–36.

27 *Our Will Rogers*, 51, 55–59, and *Papers*, 1: 154–155, 175.

28 *Autobiography*, 11–12; *Papers*, 1: 208–209; and *Story of His Life*, 58–59.

29 *Papers*, 1: 387, and Eddie Cantor, *As I Remember Them* (New York: Duell, Sloan, and Pearce, 1963), 142–143.

30 *Weekly Articles*, 3: 233, and Ben Dixon MacNeill in *Folks Say*, 116–117.

31 *WR Biography*, xii, and *Cherokee Kid*, 3.

32 W. E. B. DuBois, *Souls of Black Folks* (Dover Publications, 1903), 2–3, and *Autobiography*, 5.

33 *Papers*, 1: 176–177; *Cherokee Kid*, 41–43; and Maude Ward DuPriest, Jennie May Bard, and Anna Forman Graham, comps., *Cherokee Recollections: The Story of the Indian Women's Pocahontas Club and Members in the Cherokee Nation & Oklahoma Beginning in 1899* (Glenpool, OK: Thales Microuniversity Press, 1976), 10.

34 *Our Will Rogers*, 59, and *Cherokee Kid*, 42. On stomp dances, see Paula J. Conlon, "From Powwow to Stomp Dance: Parallel Dance Traditions in Oklahoma," in Anthony Shay and Barbara Sellers-Young, eds., *The Oxford Handbook of Dance and Ethnicity* (New York, 2016).

35 *Papers*, 1: 184–186 and 2: 315–318.

36 Arthur Martin Hitch, *Will Rogers, Cadet: A Record of His Two Years as a Cadet at the Kemper Military School* (Boonville, MO, 1935), 16–17, and *Our Will Rogers*, 41.

37 *Boy's Life of Will Rogers*, 73–76, and *Papers*, 1: 507.

38 "Rogers Pleads for Landmark," *Tulsa Daily World*, March 19, 1926; *Weekly Articles*, 4: 142–143, 129; and *Radio Broadcasts*, 18.

39 *Papers*, 1: 147–152, and *WR Biography*, 35.

40 *Story of His Life*, 49, 59, 60–61, and *Autobiography*, 56.

CHAPTER TWO

1 *Weekly Articles*, 3: 76.

2 *Papers*, 1: 178–179, 518–519, and *Autobiography*, 13–14.

3 Spi M. Trent, *My Cousin Will Rogers* (New York: G. P. Putnam's Sons, 1938), 163, and *Weekly Articles*, 3: 76.

4 *Autobiography*, 16, and *Story of His Life*, 61–63.

5 *Papers*, 1: 237–238, 249–250.

6 *Autobiography*, 17–18, and *Papers*, 1: 238, 251, 254.

7 *Papers*, 1: 239–240, 276.

8 *Papers*, 1: 276–277, 301–303, and *Autobiography*, 19.

9 *Papers*, 1: 305–306.

10 *Autobiography*, 19, and *Papers*, 2: 305.

11 *Papers*, 1: 324–325, 334, 354–355, 365.

12 *Papers*, 1: 355, 361–362.

13 *Papers*, 1: 324–326, 355, 376.

14 *Papers*, 1: 355, 357.

15 *Papers*, 1: 327–328, 334–335, 346, 364, and *Our Will Rogers*, 79–80.

16 *Our Will Rogers*, 81–82.

17 *Papers*, I: 559–561.

18 *Ibid.*, 328–329, 384, 389, 418, 420–421, and *Autobiography*, 23.

19 *Papers*, 1: 390–391, 403.

20 *Papers*, 1: 384–385, 387, and *Autobiography*, 23.

21 *Papers* 1: 408–409, 446, 404, 406.

22 *Ibid.*, 443.

23 *Ibid.*, 458, 449.

24 *Ibid.*, 449, 458.

25 *Story of His Life*, 80; *Papers*, 1: 465–466; and *Autobiography*, 24–25.

26 *Story of His Life*, 80.

27 *Papers*, 1: 281, 279, 357.

28 *Ibid.*, 1: 449–450, 318.

29 *Ibid.*,1: 318–319.

30 *Ibid.*, 1: 467.

31 For general treatments of the St. Louis World's Fair, see Joe Sonderman and Mike Truax, *St. Louis: The 1904 World's Fair* (Charleston, South Carolina: Arcadia Publishing, 2008) and Elana V. Fox, *Inside the World's Fair of 1904*, Vols. 1 and 2 (St. Louis: 1st Books Library, 2003). For a contemporaneous overview, see Bennitt, Mark, et al., eds., *History of the Louisiana Purchase Exposition* (1905; reprint, New York: Arno Press, 1976).

32 *Papers*, 2: 41–43, 52, and Robert W. Rydell, *All the World's A Fair: Visions of Empire at American International Expositions, 1876–1916* (Chicago: University of Chicago, 1984), 160–164.

33 Quoted in *All the World's a Fair*, 155.

34 *Autobiography*, 26; *Our Will Rogers*, 93; and *My Cousin Will Rogers*, 163.

35 *Papers*, 2: 44, 46–49.

36 *Weekly Articles*, 5: 77, and *Papers*, 2: 57, 59–61.

37 *My Cousin Will Rogers*, 83, and Amy M. Ware, *The Cherokee Kid: Will Rogers, Tribal Identity, and the Making of an American Icon* (Lawrence: University Press of Kansas, 2015), 55. 55. On Buffalo Bill, see Joy S. Kasson, *Buffalo Bill's Wild West: Celebrity, Memory, and Popular History* (New York: Hill and Wang, 2000).

38 *All the World's A Fair*, 178–179, and *Papers*, 2: 44–45, 4.

39 *Mulhall Enterprise*, June 24, 1904; *St. Louis Republic*, June 22, 1904; and *Papers*, 2: 49.

40 *Papers*, 2: 64, 94–95, 79, 68, and *Our Will Rogers*, 94–95.

41 *Autobiography*, 28; Papers, 2: 492; and *Story of His Life*, 85–86.

42 "Two Cowboys Will Try to Take Big Prize," *Washington Times*, April 23, 1905.

43 *Papers*, 2: 107–117, and New York *Morning Telegraph*, April 25, 1905.

44 *New York Herald*, April 25, 1905, and New York newspaper clipping, ca. April 28, 1905 in *Papers*, 2: 118–119.

45 *Autobiography*, 30, and *Papers*, 2: 119.

46 *Papers*, 2: 122, 123, and *Autobiography*, 30–31.

47 *Story of His Life*, 86; *Our Will Rogers*, 102; and *Papers*, 2: 123–124.

48 *Autobiography*, 30–31, and *Papers*, 2: 133–134, 144–147, 142–143.

49 *My Cousin Will Rogers*, 165, and *Papers*, 2: 139.

CHAPTER THREE

1 *Story of His Life*, 115.

2 *Our Will Rogers*, 108–109, based on an interview with Buck McGee.

3 *Papers*, 2: 129–133, and David Nasaw, *Going Out: The Rise and Fall of Public Amusements* (Cambridge, MA: Harvard University Press, 1999 [1993], 19–33. For a host of compelling images, see Bernard Sobel, *A Pictorial History of Vaudeville* (New York: Citadel Press, 1961).

4 *Going Out*, 24–25.

5 *Ibid.*, 21–23.

6 *Ibid.*, 25–27, and *Papers*, 2: 132–133.

7 *Papers*, 2: 128, 130–133, 160, 174.

8 *Autobiography*, 33, and *Papers*, 2: 273–276.

9 *Papers*, 2: 306, 518–519, and 3: 91; *Story of His Life*, 90; and *Our Will Rogers*, 103, 107–108.

10 *Story of His Life*, 90–92, and *Our Will Rogers*, 103–104.

11 *Autobiography*, 32.

12 *Ibid.*, 31–32.

13 *Papers*, 2: 195–197, and *Our Will Rogers*, 106.

14 *Papers*, 2: 163, 174, 371–373.

15 *Ibid.*, 3: 43, and 2: 212–213, 316–318.

16 *Ibid.*, 2: 434, 440–441, and 3: 177–180.

17 *Ibid.*, 2: 236–237, 239, and 3: 56.

18 *Ibid.*, 2: 335–337.

19 *Ibid.*, 2: 417–418.

20 *Our Will Rogers*, 106–107, and *Story of His Life*, 110, 116–117.

21 *Papers*, 3: 125–127; *Our Will Rogers*, 125–126; and *Story of His Life*, 110.

22 *Papers*, 3: 212–213.

23 *Ibid.*, 3: 214–215, 355–357, 331.

24 *Ibid.*, 3: 226, 246.

25 *Ibid.*, 3: 265–267, 269–270, 279, 282, and *Our Will Rogers*, 132–133.

26 Eddie Cantor, *Take My Life* (Garden City, NY: Doubleday, 1957), 104; George Jessel, *World I Lived In* (Chicago: Henry Regnery, 1962), 18; and *Papers*, 3: 313, 321, 325, 328.

27 *Papers*, 3: 344–353, 366.

28 Fred Roach, Jr., "Will Rogers' Youthful Relationship with His Father, Clem Rogers: A Story of Love and Tension," *Chronicles of Oklahoma*, vol. 58 (1980), 336; *Our Will Rogers*, 119–120; *Story of His Life*, 27, 119–120.

29 *Papers*, 3: 62–63.

30 Jim Hopkins Oral History, WRM.

31 *Papers*, 1: 127–131, 564.

32 *Ibid.*, 1: 211–213, 155, 402–414.

33 *Ibid.*, 1: 380, 365, 396–398, 489–490, and *Our Will Rogers*, 55, 342–343.

34 *Papers*, 1: 411, 423–424.

35 *Ibid.*, 2: 516–518; *Weekly Articles*, 5: 77–78; *Autobiography*, 27; *My Cousin Will Rogers*, 160; *WR Biography*, 69.

36 *Papers*, 3: 97, 52, and 2: 330–331, 334.

37 *Ibid.*, 2: 135–137, 480–485.

38 *Story of His Life*, 14–16, and *Papers*, 1: 155.

39 *Papers*, 1: 184–187, 189–191.

40 *Papers*, 191, 531, 156; *Our Will Rogers*, 70; and *My Cousin Will Rogers*, 177–178.

41 *Story of His Life*, 20–21.

42 *Ibid.*, 82–84; *Papers*, 2: 80–83; and *Our Will Rogers*, 93–94.

43 *Papers*, 2: 91, 92, 94, 143, 187.

44 *Story of His Life*, 94–96.

45 *Ibid.*, 96–98, and *Papers*, 2: 247–248, 324, 388–389.

46 *Papers*, 2: 172, 330–334, 397, 402–403, 479–480.

47 *Ibid.*, 2: 405–407.

48 *Story of His Life*, 101–102, and *Papers*, 2: 402, and 3: 65–66, 69, 70, 78.

49 *Story of His Life*, 102–103; *Papers*, 80, 83–84; and *Autobiography*, 35.

50 *Story of His Life*, 104–106.

51 *Ibid.*, 106–107.

52 *Story of His Life*, 108; *Our Will Rogers*, 118; and *Papers*, 3: 97–99.

53 *Papers*, 3: 242, 248, 218, 258–260, 390–391, and *Story of His Life*, 109, 124, 126.

54 *Papers*, 3: 362–363.

55 *Story of His Life*, 126–127, and *Papers*, 3: 363–364, 387, 392.

CHAPTER FOUR

1 *Papers*, 4: 108, 113; "Ziegfeld Follies of 1917" on Internet Broadway Database; and program for "Illinois Theatre, Ziegfeld Follies," December 23, 1917.

2 "The Playbill," Joseph Urban Papers, Columbia University Libraries, Series III, Zeigfeld Productions, 1915–1932.

3 *Papers*, 4: 81, 116–117, and *Rogers at the Follies*, 9, 51.

4 *Papers*, 4: 121–122, and *Rogers at the Follies*, 89–90, 9.

5 Percy Hammond, "Ziegfeld and His Follies," *Chicago Tribune*, Dec. 24, 1917, and *Papers*, 4: 10–11. See another Percy Hammond review of the 1917 show in "Follies of 1917 is a Fine Spectacle," *New York Times*, June 13, 1917, p. 11.

6 Florenz Ziegfeld, Jr., "Beauty, the Fashions, and the Follies," *Ladies Home Journal* (March 1923), 17. The best treatments of Ziegfeld's life are Cynthia Brideson and Sara Brideson, *Ziegfeld and His Follies: A Biography of Broadway's Greatest Producer* (Lexington: University Press of Kentucky, 2015); Ethan Mordden, *Ziegfeld: The Man Who Invented Show Business* (New York: St. Martin's Press, 2008); and Richard Ziegfeld and Paulette Ziegfeld, *The Ziegfeld Touch: The Life and Times of Florenz Ziegfeld, Jr.* (New York: Henry Abrams, 1993).

7 *Rogers at the Follies*, 10–13.

8 *Ziegfeld and His Follies*, 75; *Ziegfeld: Man Who Invented Show Business*, 180–183; and *Ziegfeld Touch*, 39.

9 *Ziegfeld: Man Who Invented Show Business*, 182; *Rogers at the Follies*, 13–14; and Richard M. Ketchum, *Will Rogers: The Man and His Times* (New York: American Heritage Publishing Company, 1973), 141.

10 Florenz Ziegfeld, Jr., "Picking Out Pretty Girls For the Stage," *American Magazine* (Dec. 1919), 34; Florenz Ziegfeld, "Beauty, the Fashions, and the Follies," *Ladies Home Journal* (March, 1923), 154; and Lewis A. Erenberg, *Steppin' Out: New York Nightlife and the Transformation of American Culture, 1890–1930* (Chicago: University of Chicago Press, 1981), 214–215.

11 *Ziegfeld Touch*, 61, 86–87.

12 *Ziegfeld Touch*, 45–46, 47, 53, 60–61, 84, 103–104.

13 *Ziegfeld Touch*, 59, 60, 73; *Rogers at the Follies*, 13; and *Story of His Life*, 139–140.

14 *Ziegfeld Touch*, 23, 121, and an array of *Follies* posters from 187–216; *Ziegfeld and His Follies*, 79, 102; *New York Telegraph*, Sept. 28, 1908; and "The Follies of Florenz Ziegfeld," *New Yorker*, March 14, 1925.

15 Florenz Ziegfeld, Jr., "Why I Produce the Kind of Shows I Do," *Green Book Album* (January 1912), 172–177.

16 *Our Will Rogers*, 135–136, and *Autobiography*, 38.

17 *Our Will Rogers*, 137–138; *Rogers at the Follies*, 6–7; and *Ziegfeld and His Follies*, 155–156.

18 *Our Will Rogers*, 136–138, based on Croy's interviews with Gene Buck; *Rogers at the Follies*, 8; and *Autobiography*, 77.

19 *Rogers at the Follies*, 35, 8, 36; *New York Times*, May 21, 1916; and *Story of His Life*, 128.

20 *Autobiography*, 37–38; *Steppin' Out*, 207, 217, 222; and "Gag Book," 1915–1916, WRM.

21 *Story of His Life*, 129; *Our Will Rogers*, 137–138; and *Autobiography*, 38–39.

22 *Story of His Life*, 131–132.

23 *Ibid.*, 132–133, 136–137; and *Rogers at the Follies*, xvii–xviii.

24 *Rogers at the Follies*, 16–18, 70–72, 75–76.

25 Marcelle Earl, *Midnight Frolic: A Ziegfeld Girl's True Story* (Basking Ridge, NJ: Twin Oaks Publishing, 1999), 245, 270, and *Story of His Life*, 137–139.

26 Eddie Cantor, *My Life Is in Your Hands* (New York: Harper and Brothers, 1928), 197; *Our Will Rogers*, 154; and Eddie Cantor, *Take My Life* (Garden City, NY: Doubleday, 1957), 110.

27 *Autobiography*, 47, and *Story of His Life*, 106, 139.

28 *Story of His Life*, 141, and Will Rogers, "The Extemporaneous Line," *Theater Magazine* (July 1917), 12.

29 *Autobiography*, 39; George Martin, "The Wit of Will Rogers," *American Magazine* (Nov. 1919), 106, 34; and "Original Follies Routine Notes," Typed Manuscript, WRM.

30 "Wit of Will Rogers," 109, and *Our Will Rogers*, 143.

31 "Wit of Will Rogers," 34, 118.

32 *Ibid.*, 109–110, and *Rogers at the Follies*, 115, 134.

33 "Original Follies Notes," WRM; *Ziegfeld and His Follies*, 169–170; and *Ziegfeld Touch*, 65.

34 *Story of His Life*, 140, and *Rogers at the Follies*, 51, 39.

35 Gladys Hall, "New 'Follies' is Prodigal," *New York Times*, June 6, 1922.

36 Daniel J. Boorstin, *The Image: A Guide to Pseudo-Events in America* (New York: Atheneum, 1962), 79, and Richard Schickel, *Intimate Strangers: The Culture of Celebrity in America* (Chicago: Ivan R. Dee, 2000 [1985]), 4, 54.

37 "Wit of Will Rogers," 34; Karl Schmidt, "The Philosopher with the Lariat," *Everybody's Magazine* (Oct. 1917), 494; *Our Will Rogers*, 148; and *Story of His Life*, 128.

38 *Story of His Life*, 133–135; "The Extemporaneous Line," 12; and *Rogers at the Follies*, 18, 62.

39 *Rogers at the Follies*, 18, 60, 73–74, and *Our Will Rogers*, 145.

40 *Story of His Life*, 133; "Philosopher with the Lariat," 494; and *Rogers at the Follies*, 73–75.

41 Cantor, *Take My Life*, 105, 115, and W. C. Fields, *W. C. Fields by Himself: His Intended Autobiography* (Englewood Cliffs, NJ: Prentice Hall, 1948), 154.

42 *Rogers at the Follies*, 85, 90, 121, 168–169.

43 "Philosopher with the Lariat," 494–495, and "Wit of Will Rogers," 110, 113.

44 Michel Mok, "The Cowboy Ambassador: A Life Story of Will Rogers," undated newspaper clipping in scrapbook, Will Rogers State Historical Park, Pacific Palisades, CA.

45 *Our Will Rogers*, 158, and *Rogers at the Follies*, 3, 19–20.

46 *Rogers at the Follies*, 230–231, 210, 214, 217–218, and *Story of His Life*, 137.

47 *Rogers at the Follies*, 231, and *Story of His Life*, 142.

48 Patricia Ziegfeld's reminiscences in *Rogers at the Follies*, 230–231, and "Will Rogers Tells One on Mr. Ziegfeld," *Los Angeles Examiner*, Oct. 25, 1931.

49 Eddie Cantor and David Freedman, *Ziegfeld: The Great Glorifier* (New York, 1934), 163, 166, and *Daily Telegrams*, 3: 189.

CHAPTER FIVE

1 *Papers*, 4: 135–137.

2 *Autobiography*, 59; *Papers*, 4: 134; *Story of His Life*, 143; and *Rogers in Hollywood*, 2.

3 *Papers*, 4: 151–153, and *Story of His Life*, 143–144.

4 *Papers*, 4: 176–178.

5 See Lary May, *Screening Out the Past: The Birth of Mass Culture and the Motion Picture Industry* (Chicago: University of Chicago Press, 1983 [1980]), for a brilliant analysis of Hollywood's emergence and its impact on American culture. A comprehensive and detailed history of silent movies appears in Richard Koszarski, *An Evening's Entertainment: The Age of the Silent Feature Picture, 1915–1928* (Berkekey: University of California Press, 1994). For an engaging and insightful analysis of Hollywood stardom, see Ty Burr, *Gods Like Us: On Movie Stardom and Modern Fame* (New York: Anchor Books, 2012).

6 "A Democratic Art," *The Nation*, August 28, 1913.

7 On Goldwyn's life, see A. Scott Berg, *Goldwyn: A Biography* (New York: Alfred A. Knopf, 1989). The quote is from page 84.

8 *Papers*, 4: 186–187.

9 No copies of the *Laughing Bill Hyde* film are known to exist, but a number of promotional photos and a musical score listing scenes and titles have survived. So, too, has Rex Beach's original short story. See discussions and descriptions of the film in *Rogers in Hollywood*, 3–5, and Amy M. Ware, *The Cherokee Kid: Will Rogers, Tribal Identity, and the Making of an American Icon* (Lawrence: University Press of Kansas, 2015), 101–107.

10 Ben Yagoda has termed it "rube melodrama" in his *WR Biography*, 165. "Rustic" seems less harsh than "rube."

11 *Weekly Articles*, 4: 75; *Rogers in Hollywood*, 20; *Papers*, 4: 189.

12 *Rogers in Hollywood*, 20–21, and Clarence Badger's "Reminiscences" in this same book, 11–12.

13 *Papers*, 4: 188–189, and *Weekly Articles*, 4: 75.

14 *Rogers in Hollywood*, 21.

15 *Story of His Life*, 145; *Rogers in Hollywood*, 36; and *Papers*, 4: 190–194.

16 The silent films discussed in this chapter are held at the WRM, while brief synopses of them can be found in *Will Rogers in Hollywood.*

17 *Rogers in Hollywood*, 35.

18 Review of *The Strange Boarder* in *New York Morning Telegraph*, April 25, 1920; reviews in *Photoplay*, Aug. 1920 and *Houston Chronicle*, January 6, 1920, quoted in *Rogers in Hollywood*, 27, 20; and *New York Times*, August 25, 1923.

19 *New York Times*, September 1918 quoted in Ralph M. Ketchum, *Will Rogers: His Life and Times* (New York: American Heritage Publishing Co., 1973), 165; *Motion Picture News*, 1920 and *Dramatic Mirror*, February 7, 1920 quoted in *Rogers in Hollywood*, 25, 23; and review of *Almost a Husband* in *Motion Picture News*, October 25, 1919.

20 Reminiscences of Charles W. Dwyer in William Howard Payne and Jake G. Lyons, eds., *Folks Say*, 69–70; *Rogers in Hollywood*, 7, 8, 12, 28; and *Story of His Life*, 146.

21 *Story of His Life*, 146; *Weekly Articles*, 2: 232; and *Rogers in Hollywood*, 40.

22 *Rogers in Hollywood*, 6, and *Autobiography of Rogers*, 64–66.

23 *Papers*, 4: 159–160, 162–166, and *Rogers in Hollywood*, 43–44.

24 *Story of His Life*, 144, 147.

25 *Ibid.*, 147–149.

26 *Papers*, 4: 185, and Arthur Mayer, *Merely Colossal* (New York: Simon and Schuster, 1953), 35.

27 *Papers*, 4: 215–216, and Berg, *Goldwyn*, 91–92, 95–96, 98–103.

28 *Papers* 4: 221.

29 *Story of His Life*, 149–150; *Evening's Entertainment*, 77–80; and *Papers*, 4: 219–220.

30 *Papers*, 4: 227–228, and *Rogers in Hollywood*, 46–50.

31 *Story of His Life*, 150, and *Papers*, 4: 220.

32 *Story of His Life*, 151.

33 Koszarski, *An Evening's Entertainment*, 210, 246, and *Rogers in Hollywood*, 74–75.

34 *Rogers in Hollywood*, 75–76.

35 Hal Roach interviews with film historian Richard W. Bann, shared with the author; Hal Roach ad for Will Rogers films, in the collections of Richard W. Bann; and *Weekly Articles*, 1: 84–85.

36 Roach interviews with Bann; *Rogers in Hollywood*, 52–53; and *Story of His Life*, 157–158.

37 *Papers*, 4: 19–22, and *Rogers in Hollywood*, 54, 59–60, 62–64, 65. (The WRM has copies of the films for Hal Roach discussed in this section.)

38 *Rogers in Hollywood*, 55–57; *The Cherokee Kid*, 113–117; and *New York Times*, January 24, 1924.

39 *Rogers in Hollywood*, 64–65, 67–68.

40 *Ibid.*, 58, 69.

41 Roach interviews with Bann, and *Rogers in Hollywood*, 56.

42 *Rogers in Hollywood*, 77–81.

43 Will Rogers, *Letters of a Self-Made Diplomat to His President* (Stillwater: Oklahoma State University Press, 1977 [1926]), 29, 41, 55, 72–73, 82, 100; and *WR Biography*, 228–229.

44 *Letters of a Self-Made Diplomat*, 113.

45 *Papers*, 4: 407, 419, 489, and *Rogers in Hollywood*, 72.

46 *Papers*, 4: 407, 418–419, 430–431, 442, 488–490.

47 *Papers*, 4: 488–490. The complete list of the travelogue films: *With Will Rogers in Dublin* (1927), *With Will Rogers in Paris* (1927), *Hiking Through Holland with Will Rogers* (1927), *Roaming the Emerald Isle with Will Rogers* (1927), *Through Switzerland and Bavaria with Will Rogers* (1927), *With Will Rogers in London* (1927), *Hunting for Germans in Berlin with Will Rogers* (1927), *Prowling Around France with Will Rogers* (1927), *Winging Round Europe with Will Rogers* (1927), *Exploring England with Will Rogers* (1927), *Reeling Down the Rhine with Will Rogers* (1927), *Over the Bounding Blue with Will Rogers* (1928).

48 *Weekly Articles*, 1: 56.

49 Roach interviews with Bann.

CHAPTER SIX

1 *Daily Telegrams*, 3: 45.

2 See Warren Susman, *Culture as History: The Transformation of American Society in the Twentieth Century* (New York: Pantheon, 1984), especially the Introduction, xix–xxx, and Chapter 13, "Culture and Communication," 252–270.

3 *Papers*, 4: 517.

4 *Ibid.*, 4: 388–389.

5 See *Elmira Advertiser*'s long account of this talk, October 2, 1925 in *Papers*, 4: 389–393, and *Weekly Articles*, 2: 95.

6 See Angela G. Ray, *The Lyceum and Public Culture in the Nineteenth-Century United States* (Lansing: Michigan State University Press, 2005), and Roger E. Barrows, *The Traveling Chautauqua: Caravans of Culture in Early 20th Century America* (Jefferson, NC: McFarland and Company, 2019).

7 *Papers*, 4: 377–380, 25–28.

8 *Weekly Articles*, 2: 109–110.

9 *Papers*, 4: 407–410, and *Weekly Articles*, 2: 188–190.

10 *Our Will Rogers*, 194, 197.

11 *Ibid.*, 191–192.

12 *Ibid.*, 196; *Papers*, 4: 340; and *Story of His Life*, 186–187.

13 *Story of His Life*, 186, and *Our Will Rogers*, 195.

14 *Papers*, 4: 533–535, 538, 553, 556, 559, 560, 563, 569, and "Lecture Routine, Season 1925–1926," typed manuscript, WRM.

15 *Papers*, 4: 316–317, 338, 340–341, and *Story of His Life*, 181, 183.

16 *Weekly Articles*, 2: 90–91, and *Story of His Life*, 183.

17 See Tom Lewis, *Empire of the Air: The Men Who Made Radio* (New York: Harper Collins, 1991), and *Papers*, 4: 466.

18 *Papers*, 4: 385–387.

19 *Ibid.*, 4: 464–466.

20 *Papers*, 4: 450, 518–523, 549, and *Weekly Articles*, 3: 125–127, 280.

21 *Weekly Articles*, 1: 230, 2: 30–31, and 3: 127.

22 *Story of His Life*, 181–182, and *Weekly Articles*, 3: 127.

23 *Papers*, 4: 273, 292–294.

24 *Ibid.*, 4: 338, 353–354, 368–369.

25 See Christopher P. Wilson, "The Rhetoric of Consumption: Mass-Market Magazines and the Demise of the Gentle Reader, 1880–1920," in Richard Wightman Fox and T. J. Jackson Lears, eds., *The Culture of Consumption: Critical Essays in American History, 1880–1980* (New York: Pantheon, 1983), 39–64.

26 *Papers*, 4: 254–257, 283–285, 291–292. Rogers' 1928 articles are assembled in Steven K. Gragert, ed., *"He Chews to Run": Will Rogers' Life Magazine Articles, 1928* (Stillwater: Oklahoma State University Press, 1982).

27 *Papers*, 4: 485.

28 *Ibid.*, 4: 339, 404–405, 419, 426–429, 447, 449, 458, 504, 515.

29 *Ibid.*, 4: 271–272, 277, and *Our Will Rogers*, 173–174, 177, 180.

30 *Papers*, 4: 248–252, 277.

31 *Weekly Articles*, 1: 1, 4, 5.

32 *Papers*, 4: 439, 273, and *Weekly Articles*, 1: xiii.

33 *Weekly Articles*, 1: 38–39.

34 McNitt quoted in *WR Biography*, 197; *Story of His Life*, 154; and *Weekly* Articles, 1: xiii.

35 *Weekly Articles*, 1: 165–166, 150, 261–262, and 2: 16–17, 10.

36 *Ibid.*, 1: 336–340.

37 *Ibid.*, 1: 45–47.

38 *Ibid.*, 1: 72–73, 3: 243, 2: 97, and Rogers quoted in Ray Robinson, *American Original: A Life of Will Rogers* (New York: Oxford University Press, 1996), 160.

39 *Weekly Articles*, 1: 30–31, 286–289.

40 Will Rogers, "The Grand Champion," *American Magazine*, December 1929 reprinted in Steven K. Gragert, ed., *Will Rogers: 'How To Be Funny' and Other Writings* (Stillwater, OK: Oklahoma State University Press, 1983), 121–122.

41 *Daily Telegrams*, 1: xiii, 1, and *Our Will Rogers*, 180–181.

42 *Our Will Rogers*, 182–183.

43 *Ibid.*, 183–184, 194–195.

44 *Daily Telegrams*, 1: 67, 30.

45 *Ibid.*, 1: 44, 90, 283.

46 *Ibid.*, 1: 176, 288, 290.

47 *Ibid.*, 1: 146, 100–101.

48 *Our Will Rogers*, 358.

49 "Educators and Leaders of Thought Might Take the Tip," *San Francisco Chronicle*, March 12, 1927; Rollin Lynde Hart, "Roping Will Rogers," *Everybody's* (June 1925), 34; Robert O. Scallan, "Ride 'Im, Author!" *Collier's* (December 13, 1924); and David Karsner, "A Writer Who Knows the Ropes," *Tulsa Daily World*, magazine section (November 27, 1927), 7.

50 *Papers*, 4: 489.

CHAPTER SEVEN

1 Will Rogers, *The Illiterate Digest* (Joseph A. Stout, Jr., editor; Stillwater: Oklahoma State University Press, 1974 [1924]), 5–7.

2 See WR's quotes from his travels abroad as a young man in Chapter 2, and *Weekly Articles*, 2: 209, 249.

3 Richard Hofstadter, *The Age of Reform: From Bryan to FDR* (New York: Alfred A. Knopf, 1959), 4–5, 11–12.

4 *Weekly Articles*, 2: 95 and 3: 172–174.

5 *Ibid.*, 1: 277, 154, 283 and 2: 59, 134–135.

6 *Ibid.*, 1: 270, 313–314.

7 *Ibid.*, 1: 346, 179 and 3: 104.

8 *Ibid.*, 2: 310 and 3: 26, 207–208.

9 *Ibid.*, 2: 311 and 3: 39, 162.

10 *Ibid.*, 3: 159–160; 1: 325–326, 136; and 2: 15.

11 *Ibid.*, 2: 274–275.

12 *Ibid.*, 2: 252, and *Radio Broadcasts*, 121.

13 *Weekly Articles*, 2: 107 and 1: 144.

14 *Ibid.*, 4: 127–129.

15 *Ibid.*, 1: 161–162.

16 *Daily Telegrams*, 1: 251–252, 150, and *Weekly Articles*, 1: 177.

17 *Weekly Articles*, 4: 101 and 3: 164–165.

18 *Ibid.*, 2: 173–174, 269.

19 *Daily Telegrams*, 1: 144–145, and *Weekly Articles*, 3: 94–97.

20 *Weekly Articles*, 1: 177, and 2: 179.

21 *Ibid.*, 1: 367–370.

22 *Political Life*, 290–291.

23 On Bryan, see Michael Kazin, *A Godly Hero: A Life of William Jennings Bryan* (New York: Alfred A. Knopf, 2006), and Jackson Lears, *Rebirth of a Nation: The Making of Modern America, 1877–1920* (New York: Harper, 2009), 174–177, 186–189, 208–209, 212, 216, 304–314, 322–326.

24 *A Political Life*, 11; *Weekly Articles*, 1: 123; and *Papers*, 1: 541 and 4: 202.

25 *Weekly Articles*, 1: 185, 265 and *Papers*, 4: 345–346.

26 *Weekly Articles*, 1: 272, 13, and *Papers*, 4: 266.

27 *Weekly Articles* 1: 76, 93.

28 *Ibid.*, 1: 123, and 2: 55–57.

29 *Ibid.*, 1: 263–265, and Stout, Joseph A., ed., *Convention Articles of Will Rogers* (Stillwater: Oklahoma State University Press, 1976), 36–38.

30 *Weekly Articles*, 2: 63–66.

31 *Daily Telegrams*, 1: 90, 91, and *Weekly Articles*, 3: 35.

32 *Daily Telegrams*, 1: 91–92, 130, and *Weekly Articles*, 3: 35, 37.

33 *Weekly Articles*, 3: 115, 85; *Daily Telegrams*, 1: 129; and *Our Will Rogers*, 221–222.

34 *Our Will Rogers*, 222–223, and *Daily Telegrams*, 3: 137–138.

35 *Weekly Articles*, 3: 35, 87, 218–219.

36 *Ibid.*, 4: 43–44.

37 *Daily Telegrams*, 1: 130, and *Weekly Articles*, 3: 36, 89, 159.

38 *Weekly Articles*, 4: 44–45.

39 WR, "The Grand Champion," *American Magazine* (December 1929) reprinted in Gragert, Steven K., ed., *"How to Be Funny" and Other Writings* (Stillwater: Oklahoma State University Press, 1983), 116–124, and *Weekly Articles*, 2: 91.

40 *Weekly Articles*, 2: 75 and 3: 122–123.

41 *Papers*, 4: 304–305; *Weekly Articles*, 1: 269–270; and Steven Watts, *The People's Tycoon: Henry Ford and the American Century* (New York: Knopf, 2005), 341, 396.

42 "The Grand Champion" in *How to Be Funny*, 117, 119, and *Weekly Articles*, 2: 98–100, 175.

43 *Weekly Articles*, 3: 243, 90, 107, and "The Grand Champion" in *How to Be Funny*, 123. On Ford's airplane projects, see Timothy J. O'Callaghan, *The Aviation Legacy of Henry & Edsel Ford* (Ann Arbor, MI: Proctor Publications, 2000).

44 *Weekly Articles*, 3: 106, 104, 107, and 4: 173–174, and *Radio Broadcast*, June 1930.

45 *Weekly Articles*, 2: 100, 102, and "The Grand Champion" in *How to Be Funny*, 121–122.

46 *Weekly Articles*, 2: 77, and 1: 44.

47 L. H. Robbins, "Portrait of an American Philosopher," *New York Times Magazine* (Nov. 3, 1935).

48 Elsie Janis, "What I Know About Will Rogers," *Liberty* (March 11, 1933), 34; *What's On the Air* (May 1930), 10; and "Nominating Will Rogers," *Motion Picture Magazine* (Spring 1931), 89–90.

49 John Crawford, "Will Rogers Knows More Than He Pretends," *New York Times* (December 14, 1924); "Will Rogers, Cowboy Comedian," *Current Opinion* (January 1923), 103; Charles W. Lobdell, "Will Rogers: The World Laughs With Him," *Liberty* (November 29, 1924), 19, 20; Charles Collins, "Will Rogers, the Cowboy Humorist: His Life Story and How He Became Idol of American Public," *Chicago Daily Tribune* (August 18, 1935); and "Will Rogers—National Spokesman," *Dearborn Independent* (February 17, 1923), editorial page.

50 "Tom Mix and Will Rogers," *College Humor* (November 1928), 46; Archibald C. Coolidge, "A Self-Appointed Diplomat," *Saturday Review of Literature* (December 26, 1926), 405; "The World Laughs With Him," 21; O. O. McIntyre, "Our Will," *Cosmopolitan* (October, 1931), 82–83; "Will Rogers Rings the Bell," *Buffalo Evening Times* (February 15, 1925); and John Carter, "Will Rogers Takes His Lariat to Europe," *New York Times* (October 31, 1926).

51 Robert O. Scallan, "Ride 'Im, Author!" *Collier's* (December 13, 1924), 48, 8; Sylvia B. Golden, "Will Rogers: The Business Man," *Forbes* (February 15, 1928); and Rollin Lynde Hart, "Roping Will Rogers," *Everybody's Magazine* (June, 1925), 166, 168.

52 J. Hector St. John de Crevecoeur, *Letters from an American Farmer* (New York, 1981 [1782]), Letter III, 67–71; "Will Rogers Literary Round-Up," *Current Opinion* (Jan. 1, 1925), 40; "Prairie Pantaloon," *Time* (July 19, 1926), 22; "The World Laughs With Him," 21; and "Will Rogers in London," *Literary Digest* (August 28, 1926), 22–23.

53 Alexis de Tocqueville, *Democracy in America* (Chicago, 2000 [1835]), 489–492; "Ride 'Im, Author!", 48; "Prairie Pantaloon," *Time* (July 19, 1926), 22; and *New York Times*, June 2 and 28, 1927.

54 "Our Will," 82–83, and W. E. Woodward, "Humor Dead or Alive," *Nation* (February 11, 1925), 160.

55 "Ride 'Im, Author!", 8; "Will Rogers Literary Round-Up," 40; George Mathew Adams, "Today's Talk: Will Rogers," newspaper column, no citation and undated, probably 1935, Clipping Scrapbook No. 1, WRM; Helen Black, "Kings as Good as Common Folk to Cowboy Humorist Who Says Funny Things Without Rancor," Colorado newspaper clipping in Scrapbook No. 2, undated but probably 1922, WRM; and Charles Collins, "Will Rogers, the Cowboy Humorist: His Life Story and How He Became Idol of American Public," *Chicago Daily Tribune* (August 18, 1935).

56 "Educators and Leaders of Thought Might Take the Tip," *San Francisco Chronicle* (March 12, 1927).

57 Clarence Budington Kelland, Reminiscence in *Folks*, 198, and *New York Sun*, April 5, 1935, quoted as an epigraph in Ben Yagoda, *WR Biography*, xi.

CHAPTER EIGHT

1 Mencken quoted in Stout, Joseph A., ed., *Convention Articles of Will Rogers* (Stillwater, OK: Oklahoma State University Press, 1976), 93–94, based on a June 11, 1928, story in the St. Louis *Post-Dispatch*.

2 *New York Times*, May 29, 1924; *Papers*, 4: 34–36; *WA*, 3: 1–2; and Jerome Beatty, "Betty Holds the Reins," *American Magazine* (October 1930), 61.

3 *Weekly Articles*, 1: 5, and *Daily Telegrams*, 1: 34.

4 *Weekly Articles*, 3: 169, 177.

5 Betty, 204; *Papers*, 4: 528–529; *Weekly Articles*, 2: 249–251; and *Daily Telegrams*, 1: 175.

6 *Weekly Articles*, 1: 75, 326–327, 2: 236, and *Political Life*, 151–152, 159–161.

7 *Weekly Articles*, 2: 22–25, and 3: 250; *Daily Telegrams*, 1: 170; and *More Letters of a Self-Made Diplomat*, 10–16, from *Saturday Evening Post*, Jan. 8, 1927.

8 *Papers*, 4: 239–242.

9 *Weekly Articles*, 1: 5–6, 78, 244–245, and 3: 220.

10 *Ibid.*, 3: 220–221, and 1: 148, 150.

11 *Ibid.*, 1: 306, 308.

12 *Story of His Life*, 166–168; *WR Biography*, 189–190; and *Weekly Articles*, 1: 62, 111–112.

13 *Papers*, 4: 518–523, 551, and *Daily Telegrams*, 1: 170.

14 Adolph Ochs, Letter of Introduction for WR on European trip, written on *New York Times* letterhead and dated April 28, 1926, WRM; see also *Papers*, 4: 421.

15 *Weekly Articles*, 2: 8.

16 *Political Life*, 78; and *Weekly Articles*, 3: 93, 4: 222–223, and 1: 368.

17 *Weekly Articles*, 2: 248–249, and Will Rogers, *There's Not a Bathing Suit in Russia & Other Bare Facts* (Stillwater: Oklahoma State University Press, 1973 [1927]), 51, 58, 84–85.

18 *Bathing Suit*, 87, 54, 73, 81.

19 *Daily Telegrams*, 2: 55–56, and *Letters of a Self-Made Diplomat*, 58, 69, 63, 68.

20 *Letters of a Self-Made Diplomat*, 64, 66.

21 *Weekly Articles*, 3: 252, 226–227, 179.

22 *Ibid.*, 2: 137, 232, 58, 82–83, and 1: 20.

23 *Ibid.*, 1: 63–64, and *Political Life*, 78.

24 *Weekly Articles*, 1: 78, 40, 313–314, and *Daily Telegrams*, 1: 214.

25 *Daily Telegrams*, 1: 301; Donald Day, in *Autobiography*, 70, claims this speech was delivered to the International Bankers Association in 1922 – Will Rogers then recorded it for Victor Records on May 31, 1923, the transcript of which is in *Papers*, 4: 305–307, where the editors suggest he may have delivered the talk to the American Bankers Association convention in October 1922; and *Weekly Articles*, 1: 322.

26 *Daily Telegrams*, 1: 251–252, 260; *Weekly Articles*, 3: 16; *More Letters of Self-Made Diplomat*, 71; and *Daily Telegrams*, 2: 160.

27 *Weekly Articles*, 2: 310–311, 79, and 3: 162, 26.

28 *Ibid.*, 3: 219, 155–156, 146–147.

29 *Ibid.*, 3: 211–212, 178, 82, 220.

30 See Chapter 2 of this book for his letters home; *Papers*, 3: 118–119; and *Weekly Articles*, 3: 248, and 2: 116–117.

31 *Weekly Articles*, 2: 34, and 3: 26.

32 *Daily Telegrams*, 1: 58; *Convention Articles*, 65; and *New York Evening Telegraph*, November 10, 1928, quoted in *Political Life*, 138.

33 *Weekly Articles*, 2: 56–57; *Papers*, 4: 275–276; "Transcript of Lecture Performance," April 16, 1928, in *Papers*, 4: 560; and Rogers quoted in *Political Life*, 140.

34 *Weekly Articles*, 4: 135–137, and 2: 33, 73–74.

35 *Ibid.*, 4: 205, 3: 179–180, 219, and 1: 181–182.

36 Richard Hofstadter, *The Age of Reform: From Bryan to FDR* (New York: Alfred A. Knopf, 1959), 271.

37 *Weekly Articles*, 2: 48, 164–165, 247, and *Bathing Suit*, xv.

38 *Weekly Articles*, 1: 97, 330, 360, and *Letters of a Self-Made Diplomat*, 114.

39 *Weekly Articles*, 3: 201–203, 219, 2: 179, and 1: 185.

40 W. E. Woodward, "Humor Dead or Alive," *Nation* (February 11, 1925), 160; "Will Rogers Rings the Bell," *Buffalo Evening Times*, February 15, 1925; *New York Times* quoted in "Will Rogers, Cowboy Comedian," *Current Opinion* (January 1923), 104; L. H. Robbins, "Portrait of an American Philosopher," *New York Times Magazine* (November 3, 1935), 4; and John Carter, "Will Rogers Takes His Lariat to Europe," *New York Times*, October 31, 1926.

41 *Weekly Articles*, 6: 2.

42 *Ibid.*, 2: 1, and 1: 307.

43 "Will Rogers – Modern Abe Lincoln," unattributed newspaper clipping, Scrapbook 18, WRM; Will Rogers to James Davenport, WRM; and *Daily Telegrams*, 1: 177.

44 *Papers*, 4: 469, 471–473. See an account of the episode in *Political Life*, 106–107.

45 *Daily Telegrams*, 1: 39, 43, 58, 64, 118–119, 120.

46 *Weekly Articles*, 3: 68, 70–72.

47 Gragert, Steven K., ed., *"He Chews to Run": Will Rogers' Life Magazine Articles, 1928* (Stillwater: Oklahoma State University Press, 1982), 1–3, 4–6, 7–9.

48 *Ibid.*, 28.

49 *Ibid.*, 34, 39, 77, 52.

50 *Ibid.*, 54–55, 73, 62, 42.

51 *Ibid.*, 10–11, 26, 27, 69.

52 Dorothy Van Doren, "Will Rogers, the Bunkless Candidate," *The Nation* (October 3, 1928), 314–315.

53 *Chews to Run*, 106, 113.

54 *Story of His Life*, 171, and *Weekly Articles*, 1: 318.

55 "Transcript of Lecture Performance," April 16, 1928, in *Papers*, 4: 560.

56 *Weekly Articles*, 2: 14, and 1: 111–112 and "Will Rogers Miffed as Harding Refuses to See His Act," United News Clipping, February 14, 1922, scrapbook at WRM.

57 *Weekly Articles*, 4: 49–50, and 1: 111; and "Transcript of Lecture Performance," April 16, 1928, in *Papers*, 4: 560.

58 *Weekly Articles*, 1: 314–315.

59 *Ibid.*, 1: 319, and W. E. Woodward, "Humor Dead or Alive," *Nation* (February 11, 1925), 160.

CHAPTER NINE

1 Robert Darnton, *The Great Cat Massacre And Other Episodes in French Cultural History* (New York: Vintage Books, 1985), 75–104.

2 E. B. White and Katharine S. White, "The Preaching Humorist," *Saturday Review of Literature* (October 18, 1941), 16, and Shane Snow, "A Quest to Understand What Makes Things Funny," *New Yorker* (April 1, 2014).

3 William Faulkner, "Foreword," *Sherwood Anderson and Other Famous Creoles* (New Orleans: The Pelican Bookshop, 1926), no pagination, and Constance Rourke, *American Humor: A Study of the National Character* (New York: New York Review Books, 2004 [1931]). For a valuable survey of the scholarship on American humor, see M. Thomas Inge, "'One Priceless Universal Trait': American Humor," *American Studies International* (April, 1987), 28–44.

4 W. E. Woodward, "Humor Dead or Alive," *Nation* (February 11, 1925), 160; Rollin Lynde Hartt, "Roping Will Rogers," *Everybody's* (June 1925), 168; D. Jay Culver, "The Humor of Will Rogers," *Dearborn Independent* (March 28, 1925), 5; "Will Rogers' Literary Round-Up," *Current Opinion* (January 1, 1925), 57; John Crawford, "Will Rogers Knows More Than He Pretends," *New York Times* (December 14, 1924), BR2; and David Karsner, "A Writer Who Knows the Ropes," *Tulsa Daily World* (November 27, 1927), 7, 15.

5 *Weekly Articles*, 2: 108, 1: 25; and WR, "How to Be Funny," in Gragert, Steven K., ed., *"How to Be Funny" and Other Writings of Will Rogers* (Stillwater: Oklahoma State University Press, 1983), 3–4.

6 *Weekly Articles*, 1: 244; *Our Will Rogers*, 267; Will Rogers, "The Extemporaneous Line," in *How to Be Funny*, 3–4; and "The Cowboy Philosopher," *New Republic* (August 25, 1935), 62.

7 George Martin, "The Wit of Will Rogers," *American Magazine* (November 1919), 34–35, 106–113.

8 Edgar C. Wheeler, "The Science of Laughter: An Interview with Will Rogers," *Popular Science* (May 1923), 31.

9 "Roping Will Rogers," 166, and "The Humor of Will Rogers," 5.

10 *Story of His Life*, 186, and "The Humor of Will Rogers," 15.

11 *Weekly Articles*, 2: 141–144.

12 *Ibid.*, 2: 159.

13 *Ibid.*, 2: 299–300.

14 *Ibid.*, 3: 254–257.

15 *Ibid.*, 1: 97–101.

16 L. H. Robbins, "American Humorists," *New York Times* (September 8, 1935), 8, and "Humor Dead or Alive," 160.

17 *American Humor*, 86, 232, and "American Humorists," 8.

18 Walter Blair, *Horse Sense in American Humor: From Benjamin Franklin to Ogden Nash* (Chicago: University of Chicago Press, 1942), v–ix, and "Homespun Philosophers," *Saturday Review of Literature* (August 31, 1935), 8.

19 See *Horse Sense in American Humor* for insightful analysis of these figures while "Homespun Philosophers" and "American Humorists," offer additional useful discussions.

20 David S. Reynolds, *Abe: Abraham Lincoln in His Time* (New York: Penguin Press, 2020), 173, 453.

21 *Horse Sense in American Humor*, 57, 175–177, 209–211, 250.

22 "American Humorists," 14; "Homespun Philosophers," 8; and Henry F. Pringle, "King Babbitt's Court Jester," *Outlook and Independent* (April 8, 1931), 497.

23 *Horse Sense in American Humor*, 266, 268.

24 See, for example, "King Babbitt's Court Jester," 496–498, and *Horse Sense in American Humor*, 270–271.

25 *Papers*, 4: 388, 490, 396–398; E. P. Alworth, *The Humor of Will Rogers* (Ph.D. Dissertation, University of Missouri Department of English, 1958) 25, based on interview with WR's sons, Will Rogers, Jr. on April 12, 1957 and James Rogers, June 6, 1957; and WR telegram to *Hannibal Courier*, February 25, 1935 quoted in *Autobiography*, 360.

26 "A Writer Who Knows the Ropes," 7.

27 *Ibid.*; *Horse Sense in American Humor*, 273; and Frederick Van de Water, "Books and So Forth," *New York Herald Tribune* (January 25, 1924).

28 Alworth, *Humor of Will Rogers*, 133, makes a similar observation.

29 Walter Blair and Hamlin Hill, *America's Humor: From Poor Richard to Doonesbury* (New York: Oxford University Press, 1980), vii, 155, 254–255, 368–369, 417–421.

30 Clive James, *The Crystal Bucket: Television Criticism From the Observer, 1976–1979* (Jonathan Cape: London, 1981), 168.

31 "A Writer Who Knows the Ropes," 7.

32 "Humor Dead or Alive," 160, and Charles W. Lobdell, "Will Rogers: The World Laughs With Him," *Liberty* (November 29, 1924), 19.

33 Will Rogers, *Letters of a Self-Made Diplomat to His President* (Stillwater: Oklahoma State University Press, 1977 [1926]), 11–13.

34 Joseph A. Stout, Jr., ed., *Rogers-isms: The Cowboy Philosopher on Prohibition* (Stillwater, OK: Oklahoma State University Press, 1975 [1919]), 11, and *Weekly Articles*, 2: 191–193.

35 *Weekly Articles*, 2: 51; 1: 330; *Daily Telegrams*, 2: 193–194; and *Letters of Self-Made Diplomat*, 109.

36 "The World Laughs With Him," 19–21.

CHAPTER TEN

1 *Story of His Life*, 210–213; Will Rogers, Jr., "Preface" to Will Rogers, *Ether and Me, or Just Relax* (Stillwater: Oklahoma State University Press, 1973 [1929]), xix; and *Papers*, 4: 499–500.

2 *Weekly Articles*, 3: 43–48; *Daily Telegrams*, 1: 100–104; and *Ether and Me*, 2, 8–9, 21–22, 28–30.

3 *WA*, 3: 45–46, and *Daily Telegrams*, 1: 101.

4 Elmer T. Peterson, "Will Rogers in His Garden," *Better Homes and Gardens* (June, 1928), 110, and Carol Bird, "Will Rogers is Funny at Home – His Wife Says So!" (November 29, 1926) unattributed newspaper clipping, Scrapbook at WRM.

5 *Papers*, 3: 218, 431, 432.

6 Mayme Ober Peak, "Mrs. Rogers and Will, and 'The House That Jokes Built,'" *Kansas City Star Magazine* (August 26, 1926), 18, and *Story of His Life*, 147–149.

7 *Papers*, 3: 432–433; *Story of His Life*, 229; Jerome Beatty, "Betty Holds the Reins," *American Magazine* (October 1930), 61; and Dorothy C. Reid, "In Miniature – Mrs. Will Rogers," *McCall's* (February 1929), 8.

8 *Story of His Life*, 267–268, 269–271, and Richard M. Ketchum, *Will Rogers: His Life and Times* (New York: McGraw–Hill, 1973), 301–304.

9 *Papers*, 3: 433; *Story of His Life*, 269; and "Betty Holds the Reins," 61.

10 WR to Jim Rogers, December 30, 1928, WRM, and *Story of His Life*, 255, 269.

11 *Papers*, 4: 392, 400.

12 "Betty Holds the Reins," 62; "In Miniature – Mrs. Will Rogers," 8; and "Will Rogers is Funny at Home."

13 "In Miniature – Mrs. Will Rogers," 66, and "Betty Holds the Reins," 114.

14 "Will Rogers Is Funny at Home," and "Betty Holds the Reins," 62.

15 "In Miniature – Mrs. Will Rogers," 66; "Betty Holds the Reins," 61; "The House That Jokes Built," 8.

16 *Story of His Life*, 262–263, and *New York Sun*, September 10, 1917, quoted in *WR Biography*, 148–149.

17 "Will Rogers in His Garden," 108–109, and "In Miniature – Mrs. Will Rogers," 8, 66.

18 "Will Rogers in His Garden," 108–109; *Story of His Life*, 148, 262–263; and Dorothy C. Reid, "Mrs. Will Rogers Talks About Her Husband," *Home Magazine* (September, 1930) 128.

19 "Betty Holds the Reins," 114; Jim Rogers Interview, July 30, 1985, Sterling Papers, WRM; and "Mrs. Will Rogers Talks About Her Husband," 128.

20 For brief biographies of the Rogers children, see *Papers*, 3: 438–447, 408–411, 431–438. For Bill's encounter with Durant, see *Rogers: Life and Times*, 309.

21 "The House That Jokes Built," 8, and "Betty Holds the Reins," 114.

22 *Rogers Life and Times*, 307–308; "Will Rogers Is Funny at Home" and "Interview with Joel McCrea," in Bryan B. Sterling, ed., *The Will Rogers Scrapbook* (New York: Grosset & Dunlap, 1976), 118.

23 "Will Rogers is Funny at Home," and "Mrs. Will Rogers Talks About Her Husband," 23.

24 *WA*, 6: 26–27, and *Rogers: Life and Times*, 308.

25 *Papers*, 4: 115–116, 5: 86, and Neal Gabler, *Walt Disney: The Triumph of the American Imagination* (New York: Knopf, 2006), 205.

26 Edward Churchill, "The Will Rogers Nobody Knows: As Revealed by Guinn (Big Boy) Williams," *Hollywood* (May 1935), 28–29, 68–69.

27 *Story of His Life*, 295–297, and *WA*, 1: 218–221.

28 *WA*, 1: 221; *Story of His Life*, 295; and *Rogers: Life and Times*, 303–304.

29 *WR Biography*, 174, and *Papers*, 4: 216–217. On Lummis, see Mark Thompson, *American Character: The Curious Life of Charles Fletcher Lummis and the Rediscovery of the Southwest* (New York: Arcade Publishing, 2001).

30 *Papers*, 4: 399; *WR Biography*, 276; and *Papers*, 5: 206, 616. On Carter, see Brian A. Cervantez, *Amon Carter: A Lone Star Life* (Norman: University of Oklahoma Press, 2019).

31 *Papers*, 5: 266; O. O. McIntyre, "Our Will," *Cosmopolitan* (October 1931), 82; and O. O. McIntyre in William Howard Payne and Jake G. Lyons, eds., *Folks Say of Will Rogers: A Memorial Anecdotage* (New York: G. P. Putnam's Sons, 1936), 213–215.

32 *WA*, 5: 187, 207–210, and *Memorial Anecdotage*, 213–216.

33 *Papers*, 5: 266–267. On Cobb, see William E. Ellis, *Irvin S. Cobb: The Rise and Fall of An American Humorist* (Lexington: University Press of Kentucky, 2017).

34 *WR in Hollywood*, 34, 147–148; Ketchum, 259; *Radio Broadcasts*, 152–155, 71–72; and Irvin S. Cobb in *Memorial Anecdotage*, 77–84.

35 *Our Will Rogers*, 122–123, and Fred Stone, "The Will Rogers I Knew," 33, unattributed clipping, Scrapbook, WRM.

36 See *Papers*, 3: 451–457 for biography of Fred Stone.

37 *Story of His Life*, 112–114; "We Need More Fred Stones," in *Weekly Articles*, 1: 37; and "Interview with Dorothy Stone Collins" in *The Will Rogers Scrapbook*, 129.

38 *Story of His Life*, 112–114, 124–125, 230; *Papers*, 3: 453–454; *Our Will Rogers*, 134; and Fred Stone, "The Will Rogers I Knew," 80.

39 *Papers*, 3: 363–364; *Story of His Life*, 135, 229–231; *Our Will Rogers*, 238–240; "Interview with Dorothy Stone Collins," 132–133.

40 "The Will Rogers I Knew," 33; Fred Stone, *Memorial Anecdotage*, 50; "We Need More Fred Stones," *Weekly Articles*, 1: 33–38.

41 *Story of His Life*, 262, 255, and *Rogers Life and Times*, 305.

42 *Story of His Life*, 275, 255–261, and *Weekly Articles*, 6: 179–180.

43 *Story of His Life*, 158–162, 256–257; *Weekly Articles* 1: 222, 4: 200; and McIntyre, "Our Will," 83.

44 *Our Will*, 358–359, and *Weekly Articles*, 1: 223.

45 *Story of His Life*, 261, and *Weekly Articles*, 1: 297–299, 2: 297 and 6: 163–164, 198.

46 *Story of His Life*, 272–274, 261, and *Weekly Articles*, 4: 13, 179–182, 2: 138.

47 *Story of His Life*, 106, 173, 264.

48 *Our Will Rogers*, 184, 194; Joseph A. Stout, Jr., ed., *Convention Articles of Will Rogers* (Stillwater: Oklahoma State University Press, 1976), 105; and "Betty Holds the Reins," 114.

49 *Story of His Life*, 276–277; *Our Will Rogers*, 188, 230; *WA*, 5: 221; and "In Miniature – Mrs. Will Rogers," 8.

50 "Interview with Dorothy Stone Collins," 133; *Our Will Rogers*, 199; Homer Croy, "Will, As I Knew Him," *Successful Farming* (January 1936), 16; *Story of His Life*, 208–209, 263; "The Will Nobody Knows," 28–29, 68; and "The Will Rogers I Knew," 33.

51 "Mrs. Will Rogers Talks About Her Husband," 22; *Our Will Rogers*, 24, 52–53, 198; Ben Dixon MacNeil in *Folks Say*, 114–115, and "The Will Nobody Knows," 29.

52 *Claremore Weekly Press*, Feb. 20, 1930, and "Interview with Dorothy Stone Collins," 129, 131.

53 "The Will Nobody Knows," 68; "Betty Holds the Reins," 62; "Will Rogers in His Garden," 112; and Kirtley Baskette, "I'll Be at Doc Law's," *Photoplay* (January 1934), 31.

54 *Story of His Life*, 172–175; "Will Rogers Is Funny at Home"; and "Betty Holds the Reins," 113.

55 *Story of His Life*, 175–176, and *WA*, 3: 47–48.

56 *Our Will Rogers*, 228, 230; "The House That Jokes Built," 18; and "I'll Be at Doc Law's," 93.

57 *Our Will Rogers*, 231, 237.

58 *Story of His Life*, 152, 292–294.

59 *DT*, 3: 247; *WA*, 2: 132–135; and *Story of His Life*, 129–130.

60 *Our Will Rogers*, 191–192, 188, 230; *Story of His Life*, 100–101; Sylvia B. Golden, "Will Rogers: Business Man," *Forbes* (February 15, 1928); Homer Croy, "Will, As I Knew Him," *Successful Farming* (January 1936), 16.

61 "The Will Rogers I Knew," 80, letter and Jim Hopkins, "Oral History," WRM, cited in *WR Biography*, 242.

62 *Our Will Rogers*, 271, and "Will, As I Knew Him," 16.

63 *Our Will Rogers*, 327; "The Will Nobody Knows," 28; Larry Swindell, *Spencer Tracy* (New York: World Publishing, 1969), 148; *Walt Disney Triumph*, 251; and Ben Dixon MacNeill, "Reminiscences," in *Folks Say*, 118–119.

64 Richard M. Ketchum, *Will Rogers: His Life and Times* (New York: McGraw–Hill, 1973), 57, 306; and Jim Rogers Interview, July 30, 1985, Sterling Papers, WRM.

65 *Story of His Life*, 297–300; Jim Rogers Interview, July 30, 1985, in Sterling Papers, WRM; and *WA*, 5: 221.

66 *WA*, 5: 44–46.

67 "Betty Holds the Reins," 62, and *Our Will Rogers*, 238, 266.

68 Homer Croy, *Country Cured* (New York: Harper & Brothers, 1943), 224.

CHAPTER ELEVEN

1 On Cantor, see *Papers*, 3: 412–416.

2 Cantor in *Folks Say*, 56–57; *Weekly Articles*, 4: 83–85; and *Our Will Rogers*, 241.

3 For statistics on the impact of the Great Depression, see Robert Heilbroner, *The Economic Transformation of America: 1600 to the Present* (New York: Harcourt, Brace, Javonovich, 1977), 179, 185.
4 *Weekly Articles*, 4: 83–84, and *Daily Telegrams*, 4: 172–173, and 2: 89–90.
5 *Weekly Articles*, 2: 136–138; Will Rogers, *More Letters of a Self-Made Diplomat*, ed. Steven K. Gragert (Stillwater: Oklahoma State University Press, 1982), 71; *Daily Telegrams*, 2: 252.
6 *Weekly Articles*, 4: 87–88, and *Daily Telegrams*, 2: 89.
7 *Weekly Articles*, 4: 89–91.
8 *Weekly Articles*, 4: 214, and *Daily Telegrams*, 2: 240.
9 *Weekly Articles*, 4: 90–91, 162, and *Daily Telegrams*, 4: 2, 3.
10 *Weekly Articles*, 4: 127–128.
11 *Ibid.*, 4: 224–226, 214.
12 *Daily Telegrams*, 2: 183, 239, and *Weekly Articles*, 4: 178–179, 166–167.
13 *Weekly Articles*, 5: 82, and 4: 220–222.
14 *Ibid.*, 4: 223–224. See *Papers*, 5: 129, for figures on Rogers' income in 1930.
15 *Weekly Articles*, 3: 42, and *Papers*, 4: 502–503.
16 *Daily Telegrams*, 2: 101–102, and *Weekly Articles*, 4: 96.
17 *Daily Telegrams*, 3: 85, 64, and Joseph A. Stout, Jr., ed., *Convention Articles of Will Rogers* (Stillwater: Oklahoma State University Press, 1976), 119.
18 *Daily Telegrams*, 2: 274–275, 228, and *Weekly Articles*, 4: 224–225.
19 *Weekly Articles*, 4: 224–226, and *Daily Telegrams*, 3: 67, 173.
20 *Daily Telegrams*, 2: 258–259, and 2: 255.
21 *Radio Broadcasts of Will Rogers*, 65–67, and *Daily Telegrams*, 3: 88.
22 *Daily Telegrams*, 3: 162–163.
23 *Ibid.*, 2: 210, and 3: 194, 70.
24 *Ibid.*, 1: 143, and *Convention Articles*, 121, 124, 126, 127.
25 *Weekly Articles*, 4: 186, and 5: 154, 189, 204.
26 *Ibid.*, 4: 204, and *Political Life*, 212–213.
27 *Papers*, 5: 249, 257–258, 332, and *Political Life*, 214–215.
28 *Daily Telegrams*, 3: 46–47, and *Papers*, 5: 332.
29 *Convention Articles*, 129–132.
30 *Ibid.*, 141, 146–147.
31 *Papers*, 5: 342–345; *Convention Articles*, 133–134; and *Political Life*, 215–216.
32 *Papers*, 5: 353–355, and *Story of His Life*, 279.
33 *Convention Articles*, 137; *Daily Telegrams*, 3: 214; and *Papers*, 5: 365, 357.
34 *Daily Telegrams*, 3: 212, 230, 232, 233, 234.
35 *Ibid.*, 3: 235; *Weekly Articles*, 5: 205; and *Papers*, 5: 365.
36 *Papers*, 5: 367–369.
37 *Daily Telegrams*, 4: 1, and *Radio Broadcasts*, 73–77.
38 *Weekly Articles*, 6: 28, 30.
39 *Good Gulf Show* broadcast, May 28, 1933, transcript at WRM, summarized in Peter C. Rollins, *Will Rogers: A Bio-Bibliography* (Westport, CT: Greenwood Press, 1984), 212; *Weekly Articles*, 6: 96–97; and *Daily Telegrams*, 4: 205.

40 *Daily Telegrams*, 4: 4, 260, and *Weekly Articles*, 6: 214.

41 *Daily Telegrams*, 4: 6, 14.

42 *Weekly Articles*, 6: 6, 188.

43 Daily Telegrams, 4: 27, 31, and *Weekly Articles*, 6: 20, 127, 85.

44 *Rogers Bio-Bibliography*, 209; *Political Life*, 234–237; and *Papers*, 5: 338, 398–402.

45 Radio broadcast transcripts on file at WRM, summarized in *Rogers Bio-Bibliography*, 216, 218, 220, 230, 222–223, and *Papers*, 5: 405, 407.

46 *Good Gulf Show*, June 4, 1933, summarized in *Rogers Bio-Bibliography*, 212, and *Daily Telegrams*, 4: 72, 166.

47 *Daily Telegrams*, 4: 91, 177, and *Weekly Articles*, 6: 146.

48 *Daily Telegrams*, 4: 77, 68, and *Weekly Articles*, 6: 103, 206. See *Rogers Bio-Bibliography*, 98, for a transcript of WR's Blue Eagle radio broadcast on August 27, 1933.

49 *Papers*, 5: 465.

50 *Ibid.*

51 Christopher Lasch, "Foreword," in Richard Hofstadter, *The American Political Tradition* (New York: Vintage, 1973), vii–xxiv. On 1930s populism, see Warren Susman, *Culture as History: The Transformation of American Society in the Twentieth Century* (New York: Pantheon, 1984), 150–183, 184–210.

52 See Alan Brinkley, *Voices of Protest: Huey Long, Father Coughlin, and the Great Depression* (New York: Vintage, 1983) for a brilliant analysis of 1930s populism.

53 *Daily Telegrams*, 4: 323, and *Weekly Articles*, 4: 129.

54 *Weekly Articles*, 5: 207, 236, 212–213.

55 *Daily Telegrams*, 3: 135, 121, and *Weekly Articles*, 5: 136.

56 *Daily Telegrams*, 3: 68, 38; *Weekly Articles*, 4: 225; and *Papers*, 5: 369.

57 *Weekly Articles*, 6: 15; *Papers*, 5: 400–401; and *Daily Telegrams*, 4: 118–119, 382 n. 2305.

58 *Weekly Articles*, 5: 65, and 6: 205, 185–187, and *Daily Telegrams*, 4: 271, 246.

59 *Weekly Articles*, 2: 139–140, and 6: 103, and *Daily Telegrams*, 4: 183.

60 *Radio Broadcasts*, 67; *Daily Telegrams*, 3: 282; and *Weekly Articles*, 2: 139–140, 257–258.

61 *Daily Telegrams*, 2: 257, 262, 268, 269, 272.

62 *Papers*, 5: 406, 438–441.

63 *Ibid.*, 5: 430–431.

CHAPTER TWELVE

1 *Weekly Articles*, 5: 44–45, and *Story of His Life*, 106.

2 Arthur F. Werthiem, "Will Rogers—Radio's Court Jester," in Wendell Mathews, ed., *Will Rogers—The Man and His Humor* (Racine, WI: Glenheath, 1991), 83.

3 *Story of His Life*, 242, and *Weekly Articles*, 6: 147.

4 Will Rogers, *More Letters of a Self-Made Diplomat*, ed. Steven K. Gragert (Stillwater: Oklahoma State University Press, 1982), xiv.

5 George Rublee, *Reminiscences*; WR quoted in *WR Biography*, 247; *More Letters of a Self-Made Diplomat*, 82, 46, 80–82; *Daily Telegrams*, 1: 158.

6 *Papers*, 4: 522, and *Daily Telegrams*, 1: 171, 172.

7 *Papers*, 5: 128–129; *Radio Broadcasts*, 4; and *Weekly Articles*, 4: 104, 114–115.

8 *Papers*, 5: 22–23, 192, 250; *Weekly Articles*, 5: 17–22; and *Daily Telegrams*, 3: 13–20.

9 *Papers*, 5: 24–25; *Weekly Articles*, 5: 80, 87–90; and *Daily Telegrams*, 3: 82–83, 91–92.

10 *Papers*, 5: 25–27, 193, 277–310. The articles addressed to Senator Borah were published in *More Letters of a Self-Made Diplomat*, 95–174. See *Political Life*, 189–210, for a survey and analysis of the journey.

11 *Papers*, 5: 25, 27, 279–280, and *Political Life*, 189–192.

12 *Papers*, 5: 25–27, 278, and *More Letters of Self-Made Diplomat*, 108.

13 *More Letters of a Self-Made Diplomat*, 119–120, 126–127.

14 *Ibid.*, 154, 158, 128, 152–153, 157.

15 *Ibid.*, 127, 146, 128, 155–156, 158, 172–173, and *Weekly Articles*, 5: 213.

16 *Daily Telegrams*, 3: 219–227, and *Papers*, 5: 30–31, 359–360.

17 *Story of His Life*, 303; *Daily Telegrams*, 4: 210–211; and *Papers*, 5: 40–41, 486–487, 494–504.

18 *Papers*, 5: 251, 494–495, 498–499, and *Folks Say*, 6–7.

19 *Letters of a Self-Made Diplomat*, 65; *Daily Telegrams*, 3: 82; *Weekly Articles*, 2: 48; and *Story of His Life*, 286.

20 *Radio Broadcasts*, 4.

21 *Daily Telegrams*, 1: 171, and 3: 108; *More Letters of a Self-Made Diplomat*, 55, 172, 99; and *Weekly Articles*, 2: 48, and 5: 20.

22 *Story of His Life*, 200.

23 *Political Life*, 125.

24 Carl Stearns Clancy, "Aviation's Patron Saint," *Scientific American* (Oct. 1929), 283–286.

25 *Story of His Life*, 203, 200; *Weekly Articles*, 2: 232; and "Aviation's Patron Saint," 284. See discussion in *Political Life*, 124–131, and in Fred Roach, Jr., "Vision of the Future: Will Rogers' Support of Commercial Aviation," *Chronicles of Oklahoma*, vol. 57, 1979: 340–364.

26 Will Rogers, "Flying and Eating My Way East" and "Bucking a Headwind," Jan. 21 and Jan 28., 1928, in the *Saturday Evening Post*, reprinted in Steven K. Gragert, ed., *"How to Be Funny" and Other Writings of Will Rogers* (Stillwater: Oklahoma State University Press, 1983), 46–60, 61–73. The quotes are from 57–59, 70.

27 "Flying and Eating," 59, and "Bucking a Headwind," 68, 73.

28 "Aviation's Patron Saint," 283, and *Weekly Articles*, 3: 159, and 5: 15.

29 *Weekly Articles*, 5: 15; Will Rogers, *There's Not a Bathing Suit in Russia*, ed. Joseph A. Stout, Jr. (Stillwater: Oklahoma State University Press, 1973), 38, 41; *More Letters of a Self-Made Diplomat*, 10, 102; "Aviation's Patron Saint," 286; and *Weekly Articles*, 3: 187–188.

30 *Daily Telegrams*, 1: 208, and *Weekly Articles*, 3: 166.

31 *Weekly Articles*, 3: 36, and 1: 308, 341.

32 *Ibid.*, 2: 27–29.

33 *Ibid.*, 1: 370–371; and *Papers*, 4: 393, 403–404. On Mitchell, see Burke Davis, *The Billy Mitchell Affair* (New York, 1967).

34 *Daily Telegrams*, 4: 137, and *Papers*, 5: 472–477. See *Political Life*, 252–254, for a lucid discussion of the airmail controversy.

35 *Weekly Articles*, 4: 71–72, 5: 51, and 6: 240.

36 Peter Rollins makes a similar point in his "Will Rogers on Aviation: A Means of Fostering Frontier Values in an Age of Machines and Bunk," *Journal of American Culture* (Spring/Summer 1984), 85–92.

37 "Aviation's Patron Saint," 284, 285; "Bucking a Head Wind," 65; and *Bathing Suit in Russia*, bookflap front cover.

38 *Bathing Suit in Russia*, 25–26, and "Bucking a Head Wind," 70.

39 "Bucking a Head Wind," 64; "Flying and Eating," 55, 58–59; *Weekly Articles*, 3: 42; *More Letters of Self-Made Diplomat*, 90; and *Daily Telegrams*, 3: 132.

40 *Story of His Life*, 201–202; "Interview with Dorothy Stone Collins" in Bryan B. Sterling, ed., *The Will Rogers Scrapbook* (New York: Grosset & Dunlap, 1976), 132; McIntyre, "Our Will," 83; and *Weekly Articles*, 2: 173, and 3: 17.

41 *Papers*, 5: 160–162, and *Story of His Life*, 181.

42 *Radio Broadcasts*, xiii, 3–62, and *New York Times*, March 30, 1930.

43 *Papers*, 5: 394–395.

44 *Ibid.*, 5: 397–398, 402–403, 408.

45 "Radio's Court Jester," 77, 78.

46 *Papers*, 5: 469–475, 571; Peter Rollins, *Will Rogers: A Bio-Bibliography* (Westport, CT: Greenwood, 1984), 213, 228–22; and "Radio's Court Jester," 88.

47 Ruth Chandler Moore, "What a Voice!" *Collier's* (June 29, 1935); "Will Rogers," *What's on the Air: The Magazine for the Radio Listener* (May 1930), 9–10; Harry Steele, "Will Rogers – Prairie Plato," *Radio Guide* (December 1, 8, 15, 1934); "Will Rogers at the Microphone," *World's Work* (June 1930), 17–18; and Homer Croy, "Will Rogers – Mystery Man of Radio," *Radioland* (February 1935), 12, 54.

48 *Papers*, 5: 455–460; and Amy Ware, *Cherokee Kid: Will Rogers, Tribal Identity, and the Making of an American Icon* (Lawrence: University Press of Kansas, 2015), 194.

49 *Rogers Bio-Bibliography*, 217, 219, and *Cherokee Kid*, 195–196.

50 *Papers*, 5: 461–462. Rogers wrote in the form of a telegram, but I have removed the caps and added normal punctuation for clarity of reading.

51 *Our Will Rogers*, 250–253, 161.

52 *Weekly Articles*, 3: 26; *Papers*, 5: 218–220; and *Daily Telegrams*, 2: 276.

53 *Papers*, 1: 381, 389, 449; *More Letters of a Self-Made Diplomat*, 140–141; and *Political Life*, 264.

CHAPTER THIRTEEN

1 *Weekly Articles*, 3: 170–172.

2 On the talkie revolution, see Robert Sklar, *Movie-Made America* (New York: Vintage, 1994), 152–155, and Donald Crafton, *The Talkies: American Cinema's Transition to Sound, 1926–1931* (Berkeley: University of California Press, 1999). The attendance figures come from Steven Mintz and Randy Roberts, eds., *Hollywood's America: United States History Through Its Films* (Malden, MA: Blackwell Publishing, 2008), 87.

3 *Weekly Articles*, 3: 198 and 4: 336, and Ken Taylor, "Talkies Offer Will Perfect Film Medium," *Los Angeles Express*, Sept. 19, 1929.

4 *Papers*, 5: 111–113, and *Story of His Life*, 234–235.

5 *Weekly Articles*, 5: 157, 69, and *Papers*, 5: 114–115.

6 *Our Will Rogers*, 236–238, 135.

7 *Weekly Articles*, 4: 69; *Our Will Rogers*, 243; and *Papers*, 5: 130, 131.

8 Cumberland MD *News*, October 4, 1929; Edwin Schallert, "Rogers Star Shines Gayly," *Los Angeles Times* (September 19, 1929); Mordaunt Hall, "Cowboy Comedian Has Best Screen Role in New Audible Feature," *New York Times*, October 20, 1929; Dan Thomas, "Will Rogers Is Superb in His First Talking Film," unattributed clipping, Scrapbook, WRM; and *Philadelphia Public Ledger*, September 18, 1929.

9 Copies of Rogers' talking films are in the possession of the WRM. A listing and synopses of these movies can be found in Bryan B. Sterling and Frances N. Sterling, *Will Rogers in Hollywood* (New York: Crown Publishers, 1984), 100–171, and Richard J. Maturi and Mary Buckingham Maturi, *Will Rogers, Performer* (Cheyenne, WY: 21st Century Publishers, 2008), 240–261.

10 *Papers*, 5: 589–591. The *Motion Picture Herald* survey is in *WR in Hollywood*, 102.

11 *Papers*, 5: 200–203.

12 WR quote on David Harum in *WR in Hollywood*, 138.

13 Among many treatments of Ford, see Joseph McBride, *Searching for John Ford: A Life* (New York: St. Martin's, 2001), and Tag Gallagher, *John Ford: The Man and His Films* (Berkeley and Los Angeles: University of California Press, 1968).

14 For an insightful view of the Ford–Rogers partnership, see Martin Rubin, "Mr. Ford & Mr. Rogers: The Will Rogers Trilogy," *Film Comment* (January–February 1974), 54–57. The quote is on p. 57.

15 *Los Angeles Times*, September 29, 1933; *Los Angeles Examiner*, September 29, 1933; Mordant Hall, "The Screen," *New York Times*, October 6, 1933; John S. Cohen, Jr., "Will Rogers in Dr. Bull, Another Eulogy of the Country Healer," *New York Sun*, October 6, 1933.

16 The career of Stepin Fetchit has aroused great controversy, with most critics and historians denouncing this character as the most notorious "Uncle Tom" symbol in the history of American culture. On the other hand, the African American critic, Mel Watkins, in his biography, *Stepin Fetchit: The Life and Times of Lincoln Perry* (New York: Pantheon, 2005) has argued that Lincoln Perry, who created and played this comic character in many movies, stood in a long line of "trickster" figures dating back to slavery who played the lazy, shiftless fool in front of whites to take their money and escape their demands. Perry, he points out, was the first African American actor to become a millionaire.

17 Ford quoted in 1972 interview, *WR in Hollywood*, 151, and *Weekly Articles*, 6: 128.

18 W. Ward Marsh, "Will Rogers at His Best in *Judge Priest*," unattributed clipping, Scrapbook WRM; Louella O. Parsons, "Rogers Charming as Judge Priest," *Los Angeles Examiner*, no date, Scrapbook WRM; *Kansas City Star*, October 21, 1934; "Presenting Dr. Rogers," *New York Times*, October 12, 1934; and *New York Herald Tribune*, October 12, 1934.

19 Andre Sennwald, "The Screen," unattributed clipping, September 20, 1935, WRM Scrapbook, and "On the Current Screen," *Literary Digest* (September 28, 1935), 26.

20 M. A. McConnell of the Emerson Theater in Hartford, Arkansas to *Motion Picture Herald* on February 25, 1933 and March 3, 1934, quoted in *The Big Tomorrow*, 39; *New York American*, December 3, 1932, excerpted in *WR in Hollywood*, 122; "Rogers Picture Wins Favor in Country Towns," unattributed clipping, Scrapbook WRM; and *New York Sun*, April 5, 1935, excerpted in *WR in Hollywood*, 156.

21 Venable interview quoted in *WR in Hollywood*, 139; Reginald Taviner, "On the Set With Will Rogers, as Told By Rochelle Hudson," *Photoplay* (August 1935), 36, 106; *Our Will Rogers*, 249; *Story of His Life*, 236–237; and *Hollywood*, May 1935 in *WR in Hollywood*, 161.

22 Borzage interview quoted in *WR in Hollywood*, 104–105; "On the Set With Will Rogers," 108; *Weekly Articles*, 4: 73; and Butler interview quoted in *WR in Hollywood*, 113.

23 "On the Set With Will Rogers," 106, 108; Thornton Sargent, "What Can You Do With Will Rogers?" *Movie Mirror* (March 1935), 107; and James M. Fidler, "Will Rogers' Cinematic Life Story," *Screenland* (July 1935), 93.

24 Ford interview, *WR in Hollywood*, 152; "On the Set With Will Rogers," 106; "Rogers' Cinematic Life Story," 92; and Peggy Wood interview, *WR in Hollywood*, 145.

25 Hal Mohr and Evelyn Venable Mohr interview, *WR in Hollywood*, 139.

26 King interview, *WR in Hollywood*, 129; "Rogers' Cinematic Life Story," 92; and Rogers quoted in *WR in Hollywood*, 126.

27 *Weekly Articles*, 6: 37, 130; "On the Current Screen," *Literary Digest* (April 20, 1935), 34; and *Film Spectator* quoted in *WR Performer*, 130.

28 Borzage quoted in WR Biography, 261, and Holloway interview, *WR in Hollywood*, 156–157.

29 Borzage quoted in Lary May, *The Big Tomorrow: Hollywood and the Politics of the American Way* (Chicago: University of Chicago Press, 2000), 40–41; Holloway interview in *WR in Hollywood*, 157; and Lew Ayres interview in *WR in Hollywood*, 128–129.

30 Borzage, Butler, and Ford interviews in *WR in Hollywood*, 105, 113, 151.

31 Ayres and Venable interviews in *WR in Hollywood*, 129, 139, and "On the Set With Will Rogers," 37.

32 WR quoted in *WR Performer*, 158; *Weekly Articles*, 4: 114; and *WR in Hollywood*, 171–172.

33 *Ah, Wilderness!* reviews listed in *WR as a Performer*, 158–161, and George C. Warren, "Humorist Scores in O'Neill Play," in *Papers*, 5: 491–492.

34 These movie flyers, ads, and posters are in the Sterling Papers, the Gordon Kuntz Collection, and various scrapbooks, all at the WRM.

35 "Will Rogers Cinematic Life Story," 92; "What Can You Do with Will Rogers?" 44; Katherine Albert, "Will Rogers – Father and Husband," *Modern Screen* (June 1934), 66–67, 98; and Thornton Sargent, "Will Outwits the Sexy Fellows," *Photoplay* (September 1934), 34, 106–107. On the movie fan magazines, see Anthony Slide, *Inside the Hollywood Film Magazine: A History of Star Makers, Fabricators, and Gossip Mongers* (Oxford: University Press of Mississippi, 2010).

36 K. C. Thomas, "Why Will Rogers is the Greatest Film Star," *Screenland* (March 1935), 96–97; "Will Outwits the Sexy Fellows," 34, 106; "What Can You Do with Will

Rogers?" 107; and George Kent, "The Mammy and Daddy of Us All," *Photoplay* (May, 1934), 33, 100, 102.

37 *Weekly Articles*, 4: 75, 5: 25, and 6: 32–33.

38 *Ibid.*, 5: 183, and 6: 131, 132–134, 233, 239–240.

39 *Ibid.*, 6: 95, 154, and 5: 197.

40 *Our Will Rogers*, 249, 261–262, 274–275, and Rogers quoted in *WR in Hollywood*, 154.

41 *Papers*, 5: 317; *Variety*, May 3, 1932, excerpted in *WR in Hollywood*, 119; *Weekly Articles*, 5: 148–149; and *Story of His Life*, 238–239.

42 *Papers*, 5: 477–480, and *Photoplay*, June 1934, quoted in *WR in Hollywood*, 141.

EPILOGUE

1 *Story of His Life*, 301, and *Our Will Rogers*, 276, 229–230.

2 *Our Will Rogers*, 276–277, and George Riedel, "Conversations with Will Rogers: 9 Intimate Days at Sea," unpublished manuscript, WRM.

3 *Papers*, 5: 39–47, 586–587.

4 James Agee, "Pseudo-Folk," *Partisan Review*, Spring 1944, reprinted in James Agee, *Agee on Film* (New York: Grosset and Dunlap, 1967), vol. 1, 407.

5 John Riddell, "An Open Letter to Will Rogers," *Vanity Fair* (October 1929), 90. On Corey Ford, see *Papers*, 5: 135.

6 *Our Will Rogers*, 279, and Macdonald quoted in *WR Biography*, 311.

7 "Two Show Figures," *New Republic* (September 4, 1935), 104; "The Cowboy Philosopher," *New Republic* (August 28, 1935), 62; and "Will Rogers," *Nation*, August 28, 1935.

8 *Story of His Life*, 301–304, 307.

9 Scott Eyman, *Print the Legend: The Life and Times of John Ford* (New York: Simon and Schuster, 1999), 132, and *Papers*, 5: 489.

10 *Story of His Life*, 305, and *Papers*, 5: 601, 47.

11 *Papers*, 5: 47–48. Accounts of the crash can be found in *Our Will Rogers*, 299–303, details of which came from Homer Croy's interviews with those involved, and in Bryan B. Sterling and Frances N. Sterling, *Will Rogers and Wiley Post: Death at Barrow* (New York: M. Evans and Company, 1993), which also provides the fullest analysis of the causes of the deadly crash. The Sterlings, after sifting through every shred of evidence, conclude that several factors converged to cause the accident: the cobbled-together plane's lack of airworthiness; dangerously dismal weather with dense fog and near zero visibility; the likelihood of a low amount of fuel with five of the six gas tanks having no gauge, a situation exacerbated by Post's habit of draining every drop from a tank before switching to another tank; and Post being accustomed to high-wing planes with highly situated tanks that supplied fuel to the carburetor by gravity, whereas the Alaska plane was low-wing with tanks placed below the fuselage with fuel being pumped upward by suction into the carburetor. These last two factors, either alone or in combination, caused the engine to stall because fuel failed to reach the carburetor. Behind these mechanical issues, the Sterlings also argue, lay the hubris of Post and Rogers, who were

careless since they "were totally convinced of their indestructibility." See *Death at Point Barrow*, pages 118, 145, 168–169, 177–178, 293, 303, 308.

12 *Our Will Rogers*, 301–305, based on interview with Dr. Greist, and Richard M. Ketchum, *Will Rogers: His Life and Times* (New York: McGraw-Hill, 1973), 391. Additional details can be found in *Death at Point Barrow*.

13 Bill Blowitz, "Notes From Humphrey Bogart," excerpted in *Papers*, 3: 409, and *Papers*, 3: 440, 436.

14 *Papers*, 5: 613–615, and "All Studios in Last Tribute to Rogers," *Los Angeles Evening Herald and Express*, August 22. 1935.

15 "Vast Throng Passes Bier, Tribute Paid by 50,000," *Los Angeles Times*, August 23, 1935, and "Silent Multitude Pays Last Respects at Bier of Rogers," *Los Angeles Daily News*, August 23, 1935.

16 "The Cowboy Philosopher," 62.

17 *San Francisco Monitor*, August 21, 1935; S. K. Ratcliffe, "Will Rogers – Philosopher-Humorist," *Spectator* (August 23, 1935), 287–288; *Tulsa Daily World*, August 25, 1935; *Variety*, August 21, 1935; "The Friend of All the World," *Minneapolis Journal*, August 25, 1935. These articles, as well as many noted below, can be found as clippings in Fred Stone Scrapbook, WRM.

18 "Will Rogers – Philosopher-Humorist," 287–288; "Rogers and Post," *Commonweal* (August 30, 1935), 416; "Will Rogers – Plain American," *World Digest* (October 1935), 870; and "Will Rogers," *Variety* (August 21, 1935), 2.

19 *New York Daily Mirror. . . .* included in "Eulogized by N.Y. Press," *Motion Picture Daily*, August 19, 1935; *Evansville Courier and Journal*, August 25, 1935; and "Where the Loss of Will Rogers May Be Most Deeply Felt," *Christian Century* (August 28, 1935), 1075.

20 Charles Collins, "Will Rogers, the Cowboy Humorist – His Life Story," *Chicago Daily Tribune*, August 18, 1935; "Will Rogers – Philosopher-Humorist," 287–288; and "Quite a Guy," *Variety* (August 21, 1935), 3.

21 *New York Evening Journal*, excerpted in "Eulogized by N.Y. Press," *Motion Picture Daily*, August 19, 1935; Charles Collins, "Will Rogers, the Cowboy Humorist – His Life Story," *Chicago Daily Tribune*, August 18, 1935; L. H. Robbins, "Portrait of An American Philosopher," *New York Times Magazine* (November 3, 1935), 4, 21; and Damon Runyan in *Folks Say*, 207.

22 FDR's remarks in *Folks Say*, 6, and *Weekly Articles*, 6: 178–179.

Index